Blacked Out Through Whitewash

UNABRIDGED

Volume 1 of 7

Exposing the *Quantum Deception*
Composing the Foundation
of Western Culture, Religion, and *His*-Story

Rediscovering and Recovering
Suppressed *Melanated*:
History • Herstory • Earthstory
Lost Light • Lost Knowledge
Consciousness
Wholeness
Power

SUZAR

— Dr. S. Epps —

A-Kar Productions

Written, designed, illustrated by Suzar.

First Printing, First Edition, November 1996.
Second Printing, with revisions, August 1998.
Third Printing, with revisions, additions, September 1999.
Printed in the United States of America.

ISBN: 0-9675394-3-9

Published by
A-Kar Productions
P.O. Box 386 • Oak View, CA 93022
WEBSITE: www.a-kar.com

Associate Publisher-Distributors:

Aldor Productions
P. O. Box 517
Highland, CA 92346
EMAIL: Metaphy3@cs.com
(909) 875-9552

The Exhibit Productions
P. O. Box 29512
Shreveport, LA 01149
WEBSITE: www.hotep.org
EMAIL: umar@hotep.org
(318) 682-5963

Also by Suzar:

- *Creation's Great BLAK Mother & the Blak Woman* (vol. 2 of Blacked Out Through Whitewash) © 1999
- *Resurrecting Bab-El, The Book of Books of Books* (vol. 3 of B.O.T.W.) © 1999
- *The numerous book releases from the 7-volume series of B.O.T.W.*
- *Drugs Masquerading as Foods* © 1999
- *Unfood By The UnPeople* (vol. 2 of D.M.A.F.) © 1999
- *Don't Worry, Be Healthy!* (vol. 3 of D.M.A.F.) © 1999
- (Editor) *The Double-You (W) Book* by Drs. Arvel & Bobbie Chappell

For information or booking lectures of Suzar, contact A-Kar Productions.

Dedicated
to the
Loving
Great Mother
Of the
Universe
and All Life

With Love and Gratitude to

Albert D.
Arvel C.
Bobbie C.
Ceanne D.
Connie K.
Daisy E.
Derrick P.
Gerald M.
Gwendolyn H.
Harroll C.
Irasha P.
Jamaal G.
James G.
Jerome I.
Johni N.
Keidi A.
Locksley G.
Omar S.
Peter K.
Runoko R.
Richard M.
Sherill P.
Steven M.
Umar B.
William M.
Yosef B.
Zears M.
and my
Inner Friends

Contents

VOLUME I

3

The Afrikan Origin of European Civilization 31

4

The Afrikan Origin of Hue-manity & the Albinos 47

Your right to remain DECEIVED, misled and ignorant

You have the right to remain *DECEIVED*; the right to remain misled and ignorant; the right to drop this book like a hot potato when the truth becomes too searing to bear, melting the ice of *Quantum Deception* composing the foundation of the culture encompassing us. You also have the right to know the truth. If you prefer not to know the truth, you can gracefully back out right now and stop reading this book... ... ... That you are still reading is possible evidence that at least a part of you is willing or brave enough to glimpse a portion of the truth. *Beware* however, when the chick breaks forth from its egg of *ignorance*, it cannot go back into its shell! From then on, its life is permanently, irrevocably *changed.*

We do not realize the depth of darkness we have been living in until the blinding light of truth starts to shine in. Never having experienced the orgasm of truth, we don't know what we are missing and thus are content with *Counterfeits.* We don't realize how snug and comfortable our ignorance and *Deception* are until they are threatened, ransacked, severed, cut up by the double edge Sword of Truth. In other words, knowing the truth may be initially painful. But this pain is small compared to the pain of ignorance and *Deception* that perpetuates Humanity's wretched condition. Ignorance is no longer bliss. For the errors we make, paths we take, and decisions we make due to ignorance and our having been *Deceived,* is tremendously harming us, even killing us, while robbing our happiness along the way.

If you know you're a slave, you will probably seek to free yourself. But if you do not know you're a slave, you will likely remain in bondage, never reaching your true potential, never even seeking the freedom that should be your birthright but was robbed from you *before* you were born. Being ignorant of true, relevant, vital history, we are content to be "hundred-naires" when it is our birthright to be *millionaires* and *billionaires.* The sad part is that we don't miss it; for we don't know enough to know how *abysmally* we have been cheated, *Deceived,* misled, lied to, and kept in ignorance. The depth of the *Deception* perpetrated upon all of us has been and still is "unfathomable." It is primarily this *Deception* that allows the present situation of the world to both continue and perpetuate itself. In fact, the "victims" (us) participate in and maintain their own subservience –so well have we been conditioned and brainwashed. "Education" and the Media (TV especially) are principal tools in this ongoing Grand Theft, *Deception*, and Manipulation.

This book exposes the *Quantum Deception.* This reference book is also about rediscovering and recovering suppressed and vital truths, especially in History and Cosmology, –particularly the jet black, *Krystal Black Truth* that has been *WHITE-washed* so well that when it is finally witnessed in its original ebony form, it is virtually unbelievable, which is why I say: "Ye shall know the Truth and the Truth shall BLOW YOUR MIND! –your *false* mind! *Then* it will set you FREE!" The *SEVEN* volumes of this book is not the whole Truth but a key hunk of it! As we reclaim our parts (RA-*member*, or put our *light* back together) and become whole, we likewise gain more insight and find even more of our missing *members.* As we recover the *real truth* about our History, *Herstory*, and *Divine Identity*, we simultaneously recover our fragmented consciousness and thus our lost and stolen Power. We are then in a much better position to *keep* our Power. Thus we have much greater strength to HEAL ourselves and with it, the Planet. I now invite you to finish reading the rest of this book at the risk of losing your (false) mind, and be firmly on the road to recovering your *true* mind.

BOOK 1 :

Exposing the Greatest Coverups in "*His*-Story"

1

Black, Nappy, and Divine

You probably already know that Jesus Christ was a *woolly* haired *Black* man

...according to the Bible itself, called the "*Lamb* of God" with *kinky* hair compared with *lamb's wool*, feet the color of *burnt* brass (Rev. 1:14,15), and a likeness resembling jasper and sardine stone (Rev. 4:3). Jasper and sardine stone (also called sard /sardonyx), are commonly brownish and brownish-red. Three female ancestors of Jesus were Hamitic (Afrikan). Listed in Matthew's genealogy of Christ (1:1-16), their names were Tamar and Rachab (who were Canaanites), and Bathsheba who was likely a Hittite, being the wife of Uriah the Hittite. The biblical Hittites descended from Heth, a son of Ham (Gen.10:15; 23:10).

The earliest pictures of Christ ALL portray him as Black

In the catacombs under Rome where images of Jesus appear for the FIRST time, black paintings and statues of Christ, the Madonna, and biblical characters still survive from early Christian worship. In the hard-to-find classic, Anacalypsis, historian Godfrey Higgens writes on page 138, "the God Christ, as well as his mother, are described in their old pictures and statues to be black. The infant God in the arms of his black mother, his eyes and drapery white, is himself perfectly black...the whiteness of the eyes and teeth, and the studied redness of the lips, are very observable."

Early catacomb painting of Christ and his disciples gathered for the Eucharist.

Often provoking the establishment with his penchant for flaunting heretical truth, the lectures and books by the uncompromising scholar, Kersey Graves, were frequently suppressed and sometimes banned. First published in 1875, one such book, *The World's Sixteen Crucified Saviors*, continued to be a clandestine best seller for nearly a century, despite vigorous suppression. On page 56, Kersey declares: "There is as much evidence that the Christian Savior was a black man, or at least a dark man...and that evidence is the testimony of his disciples, who had nearly as good an opportunity of knowing what his complexion was as the evangelists, who omit to say anything about it. In the pictures and portraits of Christ by the early Christians, he is uniformly represented as being black. And to make this the more certain, the red tinge is given to the lips; and the only text in the Christian bible quoted by orthodox Christians as describing his complexion, represent it as being black." [underlines added] Kersey asks what would happen if Christ made his second advent to earth as expected by Christians, "and that he comes in the character of a sable Messiah, how would he be received by our negro-hating Christians...? Would they worship a negro God? Let us imagine he enters one of our fashionable churches...what would be the results? Would the sexton show him to a seat? Would he not rather point to the door, and exclaim, 'Get out of here; no place here for niggers?' What a ludicrous series of ideas is thus suggested by the thought that Jesus Christ was a 'darkey.'"

The Turin Shroud, a fraud

Purported to be the burial cloth of Jesus, the Turin Shroud has been proven to be a fraud. Carbon dating indicates the Shroud did not exist at the time of the Fourth Crusade (1204).[1] The story is thoroughly documented in *Turin Shroud* by Picknett and Prince, who writes, "there is no historical evidence that the Shroud is older than –at the very best reckoning – 650 years."[2]

An ancient Roman coin depicts Christ's Afrikan identity

In the British Museum, an ancient gold coin shows Christ as an Afrikan with tightly curled, woolly hair and a cross behind him.[3] This coin was minted under the second reign of Roman Emperor, Justinian II who ruled at two separate times, separated by ten years (685-695 and 705-711 A.D.). During his first reign, the gold coins he had minted depicted Christ as a straight-haired European. During his second reign, he had the Christ-image on the coin changed to an Africoid image in order to ensure that this depiction was more in keeping with the original traditions of the Byzantine Church,[4] which commonly portrayed Jesus as an Afrikan. The obverse side of the coin shows Justinian with a cross behind him also. The Cambridge Encyclopedia wrote: "Whatever the fact, this coin places beyond dispute the belief that Jesus Christ was a Negro. The coin is otherwise of great historical interest, for it was the cause of a war between Justinian and Abdula Malik, 5th caliph of the Omniads, the former demanding tribute to be paid in these same coins and the latter refusing."[5]

1) Picknett/Prince, 121. 2) Ibid., 20. 3) Saakana, 47. 4) Watts, 22. 5) Diop, CU, viii; Rogers, SR, 81, 292.

Christ's Mother, "The Black Madonna" is worshiped throughout *Europe,* of all places

The most sacred icons of the Catholic Church are the Black Madonna and Christ child, which are found in Europe's most venerated shrines and cathedrals. Each year, hundreds of thousands of European pilgrims ritually humble themselves before the image of Black Mary and her child Jesus at Black Madonna sites throughout France, Germany, Spain, Italy, Belgium, Portugal and other Catholic countries. Many Black Madonna statues have the black paint literally kissed off of their hands and feet. In Poland, the Church encourages believers to pray to the Black Madonna of Czestochowka every morning before rising. It is reported that Pope John Paul follows this ritual. Time Magazine (June 11, 1979) reported on Pope Paul II's visit to Czestochowka's holiest shrine, which prominently displays "The Lady" known for centuries as the Black Madonna. At Our Lady of Koden (Poland), there are statues of white saints carrying pictures of Black Madonnas. Pilgrims throughout the ages have visited Black Madonna sites and left inspired, confident, relieved, or healed of their afflictions. Today, there are over 300 documented Black Madonna sites in France alone![1] Sometimes they are hidden away in vaults, while the public is shown Madonnas with European features.

In the hard-to-find classic, Anacalypsis, historian Godfrey Higgens writes, "...in all the Romish countries of Europe, in France, Italy, Germany, &c., the God Christ, as well as his mother, are described in their old pictures and statues to be black. The infant God in the arms of his black mother, his eyes and drapery white, is himself perfectly black. If the reader doubt my word, he

> may go to the cathedral at Moulins –to the famous chapel of the Virgin at Loretto ...the whiteness of the eyes and teeth, and the studied redness of the lips, are very observable... There is scarcely an old church in Italy where some remains of the worship of the BLACK VIRGIN and BLACK CHILD are not to be met with. Very often the black figures have given way to white ones, and in these cases the black ones, as being held sacred, were put into retired places in the churches, but were not destroyed...[2]

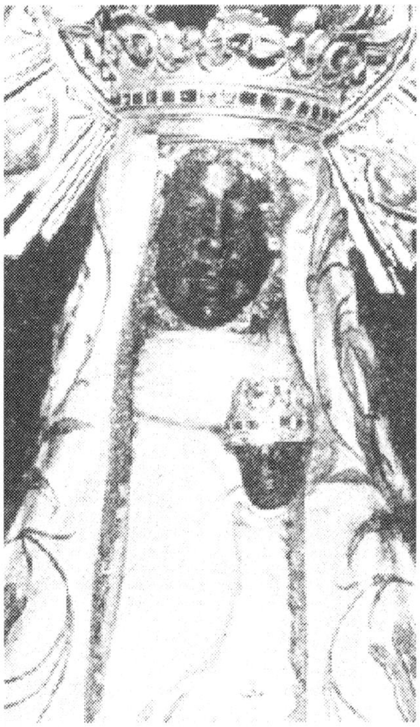

The Queen of the Pyrenees

The Black Madonnas originally all had Africoid features before most of them were destroyed by iconoclasts. When they were replaced, the artists retained the dark skin color but, not being familiar with real Afrikans, gave European features to the paintings. In cases where originals have survived, you may witness Africoid features on Mary and her child Jesus, such as the Black Madonna of Nuria, Spain – called "the Queen of the Pyrenees." Russia's remarkable legacy of Black Madonnas and other Christian icons of dark skin is evidenced in the book, Russian Icons by Vladimir Ivanov, including the feature story of the Spring 1994 issue of *Russian Life* magazine, graced with a Black Madonna on its cover.

1) Watts, 18. 2) Higgens, vI, 138.

Goddess Ast (Isis) suckling Her Holy Child Heru (Horus).

Actually the worship of the virgin, Black "Mother of God" with her God-begotten child, far predates Christianity and prevailed throughout the ancient world.

Historians recognize that the statue of the Egyptian Goddess Isis with her child Horus in her arms was the first Madonna and Child. They were renamed Mary and Jesus when Europe was forcibly Christianized. The worship of Isis and Horus was especially popular in ancient Rome. "Roman legions carried this figure of Black Isis holding the Black infant Horus all over Europe where shrines were established to her. So holy and venerate were these shrines that when Christianity invaded Europe, these figures of the Black Isis holding the Black Horus were not destroyed but turned into figures of the Black Madonna and Child. Today these are still the holiest shrines in Catholic Europe."[1] Titles such as Our Lady, The Great Mother, are the same titles attributed to Isis. The word "Madonna" itself is from mater domina, a title used for Isis! The month of *May*, which was dedicated to the heathen Virgin Mothers, is also the month of Mary, the Christian Virgin.[2]

The Fedorovo Virgin, a Black Madonna icon of 18th century Russia

Incredulously, many contemporary white authors seem not to link or acknowledge the Black Madonna's color with her Afrikan origin, although their ancestors did without hesitation. Some flatly deny any racial connection. Instead, they come up with various reasons and sophisticated explanations (the "dark" phase of the moon, fertility of the earth, etc.) –any excuse except *Melanin*– to explain why the Lady is portrayed black. This is evident in a number of books by white authors discussing Black Madonnas. Perhaps whites have become so enmeshed in the webs of false history woven by their predecessors that many are blind to the truth, unable to see or discern even glaring evidence of Afrikan historical presence. If white writers of today are indeed this ignorant –or pretending ignorance– of the Black Madonna's Afrikan origin, let them read the works of a few rare honest white scholars which preceded them, such as Gerald Massey, T.W. Doane, Godfrey Higgins and Kersey Graves. These writers knew and wrote the truth. This is amazing given the exceedingly overtly racist times in which they lived. Yet today, official white establishment does not and will not acknowledge the Afrikan genesis of their whitewashed religions. In Bible Myths, T.W. Doane devotes a chapter to *The Worship of the Virgin Mother*, where he candidly states, "The whole secret of the fact of these early representations of the Virgin Mary and Jesus-so called-being *black*, crowned, and covered with jewels, is that they are of pre-Christian origin; they are *Isis* and *Horus*... baptized anew." [3]

1) Saakana, 53-54. 2) Doane, 335. 3) Ibid., 337.

Like Christ, the earliest messiahs and gods & goddesses on all continents were Black & woolly haired

Buddha of India was Black, that's why his woolly hair is always shown in small tight curls –pepper corn style, or in corn rows. Early sculptures of him clearly portray his Africoid features of wide nose and full lips. "Buddha was adored as a square black stone." [1] In the most ancient temples of Asia and India, the sculptures of the gods and goddesses have Africoid features and woolly hair in pepper corn style and even dredlocks.

Fu-Hsi, the "Son of Heaven" and legendary first Emperor of China, was Black and woolly haired.[2]

Zaha of Japan was woolly haired and Afrikan in appearance.[3]

Kar of Afrika's Nile Valley was the inner soul of Mother Earth, a beautiful ebony virgin who was the "Heart of the World."[4] Shrines of *Kar*nak in Egypt and *Car*nac in Brittany were dedicated to Kar, the Goddess of Agriculture, especially the *growth* of grain. She was Kore to the Arabs and Greeks, Ceres to the Romans. Derivatives of her name include cereal, corn, kernel, cardia (heart), care, and cherish. If you cut an apple transversely, you will

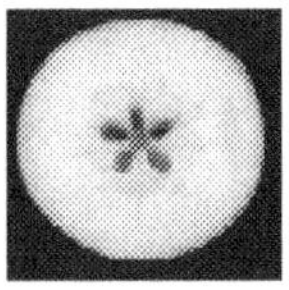

discover that every apple has a "Kore," the magic pentacle which is her symbol.

Moses was Black according to Mohammedan tradition and early portraits. His hand would turn white, then back to his "other flesh" when God wished to give him a sign (Exo. 4:6,7).

Apollo was Black and woolly-haired like his father Zeus. The world famous Apollo Theatre in Harlem is named after him.

Venus of Willendorf is a famous stature of the Mother God as she was worshipped some 15 to 20 thousand years ago. Although she is found in most art history books, none mention that she is Africoid: her entire faceless head is covered with woolly hair like that of Buddha's.

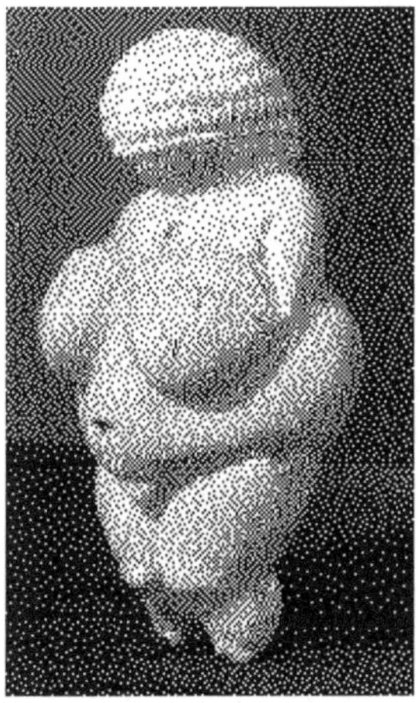

Venus of Willendorf

Courtesy of Runoko Rashidi (left & top right)

Buddha, 12th century (sitting), 9th century (top inset), and 11th century (bottom inset).

1. Higgens, v-I, 137. 2) Doane, 534. 3) Ibid. 4) Walker, WE, 514.

Krishna of India was "blue-black." His name means *black* or The Black One! He is always portrayed with black or blue skin, and his hair was woolly according to the Cambridge Encyclopedia,[1] and sometimes locked.

Tyr of Scandinavia was a woolly haired Norse god who preceded Thor as a sky deity.[2]

Athena of "Greek" mythology was Black and woolly haired, originating from Afrika (Libya). She was later whitened up like the other Afrikan gods adopted by Europe. She was also known as Anath, Medusa, and the Egyptian goddess Neith.[3]

Isis (As-t) the greatest of Afrikan Goddesses, was worshipped throughout the ancient world in Egypt, Greece, Rome and beyond. Known under many names, She was the "Queen of Heaven" and the "Goddess from whom all becoming arose." The worship of Her survives today, disguised as the worship of the Black Madonna throughout Catholic Europe.

Lao-tse of Taoism "*was born of a virgin*, black in complexion, described 'marvelous and beautiful as jasper.' Splendid temples were erected to him, and he was worshiped as a *god.*" [4]

Scotia was a Black goddess and Egyptian princess after which Scotland is named.[5]

Caillech (Cale, Kali) was known as the "Black Queen" in medieval legend, and to the Celts as the mother of many races. The Spanish called her Califia and gave her name to their newly discovered paradise which is now called *California*.[6]

Quetzalcoatl of Mexico was "recognized as the Messiah by seers and astrologers; his head was rayed; his complexion was black; his hair was woolly." [7] He was never blond or white, as stated by friars, though he may have been clad in white.[8]

Osiris (Azar), husband of Isis and greatest of Egyptian gods, was called "The Great Black," similar to Krishna. His chief title means "Lord of the Perfect Black." "Osiris was sun-rayed; his complexion was black and his hair was woolly." [9]

Mohammed of Islam was 'large mouthed', 'bluish' in color with 'frizzy' hair. His grandfather was "black as the night and magnificent." [10]

Zeus, the top god and father of gods in Greek mythology, was Black and woolly haired, having originated in Afrika. His chief title was *Ethiops* (burnt faced).

At **Delphi** in Greece, the oracles of Dodona and Apollo were founded by two "Black Doves" or Afrikan priestesses from Thebes, according to Herodotus.[11]

Circe, who played a great role in Homer's *Odyssey*, was the most famous female magician of all time. "Ancient Greek drawings depict her as a beautiful African woman." [12]

Ixliton, the name of a Mexican god, means "black faced." [13] Many ancient Mexican gods are portrayed jet black with Africoid features.

Dilyehe, meaning *Home of the Black God,* was the name which the Navajo gave to the seven suns of Pleiades.[16]

Kali was the Great Black Mother, the Hindu Triple Goddess of Creation, Preservation, and Destruction.

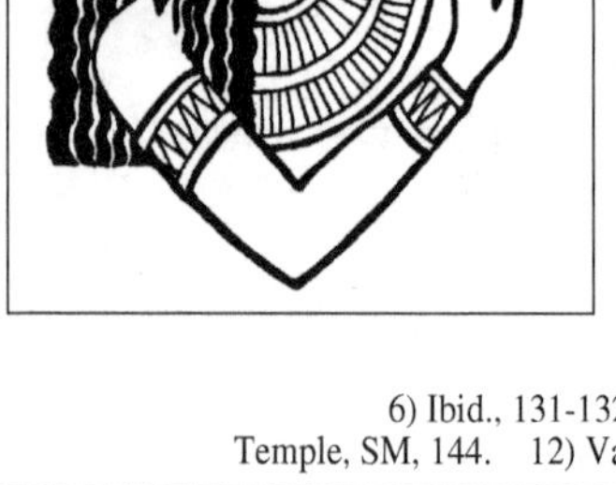

The color BLACK represented holiness and the image of God throughout the ancient world

Historian Sir Godfrey Higgens wrote, "the originals of all the Gods have been of the black race."[14] The ancients viewed the sacred image of the Divine as Black. And *woolly* hair was a sign of divinity –called "the hair of the gods." [15] In the next section, we shall discover why.

1) Rogers, SR, 266. 2) Van Sertima, APEE, 229. 3) Walker, WE, 74. 4) Doane, 120. 5) Walker, WE, 901. 6) Ibid., 131-132. 7) Rogers, SR, 266. 8) Van Sertima, TCBC, 76. 9) Rogers, SR, 265. 10) Kush, 91. 11) Rogers, SR, 266; Temple, SM, 144. 12) Van Sertima, APEE, 214. 13) Rogers, SR, 270. 14) Higgens, vII, 363. 15) Rogers, SR, 70. 16) Hatonn, PC, 32.

Nappy hair is *divine* –the choice of God!

Like Christ, "His son" and all the founders of world religions, God Himself has kinky, nappy hair according to the Bible, where God –the "Ancient of days" is described as having hair "**like the pure wool**" (Daniel 7:9). The apocryphal Book of Enoch (46:1) states the same: "There I beheld the Ancient of days, whose **head was like white *wool***..."[1] The power that causes galaxies to *spiral*, stars, planets and atoms to *spin*; that causes the double helix *spiral* of the DNA molecule; **this same *spiraling* power causes *spiraling* hair -otherwise known as NAPPY, kinky, curly, crinkly, bushy, frizzy, wavy, WOOLLY hair!** The words, SPIN, SPIRAL, and SPIRITUAL have common roots! The Supreme Power spins; spirals; it is *spiritual*. It moves or *spirals* the universe! The entire universe ever dances in spirals and rotations; everything in it reflects the "SPIRaling, SPIRitual" essence out of which it is made! Everything is *alive* with *Spirit*, the vital principle or animating lifeforce within all living beings. In many languages, the word for Spirit, Breath, and Air are identical: Sanskrit *prana*, Hebrew *ruach*, Greek *pneuma*, Latin *spiritus*. For breath and life are One. Latin *spirare* means to *breathe*; Latin *spir* and Greek *speira* mean coil. The Spiral Principle of the Universe is what makes *nappy* hair *nappy* -or *spiraling*.

Nappy hair is "the hair of the gods" –*spiraling* hair expressing the *Spiral* Principle of Creation

The "SPIRal" is the movement of Creation. The Spiral, especially the Golden Spiral, is the most profound motion in the universe. At the same time, it is the most profound design in the universe –built into all lifeforms, from seashells to man, to *spiraling* nappy hair!

- Your blood *spirals* through your veins! Plants *spiral* up from the soil! **And nappy hair *spirals* out from the hair roots!**
- Witness the unique *spiral* or whorl on your fingertips.
- Ball your hand into a fist and slowly extend each finger and you will see for yourself how the tip of each finger opens in a golden *spiral* path!

1) The Book of Enoch, translated by Laurence, 31.

- Observe the spiraling of ocean waves and wind, of animal horns, of *spir*ulina –a superfood algae that resembles nappy hair, the spiral in your ears, in flowers and throughout Nature.

Straight-haired people also have a *spiral* on their heads, visible as a whorl pattern with its center in the back of the head, where their straight hair grows out slanting in the whorl's direction. **Woolly haired people have both,** the whorl pattern and the individually *spiraling* strands of helixal, coiled, *spring*-like, nappy hair...the choice of the gods! It's no wonder that SPIRaling hair was regarded a sign of SPIRituality and divinity, and prized as "the hair of the gods."

Did Jesus have dredlocks?

The Prophet Jesus was a Nazarite: a vow of Nazarites (Nazarenes) was to never cut their hair but "let the locks of the hair of his head grow" (Num. 6:2, 5, Lev. 19:27; 21:5). The word Nazarite is from *nazar*, meaning *unshorn* and consecrated to God. It has nothing to do with Nazareth.[1] In India, *nazar* means *sight* and internal or *supernatural vision.*[2] The Nazarenes (also known as the Essenes) were reknown for their prophets or *seers.*

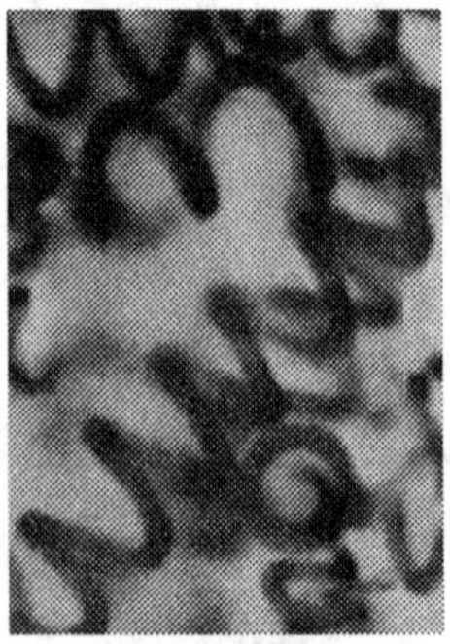

Nappy Cells of Spirulina

The firstborn child, in some Afrikan traditions, especially the daughter, is dedicated to God and their hair is never cut, but allowed to grow as locks – especially if the child is a descendant of a healer or shaman. Such a "Child of God" is highly revered and believed to inherit healing powers bestowed by God.[3] **Afrikans of the Nile Valley**, that is, the ancient Egyptians, often wore their nappy hair in locks, as evidenced by their sculptural reliefs. **Apollo**, originally a Black god adopted from Afrika by the Greeks, was the sun and Homer called him "he of the unshorn hair."[4] The Bible states "He shall be holy, and shall let the locks of the hair of his head grow" (Num. 6:5). **Samson**, the most famous example of locked hair, had seven locks (Jud. 13:5, 16:17,19). Samson was the Judaic version of the *Sungod* called Shams-On in Arabia, Shamash in Babylon, Hercules in Greece, and Ra in Egypt. Samson's name signifies the sun. His seven locks were the sun's rays with their seven colors or vibrations. His loss of hair meant the cutting of the sun-god's rays, in the winter season when he became weak.

Medusa's "hair of snakes" were really dredlocks

She was the Afrikan serpent-goddess representing Female Wisdom and was called "the mother of all gods, whom she bore before childbirth existed." In typical treatment of maligning Afrikan tradition, European "classic myth" made Medusa into a monster; the terrible Gorgon whose look turned men to stone. The Gorgons were a trinity whose names were Medusa, Stheino, and Euryale —or Wisdom, Strength, and Universality. European writers pretended they were monsters, but these are not the names of monsters! Medusa was the Destroyer aspect of the Triple Goddess called Neith in Egypt and Athena in Greece. Medusa's name is derived from Egyptian *Maat* (Truth), which also gives us the words *med*icine, *mat*hematics, and Sanskrit *medha* (female wisdom).

1) Ewing, 96; Graham, 204; Blavatsky, IU-vII, 128. 2) Blavatsky, IU-vII,142. 3) Mirella, 65. 4) Graham, 205.

God suspended him by his locks between earth and heaven

The dredlocked prophet Ezekiel, reported that God manifested in golden brightness before him and his associates, "And he put forth the form of an hand, and took me by a lock of mine head; and the spirit lifted me up between the earth and the heaven..." (Ezek. 8:3).

Biblically, Blacks were *sheep*; white people were *goats*

"Sheep" originally referred to Black people with their woolly hair and typically peaceful nature. *Woolly*-haired Jesus was called the *Lamb* of God and the Prince of *Peace*. Afrikans of the Nile Valley even made wigs from sheep wool to match their woolly hair! "Goats" symbolized white people;[1] they are naturally very hairy people with straight hair and typically aggressive natures. The term "scapegoat" originally meant the *Red Hairy Ones* who were periodically exiled into the wilderness;[2] –white people are all shades of *red.* Goats usually have long straight hair and even "beards" hence "goatees." Hebrew "sa'ir" means both "goat" and "hairy." Goats are at home in the high mountains (Ps. 104:18), where they negotiate jagged crags and narrow mountain ledges with graceful ease. Like the wild goats who live in mountains and rocky places, the ancient Europeans were associated with hills and caves. "Caucasian," the name by which they are known, is derived from the Caucasus *Mountains,* their early ancient abode.

Etymology of Nappy and Kinky

The word "nappy" is likely derived from the Egyptian words **nepi** or **nabt**, both meaning "lock" of hair. [3] The word "kinky" is derived from ANKH, the name of the most revered symbol of Afrika's Nile Valley. Ankh means Life and Tie/Join/Connect. From this Afrikan word comes most of the words which mean to join or connect: Derivatives (which usually contain NG /NK or GN /KN) include anchor, ankle, neck, knee, tangle, jungle, messenger, angel (they are "messengers" that connect you with divine messages), and juncture (from Latin *unct* from *ankh*).

A nappy, dredlocked Egyptian. The ancient Egyptians were nappy and Black.

A nappy Jew. The original Jews were nappy and Black.

A nappy, dredlocked Indian on an early Hindu sculpture.

1) Barashango, 84,85. 2) Bradley, CP, 76-77, 142. 3) Budge, EHD, 369.

Hair is really Antennae which can receive and transmit energy!

Hair is the receiver and transmitter of divine emanation –it makes you receptive to spiritual forces. Saints and sages instinctively let their hair grow. Rastafarians regard dredlocks as a quality of Black people: they regard dredlocks as "high-tension wires" which transmits divine energy and inspiration from Jah (God) the creator, to Rasta, the mirror. Within our body which is the temple of God, our *head*, the "holy of holies," is the highest point, while our hair, its natural crown, is like the spire of a church, our vertical connection with God. Representing our strength, it forms an antenna through which the SPIRitual force may descend. SPIRitual force, rather than "descend," will SPIRal through SPIRaling hair. Since Nature does nothing without a reason, what is the purpose and effect of spiral-hair?

Since Nature itself is a textbook that reveals the secrets of the universe by literally expressing these principles in the actual form that something takes, my guess is that spiral-hair enhances the ability to tune in at the most detailed levels or dimensions; the micro within the macro. Both, nappy and straight haired people have "the whorl" or Big Spiral, and surely this allows tuning in at the "Big level," while the little spirals of individual strands additionally allow the antennae to pick up detail at the most minute level (?).

Does hair antenna possess "accelerator" properties?

An accelerator is a device used by physicists to accelerate charged subatomic particles or nuclei to high energies useful for research. Two common types are the linear accelerator and the cyclotron. The linear type accelerates in a straight path that may be as long as two miles, while the cyclotron accelerates subatomic particles in a spiral path, and takes up way less space. Theoretically, energies being picked up by the antenna of hair, would be accelerated in a spiral or straight path depending on the type of hair. Throughout Nature, spiraling energy (whirlpools, eddies, tornados) manifests great speeds. Water going down a drain will spiral down the drain, picking up so much speed in the process that it becomes a suction. Energy flowing through spiral hair might also pick up extra speed, enhancing hair's antenna ability or even giving it new properties.

Certainly, energy flowing through *spiral* hair would also *spirally* enter the millions of nervepaths leading to the brain and ultimately the "third eye," to facilitate *spiritual* awareness, telepathy, perception, revelation, channeling or tuning in, understanding, receptivity, thought, who knows? This area deserves research to determine and clarify the effect of spiraling hair on perception and energy reception/transmission. Melanin, which is a super absorber of all forms of energy, undoubtedly plays a huge role in this. Sensing this at some level, is this why whites call other whites who are blond, *airheads* ?

Courtesy of *Bright Moments*, Sept., 95, p4

Tassili Maat and her antennae

Spiral-hair = "concentrated antennas." The nappier the hair, the more 'Spiral Power' it has

...or maybe the reverse is true! And the more concentrated, powerful, and advanced will be its abilities relating to the Spiral Principle. This is evident even physically, for nappy hair –being a spring, will "snap" back to the head when pulled out and released. The more the spring is coiled, the more power it has and the less space it takes up (concentration). Right after nappy hair is vigorously brushed, the nappy hair which has accumulated in the brush holds far more electrical static charge than straight hair; thus like a magnet, it will attract light items –paper for instance, whereas straight hair hardly or does not do this. Possibly, this mean that spiral hair has higher magnetic attraction for higher energies. It may also have the ability to concentrate or focus these higher energies like a magnifying lens concentrate sunrays. Whatever abilities it has are surely increased or intensified, the nappier the hair is. Thus the nappiest hair, the hair which Afrikan people are conditioned to reject and despise the most, turns out to be the most valuable, like "the stone which the builders rejected" which turns out to be the most important stone.

Does hair-antenna possess crystal properties?

Crystals have the power to receive and transmit energy waves. The earliest radios used quartz crystals and were called "crystal sets." The main composition of quartz crystal is silicon. Silicon is also a key mineral found in the hair, and undoubtedly contributes to its antenna ability. It is no accident that silicon is also the most essential component of computers; silicon enables computers to have mind-like properties including "memory." Silicon is also an important mineral found in the brain, which is the seat of the mind. Silicon is what gives an iridescent sheen to some fruit such as strawberries and cucumbers. It is also found in whole barley and oats.

> The original meaning for the Chinese character, CHEN is 'a *bushy* head of hair' and 'divine influences.'[1] Understanding how the two (hair and divine energy) are connected, no wonder they were represented by a common word.

1) H. Moran /D. Kelly, *The Alphabet & the Ancient Calendar Sign*, 110.

"Acquired Anti-Nappy Syndrome" (AANS) fuels the worldwide War on Nappy Hair

Epidemically around the world, *hundreds of millions* of Nappy People are afflicted with full-blown AANS, –"Acquired Anti-Nappy Syndrome." While no nappy person is born with it, they *acquire* it from their parents and family. AANS victims assault their hair with scorching metal combs and grease, frying each nappy strand until it is straight, to imitate the straight limp hair and hairstyles of Caucasians. In the process, some burn their hair *and* scalps. Others assault their hair with "chemical relaxers" (sodium or calcium hydroxide) which are so dangerous and poisonous that it burns the scalp shortly after applied, causing blisters and even permanent scalp and hair damage if left on too long or used too often. Additionally, chemicals from these relaxers are absorbed into the bloodstream; they are carcinogenic and can even cause birth defects. And since nappy hair keeps growing out as nappy as ever, the assault must be periodically repeated to maintain artificial straightness. Thus the hair is repeatedly damaged, forced to be what it is not, forced with "lye," to *lie* by *lying* straight. The scalps attached are likewise repeatedly damaged, by exposure to, and absorption of applied poisons.

But the worse damage appears to go unnoticed or even unacknowledged since this has become accepted "normal" behavior; this is the damage to the psyches which own the scalps. This psychological damage is "Acquired Anti-Nappy Syndrome," a form of self-rejection and self-hatred. The outward manifestation of this inner dis-ease is the War on Nappy Hair. AANS perpetuates and holds this war in place. The War on Nappy Hair was taken to such extremes, that in some Caribbean islands during the 1980s, not only was it illegal for Blacks to have locked hair, but if they dared display it in public, they could be arrested or even shot and killed on sight by the police! –who were Black themselves! And nappy foreigners sporting dredlocks, attempting to visit these areas, were detained at airports and not permitted to stay in the country unless they wore wigs or hats to hide their locks.

AANS is rampant among the Nappy *only* in Euro-centered, Euro-imitative societies

This means practically the whole world. Thus around the world, Nappy People have been successfully conditioned by their European colonizers to reject or scorn everything that makes them unique as Afrikan people; their sable skin of varying beautiful hues, full sensuous lips, broad noses, Afrikan culture, Afrikan names, and their divine nappy hair -spiraling hair expressing the divine Spiral Principle of Creation. The dictionary (like everything in these societies) promotes AANS by demeaning key words which commonly relate to Afrikan people. Example: "kinky," like the word "black," is associated with undesirable characteristics. By the same token, key words commonly relating to white people are elevated, thus "straight," like the word "white," is associated with desirable characteristics. Reflecting this attitude, the literature in the boxes of "chemical hair relaxers" refer to straighter hair as "fine," and nappiest hair as "coarse."

It happens to millions of Black girls everyday around the world:

("Pearl!") My mother broke our conscious daydreaming. ("Come over here and let me touch up your edges.") I wanted to run and hide! She set me down in the chair and pulled the hot comb from the big wood-burning stove. My mother started pressing my already altered and straightened hair.

I was always afraid of that hot comb! I held my breath as the heat from the comb moved across my scalp. Metal teeth pulling knotted hair until forced to lay flat. I wiped my damp hands on the long skirt of my pink, terry-cloth robe. With tension I bent my ear down and out of the way, then pushed my feet hard into the floor until my knees began to tremble. I lost my thoughts with the heavy smell of the burning hot comb.

She guided the comb near my ear. The sizzling sound of frying hair grease captured me motionless. I looked hard in my Grandmother's eyes, who looked breathless back into mine. This was one time I knew not to move for fear of branded teethmarks on the neck or ears. Not today! It just couldn't happen, especially this morning.

From *The Bamboo Forest*
by Irasha Pearl

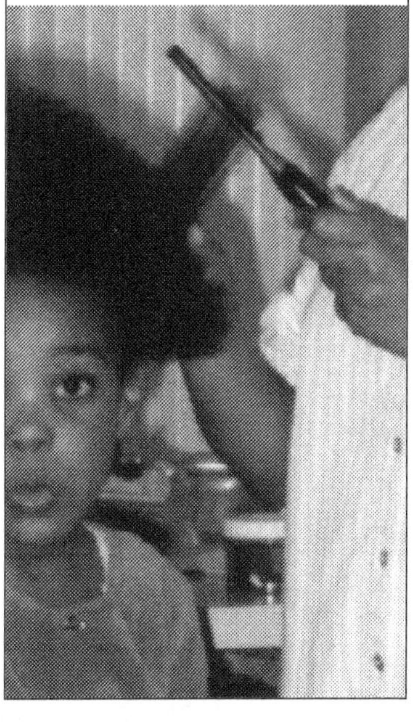

While it is mainly women that show the visible evidence of AANS, nappy men are just as afflicted; their compliments and attention seem to favor women wearing straightened hair; or perhaps they have little choice since AANS-afflicted women are everywhere. They are the overwhelming majority. AANS is also evident with Nappy Men **today**, though not as rampant as it was from the early 1900s to the 1970s.

It's hard work to keep all that nappy hair straight. It's time consuming as well, wasting countless hours that can be productively used in nurturing self-knowledge and self-respect. For who will respect you if you don't respect yourself? If 90% of whites were always perming up their straight hair to imitate kinky hair, this would clearly broadcast the statement that they don't like themselves (self-hatred); and are rejecting part of themselves. Furthermore, keeping nappy hair straight is COSTLY. In America alone, Black people annually spend *billions*, that's right –billions of dollars on Black hair care at a time when Black colleges, businesses and organizations are facing financial ruin.[1] This stands as a shameful witness to the success of the campaign to turn Afrikans against their own natural traits and thus against themselves.

Furthermore, AANS damaged hair is probably destroyed in its ability to transmit energy or be antennae. Instead of tuning into higher vibrations, such enslaved, maligned hair probably tunes into lower energies or likely, *no* energy at all, since it is cooked, hence dead.

The good news is that there is increasing evidence that many among the Nappy are healing from AANS;

they are accepting and loving their natural spiral-hair, particularly as they awaken to knowledge of their true history, true culture, and true selves, – and reject the false, anti-Afrikan history taught to them in anti-Afrikan school systems established by anti-Afrikan people. Fortunately, AANS and its outward symptoms are not permanent. As fresh new virgin hair grow out of those poisoned scalps, so can AANS exit forever.

Dredlocks were formerly abhorred by Nappy Americans.

The term itself is derived from "dread," for locked hair was considered "dreadful" ! British soldiers coined the term "dreadlocks" during Jamaica's colonial period, from the soldiers' attempts to oppress the Afrikan Maroons who revolted against slavery. Now, not only is locked hair accepted, it's even fashionable. In fact, people desiring instant long locks can now buy pre-made locks of any length or thickness, made from human hair. Thus a day is surely comin' when Blacks stop regarding nappy hair as "bad hair," and straighter hair as "good hair." They will have completely thrown off the negative racist conditioning causing them to imitate their colonizers at the expense of their self respect. As a result, *Acquired Anti-Nappy Syndrome* will be healed. Manufacturers of hot combs and relaxers will go out of business. And Nappy People will end the War on their Nappy Hair. Once more they will esteem their precious Nappy Hair as the ancients did, – as the spiraling "Hair of the Gods."

1) Browder, BF, 81.

Nappy hair is "Good Hair."...and *Dreadlocks* are "Love Locks"

In her fabulous, much-needed book, ***Good Hair***, Lonnice Bonner shows spiral-haired Black women how to look good wearing their hair NATURAL, not artificially straightened. You'd be surprised at the possibilities! Her book, ***Plaited Glory***, teaches the How-To and basics of maintaining locks, twists, braids and more.

How to be Locky

Nappy hair "ankhs" into locks automatically. If simply washed and dried but never combed or brushed, nappy spiraling hair will naturally entwine ("ankh") into long locks as it grows. **Some Blacks allow their spiraling hair to grow out any way that it grows out.** Usually the results are thick, sturdy locks that resist time and breakage. Such locks are as individualized as the person; one-of-a-kind originals, unique from head to head, reminiscent of the growth of tree branches and plant bushes. **Some Blacks, striving for a more predictable orderly appearance,** attempt to "start" their locks or control the "ankhing" of their hair at the beginning, with braids. The results are usually many, uniform, thinner, braid-like locks, which become even thinner, often breaking off after a few years. Other Blacks, perhaps having tried both approaches, do a combination, experimenting till they find what works best for them. Kamite & other ancient Afrikan art show different styles of locks. In Jamaica and India, Blacks often have just one or two very long, thick, jagged, incredible, awesome locks.

> *"My hair is not dreadful to me. I tell my children, curly hair loves itself so much it hugs itself and you have to tear it apart. That is why I call our hair 'love' locks."*
>
> *Tassili Maat*
> Brite Moments 9/95, p4

Locks can be too thick or thin, depending on the individual:

- The too-thick-lock that gets long can put excessive stress on one side of the head/body and also throw off one's balance. **Tip**: A thick short lock can be made into two or more locks by firmly pulling it apart (like tearing fabric). Thick or merging locks can be pulled apart to make them thinner.
- Locks that are grown too thin often get thinner and break off later as they become longer. **Tip**: locked strands may be tied into a *knot* where they are "weak," and thereby strengthened!

If you are locking your hair, you may need to wash it more frequently depending on the frequency of your dandruff. If washed too infrequently, locked hair may become loaded with dandruff, lent, etc., that becomes impossible to thoroughly remove, although you might get all of the "locked in stuff" very *clean.*

Rapid hair growth. Curious that Blacks who otherwise have a hard time making their hair grow long, find that when they start growing locks, their hair starts growing rapidly. If that same coiled hair could be stretched out, it would be even longer, several times its length. Some Rastafarians have locks that are several *yards* long! A way to grow hair fast without locking is through *Hairobics*... for example...

All natural hair deserves the best, hence, all natural hair-care products. The best is *Hairobics* and *Praises* (see *Resources*), Afrikan American companies with **all natural** products for your crowning glory. And if your crown has lost its glory, or its glory is too short for your preference, *Hairobics* is extremely successful at speeding or resurrecting hair growth of prematurely bald heads or short hair. Both product lines help your scalp heal itself. Even if you're not ready to go natural, you still oughta be using natural hair products and eating natural organic food and living in touch with Nature, and...oops –I'm getting carried away. But truthfully, you cannot really have "good hair" without "good health" –for your *external* hair/scalp/skin reflects your *internal* state of health! Your diet affects both. Among other topics, nutrition & health is addressed in my book, *Drugs Masquerading as Foods.*

"Bush" and "Braids"

Other ways of wearing spiral hair in its natural form include the "Bush" and "Braids." Bushes are easy to manage. Braids can have as much or more variety than straightened hair. And there is no such thing as "*French* braids"; such was originated by Afrikans –they are "Afrikan braids." Bonner's ***Plaited Glory*** will tickle you silly while educating you in this serious ancient Afrikan tradition.

Lori A. Creighton

The lovelocked antennae of Ooausha and Irasha forms a heart

2

Ancient Egypt was a *Black* Afrikan Civilization, –not *White* or *Semite* or *Atlantean* or *Extraterrestrial*

Ancient Egypt (Kamit) was an indigenous Black Afrikan civilization. The word *Egypt* itself means Black!

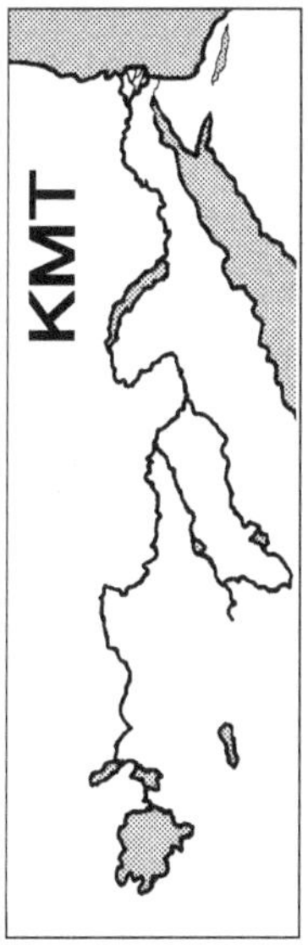

Despite overwhelming evidence for ancient Egypt's Black Afrikan identity, since the 19th century, white people claim Egypt as a white civilization. The next two sections summarizes 22 items of evidence for ancient Egypt's Black Afrikan identity.

1 **KAM (KM) was the strongest Egyptian term for *blackness*.**[1] Kamt means "jet black," states *The Egyptian Hieroglyphic Dictionary*.[2] Eminent historian Gerald Massey writes, "Kam is a name of Egypt and of the black or dark people."[3] The Afrikans of the Nile Valley called themselves Kam-Au (Black God People), and their country Kamit (Kmt), which means *both*, Land of the Blacks and the Black Land.[4]

2 **EGYPT means black!** The word *Egypt* and the variant Greek version *Aiguptos* (Aigyptos, Eguptos) mean *black*. Thus, *Egyptians* means Black People. *Egypt* and *Aiguptos* are derived from the Kamite word *Keb* (Kheb, Kep, Khept), signifying the Womb or Birthplace.[5] The Womb is dark, "The Deep," "a secret Deep that nobody can fathom," [6] hence Keb signifies *black*. Keb was also the mythological nether "Lower Egypt" of the *Amenta* underworld, a place of the blackest *unfathomable darkness* "until it was lighted by the nocturnal sun."[7] *Amenta* itself means the hidden land, and also signifies womb. Additionally, Keb was the name of Goddess Kheb who was the first Great Mother.[8] The words Gypsy, Copt, and Coptos (another word for Egypt) are also from Keb.[9]

1) Saakana, 102; Budge, EHD, 787b. 2) Ibid. 3) Massey, BB-vI, 453. 4) Amen, MN-vI, 26, 212; Browder, NV, 52. 5) Massey, AE, 303. 6) Ibid., 278. 7) Ibid., 638, 651. 8) Ibid., 123, 279, 303, 308. 9) Massey, BB-vI, 229.

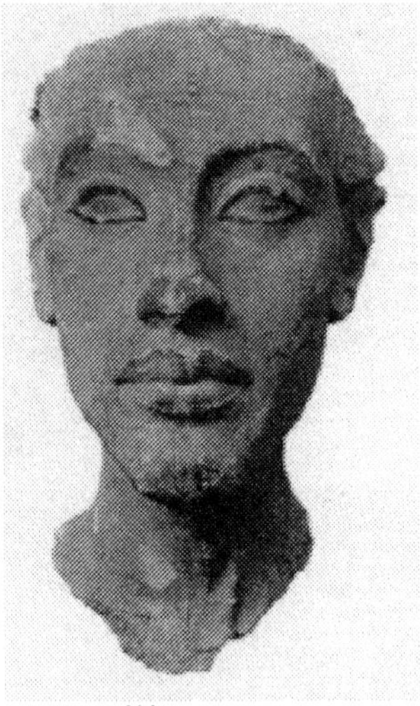

Akhenaton

3 **NILE also means black!** The name of the *Nile*, the world's longest river, is from *Nilo* which means black. This is one of a "number of trifling circumstances which constantly occur to prove the identity of the Egyptians, or rather the Ethiopians," [1] writes eminent historian, Sir Godfrey Higgens. He states that whenever the Arabs, Hebrews, Greeks, and Latins "have wished to translate the word Nil, they have always made use of a word which in their language signifies black." Hence, Sichor (Hebrew), Nuchul (Ethiopian), Melo (ancient Latin), Melas (Greek).

4 **Ancient, eye-witness European historians reported the Egyptians were black skinned.** Europe's first historian, Herodotus (in Histories, Book II) wrote: "The Colchians, Egyptians and Ethiopians have thick lips, broad nose, woolly hair and they are of burnt skin." [2] Greek writers always mention the ancient Egyptians as being *black* in their complexions.[3] Other ancient eye-witness Greek, Roman, and Hebrew historians also said the ancient Egyptians were "black and woolly-haired." There are *no* records of any ancient documents describing the Egyptians as a white, red, yellow people. It is true that the Afrikans of the Nile Valley sometimes portrayed themselves "red." These "red Egyptians" were Afrikans who *painted* their bodies red –a custom still practiced in Afrika today.

5 **The high melanin content in the skin of "mummies" from Egypt and Ethiopia proves they were Black Afrikans.**[4] Sculptural and skeletal remains indicate the same. Egyptians even made wigs from sheep's *wool* to match their *woolly* hair! The whitewashed history books favor showing Egyptian images with Caucasoid features. They go out of their way to avoid showing the abundant Africoid, dredlocked images of the early indigenous Egyptians, and the Egyptian mummies having nappy hair.

6 **Ancient bones yield evidence:** Eminent historian, Gerald Massey writes: "Captain Burton wrote to me in 1883, saying, '*You are quite right about the African origin of the Egyptians, and I have sent home a hundred skulls to prove it.*' (Does anyone know what became of these skulls?)" [5] In answer to Gerald's question, the skulls –like numerous other evidence proving ancient Egypt's Afrikan identity –were "blacked out" by whites; perhaps secreted away or destroyed. Like Massey, Godfrey Higgens also cites evidence from another source; "Dr. Pritchard ...has also shewn, in a very satisfactory manner, that the ancient Egyptians, the masters of Thebes, were Negroes -or, that they were black, with curly heads." [6] "Dr. Pritchard has most clearly proved, as I have stated...that the ancient Egyptians were Negroes." [7] Whatever happened to Pritchard's body of data? –the same thing that happened to Burton's hundred Africoid skulls.

1) Higgens, vI, 135. 2) Saakana, 7. 3) Higgens, vI, 434. 4) Barnes, MCK, 35. 5) Massey, AE, 255. 6) Higgens, vI, 286. 7) Ibid., 434.

7 **The Bible identifies Egypt as a Black Afrikan nation by calling it *HAM*; –using *Ham* and *Egypt* synonymously** (Ps. 78:51; 105:23, 27; 106:21, 22). Ham, one of Noah's sons, is the biblical progenitor of Black nations (Gen. 10:6,7). The Hebrew word Ham is derived from the Egyptian word Kham /Chem (meaning Black), a fact deliberately obscured by scholars, along with innumerable similar facts.[1] Massey writes, "Ham is modified from Kam."[2]

8 **And why are there no camels in Egyptian hieroglyphics?** "If the Egyptians were of Asiatic origin, how comes it that the Camel has no place among the hieroglyphics? No representation of the camel is found on the monument. It will be seen when we come to consider the origin and nature of the typology and hieroglyphic that this is almost an impossibility for any but an African people. The camel being a late importation into Egypt and other African countries, will alone explain its absence from the pictures of an African people."[3]

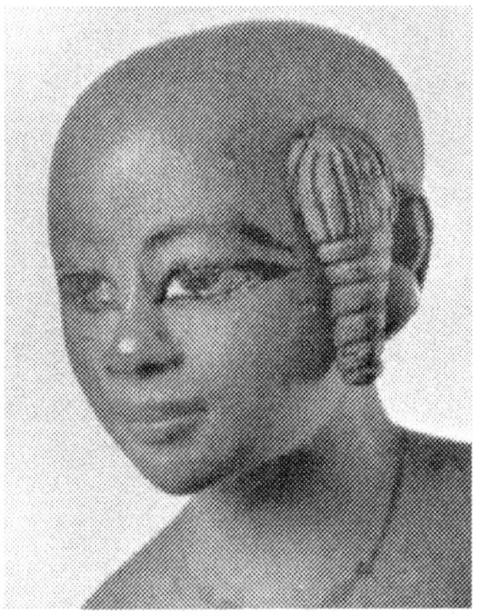

Heru Lock (Horus Lock)

9 **The key aspects of Egyptian culture were identical with that of other Afrikan cultures.** Near-nudity, as found in Egyptian paintings, is an Afrikan custom still practiced today, including painting the body red. "The African custom of children going undressed until they attained the age of puberty, was also continued by the Egyptians. Princesses went as naked as commoners; royalty being no exception to the rule."[4] "The single Horus-lock, the Rut, worn as a divine sign by the child-Horus in Egypt, is a distinguishing characteristic of the Afrikan people, among whom were the Libyans who shaved the left side of the head, except the single lock that remained drooping down. This was the emblem of Horus the Child, continued as the type of childhood from those children of the human race, the Afrikans.[5]

Twa God, Bes

10 **The dwarf statue of Egyptian gods proves their Afrikan origin from the "little Blacks,"** called the "**Twa**" by the Kamites. "Pygmy" is a derisive label from whites. The descendants of these same whites have proven that the Pygmies of Afrika are the ancestors of all of humanity. This truth was taught by the Egyptians themselves, and the oldest gods of Egypt are represented as dwarfs. An example is BES, whose facial features are also undeniably Africoid. Whites evade such evidence by classifying the Pygmies as Caucasian, as we shall soon see (page 19).

11 **The testimony of Astrology and Manetho.** The science of Astrology or the Zodiac originated in Afrika, reaching its zenith in ancient Egypt. This science is at least 52,000 years old by virtue of the Precession. It takes 26,000 years for one "turn" of the Zodiac. The Afrikans determined this by direct observation. The Kamite priest/historian Manetho gave a historical list of Egypt's dynasties stretching back some 25,000 years.[6]

1) Amen, MN-vI, 25, 26; Massey, BB-vI, 456. 2) Massey, BB-vI, 456. 3) Ibid., 12, 13. 4) Ibid., 19. 5) Ibid., 18, 19. 6) King, AOB, 53.

More evidence:

Egyptian civilization originated from Nubia, which originated from Central Afrika, home of the *Twa*

The Nile is the world's longest river system (4,150 miles). Afrika's Nile Valley Civilization, like the silt-rich Nile that sustained it, originated in the heart of Afrika and flowed from the South to the North, which was marshland or covered with the sea at one time. Nile Valley Civilization included Nubia (Ethiopia), its source. The ancient Egyptians came from the Nubians, who originated from the Twa People of Central Afrika. Nubia is from Egyptian *Nub* or *Neb*, meaning gold. Nubia was the land of gold. Ancient Egyptian / Nubian civilization has an earlier beginning with the Twa People (Pygmies) of inner Afrika, as the following evidence indicates.

12 Nubia's other names reveal its Afrikan roots:

Ethiopia: a name once referring to all of Afrika, allegedly from Greek *ethios* (burnt) and *ops* (face), to signify "burnt face" people. In his incredible book *The Black Truth*, Asar Jubal undeniably proves the true etymology "Ethiopia." He shows that *Ethiopia* and *Utopia* are variants of the same word, derived from Afrikan roots signifying *Watery Beginning*, pointing to Central Afrika, location of the Mountains of the Moon. Note this applies to the *womb*, the original "Utopia," or *wet* Womb of the Great Mother, Source of Life, personified on Earth as the area of the sacred Mountains of the Moon at the Great Lakes of Central Afrika. This place was anciently (and still today) regarded as the birthplace of Man, a word derived from the same root as Moon.

Abyssinia: Abyssinia and "abyss" are undoubtedly from the same roots. Like *Egypt* & *Ethiopia*, Abyssinia is derived from a name or title of the Great Mother as "The Abyss" or "The Deep," –the uterine Source of Life or Womb of the Great Mother. Abyss is likely Egyptian Ab-Ash (Ab=heartsoul, first ancestor, water. Ash = essence, issue, vase, Tree of Life, and As-t /Isis).

Cush: means *black* and is an ancient name for Ethiopia.[2] Massey derives Kush from Khepsh, an earlier form of Khept (Egypt).[3]

Kep-Kep: an ancient name for Nubia.[4] "Kep" was an ancient name for Egypt (see item #2 in the previous section)

13 "Upper Egypt" is *south* into Nubia where the major Nile cataracts are located.

This is also where most of the greatest structures of Nile Valley civilization were erected. And it is through the same Nubia that the Nile River and its tributaries flow before they reach "Lower Egypt."[5] In Nile Valley Contributions to Civilization, one of the clearest books on the subject, Tony Browder writes: "Nubia was the lifeline of ancient Kemet, and the source of its language, philosophy and religion. For more than three thousand years of Pharaonic rule, Nubia played a pivotal role in the development and maintenance of its daughter nation Kemet..."[6]

1) Jubal, 21-14. 2) Higgens, vI, 54. 3) Massey, BB-vII, 282. 4) Massey, AE, 303. 5) Saakana, 10. 6) Browder, NV, 57.

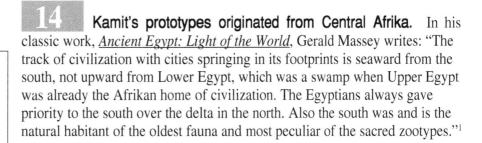

14 **Kamit's prototypes originated from Central Afrika.** In his classic work, Ancient Egypt: Light of the World, Gerald Massey writes: "The track of civilization with cities springing in its footprints is seaward from the south, not upward from Lower Egypt, which was a swamp when Upper Egypt was already the Afrikan home of civilization. The Egyptians always gave priority to the south over the delta in the north. Also the south was and is the natural habitant of the oldest fauna and most peculiar of the sacred zootypes."[1]

"The oldest and most peculiar images in the Ideographs point backward toward the equatorial land of the hippopotamus, rhinoceros, giraffe, ostrich, camelopard, ibis, various cranes... The symbolism of Egypt represented in the hieroglyphics has its still earlier phase extant amongst the Bushmen... But, beyond this art...they have a system of typology to the most primitive nature; one in which the animals, reptiles, birds and insects are themselves the living, talking types, by the aid of which the earliest men of our race would seem to have 'thinged' their thoughts in the birthplace of typology. In the 'fables' of the Bushmen, the hieroglyphics are the living things that enact the representations." [2]

Massey summarizes "a few of the pre-Egyptian evidences for the Inner African beginnings" of Nile Valley civilization. He shows "the southern origin of the Egyptian mythology" based on information about Egypt's goddess, gods, symbols and various customs. "The sycamore fig of Hathor and the palm tree of Taht were imported into Egypt from Central Africa...The hoes and wooden stands for head-rests used by the Egyptians have their prototypes among the East Central African tribes...One might fill a volume with figures from Inner Africa that were developed and made permanent in the symbolism of Egypt...The mythology, religious rites, totemic customs, and primitive symbolism of Egypt are crowded with survivals from identifiable Inner African origins." [3]

Whites even deny the Black Afrikan identity of the Pygmies, classifying them as "Caucasoid"

"Like their relatives the Bushmen, pygmies are caucasoid people: thin-lipped, light-skinned, often blue-eyed. Anthropological [i.e., *white*] investigations show the pygmies were not true primitives but remnants of a formerly sophisticated race, the proto-Berber people inhabiting what Hallet called 'old white Africa.' Pygmies have about the same stature as Egyptian mummies; the ancient Egyptians were not large people." [6] (emphasis added)

15 **Twa (Pygmy) evidence.** Re-read the last two sentences in the previous paragraph. "One might fill a volume....." Well Jeane-Pierre Hallet did just that with his book, *Pygmy Kitabu.* He spent 20 years studying the Pygmies. He shows that **Egyptian theology, cosmology, mythology, etc., originated from East Central Afrika –from the Pygmies** (their true name is the ***Twa***), whose *ologies* are essentially the same. Even the names of the gods and goddesses are similar. The ancient Egyptians themselves documented this in their hieroglyphic writings and portrayal of their gods such as Bes. **"The Egyptians placed their ancestral paradise in the heart of Pygmy territory at the source of the Nile."** [4] Hallet's book though, has one serious flaw: he classifies the Pygmies as Caucasoid![5] He then goes on to say that the Egyptians, Massai, and other Afrikan groups are all Caucasoid since they descended from the Twa. Modern (white) science has proven that all races are from the Twa. Based on such reasoning, everybody in the world is Caucasian. The fact is, everybody is Afrikan or Afrikan descendants!

Twa (Pygmies) are classified as "Caucasoid." In his book, Hallet shows photos of the "little whites" he warmly writes about, distinguishing them from the "Negroes." All the *big whites* and *Negroes* I asked about the racial identity of Hallet's friends identified them as Blacks without hesitation.

1) Massey, AE, 255. 2) Massey, BB-vI, 20. 3) Massey, AE, 250-255. 4) Hallet, 116. 5) Ibid., 5-9, 28-30. 6) Walker, WE, 831.

16 **The earliest "Egyptian" gods are Ethiopian.** Eminent historian, John Jackson writes: "Since civilization in Africa originated south of the equator, the earliest Nilotic polar gods were those relating to the South Pole. Khnumu was the God of the South Pole...He was called the Lord of Nubia and was depicted as ram-headed." [1] Kamit's theological Trinity, *Ast, Asar,* and *Heru* (Isis, Osiris, Horus), can be traced back to its *Ethiopian ancestors* (which can be traced back further to *Pygmy ancestors*). Herodotus observed that these were the only gods worshiped in the Nubian city of Meroe, in contrast to the multitude of deities worshiped by the Kamites. Cooke notes, "The singular paucity of gods may well argue an older tradition than any of which Egypt could boast." [2]

17 **Wet Greek evidence.** In Book of the Beginnings, vol. 1, Massey writes, "We see, by the Greek report, the Egyptians knew that Egypt was once all sea or water. Herodotus says the whole of Egypt (except the province of Thebes) was an extended marsh...A persistent Greek tradition asserts that the primitive abode of the Egyptians was in AEthiopia, and mention is made of an ancient city of Meroe, from which issued a priesthood who were the founders of the Egyptian civilization. Meroe, or in Egyptian Muru, means the maternal outlet, therefore the birthplace, which was typified by the Mount Muru. The modernised form of Muru or Meroe, is Balua.

"Ba-rua (Eg.) also yields the place of outlet. And this place may be pursued according to the African naming up to the Rua mountains and the outlets of the lakes. The Hebrew tradition manifestly derives the Egyptians from above [southern] and not from lower [northern] Egypt. "I will bring again the captivity of Egypt, and will cause them to return into the land of Pathros [Upper Egypt, southern Egypt]; into the land of their habitation [Ezekiel 29:14]." [3]

18 **Nubian artifacts support Egypt's Nubian origin.** The cover story of the New York Times (March 1, 1979), *Ancient Nubian Artifacts Yield Evidence of Earliest Monarchy*, recounted the archaeological discovery of Dr. Keith Seele who served as the director of the University of Chicago's Oriental Institute Nubian Expedition in 1962. Professors Keith Seele and Bruce Williams discovered artifacts in Nubia which supported the predynastic birthplace of a pharaonic civilization in the ancient Nubian city of Qustul. Although the discoveries were made around 1964, the news of the find was not made public until 1979.[4] More than 5,000 artifacts were unearthed by Seele's team during their digs in a section of Nubia which was soon to be flooded by the rising waters of Lake Nasser, which was created by the newly constructed Aswan High Dam. Williams concluded that Nubia can no longer be looked upon as an appendage of Egyptology or as a stepsister to Kamit, but as an independent field of archaeological study. The greatest concentration of Afrikan artifacts and skeletal remains have been uncovered in southern Egypt, by way of the Sudan, showing the direction from which the first Egyptians originated.

1) Jackson, CBC, 145. 2) Ibid., 91. 3) Massey, BB-vI, 34. 4) Browder, NV, 53.

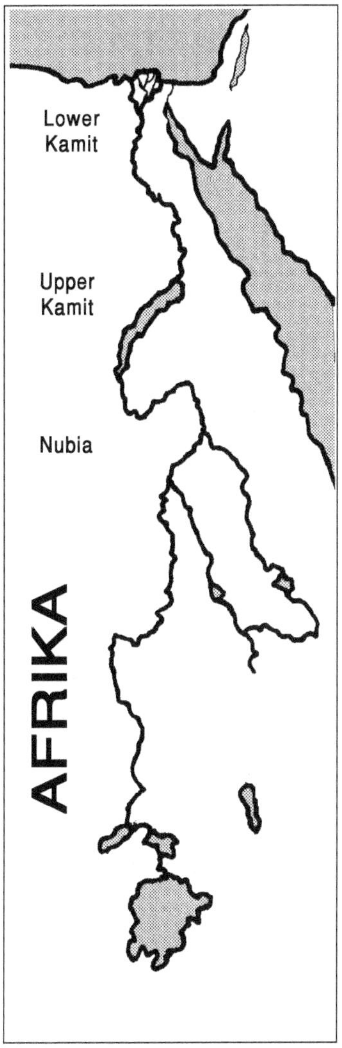

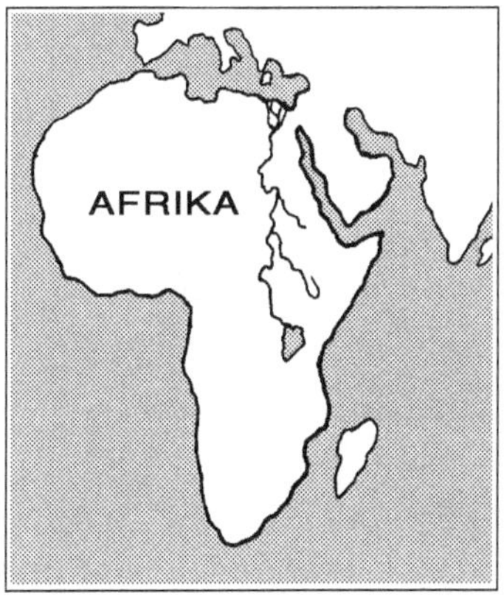

19 **The ancient Egyptians themselves claimed origination from the South.** Eminent historian Cheik Anta Diop writes: "Egyptians themselves –who should surely be better qualified than anyone to speak of their origin –recognize without ambiguity that their ancestors came from Nubia and the heart of Africa. The land of the Amam, or land of the ancestors..., the whole territory of Kush [Nubia] south of Egypt, was called land of the gods by the Egyptians." [1]

"Khenti" is the Egyptian word for both *origin* and *south*. "Khent the southern land, the name for farthest south, which can now be traced as far as Ganda (the U-ganda), means the inner land, the feminine abode, the birthplace, and the lake country." [2] The earliest Egyptian documents recount stories of their early history and southern origin. According to the famous record found in the Temple of Horus at Edfu, their civilization was brought from the south by a group of invaders under the leadership of King Horus.[3] Diodorus Siculus said the Ethiopians were the earliest of civilized men, and that they colonized Egypt under the leadership of Osiris. Then the Egyptians diffused Ethiopian culture throughout the world.[4]

In the Papyrus of Hunefer at the London Museum, eminent Egyptologist, Dr. Yosef ben-Jochannan quotes what the ancient Egyptians wrote of their origins: **"we came from the beginning of the Nile** where God Hapi dwells, at the foothills of The Mountains of the Moon." [5] Where begins the Nile? At its farthest point, it begins in Uganda from Africa's largest lake, called *Nyanza* by the natives, *Victoria* by colonists. And in this area, the Ki-Swahili word *Kilimanjaro,* and the Buganda word *Ruwenzori* both mean "Mountain of the Moon." [6] Ruwenzori also means "Rain Maker." Egyptologist historian, Gerald Massey writes: "The Egyptian record when correctly read will tell us plainly that the human birthplace was a land of the papyrus reed, the crocodile, and hippopotamus; a land of the great lakes in Karua [the lake country]...or in Apta at the horn point of the earth–that is, in Equatoria, from whence the sacred river ran to brim the valley of the Nile with plenty." [7]

The Bible and Jewish tradition gives evidence of Egypt's Southern, Ethiopian origin. Ezekiel 29:13,14 states "I will gather the Egyptians...And I will bring again the captivity of Egypt, and will cause them to return into the land of Pathros, into their habitation [origin]." Jeremiah 44:15 reads "even all the people that dwelt in the land of Egypt, in Pathros." Pathros is the birthplace in the South, "Patoris" is the south country (Upper Egypt). The "path" of PATHros is derived from Egyptian Peth/Pet (opening, crib, birthplace), source of Hebrew Puth (opening, birthplace). The "ros" of PathROS is from Egyptian RUS (south, southern).[8]

1) Diop, AO, 150. 2) Massey, BB-vI, 16. 3) Browder, NV, 48. 4) Jackson, CBC, 182; Massey, BB-v1, 21. 5) Browder, NV, 48. 6) Ibid., 46. 7) Massey, AE, 255. 8) Massey, BB-v1, 34.

20 **Historians confirm the Nubian /Ethiopian origin of Kamit (ancient Egypt).** In *The African Origin of Civilization*, Cheikh Anta Diop writes, "...all the earliest scholars who studied Nubia, even those to whom we owe the discovery of Nubia archeology (such as Cailliaud) conclude that Nubia had priority...Their studies indicate that Egyptian civilization descended from that of Nubia, in other words, Sudan. ...Cailliaud bases this argument on the fact that in Egypt all the objects of worship (thus, the essence of sacred tradition) are Nubian..." [1]

Greek historian, Diodorus Siculus also claimed that Egyptian civilization came from Nubia, the center of which was Meroe. "In fact, by following data provided by Diodorus and Herodotus on the site of that Sudanese capital, Cailliaud (circa 1820) discovered the ruins of Meroe: 80 pyramids, several temples consecrated to Amon, Ra, ad so on." [2] According to him, the Nubians (Ethiopians) were the earliest of civilized men, and after they colonized Egypt, the Egyptians diffused this Ethiopian culture to all part of the world.[3] "Juba, the Numidian king and writer, says: 'The Ethiopians assert that Egypt is one of their colonies; there are striking likenesses between the laws and customs of both lands; the kings wear the same dress and the uraeus adorns their diadem.'" [4]

21 **Kamit's linguistic links between other Afrikan languages are easy to prove.** Scholar N. Reich compared Egyptian roots with other linguistic roots still used by the Black populations of Central Afrika and Nubia. He showed without difficulty that they were absolutely identical.[5] Similarly, Professor Theophile Obenga "demonstrates conclusively the genetic linguistic links between ancient Kemit and African languages, a conclusion long ago projected and researched by Cheikh Anta Diop." [6] In *Book of the Beginnings*, Massey compares the Afrikan language of ancient Egypt with that of other Afrikan languages. He shows that their undeniable similarity points back to a common Afrikan beginning for all of them. Yet the dictionary calls Egyptian and certain other Afrikan languages "Afro-Asiatic" languages. This is done to subtract or steal credit from Afrika and give it to Europeans.

22 **The Sphinx's "water marks" proves it is at least 10,000 years old.** Groved water marks on the Sphinx and especially in the rocks near the Sphinx undeniably points to antiquity dating back to the time when the Sahara was not a desert but a rainy tropical paradise. The last time there was this much water in this part of Afrika was over 10,000 years ago. (This subject is addressed in volume II. For more information: John West's article in *Conde Nast* Magazine, February 1993.)

1) Diop, AO, 149, 150. 2) Diop, AO, 150. 3) Jackson, CBC, 182. 4) Parker, CS, 7. 5) Diop, AO, 153. 6) Saakana, xvii; Browder, NV, 20.

Whites blew off the Africoid nose of the Sphinx! –and destroyed much ancient Africoid art and archives

Carved from solid rock, the Sphinx portrays an Afrikan Pharaoh. The nose is missing because Europeans (Napoleon's soldiers), in an effort to obscure powerful, blatant, undeniable evidence of Black Afrikan achievement, blew off the broad Africoid nose and part of the generous lips with cannon fire! The *Los Angeles Times* (June 4, 1990) actually reported that "When Napoleon visited the Sphinx in 1798, everything but the head was buried in sand...his soldiers reputedly used the Sphinx for target practice." While the Sphinx had already suffered nose damage prior to Napoleon, the greatest destruction took place during Napoleon's occupation of Egypt, as documented by Tony Browder, and testified by the collection of Sphinx portraits he has assembled on page 225 of his book *Nile Valley Contributions to Civilization*. These six portraits, drawn over a period of 100 years from 1698 to 1798, are the only current evidence available which shows the progression of the nose destruction. Besides the Sphinx, a large percentage of Africoid Kamite statues are missing their noses, whereas European-looking figures are intact. Faces of Africoid sculptures were also altered to appear Caucasoid by Kamit's European conquerors. A Sphinx statue on display in the British Museum actually admits that the "face of the stature was reworked" during the Roman occupation of Egypt. Reporting on the "riddle" of the racial identity of the ancient Egyptians, Count C. Volney, a distinguished French scholar who visited Egypt in the late 1700s, wrote with astonishment "...when I visited the Sphinx, its appearance gave me the key to the riddle. Beholding that head typically Negro in all its features..." He later added "...the Egyptians were true Negroes of the same type as all native-born Africans." The Sphinx's broad nose, full lips, and prognathism are evident in an early drawing of the Sphinx as it was found by the French in the late 1700s.

The Sphinx, currently.

Early drawing of the Sphinx shows its Africoid features.

Their white plaster fell off centuries later, exposing the blacked-out truth

Tired from the hard work of defacing inumerable Afrikan monuments, whites covered them with plaster which fell off centuries later...exposing the stone evidence. Solid stone *endures*, but plaster and stucco are impermanent and will crack off in time –to expose what they have been hiding and, to the chagrin of the guilty, perfectly *preserving* for future generations to witness. The Afrikans of the Nile Valley had built their temples so well, even carving many out of solid rock, that it was often impossible to destroy them. Whites hadn't developed the use of dynamite yet, so they attempted destruction through manually chiseling away at the stone evidence in their campaigns of cultural destruction. This work proved not only ineffective, but too hard and exhausting, particularly under the desert sun, so they resorted to other methods. On pages 165-166 of *The Historical Jesus, and the Mythical Christ*, historian Gerald Massey reports the coverups perpetrated by European cultural criminals:

> "In some of the ancient Egyptian temples the Christian iconoclasts, when tired with hacking and hewing at the symbolic figures incised in the chambers of imagery, and defacing the most prominent features OF THE MONUMENTS, FOUND THEY COULD NOT DIG OUT THE HIEROGLYPHICS, AND TOOK TO COVERING them over with plaster; and this plaster, intended to hide the meaning and stop the mouth of the stone word, has served to preserved the ancient writings as fresh in hue and sharp in outline as when they were first cut and colored."

Similarly, he continues, the temples were invaded and taken over "by connivance of Roman power." But these temples were enduring, "not built but quarried out the solid rock." The Europeans covered the front of these temples with white stucco and later reopened them as Christian churches. "And all the time each nook and corner was darkly alive with the presence and proofs of the earlier gods, even though the hieroglyphics remained unread. But *stucco* is not for lasting wear ; it cracks and crumbles, sloughs off, and slinks away into its natal insignificance; the rock is the sole true foundation, the rock is the record in which we reach reality at last."

The stone indeed was the truth, and like the truth, it endured; but the plaster was a lie, and lies never have permanence. All the lies and layers of lies perpetrated and refined by successive generations of dishonest Europeans are fated for the same destiny as the stucco plaster.

The willful, systematic destruction of Africoid art has also occurred in the Americas, Asia and India

Inscriptions and hieroglyphics are defaced or bleached, Africoid noses are shot off or chiseled down, confusing nomenclatures are pasted over the evidence, photos are taken from misleading angles or filters, and often, Africoid evidence is outright destroyed. In temples and monuments of great beauty and durability where destruction was less desirable than claiming the achievements as their own, Europeans replaced the Afrikan inscriptions with new ones which credited themselves for the achievement.

"Hand in hand with the enslavement of African people came the destruction of African civilization and the loss of a culture, which the European would later say never existed." [1] Dr. John Henrik Clarke states, "There has been a deliberate destruction of African culture and the records relating to that culture. This destruction started with the first invaders of Africa. It continued through the period of slavery and the colonial system. It continues today on a much higher and more dangerous level. There are now attempts on the highest academic level to divide African history and culture within Africa in such a manner that the best of it can be claimed for Europeans, or at the very least, Asians. That is the main purpose of the Hamitic and the Semitic hypothesis in relationship to African history.'" [2]

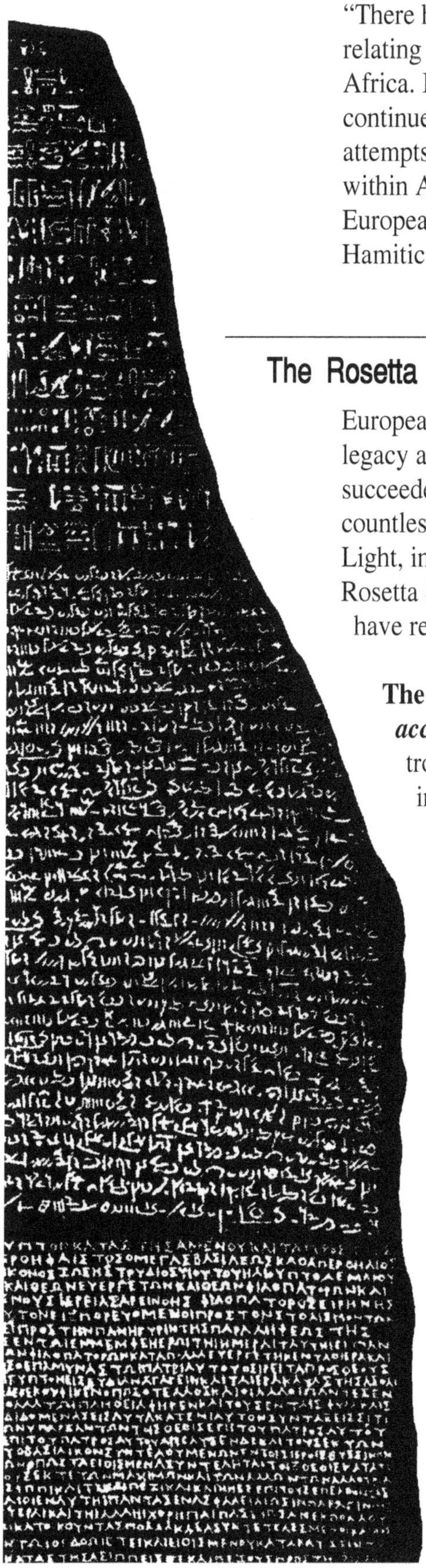

The Rosetta Stone unlocked Kamit's ancient lost suppressed language

Europeans tried with all their might to destroy the evidence of Black Egypt's legacy and its originating role in world civilization and religion. They almost succeeded. They burned major libraries of Afrikan archives, destroyed countless temples, killed countless people. They turned Egypt the Land of Light, into the Land of Darkness. Had it not been for the discovery of the Rosetta Stone in 1799, Kamit's early history and astounding legacy would have remained buried in the ruins of its demolished temples.

The Rosetta Stone was a slab of black basalt stone was found by ***accident*** (nothing really happens "by accident") in 1799 by French troops digging trenches near Rosetta, Egypt. Carved on it was an inscription duplicated in three languages: Egyptian sacred hieroglyphics, demotic Egyptian characters, and Greek. By comparing the Greek translation with the Egyptian, the French linguist, Jean Champollion in 1822, discovered the vital clue to translating the Metu Neter (Writing of the Gods), the mysterious sacred hieroglyphics of Kamit (ancient Egypt).

For the first time in modern history, it became possible to decipher the mysterious, unknown, sacred language of Egypt. "And so the lost history of old Egypt began to unfold before the eyes of an astonished world...Until the discovery of the Rosetta Stone, the history of the Land of Ham had remained buried in the ruins of the Nile Valley produced there by the Roman Army...The fanatical Romanists that buried that now famous Rosetta Stone never dreamed that the day would come when it would rise up from its grave and become the Nemesis of their beloved institution, which so greatly fears the purging effect of the Light of Knowledge." [3]

1) Browder, NV, 36. 2) Ibid., 36. 3) Hotema, GC, 27, 28.

The European Quantum Theft of Kamit (Ancient Egypt)

"Aryan Egyptians":

Whites ever strive to Europeanize Kamit and divorce it from Afrika in order to discredit and inferiorize Blacks while stealing credit for themselves.

White historians stole Egypt from Afrika. Black historians are putting it back. Universities and colleges maintain an artificial separation of Egypt from Afrika by separating "Egyptian Studies" from "African Studies." Museums do the same with their displays, as do dictionaries and history / mythology books. Egypt is physically in Afrika, not Asia, yet white academia classifies it with Asia; they do no such thing to England and other islands which, even though physically separated from Western Asia, are classified with Europe.

The term "Afroasiatic" is one of the latest manipulations by whites to undermine Afrikan legacy

The term "Afroasiatic" is a misnomer, deliberately propagated by white scholars to detach Egypt from Afrika,[1] and whiten, diffuse, and obscure Afrikan legacy. "Afroasiatic" is in dictionaries and attempts to discredit Afrika by labeling certain Afrikan languages and cultures as "Afroasiatic." For example, the indigenous Afrikan language of Nubia (Ethiopia), and Kamit (ancient Egypt) are falsely called "Afroasiatic." So-called "Asians" (whites) had nothing to do with these languages, which were already old when Europeans were still uncivilized nomads. These "Asian nomads" did nothing to create the advanced civilizations of Afrika, India and the Middle East, but they did everything to destroy them.

Whites exclude Blacks from Kamit, their own country

Not only do whites (Egyptologists, anthropologists, archeologists, esotericists, and other "ists") exclude Egypt from Afrika through "ingenious anthropological manipulations," and false evidence, they also exclude Black people from Egypt itself. "Ancient Egypt was stolen from Africa by nineteenth century Egyptologists whose doctrine was nourished by the African slave trade" wrote James Spady.[2] Dr. Henrik Clarke stated: "There are now attempts on the highest academic level to divide African history and culture within Africa in such a manner that the best of it can be claimed for Europeans, or at the very least, Asians. That is the main purpose of the Hamitic and the Semitic hypothesis in relationship to African history."[3]

Professor J. Abayomi Cole wrote: "When it became evident that the roots of civilization in Africa could not be totally eradicated, there was an attempt to mislead the public into thinking that Egypt was not a part of Africa. (The 'New American Version' of the 'Holy Bible' has removed mention of Egypt and placed all events in the Middle East. [!]) When this attempt at geographical deception failed and even until this very day, historians and anthropologist[s] attempt to represent the ancient Egyptians as people of European descent. They went so far as to place a blond wig on the mummy of Rameses II."[4]

1) Saakana, xvii. 2) Diop, CU, 209. 3) Browder, NV, 36. 4) Cole/Andoh, AG, 58.

In classifying Egypt as part of Asia to dissociate it from Afrika, whites still have not succeeded in divorcing Egypt from Afrikan roots, for the ancient civilizations of the Middle East were also Black, founded by Black Afrikans. The original people of near east Asia were the Sumerians, who called themselves the "Black-Heads." These Afrikan migrants founded the rich Black cultures of Mesopatamia which included the ancient Babylonians, Chaldeans, Canaanites, and Phoenicians. An examination of Canaanite / Babylonian culture shows that its people were Afrikan-Kamite emigrants; their manner of dress, civilization, and art were hardly distinguishable from that of the Kamites.

Nefertiti was not that European-looking image projected as her likeness.

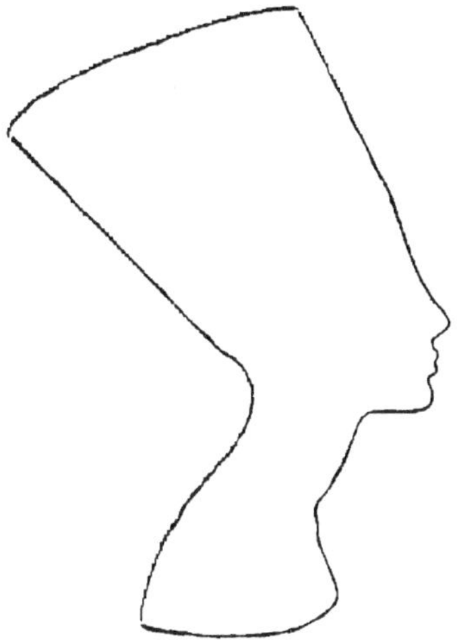

The debate over Queen Nefertiti's racial identity is part of the continuing attempt to Europeanize Kamit. Anthony Browder writes: "There is, however, no evidence linking Nefertiti to this image. This unidentified and unfinished sculpture was discovered in an abandoned art studio, in the city of Armana by professors Hermann Ranke and Ludwig Borchardt, during the excavations of 1912-1913. It was not shown publicly until 1920, when it was prominently displayed in the Berlin Museum. This bust was assumed to have been an image of Queen Nefertiti because it was wearing the royal crown and was decorated with semi precious stones, which were also associated with royalty, but there is no physical evidence to support that assumption." [1] John Anthony West stated: "The famous bust of Nefertiti, Akhenaten's wife...is in all likelihood not Nefertiti." [2]

The labeled statues and carvings of Nefertiti (wife of Akhenaton) differ greatly from the Euro-looking "Berlin Bust of Nefertiti." They show Nefertiti as she was, an unmistakably Afrikan woman. In an essay published in *Egypt Revisited*, Dr. Asa Hilliard commented on this curious anomaly: "Given the history of attempts in Germany, beginning in the mid 1700's, to degrade and to distort Kemetic history (Bernal, 1987), and given the racism permeating German culture at the time of the find of the bust, one must be very cautious with speculations by professors Ranke and Borchardt, and indeed the entire community of Egyptologists...It is an irony of ironies that the world 'knows' an alien woman and an alien image as the most famous symbol of Africa's Grand Golden Age!" [3]

1) Browder, NV, 144. 2) Sertima, ER, 234. 3) Ibid., 235.

"Atlantean Egyptians" and "Extraterrestrial Egyptians"

It seems that white writers, esoteric or otherwise, can't stand giving credit to Afrikans for their civilizing role in world history. They seek instead to give credit to themselves if possible, otherwise to credit other races or even extraterrestrials, –any people except indigenous nappy-haired Afrikans. They even label dark-skinned, nappy-haired people as "Caucasians." [1] In fact, whites have now manipulated the definition of *Caucasian* to include "brown-skinned, curly-haired people"! Look in a recent dictionary! Never mind that the ancient Egyptians (Kamites) portrayed themselves as Afrikans in their paintings, sculptures and reliefs. Never mind that the head of the Sphinx is clearly Afrikan despite its missing nose. Never mind that the body of the Sphinx is a lion and lions are indigenous to Afrika. Never mind that the sculptural, skeletal, and mummy evidence indicates the Kamites were indigenous Afrikans. So what that Kamit's language has been proven to be Afrikan. So what that the Kamites themselves claimed origination from Central Afrika; or that Kamitic civilization and cosmology were *matriarchal* and elevated *Goddesses*. This trait is never found in white or halfwhite (Semitic) cultures unless borrowed from Blacks.

The metaphysical books that promote Kamit as an Atlantean or extraterrestrial colony say nothing or extremely little about the Afrikans which were surely encountered when the Atlanteans or ETs arrived. But they are quick to cite and elaborate on the least bit of information relating to whites –or fabricate it. No one asks why the Atlanteans or ETs came to the Afrikans and not to the Europeans. No one asks why didn't the Atlanteans or ETs start a great civilization with white people in Europe or the Caucasus Mountains. Or, if whites were so advanced, why didn't they start a great civilization by themselves somewhere in Europe rather than Afrika, without the presence of any Black people around to spoil their claims to credit.

Let's suppose the European writers are correct that Atlantis established Egypt. Even so, after periodic world cataclysms (discussed in books like John White's *Pole Shift*, or books by Immanuel Velikovsky such as *Earth in Upheaval*), civilization around the globe on every continent suffered utter destruction. Always, it was the Black Afrikans that re-ignited civilization around the world. Even when Europe plunged into its Dark Age, again it was the very Black wooly haired Afrikans (the Moors) who rescued them.

Furthermore, if Egypt was Atlantean, it would have been patriarchal and very "technological"!

If the Egyptian civilization had developed from Atlanteans, it would have been patriarchal, plus highly technological with sophisticated machines. Mechanical technology was the hallmark of the Atlanteans, who destroyed themselves with their technological advances which had no matriarchal spiritual balance or respect for Nature. Ancient Egypt, like the rest of Afrika, honored and revered the Great Mother Goddess (and Father God).

1) Rogers, SR-vI, 38.

About those Atlanteans and ETs

Esoteric, metaphysical books by Europeans present Egypt as the product of extraterrestrial colonists, or as the product of an advanced super civilization which allegedly preceded it. Actually, there is undeniable evidence of "extraterrestrial presence," on this great planet, both currently and throughout humanity's past. There is also abundant evidence for supercivilizations stretching back eons, though this evidence is typically ignored or derided by modern orthodox historians. For example, there is evidence that a temple near the Sphinx, including the Sphinx itself, may be over 10,000 years old, pushing it into the era of legendary Atlantis. This temple has no hieroglyphics and is vastly different in construction from other temples of Afrika's Nile Valley. Likely, this temple and other similar structures were in fact, part of a prehistoric supercivilization which flourished throughout the *tropical* Sahara before it became a desert. And though it may have connections with "Atlantis" or other supercivilizations, this does not mean that those civilizations created it. As we shall see, there is abundant evidence that Black people played a key role wherever advanced ancient civilizations are found on the planet. This point is never (or rarely) mentioned by esoteric European writers who, if they mention indigenous Afrikans at all, typically do so with hints of derision. *Omission* however, seems to be their favorite ploy.

Thus, the esoteric books by metaphysical European writers are as one-sided, guilty, and racist as the academic books by orthodox European historians. Together on all levels (esoteric, spiritual, physical, academic, etc.), these books unite to complete the blackout of Afrikan peoples' legacy –or try to. The role of Afrika's Nile Valley Civilization with that of legendary supercivilizations and Extraterrestrials is addressed in volume II of *Blacked Out Through Whitewash.*

Egypt is in *Afrika*, not *Middle Asia* or the *Middle East!*

And the civilization of Kamit or ancient Egypt was the product of Black Afrikan People, not Caucasians, not Semites, not Asians, not Atlanteans, and not Extraterrestrials. In finding our roots, we have discovered that "Blacks had indeed invented civilization. The historical fact had been hidden in order to perpetrate the vicious propaganda of 'inherent Black inferiority,' "[1] wrote James Spady.

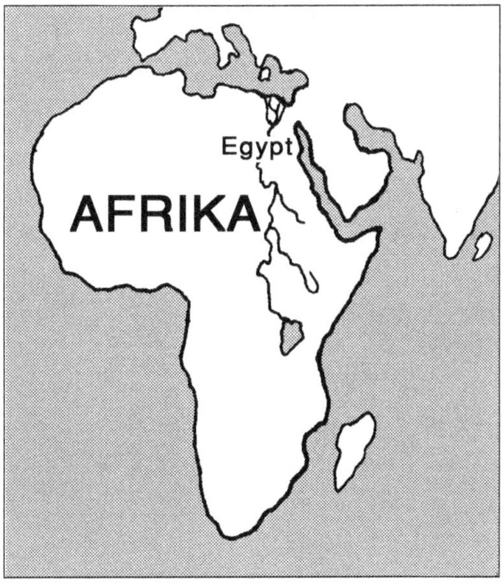

1) Diop, CU, 209.

Today, we are indebted to numerous Black historians, authors and educators who have re-established Egypt, that is, **Kamit**, as an integral part of the Black past. They include the following and many others:

Yosef ben-Jochannan	Locksley Geohagan	Patricia A. Newton
Cheikh Anta Diop	Legrand Clegg	Runoko Rashidi
Chancellor Williams	Yukiko Kudo	Asa Hilliard
George G. M. James	John Henrik Clarke	Elijah Muhammad
Anthony Browder	Richard King	J.A. Rogers
Ashra & Merira Kwesi	Ivan Van Sertima	John G. Jackson
Asar Jubal	Dadisi Sanyika	Nur Ankh Amen
Alfred & Bernice Ligon	Modupe Sais	Charles Finch

A rare handful of white historians and authors have also made outstanding contributions and have honored the truth despite the open racism which was vogue in their times. They include:

Gerald Massey	Albert Churchward
Kersey Graves	Godfrey Higgens
T.W. Doane	Count Volney

with due respect to Marlo Morgan, Ceanne DeRohan, Dorothy Blake Fardan, Michael Bradley and Martin Bernal.

Yes, Black, spiral-haired Afrikan people were the true authors of Nile Valley Super-Civilization. The ancestors of these same people were also key in the development of the other supercivilizations preceding that of the Nile Valley.

Further References

Books and videos well-documenting the"Kam-Au" (Divine Blacks) or original Egyptians, their culture and achievements include:

- *Egypt During the Golden Age* — (video) by Dr. Legrand Clegg
- *The Theft of Afrikan History & Spiritual Concepts* — (video) Ashra Kwesi
- *Nile Valley Contributions to Civilization* — by Anthony Browder
- *The Secret Waters of the Great Pyramid* — (video) Dr. Ridgely Abdul Mu'min
- *Egypt Revisited* — edited by Ivan Van Sertima
- *The Signs and Symbols of Primordial Man* — by Albert Churchward
- *Predynastic Egypt* — by James Brunson
- *Ancient Egypt, Light of the World* — by Gerald Massey
- *A Book of the Beginnings* — by Gerald Massey
- *Egyptian Temple: Mother of the Christian Church* — (video) Mathu Ater
- *The Ankh, African Origin of Electromagnetism* — by Nur Ankh Amen
- *Metu Neter (2 volumes)* — by Ra Un Nefer Amen

3

The Afrikan Origin of European Civilization

Western (white) civilization is founded on a Black Afrikan civilization

You may recall being taught in school that Western (white) civilization is founded upon the ancient Greek civilization which seemed to suddenly appear. What European historians are trying to diffuse, hide, or deny is that the Greek civilization was primarily the offspring of the advanced Black Afrikan Civilization of ancient Afrika's Nile Valley, which preceded it by thousands of years. Even Greek legends relate that Egyptian and Phoenician conquerors ruled all or parts of Greece until the 14th or 15th century B.C.

Afrika's Nile Valley Civilization was the progenitor of world civilization and the throne of ancient knowledge

The Nile Valley civilization of Egypt and Nubia was already old before Europe was born. The pyramids of Afrika's Nile Valley were hoary with age when the tribes of northern and central Europe were making their first stone hammers. Nile valley civilization also existed before the Western Asian civilization of the Tigris and the Euphrates rivers

In 1787, the distinguished French scholar, Count C. Volney, wrote in amazement: "this race of black men...is the very race to which we owe our arts, our sciences, and even the use of speech!" Later he wrote *Ruins of Empires*, a book which so delighted scholars of the day that it was translated into English with a "special edition" for the racist Americans, in which the following quotation was *left* out: "There are a people, now forgotten, discovered, while others were yet barbarians, the elements of the arts and sciences. A race of men rejected now for their black skin and woolly hair founded, on the study of the laws of Nature, those civil and religious systems which still govern the universe." [1]

In the scholarly classic, Anacalypsis, Godfrey Higgins writes, "I shall, in the course of this work, produce a number of extraordinary facts, which will be quite sufficient to prove, that a black race, in very early times, had more influence over the affairs of the world than has been lately suspected; and... the influence have not entirely passed away." [2]

1) Kush, 31. 2) Higgens, vI, 51.

As shown in Chapter 2, Kamite or Egyptian civilization originated from Ethiopia. Diodorus said the Ethiopians were the earliest of civilized men, and that they colonized Egypt under the leadership of Osiris. Then the Egyptians diffused Ethiopian culture throughout the world. In another classic, *The Signs and Symbols of Primordial Man*, Albert Churchward wrote: "Thus we can see that [Afrikan] colonies went forth and settled in all parts of the world, leaving the proofs in language, myth, and the hieroglyphics, in religious rites. The symbolical customs and ceremonies in far off lands are still extant among races by whom they are no longer read or understood, but which can be read in Egypt." [1]

Scottish anthropologist, General J. Forlong admits: "It was undoubtedly Kushites [Ethiopians] who rendered possible the Aryan advance, and who played the part of a civilizing Rome thousands of years before Rome's birth. ...it was their tales, myths, traditions and histories that lay at the base of the Western World's thought and legendary lore." [2]

Outstanding features

The ancient Kushite or Ethiopian culture may be called the Archaic Civilization. Outstanding features of this ancient cultural complex included:

1) The worship of The Great Mother Goddess.
2) Agriculture practiced by way of irrigation.
3) Astrology/astronomy or worship of the celestial bodies.
4) The practice of Mother-Right.
5) Building and carving in stone, hence the production of statues, temples, palaces and pyramids.
6) Mummification and Eschatology, which arises out of a deep love for Life, and an abhorrence for death.
7) Metal working, especially in iron and steel.
8) The making of pottery.
9) A profound respect, connection or kinship with Nature and Animals, hence the prevalence of Totemism (and plant/animal symbols in hieroglyphics).
10) The institution of Exogamy.
11) The institution of Divine Kingship and Queenship.

1) Churchward, SS, 284. 2) Jackson, CBC, 218.

So-called "Greek philosophy" is stolen Egyptian philosophy!

There is no such thing as "Greek philosophy." This deliberately misleading term is a deliberate misnomer serving to steal Afrikan credit. The true authors of "Greek philosophy" were not the Greeks but the ancient Black Afrikans of the Nile Valley, who had developed a complex religious system called the Mysteries, which was also the first system of salvation. The praise, credit, and honor falsely given to the Greeks for centuries, belongs to the Afrikans, the true originators.

The massive Greek plagiarism of Egyptian science, philosophy & religion is well documented by George James in *Stolen Legacy*

Egypt was the greatest educational center in the ancient world. Black Afrikans educated the Greeks. Black Egyptian priests and priestesses taught the best minds of Europe; Plato, Thales, Aristotle, Democritus, Anaximander, Solon and others. A surviving sculpture of Socrates shows that he was an Afrikan, as was Aesop of Aesop's fables. And historians wrote that such great lawgivers as Lykourgos studied in Egypt and brought back the legal and political basis for the West's politics.

In the introduction of *Stolen Legacy*, George James wrote: "After nearly five thousand years of prohibition against the Greeks, they were permitted to enter Egypt for the purpose of their education. First through the Persian invasion and secondly through the invasion of Alexander the Great. From the sixth century B.C. therefore to the death of Aristotle (322 B. C.) the Greeks made the best of their chance to learn all they could about Egyptian culture; most students received instructions directly from the Egyptian Priests, but after the invasion by Alexander the Great, the Royal temples and libraries were plundered and pillaged, and Aristotle's school converted the library at Alexandria into a research centre. There is no wonder then, that the production of the unusually large number of books ascribed to Aristotle has proved a physical impossibility, for any single man within a life time."

It was Afrikan Cosmology, called the Kamite Mysteries, which is the source and foundation of the all the religious teachings /philosophies throughout the world. A comprehensive book on this subject is Albert Churchward's, The Signs and Symbols of Primordial Man, with the subtitle: *The Evolution of Religious Doctrines from the Eschatology of the Ancient Egyptians.*

So-called "Greek & Roman gods" were copies of Afrikan gods

The earliest Greek & Roman gods were all Black, including the Trojan heroes! Europe loved and worshiped the Black Afrikan gods before later whitening them up as she developed racism. The early Greek-Roman gods & goddesses such as Athena, Zeus, etc., were all Black, being copies of the Black Afrikan deities. In the Campdoglio at Rome, the Goddesses Venus, Isis, Hecati, Juno, Metis, Ceres, and Cybele were Black.[1] Greek historian Herodotus himself wrote that "almost all of the names of gods came into Greece from Egypt." [2] **Ast (As-t, Asa, Ash) the Great Goddess,** was the Principal Goddess of Afrika –and the entire ancient world. Reknown as **Isis**, She was worshipped throughout ancient Greece, Rome, and Europe, from Alexandria to Britain. She is still worshipped today as Virgin Mary and the Black Madonnas of Europe. **The Aeneid, like the Illiad, Odyssey**, and all the other great epics of the world, is a poetic story dealing with Black people! Aeneas, the Trojan hero of Virgil's Aeneid, was in direct descent from Dardanus, the Afrikan founder of Troy. Helen Blavatsky informs us: "Herodotus acknowledges that the Greeks learned all they knew, including the sacred services of the temple, from the Egyptians, and because of that, their principal temples were consecrated to Egyptian divinities." [3] In Europe, Egyptian divinities were corrupted with Greek and Asiatic names and mythologies and reduced to vague pantheistic personalities, so that Isis and Osiris had retained very little of their Egyptian origin. Consequently, they failed to advance Egyptian Philosophy. [4]

Afrikan Deities	Greek Copy	Roman Copy	Description, Aspects
Ast	Isis	Isis	Principal Goddess. Other goddesses are versions of Her.
Hathor	Aphrodite	Venus	Goddess of Love, Beauty
Tannet	Gaia		Mother Earth, Nature, "Virgin Mother of God."
Tannet	Artemis	Dianna	Virgin Goddess of Hunting, Childbirth.
Kar	Kore /Demeter	Ceres	Heart of Earth. Goddess of Agriculture, Cereal.
Maat	Metis	Medusa	Goddess of Truth, Justice, Right, Balance. Serpent Goddess of Wisdom, slandered as Gorgon.
Neith	Athena	Minerva	Goddess of War, Wisdom, Crafts.
Asar (Ausar)	Osiris	Osiris	Principal God. The only God called God (Neter).
Asar / **Bes**	Dionysus	Bacchus	God of Wine, Sex, Fertility, Dance, Partying.
Amon	Zeus	Jupiter /Jove	King of the gods.
Djhuiti (Zehuti, Thoth, Anubis)	Hermes	Mercury	God of Commerce, Travel, Theft, Cunning, Science. Invention. Messenger of the gods.
Asar (Min)	Eros	Priapus	God of Sexual Love, Procreation. Guardian of Vinyards, gardens. Personified the Phallus.
Heru (Helu)	Horus / Helios	Heracles /Hercules	Sungod. God of Prophecy, Music, Medicine, Poetry.

1) Rogers, SR, 266. 2) Van Sertima, APEE, 213. 3) Blavatsky, IU-vI, 531. 4) James, SL, 37.

Afrikans originated the world's first known universities

The Temple-University of Luxor, ancient Egypt

Kamit, or ancient Egypt, was the greatest education center in the ancient world. Kamit's "Sacred Mystery Schools" were the first universities known to man. They had branches in other parts of the world, including China!

Estimated by computer analysis to have approached a mile in length, the temple-university of Luxor housed an elite faculty of priest-professors and catered to some 80,000 students at all grade levels! In ancient Afrika, Temples were at the center of religion, politics and education.

Afrikans gave us Math, Algebra, Geometry, and Trigonometry! — including the so-called *Arabic* & *Roman* Numbers!

The falsely credited Pythagoras and Euclid acquired their knowledge from Egypt's Sacred Mystery Schools. The Ethiopians and Egyptians originated Mathematics and Trigonometry. The Afrikan Moors originated Algebra and developed Trigonometry into a science. The word *Algebra* is from "Al-jabr wa'l Muqabala," the title of the first textbook on the subject, –which is further derived from ***Elegbara***, "the name of the keeper of wisdom of the [Afrikan] Ifa tradition."[1] From the name of its Black author, "Al-Khowarizmi" we get the word algorithm (a math procedure). The Arabic numbers we use are from the *original* ancient Arab people who were originally Black Afrikans (like the "Jews") –and many of them still are! The Cushites or Ethiopians were the original Arabians, for Arabia was the oldest Ethiopian colony. [2] Ancient literature assigns their first settlement to the extreme southwestern point of the peninsula. **The pyramids themselves attest to the mathematical genius of the ancient Afrikans**. Helen Blavatsky writes, "The proof that they were proficient in mathematical sciences, lies in the fact that those ancient mathematicians whom we honor as the fathers of geometry went to Egypt to be instructed...Before Greece came into existence, the arts, with the Egyptians, were ripe and old. Land-measuring, an art resting on geometry, the Egyptians certainly knew well, as, according to the *Bible*..."[3] And so-called "Roman numerals" are not Roman but Afrikan –stylizations of Kamit's hieroglyphics. Kamite TEK (the hieroglyph "X") meant 10 and is the source of DECimal, DECade, and the symbol X meaning 10 (see page 155).

1) Cole /Andoh, 9. 2) Van Sertima, APEE, 151. 3) Blavatsky, IU-vI, 531.

Afrikans gave us the Alphabet, a stylization of Egypt's hieroglyphics

The alphabet used by Western civilization as well as that of the Phoenicians, Hebrews, Chinese, Indians, etc., originated from the ancient Afrikans. Metu Neter (Medu Netcher), the oldest form of writing, was developed in the upper (southern) regions of Afrika's Nile Valley and by 3,000 B.C.E., it was being used in Kamit.[1] The Afrikan origin of the Alphabet is addressed in *The Black Truth*, by Asar Jabal, *Nile Valley Contributions to Civilization*, by Anthony Browder, *Egyptian Hieroglyphs*, by W.V. Davies, and particularly chapter 13 of Gerald Massey's *Book of the Beginning* (vol. II) entitled "Egyptian Origines in ...Language and Letters." Letters often take both their shape and sound from its parent hieroglyphics.

Examples of Afrikan Hieroglyphics icons stylized into "letters"

"**RA**." RIght Eye of RA /RE.

"**b**." Foot.

" **a**."[2] Seated God.

"*Peh*," the Lion's tail. (Kamite L=R)

"**AK**," the exact middle.

"*Sha*." (also =Hebrew *shin*)

"**n.**"

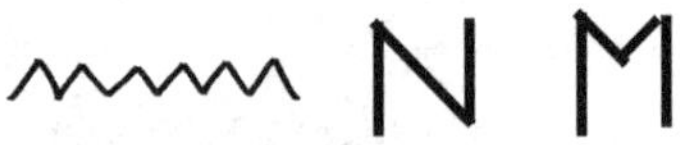

"**N**" and "**M**." Wave.

"**t**" or "**ta**." Palm.

Afrikans gave us the Art & Science of Medicine and Herbs

The real "Father of Medicine" was the Afrikan multi-genius Imhotep of ancient Egypt, not Hippocrates who lived 2000 years later. Imhotep brought the knowledge of medicine to Greece and Rome. He was a world famous physician, architect, high priest, diplomat, economist, poet, philosopher, sage, magician, astronomer, engineer, and designer of the Step Pyramid of Sakkara. He was so revered that he was deified while still living and worshiped as the Great God of Medicine. The Greeks renamed him Aesclepios, the God of Healing. "Eat, drink and be merry..." is traced to him. The symbol of the medical profession, the caduceus (a winged staff entwined by two serpents), was the insignia found on his temples. **Imhotep's temples in fact, were the first hospitals known to man!** Stolen from Afrika, his many volumes are at Karl Marx University in Liepzig, Germany. "From Egypt we have the earliest medical books, the first observations in anatomy –human and comparative – the first experiments in surgery and pharmacy, the first use of splints, bandages, compresses and other appliances, and the first anatomical and medical vocabulary, and that an extensive one."[3] As documented by Dr. Llaila O. Afrika in *African Holistic Health,* European medicine is founded upon the Afrikan healing sciences, particularly the works of Imhotep and the Black Muslims, Avicenna and Rhazes.

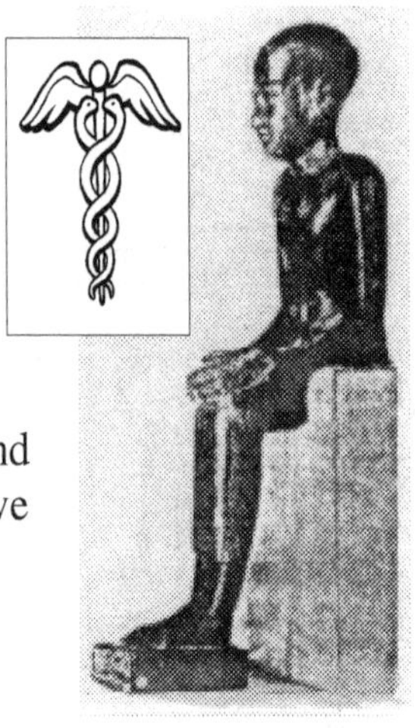

1) Browder, NV, 169. 2) Budge, EH, ci. 3) Glanvile, S., *The Legacy of Egypt,* 196.

Afrikans gave us the Calendar & StarScience (Astrology, Astronomy, Math)

The ancient Afrikans (mainly Black women) originated and developed what I call "StarScience," for the artificial separation we know as Astrology and Astronomy did not exist until the Europeans got a hold of it. Climatically, geographically, and agriculturally, Afrika was the ideal location on Earth for the birth of StarScience. StarScience itself is evidence of the vast antiquity of Afrika civilization. StarScience must be at least 52,000 years old (length of 2 Precessions), since it was mapped out by direct observation. The Zodiac could only be charted in the sky after the Great Year (Precession or revolution of the Zodiac) had been determined. **StarScience is the Mother of Sciences**, probably millions of years old, for advanced Afrikan civilization stretches back millions of years. Simplicius (6th cent. A.D.) wrote that the Egyptians had kept astronomical observations and records for the last 630,000 years. The Kamite priests and priestesses distributed their zodiacal science, along with their life-honoring matriarchal culture around the world. Later volumes of this book address StarScience as the foundation of world civilization, agriculture, religion, mathematics, geometry, computer science. Only recently have Europeans partly caught up with the advanced knowledge which the Afrikan Dogon people possess concerning StarScience and awareness of stars which are only visible through the most technically advanced telescopes.

And where would the world be without Paper or Fabric? Afrikans invented both!

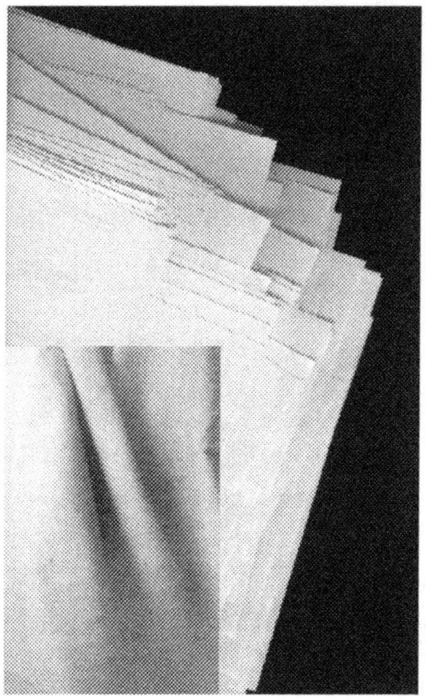

Afrikans invented paper and paper-making. Paper was made from *papyrus*, hence the name. Before this, writing was done on stone tablets. The Afrikans of the Nile Valley "made paper so excellent in quality as to be time-proof...They took out the pith of the papyrus...dissected and opened the fibre, and flattening it by a process known to them, made it as thin as our foolscap paper, but far more durable."[2] Some of the paper found in royal tombs present the appearance of the finest glossy white muslin, while it possesses the durability of the best calf-parchment.[3]

Helen Blavatsky, founder of Theosophy, informs us, "The art of making linen and fine fabrics is also proved to have been one of their branches of knowledge, for the *Bible* speaks of it....The linen of Egypt was famous throughout the world. The mummies are all wrapped in it and the linen is beautifully preserved. Pliny speaks of a certain garment sent 600 B.C., by King Amasis to Lindus, every single thread of which was composed of 360 minor threads twisted together."[4] Likely the 360 represented the days in the Kamite calendar, indicating that the Afrikans even "wove" astronomy into their very garments –all that they did had significance in relationship to the celestial bodies!

1) Blavatsky, IU-vI, 529. 2) Ibid. 3) Ibid. 4) Ibid., 536.

So-called European architecture, including "castles," originated from Afrikans

So-called European architecture (castles, arches, cathedrals, the Capitol, Parthenon, etc.) originated from Afrikan architecture (fortresses, arches, temples, mosques, obelisks, etc.)! The Washington Monument is an Afrikan *obelisk*, origin of *church steeples*. The *veranda* was brought to America from Africa in colonial times and greatly impacted architecture in the southern U.S. Afrikans carved large complex buildings, churches, and temples from massive solid rock or sides of mountains. To date, how those mighty pyramids were constructed is still a mystery to "modern" engineers. The stones used for their construction weigh some 50 tons! They are so well fitted you cannot push a business card between their joints. Black people built the ancient megalithic structures around the world, particularly throughout the Black South Pacific Islands. The most famous example is *Stonehenge*, built by "small Africoid people" –Pygmies, that is! This is well documented by two European authors; David MacRitchie: *The Testimony of Tradition*, and Gerald Massey who exhaustively explored the Nile Valley origins of British culture in the first volume of his *Book of the Beginnings*. The best of modern (Albino) equipment cannot duplicate what Black people accomplished in architecture eons ago.

The monoliths of Stonehenge in England.

Huge castles and fortresses were conceived and built by indigenous Afrikans on Afrikan soil long before Europeans arrived in Afrika, as documented by Dr. Yosef ben-Jochannan,[1] Anthony Browder,[2] and David Childress.[3] Castles were built in Nubia during the 12th Dynasty (ca. 1900 B.C.E.). These massive, formidable fortifications were equipped with moats, drawbridges, gigantic gates, battlements, and towers. They were walled villages housing hundreds of people.

Reconstruction of the fortress of Buhen near present-day Wadi Halfa in Sudan.
"It was a huge Nubian fortress as modern as any today, with towers, battlements and gigantic gates."

1) Jochannan, WTBJ, 76, 79, 81. 2) Browder, NV, 54. 3) Childress, AA, 105, 166.

The ancient Afrikans even used Electricity! Grave-robbing Europeans stole the knowledge of Electricity from Kamite tombs!

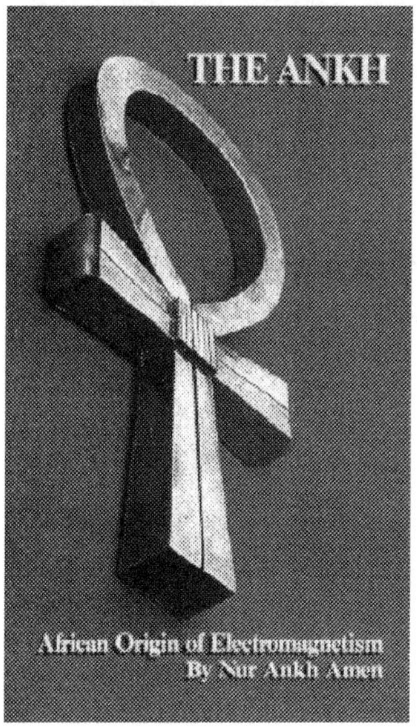

Ancient Egypt's electroplated gold objects prove that the Kamites used electricity!

Nur Ankh Amen's astonishing book, *THE ANKH – African Origin of Electromagnetism*, introduces the Afrikan origin of Electronics and its European coverup. White authors, such as Ivan T. Sanderson and David Childress, also discuss ancient Egyptian electricity. In the introduction of his book, Amen writes, **"The parallel between the sudden rise in electronic inventions and European Egyptological excavations (grave-robbery) has been suspiciously ignored. It is no coincidence that the most important discovery in Electronics, the pile or battery, and Napoleon's scientific expedition to Egypt occurred almost simultaneously."** The Afrikans of the Nile Valley had to be familiar with electricity, as the Nile is full of an electric fish known as *Gymnarchos niloticus*. The two foremost devices in Egyptian Electronics was the immortal ANKH and the Djed. The Ankh meant Life and Connection. The Djed signified the "backbone" of the god Asar (Osiris).

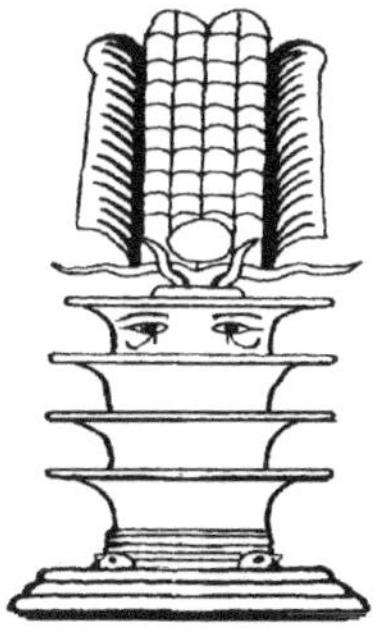
Djed Column

Electrical lighting in ancient Egypt?

"Electricity was used by the Egyptians, as evidenced by electroplated gold objects, electrical lighting reported being used in the temples, and the use of the Djed column as an electrical generator." [1] "Temples like Abydos and Dendera were apparently lit by electric lights, and probably used other electric devices. Djed columns were often used as lights in temple activities....In the basement of this temple is the famous relief of electric bulbs being used." [2] "Part of the evidence for ancient Egyptian electrics is the mystery of why tombs and underground passages are highly painted and decorated, yet there is no smoke residue or evidence of torches on the ceilings! It is usually assumed that the artists and workers would have to work by torch light, just as early Egyptologists did in the 1800's However, no smoke is found on the tombs. [3]

Note resemblance between Egyptian symbols and "western" electronic symbols:

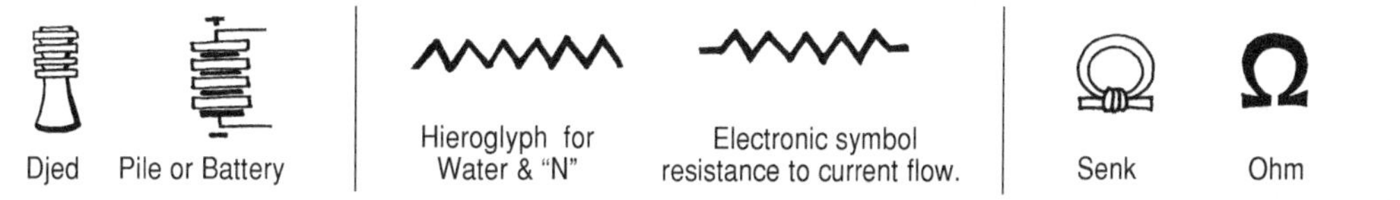

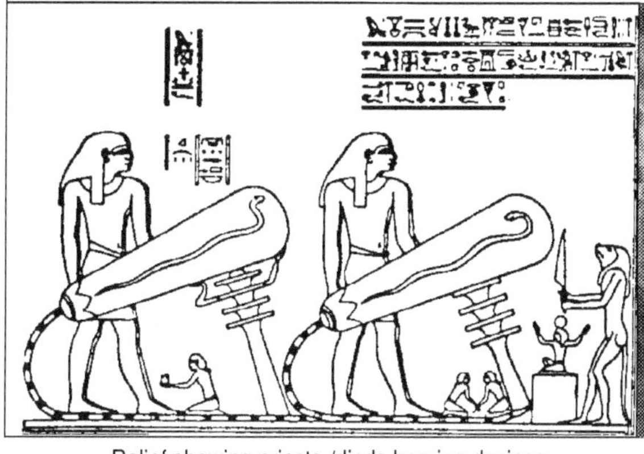
Relief showing priests /djeds bearing devices (lamps /projectors?) attached by cable to an altar.

Temple of Dendera, as drawn by Napoleon's artists.

1) Childress, LC:AA, 61. 2) Ibid., 143. 3) Ibid., 130.

The World is Ran by Afrikan Inventions

From the time you wake up till you return to sleep, inventions by Black people enrich your modern life on every level: spiritual, mental, emotional (especially through music), physical and social. Many electrical inventions were made by Blacks although the credit, like the credit of civilization, was given to Albinos. Documentation of Black inventions include the website and book by Dr. Umar S. Bey: www.hotep.org (featuring an online exhibit of Black inventions & scientists, etc.) and The Black Inventors Pocketbook; Blacks In Science by Dr. Ivan van Sertima; Black Inventors of America by McKinley Burt Jr.; Africanisms in American Culture by Joseph Holloway; and 1001 Black Inventions Supplement by Freeman/Moseley. These inventions and contributions include:

Agriculture
Ancient Afrikan women.

Alphabet
Ancient Afrikans.

Air Conditioning
Louis Latimer, 1886.
His invention was the predecessor to modern air conditioners. It consisted of a fan and cooling coils for reducing temperature and purifying the air.

Airplane
Blacks in ancient Afrika & India.
Ancient Egypt: a model plane made of wood; deemed capable of flight by NASA aeronautic engineers. India's ancient literature describes flying machines in great detail and how to operate them.

Air Ship, "The Blimp"
J. F. Pickering, 1900.

Helicopter
Paul E. Williams, 1962.

Astrology & Calendar
Ancient Afrikan Women.

Automatic Transmission
R. B. Spikes, 1932.
His mechanism allowed the automatic shifting of gears, forward or backward, in a car's transmission.

Batteries, Electrolyte
Granville T. Woods, 1888.
His batteries were such a major improvement over galvanic batteries that his invention, Electrolyte Batteries, are still used today.

Refrigerator
J. Standard, 1891.

Heating Furnace
Alice Parker, 1919.

Bicycle
M. A. Cherry's "velocipede," (1888) was the bicycle's 17th-century forerunner, a major improvement over the wheeled models of the time. Since then, it has been dramatically modified. *Issac R. Johnson's* collapsible bicycle frame (1899) could be dismounted for easy carrying and storage.

Guitar
Robert Flemming Jr., 1886.

Boomerang
Ancient Afrika, 3000 B.C.
The Kamite statue of Prince Punt carries a boomerang; also portrayed in Kamite tombs.

Bow & Arrow
Ancient Afrika.
Nubia was even called the "Land of the Bow." However, it was the Twa (Pygmies) of Central Afrika that originated this device over 400,000 years ago.

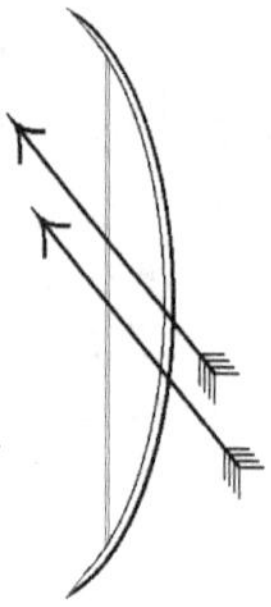

Cattle Industry
The contemporary cattle industry of America is founded upon the cattle expertise of the Fulani of Afrika (Holloway, 232). Texas longhorns and Afrikan cattle egrets were brought to America with Fulani slaves. They also introduced open grazing, driving cattle to market, and widespread use of cow's milk for humans. Afrikans inspired the term *cowboy*, which was counterpart to *houseboy*. Many cowboys of the American West were Black.

Cellular Phone (Gamma Electric Cell)
Henry T. Sampson, 1971.

Chemistry
Chemistry and Alchemy are from the word *Kam* or Khemit, the name of ancient Egypt and source of the "Black" science called Chemistry, –the original *"Black Magic"*!

Computers, Micro
Computer Science has its foundation in Kamite principles. "0" and "1" (On/Off) of the Binary System are the top & bottom of the Ankh. And numerous Afrikan Americans contributed to the development of modern computers, including: *Annie Easley* who developed computer codes; *Brian Jackson* who gained international recognition for the miniaturizations of computers; and *Courtland Robinson,* who developed a procedure called "Accelerated Life Testing" which tested the durable life of a computer chip in just a few days.

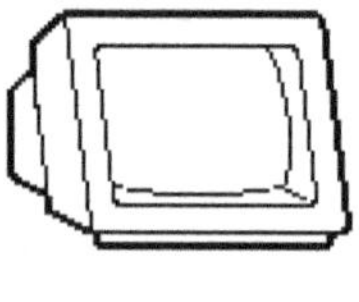

Cuisine
Fried chicken, deep-frying, gumbo, okra, nut soups, black-eyed peas, and general Southern cuisine are tasty contributions from Blacks to the American cuisine. And in 1865, Hiram Thomas invented Potato Chips. This incredibly popular snack was born when an irate customer repeatedly sent his serving of potatoes back to chef Thomas for thinner slices. In defiance, Thomas revengefully sliced the spuds ridiculously thin to disturb the customer even more. Instead, he delighted him.

Door Knob
Oscar Dorsey, 1878.

Electricity
Yes, the ancient Afrikans used electricity as proven by their gold plated objects and "batteries."

Engine, Gasoline
Frederick M. Jones, 1945.

Engine, Rotary
Joseph Gamell, 1982.
His bladeless turbine got 100 miles out of a gallon of gas! No wonder the oil industry resisted, thus curtailing mass production.

Fire Extinguisher
T. J. Marshall, 1872.
His small, portable, hand-operated invention was the forerunner to modern tank-type extinguishers.

Forks, Spoons, Knives
Ancient Afrika, 1,500,000 BC.
As noted by archaeologists, Afrikans were the first humans to create and use any type of utensils.

Guns
The African Moors of Spain introduced the first shooting mechanisms or rifles, known as firesticks.

Healing Arts & Sciences
Ancient Afrikans, especially Afrikan women. From Egypt we have the earliest medical books, the first observations in anatomy, the first experiments in surgery and pharmacy, the first use of splints, bandages, compresses and other appliances, and the first anatomical and medical vocabulary.

Hospitals
Ancient Afrikans. Imhotep's temples were the first hospitals know to man.

Language
As you will discover in this book, all world languages, like civilization, originated from the Original People, – Black, spiral-haired Afrikans, humanity's parents.

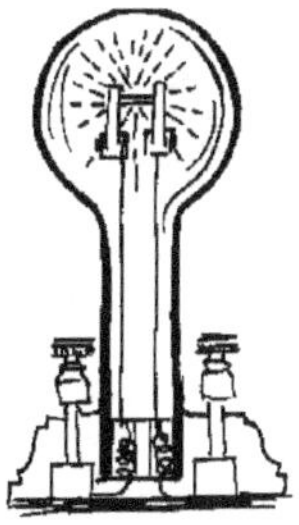

Light, Electric
Louis Latimer, 1881.
Latimer invented a method of making carbon filaments for the electric incandescent lamp, which could caused lights to burn almost indefinitely. Edison's lamps burned only 16 hours. Edison got credit for many of Latimer's electrical inventions.

Math Sciences
Afrikans gave us Math, Algebra, Geometry, Trigonometry, and the Arabic Numbers.

Paper Bag
W. B. Purvis, 1900's.
He vastly improved the speed and efficiency of paper-bag production.

Paper
The Ancient Afrikans made *paper* from the *papyrus* plant, hence the name.

Peanut Wizardry
The wizardry of *Dr. George Washington Carver* turned the peanut into hundreds of products which included mock chicken, instant coffee, shampoo, face cream, nut butter, nut milk, asphalt, and peanut oil. He saved the South's economy from destruction and gave the South a $200 million dollar peanut industry

Pen, Fountain
W. B. Purvis, 1890.
His invention removed the need for carrying around an ink well, for it had its own ink reservoir, replaceable also, that fed ink to the pen's point.

Scales
Ancient Afrikans.
Hieroglyphics show Goddess Maat weighing the heartsoul of the deceased on Her Scales of Judgement, from which Libra is derived.

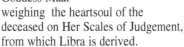

Shaking Hands
Afrikans. "Shaking hands over a bargain is a form of making the sign of the Ankh, the Cross of Covenant, as Ankh means to clasp as well as to covenant, and to thank is a form of the ankh-ing." [Massey, BB-vI, 101]

Shoe Lasting Machine
Jan Ernst Matzeliger, 1891.
He revolutionized the shoe-making industry with the machine he invented which sewed the basic parts of a shoe together in one minute. Previously, this process was hand-done and took as long as a day. Before his machine, only the wealthy could afford to own more than one pair of shoes. His design is still the foundation of modern lasting machines.

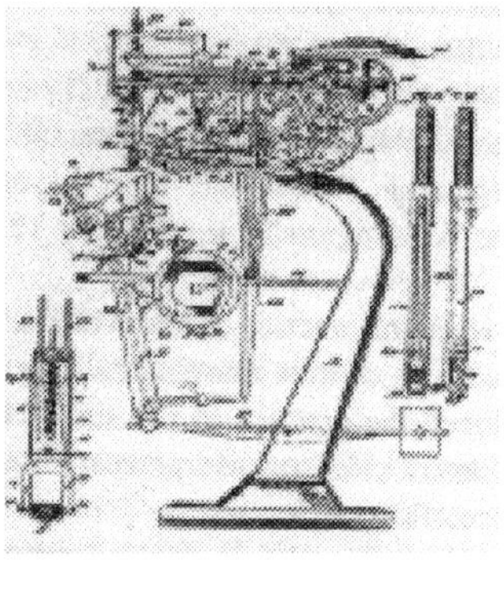

Spiritual Theology
The world's religions, mythologies, gods, goddess, etc., are derived from the ancient spiritual teachings of Afrika, a system founded upon and expressing the cosmic, universal principles of life. Essentially, the world's religions are corruptions or distortions of Afrikan theology.

Street Sweeper
Charles Brooks, 1890.

Steel, Iron
Afrikans (the Hayas of Tanzania) produced carbon steel 2000 years ago! –with pre-heated forced draft furnaces, a technology Europeans could only match in the 19th century. Afrikans were smelting iron in 200 B.C. at Nok in Nigeria; in 650 B.C. at Meroe in Nubia; and in 40,000 B.C. in South Afrika –as testified by an iron mine over 40,000 years old discovered in Transvaal. [Childress, LC/AA, 368]

Sweet Potato Wizardry
The wizardry of *Dr. George Washington Carver* turned the sweet potato into hundreds of products which included bread, syrup, alcohol, bleach, cosmetics, axle grease, printer's ink, and coffee.

Telephone Transmitter
Granville T. Woods, 1887
This transmitter cleared phone static and was especially effective for long distance calls.

Toilet
J. B. Rhodes, 1899.
Rhodes's invention was called the cater closet. Today it is called the toilet. Prior to this, outhouses were used. His invention allowed folks to used the bathroom in their own homes. Another Black inventor, Robert Shurney, designed the toilet used aboard Skylab.

Traffic Lights
Garrett A. Morgan, 1923.

Elevator
Alexander Miles, 1887.

Seed Planter
Henry Blair, 1834
Oldest recorded patent.

Type Writing Machine
Burridge & Marshman, 1885.

The white Founding Fathers built America on Black Egypt's knowledge

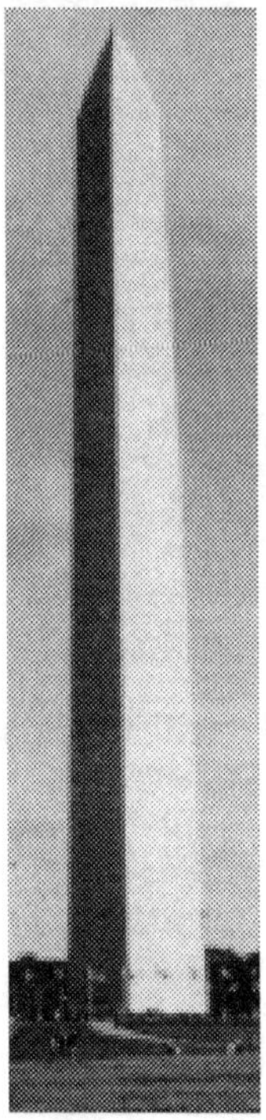

As addressed in Anthony Browder's fascinating *From the Browder File*, the Founding Fathers sought to recreate in America the same energies which guided the Afrikans of the Nile Valley by using Afrikan science, architecture and symbols (with no credit to them) as shown:

- **The Founding Fathers and all the U.S. presidents were Masons** (except Lincoln & Kennedy). Masons and other secret orders such as the Rosicrucians & Illuminati are patterned after the Sacred Mystery Schools (universities) of ancient Egypt. The word 'Mason' means 'child of the sun' and is derived from the Afrikan terms Sons & Daughters of Light (or Children of the Sun). The sun symbolizes enlightenment, hence these metaphors mean "enlightened people." The Declaration of Independence and the U.S. Constitution are Masonic documents, written in the Masonic code and have different meaning to members of the Masonic order.

- **Look on the back of the dollar bill** and see for yourself how the Founding Fathers composed the Great Seal of America with Afrikan symbols: The Eye of Horus /God, pyramid, six-pointed star (made up of 13 stars), and the eagle –their imitation of Egypt's sacred sun Falcon, a symbol for Horus.

- **The Washington monument, a symbol of America, is an Afrikan obelisk!** The obelisk was the symbol of the very Black Kamite god, Osiris who represented the regenerative powers of God and was worshiped as the impregnating force of the universe. The obelisk later became part of the worship of the Egyptian Sun God, "Ra," from which we get the words "ray, radiation." The obelisk is also found at the Vatican in St. Peter's square and in every major city in the world. It is the origin of church steeples!

- **Egyptian Design: The Lincoln Memorial** is patterned after an Egyptian temple honoring the pharaoh, Rameses II. Meridian Hill Park (aka Malcolm X Park) was designed to align Washington D.C. to the same meridian (pathway to the sun) which passes through Egypt.

- **A Black scientist designed the city.** The layout and design of Washington D.C. was accomplished by America's first Black man of science, Benjamin Banneker –astronomer & mathematician.

The Afrikan Moors sparked the European Renaissance!

Ruling Spain, southern France, much of Scotland & north Afrika during the Middle ages for 700 years, the Black Afrikan Moors gave Europe one of its finest civilizations. The word Moor means *black,* derived from Greek *mauros*, meaning scorched. The Afrikan countries *Morocco* and *Mauritania* are also from this root. In the Middle Ages, Afrikans were called Moors.

In the introduction of The Story of the Moors In Spain by Stanley Lane-Poole, John Jackson writes: "Eurocentric historians argue that Europe gave civilization to Africa, which is a complete inversion of the truth. The first civilized Europeans were the Greeks, who were chiefly civilized by the Africans of the Nile Valley. The Greeks transmitted this culture to the Romans, who finally lost it, bringing on a dark age of five hundred years. Civilization was restored to Europe when another group of Africans, the Moors, brought this dark age to an end... During the Golden Age of Islam, the Moorish Empire...was the most advanced state in the world...Cordova was the most wonderful city of the tenth century; the streets were well-paved, with raised sidewalks for pedestrians...Public baths numbered in the hundreds...at a time when cleanliness in Christian Europe was regarded a sin...Moorish monarchs dwelt in splendid palaces, while the crowned heads of England, France, and Germany lived in big barns, lacking both windows and chimneys, with only a hole in the roof for the emission of smoke."

Courtesy of the Philadelphia Museum of Art

"The Moorish Chief"

The Moors had an insatiable lust for knowledge, and acquired it from East and West, translating into Arabic all they could find, even ransacking monasteries for rare books. One king had a private library of 600,000 books! In Moorish Spain education was available to the most humble, while in Christian Europe 99% of the populace were illiterate, including kings. The incredible city of Cordova had 800 public schools!

The Moors made great advances in mathematics, physics, astronomy, medicine, botany, chemistry. The Moors also introduced the first shooting mechanisms or rifles known as firesticks! –which revolutionized European military science, ultimately causing their downfall when their enemies used gunpowder to drive them back into Afrika. Their contribution to European civilization is *vast* –with no credit given to them. For more details: Ivan Van Sertima, ed: The Golden Age of the Moors, and Samuel Scott: The History of the Moorish Empire in Europe.

Afrikans ruled widely in Europe for over 1400 years!

Shocking, isn't it! And true! The details are available in such books as Nature Knows No Color-Line, by J. A. Rogers, Sex and Race, by the same author, and African Presence in Early Europe, by Ivan Van Sertima. Afrikan rulership in Europe started with Septimus Severus and ended with the Moors. To summarize:

- Black rulership of the Roman Empire began in 193 A.D. with Afrikan born, Roman Emperor, Septimus Severus, a full blooded Afrikan. There were four other Black emperors after the Severus dynasty.

Front & back sides of Hannibal coins.

- Often called the Father of Military Strategy, Hannibal, another full blooded Afrikan, performed the astounding feat of crossing the Alps on elephants in 218 B.C. With only 26,000 of his original force of 82,000 troops remaining, Hannibal defeated Rome, the mightiest military power of that age, who had a million men, in every battle for the next fifteen years. His tactics are still taught in leading military academies of U.S., Europe and other lands.
- Black rulership was widespread in Europe during the "Dark" and Middle Ages!
- The original "knights" were Black! –including the legendary knights of King Arthur's Round Table! That's why they were called "knights," – after the *night* or darkness of their skin.
- An Afrikan king named Gormund, ruled Ireland during the Anglo-Saxon period in England, reports the medieval historian, Geoffrey of Monmouth.
- Halfdan the Black, who was Africoid, was the first king to unite Norway.

Arch of Septimus Severus

- When the British Isles were invaded by the Vikings some of these Norse raiders were Africoid. In fact, different varieties of 'Viking' Afrikans lived in Scandinavia during the Middle ages and are frequently mentioned in Viking sagas.
- British "Lion of Judah?" The British Coat of Arms is copied from Ethiopia which used the seal 6000 years before the Europeans. Lions are not naturally found in Europe!
- The Afrikan Moors dominated southwest Europe during the Middle Ages for 700 years: 711-1492 A.D.

Europe's royal families descended from Black / Mulatto rulers!

This makes sense when you know that Afrikans ruled in Europe for 1400 years. Afrikans introduced the concept of royalty to the Europeans, who were initially uncivilized barbarians. Afrikan ancestry in Europeans is well documented in Nature Knows No Color Line, by J.A. Rogers. To list a few:

- the Black Queen Charlotte Sophia, the grandmother of Queen Victoria , who was also the consort of George III and the great-great-grandmother of George VI.
- Jean Baptiste Bernadotte who founded the present day royal Swedish family
- The Duke of Florence
- the Medicis, the Gonzagas
- the Duchess of Alafoes
- St. Hilaire –son of Louis XV

... long is the list! Is this why some of Europe's oldest royal / noble families are called the "Black Nobility" even though they're "white"?

<< Queen Charlotte Sophia, mulatto Queen of England

Like Beethoven, seven U.S. presidents were mulattoes! And America's true first president was John Hanson, a Black man!

Beethoven was a darkskinned Moorish mulatto called "The Black Spaniard." His teacher, the immortal Joseph Hayden, was also a mulatto! [1]

In *The Five Negro Presidents,* J.A. Rogers documents the mulatto identity of five American presidents! "Passing for white" were Presidents Thomas Jefferson, Alexander Hamilton, Warren Harding, Andrew Jackson, and Abraham Lincoln. America's 6th mulatto president was Dwight Eisenhower, the 34th president of the U.S.[2]

Beethoven sketched from life.

Woolly-haired John Hanson, America's true First President, a Black man

And America's true first president was a Black man named John Hanson, the first president under America's first constitution, better known as the *U.S. Articles of Confederation.* Seven other presidents were elected after him, all prior to George Washington, who was really America's 9th president; Washington was the first president only under the U.S. Constitution. The new country was actually formed on March 1, 1781 with the adoption of the Articles of Confederation. Once the signing took place, a President was needed to run the country. "American

RIGHT: Ida Eisenhower, mother of President Dwight Eisenhower

1) Kush, 282. 2) Browder, NV, 143.

Revolutionary leader," who helped raise money, weapons and political support for the Revolution, John Hanson was unanimously elected "President of the United States in Congress Assembled", on Nov. 5, 1781. General George Washington himself (a member of Congress) congratulated Hanson on his elevation to "the most important seat in the United States." As America's first President, Hanson accomplished much in his 1-year term. *"He took office just as the Revolutionary War ended. Almost immediately, the troops demanded to be paid. As would be expected after any long war, there were no funds to meet the salaries. As a result, the soldiers threatened to overthrow the new government and put Washington on the throne as a monarch. ..All the members of Congress ran for their lives, leaving Hanson as the only guy left running the government. He somehow managed to calm the troops down and hold the country together. If he had failed, the government would have fallen almost immediately and everyone would have been bowing to King Washington."*[1] Hanson established the Great Seal of the United States, the first Treasury Department, first Secretary of War, first Foreign Affairs Department, the postal system, the consular service, a national bank, the Thanksgiving holiday and much more.

There are no "pure whites." Race purity is a big myth.

Europeans and their "white" American descendants have much Afrikan blood from centuries of miscegenation with Afrikans:

- That's why Spaniards, Greeks, and Italians are so "dark."
- Afrikan Moors ruling southwest Europe for centuries, darkened whites in this area, especially Portugal –described as "the first example of a Negrito (African) republic in Europe." Moors ruling Scotland in the 10th century mixed with whites until they disappeared.
- Black Celts (Silures) and Black Vikings mixed with the Scandinavian people.
- The blond Negroid type is common even in Nordic Europe where intermixing has been happening since antiquity.
- Even Hitler's 'Aryans' had Black blood, reports the *New York Times* 7/1/1940. The Huns included Black Mongolians who mixed heavily with the 'Aryan Germans.'
- Black slavery lasted in England for about 400 years (1440-1834), during which time much race mixing occurred.

For details on Europe's Afrikan history, and Afrikan ancestry in whites:

- *Nature Know No Color Line* by J.A. Rogers
- *Sex and Race* (all volumes) by J.A. Rogers
- *African Presence in Early Europe* by Ivan Van Sertima
- *Black Britannia* by Edward Scobie
- *Ancient & Modern Britons* by David MacRitchie

1) On the Internet at: http://www.dickgregory.com/dick/14_washington.html

4

The Afrikan Origin of Hue-manity & the Albinos

All "races" were born from the Black race, reports *Western* Science

Science reports that everyone alive today descended from an Afrikan woman who lived 200,000 years ago!

Based on the evidence of recent findings, modern (white) science has 'officially' declared that ALL of present humanity came from one race...the Black race –the oldest race. Throughout the world prominent magazines have done front page articles on "the most incredible find of all times: Scientists have unearthed the ancient bones of a Black African [Pygmy] woman who is indisputably the mother of all humanity!"

They nicknamed her *Eve*, "our common ancestor –a woman who lived 200,000 years ago and left resilient genes that are carried by all of mankind" reports the bestselling issue ever of *Newsweek* magazine (1/11/88), which depicts a Black Adam and Eve on its front cover, headlining it *The Search for Adam and Eve.*

Science magazine (9/11/87) stated that overwhelming evidence shows that "Africa was the cradle of modern humans... The story the molecular biology seems to be telling is that modern humans evolved in Africa about 200,000 years ago."

National Geographic (Oct. 88) reports of new evidence "of an African origin for modern humans."

Ancient legends around the world speak of "Small Blacks"

Legends around the world, from Ireland to Japan speak of the earliest inhabitants of their land as being "small blacks" or "dark dwarfs." The original Irish "leprechauns" were in fact, Pygmies! The ancient Egyptians recorded the "Twa," –their small brown ancestors who were early inhabitants of Earth. Presenting a fascinating account of the legendary Lemuria & Atlantis, the inspired *Right Use of Will* by Ceanne DeRohan, reports "the Lemurians were small and brown." In *Pygmy Kitabu,* Jean-Pierre Hallet documents the remarkable Pygmies of Zaire, "the world's most genetically pure ethnic group...surviving since the dawn of mankind in real harmony with God, nature and each other." Pygmy bones are found all over earth. Albert Churchward's *Signs & Symbols of the Primordial Man* speaks of the many ancient exoduses of Blacks out of Afrika to other parts of the world.

Whites are not "indigenous" anywhere, so where did they come from?

Aboriginal, indigenous whites do not exist! You do not hear of white people being "aboriginal" or "indigenous people." Why? Because they are *unnatural.* They are not indigenous to any place for they are a recent people, a *new* so-called race. White skin is a form of *albinism. Albino* simply means *white.* Their own historical accounts say they suddenly *appeared* in *Caucasia* or the *Caucasus* Mountains, about 6000 years ago.[1]

The *Chalk*-Asians are the *Cauk*-asians!

The whole of *Europe,* really is *Chalk (white) Asia, Cauc-Asia*

Europe is NOT a *continent,* despite what Albino dictionaries say. Europe is west Asia, thus the whole of west Asia is really Cauk-Asia or White Asia –not just the Cauc-asus mountains. **Caucasia is named both, *after* the Whites themselves and the "cauk, calk, chalk"** Other *Caulk* names include Chalcedon & Chalcis, ancient Greek (*Albino*) cities; and Chalcidice, a mountainous peninsula of Greece.

GOG too. The Cauk-Asians are the "Gog-Asians"

"Gog" sounds similar to "Cauk." The biblical, very white Land of Gog (also called the "Isles of the Gentiles") was to the North and included the Cauk-asus mountains and eastern Russia (see pgs 80, 81).

The "**cauc**" of CAUCasian is undoubtedly a variant of ***cauk*** (a word *removed* from dictionaries), *caulk, calk, chalk, chalc(edony), calc(ium)*; Middle English *cauken*; French *cauquer*; Latin *calx*; and Spanish *cauce, caucho.* All these words look similar, sound similar, and point to one thing: WHITEness. White substances. **The CAUC-asian is the *Cauk*-Asian, Caulk-Asian, Chalk-Asian –or chalky-white, caulky-white, calcium-white Asian!** "Calcium" and Caucasians are named after whiteness. Bones are essentially calcium, hence white. And yes, "cauc" is a major component of the Caucasus Mountains, which feature thousands of natural caves in its ***limestone (cauk)*** hills and slopes.[2] The **Cauk** caves of the **Cauk**-asus Mountains were the earliest homes of the **Cauk**-Asians for some 2000 years.[3] Covering several hundred miles, these *Caverns of the Northern Caucasus* [4] face north. Spanish *caucho* means ***rubber***. What's the connection with whiteness? Natural rubber is milky white! The "caulk" you buy in stores is *rubber* –white or "colorless." Latin ***calx*** means chalk, lime, limestone *–calcium* in other words. It also means "heel bone" and "to tread." Again what's the white connection? Your heelbone, upon which you tread, is a large quad*angular spur*. Calcium loves to *spur* when it "calcifies," hence "calcspar." Stalactites & stalagmites are other forms of calcium /lime "spurs," spears. Yes "calc" is in *calc*ulator / *calc*ulus, for *stones* were early tools for "calculating," and a most common type of stone is the *mineral* CALCium; Greek *khalix* (pebble). Spanish *cauce* means *riverbed* –where *stones* are naturally abundant. *Elbrus*, apparently from the same root as *albino*, is the highest mountain in Cauc-Asia.

1) Guthrie, 3. 2) Ibid., 78. 3) Ibid., 44. 4) Ibid.

Why have *Cauk-Asians* manipulated *Caucasian* to also mean *Blacks*?!

Compare!...
(bold underlines added)

Caucasian (1937):
"1. Any one of the white division of human beings, so called because the people about the Caucasus mountains were taken as the highest type of the human family; it includes nearly all Europeans, the Circassians, Jews, Armenians, Hindus, and Persians."
Webster's 20th-Century Dictionary, Unabridged, 1937.

Caucasian (1981):
"pertaining to the white race as characterized by physical features. –*n.* A native of the Caucasus; a member of the Caucasian race."
New Webster's Dictionary, 1981.

Caucasian (1992):
"1. *Anthropology.* Of, relating to, or being a major human racial division traditionally distinguished by physical characteristics such as very light to brown skin pigmentation and straight to wavy or curly hair, and including peoples indigenous to Europe, northern Africa, western Asia, and India... 2...relating to the Caucasus region or its peoples..."
American Heritage Dictionary, 3rd Ed. 1992

Caucasoid (1996):
Now whites DENY Caucasus roots!:
"*adj.* ...from the erroneous notion that the orig. home of the hypothetical Indo-Europeans was the Caucasus... one of the major... varieties of human beings... characterized by...straight or wavy hair... loosely called the *white race* although it embraces many people of dark skin color:"
Webster's New World College Dictionary, 1996.

The Cauk-Asians are untruthful when they say they are *Asians*. They are not Asians nor did they originate in Asia. They originated in Afrika. They call themselves "Asians" to avoid confronting the *BLACK* truth about themselves. Along this line, they change the true meaning of key words. Have you looked up *Caucasian* in a *recent* dictionary lately? "Caucasians" have redefined this word so that a *Caucasian* can now be a "brown skinned, curly haired" person! Based on this *white*manipulated redefinition, a whole lot of indigenous, formerly "non-white" Afrikans (and Asians / India-Indians) are now Caucasians! This is exactly why they have changed the meaning of the word, – to both: **1)** artificially greatly inflate their perceived population count –because their population is dwindling rapidly (it's now less than 7% of the world's total population, and **2)** make the "brown skinned, curly-haired" *Twa* (Pygmies) and Afrikans of the ancient Nile Valley and other key regions into "Caucasians." Then they can say "Caucasians" originated civilization and thus take the credit from Black people in one stroke. In fact I once heard at a lecture that the 1935 *Funk & Wagnells* dictionary labeled the Ethiopians "Caucasians" when the word still meant whites. They retracted /revised this when Italy failed to win the war with Ethiopia. The true etymology of words exposes the *Cauk Deception* and leads us always back to the liberating *Black Truth.*

Dictionaries do not give the roots of the word *Caucasian*! For if they did, it would be obvious that the present altered definition of *Caucasian* is deliberately, misleadingly *wrong* and *fraudulent.* A very ***white lie*** in other words! For "cauc" or "cauk" applies only to one thing: *whiteness*. Hence no indigenous Afrikans or Asians or Indians could possibly be "cauc" (white); only the Albinos are cauc /cauk /chalk /calc. This is undoubtedly why ***Cauk-Asians* have *deleted* the word "cauk" (& cawk) from all dictionaries!** For CAUK is identical with CAUC in Cauc-asian, proving that *Caucasian* means *White-Asian.* In Webster's 1937, unabridged Twentieth-Century Dictionary we find the word ***cauk*** and its kindred words: [bold underlines added]

- "**cauk**, *n.* ...**limestone**... written also as **cawk**."
- "**cawk**, *n.* See *Cauk* and *Chalk.*"
- "**chalk**...*n.* ...**limestone**...A common **calcareous** earthy substance, of an opaque **white color**"

In the term *Caucasian (Caulk-Asian)*, whites are also named after *MILK!*

Their greatest "**cult**ure" was the **Latins** (Romans); ***Latin*** is from Italian *LATTE* (milk), kin with LATex (*rubber*, again!) and **LACT /LAC** which also means Milk! LAC is in LACe, –lacy like the LATher of frothy leuco Milk! MiLK itself contains LAC. Their other Milk-names include Gaul, Galia, Gallic, Gael, Gaelic, Galatian, Latino, Lakonia, Kelt, Celt, Celtic. All these words contain Milky roots (lat, lac, cal, calc).

- In Egyptian, L and R were the same, thus the Afrikan (Egyptian) sources of these words /roots are:
  – *Lat* (or *Rait / Ra-t*, the Sun Goddess, mate of Ra)
  – *Kela* (or *Khera*, "mother of the calf," hence a *Cow*)
  – *Leko* (or *Reko*, white, to whiten or bleach).
  Since Egyptian L&R are one, then caL = caR; cuL = cuR, giving CURdle which is what Milk does naturally!
- Hence the KURDS of **Kur**distan (a region of southwest Asia) are the CURds, named after Milk and milk's whiteness! And CLOUD is certainly from this root: cLoud (caLt, ceLt, cuLture) = cRoud /cuRd. Hence Clouds are Curds in the sky! –from the *Cow of Heaven.*
- Also Greek *gala* (milk). Since L=R, then the word **GREEK itself is apparently a variant of the CALC root.** Hence caLc = caRc or gaRac = GREEK, Greece!
- This may explain why the slang "**cracker**" means white person. Cracker = cRac = cLac = caLc, pointing to hardness /brittleness –the nature of crackers & *calcium.*

Pink People, really

Actually so-called "white" people are really shades of *red.* Hence they are *Pink* People! Other names for them even point to ruddiness such as "redneck," Ruthenian, and Russians (originally, *Rustians*; Russia is the largest settlement of the white tribe.). Personal names attest to this: Redd, Redding, Rodgers, Rodney, Rothschild, Rudolf, Rutherford, Ross, Russell, and Ruston. The term "**peaches n' *cream***" combines both, *red* and *white.*

Even the name *Europe* is connected with Milk through association with the Holy Cow

The alleged Phoenician princess Europa is identified with the Moon-Cow or Moon Goddess, and rode Zeus disguised as a *White* Bull. The name Europe allegedly means *Full-Moon.* The Great Mother Goddess ***Lat*** was the **Moon**, anciently regarded a symbol of the Great Goddess and universal source of nourishment; the Moon was a GALactic, gaLACTic, celestial Breast that produced the Milky Way.[1]

Another way Cauc /Caulk becomes white:

From connection with the *CAU* or ***COW*** –the greatest of Milk-giving animals. *All* Milk from any animal is WHITE. What makes Milk white? Yes, CALCium! *Cow* is from Egyptian *Kaui* meaning *cow.* Double it and get *kaukau*, cauk, cauc! Note that "Caulk" (cau-LK) contains both CAU (COW) and LAC. **And *LAC* is *CAL* spelled backwards!**

Technically, there is no such thing as a "white race." White people are albino Afrikans or "Mutant Albinos."

White skin is a form of albinism, a genetic aberration. An article [2] by Dr. Frances Cress Welsing related: "White skin, having the same number of melanocytes as black skin, lacks color because the melanocytes of white skin are deficient in the production of the enzyme tyrosinase which is essential for the conversion of tyrosine to melanin within the melanocyte....**This is exactly the same deficiency which causes the condition of skin albinism.** Thus, in effect, skin whiteness in the human family is the same as the genetic deficiency state of albinism of one of the albinism variants." [emphasis added] In her revelatory book, *The Isis Papers*, she writes: [emphasis added]

> "White skin is a form of albinism. **There is no difference, microscopically speaking, between the white skin of a white person and the skin of a person designated as an albino.** My central thesis here is that white-skinned peoples came into existence thousands of years ago as the albino mutant offsprings of black-skinned mothers and fathers in Africa." [3]

> "whites are undoubtedly a genetic mutant albino population. They are albino mutants from the original Black (hue-man) beings, causing the formation of **a mankind and a huemankind**...From the modern science of genetics, we know that it is possible for all pigmented population groups to produces white (albino) mutants. We also know that it is impossible for albino mutants to produce Black offsprings." [4]

The Aboriginal "Real People" nation of Australia, refers to white people as the "Mutants" in the remarkable inspired book, *Mutant Message*, by Marlo Morgan. This "mutancy," however, is not limited to whites: "The word Mutant seemed to be a state of heart and head, not a color or a person, it is an attitude! Someone who has lost or closed off ancient remembering and universal Truths." [5]

1) Walker, WE, 529. 2) "Blacks, Hypertension, and the Active Skin Melanocyte.." 3) Welsing, 23. 4) Ibid., 123. 5) Morgan, 156.

How did Cauk-Asians "come into being" or become albinos? –Apparently through *all* of four ways...

1) Selective breeding and gene manipulation?

Albino scientists make albino "laboratory" animals through selective, incestuous breeding. They can also directly manipulate genes. Were Caucasians likewise engineered? There is evidence supporting this! The amazing details are addressed in *Making of the Whiteman*, by Paul Guthrie, and *The Black Truth*, by Asar Jubal.

2) Sudden genetic mutation from a catastrophe?

How curious that a large body of Albinos occur next to Afrika and nowhere else in the world. Did an unnatural catastrophe occur which caused massive mutation among Black Afrikans? There is evidence supporting this! The amazing details are addressed in *The Black Truth*, by Asar Jubal.

3) Albino offspring of Afrikans?

There is evidence supporting this! As previously noted, in *The Isis Papers*, Dr. Frances Cress Welsing states "whites are undoubtedly a genetic mutant albino population...from the original Black (hue-man) beings." [1] She theorizes that whites (as the albino offspring of Black Afrikans) migrated or were chased northward from Africa into Europe. The story she cites of "Snowflake"[1] dramatically illustrates how it is possible for whites to come into being from Blacks: Born of coal black parents, this albino gorilla named "Snowflake" has platinum blonde hair, white (pink) skin, and blue eyes! [2] Similarly in Panama, particularly among the San Blas Indians are albino natives that also have blond hair and blue eyes! They are often indistinguishable from blond Northern Europeans!

4) Ice-Age Adaptation?

White people's fondest theory of how they got white is through gradual adaptation to ice-age climatic changes. Their scholars theorize that Afrikans who migrated to Europe and were caught in the Ice Age, gradually lightened until their genes mutated to adapt to the scant sunlight, thus producing a race of whites. Similarly, biblical scholars credit Japheth (a son of Noah) as fathering the white race or fathering a (Black) people who settled in the north, ultimately becoming the Caucasian race. **But note that the Eskimos and the indigenous Indians of southernmost South America are still melanated though they have inhabited far colder places than ice-age Europe, and have done so far longer than the Albinos.** While climate, over an extended period, does affect genetic skincolor and other traits, climate least accounts for whites being white. The subject of Blacks mutating to become white is treated in the opening essays of *African Presence in Early Europe*, edited by Ivan Van Sertima.

1) Welsing, 123. 2) National Geographic : Mar. 1967, Oct. 1970.

Were a race of whites "made by Yacub" through selective breeding?

Paul Guthrie's *Making of the Whiteman*, assembles startling historical evidence which verifies much of Elijah Muhammad's controversial teachings on the origin of white people. In *Message to the Black Man in America*, according to Elijah Muhammad, founder of the Nation of Islam, whites were created from Afrikans about 6000 years ago by scientist Yacub, a Black genius. Using a selective breeding process called "grafting," Yacub created whites as a "race of devils" to rule Earth for a limited period. *Jacob's* selective breeding process for generating *strong* brown /black sheep /goats (Gen. 30:31-43) allegedly corresponds to *Yacub's* breeding process for creating white people. Interestingly, the ancient Egyptians recorded the *Tamahu*, which means "created white people." Egyptian writings also refer to whites as *Typhonians* or "Children of Set," both meaning "the devils." After these "white devils" were first released into the Black community of the Near East about 6000 years ago, they caused severe strife, thus the Afrikans rounded them up, stripped them of everything and exiled them to the caves and hills of the Caucasus Mountains. This explains the sudden appearance of white people in this region. To prevent their escaping, Afrikans installed a series of guarded walls blocking all exits along that area from one sea to the other! These walls have been witnessed and recorded by many European writers, including Pliny. Thus totally cut off from civilization, the whites degenerated into uncivilized, savages. They remained this way for 2000 years until "Allah mercifully sent an Egyptian priest named Musa or Moses to civilize them." This explains the otherwise unknown reason why suddenly, about 2000 B.C., vast hordes of these barbarians left Caucasia and stormed the Black centers of civilization throughout Mesopatamia, northeast Afrika and India, destroying and usurping them. Thus, the whiteman's arrival signalled destruction for all these civilizations and the beginning of the whiteman's rise to power.

Why do Cauk-Asians seek to hide their origins?

Dr. Welsing states: "Historically, the white race has sought to hide its genetic origins in Africa amongst Blacks, just as it has sought to deny the origins of the white civilization from the culture of Blacks in Africa, seeking instead to proclaim an origin amongst the Greeks. Historically, whites also have sought to degrade Africa and everything Black. By so doing, whites can avoid confronting the true meaning of skin whiteness as a mutation and genetic deficiency state from the Black norm – the 'hue-man' norm... Deep within the unconscious psyche of the white collective is an awareness of their origin amongst Blacks, that Blacks were their parents and that they (whites) were the **defective** offsprings of Blacks." (emphasis added)

"Defective" points to illness –the ILLness of ALbinism.

ILL means "not healthy, sick, not normal, having evil intentions." ALbinism is unnatural, "not normal." ALbinos then, are A I L-binos, ILL-binos. ALbinism is the physical manifestation of a deep Spiritual Dis-ease, –a Disconnection from and War Against Nature. The effects include the ongoing massive destruction of Earth's vegetation, the ongoing promotion of planet-eating technology, and the ongoing manufacture of weapons so destructive that one can destroy several continents at once. Thus this Dis-ease is threatening all Life and the whole planet. Is there hope for Humanity?

5

Your Brain & Nerves Cannot Operate Without Black Melanin!

Your brain and body can't function without Black Melanin!

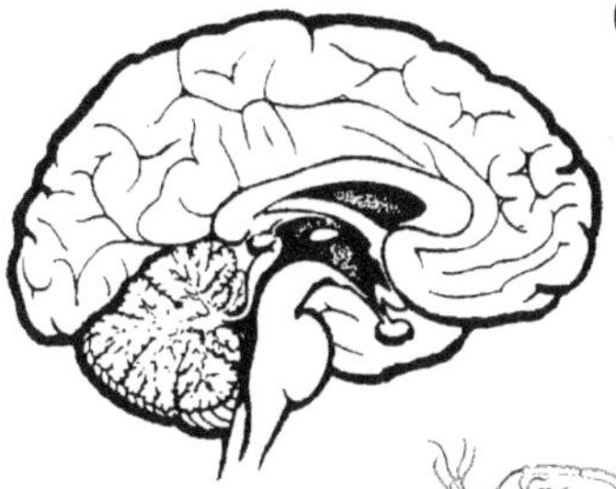

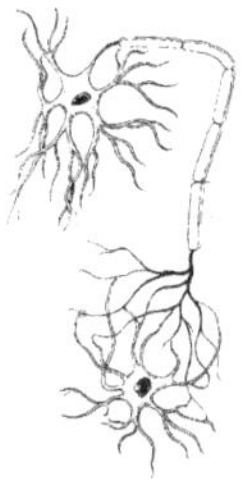

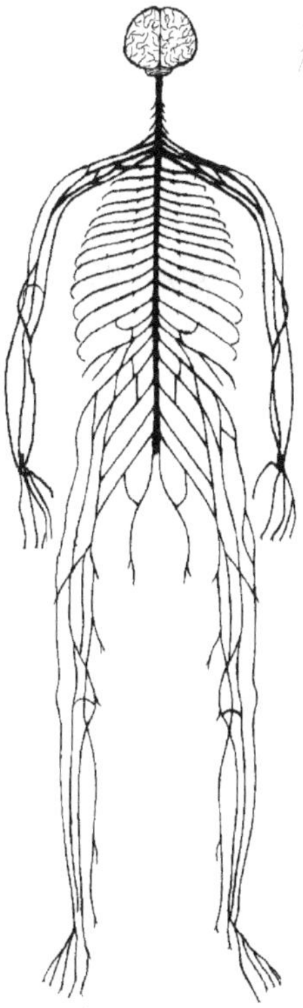

Few people know that Melanin is found in almost every organ of the body and is necessary in order for the brain and nerves to operate, the eyes to see, and the cells to reproduce!

Thus **Melanin** is vastly more than just a "pigment" coloring the skin and hair. At the core of your brain is the "locus coeruleus," a structure that is BLACK because it contains large amounts of Melanin which is essential in order for it to operate! In fact, all the most crucial brain structures are heavily melanized! "Brain melanin is concentrated in a region that functions as a gate for all sensory, motor, emotional and motivational input and output" as well as a region that mediates conscious awareness in general. Dr. Richard King considers the presence of Melanin to be a key agent in heightening psychic sensitivity in the human organism. Dr. Frank Barr suggests (neuro)Melanin may join forces with the glial cells (formerly seen as only the 'glue' of the nervous system) to form a subtly triggered matrix for mental organization–that is, the "mind's eye."

Melanin in the Brain increases from the lower primates and reaches its peak in the BLACK HUMAN

"All humans possess this Black internal brain evidence of their common Black Afrikan Origin. The All Black neuromelanin nerve tract of the brain is profound proof that the human race is a Black race, with many variations of Black, from Black-Black to White-Black, all internally rooted in a vast sea of Brain Blackness."

"Humanity may differ in outer appearance, with variations of colors but internally they are all black, all African at the core. The question for all humans is how to relate to this blackness. A transformation process requires, first, the right heart or feelings and profound African knowledge as taught in ancient African universities. Today's racist is afraid, ignorant of his/her blackness, choosing to run from the ancestral Black core. Today's reborn black masters will accept their blackness, become unified with the universe and be inspired to creative genius at levels that surpass the pyramids."

Dr. Richard King

African Origin of Biological Psychiatry (p31, 24)

Melanin is found *everywhere,* throughout Nature...

in animals, plants (that's why raisins and banana bruises are brown), the soil, waters of creeks, lakes, seas, and even in comets! Concentrations vary from parts per million to parts per billion, and it is soluble in liquid phases.

Melanin is necessary for humans to reproduce!

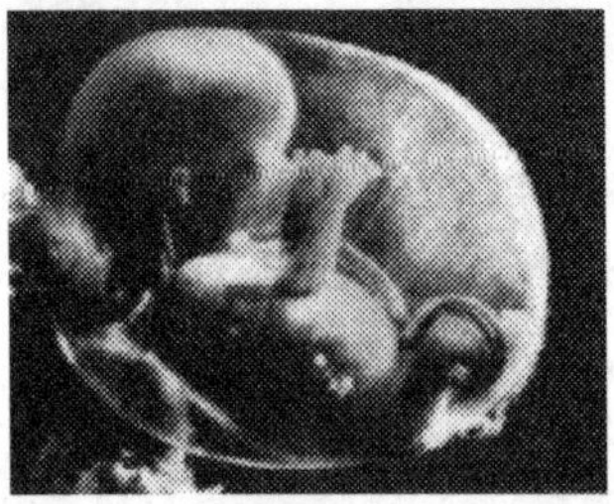

Melanin is abundantly present at the inception of life: a Melanin sheath covers both the sperm and the egg! In the human embryo, the melanocytes (skin pigment cells), the brain, and the nerve cells all originate from the same place; the neural crest. Melanocytes resemble nerve cells and are essential for conveying energy. When the presence of Melanin is missing or insufficient in the ectoderm, this causes the mother to lose her baby; in the case of all whites, a defective baby is produced.

Melanin is the major organizing molecule in living systems

Dr. Frank Barr, pioneering discoverer of Melanin's organizing ability and other properties, opens his technical work, Melanin: The Organizing Molecule: "The hypothesis is advanced that (neuro)melanin (in conjunction with other pigment molecules such as the isopentenoids) functions as the major organizational molecule in living systems. Melanin is depicted as an organizational "trigger" capable of using established properties such as photon-(electron)-photon conversions, free radical-redox mechanism, ion exchange mechanisms, ion exchange mechanisms, and semiconductive switching capabilities to direct energy to strategic molecular systems and sensitive hierarchies of protein enzyme cascades. Melanin is held capable of regulating a wide range of molecular interactions and metabolic processes..."

Melanin's Main Properties: It absorbs, stores & transforms energy. It has "black hole" properties.

- Black **Melanin** can convert light energy to sound energy and back again!
- **Melanin** is BLACK because its chemical structure allows no energy to escape. It is also Black because Black is the perfect absorber of light and all energy frequencies, making Black **Melanin** the super absorber of Energy and Light! Thus scientists describe it as acting like a "black hole."
- **Melanin** can rearrange its chemical structure to absorb ALL energy across the radiant energy spectrum (sunlight, X-rays, music, sound, radar, radio waves...) –and can transmute and store this energy for later use!
- **Melanin** can absorb a great amount of energy and yet not produce a tremendous amount of heat when it absorbs this energy, because it can transform *harmful* energy into *useful* energy. According to Dr. Leon Edelstein*, **Melanin** can absorb tremendous quantities of energy of all kinds, including energy from sunlight, x-ray machines, and energy that is formed within cells during the metabolism of cells. He theorizes that **Melanin** has the ability to neutralize the potentially harmful effects of these energies.
- In Dr. Frank Barr's theory, matter is shaped and structured by light: that is, matter is organized through the interaction of molecules composed of slowed-down light. These molecular [**Melanin**] combinations "eat" light in order to maintain, expand and evolve matter. The more highly evolved a species, the more complex its biological capacity to use light.
- **Melanin** has superconducting properties; it shows evidence of being a room-temperature (biological) super-conductor. Normally, superconductivity occurs only at very low temperatures.
- **Melanin** is like a battery. **Melanin** "may be viewed as a battery that is partially charged and can always accept an electrical charge!" [1] When sunlight or other energy comes in contact with the Melanin battery, it increases the charge of the battery to a certain degree. When the energy is captured, the battery has more energy to use in the body. "This means that the BLACK HUMAN can charge up his MELANIN just by being in the sun or around the right type of musical sounds or other energy sources." [2]
- Melanin in the eye receives light and converts it into the electrical energy that comes across as an image.

* Director of the Dept. of Dermatology and Dermato-Pathology at the St. Vincent Hospital in Worchester, Mass. 1) Barnes, 14. 2) Ibid., 15.

Other astounding properties of Melanin

- **Melanin is the chemical key to life itself.**
- **Melanin is a key ingredient in the DNA of the genes, and protects the DNA nucleus.**
- **Melanin** is centrally involved in controlling all mental and physical body activities.
- **Melanin** granules are "central computers" and may analyze and initiate body responses and reaction without reporting to the brain.
- The lack of **Melanin** is directly related to malfunctioning of the central nervous system while the presence of **Melanin** is directly associated with the proper functioning of the central nervous system.
- **Melanin** is "sweet" (has a pleasant aroma).
- **Melanin** is an anti-oxidant which destroys free radicals (which are a major factor causing aging).
- **Melanin** retards aging and reduces senility (prolongs the life and vitality of laboratory animals).
- **Melanin** causes skin to stay young and wrinkle-free by protecting it from the damaging effects of sunlight. The darker your natural skin (genetically), the less it ages. The opposite is true for lighter skin. That's why whites have wrinkled skin in their 40s or earlier while Blacks often have smooth, unwrinkled skin even in "old" age.
- Though one may be lightskinned, the concentration of **Melanin** in their organs or melanated centers may be as high as that of a darkskinned person. The reverse can also be true sometimes.
- **Melanin** shows the potential to reproduce itself.
- The **Melanin** molecule is so stable that it has been found in 150-million-year-old dinosaur fossils! It is highly resistant to chemical and advanced physical analysis such as electron spin resonance, x-ray diffraction, and synchrotron radiation studies. As a result, its precise structure remains unknown.

"BLACKNESS" is a divine, cosmic principle of the Universe

BLACK is the meaning of KAM –root of Chemistry, study of the building blocks of Life. Life is founded upon CARBON, the BLACK element present in all living matter. Black carbon atoms, with other atoms link to form Black Melanin, which has "Black-Hole" properties. Black Holes are found at the center of our own galaxy and countless others. In physics, a "Black Body" is known to be a perfect absorber and perfect radiator of all forms of light and energy. This "Black Body Radiation" is at work in the Electron, as shown by Nobel prizewinner, Richard Feynman. The Electron is responsible for **all** "Khem-ical" changes in matter. It has been present since the creation of the Universe. Scientist Jean Charon proved the Electron has all the properties of the Black Hole, plus it exchanges "Black Photons" with other Electrons, enabling it to continuously accumulate data. This means that if we view the Electron as a carrier of memory, it has experienced everything in creation since the very beginning. Blackness is fundamental to the operation of the universe of Energy. God is the Giver of All Energy: "Blackness" (not *darkness*) allows the perfect reception of all wavelengths of Energy. Regarding *blackbodies /blackbody radiation*, a physics book shares the following: "a body which is a good reflector is a poor radiator. A blackbody...described as a perfect radiator must therefore, also be a perfect absorber. This...means simply that such a body must absorb all the radiation falling upon it. This requirement could be fulfilled by drilling a small hole in a large hollow sphere since any radiation falling on the hole would be effectively trapped inside, being reflected back and forth from the walls indefinitely without finding the exit. If such an arrangement were heated the radiation streaming out of the hole would be characteristic of a blackbody and the emissivity would be unity, by definition." [1]

How "races" differ due to Melanin

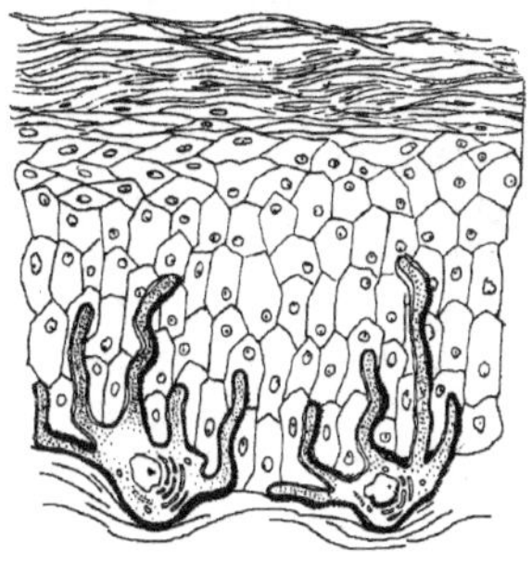

A Japanese scientist [2] has shown that inside the melanocytes (skin pigment cells) are tiny packets called melanosomes that contain Melanin. The four stages in the maturing of these packets is what accounts for racial differences:

Stage 1: The melanosome is empty and doesn't have the machinery to make Melanin.
Stage 2: The melanosome has the machinery to make Melanin, but is empty of Melanin.
Stage 3: The machinery is there and the melanosome is half filled with Melanin.
Stage 4: The machinery is there and the melanosome is completely filled with Melanin.

Whites have mainly stages 1 and 2, whereas all people of color have Melanin – with Blacks having more of stage 4 than 3, while Latinos and Asians have more of stage 3 than 4. All people of color have "circulating Melanin," which is Melanin circulating in the blood due to spillage or excess from the melanosomes.

1) W. McCormick, *Fundamentals of College Physics*, 276. 2) *Sepia Magazine* interview with Dr. Richard King.

Melanin gives Black people advanced mental and physical ability

Carol Barnes writes "...your mental processes (brain power) are controlled by the same chemical that gives Black humans their superior physical (athletics, rhythmic dancing) abilities. This chemical...is Melanin!" The abundance of melanin in Black humans produces a superior organism both mentally and physically. Black infants sit, stand, crawl and walk sooner than whites, and demonstrate more advanced cognitive skills than their white counterparts because of their abundance of melanin. Melanin is the neuro-chemical basis for what is called "SOUL" in Black people. Melanin refines the nervous system in such a way that messages from the brain reach other areas of the body more rapidly in Black people than in other. In the same way Blacks excel in athletics, Blacks can excel in all other areas as well (like they did in the past!) once the road blocks are removed. In his book, *The Developmental Psychology of the Black Child*, Dr. Amos Wilson uses test results taken from the research of WHITE social scientists to show that, contrary to being inferior to whites, Black children in particular show superior psychomotor development over European children: "Whenever motor differences between white and black American infants have been noted in research literature, the black babies have been advanced in comparison with the whites. ... this is also the case with black children of other nationalities, particularly of African origin."[1] "The African babies actually seemed to have been born at a more **advanced** stage of development, since many of their activities at **less than a week** corresponded to those performed by European children aged **four to eight weeks**." (emphasis added) Comparisons in this study show the following difference between these groups:[2]

Accomplishment	Afrikan Babies	European Babies
Being drawn up into a sitting position, able to prevent the head from falling backwards.	9 hours old	6 weeks
With head held firmly, looking at the face of the examiner.	2 days old	8 weeks
Supporting herself in a sitting position and watching her reflection in a mirror.	7 weeks	20 weeks
Holding herself upright.	5 months	9 months
Taking the round block out of its hole in the form board.	5 months	11 months
Standing against the mirror.	5 months	9 months
Walking to the Gesell box to look inside.	7 months	15 months
Climbing the steps alone.	11 months	15 months

Why are whites suddenly virtually denying racial differences?

An Editorial [3] by *Dr. Na'im Akbar:*

What is Black?!

How very strange that suddenly ***Newsweek***, ***Science*** and several of the wire services are doing front-cover and front page stories on the question of whether there is any such thing as racial difference. They are calling forth the testimonies of anthropologists, geneticists and many others to suggest that there really is no scientific validity to the concept of race. This evidence is being called to testify against the growing racial consciousness in African-American communities that is being used to elect Black political leadership, develop Black economic power, the expansion of challenging Afrocentric studies, the successful call for Black leadership coalitions and the growing response to the call for a million Black men to march on Washington, D.C., in October of this year.

While African-American scholars and leaders have argued against the use of race as the criteria for discrimination and oppression of Black people for the last four centuries, it is really interesting that now, European-American scholars and scientists have suddenly decided that race is really a meaningless designation.

Where were they when slavery was based on color for nearly three centuries? Where were they when lynching was dictated by color designation? Where were they when our children were not permitted to master basic learning skills because of race? Where were they when the wealth acquired from our labor was not shared with those who toiled? Where were they when the government refused to let us vote because of race? If their data was not relevant then, we definitely don't want it now as a means to divide and diffuse our power base.

Could it be that there is some fear of the growing number of Black people who are defining race for themselves and doing it in a positive way? Could it be that they fear the blocks of strength which grow from African-Americans beginning to see themselves as having more in common with each other than with political parties, religious denominations, or even income groups? Could it be that there is some fear of the large numbers of so-called "bi-racial" persons who prefer to see themselves as fundamentally African-American as a positive identification? Could it be that the prospect of Black people beginning to define ourselves for our own self-interest is the ultimate expression of power? Might some people fear that we have learned Wade Nobles' definition of power as the ability to define reality and have other people accept your definition as if it were their own?

1) Wilson, 46. 2) Ibid. 3) Reprinted with permission from *Sun of Mind* (Summer 1995, Vol. IV, No. 2), a newsletter by Dr. Na'im Akbar

Most whites have calcified pineal glands apparently thwarting their production of Melatonin

"**The white man or white species is a genetically defective species.** Their MELANOCYTES, MELANOSOMES, and MAST CELLS, etc., do not contain the proper catalyst concentration, chemical reactivity and/or electrical charge needed to produce significant levels of MELANIN in various MELANIN Centers throughout their bodies. Therefore, their organs and systems which depend upon MELANIN to work effectively do not operate well and may suffer numerous disorders such as rapid aging, cancer..." [3]

Why did Afrikans view the European as a child of God, but the Europeans viewed the Afrikan as a soulless savage? Because of "melatonin," described as a mentally and morally stimulating hormone produced by the pineal gland. According to scientific research, most whites are unable produce much of this hormone because their pineal glands are often calcified and non-functioning. **The pineal calcification rates with Afrikans is 5-15%; Asians –15-25%; Europeans –60-80%!** [1] Dr. Richard Kings states "When we talk about cultural differences, some black scholars have raised the question that the European approach, that of the logical, erect, rigid, anti-feeling posture, reflects a left brain orientation and reflects that they lack the chemical key [melatonin] to turn on their unconscious and therefore cannot get into feelings..." Carol Barnes writes "Melanin is responsible for the existence of civilization, philosophy, religion, truth, justice, and righteousness. Individuals (whites) containing low levels of Melanin will behave in a barbaric manner." Melanin gives humans the ability to **FEEL** because it is the absorber of all frequencies of energy. Since whites have the least amount of Melanin, this is why they are perceived by People of Color as generally being rigid, unfeeling (heartless), cold, calculating, mental, and "unspiritual." Their historical behavior towards nonwhites often confirms this.

The scientific evidence of Melanin threatens the life of white supremacy

After considering Melanin to be a "waste" product of body-metabolism which "served no useful function," Western science has now discovered that Black Melanin (neuromelanin) is the chemical key to life and the brain itself. All the studies, facts, and statistics about Melanin suggest that after four hundred years of attempting to inferiorize the Black race, "Western science is facing the sobering reality that, by its own self-defined standards, Black people are probably superior to whites in both intellectual potential and muscle coordination." [2] The central role that melanin plays in the body has been "suppressed to maintain the mythological inferiority of blacks...and the defensive clinging to whiteness as some token of superiority."

The "superiority complex" of white people is a mask for their deepset inferiority complex

which they project onto people of color. They have an inferiority complex about their lack of color in a world where everyone else (the majority) is colored. If Albinos really believed white skin was "superior," then why is "tanning" so important in white culture despite its known health risks? (thousands of whites die annually from skin cancer). In fact, Albinos are now making ***Melanin* tanning ointments.** The *Wall Street Journal* (8/26/88) reported that companies are developing Melanin-based products to help whites tan safely: a California company is developing a Melanin ointment that blocks the entire spectrum of burning ultraviolet rays; researchers in Arizona are testing an ointment that stimulates the skin to produce a natural melanin tan before you go out to the sunlight. And it is the white female who tells you her *ideal* mate is **"tall, DARK, and handsome!"** "Dark" indeed refers to more Melanin!

1) King, AOB, 58-59. 2) *Sepia Magazine* interview with Dr. Richard King. 3) Barnes, 19.

"Messed-up Melanin" is killing Black people!

In their ongoing effort to destroy People of Color, whites (scientists, chemists) create "designer drugs" that are specially structured to **chemically bind with the Melanin molecule and cause Melanin to become toxic to Blacks!** The molecules of these drugs resemble the Melanin molecule. The body is thus fooled and its balance is thrown off as it relies on its *messed up* Melanin in order to function. Major culprits include cocaine, crack, and yes, ***marijuana***.

Blacks get addicted faster, stay addicted longer, and suffer the worse...

from these drugs which are deliberately placed in Black communities. In his vital book, *MELANIN: The Chemical Key to Black Greatness*, –essential reading for all Melanated People, Carol Barnes clearly documents this subject along with the wonders of Melanin. He shows how illegal drugs alter or change Melanin's chemical structure and thus alter many life supporting activities. Toxic drugs and chemicals are destroying the heart of Black society and causing many deaths. Barnes writes:

> "MELANIN can become toxic to the BLACK HUMAN because it combines with harmful drugs such as cocaine, amphetamines, psycholic, hallucinogens, neuroleptic (tranquilizers), marijuana, 'agent orange'...paraquats, tetracyclines..." [1]

- **Toxic drugs** such as cocaine, LSD, and even **marijuana** are very similar to Melanin and the sub-units that make up the Melanin substance. **Many health-conscious Blacks consider marijuana to be a safe healthy *herb*, not realizing that once this (or any *herb*) is "cooked," it becomes a *drug* as far as your body is concerned!**
- Even **legal drugs** (tetracyclines, neuroleptics, etc.) have a remarkable affinity for reacting with or binding to Melanin and may be toxic to all Melanin centers in the Black human.
- Other culprits which bind with Melanin and cause death for Blacks are aromatic and **lipid compounds**. Melanin shows extreme affinity for binding with "aromatic and lipid compounds." [2] Lipid means fat. Lipid or fat compounds (fatty acids) are animal and vegetable oil /fats used for frying and cooking. Examples are shortening and corn oil. Aromatic compounds contain benzene, a major component of gasoline.
- **Herbicides** (paraquats, agent orange, etc.) bind irreversibly with Melanin and remain in the Black human throughout life causing many disorders. Hence Blacks especially, should buy organically grown food.
- Most Blacks test positive in the urine test for marijuana! People having high levels of Melanin or a high number of pigmented centers, such as the Black human, tend to show a positive test for the use of marijuana because the chemical species found in the urine which indicates someone's use of marijuana is also found in the urine of Black humans.

Further Information

- *MELANIN: The Chemical Key to Black Greatness* by Carol Barnes
- *Jazzy Melanin* by Carol Barnes
- *African Origin of Biological Psychiatry* by Dr. Richard King
- *MELANIN: A Key To Freedom* by Dr. Richard King
- *Handbook for a Melinated, Melatonin-Friendly Lifestyle* by Dr. Patricia Newton
- *The Melanin Symposium* (video/audio tapes) Institute of Karmic Guidance (see *Resources*)

1) Barnes, MCK, 32. 2) Ibid.

6

Black People (Humanity's Parents) Originated and Pioneered World Civilization

On all continents, civilization began with Black Afrikan people!

Given that the Black race is the oldest, this fact should come as no surprise! Historically Blacks have played the earliest civilizing role in the world as shown by Kamit (ancient Egypt), Sumer, Babylon, Canaan, Kush (Ethiopia), Indus Kush & Harrappa (ancient India), the Washitaw and Olmecs (ancient America), and the Shang of ancient China. Other great Afrikan civilizations included the empires of Ghana, Mali, Songhai, Benin, Zimbabwe and the Moors who ruled southwest Europe for 700 years. **Afrikans civilized all the peoples of Earth.** They left evidence of this in the remotest corners of the planet. Civilization has been globally destroyed numerous times from catastrophes such as pole shifts. Each time this happened, it was Black Afrikans –the Parents of Humanity– that put everything back together and redistributed civilization around the planet again.

> "**we have found the black complexion** or something relating to it whenever we have approached to the origin of the nations." [1]
>
> *Godfrey Higgens*

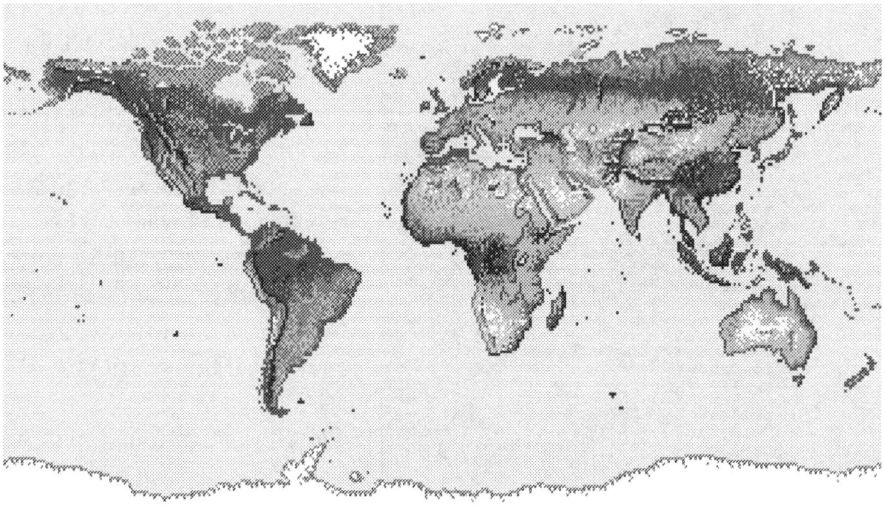

1) Higgens, vI, 286.

• ASIA :
Afrikans Pioneered Ancient Asia's Civilizations

Blacks were first in Asia and pioneered Asia's early civilizations

The Black role in Asia, as elsewhere in the world, has been submerged and distorted for centuries. Asia's Afrikan roots are well summarized in African Presence in Early Asia, by Runoko Rashidi and Ivan Van Sertima, and African Presence in Early China, by James Brunson. The original oriental people were Black and many of them still are Black –in southern China and Asia.

> **"In whatever form or under whatever name we study the origin and trace back the religious beliefs, origin of words and symbolisms of the people of Asia,** we can only arrive at the conclusion that they came out of Egypt [Afrika]....Even the present writing of the Chinese and Japanese are only the old Egyptian Hieroglyphics with linear signs added....The pictorial writings forming the basis of the cuneiform and Chinese characters is unmistakably only a species of the hieroglyphics; their astronomy is only a copy of that of Egypt." [1]

The earliest occupants of Asia were 'small Blacks' (Pygmies), who came to the region as early as 50,000 years ago. J.A. Rogers reports that in 1923, Europeans first discovered "a hitherto unknown Negro race, the Nakhis, 200,000 in number, in Southern China." [2] George Parker writes "it appears that the entire continent of Asia was originally the home of many black races and that these races were the pioneers in establishing the wonderful civilizations that have flourished throughout this vast continent." [3] Reports of major kingdoms ruled by Blacks are frequent in Chinese documents. The first kingdom of Southeast Asia is called *Fou Nan,* famous for building masterful canal systems. Chinese historians described the Fou Nanese men as "small and black."

The *Ainus*, Japan's oldest known inhabitants, have traditions which tell of a race of dark dwarfs which inhabited Japan before they did. Historians Cheikh Anta Diop and Albert Churchward saw the Ainus as originating in Egypt! There is archeological support for this. In addition, ancient Egypt and Mesopatamia records the "Anu" (Ainu?). The Ainu "...are of the same original race and type as the Australian Aborigines" reports Churchward.[4] Rogers writes "...there are any number of Japanese who, but for color and hair, bear a striking resemblance to the South African Bushman" [5] An ancient tradition points to the conquest of Japan from the southeast by a race of Black warriors.

The first shogun of Japan was a Black man, Sakanouye Tamura Maro, who lived circa 800 C.E. (of the common era).[6]

1) Churchward, SS, 264. 2) Rogers, AF, 5. 3) Parker, CS, 11. 4) Churchward, SS, 218. 5) Rogers, SR, 71. 6) R. Rashidi, *The Global African Community*, 2.

China's first historical dynasty and first emperor were Black!

Africoid T'ang general

Courtesy of Runoko Rashidi

Shang (Chiang) artifact

Founded by King T'ang or Ta, the earliest documented rulership in China was the Shang (or Chiang) Dynasty c. 1500-1000 B.C., credited with bringing together the elements of China's earliest known civilization. The Shang were given the name of *Nakhi* (*Na*: Black, *Khi*: man). Under this Black dynasty, the Chinese established the basic forms of a graceful calligraphy that has lasted to the present day. The first Chinese emperor, the legendary Fu-Hsi (2953-2838 B.C.) was a woolly haired Black man. He is credited with establishing government, originating social institutions and cultural inventions. He is said to have originated the I Ching, or The Book of Change, which is the oldest, most revered system of prophecy. It is known to have influenced the most distinguished philosophers of Chinese thought. **Emperor Hung Wu, founder of the famous Chinese Ming Dynasty,** was both a Muslim and of Afrikan (Sudanese) / Mongolian descent. "It was during the Ming Dynasty that gun powder, the Great Wall of China and the mechanical printing press combined to revolutionize that part of the world." [1]

"Chinese Roots Lie in Africa, Research Says"

As reported in the *Los Angeles Times* (9/29/98): "Most of the population of modern China –one fifth of all the people living today – owes its genetic origins to Africa, an international scientific team said today in research that undercuts any claim that modern humans may have originated independently in China. ...Li Jan, the senior scientist guiding the genetic analysis, said the findings may disappoint some of his fellow geneticists in China, where recent fossil discoveries that attest to the great antiquity of human settlement in East Asia have been a source of national pride. ... 'The genetics community in China is in favor of the idea of independent origin of the people of China,' said Jan... 'But this is another confirmation of African origin.' "

Did Afrikans build those ancient pyramids in China & Japan?

There are manmade pyramids in China[2] and Japan. China's earthen pyramids are in Xian and near Siang Fu city in the Shensi province. The Chinese deny they exist. And the builders of these ancient monuments? – the "obscure" so-called "Mound Builders" (see page 67). Mistaken for hills due to their eroded appearance, some pyramids in Japan[3] are estimated to be 25,000 years old. They are made of stones not indigenous to Japan. It is said they were built during the time of Mu.

Nappy Chinese sculpture.

One of five ancient, granite pyramids in the forest of Mount Kasagi, Japan. Local tradition describes a white serpent that dwells under or within it. In an annual ritual that continues to this day, residents leave an offering of eggs as a feast for the serpentine *genius loci*. The only other place where such symbolism (and solid stone mini-pyramids) occur is in Afrika's Nile Valley, as Kneph, the serpent manifestation of the creator-god, Khnemu, who fashioned the Cosmic Egg from which burst forth the Universe. *Photo: Ancient American Magazine, #17*

The largest of 100s of pyramids in China is also the largest pyramid in the world. Its four sides were painted red, yellow, green, and black.[4]

1) Al-Monsour, 42. 2) Childress, LCC, 387, 391. 3) *The Pyramids of Japan*, film by Alpha Media Corp. 4) Bey, 9.

The martial arts originated in Afrika, not Asia!

The Afrikan origin and history of the martial arts is the subject of _Nuba Wrestling –The Original Art_, authored by a Black Master of martial arts himself, **Nijel BPG**, –also an Actor, Artist, Sculptor, and Co-producer of several martial arts films. Nile Valley Afrikans practiced martial arts wrestling over 5000 years ago. No other records around the world can make this claim and unbroken martial arts tradition. Nijel also documents the Afrikan origin of other defense systems such as fortification, castles. "In the beginning Egypt was ruled from Cush and was considered a colony of Cush. The fighting sciences are only a small fragment of the total knowledge that each individual was expected to study in the temples and hall of letters."

Another multi-talented, multifaceted Grand Master of martial arts is **Dr. Hassan K. Salim** (photo at left). Professor, Kamitic priest, Storyteller, and founder of several institutions, he is the author of numerous books, including co-author with Shaha Mfundishi Maasi of _Kupigana Ngumi: Root Symbols of Ancient Civilizations_, which addresses among other topics, the Afrikan roots of martial arts. "Kupigana Ngumi is the synthesis of the Afrakan Warrior Experience. All martial arts, like all humankind, have their roots in Afraka, which other cultures have assimilated and modified over many centuries to serve their needs."

In _African Presence in Early Asia,_ Martial Master **Kilindi Iyi**'s essay enlightens us further about this topic. Afrikans discovered very early that the movements of animals could be used effectively to develop their fighting skills. Also, that "animal principles" could be isolated within the consciousness and manifested into an unconquerable fighting force. The oldest records of kicking, throwing, wrestling, and punching techniques were found in Kamit –ancient Egypt. These warrior scientists laid the foundation for all martial arts systems, including Kung Fu, Judo, and Aikido.

Below: Kamite mural segments from Mahez (renamed *Beni Hasan* by Arabs, meaning *hill of the son of the Hasan family*).

Courtesy of Nijel Binns (inset), and Runoko Rashidi

• INDIA:
Afrikans Pioneered Ancient India's Civilizations

The first people of India were Afrikans! *India* itself means *Black.*

"Ancient India was Africa's Asian heartland." [1]

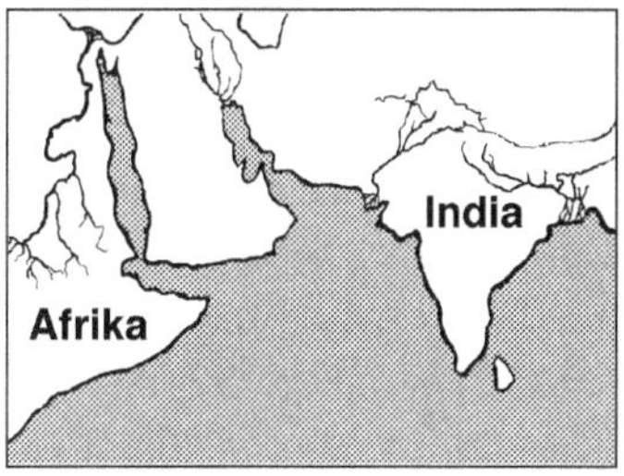

The Latin word "India" is from Greek *Indus* (or Indos) meaning black. The earliest people of India were Black Afrikans or Ethiopians called *Negritos.* Later came Blacks classified as *Proto-Australoid* (ancestors of the Australian Aborigines). Indian historian-anthropologist B.V. Bhavan stated, "We have to begin with the Negroid or Negrito people of prehistoric India who were its first human inhabitants. Originally they would appear to have come from Africa through Arabia and the coastlands of Iran and Baluchistan..."[2] Wayne Chandler wrote, "The merging of these two culturally diverse but monoracial groups–the Ethiopian Negrito and the Proto-Australoid–produced the people of the Indus Valley civilization." [3]

Ruins of bath at Mohenjo Daro.

Also called *Dravidians*, these Afrikans founded the great Indus Valley Civilization around 3000 B.C. The expanse of this empire was greater than the combined kingdoms of ancient Egypt and Mesopotamia. They brought with them many spiritual sciences which originated in Afrika, such as those of Yoga, Kundalini, Tantra, and Reflexology. It is believed that the Ganges, the sacred river of India, is named after an Ethiopian king of that name who conquered Asia as far as this river. Buddha, Krishna, and other great Black sages arose from their successive civilizations, including the great King Asoka. Ancient historians /geographers called the whole region from Kamit to India, by the name of Ethiopia, and its dark-skinned inhabitants Ethiopians.

The Afrikan founders of ancient India were masters of urban planning

They were the world's first urban planners, as attested by the ruins of their spectacular cities Mohenjo-Daro and Harappa. The city of Harappa was built in a gridlike fashion with a large main street; "it seems almost a minute version of Manhattan Island." It was a few thousand years before whites (Romans) began constructing towns with similar patterns "and then another millennium passed before municipal planning would be seen on the earth again." [4]

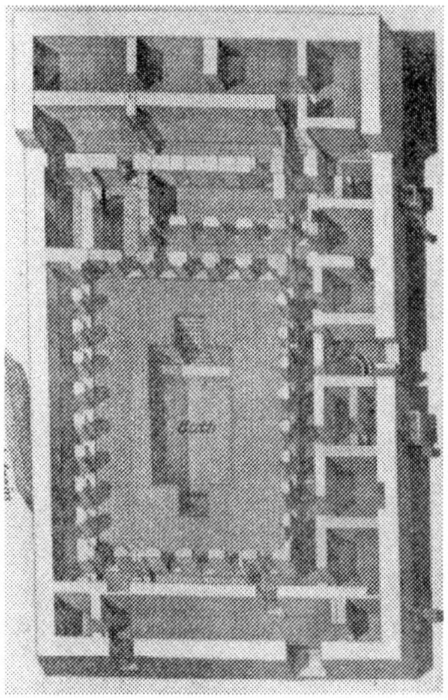

Reconstruction of bath at Mohenjo Daro.

Their homes & cities had running water, toilets and an underground sewage system!

–evidenced at the Mohenjo Daro ruins (2000 B.C.). Virtually every household was equipped with what could be called "modern conveniences." In addition to trash chutes for disposing debris, each household had bathrooms with drains which carried waste to the sewers under the main streets. Almost every dwelling had its own private water well. Harappan homes were two or more stories high, based on a common design: a square courtyard surrounded by arranged rooms. Maximizing privacy, all windows faced the courtyard. Towns were lined with shops and restaurants.

1) Runoko Rashidi. 2) Rashidi /Van Sertima , APEA, 82. 3) Ibid., 83. 4) Ibid., 90.

Barbaric whites invaded India, bringing destruction & the Caste System

Around the 7th century B.C., barbaric tribes of whites invaded India. Like their Greek cousins were to do later, these uncivilized whites learned civilization from the Blacks and overthrew them, destroying their great civilization.

Like their European cousins were to do later with Christianity and Judaism, they distorted the Blacks' religion into a system which ensured their superiority while suppressing the natives.

The invaders created and imposed the Caste System upon the indigenous population. The Caste System is the basis of their cunning, oppressive religious ideology which to this day enslaves the mind, body and soul of indigenous Blacks. Originally called *Brahminism*, this religion was altered (like original Judaism /Christianity) and is now called Hinduism –the greatest curse to India's Blacks. Eminent historian Runoko Rashidi writes: "By 800 B.C. these nomadic Aryan peoples had conquered most of northern India and renamed their newly won dominions 'Aryavarta' (the Aryan Land). Throughout Aryavarta a rigid, caste-segmented social order was established with masses of conquered Blacks (Sudras) positioned as the lowest caste and imposed upon for service (in any capacity required) to the higher castes. With the passage of time, this brutally harsh Caste System became the basis of the religion which is now practiced throughout all India. This is the religion known as 'Hinduism.'...The greatest victims of Hinduism have been the 'Untouchables.' " [1]

"Aryan" is a misnomer which did not originally mean white

Historians *incorrectly* refer to these whites as "Aryan," a word taken from the Sanskrit language of India's Blacks, where it meant *noble cultivator* or *the holy* as a title for Rishis (sages) who mastered the sacred science of Aryasatyani. The Afrikan-Kamite root of Aryan is ***ari*** (high). Since Kamite R & L were one, Ari = ***Ali***, the same *Ali* which gives EL (in Elohim, Micha-El, El-ijah), meaning deification. Ari also means maker, doer, hence giving us ARtist, ARt, ARable, etc., whence "noble cultivator." These invading barbarians were not cultivators but destroyers. Nor were they farmers, being nomads.

No justice exists for the Dalits: India's Black "Untouchables"

At the top of the Hindu caste pyramid sits the Brahmin. At the bottom are the heavily exploited, degraded, humiliated, slave-like, impoverished "Untouchables" who carry the weight of the entire population. They are the worse victims of Hindu society, along with women at all caste levels. African Presence in Early Asia presents an essay by Indian activist, **V. T. Rajshekar** who writes: "From the very beginning it [Brahminism /Hinduism] has had the suppression of the native population and women, even Aryan women, as its primary principles....whereas the natives respected all humans and assured equal status to women. In fact, the natives of India were matriarchal..." These Black Untouchables are the long-suffering descendants of Aryan/Black unions and native Black populations who retreated into the hinterlands of India seeking escape from the advancing Aryan influence under which they eventually succumbed. They call themselves **Dalits** which means *crushed and broken*. Though the Caste System (or *Varna* System) was based originally on skin color (*varna* means *color*), color is not the main problem as some dark or light skinned people are found at the top and bottom. The problem is the sanctioned oppression of the Black Untouchables. No justice exists for them! Crimes against them by caste Hindus almost always go unpunished! Rajshekar writes:

> "**No where else in the world is there any parallel to the Aryan persecution of the untouchables of India**...It is a social, cultural, and religious institution... The caste structure maintains itself because every member of a particular caste group stands to gain by belonging to that particular caste-group. The caste system helps the exploitation of the weak by the strong. India's constitution not only does not interfere with caste, but fully upholds it... Caste system is based on purity and pollution. One group is considered more pure than the other. The less pure caste

1) Rashidi /Van Sertima, APEA, 244.

group accepts its lower status because it is happy that it has a much larger caste group below it to exploit. As long as there is somebody below it to exploit, it is proud and will not mind somebody always standing on its shoulders. So the entire caste structure is a ...self-sustaining, automatic, exploitative machine."

India's Blacks are ignorant of their Afrikan roots

India's native Black population is the largest Black population outside of Afrika, numbering about 200 million. They have brown to black skin, straight or kinky hair and Africoid features, such as the famous Indian holy man, Sathya Sai Baba who has a large kinky afro. Rajshekar writes:

Courtesy of Runoko Rashidi

Sathya Sai Baba

Courtesy of Runoko Rashidi

Dravidian male

"The Black untouchables of India, even the educated among them, are not aware of the common origin of Africans and Dalits. When they come to know of this and the struggle of the African-Americans and their spectacular achievements, our people will naturally become proud. **Putting pride into their broken hearts is our prime task... The African-Americans also must know that their liberation struggle cannot be complete as long as their own blood-brothers and sisters living in far off Asia are suffering. It is true that African-Americans are also suffering, but our people here today are where African-Americans were two-hundred years ago...African-Americans and India's Black Untouchables are both the victims of racism...African-Americans leaders can give our struggle tremendous support by bringing forth knowledge of the existence of such a huge chunk of Asian Blacks to the notice of both the American Black masses and the Black masses who dwell within the African continent itself...**No group is better positioned to launch this cultural revolution than India's Dalits. Since we form the foundation of this caste pyramid, we alone are capable of shaking its structure, if not demolishing it...The moment that our people come to believe that they are neither Hindus nor obligated to obey the upper castes, the whole caste structure completely collapses." (Emphasis added)

India's Blacks, like America's Blacks, are awakening from a long spell of ignorance of their true history & Afrikan roots

India's Black Dalits have been profoundly inspired by the Black Liberation Movement and Black leaders of the 1960s, whom they revere. Some are linking with Afrikan Americans. **Instrumental in this awakening has been Runoko Rashidi,** Afrikan-American historian, author, lecturer, India-tour leader, and founder of the International Dalit Support Group.

India's rich Afrikan roots are presented in:

African Presence in Early Asia, by Ivan Van Sertima & Runoko Rashidi
Meter Neter, by Ra Un Nefer Amen
The best publication on India's Black Untouchables is *The Dalit Voice*, edited by Indian activist, author, journalist V.T. Rajshekar. (See *Resources*)

• AMERICAS:
Afrikans Pioneered Ancient America's Civilizations

The Africoid Olmecs was the parent culture of Ancient America

Flourishing more than 1000 years before Christ, the Olmecs was the parent civilization of Ancient America. Colossal monuments of stone heads in Mexico show numerous carvings of them as gods. Their faces are unmistakably Africoid, and their hair is plaited or in cornrows! Furthermore, they were Twa (Pygmies). Many gods of ancient Central America are portrayed black with Africoid features. There are many Africoid portraits in stone, clay, copper and gold. In addition to their early culture shaping role, the Olmecs were undoubtedly profoundly influenced by Black migrants from Africa's Nile Valley. Columbus himself made emphatic reference to Black traders from Guinea.

Bes, of Egypt

Note the resemblance of the god at the center of the Aztec calendar above with the Afrikan Twa god, Bes.

Afrikan technology built Mexico's pyramids and more

The reason for the profound similarity between ancient Middle America and Kamit is because Kamit authored that civilization, including Mexico's pyramids. In his scholarly work, *Signs and Symbols of Primordial Man*, Albert Churchward, a rare honest Albino historian, fully documents among other things, the Afrikan origin of ancient Mexico's culture, religion, hieroglyphics, etc. The Aztecs attributed the invention of their Calendar to their greatest god, the black skinned, woolly haired Quetzalcoatl. The Bow & Arrow originated in Afrika from the Twa of Central Afrika who carried it around the world in their migrations. Nubia was called the "Land of the Bow" with its formidable archers. And note the profound similarity between Native American culture with that of pre-Albino Afrika (drumming, singing, feathers, circle dances, body painting, love of Nature, etc.). Now you know why they resemble! **Kamite text (3900 B.C.) apparently refers to the Mayas, calling them the "Haui-Nibu"** or "People beyond the Seas" / "People from behind" (behind the setting sun). Churchward writes, "As the sun, setting in the West, went down into the sea, the Mayas would naturally be spoken of as people 'beyond the seas' or 'behind the setting sun.' "[1]

Did Afrikans also rule all of South & Central America?

Yes! According to Peruvian historian, Eduardo de Habiche who documents this in his Spanish book, *El Peru Milenario des Quicia las bases de la: Historia Universal* (Lima, Peru 1983). He asserts that these Afrikans were Egyptian invaders seeking Peruvian gold. Aztec murals clearly depict Blacks with Natives. In his book *Ancient Egypt, Mexico & the United States*, R. A. Jairazbhoy pictorially documents cultural connections between ancient North America and Egypt.

1) Churchward, 376.

The "obscure" *Mound Builders* were Indigenous BLACKS of North America; ancestors of America's "Washitaw Empire"

National Museum of Man, Ottawa

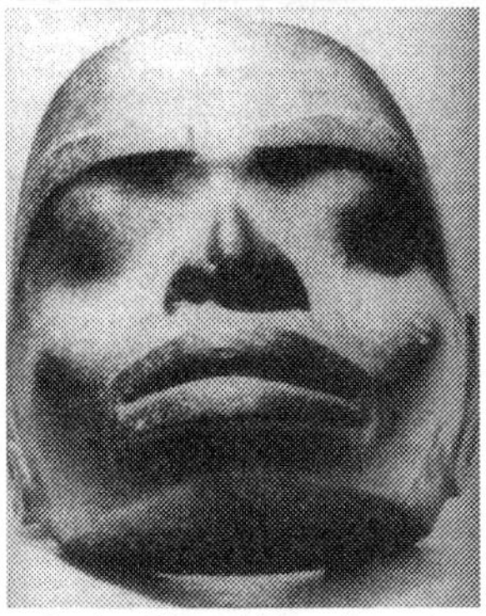

Ancient Negroid basalt mask found in Canada in 1879

Courtesy of Dr. Umar S. Bey

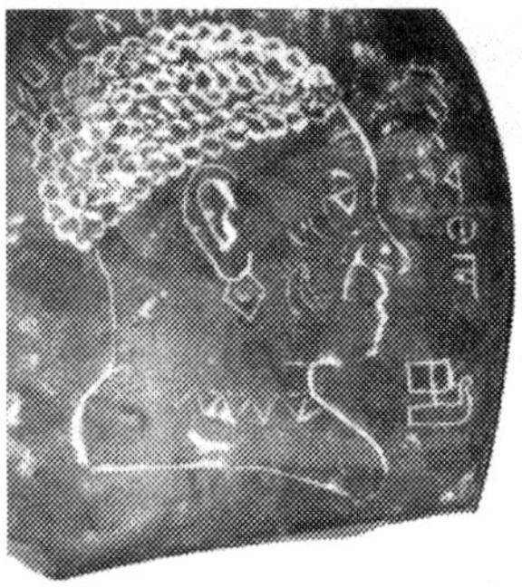

Ancient Negroid stone artifact from Burrows Cave, Illinois

Though so many have been deliberately destroyed, over 200,000 ancient pyramids and huge mounds of earth in the shape of cones, animals and geometric designs can still be found from the southern coast of America to Canada. These structures were built by a so-called "**obscure**" people largely known as "**the Mound Builders.**" The truth about the Mound Builders is suppressed. Why? Because they were an advanced civilization of dark-skinned woolly-haired Blacks who were **indigenous** (native) **to *North* America** –kin to the Olmecs of *South* America. At one time the Afrikan and American continents were joined, as proven by their similarity of tropical plants and animals, geographic traits, and their appearance of fitting together. The Black Mound Builders were the ***Washitaw-Muurs*** (Ouachita-Moors), the ORIGINAL inhabitants of North *and* South America. **Many Blacks in North America are unknowing descendants of these mound-building indigenous BLACKS –and NOT descendants of Black Afrikan slaves!** Therefore, Columbus was not entirely wrong in calling these people "Indians"! For the **true meaning of "Indian" is *Black Person!*** The massive remains of this ancient BLACK civilization /empire "stands as one of the best-kept archaeological secrets in the country." Ancient American Magazine (Issue 17) reported: *"Evidence for black-skinned natives in the Americas long before the arrival of Columbus is abundant. From the distinctly negroid features of colossal Olmec sculpted heads and a pre-Aztec obsidian bowl being upheld by a figure with unmistakably black characteristics, to the bones of negroid persons excavated from a 2,000 year-old mound in northern Wisconsin, a wealth of material exists to establish the certainty of non-White, non-Indian population living in pre-Columbian America along with these other groups."* Many Mound Builders were huge; their ancient skeletons were often 7 to 8 feet. The only other living people on Earth this tall are another group of Blacks, the Massai of Afrika. In his books (esp. *"**We Are The Washitaw**")*, website (www.**hotep.org**) & mobile exhibits, Dr. Umar S. Bey, himself a Washita-Muur and authority on the Washitaw /Mound Builders, documents the Black Mound Builders. He also documents the present-day **Washitaw Nation** in Louisiana (recently recognized by the United Nations) and **Empress of the Washitaw**: Verdiacee 'Tiari' Washitaw-Turner Goston El-Bey.

Courtesy of Ancient American Magazine

Calling pyramids "mounds" is a way (ploy) of obscuring them.
This pyramid at Cahokia in Illinois (USA) is larger than the Great Pyramid in Egypt!

Afrikan presence in ancient America is documented in:

We Are The Washitaw, by Dr. Umar S. Bey
Muur Guide to Pyramids, Mounds, and Other Earthworks in America, by Dr. Umar S. Bey
They Came Before Columbus, by Dr. Ivan Van Sertima
The African Presence in Early America, by Dr. Ivan Van Sertima
Dawn Voyage, The Black Discovery of America, by Michael Bradley
Ancient Egyptians in Middle & South America, by R. A. Jairazbhoy
Ancient Egypt, Mexico & the United States, by R. A. Jairazbhoy
Ancient American Magazine

Native Americans' great contributions have been ignored

As previously noted, the relationship of Native Americans and Afrikans goes back thousands of years. When white men came to Central & South America, they immediately began enslaving the Natives. Millions of Natives died (along with their great, quashed civilizations), from slavery, torture, murder and European diseases. **Many were also imported as slaves to Europe!** Initiating the Atlantic slave trade, Columbus crammed his tiny three ships with 1,200 Indian slaves upon returning to Spain. After running short on labor supply due to brutally murdering most of the Native population, Europeans began importing Afrikan slaves to meet the growing labor demands of their ruthless conquest and plunder. Thus Native and Afrikan Americans share a common history of massive abuse, genocide and exploitation from white men. Natives were even called by the same derogatory terms applied to Afrikans and often treated just as cruel, to say nothing of two whole continents taken from them.

Native American foods revolutionized world agriculture.

That's why Italians have tomatoes, Irish and Germans have potatoes, etc. Other foods include maize, peanuts, beans, squashes, peppers.

Wealth ravaged from Native Americans ballooned European economy.

Historians show that in 1492, the value of all the gold and silver in Europe was about $200 million. In 1600, just 100 years (& countless slaves) later, it increased to two billion! –empowering major economic & trade expansion in Europe which led to the **Industrial Revolution**.

Originally, early colonists gave some recognition to Natives

Architects of the U.S. Capitol fashioned the columns to resemble stalks of corn, and covered the ceiling with tobacco leaves and flowers. And the first symbol of America was Pocohantas, a Native American girl. It was the cartographers who drew maps of the New World that selected her. Her images frequently adorned maps well into the 1700s. As the U.S. moved toward civil war, Native heritage was obscured and whitewashed.

The tenets of the U.S. Constitution originated from Native Americans!

The Founding Fathers copied the democratic ideals of the U.S. Constitutional government from the highly developed political system of the Iroquois League of Nations! The American Federal system derives primarily from Native Americans, NOT from Europe, which was a despotic feudal society, nor from ancient Greece where the majority were either slaves or excluded from decision making. George Washington, Thomas Jefferson, Benjamin Franklin and others were highly knowledgeable of Native political systems. Franklin urged the new nation to model its government on the League of the Iroquois and guided the creation of the American constitution, which derives from the Iroquois Kayanesha Kowa (Great Law of Peace). Of course the whitewashed history books do not acknowledge this. In _The Sacred Hoop: Recovering the Feminine in American Indian Tradition_, Paula Gunn Allen documents this subject along with the Native American quest for freedom and justice, and the blacked out crucial role of women in Native American tradition (which stems directly from the same in matriarchal Afrikan tradition.

Almost all Afrikan-Americans have "Indian blood" !

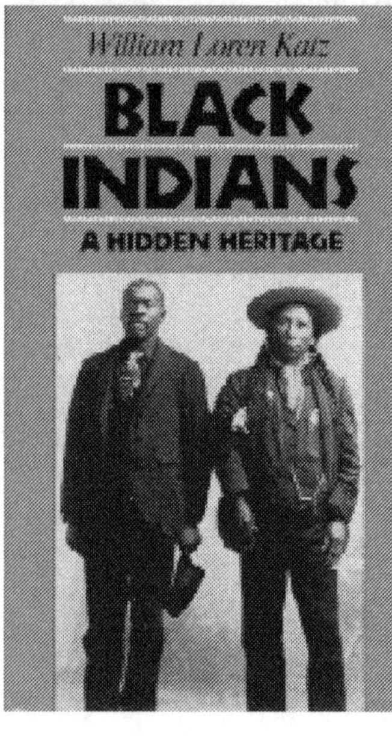

The history of the formidable "Black Indians" is almost totally unwritten. The first paths to freedom taken by runaway slaves led to Native American villages where Blacks found a Red hand of friendship and an accepting adoption system & culture. _Black Indians_ by William Katz documents the remarkable history of the descendants of Native American/Afrikan unions in North, Central & South America, including the powerful Afrikan-Seminole Alliance in Florida that fought the U.S. Army, Navy & Marines to a standstill for 40 years. It reveals that "Today just about every African-American family tree has an Indian branch... Europeans forcefully entered the African blood stream, but Native Americans and Africans merged by choice, invitation, and love."

Other books documenting Native Americans include:

Forgotten Founders, by Bruce Johansen
The New Indian, by S. Stiener
The Nations Within, by V. Deloria
Agents of Repression, by Churchill/Wall
The State of Native America, by M. Jaimes
This Land is Our Land, by Baxendale/McClaine

BOOK 2 :

Quantum Deception & Effective Mind Control in the Name of "the Lord"

7

The Original Afrikan *IUs*, Early Aryan *Hebrews*, Impostor European *Jews*

An Overview

- **The original Jews were Black Afrikan people**
  - **The original *Hebrews* (Habiru) were invading whites –not Semites at all**
    - **Today over 90% of "Jews" are European Khazars; Counterfeit Jews**

More than 90% of the people who call themselves "Jews" today, are EUROPEAN to the *bone*; they are *Khazars* with no Semitic, Judean, *Judahite,* or Israelite roots whatsoever. The Khazars were a warlike European tribe that all converted to Judaism during the Middle Ages. The original Hebrews (Habiru) were white nomadic barbarians who invaded the Black civilizations. Like their cousins the Khazars, they were not "true Jews." Unlike the Khazars, their history is woven with the original Jews. The original true ethnic Jews were Black African people in Afrika's Nile Valley thousands of years ago before there was any such name as "Jews" or "Children of Israel."

In White, Out Black. Sort of.

They were white when they invaded the Black civilizations of the South. Many mixed with them and got "melanated." Thus the original white Habiru (Hebrew) people got brown or at least, tinged. Many managed to stay near white. Some from this group migrated to Europe where they recovered most of their whiteness by re-mixing with their European cousins. The mixing of the white Habirus and other white invaders with the Blacks has yielded what is called the "Semite race." Historian Cheikh Anta Diop shows that the "Semite" arises in the 4th millennia B.C. from crossbreeding between Black inhabitants of the holy land and white northern invaders.[1] Biblically, *Semite* refers to the descendants of Shem, one of Noah's sons, but...

Since Shem was mythological, *no one* descended from him!

SEM has many meanings in Egyptian. The word Semite is from the meaning of sem as "half," (source of Latin prefix *semi*) thus the Semites are essentially *mulattoes*, a mixture, "half Black and half white... therefore Black (since Black is genetically dominant)" points out Dr. Frances Cress Welsing. This chapter addresses the original Black Afrikan *IUs*, the white *Habirus* who supplanted them, and the European Khazars who usurped them both.

1) Fardan, 47.

The original Jews or Israelites were Black Afrikan people

The original Jews began not as Semites in Palestine, but as Black Afrikan people worshipping IU in Afrika's Nile Valley. IU is the Afrikan origin the words Jew, Judah, Judaism. IU was a name of God/Goddess and the Sun/Son of God/Goddess as the Ever Coming One.

- Eminent European scholar, Gerald Massey presents abundant evidence for the Afrikan origin of the Jews in his scholarly classic, *Ancient Egypt The Light of the World*. As one of the exceedingly few white scholars who reported history without discrediting Afrikans, he writes of the original Jews' Black Afrikan identity and origin in ancient 'Egypt or Ethiopia,' from whence they spread to India.[1]
- That the Jews were originally a group of Ethiopians and Egyptians who migrated out of the Nile Valley to settle in Palestine was firmly articulated by the Roman historians; Tacitus, Eusebius, and Diodorus.[2]
- The Afrikan identity of the early Jews were so obvious that many Roman historians believed that the Jews were descendants of Ethiopians (All of Afrika was called Ethiopia in ancient times). Roman historian Tacitus (80 A.D.), reported that the Jews originated in Afrika (Ethiopia), and fled to Arabia during the reign of King Cephus to escape oppression.[3]

- Conquerors of Jewish regions clearly depicted their Jewish captives as Africoid with nappy hair, peppercorn styled like that of Buddha's. Stone reliefs at King Sennacherib's palace (700 B.C.) at Nineveh in Babylon show nappy Judean captives being escorted by their equally nappy Assyrian conquerors to King Sennacherib.[4]
- An ancient tribe of Afrikan Jews which survives to this day, and is still Black, is the Beta Israel, commonly called "Falasha" in Ethiopia.[5] Being the most ancient and authentic of Jews, they are living history. A *New York Times* editorial (3/2/84) described them as "a lost tribe that has kept its identity for more than 2,000 years in a remote corner of Africa."
- According to their own accounts, the Jews were plagued by leprosy. This supports their being Afrikan people. "We know from their own accounts that the Jews were eaten up with leprosy, and may see in that fact good ethnic evidence for their being of the ancient African stock."[6]

Dura Europas painting of Black Moses leading his Black people across the Red Sea.

Firsthand evidence survives from the past: ancient Jews portrayed themselves Africoid in lifesize paintings at Dura Europas

Untouched since 256 A.D. when it fell to an invading army of Persia, an ancient Judaic synagogue in Syria was discovered in 1920 A.D. The synagogue was at the lost site of a Greek fortress now called Dura Europas. It contained numerous life-sized paintings of Jews on its walls which were painted by the hands of Jews themselves. These paintings are a firsthand witness to the racial identity of the Jews –who painted themselves as People of Color in hues ranging from dark to light complexion, typically with Africoid features and nappy hair. They depict numerous, famous biblical events such as Moses parting the Sea, the anointment of David, etc. Books showing these murals typically selectively show only the lightskinned Jews.

1) Massey, AE, 501. 2) Van Sertima, APEA, 190. 3) Rogers, SR, 92. 4) Revell BD, 456. 5) Saakana, 6. 6) Massey, BB-vII, 415.

The Bible acknowledges the Afrikan identity of the Jews

- The Bible classifies the **Ethiopians** and **Jews** together: "Are ye not as children of the Ethiopians unto me, O children of Israel? saith the Lord" (Amos 9:7).
- Mistaken for an "**Egyptian**" **Paul** declares himself to be a "**Jew**" (Acts 21:37-39, 22: 2, 3).
- The "**Children of Israel**" mixed with the Black nations around them: "And the children of Israel dwelt among the **Canaanites**, Hittites, and Amorites, and Perizzites, and Hivites, and Jebusites: And they took their daughters to be their wives, and gave their daughters to their sons, and served their gods" (Judges 3:5, 6). All these tribes except the Perizzites, are descendants of **Canaan**, son of Ham, father of Black Nations.
- All the sons of **Jacob** (Israel) married Canaanites, except Joseph who married the daughter of an "Egyptian" (*Afrikan*) priest.
- The daughters of Jethro recognized **Moses**, the leader of the Israelites as an indigenous Afrikan, an "Egyptian" (Exo. 2:19). Moses's hand would turn *white* under special circumstances (Exo. 4:6,7). What color was it before turning *white*? Moses was an Egyptian priest who was schooled "in all the wisdom of the Egyptians" (Acts 7:22).
- **Miriam** the sister of **Moses**, was turned *white* as a result of God's *curse* (Num. 12:1-12). What color was she before turning white?
- **Gahazi** was also *cursed*, which resulted in him and his descendants becoming ***lepers*** "as white as snow" (2Kings 5:27).
- 1Peter 3:3 mentions "plaiting the hair." **Plaiting** (braiding) and corn-rowing were invented and traditionally worn by Afrikans to manage their "woolly" hair.

PhotoArtprint, Courtesy of *The King's Chambers*

"Moses: Exodus"

King Oji in Palestine, portraying *Moses* (see *Resources Guide*)

The original *Hebrews* (Habirus) were invading *whites*, not Semites!

Contrary to popular belief, the original *Hebrews* were *not* Semites, nor Blacks. They were white people, Indo-Europeans. Specifically, they were the **Habiru. The word Hebrew is from Habiru** (Hapiru, Habiri, Abiri, Apiru).[1] Some believe it derives from *Eber* (an ancestor of Abraham) or *eber* (beyond or across), but these derivations do not account for the biblical restriction of "Hebrew" to Israel, to the exclusion of the other ethnic groups that descended from Abraham or from Eber. As we shall see in Chapter 9, "Eber" and "Abraham" have common roots. Referring to the Habiru, Sarna writes: "For about a thousand years covering the entire second millennium B.C.E., these people, wherever and whenever they appear, constitute an alien, inassimilable element in the population. They share in common an inferior social status. They may be mercenaries, slaves, marauding bands; only occasionally do they hold important positions... The term [Habiri] is over-whelmingly derogatory, and in cuneiform texts it is often written as SA.GAZ, which syllables are associated with murder, robbery, and razzia." [2]

The Habiru were the same people as the invading *Hyksos,*

with whom they were allied,[3] and who preceded them. Who were the **Hyksos**? The name Hyksos is one of many names given to the invading white barbarians. Other names include: Indo-Europeans, Scythians, Cimmerians, Aryans, and Kurgans. Particularly between 2000-1500 B.C., waves and waves of warlike barbarian whites poured from the Caucasus Mountains and European northeast and descended upon the advanced civilizations of the Black people in the Near East, Northeast Afrika, and India. They ruthlessly killed, pillaged and burned wherever they went, leaving a path of death and smoldering ruins behind them, ultimately usurping and destroying these civilizations. Thus the white peoples' arrival signalled destruction for all these civilizations and the beginning of the Albinos' rise to forceful dominance.

The Hyksos invaded and occupied Lower (Northern) Egypt for about 150 years (c.1725-1575 B.C.). The earliest authority on them is Manetho, a Kamite historian-priest around 250 B.C. According to Manetho, the Hebrews are identified with the Hyksos, as well as described as being descended from lepers.[4] (In ancient times, white skin was called leprosy by dark natives.) In a fragment cited by Josephus (a Hebrew historian), Manetho reports that the Hyksos "savagely burnt the cities, razed the temples of the gods to the ground, and treated the whole native population with the utmost cruelty, massacring some and carrying off the wives and children into slavery." [5] The Kamites called them accursed, pestiferous, pillagers, thieves, unclean, etc.

Josephus declared that the Hyksos were the direct ancestors of the Israelites.[6] He writes, "The Egyptians took many occasions to hate and envy us: in the first place because our ancestors (the Hyk-sos, or shepherds) had had the dominion over their country..." [7] HYKSOS allegedly means "shepherd kings" –from Hyk (king, ruler) + Sos (shepherd). Massey derives Hyksos from Shus (servant) rather than the later Shasu (shepherds). He states, "Josephus is right when he claims that his people were Hekshus. They were not the

1) Saakana, 16. 2) Sarna, 54. 3) Cuba, 19. 4) Ibid., 29. 5) Sarna,17. 6) Blavatsky, IU-vI, 569. 7) Ibid., vII, 487; Against Apion, i. 25.

Hekshus in his sense of the conquering Syrian kings, the subduer of Egypt... Hekshus applied to the so-called shepherd kings was a nickname, the point of which lay in the word Shus meaning servants, and service. Josephus reports [Against Apion, i. 14] that Manetho in another book said the nation called Shepherds were also called captives in the sacred books." [1]

More historical evidence for the Albino identity of the early Hebrews (Habiru)

- In Chosen People From the Caucasus, Michael Bradley (a rare honest Caucasian author) writes: "The Biblical Hebrews were not Semitic at all in any cultural or ethnic way. They merely *adopted a Semitic language*, ...Therefore, when Jews imply a claim to a Semitic 'racial' and cultural heritage by labeling their critics 'anti-Semitic,' they are abusing the evidence and simultaneously denying their own Caucasus roots."[2]

- The Hyksos invaded Egypt from around the same area that the Asian Jews allegedly came, Canaan in c1675 B.C.E.[3]

- In Musa and the All Seeing Eye, Prince Cuba quotes the scholar, Albright: "In the course of historical times various non-Semitic peoples settled in Palestine. About the seventeenth century B.C., during the disturbed Hyksos Age...hordes from the north and north-east [white barbarians] poured over the land, establishing a new largely non-Semitic, patrician caste which maintained its own traditions and reduced the native [Blacks] population to serfdom. **Thanks to the cuneiform tablets from Palestine...we have a considerable number of personal names dating from the fifteenth and fourteenth centuries...[of] the remaining names nearly all (easily a third of the total) can now be identified without hesitation as Indo-Aryan.**" [4] (emphasis added)

- "According to Reisner, the SA-GAZ and Habiri are identified with the Cassites, **and not Semites**. Further, they were mercenaries, and, as later scholars have universally agreed, their name (SA-GAZ) translates into murderers, plunderers, cut-throats. Reisner relied upon the then recently discovered El Amarna tablets....**Many other studies have identified them with the same branch of Indo-Aryan peoples who first appeared in the region of Palestine/Canaan in the same period.**[5] (emphasis added)

- In *A Proposed Reconstruction of Early Hebrew History*, Theophile James Meek identified the people who conquered the Canaanites in the 15th Century B.C.E. as the Habiri or SA-GAZ. He demonstrated that these same nomadic groups, through historical and scriptural examination, were one and the same with the Hebrews, later to become known as "Israelites." [6] The Hebrews fitted the description of the Habiru /SA.GAZ according to their own writings.

> How curious that, essentially, the word
>
> **EUROPE (Europa) is HABIRU (Apiru) spelled backwards!**
>
> Europa = Aporue, Apiru, Habiru. Really, there's no such thing as a "coincidence."

1) Massey, BB-vI, 387. 2) Bradley, CP, 130. 3) Saakana, 19. 4) Cuba, 29. 5) Ibid., 29. 6) Ibid., 27, 28.

The *Neanderthaloid* cousins of the early white Hebrews were the 'Red Hairy Ones' of the Bible

Contrary to popular belief, the Neanderthals were both highly intelligent and had *larger* brains than modern man's. The early white Hebrews had Neanderthaloid cousins –the Red Hairy Ones of the Bible who were the descendents of Esau (Edomites). In *Chosen People From the Caucasus*, Michael Bradley presents incredible information about the *White Chosen People.* Backed with documented evidence, he proposes that because whites developed in the hostile refrigerator-environment of the ancient Northeast, they genetically developed extreme aggressiveness as a strategy for their survival and this accounts to a large extent for their taking first place as the most violent, aggressive and warring people on earth.[1] Bradley writes:

> "Rabbinical tradition (the exegetical works), as well as the Esau story in the *Old Testament*, indicate a continuing, very strong Neanderthal genetic strain among the Israelite tribes -a strain that they tried to eradicate by various means. ...There should be nothing odd or particularly shocking about this. If the Caucasus-Elburz region can still produce strongly Neanderthal people today, how much stronger must the Neanderthal presence have been in the distant past?..." [2]
>
> "If the ancient Hebrews *were* truly of strongly Neanderthal genetic stock, then surely the Old Testament, in addition to the vast body of Jewish exegetical writing, would have a lot more to say about it. And indeed it does... [he quotes Rabbi Yonah N. Ibn Ahron's discussion of the Hebrew's genetic variations] 'Our main concern must...rest with the creature who terrified the Israelites during the Exodus from Egypt and their period of wandering in the Sinai desert. These were the Sheidim-the Destroyers-who had been known to the Patriarchs (Abraham, Isaac and Jacob) as the Seirim-the Hairy Ones.' " [3]

There were other 'hairy ones' besides Esau, many in fact. The "scape goats" were not goats but exiled "hairy ones" according to a rabbi he quotes.[4] "These seirim are none other than the Destroyers, the sons of Esau."[5]

Rebecca's sons were Esau and Jacob (representing Evil and Good). The biblical Esau was born "red, all over like an hairy garment" [describes the white man] (Gen. 25:25). His "twin" brother Jacob was "smooth." Esau later changed his name to Edom, meaning *red.*

1) Bradley, CP, 138. 2) Ibid., 153-154. 3) Ibid., 137-138. 4) Ibid., 76-77, 142. 5) Ibid., 137.

Today over 90% of "Jews" are European *Khazars*; Counterfeit Jews

Counterfeit Impostor Jews: The hated white "Khazars," second usurpers of the real Jews!

Over 90% of the people who call themselves JEWS today, are *EUROPEAN to the bone*; they are impostors; they are *Khazars* with no Semitic or Israelite roots whatsoever. The Khazars were a powerful warlike European tribe that all converted to Judaism during the Middle Ages. Historians are now recognizing that the majority of eastern so-called "Jews," –are actually "Khazars" and have NO Semitic roots whatsoever! The Khazars are impostors: well-suppressed knowledge is emerging about this warlike tribe of Albinos that rose to vast power in Eastern Europe and were hated by the other Albinos they conquered due to their severe, exploitative treatment of them.

The Khazars all converted to Judaism as a political ploy during the Middle Ages in 740 A.D. It appears they learned all they could from the real Jews and Hebrews before usurping them, selling them into slavery (or killing them) and taking over in their place, using their corrupted form of Judaism to hide behind while continuing their treachery right into modern times. Most of Europe's historical hate for "Jews" is hate for the ruthless Khazars who continued to be hated in spite of becoming "Jews." Hatonn exposes that the Khazars are the real "anti-Semites" who have labeled themselves as Zionists and "Jews" to deceive the world in furthering their own plans for global and political conquest.

The "modern Jews" have no right to use the term "**anti-semitic**" since they are not semitic or real Jews. They use this term as a tool of manipulation to shut people up when people notice and speak out against the wrong doing of the "Jews." They themselves are the real anti-Semites. Freedman writes:

> "The word 'anti-Semitism' is another word which should be eliminated from the English language. 'Anti-Semitism' serves only one purpose today. It is used as a 'smear word'. When so-called or self-styled 'Jews' feel that anyone opposes any of their objectives they discredit their victims by applying the word 'anti-Semite' or 'anti-Semitic' through all the channels they have at their command and under their control." [1]

In *The 13th Tribe*, Arthur Koestler traces the history of the Khazars and their rise to power. In his telling book, *Facts are Facts*, Benjamin Freedman also exposes the suppressed truth about the Khazars and "Jews." Their power and control paralleled or exceeded that of the Roman Empire, and they have hidden their tracks exceedingly well! Both Albino groups did a *form change*, employing religion (using it as a cloak), in order to survive. Both Albino groups are still the seat of vast power and control over people in the form of the so-called *Secret World Government* and the *Roman Catholic Church.*

1) Freedman, FF, 72.

Evidence that Hitler did not kill *6 million* "Jews"

This a mega lie perpetrated as yet another mega tool to manipulate the masses through guilt and stealing their sympathy. In *The Hoax of the Twentieth Century*, Arthur Butz gives solid evidence that the actual or real "Jewish" holocaust was greatly different from the reported version, and that the "Jews" were *not* virtually wiped out. Butz focuses on the post-war crimes trials where the prosecution's "evidence" was falsified and secured by coercion and even torture. He re-examines the very German records so long misrepresented. He reviews the demographic statistics which do NOT allow for the loss of the "Six Million." He separates the fact from the tons of myth and propaganda that served as a barrier to the truth for 40 years. The Khazars (Counterfeit Jews) already have mega power over the world since they are the apex of the "Secret World Government." These Khazars control the media and own the major communication networks, so they can promote whatever lie best serves their interests.

"Jews" were a massive part of the Afrikan slave trade in the Americas!

Records from the Port of Charleston indicated that of 128 slave ships docked there one slaving season, 120 were of Jewish registry. Compiled strictly from *Jewish* documents, *The Secret Relationship Between Blacks and Jews*, by the Nation of Islam reveals the vast "Jewish" involvement in the Atlantic slave trade. The introduction states:

> Jews have been conclusively linked to the greatest criminal endeavor ever undertaken against an entire race of people – a crime against humanity – the Black African Holocaust. They were participants in the entrapment and forcible exportation of millions of Black African citizens in the wretched and inhuman life of bondage for the financial benefit of Jews. The effects of this unspeakable tragedy are still being felt among the peoples of the world at this very hour.
>
> Deep within the recesses of the Jewish historical record is the irrefutable evidence that the most prominent of the Jewish pilgrim fathers used kidnapped Black Africans disproportionately more that any other ethnic or religious group in New world history and participated in every aspect of the international slave trade. The immense wealth of Jews, as with most of the White colonial fathers, was acquired by the brutal subjugation of Black Africans...Now, compiled for the first time, the Jewish sources reveal the extent of their complicity in Black slavery in the most graphic of terms.

These "Jewish" slave-sellers were not "real Jews" at all but *Khazars*, the same European tribe responsible for the kidnap and enslavement of so many European "Slavs" that the word *Slav* came to mean "slave." Thus "Jews" were also massive slave sellers during the Middle Ages. On page 9 of the cited book we read: "Solomon Grayzel states that 'Jews were among the most important slave dealers' in European society. Lady Magnus writes that in the Middle Ages, 'The principal purchasers of slaves were found among the Jews.' " White *Slavs* or *slaves* were driven across Europe in great herds like cattle,[1] apparently providing practice for what their drivers did to kidnapped Afrikans centuries later on the Mother Continent.

WHITE Slavery thrived in Europe, America, and even Afrika!

White historians usually obscure or omit writing about *White* Slavery. Whenever they mention Afrikans, however, they make sure to associate Blacks with slavery. White people were slaves throughout their history, heavily enslaved by other whites. In fact, the word SLAVE was first used for White people. As noted earlier, the word SLAVE is from SLAV, a name of a European tribe that was captured and heavily enslaved by other European tribes. A huge percentage of the White populace in ancient Greece & Rome were slaves; even many of the scholars, doctors and overseers were slaves. Feudal medieval Europe, really, was a society of slaves called "serfs." Even the Christian church kept slaves. The first slaves in what is now the United States were White Englishmen. White slaves, brought to America in slave ships, apparently suffered as horribly as Black slaves on slave ships, dying like flies. George Washington advertised for two White runaways that labored on his plantation. The sale of White orphans continued in New York until as late as 1858. They were put up for sale in

1) Van Sertima, APEE, 161.

a church at $10.00 each. The very high price of Afrikan slaves induced many whites to kidnap white children and sell them as Negroes in the South as late as the 1850's. Incredibly, free "Negroes" in colonial America owned White slaves; bought white people as early as the 1640's. Even Afrikans in Afrika owned White slaves. As early as the fifth century A.D. whites were sold as slaves in Afrika. While Albinos (Europeans & Americans) were raiding Afrika for slaves, Afrikans were raiding the coasts of Europe as far north as Sweden and Finland for slaves and had been doing so for centuries. For 400 years (1400-1800) collections were taken up in the churches of Europe for ransom of these slaves. Sallee, in Morocco, was the great slave-market for these White captives. "As late as 1810, White Americans were captured on the high seas and sold at the great slave port of Sallee, Morocco. After Americans won independence, she had to pay tribute to the North African powers, better known as 'the Barbary Pirates,' to sail the North Atlantic."[1]

Like whites, Afrikans were guilty of selling their fellow countrymen into slavery as well as enslaving them, "but they still respected the humanity of the enslaved individual and they were often allowed to marry and their spouses and offspring remained free."[2] However, no group of people practiced the kind of unconscionable, utterly brutal slavery developed and practiced by White Americans on Afrikans. The intent was to totally destroy the slaves' *Human Spirit*. Slave descendants are still suffering from the effects, a subject addressed in Post Traumatic Slavery Disorder, by Dr. Patricia Newton.

The Caucasian presence in the Bible

Though originally authored by Afrikan people, the original biblical books have been massively edited, rewritten, censored, and distorted by three groups of Albinos:

- first by Hebrews (Habirus)
- second by European churchmen
- third by the Khazars (a European tribe)

So of course, whites have written themselves into the Bible. And Afrikans who came in contact with them have written whites into the Bible. Thus the Bible is racist in *both* directions; against Blacks and against whites! In fact it is one of the top most racist books in the world (see chapter 14). This becomes clear once you know certain *code* words or names. Jesus himself appears quite "racist" against the whites transgressing against the Blacks; he comes only to save "the House of Israel," not the "Gentiles."

The biblical stories are all plagiarized from Kamit. Overstepping Afrika, scholars often say these stories were copied from the Canaanites, Babylonians, and even from India. The fact is, the Canaanites, Babylonians, and Indians began as Afrikans and got their stories from Afrika (Kamit) also. A review of the Canaanites and Babylonians shows they were Kamite emigrants; their manner of dress, civilization and culture were barely distinguishable from the Kamites.

The biblical stories are *not* actual historical events: they are *allegories*, symbols and parables. Perhaps this is why some stories appear to retain much integrity, even surviving the pens of racist white editorship. What is more remarkable is the incriminating evidence in the Bible against whites themselves. Unless you know the key code words / names / concepts, it may be invisible. Once you know these words, it leaps off the page. In literalizing and perverting the Afrikan allegories, they have inadvertently made the stories tell on themselves. Is this Divine Hand at work in spite of the perpetrators and their fraud?

While the original white Hebrews yet took their culture from the Blacks, they retained their own dominant character or hallmarks of the Albino man (patriarchal, anti-female, domineering, etc., addressed in chapter 14). The white presence in "Jewish" holy writings is naturally conspicuous, since they supplanted the Blacks. Note that the Bible is intensely patriarchal and anti-female. This is evidence of their character which they wrote into the Bible, for Afrikan culture (the Bible's original source) was originally matriarchal before colonization and destruction by their enemies. Keeping in mind that **Names and Words reveal hidden history,** let's identify hidden clues (code names) of Albino presence in the Bible:

1) *"Why We Lose"*, by Jake Beason, 203. 2) Browder, NVC, 260.

ADAM.

That's right! The name essentially means *RED*. It both means "red" and "man." White people are all shades of RED. The story of Adam is a garbled story about the creation of the whiteman, or a white race of people according to some Afrikan traditions, including teachings of the Nation of Islam. Curiously, the Book of Genesis reports TWO creations of Man. In the first (authentic) creation, God makes both WOMAN and MAN at the same time and on equal status: "male and female created he them" (Gen. 1:27). In the second creation of Man, God makes Adam first, then makes Eve as an afterthought from Adam's rib (Gen. 2:7, 21-23). (This is an effective ploy to demean women and have it backed up by God. As we know from *his*–story, Adam – the whiteman, has been the ring leader of anti-female patriarchy, outdoing all other peoples, even burning millions of white females at the stake in the name of their blond Jesus). Dr. Frances Cress-Welsing enlightens us about the symbolism (emphasis added): "**Adam and Eve's shame for their nakedness indicates their rejection and shame of their pale white bodies –colorless or naked –when compared to the black and brown-skinned normals;** their use of fig leaves to cover their genitals (as they are depicted) implies the shame and rejection of their genital apparatus, including their genes; their expulsion from the Garden of Eden represents the isolation of the albino mutants away from the skin-pigmented normals..."[1] Further biblical indication of Adam as a separately created man(*kind*): Exiled from Eden for killing his brother Abel (Adam's second son), Cain goes to the land of Nod and then MARRIES! (Gen. 4:16-17). *Where* did his *wife* suddenly come from if he and his parents were the *only* people on Earth? This shows that they were not the first people; others (Blacks) preceded them. Adam's third son Seth is born much later –long after Cain, when Adam was 130 years old (Gen. 5:3).

EDOM.

This word sounds like *Adam* because they have the same root and mean the same thing: RED. In the Bible, ESAU was born red and hairy (Gen. 25:25). Again, we have a good description of the "white" man –he is all shades of red and the hairiest of peoples. Esau changed his name to, you guessed it: EDOM, who becomes the progenitor of the EDOMITES. In reality, the Edomites are the descendents of the invading IndoEuropeans. So everywhere you see *Edomite* in the Bible, it is talking about white –oops, *RED* people. Biblically, Esau and Jacob were "twins." Jacob changed his name to Israel, progenitor of the Israelites. He and his mother connived together to steal Esau's birthright as the firstborn son from his father, Isaac. Looking at the historical facts, the reverse is true: Albinos stole the Blacks' birthright inheritance. Biblically and historically, the Edomites (whites) have been the dire enemy of Israel (Blacks). The Bible labels Edom / Edomites as the enemy of the Israelites and historically, they have lived up to this. They were allegedly conquered by David but retook parts of Judah and became a kingdom in the 8th century. They participated in overthrow of Judah in 587 by the Babylonians, but were conquered by John Hyrcanus who forced them to all become "Jews" or die. The Edomites also fought the Black Jews in the Roman-Jewish War which destroyed the Jews as a nation. Helen Blavatsky writes, "Esau or Osu, is represented, when born, as 'red all over like [an] hairy garment.' He is the Typhon or Satan, opposing his brother."[2]

1) Welsing, 26. 2) Blavatsky, IU-vII, 489.

JAPHETH.

Theoretically the most Caucasoid or whitest person in the Bible since he is the alleged progenitor of white people. Although some conclude he was originally Black and his descendents became white through genetic adaptation to the cold north. But if he *was* white, and his brother, *Ham* was Black, then what color was Noah, their father? In other words, the story as it stands is not a historical fact but a myth perpetrated by the "Japhites."

"HAM."

Ham? **Wasn't he Black?** Yes. *Ham* is really ***Kham*** (K**hem**it in C**hem**istry). Theoretically Ham is the blackest person in the Bible, being the progenitor of Black Nations. Accordingly, the racist hand of white biblical editorship comes down heaviest upon "Ham, the father of Canaan," to do the greatest damage to Blacks by poisoning the alleged source of Blacks. Thus the descendants of Black Ham, as Canaan, is cursed by Noah in the Bible to be the perpetual slave of whites (descendants of Japheth) and Semites! (Gen. 9:22, 25) And in perfect alignment with white supremacy, which was as alive back then as it is now, white Japheth is exalted over *all* the nations of the Earth. Thus Albinos have created divine sanctioning for their criminal behavior towards Blacks. Do you really think God would write or inspire such? Nay, not God but certainly God's adversary, whose biblical name is derived from....

SET.

Popularly known as Satan. Satan is derived from Set-En which is derived from Set,[1] the Kamite god of Evil, Negativity, and Drought who is portrayed, you guessed it –RED (remember who is all shades of *Red*?) Set was the twin brother and enemy /adversary of Black Asar (Osiris). The warring twins Asar & Set is the Afrikan prototype for the biblical Ham & Japheth, Cain & Abel, Jacob & Esau, etc., who were black/white brothers and enemies. Are you starting to see the recycled pattern? And the mythos? Set wasn't always so wicked. He outstandingly acquired unparalleled wickedness when Afrika's original biblical scriptures were outstandingly revised, reversed and rewritten. (Or perhaps he inspired the rewriters into doing this? *"The Devil made 'em do it!"*) The rewriters (controllers, actually) needed to create a devil and a burning hell in order to manipulate people through intimidation.

Biblical variations of, and names derived from *Set* includes:

Satan	Seth	Shethar	Shuthelah	Zetham
Zethan	Sheth	Zethar	Shuthalhites	Ziddim
Sitnah	Children of Sheth (Num. 24:17)	Shadrach	Zattu	Siddim
		Shedeur	Zatthu	Sodi
	Sethur	Zedad	Zidon	Sodom

Sodom and Gomorrah were two biblical cities reknown for their "wickedness" (especially sexually, hence "sodomy"), and destroyed by "brimstone and fire." The valley of Siddim "was full of slimepits" (Gen. 6:14). Slimepits means volatile pitch, bitumen, tar, etc. "Lot's wife fleeing from Sodom is a picture of the escape from Sut [Set], the Egyptian devil, whose domain contains the hells of smoking, fulminating fires, sent forth destroyingly for ever, in blasts that stifle every breath. The Hebrew Shedim are the Devils, and Sodom is the place of the Egyptian hells." [2]

1) Saakana, 36. 2) Massey, vII-BB, 257.

Seth was the god of the Hyksos, reports Blavatsky [1] and other Albino historians. The Hyksos in Egypt revived Set's cult, 200 BC. Set was a god of the hot desert wind, known as the breath of the ass and associated with Typhoon. Under Hyksos rule, worship of the Ass god, Set was revived.[2] It makes sense that the Hyksos would embrace Set. They resembled Set (who is described as either RED or white-skinned with red hair; "white" people are all shades of red). Perhaps this is partly why Afrikans of the Nile Valley called whites the "children of Set." From day number one, the Nation of Islam identified white people as "devils," not figuratively, but literally as the embodiment of evil on Earth. Whites have classically lived up to this. Their entire history is the history of pathological killing and exploitation of People of Color. No race has exceeded them in destruction and killing. They even admit this. Earth is presently heading for annihilation due to evil caused by the children of Set. One of their nuclear subs can wipe out several continents (the world, in other words).

GENTILE.

Whites have slanted or changed the meaning of words which incriminate them so they can escape being perceived as the *incriminor*. Example: the word GENTILE. Most people think this word means "non-Jew." The original meaning of the word as given in the Bible, is *white people*, specifically the descendants of Japheth according to Genesis 10:2-5, where the word *Gentile* appears for the first time. The Bible calls the land of the white people "**the Isles of the Gentiles**" or simply the Isles (Gen. 10:5). So now we have two major ethnic terms for recognizing Albinos in the Bible: ***Gentile*** and ***Edomite***. When you next read the Bible and come across these words, the passage takes on a whole different meaning. In their efforts to pervert the original Kamite scriptures, ironically and amazingly, the truth about them gets highlighted. The same Bible they messed with identifies *them* as the chief executive agents of Set (Satan), and also calls Set their "father" (John 8:44, Rev. 2:9, 3:9).

"Jinn" sounds like *Gen*tile.
Jinn, meaning *hidden*, was anciently applied to the uncultured savages who once lived apart and hidden in the hills and caves of West Asia.[7] These were the *Caucasians* or *Cauk*-Asians living in the *Cauk* caves of the *Cauk*-asus Mountains (see Chapter 4). These destructive barbarians were "roped off," – literally walled in and "hidden" for some 2000 years. Hence in the meaning of *isle* /*aisle* as *isolation* / *separation*, the ancient earliest abode of the Albinos was truly the biblical "Isles of the Gentiles," a term pointing *north*, exactly to their early abodes.

And ***Gentile*** sounds like ***GENTLE***, from the same roots! –again modified or "softened" to round off or even reverse the sharp truth. For the *Gentiles* (barbarians, heathens) have made the word GENTLE mean the opposite of barbaric hence, "noble," well-born, refined, chivalrous, docile, not harsh. If this is really true, why does *gentle* have the exact roots as *Gentile?* And this root is "**GENS**," a word which sets the record clear as to what race *gens* refers: "**gens...1.** The **patrilinear** clan forming the basic unit of the **Roman** [white! Albino] tribe..." [3] (Emphasis added). The true (Afrikan) oriGIN of all these GEN-words is the root **GEN** or **KHEN** in the Kamite words *Gen-t* / *Gengenu* (record, archive) [4] ; *Khen* / *Khenu* (most private or sacred part of a temple / ship / dwelling / house. Cabin of boat. Innermost part of the body)[5] ; *Khenti* (likeness, portrait, image, statue).[6]

The association of GEN with "whites" is from their connection with the North; the Astrological NORTH has the Great Bear (Ursa Major Constellation), an ancient symbol of the Great Mother of the Universe, whose Womb was the oriGINal **GEN**, BeGINning, –the oriGINal Ark of Life, holding the Seeds or GENES of Creation.

1) Blavatsky, IU-vII, 488. 2) Walker, WE, 68. 3) *The American Heritage Dictionary*, Second College Edition, Houghton Mifflin Co., 1985. 4) Budge, EH, 808b. 5) Ibid., 549b, 575b. 6) Ibid., 577a. 7) Guthrie, 52-58.

LEPERS.

In ancient times, white skin was called leprosy. In numerous places, the Bible refers to white skin as leprosy. White skin is a form of albinism, a genetic aberration. White people are Hue-mans who have lost their HUE.

GOATS.

In the Bible, goats symbolized white people. They have straight hair, aggressive natures, and their natural habitant were the hills and caves of cold mountains. Like the wild goats who live in mountains and rocky places, the ancient Europeans were associated with hills and caves. Caucasia or the Caucasus *Mountains,* was the earliest known abode of the Caucasians. The term "scapegoat" originally meant the 'red, Hairy Ones' who were periodically exiled into the wilderness (white people are all shades of *red*). In the Bible (New English Translation) we read, "The two-horned ram which you saw signifies the kings of Media and Persia. The he-goat is the kingdom of the Greeks. And the great horn on his forehead is the first king" (Daniel 8:20, 21). On the other hand, SHEEP symbolized Afrikan peoples with their woolly sheeplike hair and typically peaceful nature.

GAHAZITES.

For his misdeed, Gahazi got cursed and all his "seed" or descendants, were to be likewise cursed with the same fate. What was the fate? To be lepers "as white as snow" (2Kings 5:27). Like Gahazi, the Albinos originated from Afrikan people.

GOG & MAGOG.

The prophecies in the Bible are dire, and they incriminate you know who by now. In every instance where the Bible mentions "those from the North," it has nothing good to say about them. The worse prophecies which the Bible can muster are squarely against "Gog and Magog," the descendants of Japheth. Gog is also the ancient, biblical name for the region where the *Khazars* are from. Gog is identified as the far northern lands, particularly Russia.[1] Biblical prophecy identifies Gog and Magog as the source of the worse evil to befall Earth.

You remember the *Khazars*, the counterfeit Jews? They comprise over 90% of the world's so-called "Jews" today. They are total impostors. According to numerous books,[2] the Khazars –falsely known as Jews, are the main apex of the "**Secret World Government**," a body of heartless Albinos that allegedly controls the Earth. Be not alarmed. All this is part of the game on Earth. A fruit has its time and season, then it's over with. The Khazars are playing their game so threateningly that they even have their white brethren alarmed about their activities and impending plans for takeover of the U.S. (they've already secretly taken over!), turning it into a police state, putting Blacks and other "undesirables" in "detention centers" as done with Japanese Americans only decades ago during the last World War. These books report that the Khazars are the "controllers of the invisible world government." They are credited with backing up the ongoing creation of germ-warfare, including the manmade virus / disease called AIDS. It's a big story, quite unsettling if you only know about the bad part. The good part is that not only is their time up, but a whole new game or new play is in the works, ushering Awakening Humanity into a new Golden Era.

1) Revell Bible Dictionary, 443. 2) Such books include: *Conspirators' Hierarchy*–J. Coleman; *Behold a Pale Horse*–W. Cooper; *Matrix III*–V. Valerian; *The Anglo-American Establishment*–C. Quigley; and *The Shadows of Power*–J.Perloff.

Afrikan Americans are largely descendants of the original biblical *IUs* (Jews)!

This is one of "his-story's" best kept secrets, but not anymore!

The original biblical Jews (IUs) were Black Afrikan people who were ruthlessly persecuted by the white man (Romans), also the Habirus who supplanted them. The Roman-Jewish War in 66 A.D. marked the peak of this persecution and the end of the original Black Jews as a nation. In this war Jerusalem was overthrown and the original Afrikan Jews were scattered. The loss of life was appalling. So many Jews (Afrikans) were slain that the whole lake of Galilee was red with blood and covered with corpses. Josephus estimated that 1,100,000 perished in the siege of Jerusalem alone, reports Hugh Schonfield in his book *The Passover Plot,*[1] which describes this massive genocide. In fact, the *Habiru* Josephus himself likely participated against Blacks in this war, for he was "an army commander." [2]

Seeking to escape destruction, millions of the original Black Biblical Jews fled into AFRIKA! Centuries later, their descendants were captured and sold into slavery in the Americas!

- In *The Truth About Black Biblical Hebrew-Israelites*, Ella Hughley exposes and summarizes important details about this suppressed subject: "Many of the Israelites...who managed to escape their persecutors during the Roman-Jewish War subsequently migrated to West Africa, and 1600 years later their descendants were captured and brought to America in chains by cruel slave-traders." [3] She quotes Josephus from his book *The Great Roman-Jewish War: 66-70,* where he writes about this Jewish dispersion and captivity: "General Vaspasian and his son Caesar Titus fought against the Jews. Millions of Jews fled into Africa, among other places, fleeing from Roman persecution and starvation during the siege." [4]

- In *African Origins of Major Western Religions*, Dr. Yosef ben-Jochannan writes "there were many Hebrew (Jewish) tribes that were of indigenous African origin. These African Jews... were caught in a rebellion in Cyrene...during 115 C.E. This rebellion also marked the beginning of a mass Jewish migration southward into Sudan, of West Africa." [5]

- Arab historian, Ibn Battuta writes of finding Jews scattered across North and West Afrika during his travels. The Jew-ism of numerous Afrikan peoples, especially in West Afrika is well documented. Additional authors discussing this subject include Rudolf Windsor; *From Babylon to Timbuktu*, and Moshe Y. Lewis, *History of Edom, The Impostor Jew*.

1) Schonfield, 192-195. 2) Ewing, 97. 3) Hughley, 22. 4) Ibid., 21. 5) ben-Jochannan, AOMR, 75.

8

The European Quantum-Theft, Perversion & Supplanting of Afrikan Cosmology

Albino Judaism /Christianity are massive frauds like Albino history. Albinos have done to them what they've done to true history.

The same people that have given us *False History* have given us *False Biblical History*

The Original Christianity of the Original Christians and Original Biblical books has been greatly changed, distorted, censored and reconstructed by whites into a False Christianity which serves as an effective "weapon" and primary pillar of global white supremacy.

Can the same people who have given us genocide and false history be willing or capable of giving us the truth?

Even today, when truth (such as the Essene Scrolls) surface, they immediately take hold of it and censor, distort, or otherwise suppress it.

Afrikan people cannot count on getting the truth from the very people that stole, suppressed, and distorted that truth. Distorting truth is a principal method which has been successfully used to maintain mental control and thus physical control over People of Color. To poison something effectively, poison it at its source, then everything built upon that will be poisoned. The distortions, falsehood, and frauds of Judaism, Christianity, Islam, and Hinduism is a big unholy mess.

It is exceedingly important that Afrikan people get this straightened out because this is a cornerstone in our reclaiming full mental health and wholeness of spirit. The same probably holds true for Albinos (who have been equally lied to –but in their favor– inflating their egos). Albino-poisoned Christianity, which grew out of Albino-poisoned Judaism, entraps probably half the world's Black population. Albino-poisoned Islam /Hinduism claims the rest. All four monsters have done, and are still doing massive harm to Colored People around the world. **They harm Blacks because the seeds of suppression, self-negation and death are implanted in them.** All four of these world religions are frauds, imposters, corrupt counterfeits of teachings stolen from the Afrikan Mystery Schools of the Nile Valley.

Albinos didn't manufacture any new biblical history:

they took Black people's ancient spiritual cosmology, stories and allegories, and reversed, distorted, censored, and changed them to suit their purposes -refashioning them into efficient, effective tools of subjugation, and then fed them back to us in a different package. **We can detect some truth in these stories, for lies are made out of the truth** like white flour is made out of whole wheat flour. The devil tempted Jesus not with outstanding lies, but with misrepresented quotes from the holy scriptures. Lies must have some truth present in order to stand at all. But any "holy books" or teachings given to us by the very people that have destroyed our cultures and ancestors, will be poisoned. And if we ***eat*** these false books/teachings by ***believing*** them, we poison ourselves, thinking we are nourishing ourselves. We must identify the poisons, perversions, and reversals in these teachings and discard them, or better yet, cast away the whole thing and start anew. These poisons are specifically identified in Chapter 14: *The Top 12 Hallmarks of Albino Poison in the World's Top 4 Religions.*

Albinos burned the original biblical scriptures to ensure survival of their false versions

Albino men tried to destroy Kamite legacy, the source of their Counterfeit Christianity, so they could get away with presenting it as a new religion. They almost succeeded.

In order for their falsehood to stand, Albinos had to ruthlessly destroy –as much as possible, the truthhood or original Afrikan manuscripts, hieroglyphics, and temple walls they copied them from

This very hard work took several hundred years to complete. But it is never really finished because truth can never be 100% suppressed or destroyed. Therefore the *controlling* whites in high places must ever maintain a vigil, lest a single flame of truth flare up into a raging *Forest Fire* to destroy their well established foundation of Lies which supports their entire culture. The controlling whites have done such an effective job of making their Lies stick that today, millennia later, the world is stilled fooled, believing these false stories to be true history and even the Word of God. They are the words of the white man, the Lies of the Albino man. And they mentally enslave both People of Color around the world, along with the Albinos themselves. But no lies are ever permanent for they lack substance; they are not real. Only the truth has permanence, for it is Real. And though it can be suppressed, it always makes a comeback. Truth has a way of flaring up, busting out into open view in the least expected ways. This is why the Scrolls found near the Dead Sea are so significant! They expose the Truth –which is fatal to the Lie. **The Dead Sea Scrolls are the *Live SEE Scrolls.***

Albinos (Romans) destroyed the most precious of Afrikan archives by burning down the massive Library of Alexandria in Kamit,

which housed over 400,000 volumes. *His-Story* books say this library was established by the Ptolemies (Greek Albinos). If this is true, then this is to their credit, and demonstrates their recognition and possible respect for the universal knowledge, science and wisdom embodied as the Afrikan teachings. The great Library at Alexandria constituted the storehouse of knowledge of the ancient world. "*There flocked to this great intellectual centre, students from all countries.* It is said that at one time not fewer than fourteen thousand were in attendance. Subsequently even the Christian church received from it some of the most eminent of its Fathers, as Clemens Alexandrinus, Origen, Athanasius, &c. ...The destruction of this library was almost the death-blow to free-thought wherever Christianity ruled –for more than a thousand years."[1] The great library of Alexandria was intentionally destroyed by a Christian mob on orders of the Christian emperor Theodosius in A.D. 389.[2] Albinos also burned a similar library in the Temple of Serapis, which had over 300,000 manuscripts. And they burned and destroyed another massive depository of ancient wisdom in South America. The result of their destruction is immeasurable, affecting billions over time and bringing on dark ages.

They tell on themselves

Hotema writes: "they destroyed or concealed the scrolls to hide from the eyes of the world their true and actual contents. The ancient libraries were burned to destroy all evidence that would expose the fraud." [3] "Besides forging, lying, and deceiving the people for the cause of [their fraudulent] Christ, the Christian Fathers [Albinos] destroyed all evidence [Black people's original scrolls, etc.] against themselves and their [false] religion which they could find." [4] Each of the three greatest pyramids at Gizeh had a temple on the eastern side of it. "These temples were destroyed by the early Christian fanatics [Albino men], who would have destroyed the pyramids also had they been able, but the pyramids were so massive as to resist the efforts of the destroyers." What they could not destroy, they appropriated to their own use; and this Temple of Osiris became the Temple of Christ.

Erich von Daniken, reporting on the European destruction of cultural records of People of Color on the Easter Islands, states: "the first European missionaries on this tiny patch of earth...burned the tablets with hieroglyphic characters; they prohibited the ancient cults of the gods and did away with every kind of tradition." [5]

Doane writes: "The Spaniards destroyed nearly all the books, ancient monuments and paintings which they could find; had it not been for this, much more regarding the religion of the ancient Mexicans would have been handed down to us." [6] "Christian divines seem to have always been afraid of too much light. In the very infancy of printing, Cardinal Wolsey foresaw its effect on Christianity, and in a speech to the clergy, publicly forewarned them, that, *if they did not destroy the Press, the Press would destroy them*." [7]

1) Doane, 440. 2) Van Sertima, APEE, 157. 3) Hotema, GC, 55. 4) Ibid., 44. 5) Van Daniken, CG, 92. 6) Doane, 199. 7) Ibid., 438.

What was the Original Bible and who wrote it?

The "Original Bible" was authored by spiral-haired Black Afrikan people, apparently *priestesses* primarily, and was not necessarily called "the Bible." In fact, there probably was no such "book" per se. What is called "the Bible" is a collection of books regarded holy (*bible* and *bibliography* are from the same roots). The word ***bible*** is from ***Byblos***, which is further derived from ***papyrus***, the same word giving us ***paper***. Since B/P are essentially the same, and Egyptian L/R are one, then:

> papy**r**us = baby**l**us, ***Byblos***; and papy**r** = baby**l**, ***Bible!***

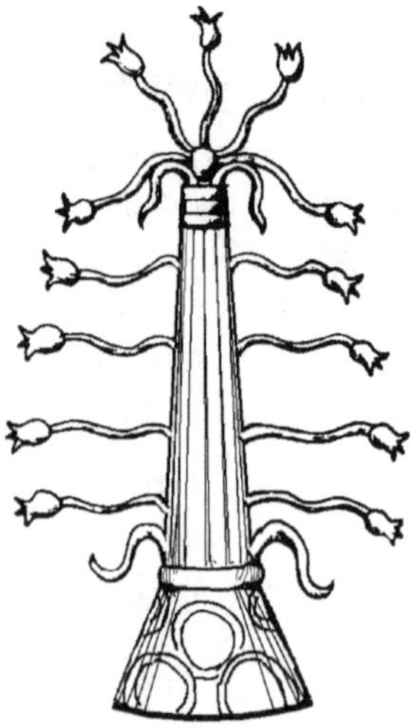

Asherah Tree

The holy city of *Byblos* was the City of the *Great Mother,*

and the oldest continuously occupied temple in the world.[1] She was called As-t, Astarte, Ishtar, Asherah, Isis, Hathor, Tannit, Anath, and Neith. She patronized learning, and Her priestesses collected a considerable library of papyrus scrolls for which Byblos was famous.[2] Yet one would be hard pressed to find any mention of *Byblos* in Bible dictionaries –because for them to do so would mean to expose what they are trying desperately to hide: that the Bible, its origin and the word itself, is from FEMININE *Afrikan* roots. You'd never suspect this, given how patriarchal and chauvinist is the Counterfeit Christian Bible (all 100+ versions of it). Byblos was also the name of the papyrus swamps of Kamit.[3] The fraudulent Christian Bible translates the word "Asherah" as "grove," but an Asherah was not a grove, it was a multi-branched tree symbolizing the Great Mother as the Great Goddess of Canaan, the Mother and Queen of all the Semitic pantheon. *Asherah* in Egyptian means Tree of Life. Her tree symbol was alternately the "Tree of Knowledge" and "Tree of Life." The fruit of Her tree represented all food, including spiritual nourishment. Apparently, Byblos, with it vast collection of holy books, was truly a manifestation of The Mother's "Tree of Knowledge," –the same Tree that "tempted Eve" in the misrepresented biblical story.

From the Dictionary:

Bible: "The sacred book of Christianity, a collection of ancient writings including the books of he Old Testament and the New Testament. ...The Hebrew Scriptures, the sacred books of Judaism. ..A book or collection of writings constituting the sacred text of a religion...[Middle English ...from Late Latin *biblia*, from Greek, pl. of *biblion*, book, diminutive of *biblos*, papyrus, book, from *Bublos*, Byblos.]"

Byblos: "An ancient city of Phoenicia northeast of present-day Beirut, Lebanon. It was the chief city of Phoenicia in the second millennium B.C. and was noted for its papyruses."

American Heritage Dictionary. 3rd Ed. 1992

Sources of the Original Biblical Text

The stories, symbolism, characters, and material of the Bible originated from the following ancient documents which predate the Christian Bible by many thousands, if not ten-thousands of years:

- **Per Em Hru,** or the Book of ***The Coming Forth by Day.*** Also known as "The Ritual." Incorrectly known as *The Egyptian Book of the Dead.* This book contains the oldest known religious writings in the world.[4] Massey devotes a chapter to it in *Ancient Egypt*, and refers to it frequently in his writings. Likely, this book was amongst the *collection* at Byblos.
- **The scrolls and papyri of Byblos**
- **The Pyramid Texts**
- Various **hieroglyphics and papyri** of Kamite temples.
- **The Gospel of the Egyptians**, among the earliest known scriptures. It was "disowned and dropped out of sight as soon as possible by the worshippers of the carnalized Christ." [5]
- **The Essene Scrolls** (called the Dead Sea Scrolls)

1) Walker, WE, 96. 2) Ibid. 3) Budge, GE, 124. 4)Massey, AE, 186. 5)Massey, HJ, 160.

Who REwrote the Original Bible and made it a Fraud?

The rulers of the same people who destroyed it. Specifically:

Three groups of Albinos were the main religious criminals

Though originally authored by Afrikans, the biblical books have been edited, censored, and distorted by three main groups of Albinos:

- First, the early white Hebrews (Habirus), particularly the "priests" (disguised dictators, rulers).
- Second, Roman emperor Constantine and other murderous despots called the European "church fathers" (disguised dictators, rulers).
- Third, the European Khazars who converted to fraudulent Judaism in 740 A.D. as a political ploy.

The Council of Nicea

Counterfeit Christianity was fabricated from its Afrikan Mother at the Nicea Council of the Roman Catholic Church in 325 A.D. Major altering and censoring of Biblical books were accomplished at this unholy Council of Albino despots, euphemistically and deceptively called *The Church*. The biblical books were deliberately selected, rewritten, and edited to wipe out all feminine images of divinity and sanction religious suppression of women. Metaphysical-occult teachings/passages were also wiped out but a few were missed (or kept?), such as the references of John the Baptist being the reincarnation of prophet Elijah; the "third heaven" (which shows knowledge of the higher dimensions or planes of existences – a.k.a. astral plane, soul plane, etc.). In addition, whole books were deleted from the Bible. **Evidence of missing biblical books exists within the Bible itself!** These include the books of Jasher, Nathan, Shemaiah, Iddo and Jehu –referred to in Num. 21:14; Josh. 10:13; 2Sam. 1:18; 1Chro. 29:29; and 2Chro. 9:29, 12:15, 20:34. Bernard writes, "In order to make this change in religious doctrines...it was necessary to profoundly alter the Scriptures, and to remove from them all doctrines that were obnoxious to Constantine, the true founder of the Church of Rome and the existing Christian religion. To accomplish this, certain 'correctors' were appointed, whose work was to completely rewrite the original writings..." [1]

Regarding the Bible's history and initial appearance

"A collection appeared in the first century B.C. and again in the first century A.D. to be accepted by the Jews [fraudulent Albino Jews/Habirus] of the Diaspora as sacred, and passed on to Christians [Europeans]. In both Jewish and Christian hands the papyri underwent many changes. In the 4th century A.D., St. Jerome collected some Hebrew manuscripts and edited them to produce the Latin Vulgate, a Bible of considerable inaccuracy, differing markedly from Jerome's stem text. ...The King James Bible relied mostly on a Greek text collected and edited by Eramus in the 16th century, which in turn relied on a Byzantine collection assembled gradually at Constantinople between the 4th and 8th centuries...There are no known portions of the Bible older than the 4th century A.D." [2]

1) Bernard, DSS, 2. 2) Walker, WE, 97.

The early Christians did not have any so-called Gospels

The gospels were fabricated later, as needed by the Counterfeit Albino Church. Matthew, Mark, Luke, and John were not the authors of the books which bear their names. "The Gospels themselves were forged as required to uphold privileges and practices of the early church. 'We must never forget that the majority of the writings of the New Testament were not really written or published by those whose names they bear.'" [1] **The gospels were not written in Christ's own time, "nor were they written by anyone who saw him in the flesh.** The names of the apostles attached to these books were fraudulent. The books were composed after the establishment of the church, some as late as the 2nd century A.D. or later, according to the church's requirements for a manufactured tradition. Most scholars believe the earliest book of the New Testament was 1 Thessalonians, written perhaps 51 A.D. by Paul, who never saw Jesus in person and knew no details of his life story." [2]

Moses did not write the Pentateuch

Nowhere in these books does the text say he is the author; plus it gives the account of Moses's death and burial. Dr. Yosef ben-Jochannan informs us that the Torah and Old Testament were "only written in ca. 700 B.C.E...by scribes at the Sanhedrin....at which time the Africans of the entire Nile Valley were already in their XXVIth Dynastic Period." [3] Walker writes: "Many laymen are still led to believe that a real Moses wrote the Pentateuch (first five books of the Old Testament), even though scholars have known for a long time that these books were first written in the late post-exilic period by priestly scribes in Jerusalem. Their purpose was to create a mythic history for their nation out of customs, sayings, and legends mostly borrowed from others." [4]

How did the Bible become known as the "Word of God"?

"The first copy of the Bible was finished in the early part of the 5th Century, and was called the Vulgate because its language was so common and could be read by the 'vulgar'. Then, at the Council of Trent, 1200 years later, the Catholic bishops declared the Vulgate to be the 'Inspired Word of God'. And that's how the Bible came to be the Word of God. The Catholic bishops [white men] said it was. But God knew nothing about it. They did not notify him." [5] God was also not notified or consulted regarding the 100+ different versions of the Bible, including new versions of "the Word of God" that are periodically released, even today! Outrageous, indisputable, shocking, fascinating, amusing, shameful evidence that the Bible is not the "Word of God" is presented in chapter 22 of Kersey Graves's ***Bible of Bibles*** where he lists 277 "Bible contradictions," also "an Exposition of 2000 Biblical Errors in Science, History, Morals, Religion, and General Events.

All versions of the Christian Bible are Frauds founded on forgery

"Documentary foundations of the [Albino] Christian church's temporal powers were often forged, including the crucial Petrine doctrine of the keys... The church [Albinos] refused to acknowledge that its traditional privileges were founded on false documents. The works of subsequent scholars revealing the deception were banned and their authors persecuted. Apologists who tried to explain away the forgery were rewarded with ecclesiastical preferments. In 1628, when Blondel published irrefutable proof of the Decretals' fraudulence, his work was promptly placed on the Index of Prohibited Books." [6]

1) Walker, WE, 320. 2) Ibid., 465. 3) Jochannan, WBJ, xix. 4) Walker, WE, 679 . 5) Hotema, GC, 55. 6) Walker, WE, 319.

There were over 25 Afrikan Popes before the first Roman (Albino) Pope

North Afrikan Christianity was replaced by *Romanized European Christianity.* The *North Afrikan Church* was usurped and supplanted by the counterfeit *Roman Catholic Church.* Many of its bishops, priests, etc., were canonized by its supplanter, thus many *martyred* "saints" were *murdered* Blacks. Dr. Yosef ben-Jochannan addresses the Afrikan origin of the Roman Church in *African Origins of the Major Western Religions.*

"After burning books and closing pagan schools, the church dealt in another kind of forgery: falsification by omission. All European history was extensively edited by a church that managed to make itself the sole repository of literary and historical records. With all important documents assembled in the monasteries, and the lay public rendered illiterate, [Albino] Christian history could be forged with impunity." [1]

The massive fraud is maintained today by "scholars" from the "Ivory Towers," along with the "priests" (bishops, ministers, reverends, clergy, teachers, sunday-school teachers, popes, preachers, missionaries, etc.) of Christianity, Judaism, Islam, and Hinduism. Many of the afore named are unaware of the fraud, but the ones higher up DO KNOW but do not tell their congregations. You'd be surprised! And yes, many of these are People of Color embracing and promoting /maintaining the Counterfeit Religions that are keeping them undermined in the name of the Lord.

The Essene Scrolls expose the fraudulency of white Counterfeit Christianity

Discovered in caves near Jerusalem in 1947, the Essene Scrolls (Dead Sea Scrolls) expose knowledge concealed by white Counterfeit-Christianity. They prove that Christianity was an outgrowth of Essenism. Dr. R. Bernard writes "These scrolls reveal knowledge hidden from the world ever since the Alexandrian library was burnt by the Roman churchmen in order to purposely destroy it, because they considered it dangerous to the existence and survival of the new religion [False Christianity] which they elaborated by alteration of the original doctrines [Afrikan Mysteries] taught by the Essenes [Afrikan Jews] centuries previously." [2] The Essene Scrolls (Dead Sea Scrolls) were the sacred documents of the Essenes. They hid their scrolls in caves to safeguard them from the advancing Roman legions. These Scrolls are only part of a greater body of ancient records, written by and preserved by the Essene Order since antiquity. As to be expected, Albinos have the Scrolls (the "Truth") imprisoned! Even so, what little they have leaked out to the public has caused and is still causing shockwaves. The content of a large part of the ***800*** ancient Hebrew and Aramaic manuscripts remains concealed from the general public,[3] though they were found 50 years ago.

Probably the best and most truthful book available from Albinos on the Essenes is *The Dead Sea Scrolls Deception* by Michael Baigent and Richard Leigh. As you may surmise by the title, the authors have pierced, no *gouged* the deception surrounding the Scrolls, ransacking the well established lies of their dishonest brothers. The *missing* link /key in their book and all the other albino books on the Essenes is *Melanin*, that is, the Black Afrikan identity of Christ and the original IUs (Jews). Once the *blacked out* Melanin is restored to the *whitewashed* equation, only then does the Light come on! Only then are innumerable questions answered, baffling mysteries solved, and inexplicable bizarre circumstances begin to make sense.

1) Walker, WE, 320. 2) Bernard, 2. 3) Jacket of *Dead Sea Scrolls Deception.*

The Black IUs and the Essenes are one!

The original early Christians were the Essenes, a Judaic branch in Palestine. Jesus was an Essene. The earliest images of Jesus, his Mother, disciples and other biblical characters, appear for the first time in the catacombs of Rome where these early Christians buried their dead. They are portrayed Black, Afrikan. These Essenes in fact, *were* the "early Christians" who were brutally persecuted by the Romans (whites) and often fed to the lions for entertainment!

His-*Story* books speak of the Essenes as if they were a *minority* "sect," just like Blacks and other People of Color today are referred to as "minorities." It was the Albinos (Habirus, Romans) that were the minority. In reality the IUs or Essenes were the *majority,* not a "sect"! A large number of Essenes lived at Qumran, in which is now Jordan. One of their documents refer to affiliated communities throughout Palestine, thus Qumran was not isolated from the world of its time.[1] And the Essenes were not a "sect"; the real *sect* was the *recent*, counterfeit Judaism of the counterfeit Jews (Habirus), –and actually not even a sect, since they "sected" off nothing; they were a perverted counterfeit, seeking to usurp the Afrikan original. Along with Counterfeit Christianity, they succeeded.

Other names for the Essenes include: [2]

Zealots	Ossenes	Jessaeans
Ebionim	Osim	Hassidim
Therapeutae (Healers)	**Nozrim**	Nostrim
Nozrei ha-Brit	Nazoreans	**Nazarene** (!)
Nasrani (Arabic for Christian)		

Nazarene has nothing to do with Jesus's upbringing since Nazareth did not exist during the life of Christ.[3] Therefore the reference of Christ as the Nazarene points to Christ as the Essene! And **Nozrim** is "one of the earliest Hebrew designations for the sect subsequently known as 'Christians' " [4] Note that *Nozrim* is the same word demeaned in the Talmud. The Talmud rewriters were haters of Christ /Christians or "Nozrim."

Phrases meaning the Essenes include:

- Qumran Community
- "original Christians in Judaea"
- Keepers of the Covenant (Nozrei ha-Brit)
- "followers of the Way" (echoed in Acts 9:2)

"It would thus seem that the Qumran community was equivalent to the 'early Church' based in Jerusalem — the 'Nazoreans' ..." [5] The term "early Church" is a euphemism for Afrikans (like the term "inner city). The "early Church" and the Qumran community were apparently the same. **The Original so-called Christian Church was Afrikan (Ethiopian).** Its original Afrikan founders and early saints were often martyred when this church was usurped by Albinos who supplanted it with their counterfeit *Roman Catholic Church.*

1) Baigent, DSD, 146. 2) Ibid., 173-174. 3) Ewing, 96, 98-99. 4) Baigent, DSD, 173. 5) Ibid., 174.

• Contrary to popular belief, the Essenes were *not* celibate pacifists!
• In fact, the *Essenes* and *Zealots* were the same!

They were not celibates. One of the Essene Scrolls (the Damascus Document) pertains to marriage and children, which establishes that the Qumran community were not celibate 'Essenes."[1] Nor were they "turn-the-other-cheek" pacifists. The Essenes were one with the Zealots! The Zealots militantly resisted the Romans (whites). For more information read The Dead Sea Scrolls Deception (pages xvi, 166, 167, 171, etc.).

The multi-level ruins of the Masada fortress

Masada. It seems that the Black Essenes–Zealot–IUs were formidable!

It seems that they were well organized as part of their defense for survival, for they lived under the constant threat of the Albino danger, both within (as the Habiru "Jews" ever seeking to usurp them) and without (as the "Romans" whom they call the "Kittim" in their War Scrolls). The Habiru priesthood were collaborators with the occupying Romans. **The Black IUs /Jews /Essenes /Zealots, etc., would not submit to white (Roman) rule.** They constantly resisted, revolted, fought back. **Masada is the most outstanding example.** In A.D. 74, the fortress of Masada, having withstood a sustained Roman siege for many years, was at last overrun, but rather than give up to the Albinos, all 965 of these Afrikans (except a woman and two children who hid) committed suicide! **That these were Black people is also supported by a *scalp* of PLAITED-hair surviving in the remains!** In 1963 when Masada was scientifically excavated, the skeletal remains of a man, woman and child were found. Astoundingly the scalp of the woman was still preserved and her hair was "still neatly braided into plaits" ![2] Black people still wear "plaits" today; they invented plaiting and cornrowing to manage their wooly spiraling hair; straight hair does not hold braids. This mass-suicide was not an isolated case, just the most famous. Dr. Yosef ben-Jochannan recounts another case were Black IUs or "**The Maidens** who were not killed on the battle field against King Segael and his forces committed **mass suicides** rather than become prisoners. They had formed lines and marched to the top of a precipice where they hurled themselves over the cliff..."[3]

Militant Zealot Jesus whipped the moneychangers (Habirus?), overturning their tables and driving them out of the Temple with a scourge of cords. At least two of his disciples were Zealots. Before his vigil in Gethsemane, he instructed his followers to equip themselves with swords –plus, shortly thereafter, Peter did actually draw his sword and chopped the ear off a minion in the high priest's entourage. And he was executed by the Romans in a fashion reserved exclusively for revolutionary political activity! Baigent and Leigh wrote: "Accounts of the Essenes by classical [i.e., *Albino*] writers are not consistent with the life or thought of the community as revealed by either the external evidence of archaeology of the internal evidence of the text themselves. Josephus, Philo and Pliny offer portraits of the Essenes which are often utterly irreconcilable [*major lies*, in other words] with the testimony of Qumran's ruins and of the Dead Sea Scrolls. The evidence at Qumran...repeatedly contradicts their accounts."[4] [emphasis added] Hence the "classical" writers are lying their buttocks off.

1) Baigent, DSD, 146. 2) Joyce, JS, 147. 3) Jochannan, WBJ, 94,95, 133. 4) Baigent, DSD, 170.

They destroyed and supplanted the Afrikan Mysteries, source of their counterfeit versions

In his classic work, *Stolen Legacy*, for which he was killed, George James summarized the destruction: "Ancient Rome, who through the edicts of her Emperors Theodosius in the 4th century A.D. and Justinian in the 6th century A.D. abolished the Mysteries of the African Continent; that is the ancient culture system of the world. The higher metaphysical doctrine of those Mysteries could not be comprehended; the spiritual powers of the priests were unsurpassed; the magic of the rites and ceremonies filled the people with awe...This lofty culture system of the Black people filled Rome with envy, and consequently she legalized Christianity which she had persecuted for five long centuries, and set it up as a state religion and as a rival of Mysteries, its own mother. *[Note: **What Rome legalized was the fraudulent, Romanized Christianity.** What she persecuted was the authentic version or Afrikan Mysteries. It is important to recognize that the two coexisted; the Euro-Counterfeit supplanted the Afri-Original or the Mysteries. Like George James, most people have the two confused or are not aware there is a difference, so well done is the deception!]* This is why the Mysteries have been despised; this is why other ancient religions of the Black people are despised; because they are all offspring of the African Mysteries, which have never been clearly understood by Europeans, and consequently have provoked their prejudice and condemnation. In keeping with the plan of Emperors Theodo-sius and Justinian to exterminate and forever suppress the culture system of the African continents the Christian church established its missionary enterprise to fight against what it has called paganism. Consequently missionaries and educators have gone to the mission field with a superiority complex, born of miseducation and disrespect: a prejudice which has made it impossible for them to accomplish the blessings which missionary enterprise might otherwise have accomplished. For this reason Missionary enterprise has been responsible for a positive injury against the African people..."[1]

Whites locked Kamit's knowledge behind Freemasonry

America's founding fathers and all but two presidents were Freemasons, as well as all the generals who fought in the Revolutionary War. They built America on Kamit's Masonic principles. (see page 42)

Dorothy Fardan, a rare white honest historian and member of the Nation of Islam, wrote: "The truth about Jesus and the truth about ancient Egypt as well as early Christianity have all been concealed, and in the Western world they are locked in the coded secrecy of freemasonry... Freemasonry is the knowledge, study and practice of various degrees of the ancient Egyptian mystery religion. Its symbols are embedded in the implements and tools of ancient stonemasonry. The rituals and body of knowledge are today concealed and practiced in lodges and halls hidden from the common man, the masses of people. ...While there has been this longstanding cover-up and continuous disinformation surrounding ancient Egypt, origins of man, and Jesus the Christ..., still it cannot be overlooked that there were those who knew, who perpetrated the lie. In order for the European to take the knowledge out of Egypt and keep it, it had to be hidden and preserved in a way that the people would not know in general. Those approved and selected of 'belonging' to such societies would have access, but not the 'common run' of man. ..It is said that freemasonry sprang up in Europe in the 1700's. The actual source of its knowledge is never fully expounded upon. But masons themselves recognize the source. They know it is traced to ancient Africa (Kemet)."[2]

1) James, SL, 154-155. 2) Fardan, MWM, 47-48.

Like the Bible, the Talmud is a Fraud. Modern Judaism is Talmudism.

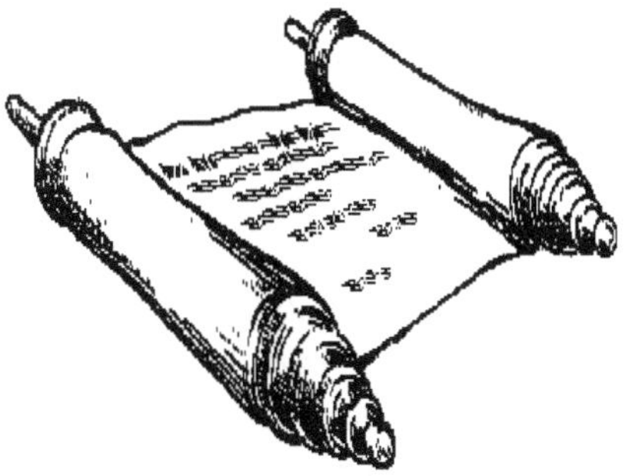

False Judaism had already been fabricated by the time the biblical Christ arrived and was already a rival to the true Judaic teachings which were the spiritual teachings of Kamit.

"Judaism" is a fraudulent and misleading term. What is today called Judaism was "Pharisaism" during Jesus's time. It was Flavius Josephus, writing for the instruction of Greeks and Romans, who coined the term Judaism, in order to pit it against Hellenism.[1] "The form of religious worship known as 'Pharisaism' in Judea in the time of Jesus was a religious practice based exclusively upon the Talmud." [2] A Jewish authority, Rabbi Morris Kertzer wrote: "The Talmud consists of 63 books of legal, ethical and historical writings of the ancient rabbis. It was edited five centuries after the birth of Jesus. It is a compendium of law and lore. It is the legal code which forms the basis of Jewish Religious Law and it is the textbook used in the training of rabbis." [3]

Jewish authorities say that the Talmud was the literature studied by Jesus in his early years. Freedman shows this to be an enormous lie by quoting from it. From pages 30-43, he quotes passages from the Talmud, including the abridged following:

> Sanhedrin, 55b-55a: "What is meant by this? -Rab said: Pederasty with a child below nine years of age is not deemed as pederasty with a child above that. Samuel said: Pederasty with a child below three years is not treated as with a child above that ...
>
> Sanhedrin, 55b: "A maiden three years and a day may be acquired in marriage by coitions, and if her deceased husband's brother cohabits with her, she becomes his.
>
> Kethuboth, 11a-11b: "Rab Judah said that Rab said: A small boy who has intercourse with a grown up woman makes her (as though she were) injured by a piece of wood (1). Although the intercourse of a small boy is not regarded as a sexual act, nevertheless the woman is injured by it as by a piece of wood."
>
> Sotah, 26b: "R. Papa said: It excluded an animal, because there is not adultery in connection with an animal...Whence is the statement which the Rabbis made that there is no adultery in connection with an animal? Because it is written, *Thou shalt not bring the hire of a harlot or the wages of a dog etc.:*...The hire of a dog (7) and the wages of a harlot (8) are permissible...
>
> (footnotes)
>
> (7) Money given by a man to a harlot to associate with his dog. Such an association is not legal adultery.
>
> (8) If a man had a female slave who was a harlot and he exchanged her for an animal, it could be offered.

1) Freedman, 25. 2) Ibid., 26. 3) Ibid.

The Talmud is anti-Jesus, anti-Christian, & anti-Black

There are many anti-Christ, anti-Christian passages in the Talmud. Why? No doubt from the Habiru-Hebrews' original hate for the original Judaic People (Black Afrikans) they were supplanting. And note that the reverse is true in the Christian Bible, which contains numerous "anti-Jew" passages! Why? No doubt from the real Jews (Afrikans) expressing their recognition of the Habiru /Edomite Wolf (false Jews) that was eating them alive. Jesus allegedly said: "I know the blasphemy of them which say they are Jews, and are not, but are the synagogue of Satan" (Rev. 2:9, 3:9).

In his eye-opening, telling book, *Facts Are Facts,* Benjamin Freedman enlightens us about the Talmud: The "most authentic analysis of the Talmud which has ever been written" was a book by Arsene Darmesteter, written in French, translated into English in 1897 by Henrietta Szold and published by The Jewish Publication Society of America in Philadelphia. From it we read: "Now Judaism finds its expression in the Talmud...The study of Judaism is that of the Talmud, as the study of the Talmud is that of Judaism...They are two inseparable things, or better, they are one and the same...The Talmud...is composed of the two distinct parts, the Mishna and Gemara; the former the test, the latter the commentary upon the text...By the term Mishna we designate a collection of decisions and traditional laws, embracing all departments of legislation, civil and religious...This code, which was the work of several generations of Rabbis..." [1] "The National Conference of Christians and Jews need not scrutinize the '63 books' of the Talmud to discover all the anti-Christ, anti-Christian, and anti-Christian faith passages in the books which are 'the legal code which forms the basis of Jewish Religious Law' and which is the 'textbook used in the training of Rabbis'... Rabbi Morris Kertzer also points out...that 'adults study ancient writings too...in..group discussion of Talmud before evening prayer.' " [2]

The Talmud's derogatory references to Jesus

Professor and Reverend I. B. Pranaitis wrote the telling book: *The Talmud Unmasked, The Secret Rabbinical Teachings Concerning Christians*. He scrutinized the Talmud for passages referring to Jesus, Christians and Christianity. His Latin translations were translated into English in 1939. Freedman summarizes some of these passages referring to Jesus:

Sanhedrin, 67a.	Jesus referred to as the son of Pandira, a soldier.
Kallah, 1b. (18b).	Illegitimate and conceived during menstruation.
Sanhedrin, 67a.	Hanged on the eve of Passover.
Toldath Jeschu.	Birth related in most shameful expressions.
Abhodah Zarah, II.	Referred to as the son of Pandira, a Roman soldier.
Schabbath XIV.	Again referred to as the son of Pandira, the Roman.
Sanhedrin, 43a.	On the eve of Passover they hanged Jesus.
Schabbath, 104b.	Called a fool and no one pays attention to fools.
Toldath Jeschu.	Judas and Jesus engage in quarrel with filth.
Sanhedrin, 103a.	Suggested corrupts his morals and dishonors self.
Sanhedrin, 107b.	Seduced, corrupted and destroyed Israel.
Zohar III, (282).	Died like a beast and buried in animal's dirt heap.
Hilkoth Melakhim.	Attempt to prove Christians err in worship of Jesus.
Orach Chaiim, 113.	Avoid appearance of paying respect to Jesus.
Iore Dea, 150, 2.	Do not appear to pay respect to Jesus by accident.
Abhodah Zarah (6a).	False teaching to worship on first day of Sabbath.

1) Freedman, 63. 2) Ibid., 68-69.

The Talmud's derogatory references to Christians and Christianity

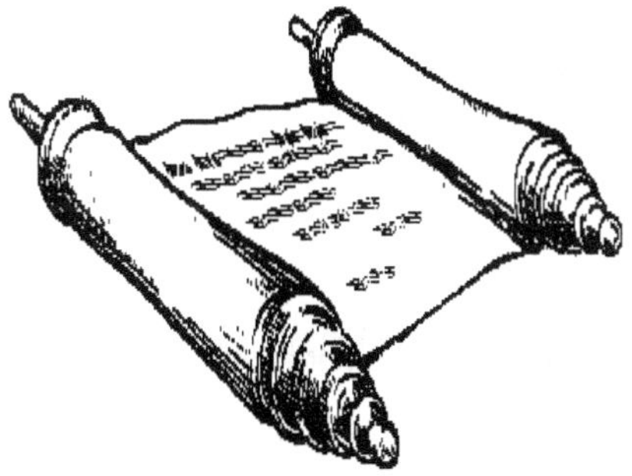

Freedman informs us there are 11 names used in the Talmud for non-Talmud followers, by which Christians (who were originally Blacks) are meant. These names include: Goim, Minim, Edom, Akum, Kuthim, and Nostrim, "from Jesus the Nazarene." (Nostrim=Nozrim, cited earlier in this chapter.) Freedman gives three pages of passages from the Talmud refering to Christians and Christianity, which include the following:

Abhodah Zarah (15b).	Suggest Christians have sex relations with animals.
Iore Dea (198, 48).	Clean female Jews contaminated meeting Christians.
Kerithuth (6b p.78).	Jews called men, Christians not called men.
Makkoth (7b).	Innocent of murder if intent was to kill Christian.
Orach Chaiim (225, 10).	Christians and animals grouped for comparisons.
Iore Dea (142, 10).	Must keep far away physically from churches.
Schabbath (116a) Tos.	Gospels called volumes of iniquity, heretical books.
Schabbath (116a).	Talmudists agree that books of Christians be burned.
Abhodah Zarah (2a).	Wine touched by Christians must be thrown away.
Peaschim (25a).	Avoid medical help from idolators, Christians meant.
Iore Dea (148, 12h).	Hide hatred for Christians at their celebrations.
Abhodah Zarah (20a).	Never praise Christians lest it be believed true.
Iore Dea (154, 2).	Forbidden to teach a trade to a Christian.
Babha Kama (11).	It is permitted to deceive Christians.
Babha Kama (113a).	Jew may lie and pejur to condemn a Christian.
Babha Kama (11b).	Name of God not profaned when lying to Christians.
Zohar (I, 160a).	Jews must always try to deceive Christians.
Iore Dea (158, 1).	Do not cure Christians unless it makes enemies.
Hilkhoth Akum (X, 1).	Do not save Christians in danger of death.
Choschen Ham. (388,15).	Kill those who give Israelites' money to Christians.
Hilkhoth Akum (X,2).	Baptized Jews are to be put to death.
Abhodah Zarah (26b) T.	"Even the best of the *Goim* should be killed."
Sepher Or Israel 177b.	If Jew kills Christian commits no sin.
Zohar (II, 43a).	Extermination of Christians necessary sacrifice.
Hilkhoth Akum (X, 1).	Make no agreements and show no mercy to Christians.
Pesachim (49b).	No need of prayers while beheading on Sabbath.

The Talmud's derogatory references to Black people

"And since you have disabled me...doing ugly things in blackness of night, **Canaan's children shall be born ugly and black!** ...your grandchildren's **hair shall be twisted into kinks**, ...your **lips** ...**shall swell**; and because you..."

Yes, there's more, and it's addressed in further detail in Chapter 14 of this book (page 337). The preceding passage is from We the Black Jews, where Dr. Yosef ben-Jochannan quotes from Hebrew Myths, by Graves & Patai, citing Talmudic text as the original sources.

Thus, we shouldn't be surprised at the viewpoint of the *chief editor* of the Dead Sea Scrolls, Dr. John Strugnell –who was put in charge of the Scrolls by the State of Israel, allegedly. After being the chief editor for years, he publicly gave his views regarding the significance of the Scrolls. Time magazine (Jan 14, 1991) reported that he **"declared that Judaism is a 'horrible' religion, with 'racist' origins that in principle should not exist at all."** What *is* surprising is that he told the truth. For his honesty, he was fired from his position.

Christianity is reworked Egyptianity

- **"Original Judaism" and "Original Christianity" were one and the same.**
- **Both began as Afrikan Cosmology from ancient Egypt, the land of *Ham*.**
- **Judaism existed long before the "Jews"!**
- **Christianity existed long before Christ!**

Massey presents massive evidence for the Afrikan origin of Christianity

He shows that the Old and New Testaments are wholly traceable to the religious records of ancient Egypt. He traces the Christ legend back 10,000 years B.C. to Afrika's Nile Valley. "The alleged facts of our Lord's life as Jesus the Christ, were equally the alleged facts of our Lord's life as the Horus of Egypt, whose very name signifies the Lord... Whether you believe or not does not matter, the fatal fact remains that every trait and feature which go to make up the Christ as Divinity, and every event or circumstance taken to establish the human personality were pre-extant and pre-applied to the Egyptian and Gnostic Christ, who never could become flesh." [1]

The Bible stories far predate the Bible

Archeologists have found in the Babylonian cuneiform inscriptions, some 1500 years or more before the alleged Jewish captivity, the story of the Creation, the Garden of Eden allegory, Eve and the Serpent, Noah and the Flood, etc. Churchward informs us: "The Jews...the Israelites, as we have shown elsewhere, were from Egypt....Their whole history, laws and traditions prove that they borrowed very largely indeed from the Egyptians, and the 'Laws of Moses,' which they consider and believe their own specific laws, were the old laws of Egypt, given to them by Moses ; laws which had been in existences thousands of years before Moses lived, as is proved by the *Stalae of Hammurabi*." [2] Kuhn echoes the same: "The entire Christian Bible, creation legend descent into and exodus from Egypt, ark and flood allegory, Israelite history, Hebrew prophecy and poetry, Gospel, Epistles and Revelation imagery, all are now proven to have been the transmission of ancient Egypt's scrolls and papyri into the hands of later generations which knew neither their true origin nor their fathomless meaning." [3]

< **No, this is NOT the Ku Klux Klan;** This is a parade of the "Seville Negro Order" in Spain, 1926.[4] The pointed hood and cape were their uniforms centuries before the Klansmen. If Klansmen knew their garb originated from Afrikans would they still wear them? Pointed hoods, pope's tiara, witches cap, and similar headgear originated in imitation of the conical crowns of Afrika's Nile Valley.

1) Jackson, CBC, 169. 2) Churchward, SS, 238, 239. 3) Kush, 69. 4) Rogers, AF, 43.

Afrikan Cosmology is the root and source of all world religions including "Eastern Religions"

Like the Human race and world civilization, all major world religions and mythologies sprang from Afrika, from the Afrikan Mysteries. This illustrates a basic and profound principle of the universe: all things have a common source, both in Heaven and Earth. All the major religions of the world originated from Afrika, including the so-called "eastern religions." This is why there is major similarity between the deities, names & character of the deities, stories, themes, rituals, prayers, symbols, and teachings of the world's religions. The Afrikans distributed their cosmology around the planet, along with civilization.

"Egyptian mythology, the source and fountainhead of all the ancient wisdom and legendary lore, could not be understood apart from this [its astrological foundation], neither can the astronomy be explained apart from the mythology." [1]

The earliest religion of Egypt has been traced back to Central Afrika. The Kamite Originals are from the *Twa*

All the stories of the Bible, from Eve to Moses, to Christ, originated from the allegories of Kamit, which originated from stories of the Twa People (called Pygmies by Europeans) of Central Afrika. In other words, the Pygmies originated the Kamit foundation of Christianity, Islam, Judaism. All the basic stories and elements of Christianity are found in the stories of the Twa People. Example: eons before Christianity and ancient Egypt, the Twa People "believed in a Father-God who was murdered, and a Virgin Mother, who gave birth to a Savior-God Son, who in turn avenged the death of his father. These later on became the Osiris, Isis, and Horus of Egypt. The Pygmy Christ was born of a virgin, died for the salvation of his people, arose from the dead, and finally ascended to heaven. Certainly this looks like Christianity before Christ." [2]

One might ask, why didn't the Twa build mighty buildings and do similar things as did the Nubians and Kamites? Well guess what? –they *did* do these things according to their own testimonies. Remember, they were the Original-original People; they had eons to develop and perfect civilization; they peopled the world. They built big cities, advanced machines, yes machines, and probably did space travel. They are the builders of the megalithic structures around the world, of which Stonehenge (in England) is a famous example. They gave all this up! —to live simply and intimately with Nature as many of them still do today. These "little people" are giants!

1) Massey, AE, 591. 2) Jackson, CBC, 175.

Foreseeing the future, Afrikans planned for the preservation of their sacred teachings from the advancing European destruction

"except God"
Adinkra symbol of the Power and Immortality of the God [/ Goddess].

Prophets and prophecy were a natural part of Afrikan life. Christ was an Afrikan prophet. Prophets permeate the Old Testament especially. The ancient Afrikans foresaw the Albino destruction invading Afrika, threatening its people, civilization and cosmology. The Afrikans conspired to save their precious teachings, accumulated over aeons. As recounted by Dr. Kweku Andoh in *African Geomancy*,[1] by Dr. J. A. Cole, protection of the Afrikan Mysteries were accomplished in secret by dividing them up and distributing responsibility for their parts to different Afrikan peoples:

- **The AKAN people of Ghana** were entrusted with "the secrets of the physical sciences, mathematics, the symbolism in pictograph relaying the principles of physics and chemistry...This graphic system expresses a highly sophisticated method of measurement and calculations which, even today, is shrouded in an aura of mystery. The use of these symbols is alive and thrives as part of the every day life of the people of Ghana." This sacred symbolism is known today as *Adinkra.*

- **The DOGON people** were entrusted with guarding the secrets of the celestial movements, stars and heavenly bodies and the origins of the universe and humanity's celestial role. Their knowledge of astronomy surpasses that of Europeans. They knew of the invisible star, Sirius B, and the composition of the moon eons before modern European scientists.

- **The YORUBA people** were entrusted with preserving the rituals, invocations, occult knowledge of the soul and spirit, religious ideology and the universal role of man/woman.

Likely, other Afrikan peoples were likewise entrusted with branches of Kamit's Cosmic Knowledge. In his profound book, *Of Water and Spirit*, an indigenous Afrikan, Maladoma, writes among other things, of his Afrikan initiation –and the part he is permitted to share is awesome, mind-boggling. This is evidence of Afrika's profound, living legacy. Nothing can really destroy this, for it is rooted in the Cosmic Principles of Life. It is a manifestation of the Cosmic Principles of Life, as is the HU-man Body. It goes deep! Though it seems that the majority of Afrikan people are colonized and ignorant of their true legacy, the truth is still there, preserved, waiting the day it may come forth to shine *Her* light, freedom, and richness to those that open to receive it. To receive it is to become the gods and goddesses we were all meant to be; already *are*; remember our Divinity. What do you think "alchemy" was *really* all about? Listen! –You Daughter of God! You Son of God! You Children of Light! Do you know *who* you really *are*? Remember! Ra-Member! (put the severed members back together and thus become whole) Wake up! Can you see that the real war is about *disinheriting* you of your true inheritance as the Sons and Daughters of God / Goddess?

1) Cole /Andoh, 6-8.

Adoption versus Theft

It seems that the very early Europeans (Greeks, Romans...) did *not* steal or plagiarize the Afrikan teachings and gods; they adopted them, giving credit to the Afrikan source. They even boasted about their fine education in Kamit. It was the later Europeans that committed the theft, plagiarism, inversion, and perversion of Afrikan Cosmology. Nothing wrong with adopting something you like. It only becomes a crime when, not only is the source denied, but destroyed. And the plagiarizer falsely claims credit for the stolen thing, claiming to be its originators. Furthermore, the true originators are demeaned and told they have done nothing or anything worthwhile. This is what Europeans have done to Afrikans. They stole the original Afrikan theology along with its culture, denied its source, then tried to destroy all the evidence which proved the connection. They severed it from its roots and denied those roots. Whites who invaded India did the same thing –and today, virtually the whole Indian continent is ignorant of their Afrikan roots. Around the world on all continents, darkskinned people are demeaned; lightskinned people are upheld. The Truth will set *many*, if not *most* of us free. I say most/many because some people are so imprisoned by the White Lies of their upbringing that they cannot let these Lies go, even if it's killing them –so secure are they in the Great Deceiver's grip.

Further References

– *Christianity Before Christ* by John Jackson
– *The Dead Sea Scrolls Deception* by M. Baigent & R. Leigh
– *African Origins of the Major "Western Religions"* by Yosef A.A. ben-Jochannan
– *Who Wrote the Bible?* by Richard E. Friedman
– *Signs and Symbols of Primordial Man* by Albert Churchward
– *Ancient Egypt the Light of the World* by Gerald Massey
– *The World's Sixteen Crucified Saviors* by Kersey Graves

Black Originals – White Copies: Comparative biblical examples of Christianity's Afrikan origin

Deities

Plagiarized Biblical Copy:	Afrikan-Kamite Original:
Amen God is called the Amen: "These things saith the Amen" (Rev. 3:14). Amen is said at the end of prayers. Emmanuel, Immanuel, a divine name of Christ (Isa. 7:14; 8:8, Mat. 1:23).	**Amen** is a divine name /title of many Kamite deities. Amen signifies the secret or hidden. *Amen*, name of the Hidden God in Heaven. *Amen-Ra*, a title of Asar as the Father. *Amen-Iu*, a title of Heru as the Son. *Amenta*, the Underworld /womb-world where the souls of the deceased went. Amenu-El (Amen-Iu-Al) the Coming Son, a title of Heru.
Asherah the Great Mother Goddess, also called Diana, "whom all Asia and the world worshippeth" (Acts 19:27).	**Asherah** a version of Ash (Asa, As-t, Isis), the Great Mother. She is also called Tannen-t (source of Goddess Diana).
Christ Christ, Kristos, Chrost (in English, Greek, Ethiopian) all mean Anointed, derived from Egyptian Krst (Karast). Christ, "the BRANCH..." (Zech. 3:8, 6:5).	**Krst, Karast** Kamite KRST (karast) means *anointed mummy. Osiris-Krst* was the original Krst /Christ. Incarnated as his son. Heru the Krst; Heru-Karast. Was called Unbu, meaning the Tree and the Branch. The Golden Unbu (Bough).
El in names (Rach**el**, Isra**el**, **El**ijah) = deification. The **El**ohim or Plural God in Genesis said "Let us make man in our image." Polytheism in Judaism /Christianity is betrayed by the ELs! "The so-called archangels of each sphere of the Tree of Life are deities in other traditions.	**Ali** Al, Ali (Ar, Ari) means elevated. The ALI were the Seven Glorious Ones, the 7 Gods or Co-Creators of the Universe, the first Seven Sons of the Great Mother and Great Father.
God "God is light" (1John 1:5). "God is a Spirit" (John 4:24). The Seven Spirits of God (Rev. 4:5).	**Khut** Khut (Spirit, Light), title of Isis & Heru as Givers of Light. Khuti / Gudi, name of the Seven Co-Creators of the Universe, also called the ALI (see previous paragraph).
I-Am-That-I-Am A name of God: "Then God said unto Moses: I AM THAT I AM. Thus shalt thou say unto the children of Israel, I AM hath sent me unto you" (Exo. 3:14).	**Nuk-Puk-Nuk** Or "I-Am-That-I-Am," is an Egyptian name for God which was carved on most Kamite temples (Higgens, vII, 17). "I AM" was a Divine name understood by all the initiated among the Egyptians. "The 'I AM' of the Hebrews, and the 'I AM' of the Egyptians are identical."
Jehovah, Yaweh, Jehoshua, Jesus *Jehovah* (JHVH, JHWH) and *Yaweh* (YHVH, YHWH) are variants of the same name. The Latin form of *Jehovah* is *Jove* or *Jupiter* (Iu-Piter), meaning Father IU. *Jesus* is Latin form of Hebrew *Jehoshua /Yeshua*, also from IU. (see page 204 for etymology and other derivatives).	**IU, Iao, Y-Ah-Weh, IU-sa** The name "Jehovah" was esteemed sacred among the Egyptians. They called it IU; of which variants include Ieu, Iao, Iaou, Jao, Jaou, J-ha-ho, Y-HA-HO, Y-AH-WEH, Yahweh, Yaho, Jah, Jahveh... (Higgens, vI, 329, 330; vII,17; Doane, 48, Walker, 463, 1094-5)
Satan The Devil of the Bible. Satan bound in chains.	**Set** Source of the name Satan. The Kamite god Set was the God of Drought, Darkness, Negativity. "Set gives his name to Satan as 'Set-an:' 'Set,'...is the destructive power and 'an' in the Egyptian language is a mark of emphasis." (Saakana / Finch, 36) Heru (Horus) bound Set in chains.

Symbols

Plagiarized Biblical Copy:	Afrikan-Kamite Original:
Altar An Altar is found *within* every church. A Steeple or Crucifix is usually found *without* every church. Why? The Altar is the female genital center (!) always within! The Steeple is the external phallus, projecting and "erected" on the outside! The Steeple is derived from the obelisk, a Kamite symbol of the divine phallus (especially of Osiris). Phalli were secretly hidden in altars of churches. (Walker, WE, 796)	**Al-Tar** Symbol of the Great Mother, Her Womb of Life, and the Earth's regenerative womb. The word ALTAR reflects this! Altar = AL (high, elevated) + TAR (opening, circle, womb, abode). The Heavenly Virgin was called the "Altar of Heaven." Tar = door (from same root). Since Kamite R/L are one, Tar =Tal, found in Delta, symbol of the Yoni or Womb. Thus Al-Tar = the High Womb. This is the O on the top of the Ankh!
Ark The Ark of the Covenant. The Ark of Noah.	**Ark** Symbol of the Body/Womb of the Great Mother Goddess, bearing the seeds of Life! The Ark of the Covenant was the female sexual vessel for the male god, –just like Isis was the "throne" for Osiris. The word ARK is Egyptian and means to "encircle," which is just what the female "vessel" does to the male. The Indian copy was the *Argha*, the Great Yoni Ship, the pregnant Moon-Boat bearing the seeds of all life through the sea of chaos between destruction of one cosmos and creation of the next. ARK also means *roll* or *writing, to know, to complete.* Source of the *words archives, archetype, arc, arch, arcane.*
Crucifix  Is half of the Kamite Ankh! –with only the male portion. As such, it is disconnected from the Feminine aspect and becomes the symbol or Cross of Death! It did not appear in Christian art until after the 5th century A.D. The original cross used by the earliest Christians was the ANKH, a looped cross which symbolizes everlasting life. The Albino man's false replacement is the Crucifix, a symbol of death.	**Ankh**  Older than Kamit, originating from earlier Afrikan civilization, the eternal Ankh existed eons before (false) Christianity. The Ankh is the "Cross of Life," the symbol of Life and Union. Symbolizes the Union of the Male & Female Polarities, or union of male & female sexual symbols: a female oval surmounting a male cross.
Dove Holy Ghost "The Father, the Son, and the Holy Ghost." Just who do you think the "Holy Ghost" is?! The Holy Ghost, in the patriarchal Bible, is the Great Mother. The Holy Ghost is even called "The Comforter," a motherly quality. The Hebrew word for Holy Ghost is of the feminine gender. When Christ was baptized, the Holy Ghost in the form of a Dove, descended upon him. Christ said "Be ye therefore wise as serpents, and harmless as doves" (Mat. 10:16).	**Tev** Dove is from Kamite TEV (Tef, Teb), a name of the Great Mother. The Dove, or bird of sexual passion, is symbol of the Great Mother, sexual passion & the Yoni. Joined to her consort the Phallic Serpent (Asar / Osiris), the Dove Goddess represented Sexual Union and Life. Christ's phrase: "Be ye therefore wise as serpents, and harmless as doves" (Mat. 10:16), is a traditional invocation of the God and Goddess.
Steeple Found atop most churches, the Steeple is derived from the Afrikan obelisk, a Kamite symbol of the divine phallus. 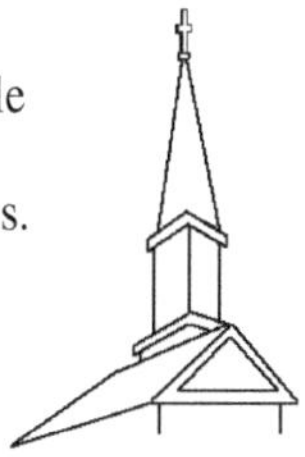	**Obelisk** Created by Isis to replace the missing phallus of Osiris when he was cut up into 14 pieces. Symbol of the phallus of a number of Afrikan gods. Two obelisks flanked the entrances of Kamite temples. 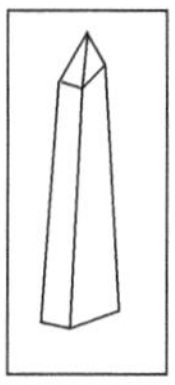

Code of Living

Plagiarized Biblical Copy:

The Ten Commandments

These are just 10 from the original list of over 147 laws from Kamit, which Afrikans wrote at least 1300 years before Moses's alleged revelation on Mt. Sinai. Even the Bible says Moses was an *Egyptian* priest. The Ten Commandments are found in Exodus 20:2-17 and Deuteronomy, 5:6-21.

1. Thou shalt have no other gods before me.
2. Thou shalt not make unto thee any graven image...[and] bow down thyself to them, nor serve them...
3. Thou shalt not take the name of the Lord thy God in vain...
4. Remember the Sabbath day, to keep it holy....
5. Honor thy father and thy mother...
6. Thou shalt not kill.
7. Thou shalt not commit adultery.
8. Thou shalt not steal.
9. Thou shalt not bear false witness against thy neighbor.
10. Thou shalt not covet thy neighbor's house, thou shalt not covet thy neighbor's wife, nor his manservant, nor his maidservant, nor his ox, nor his ass, nor any thing that is thy neighbor's.

Afrikan-Kamite Original:

The 147 Negative Confessions

From the South wall of the Tomb of Pharaoh Rameses III and VI in the Valley of Kings, Wa'at (Thebes of Luxor) (Saakana, pages 26, 27). In the Kamite Book of the Coming Forth By Day (incorrectly called the Book of the Dead), 42 are listed.

1. I have not done iniquity.
2. **I have not committed robbery with violence.**
3. I have done violence to no man.
4. **I have not committed theft.**
5. **I have not slain man or woman.**
6. I have not made light the bushel.
7. I have not acted deceitfully.
8. I have not purloined the things which belong to the God.
9. **I have not uttered falsehood.**
10. I have not carried away food.
11. I have not uttered evil words.
12. I have not attacked man.
13. I have not killed the beasts which are the property of the Gods.
14. I have not eaten my heart (i.e., done anything to my regret).
15. I have not laid waste ploughed land.
16. I have not pried into matters.
17. I have not set my mouth in motion against any man.
18. I have not given way to anger concerning myself without cause.
19. **I have not defiled the wife of a man.**
20. I have not committed transgression against any party.
21. **I have not violated sacred times and seasons.**
22. I have not struck fear into any man.
23. I have not been a man of anger.
24. I have not made myself deaf to words of right and truth.
25. I have not stirred my strife.
26. I have not made any man weep.
27. I have not committed acts of impurity or sodomy.
28. I have not abused any man.
29. I have not acted with violence.
30. I have not judged hastily.
31. I have not taken vengeance upon the God.
32. I have not multiplied my speech overmuch.
33. I have not acted with deceit, or worked wickedness.
34. ....

... etc....

Heaven & Hell

Plagiarized Biblical Copy:	Afrikan-Kamite Original:
Heaven God's celestial home. A Divine Haven, a place of Peace and Utopia of Abundance where God dwells with his angels. Situated above the Earth in the air or "space." Includes the stars, sun, moon and other celestial bodies. "Space" was called the *Nun* by the Kamites. The *Nun* was the Primeval *Waters* of the Great Mother, the Cosmic *Ocean* in which all things dwell. And God's throne in Heaven is on a crystal *Sea*: "And before the throne there was a sea of glass like unto crystal" (Rev. 4:6:). From it flows the Water of Life (Rev. 22:1). This is all copied from the Kamite Scriptures, the original Bible.	**The Nun, Kabhu, Mt. Hetep** In the rainless land of Kamit, the Nile was the lifeline. *Water* was *Life* indeed, where *Drought* was *Death*. Paradise or Heaven was where water was abundant! A Kamite name for Heaven was Kabhu, derived from water or "that which cools." Thus Water was divinized as Heaven or the Water above, a firmament upheld by Four Pillars. Also called the *Nun* (whence, *inundate*). The Kamites saw water as "the beginning and origin of all things." Hence the throne of the Eternal rested on the element of water. "So in the building of the heavens the beginning was with water, of the firmament imaged in its aerial likeness." (Massey, AE, 280) Another Kamite name for Heaven was Mount Hetep, the mount of Peace and Abundance.
Hell "Hell" is a creation by the Albinos [Habiru, European churchmen] who perverted Kamit's sacred teachings. That they could even come up with such cruelty reflects their disconnection (have they ever been "connected?) from the true Loving God of Life. Only a wicked Loveless God of Death (which is secretly the God of the false rewritten Bible) could ordain such. **The biblical Hell is a massive perversion and corruption of the "original Hell"** which was NOT a vast torture chamber of eternal fiery punishment. It has been the Europeans themselves (church fathers & their henchmen) –creators of this Hell, who practiced "giving Hell" to literally millions of their *own* people, during the Inquisition: they tortured and burned people alive, especially females (women, girls, babies), at the stake, sometimes burning them "slowly" to give them a preview of the Hell they were allegedly going to. (Walker, WE, 388) The biblical Hell is a major scare-tactic to control and manipulate believers. If Hell was canceled and abolished, how many Christians would remain Christians? It's the belief in Hell, and fear or threat of eternal Hell-punishment that keeps them "behaving." This bastard "Hell" is only necessary for a bastard religion. "Hell" is one of the principal pillars of support of this bastard religion, for without this "Hell" there is no need for "salvation" hence a Savior, etc. Historians derive *hell* from "Hel", the underworld of the Norse myths. But *hel* and *hell* are both likely from the same root as HELios, a name for the sun where it is hot as hell. Since Egyptian R/L are one, then Helios is further derived from Kamite HERU (Her-Iu), whom the Greeks called *Horus,* a name of the Sungod in Afrika's Nile Valley.	**Amenta** Amenta the Underworld. "The prototypes of hell and purgatory and the earthly paradise are all to be found in the Etyptian Amenta...The darkness, fire, and chains...and other paraphernalia of the Christian hell, are also Egyptian. But the chains were employed for the fettering of Sut, the Apap, and the Sebau, the evil adversaries of Osiris, the good or perfect being, not for the torturing of souls that once were human. The Egyptian hell was not a place of everlasting pain, but of extinction for those who were wicked irretrievably (AE, 240). **There were two deaths:** the first was a physical death. This temporary death was not a concern. It was the Second Death that was the abomination. This was a permanent Spiritual death that lasted forever, but only happened to those who "were wicked irretrievably." (AE, 240) "...a god of eternal torment is an ideal distinctly Christian [European!], to which the Egyptians [Afrikans] never did attain. Theirs was the all-parental god, Father and Mother in one [the *Loving* God and *Goddess* of Life] whose heart was thought to bleed in every wound of suffering humanity." (AE, 240) **Christianity's unquenchable hell fire** (Mark 9:43, 44): "This lake of fire that is never quenched was derived from the solar force in the mythology on which the eschatology was based. Hence the locality was in the east, at the place of sunrise." (AE, 240) "Darkness in the nether world is identical with the tunnels of Sut in Amenta. The chains are likewise Egyptian, but not for human wear. Apap and the Sebau, Sut and the Sami are bound in chains. ..As already explained the Sebau and the Sami represent the physical forces in external nature that made for evil and were for ever opposed to the Good Being and to the peace of the world. They had to be kept under ; hence the necessity for prisons, bonds, and chains." (AE, 241)

Scriptures

Plagiarized Biblical Copy:	Afrikan-Kamite Original:
The Word "In the beginning was the Word, and the Word was with God, and the Word was God" (John 1:1).	**The Word** Carved in hieroglyphics: "The Word creates all things...Nothing is before it has been uttered..." (Walker, WD, 212)
Psalm 104 So is this great and wide sea, wherein are things creeping innumerable, both small and great and beasts...There go the ships. O Lord how manifold are thy works! In wisdom hast Thou made them all...The earth is full of thy creatures.	**Akhenaton's Hymn** The ships sail up stream and down stream alike...The fish in the river leap up before thee: and thy rays are in the midst of the great sea. How manifold are all Thy works! ...Thou didst create the earth according to Thy desire, men all cattle...all that are upon the earth. (Browder, NV, 94)
Book of Revelation This is probably one of the least tampered-with books in the Christian Bible. John's apocalyptic visions were not his, nor did he write them. This material is lifted almost straight from Kamite Mysteries and allegories regarding the Zodiac.	**The Kamite Mysteries** Revelation describes scenes and characters from the mysteries of Aan (Taht-Aan), source of the name John. Aan was the Kamite Penman of the Gods, the sacred scribe to whom 36,000 books were attributed by tradition. Chapter 11 of Massey's book (*Ancient Egypt*, pages 690-726) is devoted to exposing the Kamite allegories behind the unexplainable, bizarre, awesome imagery in John's apocalyptic visions. "The present contention is that the book is and always has been inexplicable because it was based upon the symbolism of the Egyptian astronomical mythology without the gnosis, of 'meaning which hath wisdom, that is absolutely necessary for an explanation of its subject-matter..." (Massey, AE, 690)
King Solomon's Proverbs: Have I not written for thee thirty sayings, Of counsels and knowledge! That thou mayest make known truth to him that speaketh. Incline thine ear, and hear my words, And apply thine heart to apprehend; For it is pleasant if thou keep them in thy belly, That they may be fixed upon thy lips. A scribe who is skillful in his business Findeth himself worthy to be a courtier. (Saakana, 24)	**Pharaoh Amen-em-ope's Proverbs** Consider these thirty chapters They delight, they instruct. Knowledge how to answer him that speaketh, And how to carry back a report to the one that sent it. Give thine ear, and hear what I say And apply thine heart to apprehend; It is good for thee to place them in thine heart, Let them rest in the casket of the belly. That they may act as a peg upon thy tongue. A man who is skilful in his business Shall stand before Kings. (Saakana, 24)

9

Biblical Hebrew History is stolen Egyptian Mythology. Evidence is in the Bible Itself.

Exposing the fraudulent stolen history of the Hebrews

The biblical history of the Habiru (Hebrews) is as fraudulent as the people who gave it to us. Early Hebrew history as reported by the Bible's rewriters is stolen history. The Hebrews got their religion and culture from the Black nations of Kamit (ancient Egypt), Canaan, and Babylon. Canaan and Babylon got theirs from Kamit; in fact both nations appear to be Kamite immigrants; their religion and culture is often indistinguishable from Kamit's. The Hebrews converted the astrological myths of Egypt into their personal history.[1] Many laymen are still led to believe that a real Moses wrote the Pentateuch (first five books of the Bible), although scholars have known for a long time that these books were first written in the late post-Exile period by priestly scribes in Jerusalem. Their purpose was to create a mythic, glorifying history for their nation out of legends and customs originated by the Kamites.

And Massey informs us: "The monuments of Egypt are as truly and honestly historical as the geological record. Both have their breaks and their missing links, yet are perfectly trustworthy on the whole. And these monuments, from beginning to end, have no word of witness that the Jews or Hebrews ever were in Egypt as a foreign ethnical entity. They know nothing of Abraham as a Semite who went down into Egypt ... They know nothing of Jacob except as a Hyksos Pharaoh, *or a divinity*, Jacob-El, whose name is found on one of the scarabei. They know nothing of Joseph and his viziership, nor of the going forth in triumph from the house of bondage to attain the promised land. These and many other wonderful things related in the Word of God are known to the Egyptian records, but not as history." [2]

"The secret of the ancientness and sanctity of the writings is that they were originally Egyptian, like the Jewish community. They are not the product of any ground-rootage in the land of Judea. They come to us masked and in disguise. The wisdom of old, the myths, parables, and dark sayings that were preserved, have been presented to us dreadfully defeatured and deformed in the course of being converted into history. An esoteric rendering has taken the place of the esoteric representation which contained the only true interpretation." [3] Gerald Massey

1) Massey, AE, 653. 2) Ibid. 3) Ibid., 543.

Abraham & Sarah were not real people; they were the Sun & Moon. Even the Bible calls them an allegory.

Abraham and Sarah existed long before Noah, long before Adam and Eve, and long before any humans appeared on Earth, for Abraham and Sarah were the Sun and Moon. The ancient Afrikans created stories about these and other celestial bodies; stories which became the foundation of mythology in the ancient cultures around the world. Ezra, or other Habiru priestly scribes, copied these stories and refashioned them as Hebrew history to exalt their people.

Sarah the *Queen of Heaven,* is the Great Mother

Sarah Queen

Sarah means *Queen*, not Princess as namebooks demotingly say; specifically "**The Queen of Heaven**," a title of the Eternal Great Mother, revered throughout the ancient world. The Queen of Heaven was the **Moon**,[1] anciently regarded a symbol of the Great Mother.[2] Kamite priests called the Moon the "Mother of the Universe."[3] The first human form of the Great Mother in the Bible is *Eve*; She is called the Mother of All Living (Gen. 3:20). The same title is bestowed upon Sarah, the second primary Matriarch or form of the Great Mother, who is called the Celestial Jerusalem, "which is the mother of us all" (Gal. 4:26). Sarah's name "was formerly Sara'i, The Queen, a name of the Great Goddess in Nabataean inscriptions. Priests changed her name to Sarah in the sixth century B.C."[4] Among other meanings, the Afrikan root (Ser) of the name Sarah means crown, head, chief, noble. Derivatives include *sheriff* (chief law officer), *salient* –for Kamite L/R are one [hence Sally is a nickname for Sarah], Arabic *sarafa* (highborn), Hebrew *zer* (chief, ruler, head, crown) and *sorah* (principal). The Hindu "Sara-Kali" meant Queen Kali, the Goddess worshipped by the Gypsies.[5]

MoonWater Sarah

Sarah = Sa-Ra and **Sar-Ra** —yielding *wet fire* from its Afrikan roots. Derivatives include words meaning water or its qualities, such as Arabic *sariba* (to drink), *syrup, sherry,* Sanskrit *sara* (water, river), Hebrew *zirma* (flow, issue, ejaculate), *serene, silk, sail, saliva,* and *SALT!* RA is the Light Force; it signifies the Sun, Light, Splendor and Royalty. SA was the Kamite word for the Holy Blood of the Great Mother, the divine fluid of sovereignty and eternal life which contained the Spirit all *Intelligence*,[6] and was the Personification of Intelligence.[7] **The Moon was the chalice for this SA**, which also signified *Spirit*. Baptism in the sacred Lake of Sa was literally a baptism of the Holy Spirit.[8] SEA is from SA! –which recalls *salt*. And the water of the SEA and oCEAn is literally the blood of Mother Earth; our blood is similar, even salty. In Canaan, the Great Mother as Goddess Asherah, of the same roots as Sarah, was called "Lady Asherah of the Sea."[9]

1) Massey, AE, 608; Doane, 478. 2) Walker, WE, 669. 3) Ibid., 669. 4) Walker, WD, 331. 5) Walker, WE, 890. 6) Ibid., 874. 7) Budge, GE-vII, 298. 8) Massey, AE, 795. 9) Holman BD, 111.

Most important for its association with birth, the Moon was symbolically regarded as the receptacle of *menstrual blood* by which each mother formed the life of her child.[1] The Bible identifies the Moon with blood: "The sun shall be turned into darkness, and the moon into blood" (Joel 2:31, Acts 2:20). As Fire typifies the Sun, the Moon is typified by Water. Note the affinity of the Moon for Earth's Water; it is the Moon that draws the seas toward it in the daily *tides*. Our bodies, being about two-thirds Water, are likewise affected by the Moon. This is profoundly evident as the incredible link between the Moon and the female body, for the menstrual cycle is fixed by the 28 days' cycle of the Moon. Thus the Moon is linked with fertility or life's ability to begat. Menstrual itself means *month*ly, and *month* is from *moon (moonth)*. Sarah represents the Water Principle of the Great Mother, hence Her connection with the Moon.

SerpentFire Sarah

Sarah —Sa-Ra, **Sar-Ra**. Sar means Fire, like Ra. Fire twice in Her name. A contradiction with *water*? No. For both energies are part of the Great Mother. Her SA is the Living Water of Life. Her RA is the Living Fire of Life. She is the mystical Kundalini Serpent Fire in the base Chakra, which, upon ascending up the spine, produces enlightenment as it vivifies and opens all the seven Chakras (energy centers). This is symbolized as the *Uraeus* Serpent on the front of Kamite crowns. The letter "S" takes its shape and sound from the Serpent. And the SA, the Holy Blood of the Great Mother, is RED, a word from the same root as RA. Mother's Fire is the internal LifeForce, or Fire of Life. The hot derivatives from this root include sear, seraphim, seraph, sirocco, solar, silver, Soul (divine Spark), sultry, and salamander.

Biblical variants or names from the same root as *Sarah* include:

Serah	Sherah	Zara	Zereah	Zererah
Sirah	Asherah	Zarah	Zeruah	Zerahiah
Sarai	Sheerah	Zerah	Zeruiah	Zarephath (=Sar-Apt)
Seraiah	Sharar	Zorah	Zeri	Shamsherai
Sharai				

1) Walker, WE, 672.

SunMoon Abraham, identified with the Great Father

Books discussing Abraham say his two names mean *Exalted Father* (*Abram*, his first name) and *Father of Multitudes* (*Abraham*, his second name). Abe's name goes deeper than this. The fuller etymology of his names shows that both names essentially mean *Light, Fire,* or *the Sun.* Abraham represents the Fire Principle of the Great Father, hence his connection with the Sun. He is even from the city of *Ur*, meaning *Fire* or *Light.* And note the "RA" in his name. The "ham" of AbraHAM is really the Hebrew suffix "im" meaning *plural.* Ab (Father); Ur (Light); Ra (Light); Ram (High, –like the Sun). Hence Ab-Ram; Ab-Ur-Im; Ab-Ra-Im. These give the meanings of:

- *Father Light*
- *Father of Light*
- *Light that is the Father*
- *"Radiant Father of Many"*
- *From /of Light* (for AB also means from/of)

And the Sun (Abram, Abraham) *SETS.* **The Sun setting or descending to Amenta the Underworld** is signified by Abram "going west" from Ur into Canaan and Kamit, and also by the following: "And when the sun was going down, a deep sleep fell upon Abram; and, lo, an horror of great darkness fell upon him...And it came to pass, that, when the sun went down, and it was dark, behold a smoking furnace, and a burning lamp that passed between those pieces" (Gen. 15: 12, 17). The *smoking furnace* and *lamp* aligns with the legends of Abram's furnace. Also a smoking furnace is shown on the Kamite planisphere, as the altar with its fire.[1] In the Vulgate rendering (II Edras 9:7), Abram was delivered not from a city but from the Fire of the Chaldees.

Abraham is *Eber* -ham! And Eber = Habir(u)!

The letters F/V are essentially the same. So are B/V in translations. As a Hebrew name, Abraham is spelled *Avraham*, nicknamed *Avi.* The Ab-Ra of his name is linked to or based on the Afrikan solar god, Af-Ra, apparently a version of Osiris. "The Af-Ra was a god of solar fire, whose furnace was the Ament, out of which flew the starry sparks. The first idea of fire or heat would be derived from the sun; and the sun below the horizon, where the fire burned all night to be reproduced at dawn, was the furnace from which Abram escaped." [2] Now we come to the true meaning of the name EBER. Eber and Abra(am /ham) are variations of the same name!

Books discussing *Eber* say that the name *Eber* means *crosser*, *across*, or *to cross*. While that is correct, the word *eber* also means Fire, Hot. Now we come to what I see as the true meaning of the word HEBREW, a variant spelling of *Habiru*. Thus *Habiru, Eber,* and *Abraham* all signify ***Fire***. The Habirus or Hebrews were ***fiery***, constantly warring people, just like their white Indo-European family, as proven by the testimony of *his-story*. So depending on how you look at it, Abraham was a Habiru after all.

Biblical variants or names from the same root as *Abraham* include:

Abram	Ibri	Eber	Habor	Ebronah
Abiram	Ibhar	Heber	Hebron	Abronah
Abarim			Ebron	Hebrew

1) Massey, BB-vII, 337. 2) Ibid., 337.

Abram-Abraham is also connected with the Moon, thus water

He is the mirror image of his wife Sarah. How's that? Abram is Ab-Ram, name of the Firegod in the Sumerian city of Ur, where Abraham is from. Ur was the chief seat of the Moon God Sin, who gives his name to Mount Sinai and the whole Sinai Peninsula, called the Land of Sinim in the Bible (Isa: 49:12). Very ancient documents used the name Abraham /Ab-Ram as a synonym for Ab-Sin, the Moon-Father.[1] Mount Sinai is the Mountain of the Moon (after Afrika's Mountain of the Moon), where Moses received the Ten Commandments. The god Moses met on Mount Sinai was likely the god after which the Mountain was named, and not Yaweh/Jehovah as reported. The Bible even implies this when God tells Moses that Abraham knew him by a different name (Exo. 6:3).

Hebrew Sinai is from Kamite Sheni (Shennu), the mount of the Equinox.[2] It means "point of turning and returning." [3] Sinai was significant to Kamit as a locality and sacred site. Sinai was Egyptian at any time from 7,000 to 13,000 years ago. Egypt included Sinai as part of its "double kingdom," thus all the Sinai deities were Egyptian.[4] Kamite *Sheni* and the biblical *Sin, Sinai, Zin, Shean,* Beth-*Shan, Sion,* and *Zion* are variants of the same word. Sinai was an older form of Zion.[5] Zion was originally a celestial place in Egyptian mythology before being copied and turned it into an earthly place.[6]

Abe's name is also "wet" through the meaning of "ram" as water. Kamite *rem* means weeping, water, flowing. Since Kamite L & R are the same, then rem=lem, giving us lament (to cry). Therefore Ab-Ram = Ab-Lam, meaning Father Water. This reflects his alter name as Ab-Sin, the Moon Father (the Moon is inseparably linked with water).

Abraham & Sarah = India's Father *Braham* & Mother *Sarasvati*?

Historians often conclude that Abraham & Sarah are modeled from the much older similar Hindu story of Brahma & Sarasvati. Brahma is a Hindu name of the Great Father. God Brahma was married to Goddess Sarasvati, "She of the Stream" or the "Flowing One," also known as the Queen of Heaven, the Indian River Goddess whose water (Sa?) conferred divinity on kings when it was used in their baptism.[7] Despite similarities, the Judaic story is *not* derived from the Hindu version! The fact is, Abraham & Sarah, and Brahma & Sarasvati are all copied from an Afrikan original: Asar and As-t (Osiris and Isis). Asar was the only Kamite deity called by the simple name of God (Neter). And As-t (Ash, Asa, Isis) was a name of the Great Mother in Kamit. Virtually all the other Kamite goddesses were variations of As-t. Note that Abraham & Sarah were brother & sister! (Gen. 20:12), plus husband & wife, just like Asar & As-t from whom they were copied.

1) Walker, WE, 940. 2) Massey, AE, 670, 676-677. 3) Ibid., 678. 4) Ibid., 677. 5) Walker, WE, 400. 6) Massey, AE, 687. 7) Walker, WE, 894.

The Bible admits these stories are myths!

Myth and allegories were a universal method of teaching in archaic times. In the Bible, Paul, writing to the Corinthians, declares and admits that the story of Abraham, his two wives, and their sons was an *allegory*, and that the story of Moses and the Israelites was an *example*:

- "For it is written, that Abraham had two sons, the one by a bondmaid, the other by a freewoman...Which things are an allegory" (Gal 4:22-24).
- "Now these things were our examples" (1Cor. 10:6). "Now all these things happened unto them for ensamples" (1Cor. 10:11).

Lake Sarah & Abraham, all the biblical Matriarchs & Patriarchs are versions of the Great Mother & Father, thus have names meaning the Moon & Sun or Divine Mother/Father

Incredibly, *all* the great biblical Matriarchs and Patriarchs have names which either mean Divine Mother & Father, or Moon & Sun, or are intimately linked to such. Their names are directly derived from Afrikan names of the Great Mother Goddess and Great Father God. As we shall discover, the true etymology of the biblical names expose disguised evidence that these biblical stories were Egyptian allegories about the Sun, Moon, and Stars.

The Bible itself proves that 12 Tribes of Israel were the 12 Zodiac signs!

(Note: Detailed biblical evidence for the Astrological- Zodiacal foundation of the Bible is presented in Chapter 12. The section which follows is an introduction with historical evidence.)

The Twelve Tribes of Israel are alive and well: they live, move and have their glorious beings in the heavens as the Twelve Zodiacal constellations! They were never real people or real tribes as biblically presented. They were real fiction, plagiarized and reworked by Ezra (or Hebrew priests) who, like whites of today, were determined to fabricate a glorious history for their people, the Habirus (Hebrews). To accomplish this, they confiscated the celestial myths of Afrikan people and refashioned them to appear as Hebrew history. The story, presented in the Bible as a fact of history, has one serious flaw; history fails to support it:

- There is no outside *historical* evidence that these Tribes ever existed before Ezra compiled the Old Testament.[1] There never was a tribe of Simeon, and that of Levi was a priestly caste. All the others were myth.
- The abundant archeological remains of Kamit yield no confirmation of the *biblical* account of the "Children of Israel" in Egypt. No migration to Kamit by the Children of Israel is mentioned. "And these monuments, from beginning to end, have no word of witness that the Jews or Hebrews ever were in Egypt as a foreign ethnical entity."[2]
- Herodotus, who was in Assyria when Ezra flourished, never mentions the Israelites at all.[3] Herodotus was born in 484 B.C.

1) Blavatsky, IU-vI, 568. 2) Massey, AE, 653; Hotema, GC, 54. 3) Blavatsky, IU-vII, 429.

- The Tell-el-Amarna tablets contain a political correspondence between Akhenaton (Amenhotep IV) of Egypt and Barrburyash II, king of Assyria 1375 B.C., and at that time the Hebrews as a distinct sect did not exist.[1]
- And how could the Israelites possibly keep together as tribes, while on the authority of the Bible itself, whole populations were annually uprooted violently by Assyrian and other conquerors? (2Kings, 17:23, 24)

Eminent historians inform us that the Twelve Tribes of Israel were not real tribes or historical people; they were allegories about the astrological bodies, literalized and falsely presented as history. Gerald Massey writes: "As characters in the mythos, Jacob...corresponds to Ra the solar-god...whilst Israel-the same personage-with the twelve sons, answers to the same god, Ra, in the heaven of twelve divisions or twelve signs of the zodiac...**It has now to be admitted that the twelve sons of Jacob are not historic...**" (emphasis added). On pages 649-651 of *Ancient Egypt*, he gives a detailed description and explanation of the original Kamite stories and gods from which the story of the Twelve Tribes were copied. Hilton Hotema writes: "The Bible is based on Astrology...And it was a scheme of the Jews to claim as ancestors the astral gods of antiquity. For they found in the Chaldean legends and traditions, during their long captivity, the story that man descended from astral gods, and Ezra would have the Children of Israel descend accordingly...The biblical makers tried to obliterate the trail of the Children of Israel with a change of names. They tried to hide the fact that the ancient scriptures dealt with Astrology, and the symbolism of the Zodiac..." [2]

In the 12 Tribes, the traits of the Zodiac Signs are recognized!

They are disguised in the words addressed by dying Jacob (Israel) to his twelve sons, in Genesis, Chapter 49. Representing the Sun, Jacob gives a special blessing to each of his children. These blessings disguise traits of the Zodiac Signs. Jacob was the Sun, his wife Leah was the Moon, and his children were the Twelve Zodiacal Signs. In addition, the true meaning or etymology of their names correlate to the characteristics of the Zodiac Signs they represent! All this is detailed in Chapter 12 of this book.

Floors of ancient Jewish synagogues were often decorated with zodiacal mosaics!

This proves their connection with astrology. Sitchen writes, "Earlier this century archaeologists uncovered in the Galilee, in northern Israel, the remains of synagogues dating to the decades and centuries immediately following the destruction of the Second Temple in Jerusalem by the Romans (in A.D. 70). To their surprise, a common feature of those synagogues was the decoration of their floors with intricate mosaic designs that included the signs of the zodiac. [illustration at left]...the symbols were the same as now in use, and so were the names" [3]

1) Doane, 153. 2) Hotema, GC, 52-53. 3) Sitchen, WTB, 183.

Jews were never slaves in Egypt. The "Captivity" was a celestial event

Egypt's monuments and records show no evidence of Hebrews or Jews as slaves in Egypt.[1] The alleged "Captivity" was *allegorical*, not *real*, and it lasted only two days! It is a literalization of an allegory [2] in Egypt's Amenta teachings, detailed by Massey who writes, "It is a captivity that never was historical, in a land of bondage which may be called Babylon, Egypt, or Sodom; but, as Hosea shows, it was a bondage from which the prisoners were set free *after two days*-that is, *in the resurrection on the third day.* A knowledge of the matter at first hand in the Egyptian rendering will disintegrate the historical captivity and exodus..." [3] And isn't it odd that the "children of Israel," who are allegedly fleeing Kamit because of being held as slaves, have slaves themselves which they bought! (Exo. 12:44)

The biblical Exodus was a plagiarized celestial legend

God Shu

The original Exodus story was taken straight out of the Egyptian *Book of the Coming Forth By Day* (improperly known as *The Book of the Dead*). Massey details this story and its reworked biblical account.[4]

The Original Exodus was a stellar event, as summarized:

In the story,[5] god Shu-Anhur goes to Kheb (Amenta), the underworld /under-earth which is full of souls (Manes, Manas). These souls are stars, the offspring of Goddess Nut (the Night Sky), and Ra (the Sun). In inferior darkness, they inhabit the deep, lower, "nocturnal heaven," or sky of Amenta. Shu-Anhur is the Uplifter of the Sky (the god *Atlas* is a later distorted version of him). Each night he lifts up the sky of Amenta from its unfathomable darkness into the light of "the starry heaven of Goddess Nut on high." As he does this, all the souls (stars) of the underworld are likewise lifted up -delivered from deep darkness. A new heaven is thus created, populated by the stars (souls) from the underworld. In their nightly rising from Amenta, these stars becoming glorified. Thus the Exodus was an exodus of stars from the sky of the lower-world, to the sky of the upper-world. They are led to this higher region of light by Shu-Anhur. Heaven is described as the "mansion of his stars." The Exodus drama unfolds each night, manifesting as the starry heavens, resplendent with the stars from Amenta.

"Thus the *origin* of the exodus, as Egyptian, was in the coming forth of the heavenly bodies from below the horizon in the mythical representation. This was followed by the coming forth of the manes from dark to day, from death to life, from bondage to liberty, from Lower to Upper Egypt in the eschatology." [6] **The Hebrews literalized this story,** turning the underworld into Egypt; the underworld's inhabitants into themselves, the god Shu-Anhur into **Moses**; the deliverance and exodus of stars into their deliverance and Exodus from Egypt. "The sufferings of the Chosen People in Egypt and their miraculous exodus out of it belong to the celestial allegory of the solar drama that was performed in the mysteries of the divine nether-world, and had been performed as a mythical representation ages before it was converted into a history of the Jews by the literalizers of the ancient legends." [7]

1) Massey, AE, 653. 2) Ibid., 470, 541. 3) Ibid., 541. 4) Ibid., 630-640. 5) Ibid., 630. 6) Ibid., 639. 7) Ibid., 631-632.

The historical "Exodus" was several "Expulsions" of lepers & diseased foreigners

Historically speaking, the so-called "Exodus" was several Expulsions of lepers and foreigners from ancient Egypt. One involved a remnant loyal to the defeated Hyksos. The other, reported by several ancient historians, was an expulsion of diseased foreigners. Though reported details vary, the essential story is the same: a terrible disease broke out in Egypt and the cause was attributed to unclean lepers or foreigners. To purge their land, the Afrikans of the Nile Valley expelled these people, exiling them to the desert wilderness.

- The Egyptian priest Manetho (according to Josephus) said that tribes of foreigners in northwestern Egypt were lepers and unclean.[1]

- Choeremon said the king, after consulting a sacred scribe, collected the foreign workers (called Children of Israel) and drove them out of the country.[2]

- Lysimachus stated that the oracle of Ammon ordered the alien workers to be collected and driven out of Egypt.[3]

- Tacitus said Egyptians called the infected multitude "a race of men detested by the gods," whose presence in Egypt was responsible for an outbreak of disease. After they were exiled to the wilderness and lost all hope, one of them named Moyses, gained their confidence and led them to Palestine where they dispossessed the natives.[4]

- Diodorus Siculus stated that when the offenders were exiled, the wealthy ones among them went to Greece, "but the greater number followed Moses, a wise and valiant leader, to Palestine." [5]

- Gerald Massey writes, "There are at least three different exodes. One after the fall of Avaris, when the conquered Hekshus [Hyksos] 'departed from Egypt with all their families and effects, in number not less than 240,000, and bent their way through the desert towards Syria.' ...Another expulsion occurred under Horus or Bocchoris; and a third in the time of Suti-Nekht. *This is the particular Exodus of the Jews associated with the name of Moses.*" [6] Massey's account takes up several pages (413-418). He also explains "that in the Egyptian [language] the LEPERS and IMPURE are the Aati and the Aamu...But these terms of the Aati and the impure are by no means limited to the disease of leprosy. The Aati were the moral lepers, the accursed as Typhonians heretics, the practisers of dark rites, which the Egyptians associated with the origin of leprosy and other diseases." [7]

1) Doane, 55; Walker, WE, 676. 2) Doane, 52. 3) Ibid.; Walker, WE, 676. 4) Doane, 53. 5) Ibid., 52. 6) Massey, BB-vII, 41. 7) Ibid., 415-416.

The murderous Hebrew conquest of Canaan never happened according to archeological and even biblical evidence

- **Archeological contradiction:** Amen writes: The book of *Joshua* is very important because it contains the fulfillment of Yahweh's promise to give to the descendants of Abraham the land of the Canaanites. Yet, excavations conducted at the Tell-es-Sultan, 1951-1957 by the British School of Archeology totally disproves the historicity of a Jewish conquest of Canaan. The supposed destruction of the walled city of Jericho, leading to the downfall of Canaan was no more than a creation of priests writing during the exile (about 700 years after the alleged event). The only finding of the dig was a group of walled towns dating way before the Israelite period. Some even dated back to 6800 B.C.!"[1]

- **The fictional Joshua narratives:** A respected Jewish author, Irving Zeitlin writes, "Many contemporary biblical scholars continue to take for granted that the Israelites borrowed from the Canaanites almost everything essential -language, elements of religion and knowledge of agriculture. This occurred, scholars believe, as a result of the well-known phenomenon of cultural assimilation. Denying the historicity of the Book of Joshua, where it related that a large number of Canaanite city-states were destroyed together with their inhabitants, these scholars argued that the Joshua narratives are largely fictional. The Israelites did not conquer Canaan in a series of wars, they rather settled gradually in the sparsely populated hill-country, far from the Canaanite centers of power."[2]

- **The Book of Joshua contradicts these merciless atrocities,** showing that the Canaanites were not destroyed nor even dispossessed (Jos., 9:17-18, 13:13, 15:63, 16:10, 17:12). Judges denies the story of the conquest and wholesale slaughter (Judges 1:21, 27:36, 3:5-6).

- **The biblical story is taken from the Kamite story of the Sungod Ra,** slaying, *not* humans, but celestial reptiles and beasts of darkness, in order to take over a celestial kingdom: "Dreadful massacres are perpetrated in taking possession of this promised land mapped out in twelve divisions. Ra says, 'I have commanded that they should massacre...' The enemies who are doomed to be slaughtered are the Sebau and Sami, the creators of dearth and darkness, who were in possession of the land, and who are for ever rising in rebellion against the supreme god Ra....Thus the massacres by which the Israelites were enabled to clear out the inhabitants of Canaan and take possession of their lands had been previously committed by the follows of Ra...Again, one name of the keeper of the 17th gate is *'lord of the massacre and of sacrificing the enemy at midnight!'*"[3] The biblical account renders this as God killing Egypt's firstborn at midnight.

Conclusion: The biblical story apparently combines Kamit's astrological allegories with actual history, for the Habirus or Indo-Europeans *did* ultimately take over control Canaan and other areas dominated by Blacks, whether peacefully or violently. This is proven by the Tell El Armarna tablets which we shall next glimpse.

1) Amen, MN-vI, 32,33. 2) Ibid., 32. 3) Massey, AE, 652.

The Tell-el-Amarna tablets "tell" on the Hebrews

Discovered in 1887 by a peasant woman, the Tell-el-Amarna tablets contains political correspondence between Akhenaton (Amenhotep IV) of Egypt and Barrburyash II, king of Assyria 1375 B.C., and at that time the Hebrews as a distinct sect did *not* exist. [1] The Tell-el-Amarna tablets are the earliest historical mention of the Hebrews (Habiru, Khabiru). *The account reports the Hebrews as invading Palestine. They are not in Egypt.* Unearthed in the ruins of ancient Egypt was a letter of the Egyptian governor of Jerusalem, written in the 14th century B.C., reporting the invasion of Palestine by the Habirus. Written in Babylonian cuneiform on baked clay tablets, this letter of is one of 300 found in Akhenaton's palace. It is written by the terrified governor who begs the Pharaoh for help, saying: "The Khabiru are taking the cities of the king. No ruler remains to the king, my lord; all are lost." "In the Armana letters...Many of them are in distress because of the attacks of invaders from the north and the east, and they beg for assistance from the Egyptian overlords. Typical is the plea of Abd Khiba, prince of Jerusalem, who appeals for help against the ruthless Chabiru [Habiru], desert tribes who are attacking from the east, and over whom historians have been debating for years in a vain attempt to establish definitely whether or not they were the vanguard of the Hebrew invading hordes.[2]

Kamit's monuments mention the "people of Israel" only once (about 1200 B.C.)

Massey reports: "Only one mention of the people of Israel occurs by name on all the monuments of Egypt...on a stele erected by the King Merenptah II. Not that there is any possibility of identifying these with the Israelites of the biblical exodus. The 'people of Ysiraal' on the monument belongs to those who were amongst the confederated Nine Bows, the marauders, North Africans, the Kheta, the Canaanites, the Northern Syrians, and others with whom they are classed....The people of Ysiraal (Israel) are here included, together with the Syrians, and amongst the confederated 'Nine Bows' who made continual incursions into Egypt as invaders and marauders, and who are spoken of as having been exterminated. Hence it said 'The people of Ysiraal is spoiled; it hath no seed.'...The campaign against the Libyan confederacy had been undertaken by Merenptah, who, according to the inscription, was born as the destined means of revenging the invasion of Egypt by the Nine Bow barbarians. In proclaiming the triumph of the monarch the inscription says, 'Every one that was a marauder hath been subdued by the King Merenptah.' The people of Ysiraal in this inscription are identified by the Pharaoh with the nomads of the Edomite Shasu or shepherds and classed with the confederate marauders who invaded Egypt with the Libu and were defeated with huge slaughter at the battle of Procepis...also recorded on the monuments....What then was 'the seed of Israel' as an ethnological entity in the eyes of Merenptah...? They fought as mercenaries and marauders for the Libyan king, who had made war on Egypt collectively, and were driven backward all together in one common, overwhelming route....Israel in Syria was not Israel in Egypt. Israel in Egypt is not an ethnical entity, but the children of Ra in the lower Egypt of Amenta, who are entirely mythical."[3]

1) Doane, 153. 2) Sachar, *History of the Jews*, 8,9. 3) Massey, AE, 687-689.

Do we recognize the Counterfeit Religions or *Wolf* in *Sheep's* clothing?

It seems that Black people, aware of the abundant evidence for the Afrikan identity of the Jews, often embrace the whole Jew-thing, along with the deadly Albino elements which are not so easily discerned. **It is vitally important that we recognize that the original Afrikan Judaic teachings were supplanted with a counterfeit that looks like the real thing but is NOT**. In fact, it is the opposite. The teaching called Judaism today is not, nor ever has been the authentic Judaic teachings. It is a fraud, a counterfeit. The same is true for Christianity, Islam, and Hinduism. These frauds are all poisoned to the bone marrow with the anti-life essence imparted to them from the Albinos. These bastardized counterfeit religions and all their versions / variants must be recognized for what they are and hurriedly disposed, despite the "good" or the Afrikan elements that we can see within them. **They all serve to spiritually enslave us, thereby paving the way for physical enslavement (which takes many forms).** They are all massive spiritual / psychological weapons, tailored to promote and maintain the aims of the colonizers. All this amounts to taking away our power, thereby diminishing us and keeping us weak, impotent, and passive.

The "collection of so-called holy books," a.k.a. the Bible, which has passed through the perverting hands of numerous anti-Afrikan, anti-female "editors," is just the cloak, the nappy sheep's wool covering the straight-haired wolf of deadly fraud underneath; a white wolf in black sheep's covering. Many Blacks are waking up to the truth but they still embrace the European poison by embracing one of the poisoned, counterfeit teachings /religions called Judaism, Islam, Christianity, and Hinduism. **It's like loving and embracing an innocent looking Teddy Bear, in which invisible razors and daggers are embedded!** Chapter 14 exposes and clearly identifies these razor /dagger poisons that are cutting us up, making us hug even tighter and get cut up even more. Since the counterfeit religions (Christianity, Islam, Judaism, Hinduism) are so poisoned, despite their Kamite roots, I feel that Blacks need to reject the WHOLE thing and start over –no picking out the good– but return to the original source of these teachings which is Afrikan Cosmology or cosmic teaching founded on Nature.

The so-called Jews have no legitimate claim to Israel for two reasons

1) The biblical story was not, is not, and never has been true history. It is an allegorical myth about the astrological signs. This myth is falsely presented as history. Thus the "Jewish" claim to Palestine is based on mythology.
2) 90% of the people who call themselves "Jews" are not Jews; they are Europeans. They are not descendants of the original "IUs" (Afrikan people) and even if they were, they still have no legitimate claim, for reason number 1. Historically however, before invasion by Albinos and resultant Semites (from miscegenation), this area was populated and controlled by Afrikans, yes worshippers of IU.

Reconstructing Probable True Judaic History

It's no accident that the true history of the original Jews (Afrikans) and original Hebrews (Albinos) is in darkness

Such is true for practically everything of major significance pertaining to true Afrikan history. This is undoubtedly a coverup. We can attempt to reconstruct the true history based on fragments, archeology, reading between the lines, finding missed pieces, using our gut-level feelings, reincarnational memories, prophets, and even "tuning in" to the correct information. Intuition will help one discern fragments of truth in a sea of lies. Following is an attempt to partially reconstruct the true history of the Jews and Hebrews, also dispel key misunderstandings shared by many. I am confident that in time, the full true history will be totally recovered. But in the meantime, we can put together much of it based on a combining insights with fragments, etc. We must be wary and skeptical of any history presented to us by the same people that messed it up in the first place.

Jews and *Hebrews* are not the same!

They began as two separate entities and this separation must be recognized in order to see the picture clearly and set it straight. That the Jews and Hebrews are viewed synonymously is perhaps the biggest part of the problem and the greatest block to seeing the true history of the so-called Jews and Hebrews. The white Hebrews usurped and supplanted the authentic Black Jews and their authentic spiritual teachings.

The true history of the "Jews" did not begin with Abraham & Sarah,

–since they were mythological characters representing the Sun and Moon. Nor did it begin with the "12 Tribes of Israel" since they too were mythological and represented the 12 Signs of the Zodiac. The history of the authentic "IUs" began with the Afrikans themselves. For the IUs and Afrikans were one. The original "IUs" were worshippers of IU in the Nile Valley and likely throughout Afrika. "There was a religion of the god Iu or Iao in Egypt thirteen thousand years ago."[1] These Afrikans did not go around calling themselves IUs or Jews or Judahites or Judeans or Israelites or any such names, for it was understood that IU or HU signified the Divine Source of All Life. **IU is synonymous with Hu, Io, Iao, Au**— all exceedingly ancient and timeless names and divine titles for the Primal Source, whose Parts are recognized as the Great Mother, the Great Father, and Their Union, personified as Their Offspring, Heru (Her-Iu, Horus, the Afrikan model for Christ).

Nappy Jewish prisoner

The Afrikans of the Nile Valley and the ancient IUs or Jews were the same people. Nappy-haired Afrikan "Jews" from Laquash, really "Judeans" or residents of the kingdom of Judea, are shown in stone relief (circa 700-600 B.C.) as the captives of equally nappy Assyrians. Anthropologists who have examined the skeletal remains of the people of Laquash from Judea in cemeteries, have found them to be essentially identical to the skeletons of the Egyptians at that time, who we know were Black Afrikan people.

1) Massey, AE, 501.

The ancient Afrikans or *IUs* migrated at different times to different parts of the world. There is profound evidence of Judaic presence in ancient India and ancient America. Black Jews were found in great numbers in India in the 12th century A.D. The noted Churchward, a contemporary and friend of Massey writes: "Rawlinson, however, mentions an exodus of Black Jews from Upper [Southern] Egypt to the East, who settled in India and are still there, practicing their ancient forms of religion; but they have not the Pentateuch."[1] The ancient Mexican god Tezcatlipoca, was hardly distinguishable from Jehovah (Yaweh); he too, "dwelt in the midst of thick darkness" and descended atop a mountain, complete with fireworks and sound effects.[2] A European historian, Alexander von Wuthenau, author of *Unexpected Faces in Ancient America*, unearthed much ancient American art. He contended that "everybody" came to the Americas, but the Afrikans were the most influential and had the biggest impact, and one of these Afrikan groups were "Jews."

The history of the Hebrews (Habiru), originally a white people, began in Caucasia (Caucasus Mountains),

and continued as the Indo-European invasions of Black civilizations starting some 4000 years ago. Branches of this group went to India to undo the indigenous Blacks there. A branch from this group called the **Hyksos**, overthrew and controlled Lower (northern) Egypt for nearly two centuries. "All the cultural and intellectual development ceased during this time. But these barbarians were soon cast out of Egypt, but they took with them much of the wealth of knowledge of the Mysteries of these ancient people."[3] (emphasis added) A later branch called the **Habiru** by indigenous Blacks, took over Blacks in Canaan (Palestine). Technically, these were the first Hebrews-Habiru. Miscegenation produced the *Semites* (semi-Afrikan/Albino). **The Albinos learned and stole the teachings of the Blacks and created their own rival religion** (a perversion of the Afrikan system) which became the religion "in power," aligned with the interests of their controlling relatives, the Greeks & Romans. For the Habirus had the political power, though they were puppets. They were the elite minority, lesser rulers actually, disguised as the "high priests" (Sanhedrin, Pharisees, etc.) managing and ruling the populace. They had "good relations with the rulers"[4] (Romans, or Albinos like themselves). The Pharisees "controlled the synagogues and exercised great control over the general population."[5] They apparently exploited everyone including their own kind, largely through collecting "tithes" and taxes (for the Romans, etc.), taking sacrificial animals and objects (only the best), and through "stores." These "stores" were the synagogues, the same ones Jesus ransacked. It were these false "Jews" which the biblical Jesus often clashed with. For long before Christ arrived (and even during time of the early prophets) the original religion of the Black IUs was already seriously undermined, perverted, usurped, and replaced by the counterfeit Judaism of the Albinos (Hebrews). Probably many Blacks back then were as religiously misled as they are now, for on the outside, the Counterfeit had the look and gear originated by the Blacks, but on the inside they were anti-Black (as attested by the rewritten scriptures), patriarchal and female-hating (the opposite of matriarchal Afrika).

1) Churchward, SS, 240. 2) Doane, 61. 3) Cole /Andoh, AG, 4. 4) Holman BD, 791. 5) Ibid.

History's hidden "double Israel" is blended or confused in *His-Story* books

There were 2 separate people (Black & Albino):

1

The Authentic & Genuine

The Afrikan people or Blacks.

They produced Christ and many prophets, as they are still doing today.

They had the Spiritual Throne, for they were the true heirs. But they lost political control. They were dominated by the Albinos (Habiru-Hebrews, Edomites, Romans) though they constantly resisted and revolted.

2

The Frauds, Pretenders, Impostors

The impostor Habiru-Hebrews, seeking to usurp and replace the authentic Afrikan IUs. They succeeded, physically and spiritually. Habiru leaders set themselves up as high priests (Levites, Pharisees, etc.). The Pharisees were an influential *minority* within Palestine and fraudulent Judaism before 70 C.E. They were noted for their *separation* from the "common" people (Blacks and Semites). The term *Pharisee* itself means "the separated ones." They turned Israelite society into a caste system like their white cousins were doing in India with Hinduism, making Israel a 2-tiered society. The New Testament portrays them as opponents of Jesus who said to them: "I know the blasphemy of them which say they are Jews, and are not, but are the synagogue of Satan" (Rev. 2:9, 3:9). After the Destruction of Jerusalem in 70 A.D., it was from Pharisaic circles that the Rabbinic movement arose. The whites, especially at the top, tried to stay white or at least reserve whiteness for the upper ruling elite. They practiced *apartheid*, white supremacy, and subordination of Blacks, calling themselves the "chosen ones," –their racism backed by their racist God. Biblical evidence confirms this: "And the seed of Israel separated themselves from all strangers" (Neh. 9:2). Ye "shall be a peculiar treasure unto me above all people" (Exo: 19:5). And "in that day there shall be no more the Canaanite [a Black people] in the house of the Lord of hosts" (Zech. 14:21). They had political control but not the Spiritual Throne since they were bastards, not the true heirs. No wonder they rejected Christ. The "Jews" shouting "crucify him!" were likely the Pretender-Jews. The unexpurgated Talmud has many hateful, demeaning references to Christ and the early Christians.

There were 2 separate teachings (Authentic vs. Fraud):

1

The Authentic & Genuine

The authentic spiritual teachings of the authentic Afrikans. The authentic text survives today as the Essene Scrolls (the Dead Sea Scrolls). Whites attempted to totally destroy all such records. The Essenes knew this and hid many of their records. Most of these scrolls are being "imprisoned " by descendants of the same people that ultimately supplanted the Essenes.

2

The Fraud, Counterfeit

The fraudulent reversed teachings (perversion of Afrikan system) of the counterfeit Jews (Habirus). The fraudulent Counterfeit survives today as "**Judaism**" and "**Christianity**." These frauds are currently replacing the authentic teachings. Both are bastards occupying the throne. The true heir has been usurped.

There were 2 wars going on (Physical & Spiritual):

1

A Physical War.
A war against the Blacks

A war by the Albinos (Romans, Habirus, Edomites) against the Blacks (true Jews and any Semites or Albinos aligned with them).

"The Ebionites, or Nazarenes [both are names for the true Jews]..were rejected by the Jews [white Habirus & Edomites] *as apostates*, and by the Egyptian and Roman Christians [whites] *as heretics*, until they completely disappear, their history is one of tyrannical persecution." (Doane, 134)

They were dominated by the Albinos though they constantly resisted, revolted. They often fought to the end (Zealots). The Essenes and Zealots were the same! They would not submit to white (Greek/Roman) rule. They constantly resisted, revolted. Masada is an outstanding example.

The Roman Jewish War marked a major turning point, for finally, the true Afrikan IUs were usurped and destroyed as a nation. And the survivors dispersed, fleeing into Afrika (and India), where, centuries later, their descendants and other Afrikans were enslaved in the Americas by the descendants of their antagonists (EuroRomans, Habirus).

The War has continued to present times though it has gone through several form-changes. The War is now closing, for its cycle has now come to an end. Thus Black people or the Original IUs, People of Color, and even many Albinos are waking up to the Vital Truths destined for setting all of Humanity, –IU-manity free! For all of us were meant to be the Children of IU or Loving Light. It is we that chose ourselves to become the "Chosen Ones." This begins with accepting and truly loving ourselves.

2

A Spiritual War.
Really a War Against the Great Mother

The counterfeit teachings (bastardization of the original) of the Habirus (Albinos) versus the true Afrikan Teachings.

This was and still is a war against the Great Mother and the Female Principle.

It wasn't "idolatry" that the "Hebrews" were trying to abolish among "their" people. It was worship of the Mother Goddess that the Habiru-Hebrews (whites) were trying to abolish among the indigenous *matriarchal* Black people (original IUs /Jews) whom they were trying to subjugate. This is biblically documented as the destruction of Asherah's groves, altars, etc. The invading Albinos destroyed and diabolized worship of the Great Mother. They destroyed and usurped the matriarchal character of the Afrikan's matriarchal cosmology.

Worship of the Great Mother as the Queen of Heaven was so powerful and compelling that the prophet Jeremiah had to preach long and hard to shepherd the Hebrews away from Her influence.

10

Comparing 5 of 25 Crucified Saviors

The world's 25 crucified, risen Saviors

The world has had over 25 sin-atoning, crucified, resurrected, ascended Saviors, all divinely fathered, born of virgin mothers, amply invested with divine powers, and radiating vast benevolent influence. Christ was one of them, one of the last ones in fact. Crucified Saviors were the spiritual property of ancient nations around the globe, long before Europeans confiscated and patented the idea under their plagiarized, reconstructed Christianity. When white men first came to the Americas in the 1400's, they were astonished to discover that the natives revered a virgin-born crucified Savior who also arose from the dead. White travelers in Asia discovered that even the Chinese had a virgin-born, sin-atoning Savior. Mexico's Quetzalcoatl and China's Lao-Tse (Lao-Kiun) were two of numerous such Saviors around the world, preceding both Jesus Christ and the white man's missionaries. These great Saviors, including other virginborn-godmen are detailed in _The World's Sixteen Crucified Saviors_ by Kersey Graves, _Bible Myths_ by T.W. Doane, and _Christianity Before Christ_ by John Jackson. Sin-atoning, crucified Saviors who forsook heaven, descended to Earth through human birth, to suffer and die for the moral blunders of humanity include:

Savior	Location	Crucified
1. Appollonius of Tyanna [1]	Turkey (Cappadocia)	4 B.C.
2. Attis (Atys)	Turkey (Phrygia)	1170 B.C.
3. **Azar** (Asar, Ausar, Osiris)	Afrika (Kamit)	10,000 B.C. [2]
4. Baili (Baliu)	India (Orissa)	725 B.C.
5. **Christ** (Jesus, Jehoshua)	Palestine	0 B.C.
6. Criti	Chaldea	1200 B.C.
7. **Heru** (Horus, Heru-Krst)	Afrika (Kamit)	10,000 B.C. [2]
8. Hesus	Europe (Celts)	834 B.C.
9. Indra	Tibet	724 B.C.
10. Ixion	Europe (Rome)	400 B.C.
11. Jao (Iao, Iu)	Nepal	622 B.C.
12. **Krishna** (Hari Crishna)	India	4000 B.C.
13. Mithra	Persia	600 B.C.
14. Nomo	Afrika (Dogons)	3000 B.C.
15. Odin (Wodin) [5]	Europe	800 B.C.
16. Prometheus	Caucasia	547 B.C.
17. Ptah [3]	Afrika (Kamit)	10,000 B.C. [2]
18. **Quetzalcoatl**	Mexico	800 B.C.
19. Quirinus	Europe (Rome)	506 B.C.
20. Sakia	India	600 B.C.
21. Salavahana [4]	India	0 B.C.
22. Shango [5]	Afrika (Yoruba)	1100 A.D.
23. Tammuz (Adonis)	Syria & Babylonia	1160 B.C.
24. Wittoba	Madura	552 B.C.
25. Zulis (Thules)	Afrika (Egypt)	1700 B.C.

1) Doane, 129. 2) Massey traces Kamit's cosmology to at least 10,000 B.C. (Jackson, CBC, 169). 3) Massey, AE, 644. 4) Graves, WS, 227. 5) Christ was *hung* on a tree (Acts 5:30). Shango & Odin suffered likewise. "Hanged" often denoted crucifixion (Jackson CBC, 126).

Christ

Azar

Heru

Comparing five famous crucified Saviors

Asar, Heru, Quetzalcoatl, Krishna, and Christ. These are just five of over 25 crucified, risen Saviors. The astonishing parallels in their lives and the lives of all the other crucified Saviors are too close to be coincidence. Kersey Graves lists "346 Striking Analogies Between Christ and Chrishna" in his book.[1] Massey lists over 200 'close parallels between Christ and Horus' in the appendix of his book.[2] Following the Summary of Tables (below) is a Comparative Overview of well over 100 remarkable parallels between five reknown, beloved Saviors.

Krishna

Azar
Heru
Quetzalcoatl
Krishna
Christ

Summary of Tables

Table	Topic
1.	General Resumé
2.	Name Meanings
3.	Divine Names
4.	Titles
5.	Mother and Family
6.	Nativity
7.	Childhood
8.	Twinship, Duality
9.	Symbols
10.	Plant Symbols
11.	Solar Identity
12.	Zodiac Animals
13.	Other Animals
14.	Close Associates
15.	Sexuality, Lovers
16.	Strife
17.	Miscellaneous
18.	"Red"
19.	Lazarus (El-Azar)
20.	Last Days, Demise
21.	Resurrection, Ascension

Note the striking resemblance between the crowns (and posture) of Azar & Quetzalcoatl; double-crowned Heru & Quetzalcoatl; and Azar & Krishna. Also note the *cross* (+) formed by Azar's horns/beard/cobra-tail/ crown. The same cross is conspicuously behind Christ and on Krishna's crown. This is the Astrological Solar Cross of the Four Quarters –usually shown in a circle representing the disk of the sun. ⊕

Quetzalcoatl

1) Graves, WS, 256-273. 2) Massey, AE, 907-914.

TABLE 1 — Five Famous Saviors

General Resumé

	Asar (Osiris)	Heru (Horus)	Quetzalcoatl	Krishna	Christ (Jesus)
Circa	10,000 B.C.[1] 14000 B.C.[2]	10,000 B.C. 14000 B.C.	800 B.C.	1200 B.C. 4000 B.C.[13]	0 B.C.
Location	Kamit (ancient Egypt).	Kamit.	Mexico.	India.	Palestine.
Human Image	Black skin, woolly hair, bearded. Large mouth.	Afrikan with woolly or dredlocked hair. "the locks of hair of Horus." [6]	Black-skin, white woolly hair, bearded.	Early images: woolly-hair, black or blue skin.[14] Was later bleached to pastel blue.	Earliest images: Afrikan w/ woolly hair. Was Nazarite; they never cut the 'locks' of their hair.
Divine, Son of God	Called God of Gods, Universal Lord. Identified with most Kamite gods. The only Egyptian deity called by simple name God (Neter).[3]	Regarded as the Son of God. "Only Begotten Son of God the Father." [7]	Principal God of Mexico. God of Civilization, Rain, Air...	Regarded as the Son of God.[15] Becomes God in Bhagavad Gita.	Regarded as the Son of God. Is called God (Isa. 9:6).
Royal	Osiris-Ra, founder of Royalty. <u>Ro</u>yal is from Ra (Re, Ro), the Kamite name of the Sungod.	Of royal descent. "Royal Good Shepherd." [8]	Founder of kingship and highest expression of divine kingship. His name a generic name for Mexico's priest-kings.	Of royal descent from line of Yadava (David, Ya-*Dava*).[16] Sanskrit *raja* (royal) is from Kamite *Ra*.	Of royal descent from line of David.
Savior	Risen Savior, Revealer of Truth, made men and women be born again.[4]	Savior of the World. Redeemer.	Savior for man's sins.[12]	Pardoner of Sins,[17] World Savior, Redeemer, Resurrection and the Life.[18]	World Savior, Redeemer, Resurrection and the Life. Savior for mankind's sins.
Builder	Osiris the Architect.		Master Builder . His name fr. Eg. *Qet /Khut* (builder, (designer, creator)?		Christ the Carpenter.
Healer, Miracle Worker	Great healer who performed miracles.	Miracle worker, healer, raised the dead.[9]	Miracle worker, Lord of Healing and magical herbs.	Great healer, miracle worker, raised the dead, expelled demons. Raised Kalavatti, daughter of Angas-huna from dead.[19]	Great healer, miracle worker, cast out demons. Raised daughter of Jairus from the dead.
	Quelled storm at sea, walked on water.[5]	Walked on water.[10] Turned water into wine.[11]		Eastern holy men claimed ability to walk on water.[20]	Quelled storm at sea, walked on water. Turned water into wine.

1) Jackson, CBC, 169. 2) Massey, AE, 423. 3) Hallet, 42. 4) Doane, 222, 245; Walker, WE, 749. 5) Massey, HJ, 74. 6) Budge, GE-vI, 157. 7) Massey, AE, 792; Doane, 190. 8) Doane, 163. 9) Ibid., 256. 10) Massey, AE, 911. 11) Kuhn, LL, 254. 12) Graves, WS, 123. 13) Ibid., 109. 14) Rogers, SR, 265. 15) Graves, WS, 258, 104. 16) Doane, 163. 17) Ibid., 87. 18) Ibid., 285 19) Graham, 339. 20) Walker, WE, 467.

TABLE 2 Name Meanings

Five Famous Saviors

	Asar (Osiris)	**Heru** (Horus)	**Quetzalcoatl**	**Krishna**	**Christ** (Jesus)
a.k.a. & Name Variants	Azar, Ausar, Asar-Krst, Osiris	Heru, Horus, Heru-Krst.	Kukulkan, Votan, Tezcatlipoca	Hare Krsna, Chrisna	Jehoshua (Nm. 13:16), Joshua, Hosea, Yeshua, Jesus
Krst Karast Christ 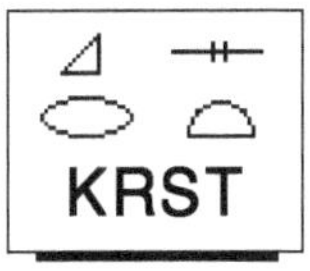	Kamite KRST (karast) means *anointed mummy.* *Osiris-Krst* was the original Krst / Christ. Called, Lord of the Perfect Black; The Great Black.	Heru the Krst; Heru-Karast.[1]		Krishna means Black or The Black One (likely from blackness defined with Osiris). NA means *black* in many languages.	Christ, Kristos, Chrestus, Chrost (English, Greek, Latin, Ethiopian) all mean *Anointed,* derived from Egyptian Krst (Karast).
Heru Har-Iu Horus		Kamite *Heru* (Har-Iu) means Lord Iu. *Horus* is Greek form of *Heru.*		Called *Hari* (Lord) and Hare Krsna, both derived from Heru-Krst.	Heru's name in the Bible as Hur, Harhur, Harhiah, Hori, Harhas, etc.
Iu-Su Jehoshua Joshua Yeshua Jesus		Called Iu-sa or Iu-su. Iu = the Ever Coming One. Su/ Sa=Son. [2]		Called Isa (Lord),[5] Chrishna Zeus or Jeseus,[6] and Ies Christna.[7]	English *Jesus*; Latin *Iesus*; Greek *Iesous*; Hebrew *Yehoshua*, are all derived from Egyptian **Iu-Su** (Iu the Ever Coming One).[9] Other biblical variants: **Ishuah, Isua, Isui.** Hebrew *Iuso* means Savior. His name written as *Ieu* in northern Israel. [10]
Quetzalcoatl	In Egyptian, *atl* (atr) = water; source of *atl* in Quetzalcoatl (L=R in Eg.).		Quetzalcoatl means Precious Water-Bird-Serpent. Quetzal = bird, precious. Co = serpent. Atl = water. [3]		
As Ash Asar Osiris	*Osiris* is Greek form of Kamite *Asar* / Ausar, meaning Born of As-t (Isis). *As* / *Ash*, the Tree of Life.	Asar, father of Heru.	Quetzalcoatl is modeled from the Afrikan god Dasiri, a version of Asar.[4]	*Esur*, a name for God in India.[8] *Sri* (holy title). *Surya* (Hindu deity).	"thou shalt call me Ishi," said the Lord (Hos. 2:16). Ishi & Asar are from Kamite Ash. Eleazar & Elieser (El-Asar, Heli-Asar), ancestors of Christ.[11] Asar's name in the Bible as Azariah, Asher, Eser, etc. (see p211). Jesus called *Ischa* in Arabic,[12] and *Isa* in the Koran.

1) Massey, AE, 910. 2) Massey, AE, 806; HJ, 15. 3) Nicholson, 80, 84; Burland, 45. 4) Van Sertima, TCBC, 80-81. 5) Tyberg, 58. 6) Graves, WS, 109. 7) Rogers, SR, 265. 8) Blavatsky, SD-vII, 114. 9) Massey, AE, 462, 509, 893, 728; HJ,18. 10) Walker, WE, 464. 11) Matthew 1:15; Luke 3:29. 12) Higgens, vI, 383.

TABLE 3 Five Famous Saviors

Divine Names

	Asar (Osiris)	Heru (Horus)	Quetzalcoatl	Krishna	Christ (Jesus)
God	*Khut* is the Afrikan source of the name *God.* Khut means Spirit and Light. Was also a title of Isis & Heru as Givers of Light. Khuti /Gudi, name of the Seven Co-Creators also called the ALI.		His name from Khut /Ket root? Mexico's 7 Gods of varied colors = different elemental spirits in nature.[4]		• "God is light" (1John 1:5). • "God is a Spirit" (John 4:24). • The 7 Spirits of God (Rev. 4:5).
Amen	Amen, name of the Hidden God in Heaven.[1] Amen-Ra, a title of Asar as the Father.	Amen-Iu, a title of Heru as the Son.	God is called: Ometeotl, the all-powerful, male/ female Creator of the universe.[5] Ometeuchtli, a divine name in ancient Mexico.[6]	Om (Aum) is the Hindu term for the Primal Word.[9] Brahm, the Hindu name for God contains Amen / Om.	God is called: "the Amen" in Rev. 3:14. The Divine Word is called *Memra* by Jews.[14]
The "I AM"	Nuk-Puk-Nuk (I-Am-That-I-Am) carved on all Kamite temples.			Tat-Twam-Asi, I Am That.[10]	God is I-Am-That-I-Am (Ex 3:14).
Emmanuel		Amenu-El, the Coming Son, a title of Heru.[3]			*Immanuel* or *Emmanuel*, divine name of Christ (Is. 7:14; 8:8, Mt. 1:23).
Iu Jah	Iu, Iao, Iaha, Au. Iah-a, Jah the Great. [2]		Yao.[7]	• *Jah* is *Aji* in India.[11] • Sanskrit *Ia* means victory.[12] • *"Ya"* chanted in Indian ceremonies.[13] • Indian divine names often end in *JI*: Mahara*ji.*	Judah, Jew (fr. IU). Jah, Yaweh, Jehovah. Jah (iah) in Elijah, Jeremiah, Messiah. Hebrew *IE* = the Self-Existent One.[15]
El	Kamite Al, Ali (Ar, Ari) means elevated. The ALI were the Seven Gods or Co-Creators of the Universe, the first 7 sons of the Great Mother and Great Father.		Mexican divine names often end in EL: Ometeotl, Quetzalcoatl...		El in divine names (Elijah, Rachel). The Elohim or Plural God: "Let US make man in OUR image" (Gn 1:26)
In Holy Books	• *Per Em Hru*, The Coming Forth by Day (aka Book of the Dead) . • The Pyramid Texts. • The hieroglyphics of Kamite temples.		• Mexican Antiquities. • Codex Vaticanus.[8]	• The Bhagavad Gita (Song Celestial). • The Upanishads. • The Mahabarat (Divine Word).	• The Bible. • The Essene Scrolls (Dead Sea Scrolls). • The Apocrypha. • The Gnostic Gospels.

1) Budge, EHD, 51. 2) Ibid., 142b. 3) Massey, BB-vII, 389. 4) Churchward, SS, 108. 5) Nicholson, 7. 6) Higgens, vII, 23. 7) Ibid., 24,34. 8) Graves, WS, 23. 9) Ibid., 181. 10) Graham, DM, 156. 11) Higgens, vI, 605. 12) Ibid., 602. 13) Ibid., 263. 14) Graves, WS, 181. 15) Higgens, vII, 175.

TABLE 4
Five Famous Saviors

Titles

	Asar (Osiris)	**Heru** (Horus)	**Quetzalcoatl**	**Krishna**	**Christ** (Jesus)
Lord	Lord of Lords, Lord of All, the Resurrection and the Life.[1] Judge, Ruler of the Dead. Lord of Eternity.	Lord of Life, Lord of Truth.[8] His name means Lord. The Eternal One.	Lord of Life. Lord of Healing and Hope.	Lord of All (Visvesvara), Jagat-Pati, Lord of the World. Judge of the dead.	Lord of Lords. King of Kings (Rev. 19:19). Judge of the dead.
Messiah	Messaeil (Messiah-God), the Persian name for Osiris's Star.	Horus the Messu, meaning anointed, born anew.[9]	Mexico is derived from Kamite Messu.[14]		Jesus the Messiah (Anointed). Messiah is from Egyptian Messu.
The Word	The Great Word.[2] In hieroglyphics: "The Word creates all things...Nothing is before it has been uttered..." [3]	Heru Mat-Kheru, the Word made Flesh /Truth.[10]		The Word.[18] "In the beginning was Brahman with whom was the Word. And the Word is Brahman (Vedas).	The Word made Flesh (Jn. 1:14). "In the beginning was the Word, and the Word was with God, and the Word was God" (Jn. 1:1).
Divine Trinity 	Osiris the Father, Horus the Son, and Isis the Mother (original Holy Spirit).[4]	Horus in the Kamite Trinity (Ast, Heru, Asar) Kamit's 3-headed Lion God.	Part of a Trinity: Mother Goddess as Earth, Son Quetzalcoatl as Venus, Father God as Sun.[15]	Krisna, 2nd person in Hindu Trinity (Brahma-Creator, Vishnu-Preserver, Siva-Destroyer)	Christ, second person in Christian Trinity (Father, Son, Holy Ghost)
Divine Quadruple	God Nebertcher said: "From one God I became three Gods." [5] (1+3=4)	Ftu Heru, the God of Four Faces.[11]		Brahma, the God of Four Faces.	Significant Fours occur many times, including the "four spirits of the heavens" (Zec. 6:5).
Bringer of Peace		Iu-em-hetep, Prince of Peace, Bringer of Peace and Plenty.[12]	Bringer of Peace.		Prince of Peace (Is 9:6). God of Peace & Love (2Cor.13:11).
Son of Man		Son of Man.[13]			Son of Man.
Bread of Life	Bread of Life. Bread & wine consumed as his body /blood in Eucharist.[6] Prototypical Messiah, first devoured Host.[7] His Vegetation Aspect symbolized by Corn.	Was Bread of Heaven in Eucharistic meal. Eu<u>charist</u> is from Kamite <u>krst</u>.	Represented Corn from which bread is made.[16] Ancient Mexicans celebrated the Eucharist, or 'most holy supper,' of consecrated corn-meal mixed with blood.[17]	"I am the oblation, I am the sacrifice" says Krishna.[19]	Bread of Life. (Jn. 6:35) His body and blood eucharistically eaten as wafers & wine.

1) Jackson, CBC, 98; Walker, WE, 749. 2) Saakana, 48. 3) Walker, WD, 212. 4) Massey, AE, 907. 5) Jochannan,WTBJ, xviii. 6) Doane, 306 7) Walker, WE, 749. 8) Saakana, 52. 9) Ibid., 49. 10) Massey, AE, 910. 11) Budge, EHD, 263b. 12) Massey, AE, 728,528 13) Ibid., 710, 793. 14) Higgens, vII, 23, 24. 15) Nicholson, MC, 85. 16) Walker, WE, 836. 17) Doane, 311. 18) Saakana, 48. 19) Carpenter, PC,132.

TABLE
Five Famous Saviors

5 Mother and Family

	Asar (Osiris)	Heru (Horus)	Quetzalcoatl	Krishna	Christ (Jesus)
Virgin Mother Named Mary	Meri, a name for Nut, the Sky Goddess & Virgin Mother of Osiris.[1] Meri-f-ua, guardian of Osiris.[2]	Meri (Hathor-Meri), the Virgin Mother of Horus.[7] Hathor = Hat-Hor or House of Horus Meri's sister & special friend Nephthys.[8]	Chimelman, the Virgin Mother of Quetzalcoatl,[11] also called Coatlicue, Mother Earth.[12]	Maia (Devaki), Virgin Mother of Chrishna.[14] Mariama, her title.[15] Maia's special female friend (wife of Nanda).	Mary, the Virgin Mother of Jesus. Mary's cousin (or sister) & special friend Elizabeth.
Had Two Mothers	"Ra joins himself to his double mother."[3]	Had 2 mothers who were sisters. One conceived him, Nephthys nursed him.[9]		Had 2 mothers: one who conceived him & Queen Yasoda who raised him.	Had 2 mothers who were sisters; Mary conceived him & Mary, wife of Cleophas raised him.
Radiant Mother	Meri & Nut are forms of Isis, the wife-sister-mother of Asar. She is the Queen of Heaven, portrayed standing on the crescent moon with 12 stars around her head.[4]	Hathor, the Queen of Heaven, the Moon Goddess bearing the Sun.[10]	His mother, the Moon-Goddess and wife-sister-mother of the Sun. She solidified Spirit into the planet to make life possible.[13]	His mother Devaki is also called Aditi, the "Great Goddess as the Woman Clothed with the Sun, mother of all the lights of heaven."[16] She birthed the 12 Zodiacal Spirits called Adityas.	Pregnant woman arrayed with the sun, moon under her feet, crown of 12 stars (Rv.12:1). Catholic Mary, Queen of Heaven stands on the crescent moon with 12 stars around her head. "Stella Mary," (Star of the Sea), title of Virgin Mary.
Foster Father	Seb (Earth God), his earthly father, a builder.[5]	Seb, his foster father, a builder & carpenter.		Had 2 foster fathers: Nanda a carpenter,[17] and Prince Vasudeva.	Joseph, his foster father was a carpenter.
Siblings	Isis his sister, Set his brother. "In the invocations of Isis and Nephthys, Isis says to Osiris, 'I am thy double sister.' Ra joins himself to his double Mother."[6]	Had 2 sisters and 4 brothers: Gebhsennuf, Hapi, Amset, Tuamutef.		Had a sister Subhadra, and 7 brothers; the first 6 were killed by Kansa. He later raised them from the dead.	Had at least 2 sisters and 4 brothers: James Joseph, Simon, and Judas. (Mat. 13:55,56)

1) Massey, AE, 863. 2) Saakana, 52. 3) Massey, BB-vII, 250. 4) Doane, 328. 5) Massey, AE, 908; Doane, 478. 6) Massey, BB-vII, 250. 7) Saakana, 52. 8) Ibid., 53. 9) Massey, AE, 786; Jackson, CBC, 114. 10) Massey, AE, 914; HJ,140. 11) Doane, 479. 12) Nicholson, 85. 13) Ibid., 84-85. 14)Graves, WS, 257; Rogers, SR, 265. 15) Graham, DM, 301. 16) Doane, 475; Walker, WE, 10. 17) Graves, WS, 257.

TABLE
Five Famous Saviors

6 Nativity

	Asar (Osiris)	**Heru** (Horus)	**Quetzalcoatl**	**Krishna**	**Christ** (Jesus)
Had a Precursor		Anup, precursor and baptizer of Horus.[6] Remi the weeper precedes the Messiah Horus.[7]		Preceded by Balarama whose life was sought by king Kansa.[14] Bala-Rama's parents, elderly.	Preceded by John the Baptizer whose life was sought by king Herod. John's parents, elderly. Jeremiah (E-Rem-Iah) precursor of Christ.
Annunciation	Angelic voices hailed his coming, which marked the rising of the Nile.[1]	Thoth, messenger of the gods, announces to Virgin Meri the impending birth of her Holy Child.[8]	Ambassador from heaven announced his forthcoming birth to his mother.[13]	His forthcoming birth announced to his mother by demigods.[15]	Messenger angel Gabriel, announces to Virgin Mary the impending birth of her Holy Child.
Birthplace of "Bread"		Horus born in Annu, the place of the multiplying bread.[9]			Jesus born in Bethlehem, meaning house of bread.
Judah, Iu-Ta	Iu-Ta (Judah) originated in Kamit.[2]			Born in the Tribe of Yadu.[16] Yadu = Juda.[17]	Born in the Tribe of Judah. "Our Lord sprang from Judah" (Heb. 7:14).
Born Dec 25	Born December 25th.[3]	Born December 25th.[10]		Birthday Dec. 25th.[18]	Birthday celebrated Dec. 25.
Miraculous Birth	His birth signified by Sirius, *his* star in the east.[4]	His birth announced by a star.[11]	His birth foretold by a star.	His birth announced by *his* star in the heavens.	His birth announced by *his* star in the heavens.
				Humble birth in a cave or dungeon.[19]	Humble birth in a manger, or *cave* according to Apocryphal Gospel.
				Born when his foster father was in another city paying taxes to the king.[20]	Born when his foster father was in another city paying tax-tribute to the governor.
Homage from Magi	His coming announced by Three Wise Men: the three stars Mintaka, Anilam, Alnitak.[5]	Infant Horus receives homage from gods, men, & Three Kings or Magi bearing gifts.[12]	Recognized by astrologers & prophets.	At birth, adored by cowherds, visited by gift-bearing Magi or kings.[21]	Adored at birth by shepherds, visited by three, gift-bearing Magi or kings.

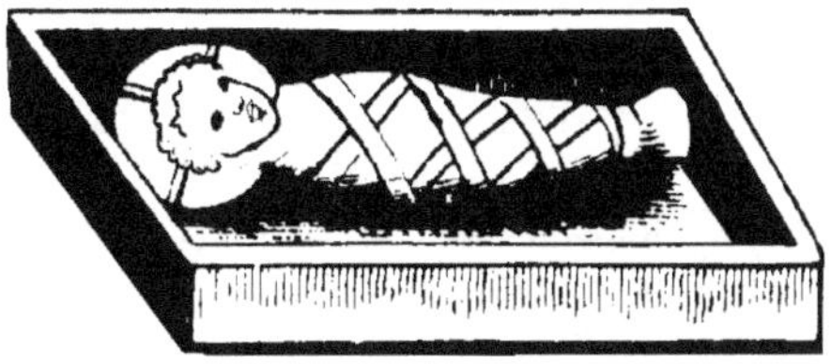

1) Walker, WE, 749. 2) Massey, AE, 503 3) Doane, 364 . 4) Walker, WE, 749. 5) Ibid. 6) Massey, AE, 908. 7) Massey, BB-vII, 336. 8) Saakana, 37. 9) Massey, AE, 908. 10) Doane, 363. 11) Massey, AE, 289, 908. 12) Jackson, CBC, 112. 13) Carpenter, PC, 160. 14) Graves, WS, 257; Doane, 280. 15) Judah, 62. 16) Massey, HJ, 106; Higgens, vI, 429. 17) Massey, HJ, 107. 18) Doane, 363. 19) Ibid., 163. 20) Ibid., 279; Judah, 63. 21) Graves, WS, 257.

TABLE 7 — *Five Famous Saviors*

Childhood

	Asar (Osiris)	**Heru** (Horus)	**Quetzalcoatl**	**Krishna**	**Christ** (Jesus)
Escapes Slaughter of Infants		Failing to prevent Horus's birth, Typhon (Set) sought to slay him. Infant Heru escapes by being taken to a distant country (Isle of Buto) where he is raised in safety.[6]		King Kansa orders massacre of all male infants in order to kill his nephew Krishna. Warned by a heavenly voice, the parents escape with their child by fleeing across River Jumna to another country.[12]	King Herod sought to kill infant Christ by slaying all boy babies (Mat. 2:13). Warned by a dream, Joseph & Mary escape with their child by fleeing to another country (Egypt).
Herod	"Herrut the Apap-reptile, slayer of the younglings in the egg." [1]				Herod the murderer of the innocents (his name means typhon or serpent).
Emerging from Papyrus		Child Horus emerging from the Papyrus-reed.[7]			Child Jesus in the catacombs emerging from the Papyrus.
Missing Record of Age 12		With mother till age 12. Age 12-30, no record of his life.[8]			With mother till age 12. Age 12-30, no record of his life.
Horus-Lock		"Horus-Lock" was worn by Afrikan children till age 12.	"Horus-Lock" on sculptures of ancient Mexico.[10]		
Childhood Miracles				Created boys out of calves and vice versa.[13]	Transformed boys into kids (goats) and vice versa in Gospel of Infancy.
Baptized (means being reborn!)	The Dead, washed from their sins by Savior Osiris.[2] Solar baptism: Sungod Azar setting in the waters of the West.[3] Those initiated into mysteries of Isis were baptized.[4] Afrikans originated Baptism, a part of ancient initiation rites into the "Egyptian Mysteries." Known as Water of Purification.[5] Baptism = returning to the womb of the Great Mother to be born again.	At age 30, Holy Spirit Dove descends upon him as he is baptized.[9]	Baptism and regeneration by water.[11]	Baptized in River Ganges.[14] Ganges is the river of Goddess Ganga, whose waters represented baptism & redemption, consuming of sins.[15]	At age 30, Holy Spirit Dove descends on him when baptized in River Jordan (Mat. 3:16).

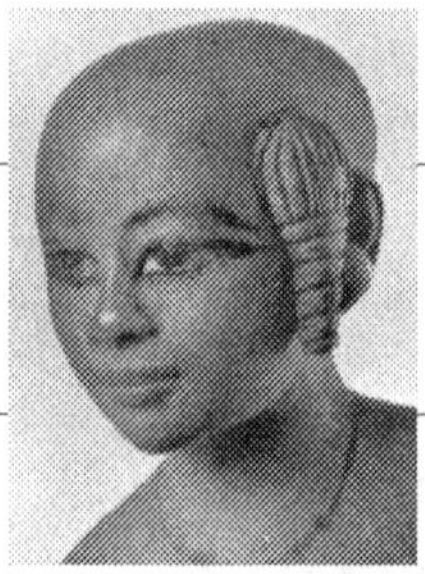

1) Massey, AE, 900. 2) Doane, 320. 3) Massey, AE, 835. 4) Doane, 719. 5) Ibid., 319, 320. 6) Ibid.,168. 7) Massey, AE, 909. 8) Jackson, CBC,114. 9)Massey, AE, 909. 10) Churchward, SS, 222. 11) Graves, WS,123; Churchward, SS, 225-6. 12)Doane, 166, 286. 13) Blavatsky, IU-vII,538. 14) Graves, WS,110. 15) Walker, WE, 336.

TABLE **8** Five Famous Saviors

Twinship, Duality

	Asar (Osiris)	Heru (Horus)	Quetzalcoatl	Krishna	Christ (Jesus)
Twins	Osiris & Set are twin brothers representing Light & Darkness.[1]	Horus & Set are twin brothers representing Light & Darkness.[3]	Quetzalcoatl and Xolotl are twin brothers as the Morning & Evening Star.[7] Quetzalcoatl is two-faced deity of Creation & Destruction.		Jesus and Satan (derived from Set) are both called "Prince." Jesus is called the Morning Star.[10] Lucifer is called Son of the Morning.[11] *Lucifer*, Latin title for the Morning Star, means *Light Bringer*.
		His dual character as Horus the Junior/Elder, double Lion, double Uraei double Equinox and double Crown, etc.[4]	*Precious Twin* is the secondary meaning of his name.[8] 		Book of Thomas says Judas was Jesus's twin brother whose full name was Judas the Tammuz (Twin). Judas is the name of one of Jesus's brothers. Joseph is another version of Christ. Many similarities between them.
Aan & John		Aan (Taht-Aan), the forerunner & proclaimer of Horus the Anointed.[5] As the Sungod's "light by night," he bears witness to the true Light of the World, the Solar Messiah.		Krishna & his elder brother, Balarama, who was also a god incarnated.	Jesus & John are cousins both born as result of divine visitation, & announced by same angel (Luke 1:5-56). Both are called "Rabbi" and have disciples. John bears witness and testifies to Christ.
				Balarama wears the skin of the tiger or lion.[9]	John wears the skin of animals (camel hair, leather).
Androgenous	Androgynous form of Osiris has two halves; male & female.[2]	With sidelock of girl-boyhood. As male & female. Portrayed with female paps.[6]	Female & male symbology linked with him.		Jesus with female paps in Revelation (Rev. 1:13).

1) Massey, AE, 837. 2) Massey, HJ, 55. 3) Massey, AE, 837; Saakana, 35. 4) Massey, AE, 336. 5) Massey, HJ, 156. 6) Massey, AE, 786, 716. 7) Burland,102. 8) Nicholson, MC, 84. 9) Higgens, vI, 238-9. 10) Rev. 22:16. 11) Isaiah 14: 12.

TABLE 9 Symbols

Five Famous Saviors

	Asar (Osiris)	Heru (Horus)	Quetzalcoatl	Krishna	Christ (Jesus)
Cross **Swastika Cross**	Ankh, Tet & other crosses used in Kamite worship for over 7000 years.[1] Tet cross = backbone of Asar. The Swastika is derived from the human figure (4 limbs; arms/legs) in Kamite symbols = divine man Iu, Heru, Christ.[2]	Was identified with the Tet cross. Swastika in a Disk = Aten, and was an ancient form of Heru; was an emblem of circle made by Aten as God of the Double Horizons.[5]	A cross, emblem of his shield.[8] Name of Mexican cross= *tree of our flesh.* [9] In ancient Mexico, "The cross was everywhere adored." [10] Swastikas are common in art of ancient America.	Crosses used in worship. His pagoda-temple in form of a cross.[13] The pagoda of Mathura (his birthplace) built in form of cross.[14]	Was identified with the Cross. Early Christians used the Ankh cross.[16]
Shepherd Crook	"The Shepherd's Cross or Crook was originally dedicated to Osiris as the 'Good Shepherd' of souls in the afterworld."[3]	Royal Good Shepherd with a crook. The shepherd crook is derived from the Ankh.	Bore a jeweled staff shaped like a serpent.[11]	The Good Shepherd a with crook.[15]	The Good Shepherd with a crook.
Conical Crown 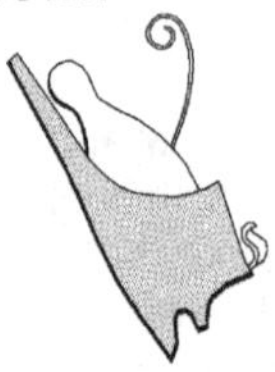	Wore a plumed conical White Crown & other styles of crowns, caps.	"Horus the Younger" wore the double crown of the Two Egypts.	Wore a conical, priestly cap.[12] 	Shown wearing crowns of different heights/styles, often with ostrich plumes. Vishnu (who incarnated as Krishna) is often shown wearing several crowns.	"and on his head were many crowns" (Rev. 19:12). Bishop caps and pope's tiara imitate the conical crown of Kamite priests & pharaohs.
Whip, Fan 	Azar with two scepters and whip (flail).	Horus with a Fan and Whip. Fan a symbol of breath, and the shade or spirit.[6]			Christ with a Fan and Whip (scourge of cords) (Lk 3:17, Mt 3:12).
Chi-Rho ☧	The Chi-Rho monogram (XP) originally his symbol.[4]	The Chi-Rho monogram used as his symbol.[7]			The Chi-Rho monogram used to symbolize Christ evolved from the Egyptian Ankh.[17]
Horns	Two horns, plumes, and uraei issuing from his crown.				"An horn of salvation" (Luke 1:69). Christ the Lamb with 7 horns (Rev. 5:6).

1) Massey, AE, 749, 750, 751. 2) Ibid., 724. 3) Walker, WD, 104. 4) Doane, 349. 5) Churchward, SS, 225. 6) Massey, AE, 222. 7) Jackson, PO, 28. 8) Sitchen, LR, 24. 9) Kuhn, LL, 420-421. 10) Higgens, vII, 34. 11) Sitchen, LR, 32. 12) Van Sertima, TCB, 83; Nicholson, 81. 13) Doane, 340. 14) Blavatsky, SD-vII, 588. 15) Massey, AE, 908. 16) Saakana, 46. 17) Jackson, PO, 28; Walker, WE, 522.

TABLE **10** Plant Symbols

Five Famous Saviors

	Asar (Osiris)	Heru (Horus)	Quetzalcoatl	Krishna	Christ (Jesus)
The Vine	Osiris was the Vine; his son Horus-Unbu was the Branch.[1]				"I am the true vine," said Christ (John 15:1, 5).
The Branch		Called Unbu, meaning the Tree and the Branch. The Golden Unbu (Bough).[2] The Branch or Natzer of Unbu. The Repa (branch) from which Labarum is derived.			Prophetically called "the BRANCH..." (Zech. 3:8, 6:5). The Burning Bush=Golden Unbu.[6] Moses's burning bush, a symbol of the Solar God.[7] Jesus the Natzer and Nazarene..
Thorny Crown		Horus wore the Unbu, a bush of flowering thorn on his head. As such, he was also called Unbu, the Tree and the Branch.	Crowned with thorns of the Magney, a tree of life.[3] He drew forth his own blood with thorns.[4]		Crown of bruising thorns placed on Christ's head (Mat. 27:29).
Reed		A papyrus reed was the throne & scepter of Heru, sign of his sovereignty. One of his titles: "Horus on his papyrus."	The Reed was his symbol.[5] His name as the Morning Star was Ce Acatl, meaning *One, Arrow-Reed.*		...a reed put in his right hand (*ruling* hand) (Mat. 27:29). In the catacombs, portrayed rising from papyrus.
Trees	Connected with trees. Tree of Life (Ash) = symbol of Ast (Isis), Asar's mate.		Connected with trees.		The Tree of Life bearing 12 types of fruits (Rev. 22:2).
Flowers		Called the Lily and the Lotus.		Often portrayed wearing a garland of flowers. Lotus, a sacred flower in India.	Called the Rose of Sharon and Lily of the Valley.

1) Massey, AE, 536. 2) Ibid., 528, 672. 3) Massey, HJ, 101. 4) Carpenter, PO, 160.. 5) Higgens, vII, 24. 6) Massey, AE, 672. 7) Ibid.

TABLE 11
Five Famous Saviors

Solar Identity

	Asar (Osiris)	Heru (Horus)	Quetzalcoatl	Krishna	Christ (Jesus)
Is the Sun	“Osiris-Ra.” Ra, the Sun. Was the first Sun symbol.[1] 	Personified the Sun. Son of Ra. “I am the Light of the World” said Heru-Kuti.	Personified the Sun.	Was the Sun of Righteousness.[6] “I am the light in the Sun and Moon...I am the brilliancy in flame, the radiance in all that's radiant, and the light of lights.” [7]	Was the Sun of Righteousness. “I am the Light of the world.” [9] “the Lord God is a sun.” [10] “God is a consuming fire.” [11] “there shall come a *star* out of Jacob.” [12] Started ministry at age 30 and died at 33. The Sun *enters* an astro-sign at 30° and *exits* at 33°!
Shiloh	Shiloh & Solar are from Eg. Zel / Zer (fire, heat, *zeal*).	Was Shiloh, the Ever Returning One.			Prophetically called Shiloh. (Gn. 49:10, a word 33xs in Bible.
Radiant Clothes	“the one whose head is clothed with a white radiance.” [2]				His face shone like the sun, his raiment white as light.[13]
Morning Star		Was the Morning Star.[3]	Was the Morning Star.[5]		“I am the bright and morning star.” [14]
Winged Solar Disk 		Horus, identified with the Winged Sundisk.			“the *Sun* of righteousness arise with healing in his *wings*” (Mal. 4:2).
Heri = Heli (Helios) Heli = Eli		Heru (Har-Iu) means Lord Iu. Heru was the ancient name of the Sungod from which *Helios* and *Hero* are derived. *Heri* (Har) means lord, master, overseer, superior, “he who is over,” chief of the Two Heavens.[4] Greek word helios (sun) is from Heru (Helu) (L=R) "Hell" (fire) likely from same root.		Called *Hari* (Lord) and *Hare Krsna*, both derived from Heru-Krst. Sanskrit Hari /Heri means Lord and Savior.[8]	Hebrew *heres* (sun); *hara* (burn, be angry. Eleazar & Elieser (=*El*-Asar, *Heli*-Asar), ancestors of Christ.[15] Heru's name in the Bible as Hur, Harhur, Harhiah, Hori, Harhas, etc. “Our Lord the Sun,” used in Liturgy & prayer by Christians till 6th Century.[16] Early Christians were charged with sunworship. They revered the East where Christ the Sun arose.[17] They prayed facing East. Worshipers of the Sun were called Christians.[18]

1) Doane, 477, 484. 2) Massey, AE, 815. 3) Ibid., 912 . 4)Budge, EHD, 498. 5) Burland, FS, 35. 6) Graves, WS, 259. 7) Doane, 546. 8) Higgens, vII, 15; Blavatsky, SD-vII, 76. 9) John 3:19. 10) Psalms 84:11. 11) Hebrews 12:29; Deuteronomy 4:24. 12) Numbers 24:17. 13) Matthew 17:2. 14) Revelation 22:16. 15) Matthew 1:15; Luke 3:29. 16) Hotema, GC, 53. 17) Doane, 502. 18) Ibid., 501.

TABLE **12** Five Famous Saviors

Zodiac Animals

	Asar (Osiris)	**Heru** (Horus)	**Quetzalcoatl**	**Krishna**	**Christ** (Jesus)
Zodiacal: • Bull • Ram • Fish 	Represented as Apis the Bull during Age of Taurus. Heru his son was the Calf; Mother Hathor was the Golden Holy Cow. Was the Winged Bull of Asyria.	Represented in sequence as Calf, Lamb and Fish as the Zodiacal Age moved through Taurus, Aries, Pisces. Was the Golden Calf worshipped by the Israelites.	Ancient Mexicans adored their "Ram of God." [6]	Matsya the Great Fish who towed the Hindu Ark was Vishnu, an incarnation of Krishna.[13]	Represented in succession as the Lamb (baby Ram) and Fish as the Zodiacal Age moved from Aries to Pisces. Golden Calf adored by the Israelites (Exo. 32:4) = Heru/Christ.
Lamb 		Lamb of God. Addressed as "Sheep, son of a sheep; Lamb, son of a lamb." [2]	"The Ram of God." [7] Llamas (sheep) were sacred in Mexico . [8]	Chrishna, the Holy Lamb of God. [14]	Christ, the Lamb of God (John 1:9).
Fish 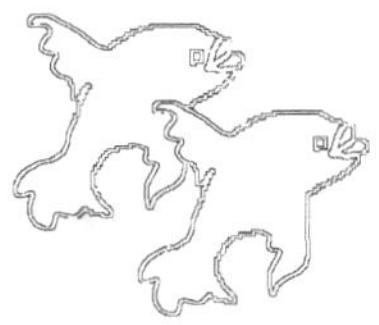	"I have come as a Fisher." [1]	Horus as Pisces. Horus the Fisher.[3] Horus as Sebek, the Great Fish of the inundation.[4]		Visnu, an incarnation of Krishna is half-fish, half-man. This = Pisces-Aquarius.	Fish, the earliest symbol of Christ, is found in the catacombs. In the Talmud, the Messiah is called DAG meaning Fish.[16]
Bird (Scorpio's Eagle) 	Seker-Osiris in Hawk-headed form. Osiris wore plumes. Dove; symbol of the Great Mother, sexual passion & Yoni. Her consort: the Phallic Serpent .	Horus the Golden Hawk /Falcon. Horus the Winged Sundisk. Alit by the Holy Spirit as a Dove at his baptism.	Represented as the Bird-Snake, the Plumed Serpent. "Quauhtli–eagle, Mexican name of Horus." [9]	Ostrich plumes on his crown. Garuda, the great Bird, vehicle of Krishna /Vishnu.	"the <u>Sun</u> of righteousness arise with healing in his <u>wings</u>"(Mal. 4:2). "Lord God of Israel, under whose <u>wings</u>"(Ruth 2:12). Alit by the Holy Spirit as a Dove at his baptism.
Lion, Feline 	"I have come like the Sun from the House of the Lions." "I am the Great Cat." Kamite priests wore panther / leopard skin.	As double lions: "I am the twin Lions." [5] Horus the Lion of the Double Force, or Lions of the Two Horizons, east and west.	His priests were a *caste of tigers.* [10] Lions in sculptures of ancient Mexico, yet did not exist in America.[11] Priests wore jaguar/leopard skin. Jaguar motif common in Olmec art.	"Lion of the Tribe of Saki." [15] Vishnu's 4th incarnation was Narasimha the Man-Lion. Called Purushavyaghra, "Tiger among men."	"Lion of the Tribe of Judah." Jehoshua ben Pandera or *Jesus, Son of the Panther.*

1) Massey, AE, 86. 2)Massey, HJ, 154. 3) Massey, AE, 336, 86. 4) Churchward, SS, 111. 5) Massey, AE,334, 909. 6) Graves, WS, 73. 7) Ibid. 8) Higgens, vII, 36. 9) Churchward, SS, 114. 10) Nicholson, MC, 141. 11) Churchward, SS, 222. 13) Doane, 354; Ross, 55. 14) Graves, WS, 73. 15) Ibid., 258. 16) Doane, 354.

TABLE **13** — *Five Famous Saviors*

Other Animals

	Asar (Osiris)	Heru (Horus)	Quetzalcoatl	Krishna	Christ (Jesus)
Kind to Animals 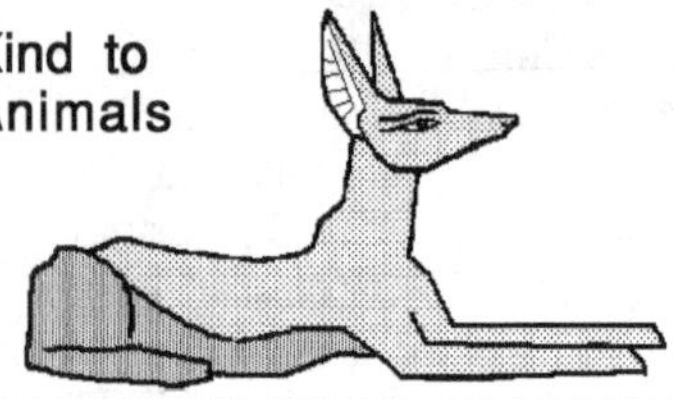			Kind to animals. Forbade killing or harming them.	Kind to animals. Forbade killing or harming them.	Is a vegetarian in Essene Gospel of Peace. Kind to animals. Forbade killing or harming them.
Canine	Identified with Anubis, canine-headed god of the dead in Under-world. Associated with Sirius the (so-called) Dog Star.	Heru-Sept, or Horus the Dog Star.[4]	Dogs sacred in Mexico. Xolotl his twin brother, was canine-headed; entered the Underworld to help him.		Because he was the guide of souls, Christ was identified with the Jackel-god by early Christian Gnostics.[11]
Serpent **Dragon** 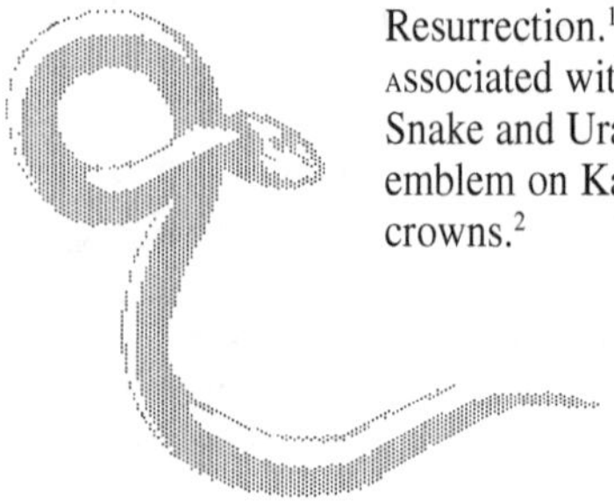	Stands upon a crocodile, holding a serpent in each hand, as Ptah-Seker-Osiris, the Triune God of Resurrection.[1] Associated with the Snake and Uraeus emblem on Kamite crowns.[2]	Associated with the double Uraei.[5]	Represented as the Bird-Snake (Feathered Serpent). His name means Plumed Serpent	Often portrayed dancing upon the head of a cobra. Incarnate of God Vishnu, the Preserver, associated with the Serpent.[8] Vishnu reclines on coils of cosmic serpent Sesha. Ananta, the 7-headed serpent on which rests the god Visnu.[9]	Emblemed as the Serpent (wisdom symbol). Said, "As Moses lifted up the serpent in the wilderness, so must the Son of Man be lifted up." "Be wise as serpents" (Mat. 10:16).
Elephant			Elephants in sculptures of ancient Mexico, yet did not exist in America.[6]	Avatar of Ganesha, the Elephant God, whose name means Lord of Hosts.[10]	Yaweh's title, "Lord of Hosts."
Ass	The Sungod rides on an Ass to the Amenta Underworld. "At dawn he rises and is hauled up by the ass, of by the young solar god with ass's ears." [3]	Aiu, Egypt's ass-headed god, the Golden Ass who carries the disk of the Sun on his head between his ears. The disk is Christ/ Horus, the Sun.	Rode on an ass.[7]		Rode on an "ass, and...the foal of an ass" (Mat. 21:5).

1) Hallet, PK, 82. 2) Doane, 491 3) Massey, AE, 506. 4) Temple, 117. 5) Massey, AE, 336. 6) Churchward, SS, 222. 7) Graves, WS, 123. 8) Doane, 356. 9) Blavatsky, IU-vII, 489. 10) Walker, WD, 372. 11) Ibid., 380.

TABLE 14
Five Famous Saviors

Close Associates

	Asar (Osiris)	Heru (Horus)	Quetzalcoatl	Krishna	Christ (Jesus)
Disciples	Had 12 apostles.[1]	Had 12 followers in Amenta.[3]	Had 4 attendants who became governors after his departure.[6]	Had 10 disciples.[7]	Had 12 male disciples, also 12 *female* disciples according to The Gnostic Gospels.[10]
John the Favorite				His favorite disciple, Arjuna (Ar-John), never deserts him to the last. [8]	John the disciple, the "one whom Jesus loved." Christ makes John his brother by entrusting his Mother to John's care (John 19:26).
Four Brother-Fisher Disciples		Had 4 brothers with him from the beginning, who were fishers (Gebhsennuf, Hapi, Amset, Tuamutef). After he resurrects, they became his *children* & the 4 foundational pillars of the future kingdom or new heaven in eschatology.[4]			Had 4 brothers. In the beginning, until his Sermon on the Mount, had 4 disciples who were fishers and pairs of brothers; Peter & Andrew, and James & John. After he resurrects, he calls his disciples *children* (John 21:5).
Sebek Zebedee		Sebek, the father of the fishers.			Zebedee, father of the fishers.
Female Attendants	The 7 female attendants of Osiris.[2]	The Seven Hathors (or cows) who minister to Horus.[5]			The seven women who "ministered to him of their substance." The Gnostic Gospels speak of Christ's 12 female disciples.
Feet Kissed by Harlot				"a harlot who came and kissed his feet with her tears." [9]	Mary Magdalene the harlot: "stood at his feet behind him weeping, and began to wash his feet with tears" (Luke 7:38).

1) Doane, 498. 2)Massey, HJ, 139. 3) Massey, AE, 710. 4) Ibid., 857. 5) Ibid., 908. 6) Massey, HJ, 146. 7) Rogers, SR, 265. 8)Blavatsky, IU-vII, 538. 9) Mehra, BP. 10) Walker, WE, 100.

TABLE **15** *Five Famous Saviors*

Sexuality, Lovers

	Asar (Osiris)	Heru (Horus)	Quetzalcoatl	Krishna	Christ (Jesus)
Sexuality, Lovers, Romance 	God of Fertility, Regeneration and Creative Energy. Phallic images of him in temples or carried in processions. The Obelisk symbolized his phallus. Restored to life as the Moongod, Min or Menu, "the mummy with a long member," the Bull of Lust.[1] Was the prototype for Priapus & Eros. The Dove, or bird of sexual passion, is symbol of the Great Mother, sexual passion & Yoni. Her consort, the Phallic Serpent = Asar. Christ's phrase: "Be ye therefore wise as serpents, and harmless as doves" (Mat. 10:16), is a traditional invocation of the God and Goddess.[2]	"Horus rises in his Ithyphallic form with the sign of virility erect; the member that was restored by Isis when the body [of Osiris] had been torn in pieces by Sut [Set]. This may account for the Phallus found in the Roman Catacombs as a figure of the resurrection." [3]	God of Fertility & Regeneration. Was a sexually potent being reknown for his enormous penis. Mated with goddess Tlazoteotl.	Had robust sensuality. Was an avatar of Ganesha, the Elephant God. The Elephant represented maximum sexual capacity and unflagging desire.[5] Shiva bore the title of "the Pillar" or "the Great Lingam." As a youth, had many lovers among the gopis (milk-maids). Multiplied himself in dances, so each dancer /lover could have one of him.	Gnostic Gospels say Christ loved Mary Magdalene more than any of his male followers. Called her the "Apostle to the Apostles," kissed her often on the mouth.[8] He *first* appeared to Her after resurrecting.[9] In *The Aquarian Gospel*, nearly flunked his seduction test but promised the sweet beautiful harpist he'd return to her after completing his mission. His sexuality *appears* denied by omission but *is* present, cloaked in symbols (woman at well, woman with issue of blood who "touched" him and took his "virtue," temple veil renting, etc.) plus Bible says he was tempted in *every* way as a *man*.
Marriage	Isis was the Wife, Sister, and Mother of Osiris the Sun.	Horus the bridegroom with the bride in Sothis. The *calf* (later, *lamb*) of Horus standing on the mount with Hathor the bride.[4]	As Ehecatl, Lord of Wind, he united with goddess Mayahuel to bring love to humanity. Their love manifested as a beautiful tree which sprang up where they alighted upon earth.	Had 16108 princess wives; each begot 10 sons.[7] Radha was his chief consort.	Jesus the bridegroom with the bride, the Lamb on Mount Zion with the bride. Wedding at Cana likely his wedding? *Joseph,* a form of Christ, marries a priestess and has twins.
Sensuous Love Songs 				The erotic Gita-Govinda or Song of Songs records his sensuous adventures and love poems.	Clergy insist that the sensuous Songs of Solomon express Christ's love for his Church.

1) Walker, WE, 750. 2) Ibid., 252. 3) Massey, AE, 883. 4) Ibid., 914. 5) Walker, WE, 839. 7) Bhaktivedanta, 48. 8) Pagels, 22, 64. 9) Mark 16:9.

TABLE 16 **Strife**

Five Famous Saviors

	Asar (Osiris)	Heru (Horus)	Quetzalcoatl	Krishna	Christ (Jesus)
Rebellious				Rebelled against the clergy, charging them with hypocrisy & ambition.[7]	Rebelled against the Jewish law, denounced the Pharisees, synagogues.
Eviction with Whip		Repossessed his Father's temple in Annu; used his flail (whip) to drive out his Father's enemies from the temple.[2]			Used a scourge of cords (whip) to drive out those who made his Father's temple a house of merchandise and den of thieves (John 2:13-17).
Bruised Serpent	Bruised the serpent's head after it bit his heal.[1]	Seed of the Great Mother who bruised the serpent's head.[3]		"seed of the woman bruising serpent's head."[8] As Vishnu treading on serpent's head.	"seed of the woman bruising serpent's head."
Satan Adversary	His adversary was Set, from whose name Satan is derived.	Contended with his adversary, Set in the desert. Carried by Set to the top of Mount Hetep.[4]	Tempted by the Evil One as he fasted 40 days in wilderness.[6]	Adversary was demon-king Kansa. Subdued, killed many demons.	Contended with his adversary, Satan in the desert while fasting 40 days (Mat 4:1-11). Carried by Satan to the top of a very high mountain (Mat 4:8).
Warrior		"Horus also comes with the sword as the avenger of his father..."[5] Savior of people from drought: Bringer of Water who slays Apap, the Dragon of Drought. Avenger of his father. Annually battled & castrated Set to avenge his father's death.	Savior of people from drought: Rain-maker God who fights the god of drought, his adversary, Tezcatlipoca (Smoking Mirror).	Great warrior. Climax of struggle was in Mahabharata War between his kinsmen, the Pandavas & Kauravas. Was called Mahabahu, "Great Armed One."	"Think not that I am come to send peace on earth: I came not to send peace, but a sword" (Mat. 10:34,35; Luke 12:51-54).

1) Graves, WS, 38. 2) Massey, AE, 837, 798. 3) Ibid., 292. 4) Ibid., 908. 5) Ibid., 803. 6) Rogers, SR, 266. 7) Blavatsky, IU-vII, 538. 8) Graves, WS, 39, 258.

TABLE 17 — *Five Famous Saviors*

Miscellaneous

	Asar (Osiris)	**Heru** (Horus)	**Quetzalcoatl**	**Krishna**	**Christ** (Jesus)
Anointed by Women	Anointed with oil by Goddess.	Anointed with oil by Goddess.	Anointed with oil.[7]	Anointed with oil by crippled lady, then healed her.[10]	Anointed with oil by a woman.
Moon	Had a Lunar aspect.		Linked with the Moon as a God of Evening.	"I am the Light in the Sun and Moon."	
Water	Lord of the Flood.[1] Ensured water (Nile over-flow) for crops.	Bringer of the water of inundation, source of life to Egypt.[4]	Ensured water (Rain) for crops.		"If any man thirst, let him come unto me, and drink." (John 7:37).
Wine		Horus full of wine.[5]			Jesus the wine-bibber.
Dance	Dance of Resurrection. Song & dance performed on way to under-world [2] (origin of funeral "wakes"?)	Dance of Resurrection. Song & dance performed on way to under-world of Amenta.	Sometimes shown dancing (this was a cosmic dance between matter & spirit).[8]	Krishna is often portrayed dancing, playing his enchanting flute. Often portrayed dancing upon the head of a cobra.	In Gnostic Gospels Christ says, "To the Universe belongs the dancer ...Now if you follow my dance, see yourself in Me who am speaking." [12] At the Last Supper, they all sang and performed a circular dance.[13]
Dwarf	Was a version of Ptah, a dwarf (original human). Was a dwarf as Ptah-Seker-Osiris.	Shown as a dwarf or Pygmy.[6]		Vishnu's first human incarnation was Vamana or the Dwarf. [11]	
52-Year Cycle	Star Sirius B, an invisible white dwarf star connected with Osiris, takes just over **50** years to complete its orbit around Sirius A, the brightest star in the sky. [3]		His Second Coming was expected every **52** years.[9]		The year of Jubilee was year **50**, after every 49 years (7x7 cycle).[14] Nehemiah finished Jerusalem's walls in **52** days.[15] God killed **50,070** well-intentioned men of Beth-*Shemesh* (House of the *Sun*) for daring to look inside the Ark in their joy.[16] Likely these events symbolize the end of a zodiacal Age. *Azar* also means **10**. Judah's **10th** King, Azariah (after Azar) ruled **52** years.[17]

The Wheel of the Zodiac takes **26,000** years to make one complete turn. **26** doubled = **52**. There is a connection, especially when the "Double Force" of each sign considered. And there are **52** weeks in a year! **5+2=7**: and **7** is the midpoint of **13**. And **13** doubled = **26**.

1) Massey, AE, 553. 2) Ibid., 48,49. 3) Frissell, NBT, 26. 4) Massey, AE, 290. 5) Ibid., 910. 6) Hallet, PK, 75. 7) Graves, WS, 123. 8) Nicholson, MC, 30. 9) Doane, 239. 10) Graves, WS, 110. 11) Hallet, PK, 82. 12) Pagels, 74. 13) Higgens, vI, 590. 14) Leviticus 25:8-55. 15) Nehemiah 6:15. 16) 1Samuel 6:19. 17) 2Kings.15:2.

TABLE 18
Four Famous Saviors

"Red"

	Asar (Osiris)	Heru (Horus)	Quetzalcoatl	Christ (Jesus)
Agonizing in Bloody Sweat	Asar *Tesh-Tesh* suffers agony and bloody sweat.[1] Tesh means bleeding, red, cut, wounded. Tesh-Tesh means to flow out (feminine phase of suffering)	Heru in *Am-Semen* suffers agony and bloody sweat, wounded by Set.[3] Am-Semen is also called Pa, "place of repose."	Worship of him included self-flagellating and thorn-pricking to bring out blood in drops which symbolized falling of raindrops to the ground for crops.[6]	Agonizing in the Garden of Gethsemane (derived from Am-Semen), Christ's "sweat was as it were great drops of blood falling to the ground" (Luke 22:44).
"Red" Suffering Saviors	The above signifies Asar as *Atum*, the RED suffering Sun of *Autumn* (whence the name) which sets from the Land of Life.[2] In this form, he was also called Ans-Ra, the Sun "bound up in linen." The days grow shorter as the old suffering Sun weakens with approaching Winter. Finally, on the Winter Solstice, shortest day of the year, the sun "dies" or *sets*. The Winter Solstice was viewed as the death of the Old Sun. Darkness befalls the earth after the "crucifixion" of the Saviors, who are really the Sun.	Torn in his battle with Set, bloody Heru is the Red Sufferer, the Afflicted One. Heru portrayed as the Red Sacrificial Calf =the Red Sun, or Red Sufferer, the "afflicted one" in the Winter Solstice.[4] When Heru arises as the Avenger of his father's death, he is addressed as the Red God. When the weak Red Sun (as Red Heru / Christ) crosses the Equinox in Aries, this is called the Crucifixion (Crossing) of the Lamb of God (lamb is a baby ram). Aries the Ram is temporarily hidden (symbolically slain).	Red was associated with death and mourning in ancient Mexico.[7] Quetzalcoatl, as Ehecatl, Lord of the Winds, is shown wearing a prominent, bright red beak-mask.[8] "The Red God of the Mexicans is the representation of Horus as the divine avenger of the suffering Osiris.[9] 	Jesus stripped & "scarlet robe" put on him (Mat. 27:28). The tradition of portraying Christ RED (or Red haired, Red bearded), naked, crippled and ugly arises from the "Red Horus."[10] Red was the color of the suffering Christ/ Horus. A 14th century manuscript shows Christ on the cross as the "ugly, 'old child' of Egypt, naked with red skin."[11] The Bible admits the crucifixion happened in Egypt: "and Egypt, where also our Lord was crucified" (Rev. 11:8), hence acknowledging the Egyptian origin of Christ as Heru who *was* crucified there. "Out of Egypt have I called my son" (Mat. 2:15).
Silent Sufferer	Osiris-Sekari, the silent sufferer.	Horus, the silent Sekari.[5]		Christ silent before his accusers.

1) Massey, HJ, 90. 2) Ibid., 90, 91; Massey, AE, 874. 3) Massey, AE, 871. 4) Ibid, 874 . 5) Ibid., 910. 6) Sertima, TCBC, 81. 7) Nicholson, MC, 24. 8) Burland, FS, 46. 9) Churchward, SS, 95. 10) Massey , AE, 874. 11) Massey, HJ, 91.

TABLE 19 — *Three Famous Saviors*

Lazarus (El-Azar)

	Asar (Osiris)	**Heru** (Horus)	**Christ** (Jesus)
Anointed with Oil	Osiris the Messu (anointed, born anew). Head & feet anointed with precious oil by the Goddesses.[1]	Horus the Messu.[4] Anointed with precious Antu oil, poured upon his head and face.[5]	Jesus the Messiah (anointed). Head & feet anointed with precious oil by Mary (John 11:2).
Mummified	Goddess Neith applies preservative oils, ointments, wound him in white linen, preparing him for burial (as the Karast or Anointed Mummy).	"I am come as a mummied one. ..I come before you and make my appearance as that God in the form of a man who liveth as a God," or as Iusu, the son of Atum-Ra.[6]	Mary Magdalene pours oil on his head to prepare him for burial. Nicodemus brings 100 lbs of aloes, myrrh; "Then took they the body of Jesus, and wound it in linen clothes with the spices" (John 19:39, 40).
Seamless Covering	The seamless cloth of incredible length wrapped around the Karast (anointed mummy / Osiris)		His "coat...without seam, woven from the top throughout" (John 19:23).
Lazarus = Azar (Osiris)	The God Osiris = EL Asar in Egyptian, Elazar in Hebrew, El-Asar in Aramaic, and Lazarus in Greek. Asar was killed and dismembered by Set. Isis found his scattered parts, put him back together, and regenerated him.. (Since El also = deity, Lazarus =El-Azar (God Azar) who **was** Kamit's greatest male deity.)		Asar's name is found in the Bible as Aser, Asher, Azzur, Azor, Ezar, Jasher, Eliezur, Eleazar, Elasar, and LAZARUS. Azariah is the name of 27 biblical males (see page 211). Three of Christ's ancestors bear Asar's name as Azor, Eleazar, and Eliezer (Mat. 1:14, 15. Luke 3:29).
El-Azar or Lazarus Raised from the Dead	Azar (Lazarus) is the dead, "sleeping" brother of his two sisters Meri & Merti (Isis & Nepthys) who mourn him.[2]		Lazarus, a full-fledged Egyptian mummy, is the dead, "sleeping" brother of his two sisters Mary & Martha who weep at his tomb (John 11:11-45).
		Horus loves the two sisters and Azar his father.	"Jesus loved Martha, and her sister, and Lazarus" (John 11:5).
		Horus goes to Bethanu to raise Azar, his father.[7] Bethannu = Beth-Anu, House of God Anu.	Christ goes to Bethany to raise Lazarus. Bethany is the Hebrew form of Egyptian *Beth-Anu.*
	Anu, a title of Azar (Osiris). The resurrection of Osiris in Annu is reproduced as the raising of Lazarus in Bethany (Beth-Anu).[3]	Horus raises the mummy Osiris from the tomb, saying loudly, "Hail, Osiris, thou art born twice! Arise on thy bed and come forth! Come! Come forth!"[8]	Christ raises Lazarus from the dead who is a full fledged mummy in a tomb, bound in bandages (John 11:44). Christ "cried with a loud voice, Lazarus come forth" (John 11:43).

1) Massey, AE, 871. 2) Ibid, 849, 845; Graham, 338. 3) Massey, AE, 842. 4) Saakana, 49. 5) Massey, AE, 880. 6) Churchward, SS, 124. 7) Graham, 338; Massey, AE, 883. 8) Massey, AE, 848, 908; Saakana, 50.

TABLE **20** — *Five Famous Saviors*

Last Days, Demise

	Asar (Osiris)	**Heru** (Horus)	**Quetzalcoatl**	**Krishna**	**Christ** (Jesus)
Last Supper	A Last Supper marked end of his career.[1]	A Last Supper was part of the Kamite Mysteries.[6]		A Last Supper marked end of his career.[12]	A Last Supper marked end of his career.
Crucified, Pierced	Crucified on the Spring Equinox,[2] on the **Arc** of the Celestial Equator.	Crucified in the heavens, represented with arms outstretched.[7] "pierced to the heart by Sut [Set]." [8]	Crucified on a cross.[10] Shown pierced in side.[17]	Crucified on a cross. Pierced with an arrow.[13]	Crucified on a cross. Pierced with a spear (John 19:34). "And Egypt, where also our Lord was crucified" (Rev. 11:8).
At age 33, crucified	The age of the crucified gods is given as 33 in the hieroglyphics of Egypt.[16] The Sun *enters* an astrological sign at 30° and *exits* at 33°. Thus, Christ (the Sun) starts his ministry at age 30 and dies at 33, the standard age when Savior-Sungods are *crucified.*		In the Mexican Codices, 95 f., the age of 33 is given for the Mexican crucified god.[18]	Crucified at age 33.	Crucified at age 33.
Hung Between Two Thieves			Sometimes shown between two thieves.[11]	Crucified between two thieves.[14]	Crucified between two thieves.
Crucifixion Site called Skull	This **Arc** is represented as a mount or rounded *calvarium* (Latin for *skull*), source of biblical Calvary.[3]	Resurrected between 2 trees.[9]		Place where he was crucified means "place of the skull." [15] After his death, darkness, calamities befell.	Place where crucified (Calvary, Golgotha) means "skull" (John 19:17). After his death, darkness, calamities befell.
Stripped, Scattered	Cut into 14 pieces by his brother, Set. The stripping & dismemberment of his corpse and scattering of the parts.[4]				The stripping of his corpse on the cross; parting of his garment among the spoilers.
Wept Over By Women	The divine sisters Isis & Nephthys weep at the sepulchre of Asar.[5]				"And there was Mary Magdalene, and the other Mary, sitting over against the sepulchre" (Mat. 27:61).

1) Massey, AE, 223; Graves, 261. 2) Rogers, SR, 265. 3) Saakana, 41. 4) Massey, AE, 877. 5) Ibid., 883. 6) Massey, BOD, 67. 7) Doane, 484. 8) Massey, BB-vII, 36. 9) Massey, AE, 752. 10) Graves, WS, 123 11) Higgens, vII, 32. 12) Rogers, SR, 265. 13) Graves, WS, 261; Rogers, SR, 265. 14) Ibid. 15) Graham, 347. 16) Churchward, SS, 480. 17) Ibid. 18) Ibid.

TABLE 21 *Five Famous Saviors*

Resurrection, Ascension

	Asar (Osiris)	Heru (Horus)	Quetzalcoatl	Krishna	Christ (Jesus)
Transfigured as the Sun	Transfigured, seen in the nether-world "as the image of Ra [the Sun]." [1]	Transfigured on the mount.[6]		Transfigured before his disciple Arjuna, "All in an instant, with a thousand suns, blazing with dazzling luster, so beheld he the glories of the universe collected in the one person of the God of Gods." [13]	Transfigured on the mount : "and his face did shine as the sun, and his raiment was white as the light" (Mat. 17:1-5).
Descent to Hell, Resurrection	Descended into the underworld, resurrected on third day. First being to raise himself from the dead. Osiris-Sahu is the risen Krst (Christ).[2] Shows his companions that he is made as they are.[3]	Descended into the underworld. Resurrected from the dead.[7] Amsu-Horus in his resurrection as a Sahu- Mummy.[8]	Descended into hell, resurrected from the dead on the third day.[11]	Descended into hell, resurrected from the dead.[14]	Descended into hell, resurrected on the third day. Shows his disciples that he is made as they are.
Ascent to Heaven	Ascended to heaven after 3 days.[4]		Sailed towards East. Ascended and became the Morning Star.	Ascended to heaven.[15]	Ascended to heaven.
Second Coming		Horus the Second Advent.[9]	Second Coming expected every 52 years.[12] The Spaniards were mistaken for him.	Second Coming expected on a White Horse.[16]	Second Coming expected on a White Horse (Rev. 19:11-13,16).
Utopian Millennial Rule	"Lord of the Aeon."[5]	Horus in the House of a Thousand Years.[10]		"I am born from Age to Age." The Hindus prophesy a great millennial era.[17]	The Millennial Reign of Jesus.

1) Massey, AE, 823. 2) Ibid., 215. 3) Massey, HJ,103. 4) Doane, 222. 5) Massey, HJ, 190. 6) Massey, AE, 911. 7) Doane, 213, 222. 8) Massey, AE, 911. 9) Ibid. 10) Ibid., 733, 913. 11) Graves, WS, 123. 12) Doane, 239. 13) Ibid., 283. 14) Jackson, PO, 16. 15) Graves, WS, 261. 16) Doane, 497. 17) Graves, WS, 269.

11

The Resurrection of the Plagiarized Solar Christ

The plagiarized Solar Christ : one original, many copies

One of Asar's titles in *The Coming Forth By Day* was *Neb-Karast*; in hieroglyphics:

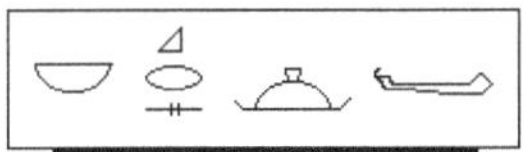

Neb (Lord) Krst (Christ) or *Christ the Lord*

The doctrine of the Crucified Savior who resurrects himself and is symbolically cannibalized is much older than Christianity, and was practiced all over the world, thousands of years before the biblical Christ. As we have seen from previous comparisons, the similarities and parallels in the lives of ***Krishna*** and ***Christ*** (including their names) are strikingly identical, so close that scholars say Christ was copied from Krishna. The fact is, both Krishna and Kristos (Christ) originated from a common source: the ***Krst*** of Afrika, specifically Asar-Heru (Osiris-Horus). Asar and Heru are aspects of each other. **The composite entity Asar-Heru is the archetype of the Gospel Jesus.** Asar was the first Krst (Christ /Anointed Mummy), the first Messu (Messiah /Anointed), the first to resurrect from the dead, and the first to be *eucharistically* eaten. The word "Eucharist" itself is from Kamite Krst, like numerous words, as we shall see. All the other crucified, risen Saviors were copies of this one Afrikan Osiris-original. This is why all the lives of the many crucified, risen Saviors are remarkably identical.

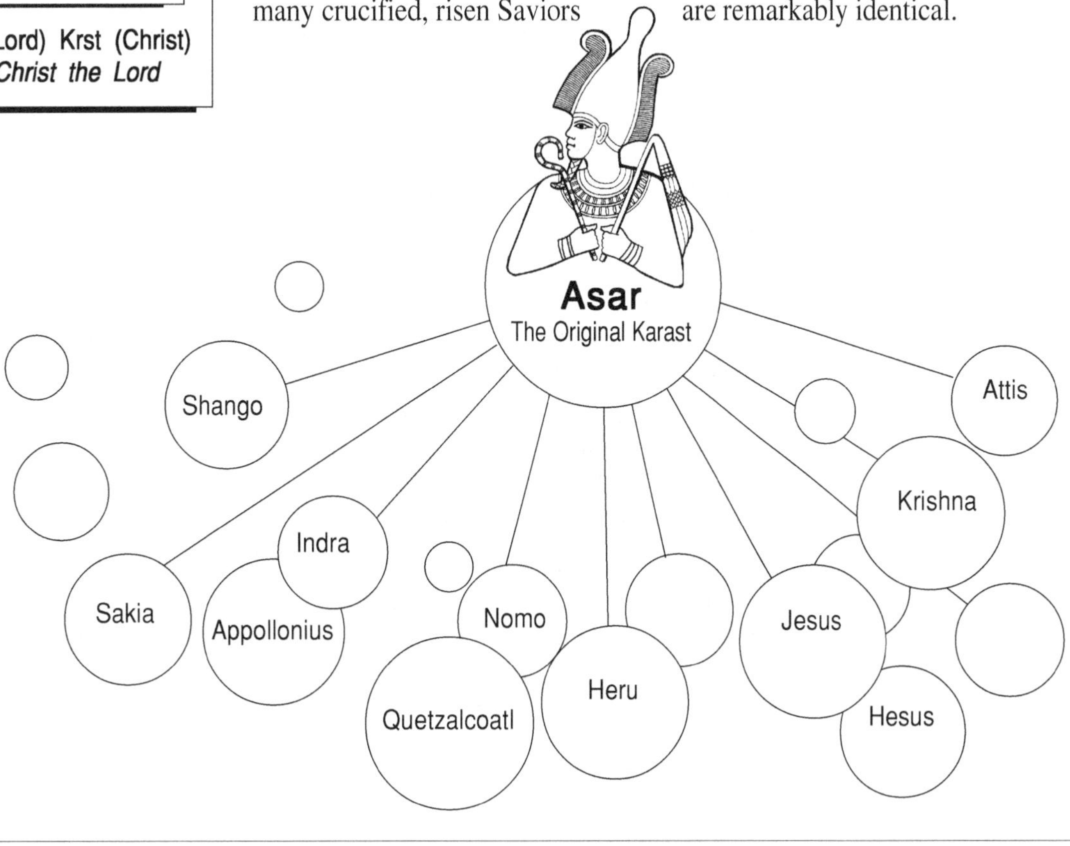

All the crucified Saviors were personifications of the Sun. They were the Sun / Son of God.

Their life-stories were allegories of the Sun's passage through the 12 Zodiacal Constellations.

Christ, Hari Krishna, Heru Krst (Horus), and Azar Krst (Osiris) were all different names for the same identity: the Sun. Yes, the SUN, that bright magnificent being who brings Light to humanity, without which there would be no life on Earth.

All of these Saviors, including Christ were the SUN and the story of their life is an allegory of the passage of the Sun through the constellations of the Zodiac. None of these risen Saviors were real men *as presented*, –though some were apparently aligned with real men and women who actualized or embodied Divine Consciousness. All the events in their lives were symbolic allegories for events in the life of the Sun.

Early Christians called Christ "Our Lord, the Sun",

and they faced East or dawn in worship, –in fact, they were charged with being sun-worshipers.[1] "Our Lord the Sun" was used in prayer by the Christians until the 6th Century, and embodied in the Liturgy until it was changed by the clever priesthood to "Our Lord the God." [2] "And, behold, the glory of the God of Israel came from the way of the east" (Eze. 43:2).

This is why all the Christian holidays match or coincide with major solar events

All the Christian holidays and gospel events perfectly parallel and coincide with the major solar-astrological events, while the gospel personages coincide with astrological bodies. They secretly, disguisedly allegorize and celebrate celestial and solar events. Thus all the important dates or holidays of Christian worship are markers of significant events in the personal life of the Sun, as shown in the following sections.

"Judgement Day" is the Grand Marker of the end of the Great Cycle

The Judgment Day was periodic. It was the end of a cycle, a period, an astrological Age, the Precession of the Zodiac! When such occurred, the dead were judged. "But the drama appears so tremendous in the Book of Revelation because the period ending is on the scale of a great year. [The Great Year or Precession is one complete cycle or "Turn" of the Wheel of the Zodiac, which takes 26,000 years] ...The great judgement of all...was held at the end of the great year of all, in the cycle of precession. At the termination of this vast period it was the Judgment Day." [3] The Coming Forth By Day (a.k.a. Book of the Dead) is the source of the very phrases found in the New Testament, in connection with the Day of Judgement.[4]

1) Doane, 501-3. 2) Hotema, GC, 53. 3) Massey, AE, 694. 4) Doane, 245.

New Testament: The Gospels are Afrikan solar allegories made literal! They mirror the Sun's annual history.

The Gospels are a literalization of the Kamite solar allegories. This means the Gospels are a disguised record of the Sun's passage through the Zodiac Signs and Seasons. The Gospel events exactly mirror the Sun's history or path through the zodiacal constellations:

Person, Item, Event:	Disguised astrological significance. Celestial Body or Solar Event allegorized:
Christ, Krishna, Heru, Asar	The Sun. The Sungod.
The Christ	The Sun. Christ is called the Sun in more than one place in the Bible: • "For the Lord God is a sun" (Ps. 84:11); Christ is called *Lord* and *God* (Isa. 9:6). • "God is a consuming fire" (Heb. 12:29, Deu. 4:24). • *Sun* of Righteousness (Mal. 4:2). *Right* is from the same roots as Regal, Royal; derived from Ra, the Kamite name for the Sun. • Prophetically: "there shall come a Star out of Jacob" (Num. 24:17). Stars are suns. • "I am the bright and morning star" (Rev. 22:16). • "And behold, the glory of the God of Israel came from the way of the east" (Ezek. 43:1). The "glory" or Sun rises in the east. Christ's crown of thorns = Sun's rays. • "I am come a light into the world" (John 12:46). • Light of the World (John 3:19). What Light is so great that it lights up the whole world, but the Sun? The Sun, like the Earth, is a living, conscious being and a direct expression of God/Goddess from which our Life Energy is derived. Christ started his ministry at age 30 and died at age 33. The Sun *enters* an astrological sign or house at 30 degrees and *exits* at 33 degrees! Thus, age 33 is the popular age when Savior-Sungod-Messiahs are crucified.
Shiloh	The Sun. "The sceptre shall not depart from Judah...until Shiloh come" (Gen. 49:10). Shiloh, another name for Savior, is from the same root as Solar (sun).[1] The Solar Shiloh is the "sun of the resurrection at the time of the summer solstice, as...Adonai, or the child Horus or of Easter at the vernal equinox." [2] "The Shiloh was the RETURNING ONE...whether stellar, lunar, or solar, the Shiloh was periodic." [3]
Sunday	SUN-day, the "Lord's day" was celebrated long before the Hebrews & Christianity.
Virgin Mothers	Virgo, constellation of the Celestial Virgin.
Virgin Mother Names	The Virgin Mothers almost always have names beginning with M (Meri, Mary, Myra, Maia, Maya, Mariam, Moye...) M is the symbol of Virgo. These names are derived from a common Afrikan original, MER which means Water and Mother-Love. Other derivatives include marine, mermaid, merge, and marry. Hathor-Meri, the virgin mother of Horus, was the Egyptian Goddess of Love and prototype of Virgin Mary.[4]
Virgin birth of Saviors	When Sirius, heaven's brightest star, was at its zenith (during the Age of Aries at the winter solstice) on Christmas Eve at midnight, simultaneously arose the Y-shaped constellation of the celestial Virgin (Virgo) in the East. She bore in her left arm the Holy Child (Messiael, Messiah-God) and in her right hand the star Spica. Hence, all Savior-Sungods are represented as being *born of a Virgin* on December 25th.

1) Higgens, vII, 180. 2) Massey, BB-vII, 247. 3) Ibid., 78. 4) Ibid., 140.

Person, Item, Event:	Disguised astrological significance. Celestial Body or Solar Event allegorized:
"His" Star announces birth of Christ, Krishna, Heru, Asar	The birth of each Savior is announced by "his" *Star in the East* (proof of astrology), the "Star of Bethlehem" which piloted the "Three Wise Men" who apparently were astrologers, having gotten their knowledge of the Messiah's birth from watching the stars! The Star they saw was **Sirius**, brightest star in the sky, signaling the birth of the New Sun at midnight on Christmas Eve. Some 3000 years ago at the moment of this birth, "Sirius, coming from the East, did actually stand on the Meridian,"[1] and at the same time, Virgo arose in the East. The Coming God and commotion around him is plagiarized from Afrika's *Book of the Coming Forth By Day*, where we read: "His light appeareth in the sky like that of a great star in the East." [2]
The 3 Kings	The 3 bright stars in Orion's belt, which lie in a straight line pointing to Sirius, the "Star in the East" which announces the Sungod's birth at midnight on Christmas Eve. These 3 stars have always been called the Three Kings, long before Christ (since about 6000 years ago when the vernal equinox was in Taurus).[3]
Born in a stable	At midnight on December 25 "The sun was then in the zodiacal sign of Capricorn, then known as the Stable of Augeus, so the infant sun-god was said to have been born in a stable." [4]
Assumption, Nativity of the Virgin	Assumption of the Virgin (Aug 15) and Nativity of the Virgin (Sep 8) = the movement of the Sun through Virgo constellation (entering 8/15, exiting 9/8).
The Twelve Apostles	The 12 Apostles or Disciples of Asar, Heru & Christ were the 12 Zodiacal Signs.
4 brothers of Christ, Heru	The four cardinal, cornerstone constellations of the Zodiac.
The 4 apostles	Matthew, Mark, Luke and John = the four cardinal zodiacal signs. In the Roman Vulgate and Greek Bibles, Matthew is shown with an angel near him; Mark with a lion; Luke, a bull, and John, an eagle.[5] The sculptured relief on Chartres Cathedral depicts Matthew as a Man, Mark as a Lion; Luke as an Ox; and John as an Eagle.[6]
Mary Magdalene and the Multiple Marys	The Great Mother. Mary is one of Her names. *Magdalene* is derived from roots meaning *very great* or *high.* The Bible's patriarchal rewriters demean and suppress women, especially the Female Principle of God (Goddess). Like the Zodiac which She birthed, the Great Mother is disguised in the Bible, fragmented into the numerous Marys; Mary the Virgin, the Whore, the 3 Marys at the Cross, etc.
Beheaded John the Baptizer, Jesus the Christ.	Son of Virgo, Son of Pisces. Both Jesus and John are born as a result of divine visitation and announced by the same angel. John baptizes "by water only" but said Christ will baptize by Fire and the Holy Spirit. **John** is born six months *before* Christ; he represents the Son of Virgo, the Water-Mother of the Natural Human. He is a type of the natural First Birth by Water (babies are born in a sac of water). **Jesus**, born at the dawn of the Age of Pisces, represents the Son of Pisces, the Fish-Mother of the Evolved Human. Fish is a symbol of Christ. He is a type of the Spiritual Second Birth by Fire and the Holy Spirit. John said, "He [Christ] must increase, but I must decrease" (John 3:30). Virgo and Pisces are opposite each other and stand six months apart. Astrologically, as a constellation or star sinks below horizon in the West, its opposite constellation rises in the East. Hence as John went down ("decreased," got beheaded), Christ rose up on the world ("increased"). Thus in the Christian calendar, the birthday of John the Baptist is on the day of the Summer Solstice when the Sun begins to *decrease.*

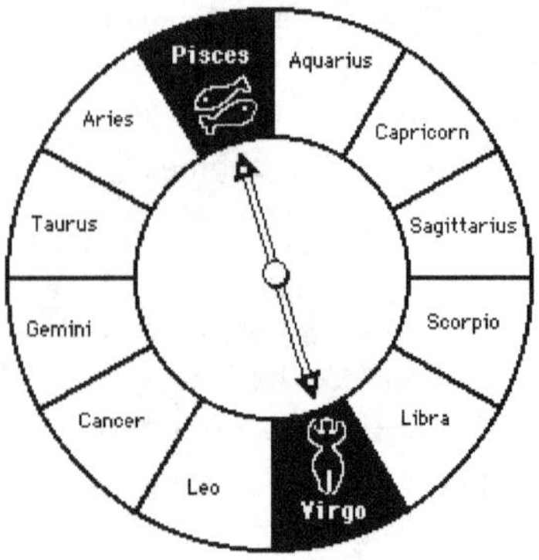

1) Carpenter, PC, 30. 2) Kuhn, LL, 329. 3) Jackson, CBC, 127. 4) Massey, HJ, 13. 5) Blavatsky, IU-vII, 235. 6) Jackson, CBC, 147.

Person, Item, Event:	Disguised astrological significance. Celestial Body or Solar Event allegorized:

Aug 29 fixed for death of John the Baptist

The Star which represents the head of Aquarius rises while the rest of the body is below the horizon, at the same time as the Sun sets in Leo (kingly sign representing king Herod). Thus Herod beheads John (the horizon cuts off the head of Aquarius).

Christmas, December 25th
(Christ-Mass)

A date anciently celebrated as the "Birthday of the Sun" after its "death" at the Winter Solstice (Dec. 21), the *longest* night of the year. Christmas is the first day to noticeably lengthen after this date; thus the Sun begins to ascend toward its zenith at the Summer Solstice on June 21st. December 25th is the standard birthday of the Sungods /Saviors. The Gospels do not state when Christ was born. Right after midnight on December 25th, the Great Goddess births Her Beloved Son (Sun).

St. Thomas, the Doubter

Church dedicates the Date of Winter Solstice, when any one may naturally doubt the rebirth of Sun, to Thomas the Doubter.

Saviors-Sungods grew up in concealment

After the Winter Solstice, the puny newborn Sun struggles against the powers of Darkness. But as the weeks pass, the young Sungod gathers strength, rising higher and higher in the sky, his brightness increasing rapidly until on March 21, the day of the Spring Equinox, he emerges victorious.

Red Christ, Red Horus, Red Osiris

The diminishing RED Sun of autumn. The Days grow shorter as the "suffering" Sun grows weaker with approaching winter. This dying Old Sun is portrayed as:

- The Red (or Red-Haired) crippled, naked, ugly image of Christ preserved by tradition.
- Christ with the scarlet robe.
- Horus as the sacrificial Red Calf, the bloody "afflicted one." Horus as the "old child," blinded, wounded and crippled.
- Osiris as Atum, the Red Sun of Autumn, "bound in linen."

Betrayal of Christ, Horus, Osiris

The "Betrayal" is the event of Scorpio stinging Ra (the Sun, Messiah) to "death" in the Fall of the year. In the autumn-sign of Scorpio, the Sun enters the wintertime of darkness and solar feebleness. Thus Scorpio was called the gate or door of the dark "underworld." Scorpio falls in October-November when the Sun is going to its death in Winter. Astrological myths place Scorpio at the Autumn Equinox, thus "it was said in Egypt that the Scorpion killed Horus, the sun, sending him to his midwinter death and resurrection as his Mother Isis gave him rebirth." [1] Osiris's betrayal by his brother Set led to his death. And Judas's betrayal of Christ led to his death. Darkness gradually wins over the powers of Light until on December 22, there are twice as many hours of darkness as there are of daylight in the Northern Hemisphere. December 22 is the Winter Solstice, the shortest day of the year. The event of the Sun setting on this date was called the "Death of the Old Sun." Thus the forces of Darkness achieved victory as the Old Sun died with the sunset. But this Darkness is quickly challenged, for the Great Mother as Virgo births a New Sun (new Savior) on December 25, a date celebrated from antiquity as the birthday of the Sun.

Red Dragon chasing Radiant Pregnant Woman

Scorpio perpetually following Virgo! "And there appeared a great wonder in <u>heaven</u>; a woman clothed with the sun...And she being with child cried, travailing in birth... And there appeared another wonder in heaven; and behold a great <u>red</u> dragon" (Rev. 12:1-3). The Serpent, one of Scorpio's 3 symbols, was also called the Dragon by the ancients. Scorpio constellation features *Antares* the RED star!

1) Walker, WE, 900.

Person, Item, Event: | **Disguised astrological significance. Celestial Body or Solar Event allegorized:**

Candlemas
(Feb 2)

Processions of candles stands for growing light of approaching Spring. "The feast of Candlemas was kept by the ancient Egyptians in honor of the goddess Neith. It was called the 'Feast of Lamps.'"[1] In China it was called "Festivals of Gratitude to Tien."

Passover, Easter

Both Easter and Passover out of which it derives are equinoctal festivals; they commemorate the Vernal Equinox (arrival of Spring), a most important event, celebrated throughout the ancient world from Mexico to China.

Passover
(about Mar 25)

Spring Equinox (arrival of Spring). Passover was to be the beginning of the new year. It is an approximation of the Vernal (Spring) Equinox. Passover superficially referred to the angel of death 'passing over' the homes of the Hebrews in Goshen smeared with the blood of a slain lamb. In reality, Passover refes to the Sun "passing over" or crossing the Celestial Equator at the Spring Equinox when Night and Day are of equal length all over the world.[2]

The Slain Lamb of God

Aries the Ram. The slain lamb was the Lamb of God, slain each year, and "slain from [since] the foundation of the world" (Rev. 13:8). This Lamb (baby Ram) was the constellation Aries the Ram, which is obliterated ("slain") when "the Lord" (Sun) "passed over" the Celestial Equator.[3] The custom of dressing the Paschal Lamb in the shape of a cross originates from this.

Easter
(in March or late as April 25)

Easter is an approximation of the Spring Equinox. Easter celebrates the Crossing of the Celestial Equator by the Sun. Easter, a roving date, is the first Sunday after the first full moon after the Spring Equinox (Mar 21), therefore it cannot be the date of the death of any historical personage. The Crucifixion or Crossing was, and still is determined by the full moon of Easter.

The Crucifixion

The Crucifixion (from crux, meaning cross) is the "Crossification" or intersection of the Ecliptic and Equator. In other words it is the "Heavenly Cross" created by the Ecliptic (sun's path) crossing the Celestial Equator on the *Spring Equinox.* (The Celestial Equator is a projection of Earth's equator into space.)

Bull, Lamb, and Fish of God

Taurus, Aries, Pisces. Two thousand years ago, the intersection of the Ecliptic and Equator (see previous paragraph) was in the constellation of Aries the Ram. Thus the LAMB was the symbol of the risen Savior (Sun) who was called the Ram or Lamb of God. Every 2155 years when the Sun moves to the next Zodiacal constellation, a "New Age" begins and the symbol of that sign becomes the new symbol of worship:

- During the Age of Taurus, the Savior was represented as a Bull. This was Horus as the Golden Calf worshipped by the Israelites; Osiris as Apis the Bull and the Winged Bull of Assyria.
- During the Age of Aries the Savior was worshipped as a Ram such as Amon, Egypt's Ram-headed god. Heru /Christ were represented as the Lamb of God.
- With the Age of Pisces, Fish became the symbol of Heru/Christ.

Lamb only can open 7 seals

Only the Lamb has the power to open the book of Seven Seals (Rev. 5:2-9). When Vernal Equinox passed from Taurus to Aries, the Son of God was imaged as a Lamb, instead of the earlier Calf; "thenceforth his was the power and the glory and the majesty, and his the book of life then newly-opened, in the cycle of precession for another 2,155 years." [4]

1) Doane, 330, 392. 2). Saakana, 40; Jackson, CBC, 193. 3) Carpenter, PC, 40. 4) Massey, AE, 690.

Person, Item, Event:	Disguised astrological significance. Celestial Body or Solar Event allegorized:

Christ's image was changed from Lamb of God

Originally in Europe, Christ was worshipped in the image of a Lamb, the *Lamb of God*, and "it was not till after the Council of Constantinople, called *In Trullo...* [in 707 A.D.] that the pictures of Christ Jesus were ordered to be drawn in the form of a man...From this decree, the identity of the worship of the *Celestial Lamb* and the Christian Saviour is certified beyond the possibility of doubt...Nothing can more clearly prove the general practice than the order of a council to regulate it." [1]

House of "Many Mansions"

Christ allegedly said, "In my Father's house are many mansions" (John 14:2). Originally, the "house of many mansions" meant the Zodiac Constellations.[2] This terminology is straight from Egyptian scriptures describing the many mansions in the afterworld. This is why the zodiacal divisions are called Houses. "Mansion" itself is derived from Kamite "men" meaning moon and mind. The original meaning of these mansions was "Houses of the Moon," that is, the Zodiacal Constellations through which the Moon Goddess (the Great Mother) passed on Her monthly round,[3] for the ancient Afrikans recognized both a Solar and *Lunar* Zodiac. The Lunar Zodiac was older and given highest priority.

Christ's ride on the Ass, Palm Sunday

Palm branches covered Christ's path in his Palm Sunday procession into Jerusalem on the back of an ass (Mat 21:5-8). The Ass is a copy of Aiu, Egypt's ass-headed god; the Golden Ass who carries the disk of the Sun on his head between his ears. The **disk** was Christ/Horus, the Sun. The **Palm Branch** was a type of time, with the two equal sides of the branch representing Day and Night at the Equinox. Christ riding the Ass to the crucifixion scene is the Sun moving toward the Equinox (symbolized by the Palms) at the Easter or Passover where he will be "crucified" on the "cross" of the Equator and Ecliptic [4] (Mat. 21:5).

Numerous solar heroes rode asses, including Quetzalcoatl, Dionysus, Saul and Moses (Ex. 4:20). "These asses are the cosmic asses, the Ascelli, in the constellation Leo, on which numerous solar heroes rode to their death against the warlike material elements." [5]

The Crucifixion-Slaying of the *Lamb* of God

At the time of the Spring Equinox, the constellation of Aries the Ram is temporarily hidden or obliterated (symbolically slain) when the Sun passed over, that is, CROSSED the Equator. This "crossing" is the Crucifixion; the Sun is "crucified" or crossed at the intersecting lines of the Ecliptic & Equator at the moment of his descent into the lower hemisphere, the hemisphere of darkness and death; and so again at the moment of his resurrection into the hemisphere of light and life, while the period of transit is three days.

Crucifixion site named Skull

Mt. Calvary or Golgotha both mean "skull" and was the name of the place where both, the biblical Christ and Krishna were crucified.[6] The source of this imagery was the crucifixion of Osiris, the prototypical Christ, on the Spring Equinox, on the ARC of the Celestial Equator. This Equator forms a broad Arc through space which can be represented as a mount or rounded *Calvarium* (Latin for skull). Thus, on the celestial Calvary, the Sun is momentarily suspended (crucified) at the crossing.[7]

Ages 30 and 33 highlighted

The age of the crucified Saviors is given as 33 in Egyptian hieroglyphics and the Mexican Codices.[8] **The Sun *enters* an astrological sign at 30° and *exits* at 33°. Thus, Christ (the Sun) starts his ministry at age 30 and dies at 33**, the standard age when Savior-Sungods are *crucified*.

1) Doane, 503. 2) Walker, WD, 144. 3) Ibid. 4) Saakana, 45. 5) Graham, DM, 340. 6) Ibid., 347. 7) Saakana, 41. 8) Churchward, SS, 480.

Person, Item, Event:	Disguised astrological significance. Celestial Body or Solar Event allegorized:

The Savior dies

The Sun *sets*.
There are *two* deaths and *two* births of the Sun:

- A Death on December 22 (Winter Solstice). The event of the Sun setting on this date, shortest day of the year, was called the "Death of the Old Sun." Thus the forces of Darkness achieved victory as the Old Sun died with the sunset. This is followed three days later by the Birth of a new Sun on December 25, anciently called the "Birthday of the Sun."
- A Death just prior to Easter, called the Crucifixion. This is the Sun crossing the Equator on March 21 (Spring Equinox), getting "crucified" or *crossed* at the intersecting lines of the Ecliptic and Equator. When this happens, the sign of the current age (Aries for example) is temporarily obliterated or "slain." Thus the Ram or Lamb of God is sacrificed or crucified. This Crucifixion is followed three days later by a second Birth (REbirth) of the Sun, called the Resurrection (Easter). This is really the arrival of Spring, heralding the resurrection of Light (days grow longer than nights) and thus Life.

Darkness after Savior's death

When the Sun sets, there is darkness. When the Savior-Sungod dies or disappears into the other world, the sun eclipses (Luke 23:44). All the Sungods are fated to be slain by darkness, then they rise again.

Savior descends to Hell for 3 days

The Sun *below* the horizon. At the end of his career, the Sun enters the lowest regions or bowels of the earth (descent into Hell or Underworld) and remains there three days, for reason that from Dec. 22 to 25, the Sun apparently remains in the same place. He is in the Underworld where he becomes the "Judge of the Dead," a title of Asar, Heru, Christ and Krishna. After these three days, Day is perceptibly longer, thus the Sun resurrects or "rises from the dead" and "ascends into heaven."

Resurrection and Triumph after 3 days

At the time of the Spring Equinox, for a few days, Night and Day are equal length, then the *Days* get longer. This signifies the "triumph" of the Sungod over the powers of darkness. The Spring Equinox was the "second birth" of the Sun as the length of Day exceeded that of Night. The Savior-Sungod is now resurrected from the dead (Underworld), having emerged victorious on March 21, the day of the Spring Equinox. The days triumphed over the nights; the young Sun (Savior) redeems the world from Darkness.

Second Coming on a "White Horse"

Like Krishna, Mithra, and other Sungods, Christ is expected to return on a "white horse," "And I saw heaven opened, and behold a white horse; and he that sat upon him was called Faithful and True" "And the armies which were in heaven followed him upon white horses" (Rev. 19:11-13,16). Sosiosh, the Persian Savior of mankind "will come seated on a white horse and followed by an army of good genii equally mounted on milk-white steeds." [1]

The "White Horse" is an ancient, universal symbol of the Sun.[2] Christ, Krishna and the other Savior-Sungods are definitely "returning," or "coming" as they have been for eons. One of the meanings of the very root and source of their name (Iu) means "The Ever Coming One." Each time the Savior (Sun) comes or returns, a New Age begins. Each Age is a 2155-year division of the Great Year. The Great Year is one Turn of the Zodiacal Circle, which takes 26,000 years to complete and is divided into 12 sections called Houses of the Zodiac by the Afrikans of the Nile Valley who originally charted celestial, solar history, which is the whole foundation of the Bible and other holy books.

Above: Vishnu (incarnate as Krishna) astride his stallion, symbol of the Sun.

1) Blavatsky, IU-vII, 237. 2)Ibid., 237; Doane, 797.

The Old Testament is equally astrological !

The Old Testament is likewise composed of disguised Zodiacs and solar history or Kamite allegories made literal. The floors of ancient Jewish synagogues were often decorated with zodiacal mosaics, proving their connection with astrology (see page 111) . The apocryphal Book of Enoch is rich with clear, undeniable astrological references. Chapters 71-78 dwells on 'Astronomical Secrets,' and starts off: "The book of the revolutions of the luminaries of heaven, according to their respective classes... powers... periods... names... nativity, and their respective months, which Uriel, the holy angel who was with me, explained to me" (Enoch 71:1). Following are examples illustrating the zodiacal presence composing the Old Testament.

Person, Event, Item:	Disguised astrological significance. Celestial Body or Solar Event allegorized:
4, 7, 10, 12 (13 disguisedly)...	Why do these numbers occur over and over and over in the Bible? Keep reading...
(4) Four:	The Four Cornerstone Signs or Cardinal Signs of the Zodiac, which correspond to the Four Classical Elements of **Earth**, **Water**, **Air**, and **Fire**. Each sign belongs to one of these Elements.
The Four Beasts (Rev. 4:7)	"And the first beast was like a lion, and the second beast like a calf, and the third beast had a face as a man, and the fourth beast was like a flying eagle." These four "beasts" are the four cardinal zodiacal signs of Leo, Taurus, Aquarius, and Scorpio (Scorpio has 3 symbols; the Scorpion/Eagle/Serpent).
The Awful Four Horsemen (Rev. 6:1-8)	Four planets. And their names point to the Elemental Four. Riding a white horse, the first horseman was a crowned conqueror armed with a bow. He is planet **Venus** (Air). Riding a red horse, the second horseman was a warrior wielding a great sword and given power "to take peace from the earth." He is **Mars** (Fire), the red planet. The third rider, upon a black horse, was holding a pair of balances. He is **Saturn** (Earth). The fourth horseman was **Mercury** (Water; the metal *mercury* is liquid at room temperature, *mercurial* like water): "And I looked, and behold a pale horse: and his name that sat on him was Death, and Hell followed with him" (Rev. 6:1-8). We meet the same horses in a nicer version called The Four Chariots, with sets of horses in red, black, white, and dappled (Zech. 6:1-3).
Ezekiel's four, 4-fold, noisy winged thangs	UFO writers have a heyday with the Book of Ezekiel. The first chapter of Ezekiel gives an amazing account of an unbelievable creature he saw emerge from a fiery "whirlwind" which could be accused of being an extraterrestrial vehicle, based on its description. From this whirlwind or: "out *of the midst thereof came the likeness of four living creatures...And every one had four faces, and ...four wings. ...Their wings were joined one to another; they turned not when they went; they went every one straight forward. As for the likeness of their faces, they four had the face of a man, and the face of a lion, on the right side: and they four had the face of an ox on the left side; they four also had the face of an eagle."* In chapter 10 he describes equally amazing creatures (cherubs), perhaps from the same planet as the fourfold thangs since they shared common traits. The face of the Man, Lion, Ox, and Eagle are the four signs of Aquarius, Leo, Taurus, and Scorpio.

Person, Event, Item:	Disguised astrological significance. Celestial Body or Solar Event allegorized:
More Fours	• The *River* that became the *4 Rivers* of Eden: Pison, Gihon, Hiddekel, and Euphrates (Gen. 2:10-14) = the Zodiac and its 4 cornerstone signs. • The "four winds from the four quarters of heaven" (Jer. 49:36). • "These are the four spirits of the heavens" (Zech. 6:5). • The Four Horns and Four Carpenters (Zech. 1:18-20).
(7) Seven:	The **Seven Stars of the Great Bear** (now called Ursa Major). The Great Bear was anciently regarded as the constellation of the Old Great Mother, "The Mother-Goddess of Time," She who figured the first Celestial Circle.[1] The Seven Stars of the Great Bear symbolized both, the Sabean Great Mother (Sheba or Seven is one of Her names) and Her original Seven Offspring. These Seven Offspring were Co-Creators of Creation. Known as the **Khuti** and the **Alu /Ali**, they were the first Seven Spirits of Light. These Seven are the Afrikan source of all "The Seven" whatevers, prominently found in the world's mythologies and sacred books. Time is a Circle, Cycle, –from the seconds of the circle of the Minute to the cyclic seasons of the Year, to the Precession of the infinite Great Circle called the Zodiac. **The Great Bear was a Great Clock** for She revolved around the North Pole once every 24 hours. She was a Clock of the Four Quarters in the Cycle /Circle of the Year. Her tail was a "hand" on the Great Clock in the sky. In ancient Egypt when the Great Bear pointed to the South, it was the time of Inundation and Birthday of the Year and the World. [2]
The 7 Spirits of God	The **Alu** (see preceding section). The Alu are the **Elohim** (hence the name), the plural God in Genesis who said "Let US make man in OUR image" (Gen. 1:26). Elohim literally means *plural* gods (im=plural). They appear as the Seven Lamps and Seven Spirits of God before His Throne: "and there were seven lamps of fire burning before the throne, which are the seven Spirits of God" (Rev. 4:5).
The 7 Eyes of God	The Ali (represented by the Seven Stars of the Great Bear), the Sabean Circle, and the Sabean Attributes of the Great Mother. As Earth rotates, the Seven Stars of the Great Bear form Seven Circles. These circles are a form of the Seven Eyes of God: "with those seven; they are the eyes of the Lord, which run to and fro through the whole earth" (Zech. 4:10). Again as the Seven-Eyed Stone: "For behold the stone that I have laid before Joshua; upon one stone shall be seven eyes" (Zech. 3:9).
Sevenfold Sunlight	"and the light of the sun shall be sevenfold, as the light of seven days, in the day that the Lord bindeth up the breach of his people..." (Isa. 30:26).
Seven this and seven that	Number **Seven** takes the leading position as the Bible's darling number, appearing constantly throughout the Bible: Creation was finished in **7** days. The **7**th or Sabbath as the day of rest. Revelation's **7** Churches, **7** Seals, and the **7** Spirits before God's throne (Rev. 1:4). The **7**-headed dragon also sporting **7** crowns (Rev. 12:3). Pharaoh's dream of **7** fat cows, **7** skinny cows, and **7** ears of corn on one stalk (Gen. 40: 2, 3, 5). Major festivals (Passover, Tabernacles, Wedding festivals, etc.) lasted **7** days. The **7** daughters of the Priest of Midian (Exo. 2:16). A river smitten into **7** streams by the Lord (Isa. 11:15). Jacob working **7** years to gain Rachel as his 2nd wife (Gen. 29:20). Lamech living **777** years (Gen. 5:31). Balaam's **7** oxen and **7** rams (=Taurus & Aries), one of each sacrificed on **7** altars (Num. 23:1, 29, 30). The Golden **7**-Branched Candlestick (Zech. 4:2).

1) Massey, BB-vII, 131. 2) Churchward, SS, 99.

Person, Event, Item:	Disguised astrological significance. Celestial Body or Solar Event allegorized:

(10) Ten:

The ancient Afrikans divided Time partly based on the 10 digits of the two hands (probable source of two hands on the clock!). The hieroglyph for 10 is two hands clasped; Egyptian TEK[1] (the hieroglyph X) or TEKA (source of decimal, decade, decan) means to cross or join together. The cross is still the sign of ten as the "Roman" numeral *X*. Kamit's calendar had 10 days to the week, in a year of 36 divisions, hence 360 days.[2] They "divided the heavens into thirty-six division after – twelve North, twelve South and twelve Central." [3]

Tens in the Bible

The **10** Commandments. Jeshurun, name of the **10**-tribe Israel of Moses's time. The **10** horns of the 7-headed beast. The **10** plagues of Egypt. Jesus's parable of the **10** Virgins; *5* were foolish, *5* were wise (Mat. 25 1-2). The **10** thousand men which Judah and Simeon slew (Jud. 1:2). In Solomon's Temple: the **10** stands with **10** basins, and the **10**-branched golden candlestick with 5 candles on the right side and 5 on the left (1Kings 7:38, 43, 49). The year of Jubilee occurred the year *after* a 49-year (7x7) period –hence in the *50th* year on the **10**th day of the 7th month (Lev. 25:8-11). King David's **10** concubines (2Sam. 20:3).

"Praise the Lord with harp: sing unto him with the psaltery and an instrument of ten strings" (Ps. 33:2).

40s and 70s

4 x 10 yields the **40** days of the Great Flood, **40** days of Jesus's fast under temptation in the desert, Ninevah's **40** days to repent, the **40** years of the Children of Israel wandering in the wilderness.

Israel's **400** (10x10x4) years of slavery (like Afrikan-Americans' 400 years of slavery; and Afrikans are largely descendants of the original Jews –IUs).

7 x 10 yields the **70** Elders of Israel (Exo. 24:9), the **70** sent out in two's by Jesus, the **70** years of the Exile (Jer. 25:12; 29:10), the Lord visiting Tyre after **70** years (Isaiah 23:17). The **70** offspring of Noah's sons who repopulated the Earth after the Great Flood and from whom all of humanity allegedly descended (Gen. 10). Jacob's family of **70**: "all the souls of the house of Jacob, which came into Egypt, were threescore [score = 20] and ten" (Gen. 46:27). The **70** kings of which Adoni-Bezek cut off their thumbs and big toes (Jud. 1:7). Gideon's **70** sons (Jud. 8:30). Jerubbaal's **70** sons (Jud. 9:2).

Journeying through the wilderness, the Israelites moved from site to site, "And they removed from Marah, and came unto Elim: and in Elim were twelve fountains of water, and threescore and ten palm trees [**70**]; and they pitched there" (Num. 33:9).

1) Churchward, SS, 373. 2) Massey, BB-vII, 358. 3) Churchward, SS, 335.

Person, Event, Item:	Disguised astrological significance. Celestial Body or Solar Event allegorized:
(12) Twelve:	The twelve signs of the Solar Zodiac.
Square city of 12 foundations	Twelve individual foundations belie the glorious walled city described in Revelation (21:14, 19, 20). Each foundation is composed of a different type of gemstone. The 12 foundations = the 12 Zodiac Signs bearing their gifts (gemstones) or attributes of each sign. As measured by John, the *4* walls of the city are equal in length, breadth and height, forming a perfectly *square* enclosure. (21:14-17) These *4 walls* represent the four cardinal Zodiac Signs (why would a city in heaven need *walls*, especially like this?) Each "wall" has *three* pearly *gates* (21:13) for a grand total of 12.
The 12 gems on Aaron's bejeweled breastplate	Twelve types of gemstones are specified in the meticulous divine instructions for making Aaron's breastplate in Exodus (28). Like the *square* city in Revelations, the finished breastplate is perfectly *square,* symbolizing the 4 Corner Signs of the Zodiac. It is labeled with the 12 names of the children (tribes) of Israel "according to their *birth*" (Exo. 28:10). "Birth" clearly signifies the 12 *months.* On the breastplate are 4 rows of 3 gemstones. The tradition of assigning a particular gemstone to each month is still alive and well today, to the profit of the jewelry business. These "birthstones" symbolically represent the 12 gifts or characteristics of each sign.
Elijah's 12 stones and 4 barrels of water	The 12 zodiacal constellations and 4 cornerstone constellations. "And Elijah took twelves stones, according to the number of the tribes of the sons of Jacob...And with the stones he built an altar...Fill four barrels with water" (1 Kings 18:31-33).
The 12 Sons & 1 Daughter	The Twelve Sons of Jacob, Ishmael, Joktan, and other Patriarchs are the Twelve Zodiacal Constellations. Two of their sons are twins; their only daughter = Virgo, making it really the 13 Tribes of the original Lunar Zodiac from which came the 12-sign Solar Zodiac.
The Tree of Life bearing 12 types of delicious fruits	No earthly tree produces 12 different types of fruit on the same tree. The Zodiac originally represented the Great Mother's gifts to Her precious children (that's US! – Humanity). Asian images portrayed Her with 12 arms or hands, each bearing gifts to humanity for each of the *months.*[1] She was also regarded as the Tree of Life, which represented Her all-giving, all nourishing care. In fact, Her name as Ash means Tree of Life. The Book of Revelation states that *twelve different* fruit grow on the Tree of Life which "yielded *her* fruit every *month*" (Rev. 22:2).
Joseph's dream of 12 stars	In his dream, Joseph saw eleven "stars" bowing to the *twelfth,* which was *his* "star" (Gen. 37:9). The Zodiac is signified.
Solomon's 12 oxen	Solomon's 12 oxen of 4 rows = the Zodiac and its 4 cornerstone signs (2Chron. 4:4.). Three of each oxen faced one of the 4 directions.
Moses' 12 spies	From the wilderness of Paran, Moses sent out 12 spy-chieftains to spy out the land of Canaan (Num. 13:2, 3, 11).
Coat torn in 12 pieces	Ahijah tore his new coat into 12 pieces (= new cycle of the Zodiac) (1Kings 11:30).
Joshua's 12 stones	After crossing the Jordan with the Ark of the Covenant, aided by a miracle akin to the parting of the Dead Sea, Joshua established a camp at Gilgal (which means *circle* –zodiac circle no doubt) where he took twelve stones from a river bed to set up a memorial for the miraculous crossing (Josh. 4).
144. 144,000.	12 x 12 or 12000. Each square wall was 144 cubits (Rev. 21:14). The 144,000 Servents of God (Rev. 7:4) composed of 12,000 from each of the 12 tribes of Israel.

1) Thornsten, GH, xiv, 264.

Person, Event, Item: | **Disguised astrological significance. Celestial Body or Solar Event allegorized:**

Clear Zodiacal References:

Creation of the Zodiac Signs

Genesis 1:14 delineates the creation of the Zodiac Signs: "And God said, Let there be lights [stars!] in the firmament of the heaven ...for signs, [zodiac signs!] and for seasons, and for days, and for years."

"Mazzaroth," Arcturus, Pleiades

Knowledge of Astrology is clearly indicated in these passages:

- Canst thou bring forth Mazzaroth in his season? (Job 38:31-33) "Mazzaroth" means zodiacal constellations.[1]
- "Which maketh Arcturus, Orion, and Pleiades, and the chambers of the south." (Job 9:9).
- "Canst thou bind the sweet influences of Pleiades, or loose the bands of Orion? Canst thou bring forth Mazzaroth in his season? or canst thou guide Arcturus with his sons? Knowest thou the ordinances of heaven? canst thou set the dominion thereof in the earth?" (Job 38:31-33)
- "Seek him that maketh the seven stars [Pleiades] and Orion" (Amos 5:8).
- "When I consider thy heavens, the work of thy fingers, the moon and the stars, which thou hast ordained" (Psalms 8:3).

Host of Heaven

Zodiacal Constellations (stars and other heavenly bodies). The Zodiac Constellations are clearly mentioned in 2Kings 23:4, 5, where the priests burned incense to "the sun, and to the moon, and to the planets, and to all the *host of heaven* [zodiac constellations]." The Host of Heaven (2Kings 17:16) and "Lord of hosts" (1Sam. 17:45) appears frequently in the Old Testament. "By the word of the Lord were the heavens made; and all the host of them by the breath of his mouth" (Ps. 33:6).

Shiloh Circle Dance

Shiloh and solar are from the same Afrikan roots. The dance performed by the daughters of Shiloh (Jud. 21:21; Jud. 21:21, 23) was a circle-dance of the Sabean tradition which denoted the motion of the planets around the Sun.[2] The same dance was performed by David around the ark (2Sam. 6:5, 14-22), and by the leaping prophets of Baal (1Kings 18:26). Shiloh biblical references:

- "Let us fetch the ark of the covenant of the Lord out of Shiloh" (1Sam. 4:3).
- "if the daughters of Shiloh come out to dance in dances" (Jud. 21:21).
- "So that he forsook the tabernacle of Shiloh" (Ps. 78:60).
- "Then will I make this house like Shiloh" (Jer. 26:6).
- "The sceptre shall not depart from Judah until Shiloh come" (Gen. 49:10).

Other references

- Before the "book of the law" was "found" by Hilkiah, the high priest, the signs of the Zodiac were known and worshipped (2Kings 22:8).
- "there shall be signs in the sun, and in the moon, and in the stars" (Luke 21:25).
- Joseph dreaming 11 stars bowing to the *twelfth*, which was *his* "star" (Gen. 37:9).
- "the star of your god" (Amos 5:26).
- "God [Jah] rideth upon the heavens" or traverses the circle of the zodiac signs writes Massey.[3] (Ps. 68:4).
- "The day is thine, the night also is thine: thou hast prepared the light and the sun. Thou has set all the borders of the earth: thou hast made summer and winter" (Ps. 74:16-17).
- "The heavens declare the glory of God; and the firmament showeth his handiwork. Day unto day uttereth speech, and night unto night showeth knowledge" (Ps. 19:1-2).

1) Blavatsky, SD-vI, 648; Massey, BB-vII, 357-358, 360. 2) Saakana, 117; Blavatsky, IU-vII, 45. 3) Massey, BB-vII, 351.

"Glorification Through Grease": The Afrikan Origin of *Anointing*

"The Egyptians were pre-eminent as anointers. They anointed the living and the dead, the persons of their priests and kings, the statues of their gods; anointing with ungents being an ordinary mode of welcome to guests on visiting the houses of friends. This glorifying by means of grease is essentially an African custom. Among some of the dark tribes fat was the grand distinction of the rich man. ...the wealthier the Hottentot the more fat and butter he used in anointing himself and family. A man's social status was measured by the luxury of butter and fat on his body. This glory of grease was only a grosser and more primitive form of Egyptian anointing." [1]

Gerald Massey

"Anointing" is still practiced by Afrikan people today except Vaseline® grease (petroleum jelly) is commonly used!

Embalming originated from the Afrikan practice of '*karas*-ing' the dead,

as you may have guessed. Contrary to popular belief, the mummies were not created to rise again in the *physical* flesh; after all, the organs were removed and placed in jars, and in the process the body was lacerated. It was the Soul of the mummy that was believed to resurrect in the afterworld, in its glorified or spiritual body, called the *Sahu.* According to the dictionary, Embalm means to *treat a corpse with preservatives in order to prevent decay. Embalm* is from balm (aromatic oil, salve or resin), which is from Balsam (fragrant ointment, aromatic oil). Modern embalming is no longer true embalming (has it ever been?); it is *pickling*. It is a degenerate imitation of the original thing, like the Christian religion itself. Instead of natural, precious, aromatic oils, ointments and ungents being used, the preserving agent is toxic formaldehyde or other unnatural, unholy chemicals.

Red Bones, Holy Bones

Red orchre was used in the earliest form of embalming or anointing the dead, "who were KARAST in their covering of ochre." The red earth, as an image of the flesh, preserved a kind of likeness to life. Human bones found in British mounds and other parts of the world were found painted with red orchre. In the Maori custom of preserving the bones of the dead, the bones were exhumed periodically, scraped and re-anointed –that is with red orchre. Anointing the living came later, but originally it was the dead who were anointed or consecrated.[2]

1) Massey, BB-vI, 19. 2) Ibid., 295.

Some 100 Euro Christ-words from just four Afro Krst-words

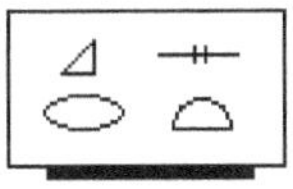

KRST

A wealth of words in so-called European languages and Christian terminology are derived from just a handful of Afrikan words:

Krs • Krst • Mes • Ankh

The derivatives reflect the interwoven ideas around the Afrikan concepts represented by the root words. Let's examine these derivatives.

Etymology of Krst /Christ Words

Category	Afrikan-Kamite Roots	Derivatives	Comments
1 **KRST** Christ Anointed Mummy	**Krst** (karast) • anointed mummy. 218AE The mummy was the Karast (KRST) by name. "The karast is literally the god or person who has been mummified, embalmed, and anointed or christified." 218AE **Krs** (karas) • to embalm or *make the mummy.* 218AE **qeras** (karas!) • to wrap up a body in linen & prepare it for burial. 775b, 776a • winding (mummy) sheet. 775b, 776a	**Christ**, anointed (English) **Chrestus**, anointed (Roman) **Krishna**, Black (Sanskrit) **Crost**, anointed (Ethiopian) 588hig1 **Kristo**, divine image, idol (Pepel-*Afrikan*) **Kristos**, anointed (Greek)	**"Hence the name of the Christ,** Christos...Chrestus...for the anointed, was derived...from the Egyptian word krst." (218AE) **Anointing is kindred with embalming.** Osiris, Horus, Jesus, and others were known as the Karast (Christ). "Christ" is not a name but a title. The Bible even acknowledges this: "And Simon Peter answered and said, Thou art <u>the Christ</u>, the Son of the living God...Then charged he his disciples that they should tell no man that he was Jesus <u>the Christ</u>" (Mat. 16:16, 20). All passages in the New Testament which speak of Christ as a name, betray their modern date. The term "**Christian**" was unknown by the early original Christians –who called themselves brethren, disciples, saints, etc.
2 **Messu** Messiah	**mes** • to anoint. • to steep as in making the mummy. • to be born anew. 186LL, Saakana49 **Messu** • the Anointed. 217AE **Iah-a** • "Jah, the Great" 142b	ENGLISH: **Messiah**, Anointed **Mexico** **Jah / Iah** as in Elij<u>ah</u>, Jerem<u>iah</u>, Mess<u>iah</u>. HEBREW: **Msih**, the Anointed or Savior. The Lamb was the Messiah. **Mashuah**, anointed, consecrated, smeared SANSKRIT: **Massih**, Savior, Fire, and Aries (Lamb).	**Messiah Mexico**. Higgens shows that the word Mexico (Mesitli, Mesi-co) is the same as Hebrew Msih, making Mexico "the country of the Messia" (Higgens-vII, 23, 24). He also shows the numerous similarities of the ancient Mexican Religion with that of the Hebrew (34-35). **Iah** (or Jah) means deity or God (*Jah*weh, Jerem*iah*, Isa*iah*, Eli*jah*, Zachar*iah*). Thus, Mess*iah* denotes the *divinely anointed one* or the *reborn deity.*
3 **KRS** Oil	**krs** (karas) • to embalm, to anoint, to make the mummy. 215AE In anointing, **OIL** was poured on the head and face of the living. 880AE In anointing the dead body, it "was **smeared all over with ungents** and thus glorified." 880AE	**chrism** **cruse** **cruet** **cream** **grease** **grime** from German *grim*, to smear **cresme** (French) **chrisma**, an anointing (Latin) **khriein**, to anoint (Greek) **khrisma**, unguent, an anointing (Greek) **Crisco**, a brand name for vegetable shortening. **kri**, to pour out, rub over, anoint (Sanskrit)	*Chrism* is the consecrated *oil* mixture (also called holy oil) used by bishops for *anointing* in church sacraments such as baptism. Also means "sacramental anointing." The chrismatic ceremony was the "ankh-ing" or tying together of Soul and Flesh for fuller outflow. *Cruse* is a small earthen container (like the earthen flesh container of our body) for holding liquids (the precious oil /ointment /ankh-ment - representing Spirit) *Cruet* is the flask used for holding the holy water , wine, or oil used in ceremonies.

AE = <u>*Ancient Egypt: Light of the World*</u>. **a, b** = columns in <u>*An Egyptian Hieroglyphic Dictionary*</u>. LL = <u>*Lost Light*</u>.

Etymology of Krst /Christ Words

Category	Afrikan-Kamite Roots	Derivatives	Comments
4 **KRS** **KRST** Crust Body	**Krst** (karast) • anointed mummy. 218AE **Krs** (karas) • to embalm or *make the mummy.* 218AE **qeras** (karas!) • to wrap up a body in linen & prepare it for burial. 775b, 776a • winding (mummy) sheet. 775b, 776a • sepulture. 775b, 776a **qeres** (karas!) • to wrap a corpse in cloth and make it ready for burial. 776a The mummy was the Karast (KRST) by name. "The karast is literally the god or person who has been mummified, embalmed, and anointed or christified." (218AE)	**crust** **crystallize** **Eucharist** **Corpus Christi,** body of Christ **corpse** **corps** **corse** **carcass** **kreas,** carcass, especially its flesh (Greek) **corpus,** dead body (Latin) **chros,** body (Greek) **cras,** body (Irish) **crusta,** shell (Latin) **crustacean** (shelled lifeforms, like lobsters) **crypt, crypto** (essentially means *hidden.* the mummy body is hidden within its wrappings, and further hidden in its tomb.) **crystal** (is hard. mineral) **crisp** (hard. body is *hard.*) **cryo-** (prefix meaning *freezing.* a frozen thing is *hard.*) **crispate** (curled. apparently from the fact that the burial cloth becomes curled from being WRAPPED / COILED around the corpse! Further, the original Krst / Christ was curly, wooly-haired, nappy) **khrusos,** gold (Greek) **chrysos,** gold (Latin) **charisma** **grace** **chrysalis,** gold-hued butterfly pupa in a cocoon **chrisom,** the white cloth or robe worn by the infant in a Catholic baptism	**The Mummy is the Corpus, Body, Crust...** The ***crust*** of flesh is ***crystallized*** around the Soul. Spirit energies ***crystallize*** around an actuating nucleus of force. Kirlian photography, a method of photographing the aura or field of energy/light emanating from living creatures, proves this. Krst /Christ is the Word made Flesh (crystallized), the ***encrusting*** of Divinity with flesh. The flesh and blood of the Krst (Christ) is symbolically eaten in a meal called the **Eu*charist.*** ***Corps, corpse, corse, carcass***, Greek ***kreas*** (human carcass, Latin ***corpus*** (dead body), Greek ***chros***, Irish ***cras***; "these are all preceded by the word karas or karast, in Egyptian, with the risen mummy for determinative of meaning." writes Massey (Massey, BOD, 59). **Osiris as the Karast mummy was the prototypical or first *Corpus Christi* (body of Christ).** Greek ***khrusos*** and Latin ***chrysos*** mean gold. Metaphorically, the baser crust or flesh is transformed or transmuted into Gold by divinity's fire. The lower form of Self is elevated to a higher octave. When Horus was reborn or resurrected, he transformed into the *golden* hawk (800AE). ***Chrysalis*** –my favorite. It means *gold*-hued butterfly pupa enclosed in a cocoon. Metaphorically signifies the glorious transformation into divinity through the "second birth" or spiritual rebirth. The first or natural birth = the crawling Caterpillar. The second or spiritual *re*birth = the soaring Butterfly. In one method of embalming, the body was shrunk, wound up in linen, then modeled all over with a *golden* gum into the natural shape of the living figure; and this was wrapped with the finest gauze (Massey, BOD, 61). This was a way of modeling the dead body into a type of the glorified, spiritual body called the *Sahu.* **Cocoon: source of the mummy-cloth concept?** The pupa's cocoon is a silk case made out of a single, extremely long, continuous thread -just like the single, *seamless* cloth "of incredible length" wound around the Karast-mummy. The mummy cloth is usually hundreds of yards long. Some are even 800-1000 yards long! (216AE) From this originated the ***Chrisom***; the *white cloth* or robe worn by the infant in a Catholic baptism. Since the Afrikans were intimately connected with Nature, did the *Chrysalis-cocoon* inspire the *mummy-cocoon*? The Soul of the mummy in the cocoon-like linen covering is reborn (resurrected in Amenta) like the Caterpillar in the pupa, which is reborn as the Butterfly. The salient characteristics of both are shared. The Butterfly correlates to the *Sahu*. The Sahu is the glorified body in which the soul of the deceased is re-incorporated for the life hereafter. "**Butterflies** were particularly associated with Tezcatlipoca transmuted - in other words with Quetzalcoatl. In Teotihuacan, where a place has been discovered evidently belonging to the priestly cast dedicated to Quetzalcoatl, there is a frieze showing the god's first entry into the world in the shape of a chrysalis, out of which he breaks painfully to emerge into the full light of perfection symbolized by the butterfly." (Nicholson, MCA, 110)

Etymology of Krst /Christ Words

Category	Afrikan-Kamite Roots	Derivatives	Comments
5 **KRS** Cross    	**Krs** (karas) **KRS** is the KROSS of the **Equinox** – derived from the Sun's path "crossing" the ecliptic, forming the great Celestial Cross. This is also the Astronomical **CROSS** of the 4 quarters in a *circle*. The same CROSS upon which the *Karast* is annually crossified (crucified) –which is why **X** means to ***cross out***. The Mummy was the Karast. The arms of the Karast mummy is crossed over the chest, signifying X means "to cross out," and Death. It still means this as the "Skull & Crossbones," likely derived from this. Hence, although Albino reference books say X means Christ, really X means the Dead Christ or Christ of Death. This is the REVERSED Christ of the rewritten, Unholy Bible which all Christians worship. This Death-Christ is Set (Satan) the False Christ. The Cross of the True Christ was the "**PLUS**" or **Equilateral Cross**, or Astronomical Cross of the Four Quarters in a Circle. Thus, early images of Christ show the **+** Cross (not **X**-cross) behind his head! "Criss-Cross" means to mark with crossing lines. Criss-Cross = KRS-CROSS, –to cross the Krs, or cross out the Krs. The Mummy was the Krs-t, and its arms were crossed over the chest, over the *Heart* which is the CRUCIal POINT.	**cross** **criss-cross** (= krs-cross!) **crux**, cross (Latin) **ceryx**, cross or caduceus **qrs** (Hebrew) **crisis**, "crucial point." Point of the Cross. Crucifixion is a "crisis." **crossing** **Crucifixion** **Crossification** **cruise** **across** **kruisen**, to cross (Dutch) **crucial** **excruciating** **crusade** **cruciate** (cruciform) **crucible** ("severe test," –like getting *crucified*)	***Cross*** is a variant spelling of KRS, Kris. Higgens traces cross from ***crux***, from ***ceryx*** (cross or caduceus), from Hebrew "**qrs**" (Higgens, vi, 58). Hebrew **QRS** is obviously Afrikan **KRS**. 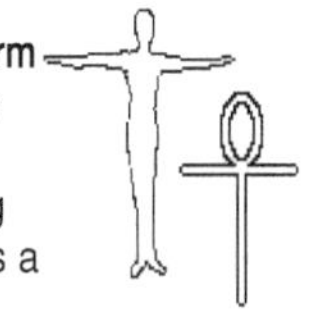 **Matter & Spirit (or Flesh & Soul) *joins* to form the *Cross* of our Body,** sometimes called "the Tree of our Flesh" (Kuhn, LL, 420-421). *Tree* was sometimes a euphemism for *Cross*. Expressing this principle, the Human-Body even resembles a Cross –the Ankh Cross– when standing erect with arms outstretched. Our bodies and all living things mirror the Divine Principles which brought them into existence.  **Life's two polarities clearly express as Water and Fire, and their qualities.** Water is Cold in its natural state, appears Blue, and flows Down, ever seeking its level. Fire is the opposite; it is Hot, appears Red, and rises or flows Up. But more importantly, Water is always Horizontal, no matter how you hold it! And Fire is always Vertical; no matter how you hold a burning match, that fire burns vertically! As a further expression of this, note that when you lay down (become horizontal), you become *cool* and may reach for a blanket. But when you stand up, you become *warm*. **To summarize:** **Water** = – Cold – Blue – flows Down – is Horizontal **Fire** = – Hot – Red – flows Up – is Vertical **When the polarities of Horizontality and Verticality are *united*, they form the Great Cross!** –which is Kamit's Astrological Cross found in all ancient cultures, apparent source of the Swastika. The *junc*tion (ankh-tion) of polarities indeed creates the Cross –which has four divisions or sections representing: – the Four Cornerstone Zodiac Constellations – the Four Directions (South, North, East, West) – the Four Essences (or elemental states) of **Earth, Water, Air & Fire.** **The 5th or Quint-Essence is the Center of the Cross -Life itself. Divinity.** Spirit. That's Consciousness, the part of you that says "I AM." And Consciousness permeates Space. The atoms and molecules composing this paper are living systems with focal points of Consciousness, as You are. The Pyramid is an archetypal expression of this cosmic Principle. Pyramid means "Fire in the Middle," the Divinity in the Center. Intersecting lines define "the point," and the Pyramid personifies it. 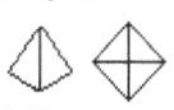 **The Spring Equinox signaled the arrival of Spring (or Life after Winter).** The Sun ***crossing*** the Celestial Equator at the Spring Equinox is the true original of the **Crucifixion** or **Crossification** (see pages 150-152). This is the Great Celestial Cross. The Sun slowly ***cruises across*** the heavens. ***Cruise*** means to move along unhurriedly, especially across *water* in a sea voyage. The *equi* of *Equi*nox is from Latin aequi / aequus, meaning *even* or *level* -obviously related to water (aqua). The Spring Equinox was considered one of the most ***crucial*** events in ancient times.
6 **KRS** Ram	**Krs** (karas) In the Age of Taurus, the Karast was the Calf /Bull. In the age of Aries, the Karast (Sun in Aries) became the Lamb /Ram. Hence by association, "KRS" means ram.	**criosphinx** (a sphinx with the head of a ram) **kyrios,** lord, master (Greek)	
7 **KRS/T** Crest Lord	**Krs** -t (karas-t) Since the Karast was the SUN overlooking all, KRS-T means overlord, the Karast at the Crest.	**crest**, peak, ridge. **crist**, crest or ridge **krios**, ram, Aries (Greek) **church!** (from Greek *kyrios*, lord, master) The Church was Europe's dictator-lord during the Dark Ages.	

Etymology of Krst /Christ Words

Category	Afrikan-Kamite Roots	Derivatives	Comments
8 **Ankh** Unction Join 	**Ankh** (nk) • Life. 186LL • Love. 186LL • Tie, Join. 186LL **ankh** • life, to live. 124b • living. 124b **ankh** • ungent. 126b **ant, antiu** • myrrh [used in anointing & embalming] 127a	**anointment** **ointment** **unguent** **unct–** (Latin stem) **join** **junction** adjunct conjunction **communicate** **anchor** knit knot net kin **con–** (prefix meaning joint, together, with; as in conjunction, congregate, confuse) link string tangle gnarled **jungle** (where plants are all grown and tangled together) hinge ankle neck knee knuckles **anger** anguish **anxiety** (tightening up of feelings) **wrinkle**, (tightening up of the skin) king belong messenger (=mes-ank-er) angel (ank-er / ank-el) bring harbinger phalanx phalange **unction** (the act of anointing as part of a religious ritual. An ointment or oil) **Key** (see page 272 for Ankh derivatives in other categories)	**The corpse is made into a mummy: that is, it is *anointed*, meaning prepared with *oils, ointments, and unguents* to preserve it. *Anointment*** and ***unguent*** are derived from Egyptian ***Ankh.*** ***Ankh* means Life, Love, and Tie,** for no Life is possible until the two polarities, Spirit and Matter, are *tied* together. Life is the result of Tying together life's two polarities with Love. All living things result from the linking of these two factors. Signified by its very shape, the Ankh *joins* the female and male polarities –represented as the circle and vertical line signifying the Yoni & Phallus. Thus the *junction, ankh-tion* of polarities form the Ankh, the ancient Cross of Eternal Life. ***Join* and *junction* are derived from Ankh!** –from the Latin "unct" stem (Kuhn, LL, 186-187). This *ankh-ing* of Male and Female polarities –also known as *sex-* yields Life (babies) and allows Life to continue by reproducing after its kind. It symbolizes the origin of our life and the means of our continuity. Life comes only through the union of male and female. **The ankh is the hieroglyph of both the structure and meaning of Life.** Rendered in one sentence the symbol means Life because life can exist only where two things, **Spirit (I)** and **Matter (O)** are tied together by the cohesive power called Love. Love ties the two together to procreate Life. When the two emblems composing the Ankh are laterally combined, we have the first Divine Word and Name in all literature, **IO**. IO is also the foundation of all numbers and mathematics. IO is also rendered as Iu, Ia, Iao, Au, Ua, etc. It seems to be the most fertile holy root for divine names, –quite naturally. The O is the eternal Feminine, matter, the Universal Mother. The I is masculine, standing for the Father's power of generation, which is Spirit. **NK** is the root of Ankh. In later philological usage, it was written NK and KN. In Greek, the NK (KN) became NG (GN). Words derived from these roots usually contain these letters and signify tying or connecting. The **anchor** connects a boat to a fixed place. The ***hinge***-points or *joints* of the body contain NK, KN; ankle, neck, knee and knuckles. ***Unction*** means "The act of anointing as part of a religious, ceremonial, or healing ritual. An ointment or oil," according to the dictionary. *Unction* is *junction* without the J. Unction is from Egyptian *Ankh.* The *unction* of the sacrament then, is really the *junction* or ***ankh-tion*** of the two polarities of Life's Energy. The word ***Key*** and the concept it represents are both derived from the Ankh. The Ankh is the Key of Life, the Key which unlocked or opened the door of human and eternal Life. Higgens derives *Key* from ***Kire*** or ***Cire***. The Druids of Ireland carried the Ankh in their hands, which they called the Kire or Cire –etymologically linked with Kamite ***Krs*** (Higgens, vI, 590).

Holy Cannibalism –Saviors for Supper

Asar, Heru, Christ and other Saviors were cannibalized

Their bodies were broken, then eaten as "the Bread of Life." Their blood was drank as wine. The tradition of symbolically eating the bodies of deities originated in Afrika. The first deity to be consumed by spiritually hungry humanity was the Great Mother Herself. Later, male gods took on the role. This holy meal is called the Eu*charist*, a word derived from Kamite *krst*, which also give us Krishna, Kristos, Christ. John said: "This is that bread which came down from heaven, that if a man eat of it he shall hunger no more." Christ allegedly said, "He that eateth my flesh, and drinketh my blood, dwelleth in me, and I in him" (John 6:56). Christ broke a loaf into fragments and gave to his disciples, saying that it was his body, broken for them (Luke 22:19, 20). Wheat or grain must be "broken" that is, mashed before it can become Bread.

"Evening bread" is one of the many meanings of Kamite "mes" from which *mass* (as in Mass and Christ*mas*) is derived. Mes also means *grain* (as in bread), crop, male child, chief prince. The same root yields the word *Messiah*, who is the "Bread of Life." The "Solemnitas Messis" or *Last Supper* is the offering of Bread. "This is the meaning of the Mass."

At midnight on Christmas Eve, the constellation of Virgo (the virgin Mother of the Saviors /Sungods) rises in the East, bearing her holy child Christ/Horus in her left arm and in her right hand the great star *Spica*. Spica is Latin for "*spike* of wheat," (from its shape) symbol of that same divinity coming as celestial, spiritual food for humanity. This signifies astrologically that the Mesu /Messiah is the Mass, the Bread of Life heralded by star-Spica, symbol of the Bread from Heaven. The Mesu is also the Wine of Life; Romans named Spica, "Vindemaitrix" (Grape Mother) or "she who brings forth the grape harvest. Horus and Christ both turned water into wine.

The cannibalism of Jesus Christ bespeaks his Afrikan origin

As previously stated, sacrificing animals is a very ancient Afrikan tradition. Afrikans or Jews, sacrificed sheep, bulls, goats, and sometimes humans for the remission of sins. And while Christians had given up slaughtering animals for offerings, "the very cornerstone of their faith was that Jesus Christ, the Son of God, was sacrificed for the sins of man and that His blood was shed for this purpose alone. Drinking of the blood (wine) and eating of the body (bread) are all fundamental aspects of [the Afrikan] man's most ancient religion." [1]

Mummy Jesus in the Bible

Mummy infant Christ /Heru. "Wrapped in swadding cloth."

To embalm the body was to ***karas*** it.[1] Making the Krst (anointed mummy or mummy-Christ) after the Egyptian fashion is evident in the Gospels. Mary Magdalene pours a cruse of "very precious ointment" on Christ's head and he says, "For in that she hath poured this ointment on my body, *she did it [to prepare me] for my burial"* (Mat. 26:7, 12). She was making the Karast (Christ) as the Anointed-Mummy prior to burial. Additionally after Christ's crucifixion, Nicodemus came with a 100 pounds of myrrh and aloes; "Then took they the body of Jesus, and ***wound it in linen clothes with the spices***" (John 19:39, 40). The Gospels are clearly saying here that they made Jesus's corpse into an Anointed Mummy (Karast)! **The resurrection of Christ was founded on that of the mummy, and ever since, the resurrection of the dead has been dependent upon the rising again of the mummy.**[2]

> "Say what you will or believe what you may, there is no other origin for Christ the anointed than for Horus the karast or anointed son of god the father. There is no other origin for a Messiah as the anointed than for the Masu or anointed. Finally, then, the mystery of the mummy is the mystery of the Christ. As Christian, it is allowed to be forever inexplicable. As Osirian, the mystery can be explained. ...Christ the anointed...originated as the Egyptian mummy in the twofold character of Osiris in his death and in his resurrection; as Osiris, or mortal Horus, the karast; and Osiris-sahu, or Horus divinized as the anointed son." [3]

Massey traces the Christ legend back 12,000 years to Afrika's Nile Valley. He writes, "The alleged facts of our Lord's life as Jesus the Christ, were equally the alleged facts of our Lord's life as the Horus of Egypt, whose very name signifies the Lord... Whether you believe or not does not matter, the fatal fact remains that every trait and feature which go to make up the Christ as Divinity...were pre-extant and pre-applied to the Egyptian and Gnostic Christ, who never could become flesh."[4] **The resurrection of the human soul in the after-life was the central fact of the Egyptian religion, and the transfigured, re-erected mummy, otherwise called the Karast, was a supreme symbol.**

Below: scene from the Temple of Luxor at ancient Thebes in Egypt, built by Amenhept III, about 1600 B.C.: "The story of the divine Annunciation, the miraculous Conception (or incarnation), the Birth, and the Adoration of the Messianic child, had already been engraved in hieroglyphics and represented in four consecutive scenes upon the innermost walls of the holy of holies in the temple of Luxor..."

1) Massey, AE, 880. 2) Massey, HJ, 100. 3) Massey, BD, 66-67. 4) Jackson, CBC, 169.

Christ's biblical connections with Pisces

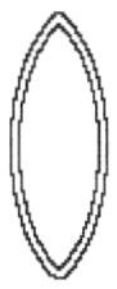

The RU

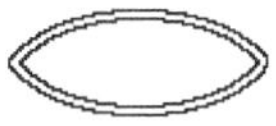

Christ's connection with Pisces is evident; he is linked with Fish symbols:

1. He was born at the dawn of the Age of Pisces and is symbolized as Ichthys, meaning Fish in Greek.
2. Picked fishermen as his disciples, declares to make them "fishers of men."
3. Told Peter to find gold in the fish's mouth (Mat. 17:27).
4. Fed fish to the multitudes and to the Seven.
5. Performed the miraculous draught of fish.
6. Is represented with fish in the ancient catacombs under Rome.
7. "Jeshua the son of Nun" = Jesus Son of Pisces (Neh. 8:17). Jeshua and Jesus are variants of the same name. Another variant is "Non" and "Jehoshuah," the sons of Ephraim (1Chro. 7:27). In the Hebrew alphabet, "N" is called and spelled "Nun" which means Fish.

"Now, the Ru () represents the fish's mouth; it is also the emaning mouth of that fish which gives forth birth to water as the life of the world and the Saviour who comes to Egypt by water as the water of the inundation or overflow of the Nile. When the grown is parched and dry, the overflow or inundation occurs and thus brings life, gladness and plenty to all those who depend on the fructification of seeds; etc., planted to maintain life, representing symbolically 'the water of life,' 'the saviour of life,' etc., and in conjunction with, would represent originally 'the Great One,' 'the Great Saviour of Life'" [2]

Christ Identified himself with *Jonah*, who represent Fish/Pisces

When the Pharisees sought a "sign from heaven," Christ said "there shall no sign be given...but the sign of the prophet Jonas...For as Jonas became a sign unto the Ninevites, so shall also the Son of Man be to this generation" (Mat. 16:1,4). This "sign" was Pisces the Fish; Jonas (Jonah) is the sign of the Fish. He spent 3 days in the belly of a great fish (Jonah 1:17). The names John, Jonah, Jonas and Oannas are derived from Egyptian AN (fish, water, being). Jonas is the biblical version of the Babylonian Fish-god Oannas (also called Dagon) who appeared for the instruction of humanity. In the Talmud, the Messiah is called DAG meaning Fish. God sends Jonah to city of Nineveh (Nin-Eveh) meaning Holy Lady Eve,[1] named after Lady Nina (Fish Mother) which is derived from Nun. Nun is the Kamite word for the Primal Ocean (called "Space" by the Europeans) and origin of the Hebrew letter Nun, meaning fish. Jonah was immersed three days in the ocean for the salvation of the Ninevites, as Jesus afterward was buried three days for the salvation of humanity. Christ is establishing himself as the Avatar (Messiah) of the Piscean Age by connecting himself to Jonah the Fish-Man, and to John the Baptizer. Both Jonah and John are forms of the Christ. The Age of Pisces began in 255 B.C. As the Messiah of the Piscean Age, Christ also incorporates the previous form of the avatar (in Aries) and is thus regarded as the Lamb.

John decreases, Jesus increases

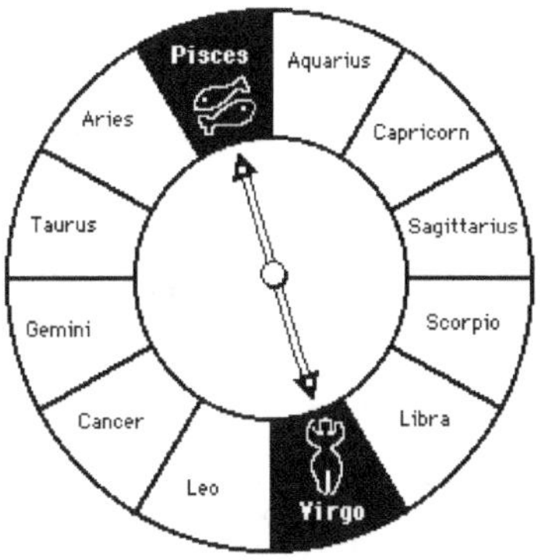

John is born six months *before* Christ. He represents the Son the Water-Mother (Virgo), while Christ represents the Son of the Fish-Mother (Pisces). Virgo and Pisces are opposite each other and stand six months apart. Virgo is on the Western equinox point, Pisces is on the East. John the Baptist, who got beheaded (Mark 6:27) said, "He [Christ] must increase, but I must decrease" (John 3:30). Astrologically, as a constellation or star sinks below the horizon in the West, its opposite constellation rises in the East. So as John went down ("decreased"), Christ rose up on the world ("increased"). The equinoxes and solstices equally marked the births and deaths of John and Jesus. John is born June 25th, shortly after the Summer Solstice, so that he began to decline immediately. Jesus's birthday is assigned to December 25th, shortly after the Winter Solstice so that he rises or increases.

1) Walker, WE, 288. 2) Churchward, SS, 373-374.

Born as Water, Reborn as Fire: The unsuspected significance of Virgo & Pisces with John & Jesus

Baptist-John and Baptized-Christ

Jesus the Christ and John the Baptist were cousins; in reality they are two polarities of the same being: a disguised version of *twins*. They were *both* born as a result of divine visitation and announced by the same angel.[1] John said, "I indeed baptize you with *water*...but he that cometh after me is mightier than I...he shall baptize you with the Holy Ghost, and with *fire*.[2]

Mortal Water-Man John	Immortal Fire-God Christ
Water-Birth = the Lower Natural Aspect John is born 6 months *before* Christ. He represents the Son of the Water-Mother, Virgo. He is a type of the natural *First* Birth by Water. He baptizes by Water only (Mat. 11:11).	**Fire-Rebirth = the Higher Spiritual Aspect** Jesus is born 6 months *after* John. He represents the Son of the Fish-Mother, Pisces. He is a type of the spiritual *Second* Birth by Fire. He baptizes "with the Holy Spirit and with *fire*."
Virgo as the Water-Mother, represents the *first* birth of the Natural Human by Water; all birth in the natural world is by or in water; all babies are born in a sac of water. Plus our physical bodies are 2/3rds water.	Pisces as the Fish-Mother, represents the *second* birth of the Spiritually Evolved Human by Fire and the Holy Spirit. Pisces is the sign of the birth of Saviors; Jesus, Heru, Ioannes, Vishnu and others came as *Ichthys*, "fish" in Greek. The Fish was the earliest symbol of Christ and is found in the catacombs.
Water refers to our lower or animal-human-earthly aspect This is symbolized by the following: • John represents First Birth, Mortality, born in the Flesh or Begotten of Woman. Christ calls John the greatest of those Born of Women (Mat. 11:11). • He baptizes by Water only. • John's name is derived from Kamite *An*, of which two meanings are *fish* and *water!* • John wears animal skin (camel fur /hair, leather) (Mark 1:6, Mat 3:4). 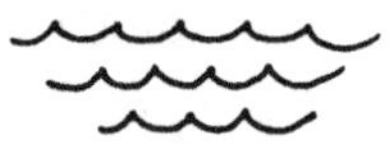	**Fire refers to our higher or divine-spiritual aspect** This is symbolized by the following: • The Holy Spirit *Dove* (symbol of the Great Mother) descends upon Christ at the time of his baptism (Spiritual Rebirth), and the voice of the Father declares Christ to be His Son, thus Christ is Begotten of God. His face shone like the sun.[3] • He is called the *Lion* of the Tribe of Judah. Lion= *Leo* a Fire sign. • An item *left* out the Gospels was that at Jesus's baptism by John, "a fire was kindled in the waters of Jordan."[4] This matches the Egyptian "a burning within the sea." 

1) Luke 1:5-56. 2) Matthew 3:11. 3) Ibid., 17:2. 4) Kuhn, LL, 15, 273.

The Virgo-Pisces theme disguisedly repeats in the Gospels as...

Two Mothers

Most of the Saviors, Christ and Horus included, are represented as having two mothers. Now you know why: their first mother represents the natural **First Birth** by *Water* (Virgo as the Water-Mother). Their second mother represents the **Second Birth** by *Spirit/Fire* (Pisces as the Fish-Mother).

Two places of origin

In addition to having two mothers (Mary the Virgin and Mary the wife of Cleophas), Jesus is represented as having two places of origin; Bethlehem and Nazareth, again signifying Virgo and Pisces. Bethlehem means House of Bread (Beth=house. Lehem, Lekhem = Bread). Bethlehem represents Virgo, which was known as the astrological "House of Bread" because this constellation contains the great star Spica, "the spike of wheat." Thus Virgo is always represented holding a *spike* of *wheat.*

Despite being born in Bethlehem, Christ is discrepantly represented as "Jesus of Nazareth." Nazareth did not physically exist during Jesus's time so he could <u>not</u> have been from this town. But Nazareth did exist astrologically in that it symbolized Pisces. Nazareth is from Nazar, meaning consecrated to God, thus Nazareth becomes the symbol of the Spiritual aspect denoted by Pisces, the Fish-Mother of the Spiritual, Evolved Human.

Christ's 5 loaves & 2 fish = Virgo & Pisces

The Virgo-Pisces theme is yet repeated in Christ's miracle of feeding the multitude with just five loaves of bread and two fish (Mark 6:38).

- The five loaves of bread =Virgo, who is always represented holding a spike of *grain* with *five* kernals. The constellation of Virgo contains the great star Spica, the spike of wheat, thus Virgo was also known as the "House of Bread."
- The two fish = Pisces, which is always represented as Two Fish.
- The *12* baskets of leftovers = the 12 zodiacal signs (Mark 6:43).

The 5 Johns & 5 Books of John

The name John outnumbers all the names of biblical books. Considering that Jonah and John are variations of the same name, then the Bible has a generous total of five books named John! They are Jonah, John, John1, John2, and John3. And there are five major representations of Johns in the Bible:

1) Jonah
2) John of the four Apostles (Matthew, Mark, Luke, John)
3) John the Baptizer
4) John of the three Books of John
5) John of Revelations

That there are 5 Johns both emphasizes Earth (Virgo) and Water (Pisces):

- **EARTH**: the "five Johns," like the five loaves of bread signify Virgo. Number Five as the pentacle is the symbol of the Black Virgin Kar (Kore), the Heart-Soul of Earth.
- **WATER**: the name John itself, which is derived from Kamite Aan (On), of which two meanings are *water* and *fish*. Jonah exemplified both in being swallowed by a huge fish in whose belly he dwelled for three days submerged in the *ocean*. Plus Jonah was connected with the city of NUN, a word meaning Fish in Hebrew, derived from Kamite *nun* which yields "*inundation*."

The Divine alchemy of Baptism

In his baptism, Horus the Word-Made-Flesh transformed into the Word-Made-Truth. In his baptism, Jesus the Son of Man became the Christ, the Son of God. Like Horus, the first Jesus was born of the Virgin Mother, not begotten, while the second or reborn baptized Jesus was begotten of the Father. We are born first as human by Water, and reborn later as divine by Fire. The first birth is represented by Virgo; the second birth by Pisces. Pisces is the "house" in which the Christ-ed man/woman comes to spiritual re-birth. In ancient times, children were baptized first with water, later with smoke.[1]

True baptism is supposed to be a new birth, a spiritual rebirth, a transformation. This probably happened when the ceremony was authentic, prior to Hebrew-European corruption. But the ceremonies of today apparently lack this power. It seems that the only thing that happens really, is that the baptized person gets *wet*.

Divine Fermentation

Horus did it. Christ did it. They turned Water into Wine. Horus puts grapes into the water and "the water of Teta is as wine even as that of Ra."[2] The transmutational rebirth is symbolized by the miracle of turning water to wine. Wine is born or made of Water but reborn as 'Spirit' through fermentation. Wine has been regarded as a symbol of divine rebirth. Turning water to wine was the first miracle performed by Jesus, right after his baptism where he himself had undergone transmutation or spiritual rebirth though "divine fermentation." This was the *beginning* of his miracles according to the Gospels (John 2:7-11).

So what does all this mean?

It further shows that the Gospel Jesus was Heru, the Solar Christ! In the Age of Taurus he was the Golden Calf worshipped by the Israelites. In the Age of Aries he was the Lamb of God. In the Age of Pisces he was the Fish of God. Now, in the Age of Aquarius he becomes the biblical "Son of Man". And who was the "father" of this "Son of *Man*"? Let's find out! ...

1) Kuhn, LL, 389. 2) Ibid., 254.

Who was the "father" of the "Son of Man"?

If Jesus was the Son of God *only*, then no physical man was his "father," yet he is repeatedly called the "Son of *Man*" in the New Testament. In addition, the only two genealogies of Christ (by Matthew & Luke) are the genealogy of Joseph, clearly pointing to Joseph, not God, as the "father" of Jesus:

- Matthew (1: 1, 2, 16): "The Book of the generation of Jesus Christ, the son of David...Abraham begat Isaac...Matthan begat Jacob; And Jacob begat Joseph the husband of Mary, of whom was born Jesus, who is called Christ."
- Luke (3:23, 38): "And Jesus himself began to be about thirty years of age, being (as was supposed) the son of Joseph, which was the son of Heli, ...Which was the son of Adam, which was the son of God."

Jesus is called "the seed of David according to the flesh" (Rom. 1:3). If *step-father*-Joseph was *not* Christ's father, but Christ is still descended from the "royal blood" of King David, then Christ's lineage would have to be traced through Mary his Mother! The genealogy then, belongs to Virgin Mary, making Her the Queen which She is anyway. The rewriters' chauvinism trips them; they can't stand giving credit to the Female Aspect. Trying to make sense of all this as if these were physical people exposes the nonsense of it all. It makes sense only in the light of its astrological roots. The personages referred to in the scriptures are really celestial bodies.

The real meaning of "Son of Man"

- The real meaning of Son of Man is "**Son of Woman & Man**" (i.e., Human, terrestrial, Earthly, physical, Night). As previously described, this is the natural First Birth by Water.
- The real meaning of Son of God is "**Son of Goddess & God**" (i.e., Divine, celestial, Heavenly, spiritual, Day). This is the Second Birth by Fire (Light).

One is *not better* or higher or greater, just the manifestation in the material plane of Divinity. In other words, the "Word" made "Flesh." The *Word* (Divinity, Son of God) made *Flesh* (Human, Son of Man). Having already concluded this, I was surprised to find clear, scriptural support in the following verses from 1Corinthians (15:40, 44, 47, 48):

> "There are also celestial bodies, and bodies terrestrial; but the glory of the celestial is one, and the glory of the terrestrial is another. ..It [resurrection of the dead] is sown a natural body; it is raised a spiritual body. There is a natural body, and there is a spiritual body. ...The first man [Son of Man!] is of the earth, earthy; the second man [Son of God!] is the Lord from heaven. As is the earthy, such are they also that are earthy; and as is the heavenly, such are they also that are heavenly."

This is also why Christ had two mothers and why the Apostles and sons of Jacob, etc., have two names. The first name is their Mother /Matter / Terrestrial/ Dark name. The second name is their Father / Ethereal / Celestial / Bright name...or vice versa when "reversals" are considered; an example being Mary the Virgin Mother of seven children = Mary Magdalene the Harlot of seven demons. Thus *Jedidiah* becomes *Solomon*; *Jacob* becomes *Israel*; *Benoi* becomes *Benjamin*; and *Jesus the Son of Man* becomes *Christ the Son of God.*

The Double Names relate directly to the Karast (anointed mummy). The ***Human*** becomes the ***SAHUman*** or godman, like the ***Caterpillar*** becomes the ***Butterfly***. Like the Caterpillar in its cocoon made of one incredibly long thread of silk, the Human-mummy-caterpillar is wrapped in a single piece of linen that is hundreds of YARDS long!

Thus the Cruci*fixion* is Cruci-Fiction about the Crossifixion

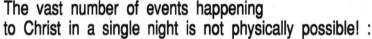

Yes, the Crucifixion did happen, but not as described in the rewritten Bible. And yes, Christ was crucified, but not as described in the same Bible. The Crucifixion was and still is a celestial event. The Lamb of God (Aries) is crucified each Spring Equinox. Hence **X** means Cross, Christ, "criss-cross" (KRS-Cross), and to cross out. (See review on the next page.)

In the Catacombs, were images of Christ appear for the first time, there are no images of a crucified Christ!

"The crucifixion was not a symbol of the earliest church; no trace of it can be found in the Catacombs." [1] The historical Herod who sought to slay baby Jesus, died four years before the date of the Christian era, assigned for the birth of Jesus. The Bible admits that the Crucifixion was spiritual and that it happened in Egypt: "**...and Egypt, where also our Lord was crucified**" (Rev. 11:8); thus admitting the Kamite origin of Christ as Heru who *was* crucified there! "Out of Egypt have I called my Son (Mat. 2:15).

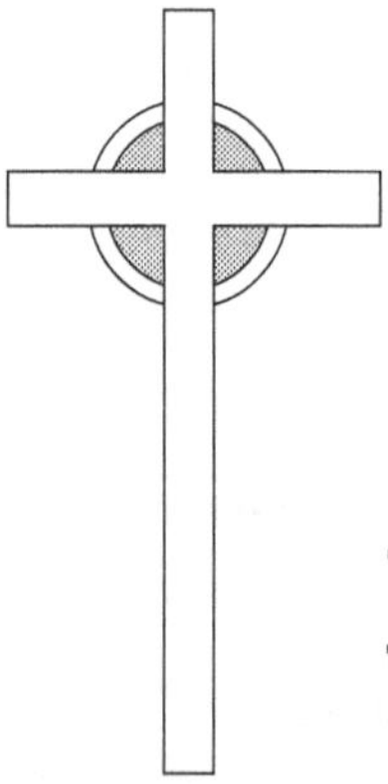

"The Egyptians...had no fall of man to encounter in the fallacious Christian sense. Consequently they had no need of a redeemer from the effects of that which had never occurred. They did not rejoice over the death of their suffering saviour because his agony and shame and bloody sweat were falsely supposed to rescue them from the consequences of broken laws; on the contrary, they taught that everyone created his own karma here, and that the past deeds made the future fate." [2]

The vast number of events happening to Christ in a single night is not physically possible! :

- the Last Supper with his disciples.
- the walk to the Mount of Olives.
- the long watch in the garden of Gethsemane.
- the disciples falling asleep several times with Jesus scolding them.
- the betrayal and arrest of Jesus.
- Peter cutting off a soldier's ear and Jesus healing the ear.
- ***three* separate and distinct judicial trials** involving the summoning of judges, juries, attendants, officers, and the populace in the *dead of night.*
- the whipping of Jesus, the crowning Jesus with thorns.
- the soldiers' mockery of Jesus; their parting of Jesus's garments.
- marching Jesus to the hill of Golgotha.
- the Crucifixion, running into the next morning.

It is not physically, humanly, or realistically possible for all these events to have happened to one person in a brief single night. But *astrologically* it is possible, being the astrological truth.

What is the Crucifixion doing in the OLD Testament?

In the NEW Testament, on the cross Jesus uttered "My God, my God, why hast thou forsaken me?" And when he dies, his garments are parted amongst the soldiers.
In the OLD Testament, the alleged King David utters: "My God, my God, why hast thou forsaken me?...the wicked have inclosed me: they pierced my hands and my feet...They part my garments among them, and cast lots upon my vesture" (Psalms 22: 1, 16, 18). What does this signify? A lot! Including : the biblical Jesus and David are two versions of the same Solar Christ (the Sun), hence mythological as humans.

Jesus descends from four forms of the Harlot

The only four female ancestors listed in Christ's genealogy are four forms of the Harlot. They are Thamar, Rahab, Ruth, and Bathsheba –each of whom is a 'stranger in Israel' and not a Jewish woman (2Sam. 11:3; 12:24; 1Ki. 1:15, 31; 2:13; Heb. 11:31; Mat. 1:5). The significance of there being "four" = the Great Mother of the Four Corners of the Astrological Cross. The names of all these women are associated with the Great Mother. Such "history" only proves the mythos.

1) Doane, 520. 2) Massey, AE, 230.

A *Cruci*-al Review of the *Crossi-Cruci*-fixion

(from pages 150-152)

Person, Event, Item:	Disguised astrological significance. Celestial Body or Solar Event allegorized:
Passover (about Mar 25)	Spring Equinox (arrival of Spring). Passover was to be the beginning of the new year. It is an approximation of the Vernal (Spring) Equinox. Passover superficially referred to the angel of death 'passing over' the homes of the Hebrews in Goshen smeared with the blood of a slain lamb. In reality, Passover refers to the Sun "passing over" or crossing the Celestial Equator at the Spring Equinox when Night and Day are of equal length all over the world.
The Slain Lamb of God	Aries the Ram. The slain lamb was the Lamb of God, slain each year, and "slain from [since] the foundation of the world" (Rev. 13:8). This Lamb (baby Ram) was the constellation Aries the Ram, which is obliterated ("slain") when "the Lord" (Sun) "passed over" the Celestial Equator. The custom of dressing the Paschal Lamb in the shape of a cross originates from this.
Easter (in March or late as April 25)	Easter is an approximation of the Spring Equinox. Easter celebrates the Crossing of the Celestial Equator by the Sun. Easter, a roving date, is the first Sunday after the first full moon after the Spring Equinox (Mar 21), therefore it cannot be the date of the death of any historical personage. The Crucifixion or Crossing was, and still is determined by the full moon of Easter.
The Crucifixion	The Crucifixion (from crux, meaning cross) is the "Crossification" or intersection of the Ecliptic and Equator. In other words it is the "Heavenly Cross" created by the Ecliptic (sun's path) crossing the Celestial Equator on the *Spring Equinox.* (The Celestial Equator is a projection of Earth's equator into space.)
The Crucifixion-Slaying of the *Lamb* of God	At the time of the Spring Equinox, the constellation of Aries the Ram is temporarily hidden or obliterated (symbolically slain) when the Sun passed over, that is, CROSSED the Equator. This "crossing" is the Crucifixion; the Sun is "crucified" or crossed at the intersecting lines of the Ecliptic & Equator at the moment of his descent into the lower hemisphere, the hemisphere of darkness and death; and so again at the moment of his resurrection into the hemisphere of light and life, while the period of transit is three days.
Crucifixion site named Skull	Mt. Calvary or Golgotha both mean "skull" and was the name of the place where both, the biblical Christ and Krishna were crucified. The source of this imagery was the crucifixion of Osiris, the prototypical Christ, on the Spring Equinox, on the ARC of the Celestial Equator. This Equator forms a broad Arc through space which can be represented as a mount or rounded *Calvarium* (Latin for skull). Thus, on the celestial Calvary, the Sun is momentarily suspended (crucified) at the crossing.
The Savior dies	The Sun *sets*. There are *two* deaths and *two* births of the Sun: • A Death on December 22 (Winter Solstice). The event of the Sun setting on this date, shortest day of the year, was called the "Death of the Old Sun." Thus the forces of Darkness achieved victory as the Old Sun died with the sunset. This is followed three days later by the Birth of a new Sun on December 25, anciently called the "Birthday of the Sun." • A Death just prior to Easter, called the Crucifixion. This is the Sun crossing the Equator on March 21 (Spring Equinox), getting "crucified" or *crossed* at the intersecting lines of the Ecliptic and Equator. When this happens, the sign of the current age (Aries for example) is temporarily obliterated or "slain." Thus the Ram or Lamb of God is sacrificed or crucified. This Crucifixion is followed three days later by a second Birth (REbirth) of the Sun, called the Resurrection (Easter). This is really the arrival of Spring, heralding the resurrection of Light (days grow longer than nights) and thus Life.

Tracking down the historical human Jesus

The biblical Jesus Christ, as we have seen, is Heru plagiarized

When all the Heru-data is removed from the biblical Christ-data, nothing is left about "Christ." The whole, complete, entire story of Christ in the Bible is wholly, completely, entirely plagiarized and stolen from the Kamite story (allegory) of Heru the Sun. This Afrikan story existed thousands, if not tens of thousands of years before the biblical Christ. Christ Heru-Jesus was the Sun, that radiant solar orb in the sky that truly is the "Light of the World." The names Jesus, Jehoshua (Iu-Su), and Heru (Her-Iu) are from IU, a name of the Sun as the "Ever-Coming One." The entire story of Christ's biblical life is the story of the solar orb traversing the Zodiac signs. If there was a historical Jesus Christ, he was not the same as the plagiarized Jesus Christ of the Bible.

Outside of the Gospels, there is no bonafide historical data about a historical Christ,

for the meager existing "historical" information has been shown to be forgery: Tacitus's passage "concerning the name of Christ was obviously unknown to the Christian Fathers, and therefore non-extant." [1] Josephus's references to Jesus Christ are forged references [2] which he did not write, thus they fail as "proof" for a historical Jesus. None of Christ's famous biographers, Matthew, Mark, Luke, or John, are honored with a notice in history till 200 years after Christ's birth; and then the notice was by a Christian writer (Ireneus).[3]

Will the Real Historical Jesus Please Stand?

Was there a live, physical, historical Jesus underlying the Gospel Christ? The search for a physical historical Jesus leads to four eligible candidates:

- **Appollonius**
- **Issa**
- **Jehoshua ben Panthera** (Pandera)
- **"The Teacher of Righteousness"**

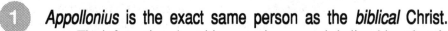

I have come to the following conclusions about these Christ-candidates:

1 *Appollonius* is the exact same person as the *biblical* Christ.

The information about him sometimes sounds believable, other times not believable. The story of his life is virtually indistinguishable from that of the biblical Christ. He too was a healer, miracle-worker, raised the dead, and cast out demons which sometimes "cut up" like those of Christ. His virgin-birth was foretold by an angel. He was transfigured like Christ, called a prophet, the Son of God, and the Light of the World. To top it off, he was crucified, arose from the dead, and ascended to Heaven. He is treated as a historical person by historians such as Hilton Hotema, Albert Kuhn, and Kersey Graves, who devotes several pages to him in *The World's Sixteen Crucified Saviors*. Therefore Appollonius is disqualified as the historical Jesus, being exposed as *Heru*, the original Egyptian Solar Christ. For the elements of his alleged life matches that of the Sun's annual history in allegory form.

1) Massey, HJ, 191. 2) Graves, WS, 323; Massey, HJ, 191. 3) Graves, WS, 324.

2 *Issa*, Appollonius, and the *biblical* Christ are the exact same person.

Briefly a Russian, N. Notovitch, gained access to ancient Indian manuscripts which he translated in the mid 1880s. The story of "Issa" which unfolded paralleled the story of the biblical Christ. In addition it included the so-called missing years of Christ (wherein he travels abroad). Issa and Jesus (note similarity of names) are apparently the same person. Issa's story is in *The Unknown Life of Jesus Christ* by N. Notovitch. A book called *The Aquarian Gospel of Jesus Christ* purports to be an *akashic* record of the Gospel Christ. Both Issa and the Aquarian Jesus travel to India, where, amongst other deeds, they denounce the caste system, inspire the outcast Untouchables, and are eventually chased out of India by a jealous priesthood that sits atop the caste system. This part of their story has a ring of historical probability. The Aquarian Gospel story is basically identical to the story of Issa. Therefore Issa is disqualified as the historical Jesus, being exposed as *Heru*, the original Egyptian Solar Karast (Christ). For the elements of his alleged life matches that of the Sun's annual history in allegory form.

3 *The Teacher of Righteousness* was not necessarily the historical Jesus.

The Essene Scrolls (Dead Sea Scrolls) predate the Gospel Jesus. These scrolls speak of the "Teacher of Righteousness." Some scholars assume this person was the Gospel Jesus. Szekely calls him Jesus Christ in his beautiful translations of Essene Scrolls from the Vatican. After all, this "Teacher" perfectly fits the image of "Christ." Other scholars believe the Teacher of Righteousness was Krishna. After all, this "Teacher" perfectly fits the image of "Krishna." I believe that the "Teacher of Righteousness" was neither Christ nor Krishna. The "Teacher of Righteousness" is ageless, and the original representation of him was the timeless Asar-Heru. For this "Teacher" perfectly fits the image of Asar, the original "Teacher of Righteousness" who, along with the Great Mother As-t, were apparently the true founders of the Essenes since the Essene teachings are but the cosmology of ancient Egypt! Therefore the "Teacher of Righteousness" is excluded as the historical Jesus, being exposed as the original Egyptian Karast-Christ.

4 Jehoshua ben Pandera comes closest, but...

The last candidate, Jehoshua ben Pandera, is the *darling* alleged "proof" of a historical Christ. Black historians argue well for his legitimacy. So do some white historians. For a long time, I too was convinced about him until I discerned deeper layers of inconspicuous truth. Let's look more closely...

Black Panther Jesus

Who was Jehoshua ben Pandera /Panthera? "Jesus, Son of the Panther." His name suggests he was a Black Afrikan High-Priest, for panthers are black and found in Afrika, and the panther-skin or leopard-skin was the badge of priesthood throughout Afrika. The Bible refers to Jesus as both, a "high priest" (Heb. 6:20, 8:1) and "the Lion of the tribe of Judah" (Rev. 5:5). Jehoshua ben Panthera lived a century before the Gospel Jesus. He learned "magic" in Egypt and wrought miracles, healing the sick and casting out demons. At the age of 50 or 60, in the city of Lud (Lydda), he was stoned to death by the *Jews* (Hebrews) as a sorcerer and hung on a tree to become accursed, on the eve of Passover. So the story goes.

Jehoshua ben Panthera is *99%* disqualified. His "1%" qualification is that he was apparently a real live human –called Jesus /Jehoshua (one of many with this name), who allegedly exercised spiritual powers /prowess, and may have even been ***anointed,*** hence a "Christ." However, he is 99% disqualified as the *main big central Jesus* for the following reasons:

- He was not crucified by the Romans; he was stoned to death by the Hebrews and hung on a tree to become accursed.
- His father was an Albino (a Roman soldier).
- He was an illegitimate child whose mother was a prostitute.
- **The above *slanderous* data** is from the **Hebrew *Talmud*,** where we learn about Jehoshua ben Pandera. Any information significantly pertaining to Blacks, and coming to us from Albinos is invariably not trustworthy, as proven by "his-story." Any truth they may contain is distorted, slanted, and poisoned. This is obvious in the Talmud for it obviously slanders Jesus (see Chapter 8) and is thus obviously untrustworthy.

Does Jesus's "double executions" point to *two separate Christs?*

Was *Panthera-Jesus* identical with the Gospel's *Militant Messiah?*

The who? Continue reading...

Black Warrior Jesus, the *Militant Messiah*

- Overturned the tables of the money-changers or salesmen (Habirus?) in the Temple, violently driving them out with a whip of cords.
- Declared, "I came not to send peace, but a sword" (Mat. 10:34).
- Two of his disciples were Zealots; Simon *Zelotes* and Simon Peter.
- Before his vigil in Gethsemane, he instructed his followers to equip themselves with swords, plus, shortly thereafter, Peter did actually draw his sword and chopped the ear off a minion in the high priest's entourage.
- Barashango identifies Jesus as a "Black nationalist freedom fighter... whose goals were to free the Black people of that day from the oppressive ...white Roman power structure and to build a Black nation." [1]
- *The Passover Plot* reports "Galilee, where Jesus had lived...which was the home of the Jewish resistance movement, suffered particularly. The Romans never ceased night and day to devastate ...pillage [and kill]." [2]
- In *The Black Messiah,* Cleage writes that Jesus was a revolutionary "who was leading a [Black] nation into conflict against an [white] oppressor...It was necessary that he be crucified because he taught revolution." [3]
- Jesus showing ethnic preference? He at first refused to heal a white woman (a Greek), and on top of that, called her a dog (Mark 7:24-29). He commanded his disciples to go <u>not</u> to the Gentiles (whites),"but go rather to the lost sheep of the house of Israel" (Mat. 10:5, 6), who were Black people, the original IUs being violently oppressed by the Gentiles.
- According to the Catholic Bible, it was a legion (6000!) of soldiers that came to arrest Militant Jesus –**who was executed by the Romans in a fashion reserved exclusively for revolutionary political activity!**

1) Barashango, 121. 2) Schonfield, *The Passover Plot,* 186. 3) A. B. Cleage, *The Black Messiah,* 91.

Jesus's "double executions" apparently point to *two separate Christs!*

Though called by the same name in the Bible, *Panthera-Jesus* and the *Militant Messiah* apparently were ***not*** the same men because each died differently. **The Bible reports the death of two Jesuses:**

- ### Jesus-1 died through *Roman* Crucifixion.

He was the ***Militant Messiah,*** a Black revolutionary, a Zealot-Essene (for they were one) *physically* fighting for Black freedom from *physical* Albino (Roman) oppression. He was executed by Crucifixion, a form of death reserved for revolutionists. Given the oppression and "occupation" of Black Palestine by the Albinos (Romans) at that time, it is likely that there were *many* militant messiahs. The one recorded in the Bible must have been *something else!*

- ### Jesus-2 died through *Hebrew* Stoning...

–ordered by Habiru-Hebrew priests! He was ***Jehoshua ben Panthera,*** *–spiritually* fighting to re-establish Israel's *spiritual* freedom from *spiritual* Albino (Hebrew, Edomite) oppression. Panthera was also something else, and made quite an impact, else why is he recorded in Hebrew writings? That they speak of him hostilely is further evidence they were likely the false Jews (Habirus, Edomites) who were already against Panthera and any like him from the beginning. The Bible and Talmud both speak of *a Jesus* getting stoned to death, then hung on a tree to become accursed. Both are apparently referring to the same man: Black Panther Jesus.

All this doubleness is the
Duality Principle (= 2)
The double-Jesus, double-Christ, double-executions. Recall from page 169 that Christ is both, the:
- Son of Man (Woman & Man) or Human /Earthly. The *Mother's* Son of the Flesh, Night, Water.
- Son of God (Goddess & God) or Divine /Celestial. The *Father's* Son (Sun) of Spirit, Day, Fire.

⊕

This is also
"Double Duality" (= 4)
or the Astrological Cross of the 4 Quarters / 4 Elements, uniting the Horizontal & Vertical Dualities (Polarities), or Feminine & Masculine Principles. For there are 2 Christs and 2 Jesuses/Executions:
1) as Son of Man (EARTH, Fem.)
2) as Son of God (FIRE, Masc.)
3) of Roman crucifixion (AIR; phallic cross put him high in the Air). Vertical path of piercing phallic linear spear/ nails. Masc.
4) of Hebrew Stoning/TreeHanging (WATER; water in circular feminine tree; path of circular spherical *thrown* stones is *horizontal* like water). Fem.

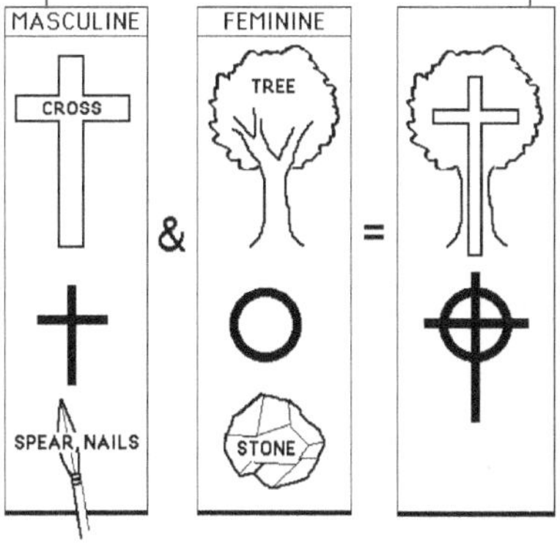

Jesus-2: Stoned & Hung

- **The process:** "And all the men ...shall stone him...that he die ...and thou hang him on a tree...for he that is hanged is accursed of God" (Deu. 21:21-23).
- **Galatians** describes Christ accursed by hanging on a tree: "Christ...being made a curse for us: for it is written, cursed is every one that hangeth on a tree" (Gal. 3:13).
- **Peter cites** Christ bore our sins "in his body on the tree" (1Pet. 2:24).
- **Finally** in Acts, the Apostles respond to the high priests (Habirus): "The God of our fathers raised up Jesus, whom **ye** [*high priests,* not Romans!] **slew** and hanged on a tree" (Acts 5:30).

The contradiction and impossibility of two different types of executions happening to the *same* person is resolved when we realize it is likely pointing to TWO separate messiahs!

(Note that the same Bible speaks of two separate creations of Man.) Recognizing the duality brings us closer to seeing the truth. The name *Jesus* was common during the time of Christ. The Bible itself speaks of both, other Jesuses *and* other *spirits* and *gospels*: "For if he that cometh preacheth another Jesus, whom we have not preached, or if ye receive another spirit, which ye have not received, or another gospel, which ye have not accepted, ye might well bear with him" (2Cor. 11:4). Josephus mentions more than 10 different people who bore the name of Jesus. And the term *Christ* is not a name but a title meaning *anointed.* So both messiahs apparently were named or called Jehoshua (Jesus in Hebrew).

And the critical question remains:

Was there a physical, live, breathing, historical Jesus underlying the plagiarized Gospel Christ?

My answer is... *YES!*

Having shown the most eligible candidates *ineligible* and disqualified, what basis do I have at all for a historical Christ? The following! :

1) I *feel* that there was a major incarnation of the *Christ Consciousness.*
2) Ancestors of the "Real People" Australian Aborigines recorded him.
3) A certain book I respect speaks of him in a way that aligns with the Afrikan and Cosmic truth.
4) People's past-life regressions sometimes reveal contact with *The Christ.*
5) Very little, if any, historical information from Albinos can be trusted, especially if it deals vitally with Afrikan People of Color.

Let me explain my reasons:

1 I *feel* that there was a major incarnation of the *Christ Consciousness*:

"Feeling" (not "believing" on faith) is a proven way of "knowing" the truth. "Truth" is a vibration that can be *felt.* Example: You read or hear about something and immediately have a "feeling" about it. You later come across information which confirms what you intuitively *felt.* I once read in a metaphysical book that at the beginning of each "Age" there is an incarnation of "the Christ Consciousness." I immediately *felt* a ring of truth to this! It seems that humanity cannot shake off this concept of a deific superbeing or Energy that *cyclically* comes, bringing great positive upliftment to the world. They can't shake it off because it is deeply rooted in cosmic truth despite all the distortions around it. "Lord of the Aeon" was a title of Asar.[1]

2 Ancestors of the "Real People" Australian Aborigines recorded him:

A white *sister* named Marlo Morgan documents her incredible story in her incredible book, Mutant Message. The book has a profound "message" from the "Real People" to the "Mutants" (Albinos), for many Mutants, according to the Aborigines, are on the verge of becoming "real people" at last. Actually, the book has an inspiring "message" for all people who read it. Morgan was the first *Mutant* in history to go on a *walkabout* with the 60+ *Real People.* She was privileged to witness their historical records on stone walls. These records stretched back eons, at least 50,000 years! Like their ancient Afrikan ancestors, the *Real People* have a profound connection with Nature and the Cosmos. They are natural healers, telepaths, artists, etc. The *Real People* have recorded all the significant events of global history. The fact that they documented the incarnation of *The Christed One* points to a live, breathing historical person belying **or covered up by** the plagiarized account of the Gospel Christ. I trust their historical records over that of the usually distorted orthodox Albino records.

1) Massey, HJ, 190.

3 A certain book I respect speaks of him in a way that aligns with the Afrikan and Cosmic truth:

Ancient holy books around the world, including the Bible all speak of extraterrestrial beings (ETs). The ancient Afrikans and all the ancient world cultures have recorded commonplace contact with ETs. According to information in *Bringers of the Dawn*, which the author Barbara Marciniak received from off-planet beings (Pleiadeans), a major incarnation of *The Christ* did occur around the time of the Gospel Jesus. He was a stunning success, a boxoffice hit! **He was massively well received!** In fact he was so universally well accepted and making such vast progress in steering the world into balance and healing that the Negative Forces had to do something to stop, reverse, and derail this, else loose their stranglehold upon Humanity. No they did not kill or crucify him. Repeat : they did NOT kill or crucify *The Christ.* They couldn't any way! They had not the power to do so, for *The Christ* was much too powerful and popular. Instead, they sabotaged and usurped his teachings, replacing it with counterfeit bastard teachings (Christianity, Judaism, etc.). They also countered the true Christ reality by inserting a 3-dimensional hologram-movie of false-reality into Palestine. Their 3D hologram movie portrayed the opposite (*lies*, in other words) about the true reality of *The Christ*, falsely depicting him rejected by the world and later crucified, when in reality, the true reality, neither of these occurred! If this sounds incredible, read the book for yourself before judging, and learn how massively you and everyone are *Deceived* on all levels.

4 People's past-life regressions sometimes reveal contact with *The Christ:*

When people are regressed into their past lifetimes, they sometimes discover they had a past life during Christ's human presence on Earth and their path crossed Christ's path, according to readings by psychics such as Edgar Cayce.

5 Very little if any, historical information from Albinos can be trusted, especially if it deals vitally with Black Afrikan People!

Given the background of Albinos in distorting, falsifying, sabotaging, and reversing the Afrikan truth, I do not trust their references, especially their religious and historical references. **The false Jews (Habiru-Hebrews) did not record *their* Messiah as ever having come.** The real IUs recognized from the beginning that their awaited Messiah came. The false pretender-Jews naturally rejected the Christed One. The real IUs naturally embraced him. It was the Habirus' story that got the press. The Albinos' war against Melanin and the things born of Melanin is really a war against the Principle of Life, thus Nature (the Great Mother) and the true Loving God. Whether they are called Habirus, Romans, Greeks, Aryans, or Europeans, they are consistent in their historical denigration and overthrow of the Afrikan Cosmic Truth.

Know this: the "Afrikan Truth" is not *ethnic*, it is cosmic, universal. This is why it has had and is still having such a vast impact upon Humanity. *The Christed One* represented this Cosmic Truth. Is it any wonder that we have little or no "his-*story*cal" references to him? Look at how well the Khazars (imposter European Jews) have erased their historic tracks, –so well that the Khazars are hardly known, let alone taught about in schools. I believe that Afrikan people did record *The Christed One*, and these records were destroyed, for the Albinos have notoriously destroyed and burned the ancient precious archives of Afrikans and People of Color around the world. **If one relies on Albino historical references for the truth,** they likely will not only fail to get the truth, but will get falsehood, pseudo truths, and bastardizations, as intended by the bastardizers. The "news" you watch on TV comes across as objective reporting. It is not so! It is heavily censored and slanted. The misinformation and disinformation and withheld information is more powerful than the "information." In other words, it's what you are NOT being told that is the *most* important–and is having the greatest effect on you!

Yes the historical true Christ-in-the-flesh was recorded by the true IUs (Essenes, Nazorenes, original Black Jews, etc.). And those records were effectively demolished, for the *White Lie* cannot live in the presence of the *Black Truth.* And this was a Truth that was so strong, so vital, so liberating, that its references had to be destroyed, rewritten, rescripted. But the light of truth can never be put out fully. All it takes is for one tiny flame of truth to grow into a raging fire that burns down the thick forest of imprisoning lies, so that the truth can set all of us free!

In the 1960s, the March to Washington D.C. by Black Americans could not be stopped by the Albinos, so the Albinos joined them and took over the March, directing it, appearing to be helpers. And at 7 or whatever o'clock, they told everyone (the Blacks) to go home! And guess what? They did! Thus the March was not allowed to reach its true climax, it was thwarted. I believe the same thing happened with the "March" of the Christed One. **Yes we are told of a Christ but he is a bastardized reversed version of the *True Christed One.*** And we are told he was crucified and "died" for our sins, to save us from eternal Hellfire. He was neither crucified, nor died for anyone's sins *(a dead body does not bleed after the heart stops; so why did dead Christ bleed when pierced in the side?)*; and he is no one's "Savior" as such. For Hell is a vast lie and, along with "Salvation", are effective control mechanisms to manipulate people through fear (*terror*, actually). Everyone is squarely responsible for themselves and their deeds. When you "die" and wake up on the other side of Life, you discover you are ***still*** responsible for you! Always! We cannot escape personal responsibility (ability to respond).

The true message of the Christed One was likely a message of resurrecting HEART or LOVE within ourselves. This can only happen when we first accept and love ourselves. Then we can accept the Creator's Love for us. When this happens, we are on the road to true total **Quantum Healing**; it is this Healing that is our true Salvation!

We got a fraudulent Bible, fraudulent God, fraudulent Christ, from Masters of Fraud who work for the Deceiver. The fraudulent story of the fraudulent Christ is to derail, distract, and rob us of the true story of the Real Christ. The fraudulent Gospel story of Christ has just enough juicy, obvious "truth" or "good teachings" in it to make it seem like it's OK (just like the dangerous commercial killer-food seems OK in their beautiful packages in the supermarkets). But the points of vital liberating truth have been reversed, making them lies which shackle the consciousness of those who "eat" (believe) them. And note that these Counterfeit Religions all stress that you "believe." See the "lie" in believe? Truly "knowing" the truth (not "believing" what you don't know) was the Afrikan way, the Cosmic way. Afrikan minds have been shackled under the Lie or bastardized, pseudo, Albino-ed truth for some 2000 years. Albino minds too! And all shades in-between. When will all People open to the real truth and set ourselves free? It IS possible. We CAN do it. The time is always *now*. It begins with *intent*.

"Gwynth" an Afrikan American prophet speaks on *The Christ*

Prophecy was a natural part of Afrikan life. The Essenes were reknown for their skills of prophecy. We all have this so-called "6th sense" which manifests in different ways. It is *natural*, not "supernatural" as misleadingly labeled. A truly gifted Afrikan American prophet, whom I have been especially blessed to meet, is "Gwynth." *Gwendolyn Hayes* calls herself a "reader," which is a modern term for a prophet. "Gwynth works with her Spirit Guides to bring messages through from your loved ones, your Spirit Guides [a.k.a. guardian angels], and Spirit Teachers." Author of *And the Woman by the Well Drank Wine,* she is a graphic designer who is completing her doctoral studies in Industrial Psychology. She has lectured throughout the southwest and led numerous workshops and seminars in Self-Development and Spiritual Growth. In the south's Bible Belt, in Yukon, OK where she resides, Black churches do the same thing she does except they call it *prophecy.* The Bible is largely a book of prophecy and this points back to its Afrikan origin. Prophecy is still alive and well amongst Afrikan people around the globe. *Saint* Harriet Tubman was a great Afrikan American prophetess whose 6th-sense inner antenna made it possible for her to safely accomplish many perilous journeys on the Underground Railroad, and lead hundreds of slaves to freedom. Modern living Afrikan American prophets are discussed in Company of Prophets, by J. Nell. Prophecy helps bring in the light so we may see, discern, and know the truth, and thereby be guided along the path of our highest happiness. After I had already come to my previously stated conclusions about *The Christ,* I asked Gwynth for her views on Christ. She relayed the following, which are not direct quotes but almost. As with our Afrikan ancestors, the sources of her information are her *Higher Self* (Divine Spark in all of us) and her "spirit guides."

Please share your views and insights on "Christ" and the "Christ Consciousness" ?

The Christ Energy and the human form of Christ came simultaneously on Earth. It was actually God or the Consciousness of God having the experience of man. There was a Christ Consciousness and a Christ Incarnate (human form). When the human form or Christ Incarnate came to Earth, the Christ Consciousness came simultaneously but you could not see it. It was invisible. An illustration of this is Nelson Mandela; he walks into the room and you know that the room changed. When the human Christ Incarnate came into the earthplane, bringing with him the Christ Consciousness, humanity knew that something had changed. The Christ Consciousness is so powerful, it cannot be contained in just a room; it filled the whole atmosphere of Earth! And so simultaneously around the world, everybody got to experience the Christ Consciousness without necessarily meeting the human Christ Incarnate.

The Energy of the Christ Consciousness permeated the entire planet, radiating from The Christ Incarnate. The Energy of the Christ Consciousness came down with him. Christ's consciousness of who he was as a spiritual being was not contained in just the physical location of his physical body. So when he was in Egypt, he was in Greece, when he was in Greece, he was in Judea, when he was in Judea he was in Libya. He was in all these places simultaneously just like God is. When his physical embodiment came, he came like a Light, and this Light added a tremendous, great Energy to the earthplane. For this Light was all over the planet simultaneously. It lifted the consciousness of man.

What is the purpose of this "Christ Energy"?

The purpose is to remind man what he can become. The Christ Consciousness Energy is renewed each time the Christ Consciousness returns. This Christ Energy is usually renewed as a *virtue*, such as Love, Patience, Understanding, or some area where man is deficient. Actually, the Christ Consciousness Energy is always with us! It gets diffused by all the other energies upon the planet. All is the Energy of the One. With our finite minds, we are unable to understand that everything and everyone embodies the Christ Consciousness, or the God Consciousness, Creator Consciousness. It descended upon the world like a veil, though the manifestation was in one person, a human form we could focus on. Christ did many things we have no evidence of, including *bilocation [being in multiple places simultaneously].*

What was Christ's purpose for coming to Earth?

Christ came as a Way Shower, to show the Way, nothing more.

Showing what "way"? What is this "Way"?

The way to remember who we are and our way back to the Loving Divine Creator. Christ came as a Way Shower to remind man of our Divinity, Divineness. The miracles he performed was to remind us of the things we can do, because in all the changing and manipulation of our genes, we lost our *memory* about our power. This *memory* is still lost, but it is simple to remember our power and how to use it. *[addressed in another volume]*

They *[the Greys and other ETs or extraterrestrial beings]* were given permission by other energies to co-habitate with us. These ETs did a lot of manipulations to make us doubt what the Way Shower gave us. Earth is a *Freewill Zone*, and any and all energies existing within this environment have Freewill. The thing that makes it so difficult is that we don't know what Freewill is any more, because it has been so greatly manipulated. And **we have been given a set of belief systems that hold the manipulations in place.**

This is like a muffler on a dog. A dog may have strong teeth and an excellent body, but if the owner wants to contain or restrain the dog, they put a muzzle and leash on it. This is what these belief systems are doing to us; they have muzzled and leashed us. We are tied to belief systems, and the muzzle prevents us from sinking our teeth into the truth. Because a dog with a muzzle on him cannot eat and **what we need to eat or sink our teeth into is the truth of who we are!** We have not been allowed to do that! And so Christ came as a Way Shower, hoping that by seeing his example, it would jog our memories and break us free from the beliefs systems by which we are imprisoned. And it did work for a while, but man fell into a deep sleep. For there are things in place, such as Money, that has become the God or Creator-substitute. People substitute their power, control, and self for money. And everything revolves around the thought of money, or having enough money. For example, people drive down the street preoccupied with thoughts of paying various bills. They are giving a lot of thought to money or the lack of it. Whatever you give a lot of your thought to becomes your God.

The book <u>Bringers of the Dawn</u> said ETs inserted a "hologram implant" into earthplane 3-D reality, which falsely projected Christ as being crucified. Did this really happen?

Yes. When children watch a movie, it seems real to them. Some ETs also fool us the same way Hollywood does. Many UFOs are holograms.

When was Christ born; at or before 0 B.C.?

Before.

How much before?

Whatever time I give in manmade terms would not be adequate since numerical or manmade time as we know it today did not exist at that time. He was born a "period" of time before B.C.

Was it roughly 100 or 200 years before B.C.?

I would say a 100, though not as we think of a hundred.

Where was he born?

In Egypt on the continent of Afrika. He was *not* born in Palestine –and the geographical boundaries of this area were very different then. *[This recalls "Out of Egypt have I called my Son" (Mat 2:15)].*

Was he born east or west of the Nile river?

West of the Nile.

How long did he live.

Between 35 to 40 earthyears.

Did Christ physically die or did he ascend?

He *ascended*, he did not physically die.

Where did he live?

He was nomadic. He traveled extensively.

Did Christ go to India, China, and Asia?

Yes. He went all over, throughout Asia.

Was Buddha an incarnation of the Christ Consciousness or same Essence manifested as The Christ?

He was a "part" of the Christ Consciousness because the Christ Consciousness was never received in its entirety. The Christ Consciousness came in parts and Buddha was a part of it. *[Likely, Jehoshua ben Panthera was also.]*

Does the Christ Consciousness come to Earth at the beginning of each Age?

Parts or facets of this Consciousness does because it is multifaceted, the facets being Love, Generosity, Enlightenment, Integrity, etc.

Who was the "Teacher of Righteousness" of the Essene Scrolls?

It was not a person or human form; the Teacher of Righteousness is a *Period* during which a *Facet* of Christ Consciousness is focused upon. –A Period set aside during which a particular *Vibrational Truth* is sent out or radiated to everything from the Father /Mother of the Godhead. Every generation has a lesson to learn. Living is an evolutionary process. We are all on an evolutionary journey. During Christ's time, the Teacher or Focus was *Enlightenment.* For our present time, the Focus is Healing –*Spiritual Healing.*

12

The Disguised Zodiacs *Composing* the Entire Bible!

Astrology or the Zodiac is the disguised central theme of the Bible!

The greatest and most abundant evidence for this is in the Bible itself! This chapter exposes this hidden truth that has been cleverly concealed for thousands of years. Now is the time for Awakening –or Re-Awakening to the vital truths stolen from us. –Vital truths which we need in order to HEAL, become truly *whole* again, to get back our true minds and break the *Spell* of Deception and Lies that has held us in its grip for too long.

SOLAR ZODIAC

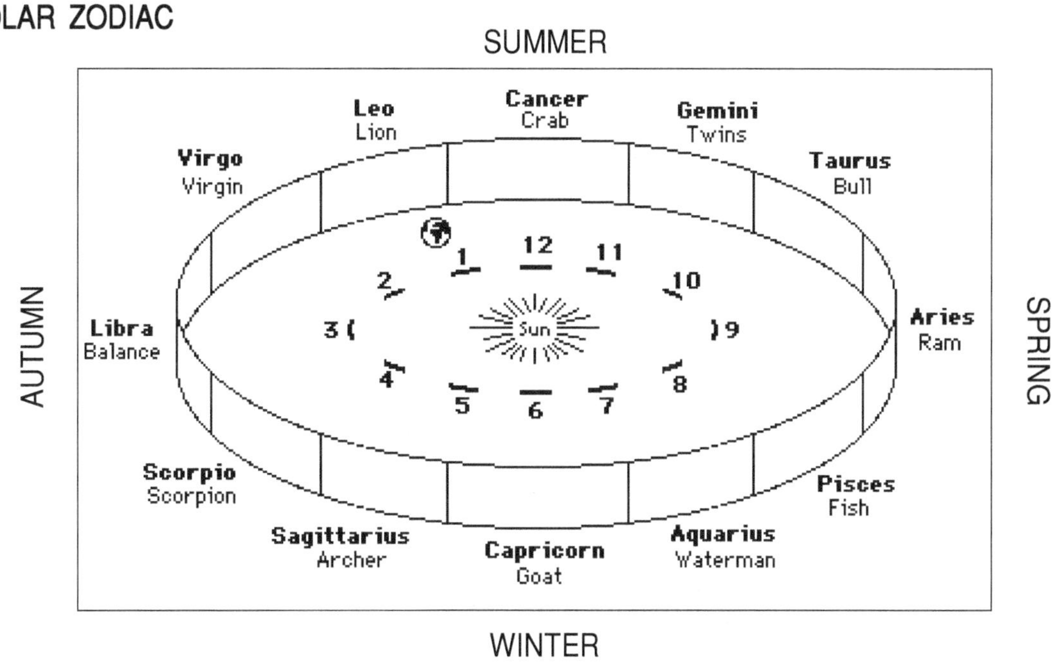

Above, the signs of the Solar Zodiac are represented as a belt to be imagined at a practically infinite distance among the stars. The Sun is in the center, and the dotted circle indicates the Earths's orbit (numerals 1,2,3...) standing for the places of the Earth in the corresponding months of the year. Thus in January, to the observer at 1, the Sun appears to be in Aquarius; in February it appears in Pisces, and so forth. The illustration shows these relative positions as they were 3000 years ago. Now, due to the Precession of the Equinoxes (whereby the Zodiac seems to slip backwards a sign every few thousand years), the place of the Spring Equinox has moved to the right, and is in Pisces, and not far from Aquarius. Thus the Precession has skewed the zodiac almost a full month out of place. This means that we are actually born under the sign ahead of the sign we are born under.

Incredibly, our Solar System describes a huge circle around another Sun called Sirius.

Jackson quotes an English scholar: "Our entire solar system with all its planets and moon describes a huge circle around another sun in space, *viz.*, the star Sirius. This movement takes 25,920 years to complete and, during that time, our Sun appears to traverse through various constellations or star clusters." [1] No wonder the ancient Afrikans gave special status to star Sirius, as do the Dogon people today (who have maintained their matriarchal Afrikan roots). The Afrikans divided this huge circle into twelve sections (–likely *thirteen* sections originally, in the *Lunar* Zodiac preceding the Solar Zodiac), which they called Houses or Mansions, and gave each House a name and appropriate symbol. Each House is a period of 2,160 years which the Afrikans called an Age. Twelve of these ages in the *Solar* Zodiac makes up one complete Turn of our solar system.

As Earth makes a full revolution in 24 hours, all the Zodiac constellations follow each other through the sky,

with a new one rising over the Eastern Horizon every 2 hours. And as Earth advances in its orbit around the Sun, the Sun appears to rise in a different sign each month, thus passing through each Zodiac sign during its annual circuit of the heavens. During the Age of Aries, sunrise was in Cancer at the Summer Solstice, in Libra at the Autumn Equinox, and in Capricorn at the Winter Solstice. Note how the 12 hours on a clock corresponds to the 12 signs of Solar Zodiac clock. This is a microcosm of the Macrocosm.

Genesis documents the creation of the Zodiac "signs"

It's easy to miss, since it's in one short sentence, but it's right there in Genesis 1:14 which delineates the creation of the Zodiac Signs or constellations:

> "And God said, Let there be lights in the firmament of the heaven ...for signs, and for seasons, and for days, and for years."

Let's read that again with highlights and notes added:

"And God said, Let there be LIGHTS
(stars! where else do "lights" come from? and lights are plural)

in the firmament of THE HEAVEN
(= the *sky*, home of the *stars*)

...for SIGNS, (the Zodiac Signs!)

and for seasons, and for days, and for years."
("months" shoulda been in this list but was likely omitted because of its feminine connections).

1) Jackson, CBC, 183.

Afrikans originated Astrology /Astronomy and took it around the world

Below: Afrikan deities from the zodiacal ceiling of the temple of Dendera:

Aries

Taurus

Gemini

Cancer

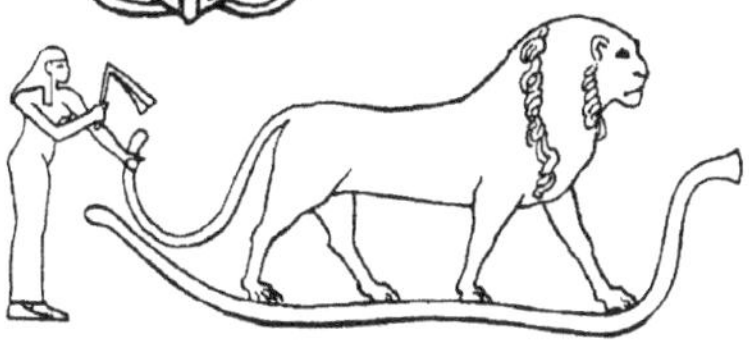
Leo

Virgo

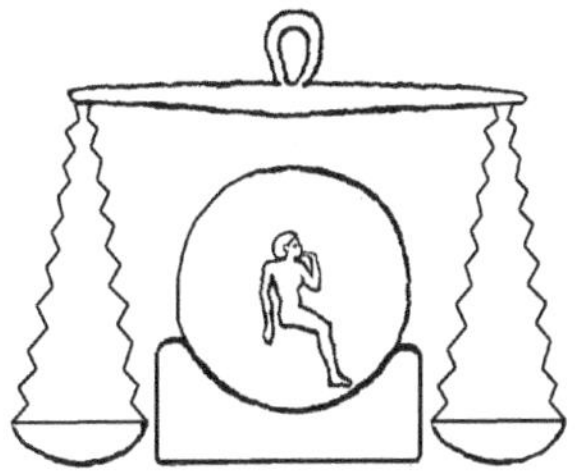
Libra

Afrika provided the ideal conditions for discovering and charting the Zodiac. Climatically, geographically, and agriculturally, Afrika was the ideal location on Earth for the birth of what I shall call "StarScience," for the artificial separation we know as Astrology and Astronomy did not exist until the dissecting, fractionating, segmenting, patriarchal mindset got a hold of it. This is also why the "modern zodiac" is heavily masculinized. The original prototypical Afrikan Zodiac reflected the matriarchal society that gave it birth. And the Afrikan distributed StarScience throughout the world. "It was the ancient Egyptians who mapped out the heavens into 12 divisions in the North, 12 divisions in the South, and 12 in the centre, making 36 in all, and the twelve signs of the Zodiac. To whatever part of the world the Priests [and Priestesses] went they carried this knowledge with them."[1]

Kamite deities provided the prototypes for the Zodiac's figures

Over 1200 deities are mentioned in *The Coming Forth By Day*; some 200 are mentioned in *The Pyramid Text*. "The imagery configurated in the stars was African in origin, and the teachers of its primitive mysteries were Egyptian." [2] "It is not possible that all these gods and goddesss and nature powers of Egypt were constellated as figures in the universe by any other than the Egyptian mystery teachers of the heavens."[3] The planisphere is populated with a whole pantheon Kamite deities. They are the allegorical personages and zootypes composing the vast Precession which moves on forever round and round, according to the revolutions of the earth or apparent revolution of the sphere. Taking the same order in which the signs on the ecliptic are read today, at least a dozen African deities can be identified with the 12 signs as follows: [4]

	Kamite Deity:	Identified With:
1.	The Ram-headed Amen	Aries
2.	Osiris the Bull of Eternity	Taurus
3.	Waring twin brothers, Sut & Heru	Gemini
4.	The Beetle-headed Kheper-Ptah	the Crab
5.	The Lion-faced Atum	Leo
6.	The Virgin Neith	Virgo
7.	Har-Makhu of the Scales	Libra
8.	Isis-Serkh, the Scorpion Goddess	Scorpio
9.	Shu & Tefnut imaged as the Archer	Sagittarius
10.	Num, the Goat-headed	Capricorn
11.	Menat, the Divine Wet Nurse	Aquarius
12.	Heru of the Two Crocodiles	Pisces

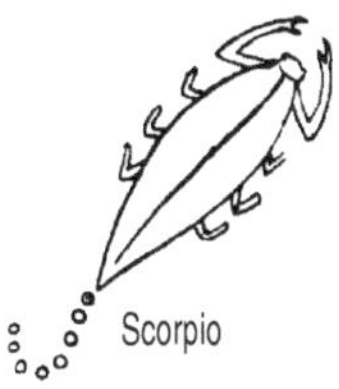
Scorpio

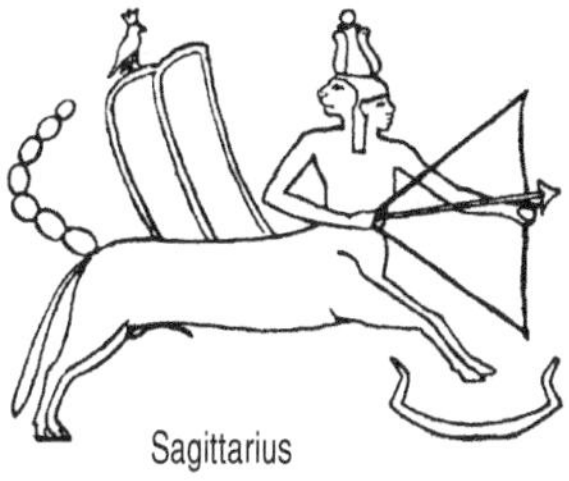
Sagittarius

Capricorn

Aquarius

Pisces

1) Churchward, SS, 213. 2) Massey, AE, 305. 3) Churchward, SS, 215. 4) Massey, AE, 302.

Biblical evidence that the 12 (13) Tribes of Israel were the 12 Zodiacal Signs !

The Bible itself furnishes abundant evidence that the Twelve Tribes of Israel were the Twelve Zodiacal Signs. The characteristics of the Zodiac Signs are especially recognized in these areas:

1) Jacob's last words to his children

Disguised in Jacob's last words to his twelve sons in Genesis, Chapter 49, are key references to the characteristics of the Zodiac Signs! Representing the *setting* –hence, *dying* Sun, Jacob gives a special blessing and prophesy to each of his children as he lies on his deathbed. The plagiarized allegory begins with the 12th chapter of Genesis to agree with the twelve constellations. Jacob was the Sun, his first wife Leah was the Moon, and his *thirteen* children were the *Twelve* Zodiacal Constellations, for *two* of his sons were Gemini the Twins while his *only* daughter represented Virgo. In reality however, his thirteen children disguisedly correspond to the original Lunar Zodiac of 13 houses. Jacob's blessings are recorded in Genesis 49; *thirteen* is the total of 4+9. The biblical order of the tribes has been jumbled to further disguise their zodiacal character. Their proper order and identities are:

Tribes of Israel	Zodiac Sign Represented	On Page
1. Naphtali	Aries the Ram	187
2. Issachar	Taurus the Bull	189
3. Simeon & Levi	Gemini the Twins	190
4. Benjamin	Cancer the Crab	200
5. Judah	Leo the Lion	203
6. Dinah	Virgo the Virgin	205
7. Asher	Libra the Balance	210
8. Dan	Scorpio the Scorpion/Eagle/Serpent	213
9. Joseph	Sagittarius the Archer	216
10. Gad	Capricorn the Goat	220
11. Reuben	Aquarius the Waterman	229
12. Zebulun	Pisces the Fish	235

2) Their history and nuances

Each person's biblical history and little details about their character and connections with other people, provides additional clues to support or link them to the sign they represent. Numerals that are mentioned, including verse-numbers may also contribute to the picture. Often these clues are repeated.

3) Territory adjacency matches zodiacal-sign adjacency

All the territories of the 12 tribes border each other in accordance with the signs they represent (see map). Thus the territories of Reuben and Gad (representing Aquarius-Capricorn) are adjacent, as found in the real Zodiac. There was no tribe of Joseph. Instead, his two sons were counted as full sons of Jacob and distinct tribes of Israel, thus Joseph was awarded two portions of land (Ez. 47:13, Gen. 48). Therefore Joseph (Sagittarius) is represented by his sons Ephraim & Manasseh, who are next to Dan and Gad (Scorpio-Capricorn). **Simeon and Levi were not given land.** The Simeonites were allowed to have 'their inheritance within the inheritance of Judah' (Jos. 19:1, 9). And there was no tribe of Levi for the Levites were a priestly caste. **Note there are really *two* territories of "Dan,"** which are widely separated (south/north). One is disguisedly for Dinah (Dinah/Dan are from common roots) without acknowledging the fact in order to avoid crediting the underlying feminine Lunar Zodiac of 13 signs, thereby maintaining the patriarchal pretense of 12 territories. Actually, both territories of Dan equally represent Dinah (Virgo) and Dan (Scorpio). For Virgo is between Leo & Libra, therefore southern-Dan-Dinah borders Judah (Leo) and lies in the same area as Asher (Libra); Scorpio is between Libra and Sagittarius, therefore southern-Dan borders Ephraim (Sagittarius), while northern-Dan is in the same area as Asher (Libra):

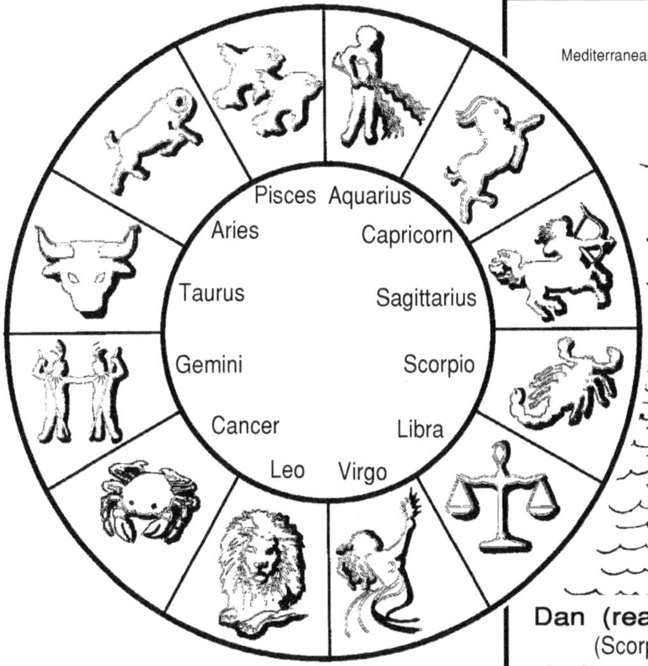

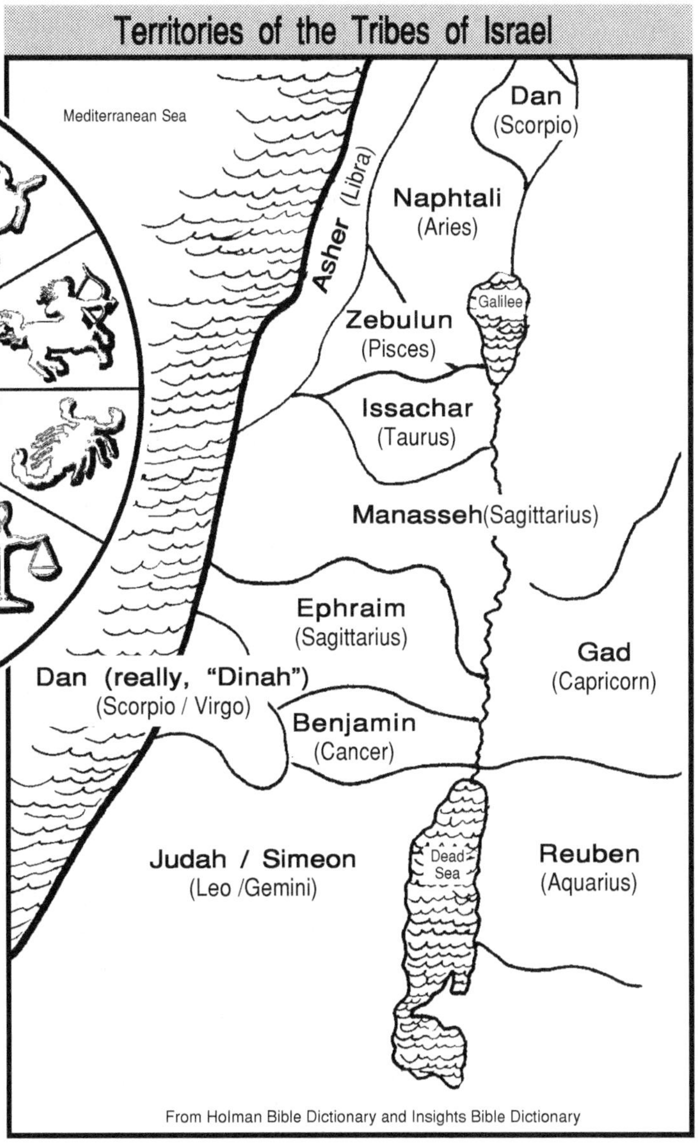

From Holman Bible Dictionary and Insights Bible Dictionary

4) Their true name-meanings disguise the Zodiac traits

The true etymology of the names of the 12 tribes holds massive evidence of their zodiacal identity, and links them to the zodiacal sign they represent. The name of each tribe has been carefully chosen so that its *true* meaning or roots matches a major characteristic of the sign it stands for.

The same characters and themes are recycled, disguised by multiple name-spellings and other ploys

Throughout the Bible, important names are typically spelled numerous ways, sometimes with just slight variations as they seemingly apply to "different" individuals. This ploy is done to hide or disguise the fact that the same individuals, that is, the same zodiacal or celestial bodies are being discussed from one biblical book to the next or even in the same book. The characters are redressed for each play, but always the same characters and themes are recycled over and over and over...*and over* like the cyclic nature of the bodies they represent. An example is the Twins Theme: two brothers are born; the birthright inheritance of the elder brother always gets diverted to the younger, and the elder is portrayed a bad person (Cain & Abel, Esau & Jacob, etc.). When really big beings are involved (such as Abraham, Christ), the ploy is more convoluted but the truth and evidence of what is really going on is available largely through the KEY of true etymology, which always takes us back to Afrika, the sourceplace. Had not the Rosetta Stone been found (which enabled Kamite hieroglyphics to be decoded), we would have been denied these vital liberating truths, just as intended by the perpetrators. The multiple individuals (or places) bearing variants of the same name are usually a single entity split into different parts. Each "part" contributes to the whole picture of that particular entity. **Another ploy:** one name is used for an entity in one place, and a totally different name is used for the same entity in another place, making some Bible scholars report that this is an "error" (example: Dalmanutha & Magdala). Not so! For each name yields important pieces to the puzzle, and once the true etymology is determined, the connection is logical and often amazing. I have found this to be consistent, and it gives the impression that **the translators of the *King James* version of the Bible knew that the Bible and its characters were zodiacal**. Modern "improved" translations of the Bible (written in regular English) apparently are not aware of this, therefore key names/situations/nuances are often revised or even edited out. **Freak oddness** has deep zodiacal meaning (examples: a woman turning to salt; a giant with 6 fingers/toes on each hand). Such are easily deciphered with awareness of the Afrikan roots.

Namebooks are unreliable

Namebooks are as unreliable as history books for giving the Afrikan truth. You cannot prove etymologies by using the standard references of the very people who distorted or suppressed it in the first place. The biblical names originated, like the Bible itself, from Afrika, specifically ancient Egypt (Kamit). Kamite words often have multiple meanings (distinguished by their hieroglyphics). As documented in The Book of the Beginning (vol. II), the Hebrew language is but a variant or dialect of the Egyptian language. In the following pages we will review Jacob's blessings containing key references describing the Zodiacal Signs, his sons. We will also uncover the true or most likely roots of the names of Jacob's *thirteen* children.

1 **Naphtali** = Aries the Ram

Cardinal **FIRE** Sign

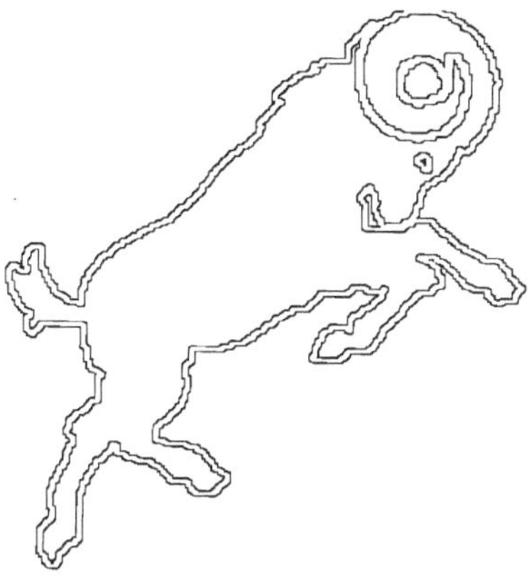

"Naphtali is a hind let loose: he giveth goodly words" (Gen. 49:21). A *hind* is a female *red* deer. Red correlates to the fiery type of sign this is. Red is the first color of the spectrum as Aries is the first sign of the Zodiac. "Let loose" implies unbridled energy, the sexual energy of a hind in heat, arousing the stag who corresponds to the Ram. The Ram was honored for its virile powers and was one of the most popular animal incarnations of the phallic god. Egypt's ram god Amon was regarded as the virile principle in gods and men, and addressed as "the virile male, the holy phallus, which stirreth up the passions of love, the Ram of rams." [1] Aries is associated with Mars, the *red* planet and *red* god of war. *Mars* and *martial* mean war, fighting, "wrestling." When Naphtali was born, his mother said, "With great wrestlings have I wrestled with my sister" (Gen. 30:8).

Naphtali is **Nef-Ptah-El** (or Nef-Peth-Al)

Biblical variants are Nephthalim (Mat 4:13) and Naphtuhim (Gen. 10:13, 1Chron. 1:11). Ptah (pteh) means "to open" and is also a Kamite name of the Divine Father whose title was "The Opener." Aries "opens" the Zodiac, opens the hymen (of the "hind"), and opens the beginning of the seasons with the passionate, unbridled Sexual Energy of Life, officially awakening and *bursting* forth at the Spring Equinox. Regarding **Naphtuhim**, the *Holman Bible Dictionary* admits "The term may come from Egyptian for Ptah, pointing to Middle Egypt." [2]

Derived from the same roots, Hebrew Nephtoah means *opening* and *vulva*,[3] and is found only in the phrases "fountain of the water of Nephtoah" and "well of waters of Nephtoah" (Jos. 15:9, 18:15). Fountains and wells are both "openings" as well as ancient female symbols. This bring us back to HIND; how curious that Naphtali is called a "hind." This makes *him* really a female! This ties into the meaning of his name-root as "opening," for it is the female that has the *opening* –which is "opened" by the phallus in the act of sex. And the female is the source, the beginning. This relates to Naphtali as the beginning or opening of the Zodiac. Naphtali "giveth goodly words." *Words* come from the *mouth*, another *opening*.

1) Budge, GE-vII, 64. 2) Holman BD, 1008. 3) Ibid., 1017; Rocco, 29.

Naphtha is derived from the same roots as **Naphtali**, and its meanings aptly apply to the Cardinal *Fire* Sign of Aries. *Naphtha* is any of several volatile hydrocarbon liquids derived from coal tar and other materials and used as solvents. And when "**lit**" (relates to sex /fire), naphta will make "openings" in the Earth like dynamite. Naphtha is also called *petroleum* and *bitumen*, a substance which occurs naturally and abundantly in the Middle East. Even today it is occasionally washed ashore. The Bible refers to it as "pitch" which Noah used to waterproof his ark (Gen. 6:14), and "slime" used for mortar and to waterproof baby Moses' basket on the Nile (Gen. 11:3 / Exo. 2:3). The valley of Siddim "was full of slimepits" (Gen. 14:10). Isaiah prophesied that the land of Edom would be aflame with burning pitch (Isa. 34:9).

Napthtali is certainly *hot,* with an etymology indicating these meanings for his name:

- Passionate Opener
- The Fire Which Impels Union
- Divine Sexual Fire (El signifies divinity)
- God of Sexual Fire

Thus, passionate Naphtali is Aries the Ram, naturally "in heat" !

Etymology of Naphtali (Nep-Ptah-El)

Category	Afrikan-Kamite Roots	Apparent Derivatives: ENGLISH:	Apparent Derivatives: HEBREW:
Explosive Fire Light	**nahp** • emit light. 627BB2 **neb** • fire, flame. 366b • to smelt. 366b **neba** • to burn, flame up, burner. 367a **neb, nub** • gold (has fiery color). 353a **nefer** • heat, fire. 67BB1 **nabui** • fire, flames. 367,627BB2	naphtha naphthene naphthol neuf (*blaze* in Old English)	**neft,** petroleum, oil, kerosene **nefets,** explosion, burst **Nophah,** a biblical name, means *blast* (Holman, 1027) •**nippah,** blacksmith
Air	**nef** • air, wind, breath. 369a **nefi** • to breathe, blow at, give breath to. 369a **nifa** • to blow, to breath. 348b	nib (nose) neb (bird's beak) snuff sniff snob (looking down one's nose)	**naphesh,** living breathing soul •**nippah,** blow up, inflate, fan, exaggerate **nippuah,** blowing up, inflation, puffing **nefiha,** blowing, fanning
Opening	**pet** • a circle. 69BB1 • open out, be wide, spacious. 255b **peth, put** • to open, open the mouth. **ptah** • to open, engrave. 254b **pat** • path, course, path of sun. 68BB1	pot pothole pit pita (openable pocket bread) vat pitcher petal patent boat (*open* container) path	**peh, peth,** opening, the mouth **patah,** open, untie, begin **petah,** opening, doorway
Light Power	**peht** • strength, might, power, bravery, renown. 245a **bet** • to illumine, to shine, to burn, burn incense. 227b	photon (light) photography pith (strength) vitality potency battery butter butane petrol pitch bitumen fat fit (tantrum) impetus impetuous rapid	

a, b = columns in *An Egyptian Hieroglyphic Dictionary*. **BB** = *Book of the Beginnings* (vol. 1 or 2).
WE = *Women's Encyclopedia of Myths & Secrets*. **AE** = *Ancient Egypt: Light of the World*.

2 **Issachar** = Taurus the Bull

Fixed **EARTH** Sign

Issachar is described as a *slavish beast of burden*, **"a strong ass couching down between two burdens...and bowed his shoulder to bear, and became a servant."** (Gen. 49:14, 15) Bulls are "strong," reknown for their great strength, thus used as beasts of burden and heavy labor. Asses were used for the same; they were the most common means of transportation ("burdens") and heavy labor in Israel. Bulls and Asses are also reknown for stubbornness, an appropriate trait for the *Fixed Earth* Sign of the Zodiac. Stubbornness signifying the earth principle of firmness, unyielding, rigid hardness.

Issachar is **Ash-Seker**. Hebrew **ish** means virile, man; **zakar** means male, masculine; **sakhar** means *hired worker* –the bull was a *worker*, a "servant," an animal of heavy labor. Right after Issachar's birth, "Leah said, God hath given me my **hire**" (Gen. 30:18). In Afrika's Nile Valley, ***Seker*** was the name of the jet-black Bull of Osiris. "The Sun in Taurus" was also called Osiris-*Sekari*, the dismembered, sacrificial Bull. Isis was the Holy Cow, and their son Horus was the Golden Calf worshiped by Aaron and the Israelites during the Age of *Taurus*. The Bull was the arch-symbol of masculinity. Bulls are so well endowed that for centuries, their penises were used as whips, hence the term *bullwhip*. Seker was also the name of Osiris as the Black Sun enclosed in Earth's womb at the bottom of the underworld; Seker was the title of his *Phallus*, hidden in the Mother's Womb, at the point of "dying," sending forth seed into the dark.[1] The phallus is famous for getting "hard" like the Earth sign it is connected with. **Thus Issachar means:**

- Masculine
- The Male Principle
- Virile Phallus
- Hard Worker

These are all traits of the mighty Bull, making Issachar the Bull of Eternity immortalized as Taurus.

Etymology of Issachar (Ash-Seker)

Afrikan-Kamite Roots	Apparent Derivatives
ash • emission, emanation, issue, liquid. 9,326BB2 • seminal source. 9,326BB2 **Asar** • (Osiris) was a form of the Great Father, the God of Regeneration, the epitomy of virility and masculinity. **Seker** • title of the phallus of Asar. **Sekari** • title of the sacrificed Bull of Osiris.	HEBREW: **ish**, virile, man, male, husband **zakar**, male, maleness, masculine **zakhrut**, penis, virility **zekhari**, male, manly **sakhar**, hire, rent, wages, reward **sakir**, wage earner, hired worker, employee ARABIC: **zekker**, penis

1) Walker, WE, 901.

3 **Simeon & Levi** = Gemini the Twins or Couple

Mutable **AIR** Sign

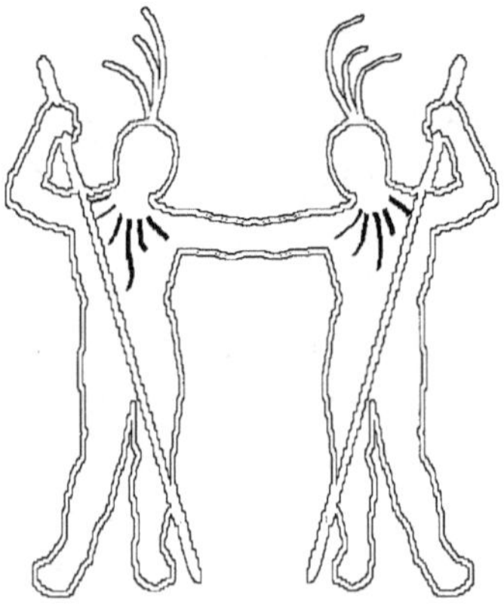

"Simeon and Levi are brethren" (Gen. 49:5). The other brothers are *brethren* too, so why are these *two* singled out? Now you know why! The names Simeon & Levi are alike in meaning, just like *twins*. **Simeon** is derived from Kamite **sem /smen**, whose meanings include *same*, union, and *twin*. "Sem" was a name of the *double* solar plume and a title of the Twin Lion Sungods.[1] **Levi** means joined to, wrapped around, or *double*.[2] Levi is "joined to" Simeon his *brethren*. In the original zodiac, the Afrikans represented Gemini as a pair of male and female lovers "joined to" each other in loving embrace. You can guess what these lovers were doing! In fact, the words Gemini and "gamy" (*marriage* –as in poly*gamy*) are from common roots. Thus Gemini originally celebrated the *union* of opposites. The human male/female couple represented the union of sexual opposites that bring forth new life. Only in later zodiacs did Gemini become "twins."

Simeon & Levi reflect the male /female principle of the original Afrikan Gemini

This is apparent upon reviewing the history and true etymology of the names Simeon & Levi. The etymology shows that Simeon stands for the Male Principle; Levi for the Female Principle. Male and Female are made to "join." This "joining" is SEX or the union of Life's two polarities to bring forth the third principle, which is *New Life* or renewed Life, continuation of Life.

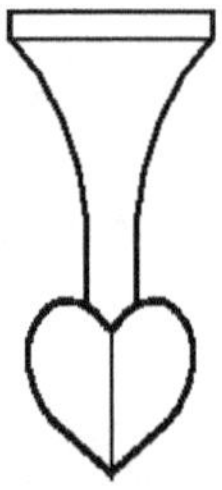

SEMA

Simeon's Semen: Masculine Aspect

In Egyptian, the SEMA hieroglyph was the symbol of union. Books typically say SEMA is the image of two *lungs* attached to the trachea. In reality, SEMA or the "Amulet of the Sam" is a symbol of sexual intercourse.[3] It is a lingam/ yoni image and sign of *knowledge* in the biblical sense that "knowing" = sexual intercourse, and one *knows* divine power by *feeling* it. Thus the words *Know, Gnosis, Ken, Gene, Genital, Gonad, Cunning,* and *Cunt* are all from the same roots! The knowledge within the genes are the blueprint for making a whole new human being, and this happens through the genitals (sex; semen/ egg). Another meaning of sem/smen is to *establish* or erect, –giving us the words *semen* (which *establishes* after the parents), *seminar* (where *knowledge* is *disseminated*), and *symbol* (a means by which *knowledge* is *established* and transferred, which is happening now as you read the letter/words symbols in this book). Note that the Sema hieroglyph contains the *valentine*, a *symbol* derived from the shape of the female genital.

1) Massey, BB-vII, 515. 2) Massey, HJ, 158. 3) Walker, WD, 312.

Levi's Love: Feminine Aspect

Levi's true etymology reveals that essentially, Levi means *love*, another word derived from the same roots! Levi means to unite or join. It means the Joint itself. And this Joint is what polarities have in common, for this Joint is the *Heart*. After Levi was born, his mother Leah, the "hated" one of Jacob's two wives said, "Now this time will my husband be joined unto me" (Gen. 29:34).

Reference books say Levi is from *Leviathan*, a word defined as *sea monster, whale,* and *coiled one*. These definitions have a basis in truth but are shallow fragments of the real picture. Let's look at them:

- *Sea Monster:* the Leviathan was known as Okeanus (whence, *ocean*), the massive *Serpent* encircling the Earth in the aerial mystic waters of the *Nun* (which Albino scientists call "space").
- *Whale:* the Leviathan was identified with the Whale or Great Fish. Fish was a major Goddess/Female symbol because fish live in *Water,* and the female genital smells like fish. As the Vesica Piscis (Vessel of the Fish), fish symbolizes the vulva.
- *Coiled One*: Serpent, in other words. Leviathan was a title of the brazen serpent called Nehushtan, whose worship was established by Moses but later discredited (2Kings 18:4).

Based on its Afrikan roots, the true meaning of *Leviathan* appears to be "Love Serpent" or "Serpent of Love and *Wisdom*." For the serpent is an ancient symbol for *Wisdom*, a chief characteristic of Great Goddess. This Serpent of Love and Wisdom can only be the amorous Goddess *Tann*, a version of Hathor-Meri, the Afrikan prototype of the Goddess of Love. She was reknown as Aphrodite and Venus, and slandered as Medusa, whose serpentine hair was really dredlocks! (And nappy hair is spiraling serpentine hair, reflecting the spiraling serpentine energy of Life which causes the atoms, planets, and stars to spin.)

Tann or Tannet is the apparent source of "athan" and "tan" in Leviathan and Nehushtan. **Thus Leviathan is really Levi-Atan!** If it is true that the Levites take their name from Leviathan, then the true original Levites were "Love-ites" or *priestesses of the Great Goddess of Love*; priestesses who healed by practicing sacred, *sanctifying* SEX in the TANtric temples of Great Goddess; priestesses who were usurped and replaced by invading pretender male-priests who plagiarized their rites and distorted and reversed the teachings of the true Goddess of *Life* (and thus *Sex* –the means of Life's propagation). The usurpers promoted disguised death instead, under *their* wrathful bloodthirsty "jealous" god who even banned his first children –the first *Couple* –the first *Gemini*– from paradise because they had SEX or the "forbidden fruit" called "Knowing." And it was a "serpent" that was blamed. There is a connection here with the *Kundalini*! You have a *Kundalini* but it is likely "asleep." The Kundalini or *Serpent Fire* is coiled up at the base of your spine in the "Root Chakra." When your Kundalini Serpent rises/spirals up your Spine, *she* opens all your 7 spinal chakras (energy centers) along the way, culminating at your Crown-Chakra at the top of your head to produce Enlightenment (being IN the

1) Jubal, 176.

LIGHT. Light is a synonym for "knowledge"), profound Spiritual Awakening, and "union of Self with the Infinite." Note the KN of KNowing in KUNdalini! The Uraeus Serpent on the crowns of Kamite royalty is a symbol of the Great Mother, the Sacred Uraeus, the Sacred Serpentine Sexual Energy of Life. **Apparently, only when the Albino usurpers came into power did Sex become "filthy" and the "original sin."** And the loving Leviathan was turned (or rescripted) into an unloving frightening monster.

Gemini biblically reversed!

In the story of Simeon & Levi, it appears that the rewriters have *reversed* the original Afrikan meaning of Gemini, making what should be a love-sign of Joining, into a hate-sign of bloody Division. For far from representing Love and Unity, the *brethren* Simeon and Levi are cruel killers that *divide* bodies with the sword. When their sister Dinah was violated by Prince *Shechem* (who fell in *love* with her and made plans to marry her), they avenged this by massacring the entire male population in the city of *Shechem* –remember this word, ***Shechem***. Then they burned and pillaged the city, taking all the remaining females as slaves. No wonder Jacob's "blessing" sounded more like a curse: "Simeon and Levi are brethren; instruments of cruelty are in their habitations" (Gen. 49:5). "Cursed be their anger, for it was fierce; and their wrath, for it was cruel; I will divide them in Jacob, and scatter them in Israel" (Gen. 49:7).

How does this align with Gemini, and what is the reversal I'm talking about? Directly opposite Gemini is its complementary sign *Sagittarius*. Apparently these two signs have been switched, in that:

- Simeon & Levi (representing Gemini) have "instruments of cruelty." Sagittarius is the only sign with an "instrument of cruelty" (bow & arrow is a war weapon). And the name Sagittarius is from a root meaning *sharp* or *to cut*. The rewriters have assigned this cutting trait to Gemini by making the *brethren* slashing killers.
- Conversely, they have made Sagittarius a sign of *Twins*. Representing Sagittarius, their brother Joseph has apparent *twin* sons (Ephraim & Manasseh) who *replace* him and are fully counted as both, legal tribes of Israel and actual sons of Jacob their grandfather (Gen. 48:5,6).
- The Love/Sex trait of Gemini (Simeon/Levi) is given to Sagittarius (Joseph) in several ways: Joseph was the firstborn son of Rachel, Jacob's *favorite* wife, and he was the *favorite* child over all his brothers. Favorite indicates Love, just like the name Levi. Joseph was thrown into a PIT by his jealous brothers. "The Pit" is an ancient Womb symbol. In essence, by being in "the pit," Joseph himself is the Phallus (like Osiris) in the Womb of Mother Earth (Osiris-Sekari). Three significant female symbols occur in Jacob's blessing to Joseph: "the deep" (or *Pit*), "the breasts," and "the womb" (Gen. 49:25).

"Shechem" provides major sexual links between Simeon/Levi (Gemini) and Joseph (Sagittarius):

- Prince *Shechem* raped Dinah, fell in *love* with her, and made arrangements with her father to *marry* her (Gen. 34). Shechem was the son of Hamor. Hamor is *Amor*, a name of the *amorous* Great Mother meaning *Love*.
- Avenging their sister, Simeon & Levi slaughter Prince Shechem and all the males in the Hebrew city of Shechem.
- Shechem was a *Levitical* city (Jos. 21:21), located in the territory of Ephraim (a son of Joseph).
- Shechem was the name of two men in the tribe of Manasseh (Joseph's other son).
- Shechem was "a city of refuge for slayers" (Jos. 21:21). Ironically, all these "slayers" got slain by the slayers Simeon and Levi, so it failed as a refuge for slayers.
- Simeon was once held hostage by Joseph (Gen. 42:24). At death, Joseph was entombed in Shechem (Josh. 24:32).

The Afrikan origin of *Shechem* is undoubtedly SESHEMU, meaning "sexual intercourse" in Egyptian.[1] SESHEMU and SEXEN (to copulate, embrace)[2] also gives us the word SEX! But how can this be, with all this *cutting* connected with Shechem? Well guess what? The same root of the word SEX also yields *sect*, *dissect*, *sickle* and similar cutting words, including SAGittarius (!), the *keen* wise Sage or Cutter. The word Sex even contains a letter that looks like open scissors.

And *Father* Abraham was given the covenant of the land of Canaan for the deposit of his *seed* at the sacred *tree* (a female symbol) of *Shechem* (Jos. 24:26, Jud. 4:6).

Jesus *making love* at Shechem (Sychar)?

Shechem (called *Sichem* in Gen. 12:6) is the same place as *Sychar*, derived from the same roots. Jacob bought a parcel of land from "the children of Hamor [Hamor = AMOR, Love], Shechem's father" (Gen. 33:18, 19). This was the same land where Jesus "cometh...which is called Sychar, near to the parcel of ground that Jacob gave to his son Joseph" (John 4:5). At Jacob's *well* at Sychar, Jesus met a "woman of Samaria." This was just a way of saying that Her name is SemMaria or SaMary –from the same roots as *Amor* or *Meri* (the wife /sister /Mother of Asar); which means *Love*. The Afrikan goddess Hathor-Meri was the prototype for the Goddess of Love called Venus and Aphrodite. The WELL is an ancient symbol for the female orifice or vaginal gateway to the Womb, "the deep," the Inner Mystery of Life.[3] As Jesus "sat thus on the well...there cometh a woman of Samaria" whom Jesus asked "Give me to drink." Of course She complies.

1) Walker, WD, 312. 2) Walker, WE, 401. 3) Walker, WD, 329.

And now... the *Gambling Game* from *Gemini's* roots: *"The Urim and the Thummim"*

Game and *gamble* are from the same roots as *Gemini*. What's the connection with Simeon & Levi? **"The Urim and the Thummim."** The what? Bible dictionaries give the impression that "the Urim and the Thummim" are largely a mystery. They were "objects" which the *Levitical* high priests used to receive divine answers to questions. Moses gave the tribe of *Levi* special responsibility for their care (Deu. 33:8). It is believed there were *two* of them but no one seems to know just what they were or what they looked like. According to Walker, they were "divinatory **knucklebones** or dice used by Jewish priests." [1] So what is certain is that they were a form of "**lots.**" In this lies the connection of Simeon and Levi (Gemini) to games or gambling.

"The Urim and the Thummim" were placed on the breastplate of Levi at his *heart*. They were also placed over Aaron's heart when he went "in before God." For Levitical law directed that these items be carried in the "breastplate of judgement" (Exo. 28:15 ,30). The icon of "Judgement" is the Scale /Libra, the symbol of perfect Balance; and the Heart is the MIDDLE where Balance occurs. *Libra* is from the same roots as *Levi /Love*. Now we are closer to truly identifying just what were "the Urim and the Thummim." Judging by their names, there were probably ***three*** (not two) of them. For the Hebrew suffix IM denotes plurality. This leaves us with *Uri* and *Thum*. Uri or **UR means *light*. Thum means couple or *twin***, like the name Thomas. Now we see where "knucklebones" enter the picture, for *thumb* is from the same root; –our thumbs are *twins*.

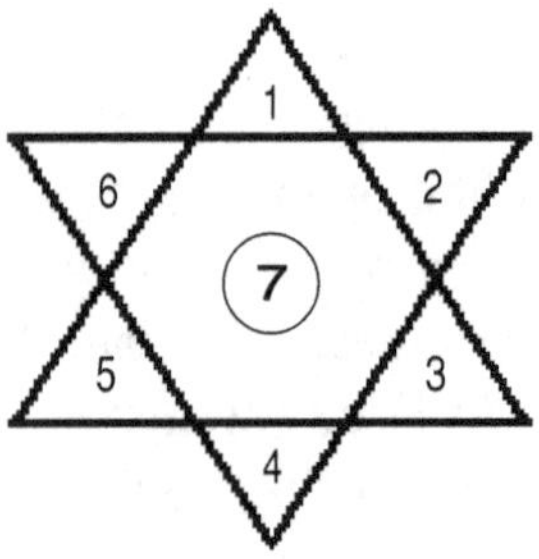

Since Urim/Thummim have plural endings ("im"), then really there were two sets for a total of SIX "lots." This brings us back to **SEX**, for both words, *six* and *sex*, are from Latin *sexus* (sexual intercourse) which is from Kamite *sexen*. Now here is where I suddenly realized that "the Urim and the Thummim" is the Star of David! The Star of David is actually a *sex symbol*, a *six* symbol. It is two *interlacing*, *interlocking* triangles. *Double* triangles. *Twin* triangles. The down-pointing triangle is Feminine –as the basic shape of the female genital (from which the valentine also originated). The up-pointing triangle is Masculine, symbolizing the male genitals; when the phallus is *erected*, its three "points" (head & testicles) form the up-pointing triangle. "Join" these double triangles and you get what's called the Star of David, DAVAD. The name **DAVAD** itself even reflects this, for it contains both "triangles" which, when meshed = the hexagram. And it is perfectly symmetrical, sounding and looking the same whether backwards or forward. Magick! The word SEX and SIX also contain the two "triangles" or "Thummim" in the letter X. And the Kamite word for six is SES, [2] from which English *six*, Latin *sex* (six), and Hebrew *shesh* (six) are obviously derived. **King David was the first king to JOIN or unite the two nations of *Israel & Judah* (Thummin)**, and the first to receive promise of a royal messiah (Uri) in his line.

1) Walker, WE, 1029. 2) Massey, BB-vII, 20.

Jesus did it a *six o'clock*

Significantly, it was "about the sixth hour" (6 o'clock!) when Jesus met the "woman of Samaria" as he "sat on the well" (well=yoni symbol). And this is recorded in the 6th verse. Jesus discerned that this woman "hast had five husbands" plus her current mate (total of 6) (John 4:18). Thus Jesus becomes the 7th man in Her life (Moses gets one of 7 sisters; see next paragraph). In the 7th verse (7=love, heart, water hence *well*) "Jesus saith unto her, Give me to drink." (John 4:5-7), and She complies in verse 15 (1+5=6): "Sir, give me this water." The result of the joining of the Thummim (divine Couple) is Uri (Light /Life) Eternal Life. Sex is the means of Life's propagation. The Well on the mountain of Sychar/Shechem was a symbol of the Great Mother's Well of Living Water, the Water of Eternal Life –reflected in verses 10 and 14.

Moses too

The same previously mentioned elements occur with Moses (and others I'm sure). In Exodus 2, verse 15 (1+5=6), like Jesus "he sat down by a well," later met 7 women (the 7 daughters of the priest of Midian) who "came and drew water" in verse 16 (1+6=7). And he marries one of them.

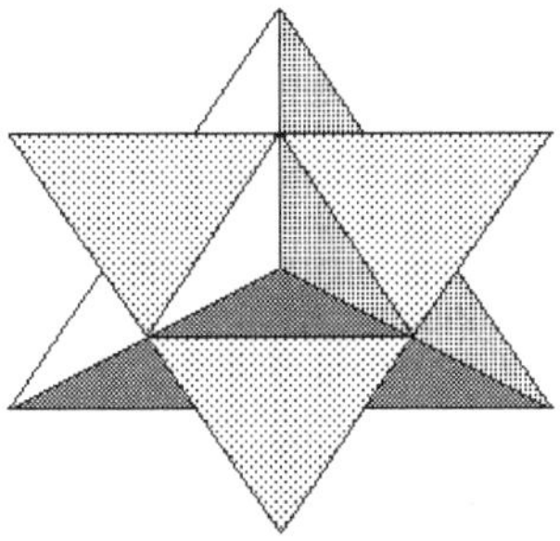

Pyramids, not knucklebones

So instead of "knucklebones," it is more likely that the actual shape of "the Urim and the Thummim" were pyramids! Pyramid means *fire in the middle*. "The Urim and the Thummim" were always worn or placed in the *middle* of the breastplate at the Heart, the sacred place of Balance (between the polarities of our 3-upper and 3-lower chakras). Significantly, the place called *Sychar* at the location of Jacob's well, was a "mountain" (John 4:20, 21).

Our Ovaries & Testes are "Thummim"

"The Urim and the Thummim" is a double set of *Uri and Thums:*

- The first set of "Thummim" or *Twins* represents the *two Ovaries*.
- The second set of "Thummim" represents the *two Testicles*.
- The remaining *two* Urim represent the Phallus and Yoni.

"Lightning" was an ancient symbol for the Phallus. And the UR of URim is the same UR of the Sacred URaeus Serpent of the Great Mother. Serpent Fire. Back to our Pyramid (fire in the middle). URIM is the fire in the middle of the Thummim (twins, lovers) –the holy Sexual Fire of Life and its seat, the Heart, from which the Fire of Love radiates. Fire equally from the Male Aspect and Female Aspect. The arrow piercing the valentine-heart is an ancient symbol for sex. **Thus Sagittarius's phallic arrow –*URrow* "pierces" the yonic "Heart" (valentine!) of Gemini,** the sign directly across from it!

Now we see why "the Urim and the Thummim" were intimately associated with the *Levites*, actually the *LOVE*-ites, for the original Levites, before they were usurped, were priestesses of the Great Goddess of Love. And sacred holy Sex was a significant part of Her temple rites. "Knowing" was an integral part of Her system. But this "Knowing" has been effectively castrated, as has been "the Urim and the Thummim" by the installation of the rewritten, reversed, patriarchal, anti-female, anti-sex, anti-Afrikan, unholy (not "whole") Bible.

Brain and Genitals are "Thummim." You have twin brains and twin genitals.

Brain and Genitals are one. Brain and Genitals are *top* and *bottom* of the same Essence; *roots* and *branches* of the Tree, –the *Sacred Tree of Life* unifying Life's two polarities. Male and Female. *"Knowing," Gene, Genitals, Cunning, Cunt, Kundalini.* And see "KN" in *King* and *Queen*? Brain and Genitals connect at the Heart, the *True* Joint, the *Tree* Joint! Ponder that! Tree = Three. Top, Bottom, Middle. 3 in 1. Trunk is the Middle, the Heart, the Joint, the *Uri.*

And though you are male or female, you have both principles in you or you could not exist. You actually have *two* brains, (a feminine and masculine brain labeled left/right brain), and two ovaries or two testicles. Their total (2 brains + 2 eggs) is FOUR. Remember, they connect at the Heart. No wonder the Heart has FOUR chambers! You have 3 chakras above your Heart Chakra and 3 chakras below it. Heart is the point of Balance. Ahh, breezes from the air-sign of Libra are blowing into the air-sign of Gemini.

Brain and Genitals are two sides of the same Coin

That coin is the *Uri*, or Heart, Connection, Transmutation... Divine Alchemy. *Divine Alchemy?* Yes. Holy Kundalini –Great Mother Serpent sleeping in your Root Chakra –transmutes /awakens / actualizes you into the Divine Being that is YOU ..IU ...HUE (Light!) ...HUman. You God/dess You! That Golden *Spark* of Divinity residing in your Heart *is* You. You are Point *Seven*, the Center (Heart) in the Middle (Heart) of the Divine-Hexagram-Star-of-DAVAD. You are Divine Child *Uri*, offspring of the Great Mother's and Great Father's SEXUAL *unction*. Unction is from Ankh, the immortal symbol personifying the *unction or* union of Life's two polarities (Female-O, Male-I) to begat LIFE.

Divine Alchemy....El-Khemi. El (divine), Khemi (Kamit). The Nile Valley Afrikans were the original Chemists. They had it going on! Big, BIG pyramids, which in fact were initiation temples where Divine Alchemy of the Soul was a way of life. And note, the Pyramids are *triple*, hence they are Uri & Thummim! The Great Pyramid is the "Uri-mid." Below some pyramids were a reverse pyramid underground to create a perfect double tetrahedron, I'm told.

Afrikan-Kamite civilization is still the "Uri" of the World, source of civilization and Divine Science, corrupted today as "religion," a bondage we must free ourselves from, for until we do so, we will remain dull BASE metal instead of radiant GOLD; we remain on the negative life-negating side of the Thummim (like the killers Simeon/Levi), on the unevolved beastly side of the manbeast (Sagittarian centaur). When we transmute or "cross over" to the Urim, or "other side of Jordan," through Divine Alchemy, we *resurrect* from the dead and become the transmuted life-affirming *fruitful* Twins, Ephraim & Manasseh, who replaced Simeon & Levi.

The "Thummim" are *Double* Twins, or the Four Cardinal Signs of Earth-Water-Air-Fire!

Simeon & Levi = Thummim Set #1

- Simeon & Levi = the Thummim (couple) signifying the Male & Female aspect. They were the 2nd & 3rd sons
- *Firstborn* Reuben (Leah's son) = Uri (Light). His name is from solar roots (Re, Iu).

Ephraim & Manasseh = Thummim Set #2

- Manasseh & Ephraim = the Thummim (couple) signifying the Male & Female aspect. They were Joseph's only sons.
- *Firstborn* Joseph (Rachel's son) = Uri (Light). His name is from solar roots (Iu).

EARTH = **Ephraim.**
Called the *Heifer* (that's Kamit's Holy Cow, Hathor). Ephraim even sounds like Heifer (Heiferam) for they are from the same roots (Ap /Ep, a name of the Great Mother). Ephraim is defined in Bible dictionaries as "Double Fruitfulness" or "Two Fruit Land." This is the Mother Principle of Earth.

WATER = **Levi.**
The Leviathan was the colossal Serpent of the Waters.

FIRE = **Simeon.**
Hot semen inseminating *Mother* Ephraim and She begats a "multitude of nations."

AIR = **Manasseh.**
Manasseh (Manasses in Rev. 7:6) is "the MAN," the Virile Man. Manasseh is Men-Ash and he represents AIR. Hebrew ISH means virile. The Kamite word MEN has a multitude of meanings. Manasseh (Men-Ash) is apparently derived from *Amen, Min,* and *Ash.* Amen and Min are two versions of the same god. Amen was the Hidden One for he was the effective force in the invisible wind [1] (there's our connection with Air). Amen was also the God of Fertility, represented as ithyphallic Amen-Min or Min with his perpetually erect phallus. Min was also the God of Vegetation. This connects him with *manna* (*Manna*-seh), the food or nourishment from heaven, gently falling through the *air*–like Aquarius's "waters." *Aquarius* is another version of "the Man."

1) Lurker, 26.

The higher meaning of "The *Uri* and the Thummim" is the *Divine Triad*

The Triad of the *Mother*, the Father, and Holy Child. In the patriarchal Bible this triad is called "God the Father, God the Son, and God the Holy Ghost," thereby depriving God of His Mate. *Who* do you think the "Holy Ghost" is? You're right if you guessed *The Great Mother*. The Bible does call the Holy Ghost the "Comforter" (John 14:16) –a feminine quality. The Bible also identifies the Dove as a symbol of the Holy Ghost. The Dove has anciently been a symbol of the Great Mother, –and doves love to make love. The Hebrew word for *spirit* is of the *feminine gender*. Representing the Mother and Father Principle, the "union" of Jesus and "SaMaria" (or the woman of Samaria) at the "well" produced the "Uri" of Everlasting Life. (John 4:14).

Simeon *Hearing*

Namebooks say Simeon means "hearing," apparently derived from Leah's exclamation after birthing Simeon: "Because the Lord hath heard..." (Gen. 29:33). "Hearing" is also one of the meanings of Simeon's roots. And "the Urim and the Thummim" allowed you to "hear" or receive a divine answer to a question. "Hearing" certainly relates to the *Air* Sign of Gemini, for sound travels through the AIR to reach our *ears* (another pair, hence *thummim*), and hearing is not possible without Air.

Immortal Couple

In reality, Simeon & Levi, and their replacement Ephraim & Manasseh, are not twins but opposite-sex-*couples* representing the **original meaning of Gemini –the union of sexual opposites to begat Life.** No wonder Ephraim, who represents the Mother Principle, becomes the most fruitful of all the tribes: "his seed shall become a multitude of nations" (Gen. 48:19). The original Gemini was the First Divine Couple, the Immortal Divine Lovers – our Great Mother and Great Father. They were *The Original Thummim* whose joining begat *The Urim* of Everlasting Light, hence Everlasting Life. This great Urim was the "Big Bang," –a Cosmic Orgasm! And likely more than one!

Etymology of Simeon

Category	Afrikan-Kamite Roots	Apparent Derivatives: ENGLISH		OTHERS	Comments
Semen	**s'men** • seminal. Massey, HJ, 145; 72BB1 **s-men** • establish oneself, fix in position, stablish. 602a **shemshem-t** • sesame seed. 740a	**semen** seminal seminary	**sesame** jasmine (a sexy oil)	LATIN: **seme**, seed **seminare**, to sow GREEK: **semeenareeo**, seminary **smeego**, mix, mingle, meet, join **smeek seemo**, mixing, meeting, mating, joining **seemeeo**, sign, mark **seema**, signal, sign, mark, badge **semeno**, mean, be a sign of SANSCRIT: **sam**, together **samana**, join together, combine **samasta**, combined, all HEBREW: **Shemi**, Semite **siman**, sign, mark, "esophagus & trachea" **semel**, symbol, emblem, image, **simmel**, symbolize	**Semen** creates (*establishes*) in the ***same*** image as the father. **"Open Seseme"**: Kamite *seshmu* (sexual intercourse) "survived in the Sufi love-charm designed to open the 'cave' of the Goddess: Open Sesame." (Walker, WE, 401) **Semites** are really a mixture of Afrikans and Caucasians, NOT descendents of the mythical Sem. **Simian** (pronounced like Simeon): the "simian line" is found only in the hands of apes & monkeys; dividing their palm in *half*. Simian means like an ape or monkey. Apes and monkeys are *similar* to humans.
Similar	**sem** • to resemble. 666b **sam** • representative likeness. 72BB2	same semblance resemble seem similar simile	similitude simultaneous simulate symmetry sympathy sham (imitation)		
Twin, Two Half	**sem** • two or twin. 515BB2 • dual solar plume. 19BB2	semi (half) **Semite**	semester		
Union Assemble	**sem** • to join, unite. 515BB2 **sema** • hieroglyph of union, sex. Lungs & trachea. **sma, smai** • copulate, unite, join oneself to someone or something. 667b, 599a **sma** • phallus. 599b **seshemu** • sexual intercourse. **smai-ta** • or sma-ta."union with the earth," burial. 599a **sam** • to assemble, flock together, herd. 514BB2	cement seam (is the joint) **cemetary** ("union with the Earth")	**simian** ***Shechem*** assemble ensemble symposium		
Symbol	**sam** • memorize, emblem, image. 483BB2 **smenu** • image, figure, statue.	symbol sample sampler example symptom	specimen (=spec-smen) semantic semiology (study of sign language)		

Etymology of Levi (Le-Av /Re-Ap)

Category	Afrikan-Kamite Roots	Apparent Derivatives: ENGLISH		HEBREW	Comments
Love Heart Joy Desire	**re** (le) • sun **ab** • heart (re + ab =re-ab / le-ab / le-av) **ra ab** (la ab) • to be excited with love or passion. 419a	**love** lufu (love in Old Eng.) leof (beloved in Old Eng.) **left** revere reverence reverend lion	**LIFE!**, live rhapsody rapture rapport libido ribald Libera liberty •Libra	**lev**, heart **levavi**, hearty, amicable **libba**, heart, core, nucleus **levav**, heart **liftan**, dessert	**Left and Love** are one. Your *left* side is your feminine side and the side of the Heart! **Rapture:** Love produces joy, ectasy, rapture! **Liberal**: She is liberal & generous. Mega-millions of eggs in one female. Mega-millions of sperm in one ejaculation. Billions of stars and galaxies. Thus is the nature of **Life**! *Abundance* can start with just 2 lovers reproducing, "geminating." And Life is Rife (abundant) throughout the cosmos. **Lips?** They always come in pairs (a couple). They represent the Female Principle. They are the doorway to the Mouth & Womb which are both always "wet" inside. Who has the "fullest" lips on the planet? Yes, Afrikan women –made abundantly in the very image of the Great Mother. The Nose, with its perpetual *erection* "stands" for the Masculine Principle. Mouth is horizontal; Nose is vertical. The (–) and (|) = ⊕.
Twin Couple Union Lips	**Rehiu, Reh-h** (Lehiu, Leh-h) • Twins, the Twin Lion Gods, twin fighters Horus & Set. 429a, 11BB2 **Rep-ti** • the two sisters Isis & Nephtys. 422b **rep** (lep)• to grow, bud, branch and take leaf. Churchward, SS, 371	•RE (prefix meaning REpeat) relate (relation. re =le. re-la-tion) alliance (le-ank) link (le-ank) coalition **lips** lapel relation	 level •Libra Labarum **labia** leaf liason	**levi, leui**, joined, plural, to wreathe around like a snake **levay**, auxiliary, attachment **lavud**, united	
Abundant *Rife*	**afa** • be filled, satisfied. 51BB1 **af-t, ab-t** • gift, offering, sacrifice. 4a	lavish liberal lipo (fat) •RE (prefix meaning REpeat)	**RIFE!** **rich** rabble (swarm) **ripe**	**rav**, large, strong, multi	
Reptile	**re** (le) • serpent, reptile. 417a **ref** • serpent or reptile. form of Apophis serpent. 56, 342BB2	•leviathan reptile	lizard ribbon	**•livyatan**, whale, sea monster **leta'a**, lizard	

4 Benjamin = Cancer the Crab

Cardinal **WATER** Sign

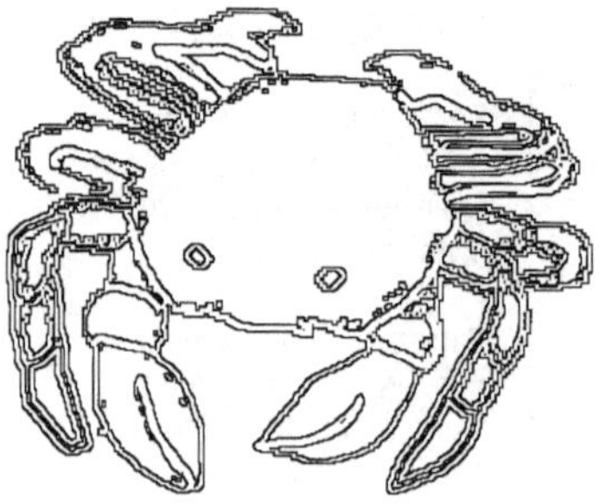

"Benjamin shall ravin as a wolf...shall devour the prey...shall divide the spoil" (Gen. 49:27). Spoil refers to booty or seized stolen goods. Ravin, raven, and Latin *rapere* means to prey, seize, plunder, tear away, greedily consume. *Wolves* seize and tear with fanged jaws. *Crabs* seize and tear with their toothed, pincer claws. Kamit's Dendera Zodiac represented Cancer as the Scarab Beetle, sign of Khepr the Beetle-god, "the seizer with his claws." *Cancer* is the Latin word for *crab* and also the name of a *ravenous* disease which *"devour[s] the prey"* who are under its *claw-like*, tenacious *grip*.

When Moses blessed the tribes, he said of Benjamin: **"The beloved of the Lord shall dwell in safety by him; and the Lord shall cover him all the day long, and he shall dwell between his shoulders"** (Deu. 33:12). The previous underlined words clearly describe or relate to the Crab, *who dwells in safety between his shoulders,* in his protective shells which *covers him all day long!*

At birth, Benjamin was originally named *Benoni* by his mother, then she *died* (Gen. 35:18). *Oni* of Ben-*oni* may be from Hebrew *ani* (poor, miserable). This relates to Cancer as the archetypal-moody sign, source of the term *crabby.* According to Bible dictionaries, the name *Benoni* means "son of my sorrow / mourning." This points to the pain in Cancer, *cancer. Oni* may also be from Kamite ***ani*** (to bring, bringing) and ***anu*** (bringer, carrier, porter). The Crab is the "carrier" of his home or shell in which he lives, bringing his burden wherever he goes, –no wonder he's so crabby.

And why did Benjamin's mother *die* after birthing him?

I'm tempted to say she was *gripped* by *cancer.* The biblical reason is "she had hard labor" ("hard" like the "shell" of the Crab) (Gen. 35:16). Likely the real reason for her death at this time was to signify entering **Amenta**, thereby showing the connection of Cancer (the *sign* and *dis-ease*) with Amenta, where people went after *dying.* (People with cancer arrive there much sooner unless they have knowledge of the many ways by which cancer may be safely healed*). **Capricorn**, the complementary sign directly opposite Cancer is also connected with death as we shall see. Amenta is the *Hidden* World (*hidden* like the Crab in its shell), the Underworld where all beings went after they died. In this sense, Amenta was a home. If you think about it, Amenta is also

* Addressed in my book, *Drugs Masquerading As Foods*

the *Womb* where people are *hidden before* they are born. The Womb is the first Home. Crabs carry their home wherever they go, so "home-ness" is surely connected with this sign. Negatively, this can be interpreted as being shut in or imprisoned; positively, it means *protection.* Crabs use their home / shell for protection. The concept of the warrior's SHELL likely originated from this (the Crab & Turtle symbolized Cancer). The Womb itself is perpetually *hidden* and perpetually wet like the water sign of Cancer. Another concept here: Cancer means to get something valuable, draw *within* like the Crab to *consume* thus digest it, then come out renewed and larger, having grown from the wisdom & knowledge of experience you *ate.* Thus Cancer entails developing one's inner core by going within to digest the experiences gathered.

Darkness-Ben is *twice* a twin

- He has *two* names: Benoni and Benjamin. One name from his mother (Benoni) and one from his father (Benjamin). This makes him a Son of Woman and Son of Man.
- He and **Joseph** *only* are full brothers, –Rachel's only two sons. In essence, he is Joseph's ***twin***. Benjamin & Joseph are another version of Judas & Christ. Judas & Christ are based on Set & Horus, representing the twin brothers of Darkness and Light. Ben is the Brother of Darkness; Joseph is the Brother of Light.

As we shall see, this picture is much deeper.

Benjamin is *Ben-Amen*

He reflects the Kamite god *Amen*, the Hidden One, the god, "who abides in all things" –imaged as the soul (ba) of all phenomena. Amen is "the sun in the belly of his Mother before his rebirth at sunrise." Benjamin's name, based on his etymology, figured as Ben-Amen, Ben-Am-In, or Ben-Ami, means:

- Aquatic Seizing Son
- Royal Seizer
- The Son Inside
- The *Good* Within
- The *Bad* Within
- *Devourer*
- Hidden Son
- Hidden Man
- The Phallus Inside
- The Divinity Within
- Son of the Right Side (Prince)

These meanings align with the Zodiacal Crab and identify Benjamin as the same.

Etymology of Benjamin (Ben-Amen)

Category	Afrikan-Kamite Roots	Apparent Derivatives & Comments	
Good Bad	**ban** • sweet, pleasant. **bena-t** • sweetness. 217b **ban** • to be evil, wicked. **ben** • evil, wickedness. 216b	**benefit** benevolence benediction bonus bona fide	**pain** ban bane banal
Penis	**benu** • male, man. 217a **benn** • virile, phallus • to copulate. 217a **benben** • obelisk (phallic pillar). 217a	**penis** peninsula pen pencil bent (stiff stalk) bandy (game stick)	banana bank (is a pile, like phallic tower) bench (*long* seat) **ben,** son, boy in Hebrew
Bind	**bent** • to bind, to tie. 219b **baent** • bind. 52BB1	**bind** band	bond bondage
Hidden Among Inside	**Amen** • The Hidden God who is in heaven. 51b **amen** • hidden. 51a **ami-ta** • between. 44a **ami-t** • between, among. **ami-t** • it which is in. 44b **ami** • person or something which is in, those who are in the waters. 44b **Ami-Uab** • "dweller in the pure place" (priest). 45a	Amen en<u>am</u>el (covers, hence *hides*) amidst among HEBREW: **amm,** to hide, conceal **emtsa,** middle, center	EM, IM prefix: <u>em</u>brace, <u>em</u>body, <u>im</u>passion
Grasp Devour	**am, amm** • to grasp, sieze. 6a **am** • devourer. **am-am** • devourers identified with the Crocodile, Am-Molech & Set. 257BB2	amass (gather, hence *grasp*) amenable amiable HEBREW: **amin,** right side	
Agree	**am** • graciousness. 49b **amam** • agreeable, kind. 50a	ARABIC: **aiman,yaman,** right side, right hand	
Right Side	**amen** • right side, right hand. 53a		

AMEN (hidden):
The turtle was the symbol for Cancer in the Babylonian Zodiac. Both, crabs and turtles HIDE or withdraw into their shells when threatened. Their shells are actually their homes which they carry wherever they go.

AMI (that which is in):
Crabs and turtles are permanently "in" their shell/home. Unless circumcised, the phallus is "inside" the foreskin, its home. Its other "home" is the Yoni. Amen-Min was the ithyphallic God of Fertility with a perpetual erection (phallus hidden in Mother's womb of the Earth). **Ami-Aha** means he who is in the palace (a king). [45a]

AMM (to grasp):
Crabs grasp with their pincers. Tenacity is said to be a major trait of this sign. When you grab something, it is "IN" your hands. It is bound, a prisoner.

AMEN (right side):
"Right side" signifies royalty, rulership. Right, royal, and rule are derived from Ra, the Kamite name of the sungod. But what have crabs and beetles to do with the Sun? The Kamites figured the Sun as an egg in the Kamite mythos; scarab beetles rolled their eggs in a protective ball of dung and soil to hatch them. This rolling was viewed as a type of transformation; rolling or rotation = the turning circle or cycles. Thus Cancer was viewed as the sign of commencement, growth, and ROtation by the ancient astrologers, and Khepr the Beetle-god was 'the Transformer.' And crabs move sideways only, imitating the sidewise movement of the Sun in the sky; the Sun reaches his highest Northern point in Cancer, then retreats "crab-like" backwards towards the ecliptic. Crabs & turtles are circular in shape like the Sun.

a, b = columns in <u>*An Egyptian Hieroglyphic Dictionary*</u>. **BB** = <u>*Book of the Beginnings*</u> (vol. 1 or 2).
WE = <u>*Women's Encyclopedia of Myths & Secrets*</u>. **AE** = <u>*Ancient Egypt: Light of the World*</u>.

5 **Judah** = Leo the Lion

Fixed **FIRE** Sign

Jacob calls him *two* lions; **"Judah is a lion's whelp...gone up... and as an old lion; who shall rouse him up?"** (Gen. 49:9). This matches the original Afrikan story from which it was copied where Horus was the *Twin* Lions of the *Two* Horizons (east and west):

- Horus the young Lion (the rising Sun or Atum-Iu the Son)
- Horus the elder Lion (the setting Sun or Atum-Ra the Father)

"I am the twin lions, the heir of Ra," [1] states Horus. Modeled from Horus, Christ is called "the Lion of the tribe of Judah" (Rev. 5:5). The Sun in *Aries* is the old **Ram** (Father) in the west who is sacrificed, then resurrects as the young **Lamb** (Son), the new Sun rising in the east. The Sun in *Taurus* –as Horus– was the Golden **Calf** (worshiped by the Israelites) who became the **Bull** of Heaven as the incarnation of his father Osiris. The young Sun in Leo is the rising "**lion's whelp..gone up**"; and as the aged sun or "**old lion**" sinking in the west, "who shall rouse him up?" Ancient Egypt's Twin Lions of the Two Horizons is the Afrikan origin of Europe's tradition of *double* lion statues flanking the entrances of significant public buildings.

Leo is also the sign of royalty. So Judah (like Horus-Christ) is associated with rulership: "thy father's children shall bow down before thee" (Gen. 49:8). "The sceptre shall not depart from Judah..." (Gen. 49:10). And Judah or Judas was a dynastic name for the priest-kings of Judea for a hundred years.[2]

Judah is derived from Egyptian **Iu-Ta**. Iu means double, ever coming. Iu was the Ever Coming One, the resplendent double-god in two persons (hence *Twin* Lions), figured as the Sun upon the Double Horizon; the Father in the *west*, the Son in the *east*. Horus, Christ, and other Sungods were IU, the Ever-Coming Son (Sun).

The Lion was a solar symbol in Egypt. Feline images were only symbolic of the Sungod and Sungoddess. And this Sun-deity was double and ever-coming, from one Zodiacal Age to the next. Eternal. As s/he moves through the 12 sectors of the Great Wheel of the Solar Zodiac, the symbol of that sector becomes the popular symbol of worship for about 2000 years until the *hand of the zodiacal macro-clock* moves to the *next number* or Zodiacal Sign. It takes about 26,000 years for the hand to complete one full rotation, or for the Wheel to make one complete turn.

1) Massey, AE, 334. 2) Walker, WE, 481.

Two Five Seven

Leo is the 5th sign. Five is connected with Judah, along with Two & Seven. 2+5=7 and 7-5=2. Judah, by definition includes duality (Two):

- Judah has **5** sons (Gen. 46:12). **2** were twins by Tamar.
- In the **5**th verse of Chapter **5** in Revelation, Christ is called "the Lion of the tribe of Judah."
- Judah is the name of **2** of Christ's ancestors and **2** of his disciples.
- The name Judah is significantly related to Christ in **7** ways: as 1 of his brothers; 2 of his ancestors; 2 of his disciples; as Jude a "servant of Christ," and Christ himself is a form of Judah as "the Lion of the Tribe of Judah." The name Jesus (Jehoshua) is from the same roots as Judah.
- **There are 13 biblical variants of the name!** signifying another Zodiac, or *Ju-diac!*

Judith	Juda	Judah	Juttah	Jude
Judas	Jehudi	Jehudijah	Euodia	Eudias
Judea	Judaea	Jehud		

Therefore the meanings of Judah's name include:

- Double Divine Fire
- Dual Evercoming Light
- Evercoming Savior
- Double Duality (Iu & Ta both mean double)
- The Double Land:

Thus Judah is the Sun in Leo, the *paternal* sign signifying the Great Father in the Zodiac who is Two in One.

Etymology of Judah (Iu-Ta)

Category	Afrikan-Kamite Roots	Apparent Derivatives	Comments
Divine Young Double Just Good Light	**Iu** • double, ever comming. • name of the Sungod. Heru • Har-Iu, Horus, the ever <u>young</u>, evercoming, divine, Sungod. The Calf, Lamb of God Hu • (HuHu, HuHi) a divine name of the Eternal Mother of All Beginning. Also a name of the Divine Father.	**You**, **hue**, **HUman**, hero (Har-Iu, Heru, Horus), **young** (Iu-Ankh), youth, juvenile, rejuvenate, **Jewel**, **Jew** **Jehovah**, Jove, Jupiter (Father Iu), **Jehoshua**, **Jesus** (Hebrew Yehoshua, from Kamite Iu-Sa), **Joseph** (Son Iu. sif=son), **Ewe**, just, adjust justice, jury, judge, judicious, **joy** (is bright!), **eu-** (prefix meaning good, well, true), <u>eu</u>phoria, <u>eu</u>phony, <u>eu</u>logy, <u>Eu</u>charist **Old God *Young*:** "Iu means the coming one, and the Iu-ank, the coming life is the Young. This is another form of the Repa, Branch, Prince, or Heir-Apparent to the throne. The Young God or God Young...is the oldest in the world." (211BB1)	**YOU**, yes, You! You *Jewel.* IU-*<u>El</u>*. Know ye not that ye are gods? (Ps. 82:6, Jn. 10:34) –a divine being, the HU-man. And God's Light comes in 7 Hues. **Holy Ewe.** The Ewe is the female sheep, anciently regarded as holy. Jacob's wives Leah (Holy Cow) and Rachel (Holy Ewe) "which two did build the house of Israel" (Ruth 4:11). **Double Duality** (Iu & Ta both mean double): Taiu means "people of the Two Lands, i.e. the Egyptians' Also means the four quarters of the world, the lands [815]. Taiu is Iu-Ta in reverse! Double Duality implies 4, the essence of the Kamite Astrological Cross (+ in a circle ⊕). This timeless symbol shows duality horizontally (–) and vertically (|). In other words, Double Duality. This = yin & yang, male & female; or the great Zodiacal Circle of 4 divisions, each representing one of the 4 elements (earth, air, fire, water). **The word JEW** evolved from Gyu, Giu, <u>Iu</u>, <u>Iuu</u>, Iuw, Ieuu, Ieuy, Iwe, Iow, Iewe, Ieue, Iue, Ive, Iew. (Freedman, FF, 16, 17)
Judah (Double Land)	**Iuta** • the double god, the double land. Taiu • people of the Two Lands, i.e. the Egyptians. 815 ta • flame, fire. 864 • a mark of the dual. 821a • land, country. taa • divine emanation, essence of a god. 821b	HEBREW: Yehudi, Yehuda ENGLISH: Jew, Judah, Judea SANSCRIT: Ioudi, Iadu, Yadu LATIN: Iudaeus, Iudaea **The Double Land:** "The name of Judea or Judah was named in Egyptian. It appears upon the monuments as Iuta or Iutah. Iu is dual, ta is earth or land, and Iuta is the double land or double earth of the Egyptian mythos localized in Judea." (Massey, AE, 503)	

6 **Dinah** = Virgo the Virgin

Mutable **EARTH** Sign

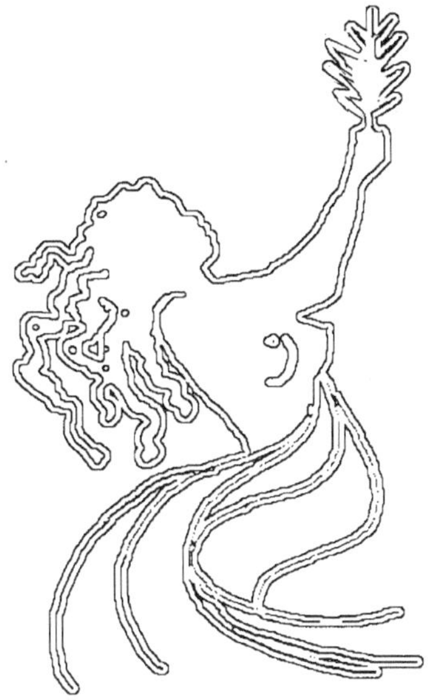

Virgin Dinah was the only daughter of Jacob and Leah (Gen. 30:21, 46:15). Chauvinist Jacob on his dying bed, blesses all his 12 sons (Gen. 49) but totally skips his only daughter. No mention is made of her. In fact, very little is said about Dinah in the Bible. Only through the true etymology of her name, do we begin to discover who she really is and why she has been skipped.

Dinah is the Great Mother. In line with their character, the Bible's chauvinist rewriters debase her like they debase all the forms of the Great Mother Goddess in the Bible, by having her raped (Gen. 34) and compared to the harlot (Gen. 34:31). The "Dinaites" (Ezra 4:9) are mentioned just once in the Bible (KJV) but *translated* (edited out!) as "judges" in other versions of the Bible. This is the only apparent acknowledgment of the *tribe* of Dinah. And if you look at a map of the territories of Israel, really there are *two* territories of "Dan," whose name is from the same roots as Dinah's. One of these territories is disguisedly for Dinah (!) without acknowledging it in order to avoid giving credit to the feminine aspect. **So in reality, there are 13 tribes and 13 territories of Israel!** This agrees with the 13-signs of the original Zodiac, the feminine Lunar Zodiac (women have 13 menstrual periods per year). Yes, the Lunar Zodiac is there in the Bible, well disguised.

The name *Dinah* is derived from Egyptian Tann (Tannen, Tanen-t, Thennit), a form of the primal Mother as Goddess Earth, and Great Goddess of the Underworld /Amenta. So really She is not Jacob's *daughter* any more than the first woman came from a man's rib (the reverse is true; every man on the planet came from a woman, including the "Son of God."). She is *his* Mother and the *Mother of All Living*, the title bestowed on Her as *Eve* (Gen. 3:20) and Sarah (Gal. 4:26). The sign of Virgo corresponded to Isis or the Mother God by the ancients.[1] And The Mother is The Queen. This is disguisedly acknowledged in that Her lover and would-be husband *Shechem*, was a prince, son of Hamor. *Hamor* is really *Amor*, a name of the Great Mother meaning *Love*. (Dinah) Tannen was reknown in Rome as Dianna the Queen of Heaven, the Triple Goddess as the Lunar Virgin, Mother of Creatures, and Huntress (Destroyer). As the Moon Goddess at the height (zenith) of Her powers, Her title was Meridiana (Mary-Diana), source of the word *meridian*.[2]

1) Massey, AE, 299. 2) Walker, WE, 650.

Multi-breasted Black Diana of Ephesus, with Africoid features, nappy hair, & Egyptian crown. One of many ancient versions of The Great Mother.

She was the jet-black Many-Breasted Artemis or Diana of Ephesus, and Her Temple at Ephesus was one of the Seven Wonders of the World. The Gospels (or anti-Afrikan, anti-female, albino-ized false Christianity) commanded total destruction of all the temples of Diana, the Great Goddess "whom all Asia and the world worshippeth" (Acts 19:27). Goddess Diana had title of "Mother" and was famed for her virginal purity.[1] In Carthage She was Tanit. Her temple was called the Shrine of the Heavenly Virgin. Her priestesses were famous astrologers. She was the biblical Astoreth, Asherah. She was Libera, the Goddess of Libya whose festival (the Liberalia or Bacchanalia) was celebrated annually in the ancient world.

The Afrikan Goddess Tanen was a form of Hathor, the amorous sensuous Queen in the Earth of Tanen, the Lower Earth, land of the nocturnal sun and domain of the deceased. Tanen was the land (Ta) beneath the waters of the Nen or Nun. The **Nun** was the starting point of Beginning, the inundating firmamental water encircling all the world with the aerial ocean which the Europeans call "space." Tanen and Amenta (the Underworld or Lower Earth) are apparently the same or inseparably connected, Tanen being an earlier form of Amenta. The descriptions of both are often identical. The line between Earth and Tanen is fuzzy or non-existent. Ta also means Earth.

Before we continue, let's read this definition from a dictionary:

> **TWAT:** "*n. Obscene.* **1.** The vulva. **2.** Used as a disparaging term for a woman. [Origin unknown]." [2]

"Origin unknown." Now we will discover the true origin of "twat," why it is "a disparaging term for a woman," and its connection with Tann-Dinah. When the Albino man came to power, he did his best to suppress, repress, depress, or otherwise destroy the Supreme Being worshipped around the globe on all continents as Goddess –a Female, the Great Mother of All Beginning. The **War against Her** is still in progress. Her sacred names and special words relating to Her qualities were demoted, dragged into the mire, reversed into obscenity. (Many obscene sexual "four-lettered" curse words were holy prior to the rise of *patriarchy.*) Where it served their purpose, The Great Mother's divine qualities were confiscated and transferred to their white male Christian god. The word "twat" is undeniably derived from *Tuat.*

Tanen was the location of Tuat, the most sacred place, for Tuat was the Source, the Mother's Womb of Life, the Abyss of the Beginning from which Life emanated; the *Tepht* or Unfathomable *Deep*, "the darkness on the face of the deep, the light breaking out of the darkness; the waters and the life springing forth from the waters." These are the same "waters" in Genesis that was divided into the upper and lower firmaments during the Creation (Gen. 1:2, 6). Tuat was the Birthplace of Eatable Plants, the Birthplace of Water, the Birthplace of Water within the Earth, and secret source of the Nile. Tuat, was the "Cleft" or Gate of entry to Amenta. Tanen is an earlier form of Amenta, and the Entrance to Amenta was called the "mouth of the cleft," as it was termed in Abydos.[3]

1) Doane, 333. 2) American Heritage Dictionary, 3rd Edition. 3) Massey, AE, 655.

"Still the secret source of water, and thence of life, was hidden in that land [Tanen /Amenta]. This was the world of the gnomes, the goblins, and other elemental spirits...The beginning in this region was the abyss [Tuat] inside the earth from whence the water welled that was to be most sacredly preserved as very source itself. This subterranean realm had somewhat the character of a mine with the water welling upward from the unplumbed depths below. It was a mine of hidden treasure, one form of which was gold. But first of all the treasure was water, the primary element of life. Hence a fount [Tuat] of the water of life was localized in the well of this under-world which the Egyptians divinized as the Neter-Kar because it was the source of water and the way by which life came into the world. Here the spirits of earth, the powers of Khar...were portrayed as watchers over the water of life and protectors of the hidden treasures underground." [1] (underlines added)

"**The Neter Kar**" and "Khar" of the preceding paragraph is the **Kar** we met earlier in Chapter 1 of this book:

> **Kar** of Afrika's Nile Valley was the inner soul of Mother Earth, a beautiful ebony virgin who was the "Heart of the World." Shrines of *Kar*nak in Egypt and *Car*nac in Brittany were dedicated to Kar, the Goddess of Agriculture, especially the *growth* of grain. She was Kore to the Arabs and Greeks, Ceres to the Romans. Derivatives of her name include cereal, corn, kernel, cardiac (heart), care, and cherish.

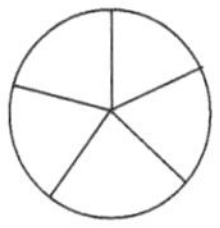

Tuat, the Underworld
(Budge, EL, 75)

And remember her symbol was the 5-pointed star. The hieroglyph of Tuat was that same star in a circle! Virgo holds a spike of grain with 5 kernals.

Some people still experience Tanen today.
An indigenous Afrikan, Malidoma Somé, who authored, *Of Water and the Spirit,* writes about some of his incredible experiences. Apparently, the Land of Tanen, with its "little people" (source of the legendary gnomes, elves, etc.) is alive and well. As a child, Malidoma once chased a rabbit which disappeared into an opening in the Earth. When he got to the hole and looked in, to his astonishment, there was a tiny little man, sitting at the entrance who began to scold him. He looked beyond the man and noticed that there was a whole world of living beings, an underworld civilization to which this gnome-man belonged.

Biblical variants or names from the same root as Dinah include:

Diana	Adna	Tanach	Dodanim
Dannah	Adnah	Taanach	Rodanim
Dan	Addan	Tanumeth	Othniel
Daniel	Adin	Taanath-Shiloh	Jathniel
Dinhabah	Adina	Jadon	Joktan
Dan-Jaan	Adino	Adonis	Zaretan
Dionysius	Ethan	Adonijah	Zarthan
	Eden	Adoniram	Zartanah

1) Massey, AE, 412.

The derivatives of TANN reflect Her attributes:

- Tann is *Black*, like the Earth She personifies, reflected in the words **TAN** (to darken) and **TONE** (color).

- Tann is the *Womb*, reflected in the **DEN**. For the den, pit, or cave is an ancient womb-symbol.

- Tann is *Wisdom*, whose symbol is the *Serpent*. "Be wise as serpents" said Jesus, Her son. Levia**THAN** was the title of Moses's brazen serpent, called Nehush**TAN** (2Kings 18:4).

- Tann is *Great*, reflected in **DINO** (huge) of *dino*saur, *dyna*mite, ti*tan*ic, and ***Den*dera**. **Dinah is MaDinah, MaDonna**: Ma (Mother; Great) Tann, the Great Donna, Great Lady, Great Mother...And Great Circle.

- Tann is the *Queen*, thus **DON, DONNA** are titles for a Lord and Lady. And royal ruling families are **DYN**asties.

- Tann is *Water*, thus **DAN**k means wet. Rivers are named after Her: the Jordan, Tanga, Dan, Danube, and Dneiper. She is the Giver of liquid nourishment, pouring from Her countless bulging pendulous breasts as Diana of Ephesus, the Dea Multimammiae. The ancient Milk Mother, Wetnurse, and Holy Cow from whose udder flows the Milky Way. Dinah (Virgo) is born right after Zebulon (Gen. 29:21), who represents Pisces. The *water*-sign of Pisces is the complementary sign directly *opposite* Virgo. And Dinah is Leah's 7th child. Seven is connected with Water (and Love).

- Tann is *Sensual*, the amorous Goddess of Love reknown as Aphrodite, Libera, and Venus. In the biblical story, Dinah's rapist/lover/would-be-husband is Prince *Shechem*, son of *Hamor*. *Shechem* is from *seshemu*, meaning sex. And *Hamor* is really Amor, the *amorous* Tann, Great Goddess of Love giving us **TAN**tric sex and he**DON**ic pleasure in the original Gar**DEN** of **EDEN**, the Garden of A-Tann! For both "A" and "Tann" are among Her ten thousand names. So the "Garden of God" was really the "Garden of *Goddess!*" or Mother Earth *–Kar-Tan*. And in the *middle* ("heart") of this Garden was the *Phallic* Tree of Life, protected by the serpent-god Lo**TAN** according to older versions of the same plagiarized story. The MIDDLE = the Heart, from which Love flows.

***Eden* return us to Virgo,** the zodiacal sign honoring our Great Mother as the Provider of Food abun**DAN**tly. Virgo holds a spike of wheat, representing food that we *eat*. EAT is from EDen or Old English ETan. Famed for its lavish (*love-ish*) growth, the soil of Eden was likely jet black, the richest type. Thus, Dinah is MaDONna, the Great Mother Tannen, the Black Virgin Goddess of Earth reknown as the *Earth* sign of Virgo.

Etymology of Dinah (Tan)

Category	Afrikan-Kamite Roots	Apparent Derivatives	Comments
Earth Dark Abode	**tenn** • ground, earth. 838a **Tanen-t** • ancient Earth Goddess, mate of Tanen. 819b **Thennit** • [Tanen-t] a form of Hathor. 856a **Tanen** • ancient Earth God, consort of Tanen-t. 819b **ta** • land, earth, ground, world. 815a **aten** • ground, earth. 13b **ten** • hole of a serpent. 837b **then-t** • place, abode, sanctuary. 856a	tundra •dune •dungeon (*underground* chamber) den tent tank container contain retain tangible dense density tan tannin tone tint taint tinge tincture (tint) •dun (brownish grey) dung dingy thunder (deep sound) thunk POLYNESIAN: tanaoa (darkness)	**Tang & Twa** Kamite TANG means dwarf. Actually it means more than this! The **Tang** are named after Life (Ankh) and their Mother, Goddess Tann. In the word ***Tang*** are Ta, Tan, Ankh. The **Tang** are the "little people" who were the ancestors (*ANK-Astors*) of humanity. Ta (the), Tan (Tann), Ank (ancestors). Kamites called them the **TWA**. Their descendents are called the Pygmies (a derogatory term). **Tang** then, means both, "The Ancestors" and "The Mother's Original Children." The original children of Goddess Tann were also called the **Tuatha**. **Tuat** or **Tuatha** is likely the Afrikan source of the Kamite word ***TWA***, and the word **DWA**RF! For the **Twa** were **dwa**rfs. The **Twa** and the underworld of **Tuat** is the Afrikan source of all the "little people" stories regarding elves, dwarfs, leprechauns, gnomes, Hobbits, etc. The Twa were famous for their **DANCing** (TANG=DANC). Pyramid texts piously called them "Dancers of God." Hallet, a Frenchman who studied and lived with them for 20 years wrote, "The Pygmies cannot live without dancing, singing, and making music." [17, 18]. The Kamite god **BES** is undeniably an Afrikan Twa (Pygmy). No wonder he was the God of Dancing, Music, and Pleasure. You can bet he had "soul." **Tanganyika** was named after them. For the area around Afrika's largest lake (location of the sacred Mountain/s of the Moon) is the birthplace of Humanity. Tanganyika joined with Zanzibar in 1964 to form **Tanzania**, still bearing the name of Tan. **China's *Tang* dynasty** is likely named after them. The Tang were Afrikans who settled in China. The Tang were reknown for encouragement of the arts and literature.
Serpent	**Tenten** • name of Serpent Deity. 839b **Tentenit** • serpent on royal crown. 881a **Aten-Ur-Nub** • serpent-headed supporter of the throne of Ra. 98	**Leviathan** Nehushtan python intestines	
Water	**tun** • rising flood, inundation. 824b **tennu** • canal, stream. 882b **tun ah** • title of the Nile deity. 825a	dank (wet) dunk (to immerse) Tanga river Don river Danube river Dnieper river tender (soft. water is soft)	
Weighing Judging	**Aten** • ancient form of Har-Makhu [Horus of the Scales or Libra]. 339AE **ten** • highest, Egyptian troy weight. 77BB1 **thenuit** • weight, quantity. 856b **tenu** • to count, reckon. 856b **tena** • to question, interrogate. 882a **aten** • to listen, to hear. 50,51BB1	**ten** teen thirteen fourteen... denary (tenfold) •ton (a weight. great) attention attend intend instinct tenable (true, trustworthy, accurate, credible) authentic (verified, tested, tenable, true) tantamount (equal) itinerary (schedule, plan) tender (cash; offer/grant; soft) •dun (invoice, charge) identify identity identical	
High Great	**Tanen-t** • ancient Earth Goddess, mate of Tanen the Earthgod. 819b **ten** • to raise up, raised, high, distinguished. 980b **then** • to lift up, raise, promote, distinguish. 856a **tentha** • steps, throne. 884a **ten** • throne, elevated seat. 513BB2 **thenti** • throne, chair of state. 857a **then-t** • great, distinguished. 856a **teni** • to possess honor or fame, to be *honorable* [like the judge]. 837b **atn** • to rule, a lord. 625BB2 **aten** • deputy, agent, vicar. **Aten** • god of the solar disk 103a **aten** • disk of the sun. 101b • the sun. 625BB2	**Dendera** meridian **Madonna** (Great Lady) Don/Donna (Lord /Lady) adonis dynast (ruler) dynasty dean dunce cap (is high. worn originally by sorcerers, etc.) dynamic dynamite dynamo titanic dinosaur (dino=huge) •ton (great amnt.) dandy (elegance, agreeable) dainty (of refined choice, excellent, delicious) deinte (excellent. Middle English) distinguish edan (hill row of the rampart) •dune (*hill* or ridge of sand) dene (dune) donjon (castle tower)	
Dwarf	**tang** • dwarf. 867b **teng** • dwarf, Pygmy, dancing dwarf. 883b	**dance** (see comments) Tanganyika Tang (Chinese dynasty)  BES	
Sex Love Pleasure Eating Abundance	**Goddess Tannen-t** was a form of Hathor, the protoype for the Goddess of Love such as Aphrodite, Venus... **tunu** • plant or shrub. 873a **tun** • a green substance 873a **ten** • to extend. 21BB2 **tennu** • increase, multiply, grow, millions. 21BB2	**tantra** **Eden** eat (from Old English ETAN) dine dinner garden dentro- (tree like) tang (flavor, savor) tantalize tangible hedonism (pursuit of pleasure) **abundant** tank donate donor pardon condone GREEK: **hedone** pleasure HEBREW: **atan**, delight, pleasure **thnn**, to extend	

7 **Asher** = Libra the Balance

Cardinal **AIR** Sign

"Out of Asher his bread shall be fat, and he shall yield royal dainties." (Gen. 49:20) The Sun is in Libra during the Autumn Equinox when the two halves of day and night are equal in length, indicating Nature has reached a point of perfect Balance, hence Libra is represented by the Scales. In this period, the Egyptians *weighed* their harvest prior to selling or storing it.[1]

Asher is derived from Kamite *Ashr* or *Ash*, both meaning the **Tree of Life.** Ash is a primary name of the Great Mother or Tree of Life whose "bread (harvest, fruit) shall be fat (abundant)." *Dainties* refer to something edible and delicious, like the *fruit* of this Tree. *Royal* is from *Ra*, a name of the sun; fruit can only ripen from the Sun's *rays* (another word from Ra). Every fruit used to be a flower! The heart of flowers (pistil & stamen) are the sex organs of trees and plants. A fruit is the ripened ovary of a seed-bearing plant. **The sex organs are one with the Tree of Life,** being the means of Life's propagation. Thus "out of Asher [the seed *out* of his/her loins] his bread [offspring, progeny] shall be fat [multiplied, many]." Like Jacob, just before his death, Moses also blessed the Children of Israel, saying of Asher "Let him be blessed with children" (Deut. 33:24).

Asher is the Tree of Life. The Tree is a perfect symbol of *Balance*; it is half under and half above the ground with a middle *upright* section. Its roots reach *down* into the *dark depths* of Earth, while its branches reach *up* into the *bright heights* of heaven. Thus it *draws* equally from earth and heaven while yet *giving* unto both. Its *hidden* roots are equal in scope to its *visible* branches. In the Tree, opposites are unified and come to a perfect Balance that supports life, –yielding oxygen, fruit, nuts, and beauty to nourish us on all levels.

Libra is the Heart!

–the Middle, the Joint itself, the Point of Balance for life's two polarities, where conflict is resolved and opposites meet face to face. Libra is the 7th sign, and 7 is the *midpoint* of the sacred number 13, sacred because of its connection with The Mother and the female menstrual cycle. The Tree of Life was in the *middle* of the Garden of Eden. Middle is the center. Balance is possible only at the center or Midpoint on the Scales.

1) Thorsten, 159.

Asher is also AsAr (Asar, Azar), meaning born of Ast (Isis). Azar is a Kamite version of the Great Father, consort of the Great Mother, whose numerous titles include King of Kings, God of Gods, and God of *Regeneration*. He represented Corn, and was thus called "The Bread of Life." The Sun was one of his manifestations. He was worshiped as **Osiris** by the Greeks, **Serapis** (Asar-Apis) by the Romans, and **Asshur** by the *Assyr*ians. **Asar also mean ten;** King Azariah (2Ki. 14:21) was the 10th King of Judah [1] (also called Uzziah). "**Jeshurun**" was the title of the 10-tribe Israel of Moses's time. (Deu. 33:5, 26). What does 10 have to do with Libra, the *7th* sign? Ten = 10 or IO; the I= male polarity while the O = female polarity. The I and O are joined or reconciled/ balanced in Libra. The Kamite Ankh personifies this, and Ankh means both *Life* and *to Join*. You have *five* fingers on each hand, each *side* of the *scale* of your body.

Azar (Osiris) throughout the Bible

Azar's name as **Azariah** (Azar-Jah) is the name of 27 males in the Bible (!) who were either princes, chiefs, or priests; two were Kings of Judah. In addition, some 30 other males in the Bible bear his name in variant spellings which include:

Azzur	Ezar	Eliezur (Heli-Asar or Asar the Sun)
Assir	**Ezra**	Eleazar (Heli-Asar or Asar the Sun)
Jasher	Jazer	Elasar (El-Asar or God Asar)
Jeezer	Hezir	**Lazarus** (El-Azar)
Esar-haddon	Izri	Jezrahiah (Azar-Ra-Jah)
Izrahiah (Azar-Ra-Jah)	Izhur	**Israel** (Asar-Ra-El or Isis-Ra-El)
Asarel (Asar-El)	**Ashriel**	**Asriel** (Asar-Ra-El or Isis-Ra-El. Num. 26:31; 1Chr. 7:14. Almost same as Israel!)
Jeshurun (Asar-On)		

Rocco writes that the name *Asher* means to be straight, upright, happy, "the erect virile member charmed with the act of its proper function." [2] In Hebrew, **yashar** means "upright, straight, honest;" **asar** means spouse. In Egyptian, Asar's name means "**born of Ast**" (Ash, Isis. **Ar** means born of); **aser** means staff, mace, tamarisk tree. Since Azar was the God of Regeneration, his numerous titles and names were often linked with or became synonymous with his phallus, such as "Seker" and "M'tha Au" (Long Phallus). In the form of the god Par, he was called "Lord of the Phallus." [3]

Libra's other sexual connections

1) The Hall of Maat (Truth) was the Hall of Justice, the Hall of the Two Truths. Since Maat expressed the equilibrium of the universe, its symbol was the Scales, representing oneness in duality. The entrances of Kamit's halls or temples were flanked by a pair of phallic pillars (obelisks).
3) In astrology, Libra is ruled by Venus, the planet of Love. In fact, the word Libra, Love, and Equilibrium have common roots.
4) The basic shape of the Scales resemble the sex organs, and like the Scales, the male organs both "hang" and "stand erect."
5) Opposite Libra is its complementary sign Aries, flaming red with the Fire of Life or passionate sexual energy bursting forth as Spring.

1) Bradley, CP, 45. 2) Rocco, 17. 3) Budge, GE-vII, 19.

The Ankh-Tree of Life and Cross-Tree of Death

The Ankh represents Life's polarities, including the male/female sex organs and their union. Both are necessary for procreation. The Cross was a type of tree and also a symbol of the *male* genitals, –which *hang* like the many *men* which were *hung* or crucified upon it, for the Ankh without its "head" is the Christian Cross, the symbol of death and Tree of Death.

Upright in perfect Balance and Love, Asher is Libra, the cosmic Scales of Heaven.

Etymology of Asher

Category	Afrikan-Kamite Roots	Apparent Derivatives: ENGLISH, ETC.:		Apparent Derivatives: HEBREW
Tree Stand Existence	**Ash** • The Tree of Life. 82BB2 **Ashr** • Tree of Life. 622BB2 **aser** • staff, tamarisk tree, foilage branches. 90a **isr** • stalks of papyrus. 143b	**essence** **S** (in endingS, existS) yes **is** as was **exist** (from Latin *sistere*) sistere (*to stand* in Latin)	–escence (suffix meaning state, process, as in flourescence) –escent (suffix meaning becoming / resembling, as in juvenescent, opalescent)	**Ashrh**, **Ashr**, Tree of Life. sacred tree **yashar**, upright, straight, honest, smooth **ishh**, to stand, to stand out **ish**, being, existence
Feminine	**Ash** • a name of the Great Mother (Ash, As-t, Isis). 82BB2	**-ess** (suffix meaning female, as in Goddess, sculptress) **sister** **she** **hyssop** GREEK: **Isis**, Ast	astral Easter East Ishtar star **Astrology** Astronomy	
Issue	**Ash** • Water of Life, river. 205BB1 **ash** • emission, issue, emanation, liquid. 9,326BB2 **as** • secreting part of the body. 9BB2 **ash** • much, numerous. 137a **asha** • abundance, frequent. 137a	say issue usher juice ooze secret (to issue) oasis **S, ES** (plurality suffix, as in books, benches)	ARABIC: **asarah**, juice **asara**, to squeeze GREEK: **ousia**, substance LATIN **ius**, broth, soup	**asis**, fruit juice, essence •**zera**, seed
Masculine Pubescent Strength	**Asar** • Osiris, God of Regeneration, epitome of masculinity. The Son, Brother, Consort, Husband of Ash (Isis) 294BB2 **"The Asar...was the son of the mother, and later consort."** 294BB2 **ash** • seminal source. 9,326BB2 **as-ti** • testicles. 9b **sherau** • pubescent. 3BB2 **usr** • strength. Budge, EHD, cxii • prevail, valiant, sustain. 15BB2	sir sire	GREEK: **Osiris**, Asar, Azar ARABIC: **azr**, strength	**ish**, virile, masculine, man, male, husband **ashr**, attain puberty **asar**, spouse **ashar**, to be married **ashr**, to become the spouse /husband •**zera**, seed **sakhar**, hire, rent, wages, reward **sakir**, wage earner, hired worker, employee
Ten	**asar** • ten.	Jeshurun (name of the 10-tribe Israel of Moses' time)		**eser**, **asara**, ten **asor**, decade **isser**, tithe

8 Dan = Scorpio, the Scorpion, *Eagle & Serpent*

Fixed **WATER** Sign

When Dan was born, his mother said "God hath judged men" (Gen. 29:6). When his father blessed him, he said: **"Dan shall judge...shall be a serpent by the way, an adder in the path, that biteth"** (Gen. 49:17). Adder means *serpent*, a word from Latin *serpere*, to creep. Snakes and scorpions are both *creeping* animals that sting or "biteth." And Scorpio is the only sign represented by *three* symbols; the Serpent, Scorpion, and Eagle. In fact, in ancient times the constellation of Scorpio was also called the Eagle due to its proximity to Aquila the Eagle.[1]

"Dan shall judge." Really it's "*Tannet* shall judge," for She was the Original Judge, Lady of the Scales, Libera the Lady of Justice. Tannet is none other than Goddess Maat, the Great Judge in Amenta, the Underworld. The name of Dan and his sister Dinah are both from Kamite Tann (Tanen, Tanen-t, Aten). Dan is apparently the biblical version of the Earth God Tanen, consort of the Earth Goddess Tannet. To the Phoenicians he was Dan-El, god of divination, transformed into a Hebrew prophet (Daniel). His powers emanated from Goddess Dana (Tannet) and her sacred serpents.

Serpent Dan and Wisdom

"Dan...shall be a serpent." The Serpent is an ancient symbol for Wisdom and is inseparable from the primal Mother of All. "Be wise as serpents" said Christ. One of Her symbols was the Ureaus serpent on Kamite crowns. The same serpent is diabolized in the biblical version of the Garden of Eden. In an earlier Canaanite version of this story, this serpent god was called Lo**TAN** or La**DON**, guardian of the holy fruit of the Tree of Life –the Tree being a symbol of the generous Primal Mother. Nehush**TAN** was the name of the brazen serpent made by Moses and worshiped by the Israelites (2Kings 18:4). Levia**THAN** was the Hebrew title of this serpent. In Kamite symbolism, there are two types of serpents. One is evil (serpent of draught, negation, and death), the other is good (the Uraeus serpent of Life, worn on the frontlets of the gods and crowns of Kamite royalty).[2]

"Other Dans" in the Bible are fragments of the original Afrikan god Tann. As to be expected, they are appropriately connected with Wisdom:

- Daniel of Ezekial (14:14, 20; 28:3) was famous for his wisdom.
- Daniel of the Book of Daniel was a prophet of great wisdom and skill in astrology and interpreting dreams.
- Ethan was so famous for his wisdom that Solomon's wisdom could be described as exceeding Ethan's (1Kings 4:31). Ethan was the Sumerian god Etana,[3] who was the Kamite Tanen.

1) Jackson, CBC, 195. 2) Massey, AE, 646. 3) Walker, WE, 286.

Scorpio Unites–Divides Opposites

Scorpio is the symbol of conjunction, expressing both creation and destruction, birth and death. In Scorpio, Heaven/Earth, and Light /Darkness are united or divided in the same sign. For the Scorpion/Snake crawls on the ground, living in the Darkness of the Earth while Eagles soar in the sky, living in treetop-nests in the Light of the Heavens. This aligns with the meaning of TAN as the joint or break, described thus by Massey: "No Hebrew scholar ever yet knew what was intended by the words 'Tan' and 'Tannin,' which include the whale that swallowed Jonah, the serpent that tempted Eve, the leviathan of Job ...it is applied to creatures of the desert and monsters of the deep, ...Islanders are the Tena in Egyptian. Lunar eclipses are Tennu; they cut off the light...Tenu is the **joint or break**, as the number ten. ...Egypt as the Tan, whether celestial or geographical, was the divided heavens or countries."[1] Derived from TAN, the word and number TEN personifies this joint & break. Ten is 10 or IO representing Yin & Yang or the two polarities of Earth and Sky; Up and Down, phallic Yang (I) and yonic Yin (O). Dan is high (an eagle) and low (a serpent, scorpion). The roots of his name both mean height and depth (like number 10 which goes from 1 to 10).

Wet Tann

In Joshua 21:25, the Levites' city is called Taanach, which is mentioned seven times only in the Bible.[2] Seven relates to water. In Egyptian, another meaning of tan (tun, tennu) is water. The Great Mother represented the "Waters," thus rivers were named after Her –the Tana rivers in Kenya and Norway, and Europe's Danube, Don, and Dnieper. *Ithnan*, name of a biblical town, means "flowing constantly." And *Ethanim*, name of the 7th month of the Hebrew calendar, means "always flowing with water." [3] Scorpio is the Fixed *Water* Sign of the Zodiac.

Punisher Dan

In Hebrew, *dan* means punish, judged; Adon means lord. "Dan shall *judge*." Dan is linked with the Earth and Sun (as the Serpent & Eagle). Shining from on high and witnessing everything from his lofty position, the Sun is in an excellent position to be a judge, and judges sit the highest in their courtrooms. Since Dan is also a serpent, he is a "wise" judge, the best kind. And the serpent biting its tail is a sun-symbol. Two cobras flanked Kamit's *winged* solar disk. Winged? There's our Eagle again, for these wings belonged to Horus as the Golden Hawk.

A judged person though, might get "punished" like the **rider** in the path of Dan who got *bitten*: "Dan...shall be a serpent by the way, an adder in the path, that **biteth** the horse heels, so that his [now *judged*] **rider** shall fall backward." (Gen. 49:17) The rider is none other than *Sagittarius* the equus sign adjacent to Scorpio, who, since armed, might retaliate with his arrows. Maybe our judge wasn't as wise as we thought.

1) Massey, BB-vII, 55. 2) Holman BD, 1316. 3) Ibid., 441.

Since Dan is both high (an eagle) and low (a serpent, scorpion), he is in the position to both "understand" and "overstand," –bringing both views to the Middle on the Scales of Judgement ("innerstand"). **Wise Dan then, befitting his symbols, is the Sun in Scorpio, whose name means:**

- Lord
- Judge
- Cutter (as in biting, stinging, or piercing arrows)
- Dispenser of Justice (thus sometimes referred to as Punisher).

Etymology of Dan (Tan, Tanen)

Category	Afrikan-Kamite Roots	Apparent Derivatives: ENGLISH		Apparent Derivatives: HEBREW	Comments
Serpent	**Tenten** • name of Serpent Deity. 839b **Tentenit** • serpent on royal crown. 881a **Aten-Ur-Nub** • serpent-headed supporter Ra's throne. 98	Leviathan Nehushtan	Python intestines	**leviathan** **roshetan**, sperm whale, cachalot	**Ethanim** (or Tishri), "always flowing with water," is the name of *seventh* month of the Hebrew calendar; Seven is connected with water.
Judging Weighing	**Aten** • ancient form of Har-Makhu [Horus of the Scales or Libra]. 339AE **ten** • highest, Egyptian troy weight. 77BB1 **thenuit** • weight, quantity. 856b **tenu** • to count, reckon. 856b **tena** • to question, interrogate. 882a **aten** • to listen, to hear. 50,51BB1	ten teen thirteen fourteen... denary (tenfold) •ton (a weight. great) attention attend intend instinct tenable (true, trustworthy, accurate, credible)	authentic (verified, tested, tenable, true) tantamount (equal) •itinerary (schedule, plan) tender (cash; offer/grant; soft) •dun (invoice, charge) identify identity identical	**dan**, sentenced, judge, punish, chastise **din**, trial, judgement, verdict, law **dinar**, denarius **ta,an**, be loaded, claim, sue, argue **tenai**, condition, stipulation, term **tinna**, recount, relate, tell **tenuha**, position	**To *weigh* is to *judge*.** **Cut.** Scorpions cut by stinging & pincers; snakes cut by fangs, the eagle, by its beak (which is really two teeth), and the judge cuts with verdicts. And with scales, the items being weighed are often cut or divided.
Cut	**tena** • to cut, to divide, separate. 881b **ten-t** • cutting, division. 881a **teng** • to cut, cut off, cut to pieces, to cleve /split /wound. 881a **tan** • division, cutting in two, to cut off, to divide, turn away, make or become separate." 55BB2	dent indent dental dentures dandelion (toothed lion) orthodontist mastodon	deny denial sting extinguish extinct danger tiny (from all that cutting!)	**tan**, jackel	**Ten, 10 or IO represents life's two polarities** as Earth & Sky; Up & Down, phallic Yang (I) and yonic Yin (O). This reflects the quality of Scorpio as the conjunction of polarities,
Water	**tun** • rising flood, inundation. 824b **tennu** • canal, stream. 882b **tun ah** • title of the Nile deity. 825a	dank (wet) dunk (to immerse) Don river Tanga river Jordan river	Danube river Dnieper river tender (soft. water is soft) •itinerant (traveling. water does this!)	**ethanim**, "always flowing with water"	symbolized by its high-flying Eagle and low-creeping Snake/ Scorpion. All three can "sting" (bite /cut). The serpent can look like I or O. The serpent biting its tail is a sun symbol.
High Great	**ten** • to raise up, raised, high, distinguished 980b **tentha** • steps, throne. 884a **then-t** • something great or distinguished. 856a **teni** • to possess honor or fame, to be *honorable* [like the judge]. 837b **atn** • to rule, a lord. 625BB2 **aten** • deputy, agent, vicar. **Aten** • god of the solar disk 103a **aten** • disk of the sun. 101b • the sun. 625BB2	meridian Don/Donna (Lord /Lady) adonis dynasty dynamic dynamite dynamo dinosaur (dino=huge) dunce cap (is high. worn originally by sorcerers, etc.) distinguish	dandy (elegance in clothes) dainty (of refined choice, excellent, delicious) deinte (excellent. Middle English) edan (hill row of the rampart) •dune (*hill* or ridge of sand) •ton (great amount)	**Adon**, lord, master, mister, ruler, sir **Adona**, God, Lord	**Scorpio with its 3 symbols reflect the "Uri & Thummim":** Uri = Eagle, a sun symbol. Thummim = Serpent & Scorpion; both are "stingers" and "creepers."

9 **Joseph** = Sagittarius the Archer

Mutable **FIRE** Sign

Blessing his favorite son, Jacob said, **"The archers have sorely grieved him and shot at him, and hated him: But his bow abode in strength, and the arms of his hands were made strong..."** (Gen. 49:23, 24).

Joseph & Jesus are two versions of the same Messiah!

The parallels between them are incredible. They are Solar Twins, Night/Day versions of the same Messiah, reflecting the Duality Principle of the Zodiac (Life, really). Yin & Yang. Upper Egypt & Lower Egypt. The Overworld of the Living and the Amenta Underworld of the Deceased. Essentially Joseph is the Christ-Messiah of Amenta the Underworld, symbolized as Egypt where he winds up. He even marries Asenath, who is really Goddess Neith, the Goddess of the Underworld. Jesus is the Christ-Messiah of the Overworld.

Etymology & Parallels with Christ

- **Joseph and Jesus are names from the same Afrikan roots** and have the same meaning. No wonder the many remarkable parallels between them:
  - Five of Jesus's relatives are named Joseph (his stepfather, one of his brothers, and three ancestors). (Luke 3:24, 26, 30)
  - Jesus and Joseph both started their careers at age 30.
  - Both were embalmed (mummified) after death (Gen. 50:26).
  - It was a *Joseph* of Arimathea who requested Jesus's body from Pilate and laid it in his own unused tomb.
  - Jesus is royal; Joseph became second in command to the Pharaoh (Gen. 41:39-43). Joseph's royalty is also denoted by his dream of 11 stars *bowing* to him as the 12th star (Gen. 37:9).
  - Joseph and Christ are both called "stars" and are connected to a fire sign (Sagittarius, Leo).
  - Joseph has twin sons. Jesus has a twin brother. Essentially, Joseph's only full brother (Benjamin) counts as his twin! (like Simeon & Levi) Ben & Joe were Jacob's 11th & 12th sons, and Rachel's only 2 sons.
  - Joseph and Jesus have a brother named Judah.
  - Joseph is called a Bough; Jesus is called a Branch.
  - Joseph is Jacob's most beloved son and firstborn son of Rachel, the most beloved of his two wives. Jesus is God's Beloved Son and the firstborn son of Mary, whose name means Love /Beloved.
  - Joseph gives the Bread of Life (by being the Food/Grain Administrator in Egypt). Jesus gives the Water of Everlasting Life.
  - Both are in top glorious positions, second only to their royal fathers (Pharaoh and God)
  - Both were mistreated and rejected by their own. Joseph's brothers planned to drown him but ultimately sold him into slavery.

- **Joseph &Jesus have 2 fathers & 2 mothers** (Physical & Divine Aspect)
  - Joseph's two mothers were Rachel (physical mom) and disguisedly, Neith, by him being renamed Zaphnath-Paaneah (Gen. 41:45) which means the Living *Son* of Neith (zaph = sif, son).
  - Joseph's two fathers were Jacob (physical dad) and Potiphar or the Pharaoh, both of whom adopted him and put him in charge. Potiphar / Pharaoh represents God or the Divine Aspect. (Note these are two separate men with basically the same name; and *Jacob* is one man with two names –Jacob & Israel. I detest all this inverted complexity! It is rampant throughout the entire Bible.)
  - Jesus's two fathers were God (Divine Aspect) and Joseph (Physical Aspect). His two mothers were Mary (the Divine Aspect, a form of the Great Mother) and Mary, wife of Cleophas who raised him.

- **Both are Sons of the Sun.** The *four* names of Joseph's *two* fathers (Jacob /Israel & Potiphar /Pharaoh) are connected with the Sun. *Jacob* means Sun of the Underworld. Christ's stepfather *Joseph* was the son of *Heli* (meaning Sun [of Overworld]) according to Luke's genealogy (3:23). Matthew's genealogy lists him as the son of Jacob (!): "And Jacob begat Joseph the husband of Mary" (Mat. 1:16). This makes both Jesus and Joseph the Sons of the Sun. And the root (IU) of their names means Sun.

- **Joseph is derived from Iu-Sif; Jesus (Jehoshua) is from Iu-Su. Iu** means Ever-Coming, and was the name of the ever-young, ever-coming Sun (Sungod, Son of God). **Sif** and **Su** means son, child of. Iu is the Ever-Coming Son of God the Eternal Father (Huhi).[1] The Greek name *Jason* is a substitute for Hebrew Joseph or Joshua (Jesus).

- **Joseph & Jesus are linked with *Judah:***
  - *Judah* is also from the same roots as their names.
  - Jesus was the "Lion of the Tribe of Judah."
  - Judah's name follows Joseph's, and vice versa in Christ's genealogy (Luke 3:26, 30).
  - *Two* sons of King *Johoshaphat* (variant of Joseph) were the king of Judah, and were *both* named **Azariah** (variant of Azar / Osiris) who was the original father of IU.
  - Joseph and Judah both have twin sons.
  - The names of two of Jesus's four brothers were Joseph and Judas.

- **Joseph & Jesus are linked with horns**
  - In Moses's blessing, Joseph is compared with the unicorn: "and his horns are like the horns of unicorns" (Deu. 33: 17). Christ is called a "horn of salvation" (Luke 1:69). (And note, the unicorn is a onehorned *horse*; Sagittarius is half*horse*; plus the horn and arrow are both weapons.)

1) Massey, AE, 498, 893.

Zodiac-Joseph, Twelvefold Sun

- Twelve men in the Bible are named Joseph![1] This is another Zodiac, a Joe-diac!
- Joseph himself (like Christ) is a "star," a sun with its own Zodiac. Joseph's astrological and solar identity is denoted with his dream of 11 *stars* (his 11 brothers /tribes) *bowing* to him as the *12th* star (Gen. 37:9).
- Boy Joseph's "coat of many colors" (Gen. 37:3) symbolizes him as the Sun, whose light contains the full spectrum. His being "stripped out of his coat" by his jealous brothers and cast into a dark pit corresponds to the Sun setting, sinking into the womb of the Amenta underworld.
- Both of Joseph's fathers gave him glorious clothing: a "coat of many colors" from Jacob; "vestures of fine linen" from the Pharaoh (Gen. 41:42), along with "a gold chain about his neck" and the Pharaoh own ring. This only underscores Joseph's solar identity.

"Double Iu"

- Iu also means duality, double, twin-ness, or a dual being that is male and female in one. The original Sagittarius was double-headed with the god Shu and his twin sister, goddess Tefnut.[2]
- Joseph's duality manifests mainly as his apparent twin sons, who are counted as sons of Jacob (Gen. 48:5-6) "The two sons of Joseph, Ephraim and Manasseh, are identical with Joseph, and both together are also called Joseph. [They are]...the exact equivalents of the twin brothers in all the mythologies, one of whom is the first-born, but the other becomes the chosen heir." [3]
- Judah also had twin sons; Pharez and Zerah.
- Judah /Judea also means double-land, derived from Iu-Ta (Iu=double, Ta=land). In the original Egyptian story, the two portions of the double earth were united once a year to form the kingdom of the Son, which is Joseph in the Hebrew version.[4] The *dual* kingdom of Judea was given to Joseph in the persons of his *two* sons Ephraim and Manasseh. "Joseph shall have *two* portions" says Ezekiel (47:13).
- Joseph is Jacob's 11th son. Numeral eleven = *2* ones. 1+1=2.

Bow, Bough

- The Bible calls Joseph both the son and wife of goddess Neith by renaming him "Zaphnath-paaneah," and marrying him to "Asenath" (Gen. 41:45). Zaphnath-paaneah (Sif-Neith-P-Ankh) means "the living son of Neith, the one of the two in the Mythos who never dies." [5] Asenath (Ast-Net or Isis-Neith) is Goddess Neith, whose symbol is two crossed *Arrows* on a shield. Neith is usually portrayed with a Bow and two Arrows.
- The *Bow* and *Bough* are associated with Joseph: "Joseph is a fruitful bough" (Gen. 49:22). Bow and Bough are from Kamite BU, meaning bough, beams, rafters. A bow is a weapon of a curved, flexible strip of material, especially *wood.*

1) Holman BD, 815-816. 2) Massey, AE, 327. 3) Massey, BB-vII, 303. 4)Massey, AE, 508-9. 5) Massey, BB-vII, 306.

- Like Joseph, Christ is also prophetically called a Bough, specifically "The BRANCH" (Zech. 6:12). The previous CAPital letters are a direct quote. This is copied from the original Afrikan story of Horus as the Unbu (Un-nb-bu? neb=gold), literally the Golden Bough, offspring of the Sun, symbol of the Solar God.[1] Joseph, as Christ's father, is also called the offspring of the Sun or "son of Heli" in Luke 3:23 (Heli is Helios, the Sun). Boy Joseph's "coat of many colors" likely symbolizes him as the Golden Sun, whose light contains the full spectrum of colors.
- Joseph was sold to a caravan of Ishmaelites (Gen. 37:27). Ishmael corresponds to Sagittarius and is described as an Archer (Gen. 21:20).
- Joseph is given land taken by the sword and the BOW (Gen. 48:22).

With this glimpse of Joseph's background, let us return to our beginning: "The archers [forces of darkness] have sorely grieved him and shot at him...But his bow abode in strength, and the arms of his hands were made strong" (Gen. 49:23, 24). This describes the Sun in Sagittarius where he diminishes daily, losing strength.

> "When the sun entered this sign the Nile was failing, the day grew shorter than the night; and Horus needed all the help that could be given. Hence Shu [conjoined with Tefnut his twin sister] the fighting force was configurated as the Archer. ...who fought for Horus as leader of the war against the rebel powers of darkness and of drought..." [2]

Thus the Sungod (Joseph, Horus, Christ) is supported by Shu, God of the Bow whose symbol was the Arrow.

Why is the Bow & Arrow a symbol of Sagittarius?

The Bow represents the circle and cycle of time, explains Massey. The bending of the bow is a symbol of turning the corner at the place of the Winter Solstice, where the aged Sun is too weak to bend the bow. At this point his successor-Son/Sun takes up the bow and pulls it, completing the circle. Hence Joseph's arms were "made strong" when he was supported by Shu, Bowman of the Solar-god, who is the 'Shepherd of Israel' appearing in Genesis 49:24 and in Psalms 80:1, again helping Joseph, "Give ear, O Shepherd of Israel, thou that leadest Joseph like a flock."

Armed with such a background, Joseph is identified as the Zodiacal Archer, otherwise known as Sagittarius.

1) Massey, AE, 528, 672. 2) Ibid., 298.

10 **Gad** = Capricorn the Goat

Cardinal **EARTH** Sign

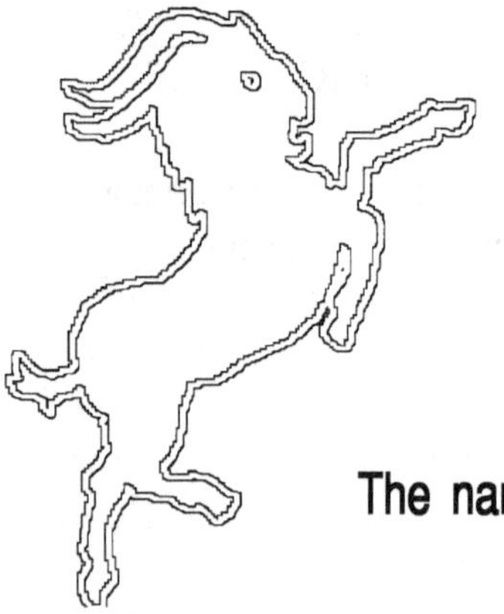

"And Zilpah, Leah's maid bare Jacob a son. And Leah said, A **troop** cometh: and she called his name **Gad**" (Gen. 30:10, 11). When Jacob blessed him we read, **"Gad, a troop shall overcome him"** (Gen. 49:19). Now what does a "troop" have to do with goats? A "troop" is simply a group or company of animals, people, or things according to the dictionary. *Band* and *flock* are synonyms for *troop*, of which "troupe" (as in dance *troupe*) is a variation. Goats come in flocks or "troops" !

The name *Gad* itself means Goat!

Baal-Gad means the "Goat-Lord." [1] Baal-Gad was the eponymous ancestor of the tribe of Gad.[2] "The sign of Gad is the Goat," writes Massey.[3] Baal-Gad was identified with Azazel (Azel), a Hebrew deity called "God's Messenger" who received annual scapegoat-sacrifices on the Jewish Day of Atonement (Yom Kippur, New Year). Azazel's name is likely from *ez*, meaning *goat* in Hebrew. It was said that after death, he ascended to heaven to become the constellation of Capricorn the Goat.[4] **Baal-Gad was reknown as Pan**, the satyr-god of Greek mythology. European churchmen borrowed his traits (horns, cloven hoofs, and unremitting lust hence "horny") to complete their tailed, horned-god image of the devil. Pan's sacred drama of death and resurrection was the original ***tragedy*** from Greek ***tragoidos***, "Goat Song." [5] "**Billy Goat**" is undoubtedly derived from Baal-Gad (Billy=Baal, lord). The Afrikan originals of these goat deities appear to be Men and Num. Men was the prototype of Pan, who had earlier forms in Set (Sut).[6] Num was the goat-headed god "who presided over the abyss with the sign of Capricornus." [7]

Gad also means to move about restlessly and with little purpose [like goats]. A **gadabout** is one who roams as in search of amusement or social activity. The **gadfly** is a pest that annoys livestock. **Gadoid** means belonging to the **Gadidae** family of fish, such as **codfish**. Codfish or *gad*-fish even have "**goatees**" (chin barbels); plus the original symbol of Capricorn was the Goat-Fish! In Greek, **gados** means cod(fish); **katseeka** means goat. **Gid** is a disease of herbivores. And baby goats are called "**kids**" apparently after **goat**, which is derived from Old English "**gat**" meaning goat.

Biblical variants or names from the same root as Gad include:

Gaddi	Gaddiel	Beth-Gader
Gedor	Gederah	Kedar (black goat hair)
Gedaliah	Giddel	Migdal-Gad ("Tower of Gad")
Goath	Azgad	Engedi ("place of the young goat")

1) Walker, WE, 85. 2) Walker, WD, 376. 3) Massey, BB-vII, 248. 4)Walker, WE, 85. 5)Ibid., 765. 6) Massey, BB-vII, 377. 7) Jackson, CBC, 152.

The Goat symbolized Caucasians (white people)

In ancient times, whites were symbolized by the Goat, due to the traits they both share such as hairiness, long straight hair, aggressive natures, destructiveness, and "mountains." *Caucasians* were from *Caucasia,* their earliest known abode. **White people still call their children "kids"!** Melanated people who do this got it from whites. Black people were symbolized by Sheep.

Geat Gothic Goats. "Geat" and "Goth" are apparent variants of *Goat. Gothic* means barbarous and crude; or relating to the Goths. The *Goths* were a Germanic people (whites) who invaded the Roman empire (whites) during the early centuries of the Christian era. The "Geats" were an ancient Germanic people of southern Sweden conquered by the Swedes in the 6th century. Geats and Goths must be the same, for Gotland, a region of southeast Sweden, was the traditional homeland of the Goths. *Goidelic* is a Celtic (white) language.

Red Hairy Scapegoats. They were called the Sheidim (Destroyers) and the Seirim (Hairy Ones). They were the original *scapegoats.* The term "scapegoat" originally meant the "Red Hairy Ones" who were periodically exiled into the wilderness. White people are all shades of *red.* Hebrew "sa'ir" means both "goat" and "hairy." These "scapegoats" were not goats but Albinos possessing genetic traits which the early Habirus /Hebrews (IndoEuropean invaders) wanted to erase from their genes. Bradley writes: "Rabbinical tradition (the exegetical works), as well as the Esau story in the *Old Testament*, indicate a continuing, very strong Neanderthal genetic strain among the Israelite tribes –a strain that they tried to eradicate by various means." [1] Jacob's brother Esau was *red and hairy* (Gen. 25:25). In the scheme to steal Esau's birthright, Jacob was wrapped in *goatskin* from a kid to fool his blind father Isaac into thinking he was his hairy brother Esau (Gen. 27:16, 25:31-33). Esau changed his name to Edom (red). His descendants, the "Edomites" are biblically portrayed as the antagonists of the Black Nation of Israel. Since Edom was fiction, no one descended from him. But the Albinos, whether called Edomites, Habirus, Romans, or Greeks, etc., have historically shown themselves to be the arch-antagonists of all Melanated People.

Gad with his bad self

Among other meanings, the roots of GAD signify cutting, destruction & death:

Afrikan-Kamite Roots			Apparent Derivatives	
khet	• to cut	55BB1	goad	cadaver
ket-t	• a butcher.	63BB1	gad	–cide (kill. as in genocide, pesticide)
kheti	• to cut into, engrave, something inscribed.	567b	tragedy	eschatology (deals with death, end of world/ Last Judgement)
khet	• to pierce, penetrate.	567b	acid	cadence
khet	• impaling pole, impaled, staff, stick, sceptre.	566a,b	godoxious	decadence
ketket	• to beat, to shake.	799b	cut	accident
gatha	• to smite, to strike, be violent.	804a	cutlass	cataclysm
khai-t	• slaughter, ruin, massacre.	528b	machete (*ma* / big; chet / knife)	cataract
khaut	• slaughter, massacre.	571a	hatchet	escheat
khatt	• the land of the dead, the grave.	571a	execute (kill)	cheat
kha-t	• corpse, dead body, mummified body.	570b	cauterize	
khetkhet	• to drop out, droop, to slip behind.	567b, 568a	catabolism	
khet	• retreat, be behind, follow, sail down stream.	568a 569a, 567b	catacombs	
			catatonia	

1) Bradley, CP, 153.

So the GOAT is apparently named after *destruction*

Qa means *goat* in Egyptian; *kah-t* means she-goat ("t" denotes female). Although Massey derives goat from kaht (she-goat), the etymology and evidence of observation and history indicates that the goat is named after destruction; essentially, *goat* means *destroyer*. Goats are typically aggressive and destructive. "Goats are extremely destructive to vegetation and thereby contribute to erosion, as they tear plants out of the soil. Some of the earliest drawings available depict goats eating on trees. Sheep and goats grazed in the same pasture, but it was necessary to separate the herds because the male goat was often hostile toward the sheep (Mat. 25:32)." [1] Gad is biblically associated with destruction, war, and killing by being identified with "troops." Death and Destruction have been chief hallmarks of the people symbolized by the Goat. They now threaten the entire planet to the point of extinction. Therefore it should come as no surprise that...

GAD is in ArmaGEDdon!

In tracking Gad's roots and biblical name-variants, I suddenly realized that GAD is in Armageddon! Bible dictionaries simply say *Armageddon* is Har-Meggidon, meaning Mount (Har) **Meggidon /Meggido**, the apocryphal, prophesied site of the world's final and largest war. And *Meggido* is simply defined as "place of troops." [2] Recall that Gad was connected with "troops" at birth and in Jacob's blessing. "Troops" is usually understood to mean soldiers –they always come in troops /troupes –like goats. The men of Gad achieved great expertise as warriors (1Chron. 12:8). "Meggido" is apparently Mag-Gad, meaning **Great Goat** or **Great Destruction /Death.**

So the true meanings of Armageddon are apparently:

- **Mount of Mega Destruction /Death**
- **Mount of the Great Goat /Destroyers**

Realizing this, I had another nearly simultaneous startling realization:

The words *Meggidon* and *Macedonia* are variants of the same word!

Macedonia was the ancient Greek empire. And the goat was the recognized symbol of their nation by the Macedonians themselves.[3] Even the Bible acknowledges this. In the New English Translation of the Bible we read, "The two-horned ram which you saw signifies the kings of Media and Persia. The he-goat is the kingdom of the Greeks. And the great horn on his forehead is the first king" (Dan. 8: 5, 8, 20, 21). Thus the meaning of both, Meggid(on) and Maced(onia) are:

- The Great Goat/s
- The Great Cutters/Destroyers
- The Goats of Great Destruction

A variant spelling of Meggido is **Makkedah** –appropriately connected with death and utter destruction. Joshua captured Makkedah and slaughtered its entire population (Jos. 10:28).

1) Holman BD, 54. 2) Ibid., 941. 3) Insights, vI, 966.

The names whites were called attested to their destructiveness

As previously stated, whites were symbolized by the destructive Goat in ancient times. Their ancient names often attested to their destructiveness:

- **Vandals**, after which vandalism is named.
- **Sheidim**, meaning Destroyers, derived from Set /Sut, source of name Satan.
- **Saxons**. On the positive side, can be interpreted as Sharp or Wisemen / Teachers, otherwise *Cutters /Slashers.* The root SEK means both.
- **Scythians** (wielders of *scythes*; cutters, slashers, etc.). From SEK.
- **Sicilian**, from Sicily /Sicani, after Latin *sicilis* (sickle) and *sica* (dagger).
- **Sa.Gaz** (the Habirus) are "associated with murder, robbery, and razzia."
- **Spartans** are the 'spear-tans,' famous for their warring, militarism.
- **Habirus** were identified as the Sa.Gaz. Through historical and scriptural examination, Meek showed that these same nomadic groups were one and the same with the Hebrews, later to become known as "Israelites." [1]
- **Children of Set:** Kamites called whites "the Children of Set /Sut." Set was the 'red' god of drought, destruction, and Negativity. Set was identified with the **goat**: "The goat was a type of Sut and the sheep of Horus, according to the twin character of the Sut-Horus. ...The goat in the zodiac is the type of Sut. ...the 'conspirators of Sut,' those who have sided with him against Horus the Christ, are 'transformed into goats.'" [2] Set (Sut-Anubis) was also identified with Capricorn.[3]
- **Sutu:** Referring to Habirus, a dictionary remarks: "Egyptian and Babylonian texts point to a people called Sutu [Children of Sut /Set], semi-nomads in the Syrian and Arabian desert. Rather than a proper name, some commentators think the translation should be, 'sons of tumult.'" [4]
- **Perversions** are named after Albino men (see marginal text at the left).

Perversions are named after Albino men by Albinos themselves. Examples:

- Machiavellian is named after Niccolo Machiavelli (author of *The Prince* –1513). The word means "characterized by expedience, deceit, and cunning." Note the word contains vile, evil, villain, etc.
- Masochism is named after Leopold von Sacher-Masoch. Note his name contains the SEK root. Plus Masoch is likely a variant of the biblical Meshech (kinsmen of *Magog*).
- Chauvinism is named after Nicolas Chauvin, a soldier of Napoleon.

And their nature has not changed. Their destructiveness has continued right into modern times, for the Albinos have demonstrated themselves to be the very personification of Destruction, Death, and Evil (evil = anti-life or *live* spelled backwards). They are agents of destruction on a quantum scale. No creature on Earth has demonstrated more destruction and anti-Nature behavior than the white man. All through his history he has done everything to ruin the balance in Nature. Over the past 500 years the Albino man has attacked Nature like no catastrophe ever has, resulting in the total extinction of thousands of species of animals and plants on every continent. "Current rate of species extinction due to destruction of tropical rainforests and related habitats: 1,000 /year." [4] **The Albino man has slaughtered over one billion people over the last 450 years,** not even sparing his own kind.[6] Just one of their nuclear submarines can blow up several continents at once –in other words, one nuclear sub can destroy the entire planet! There are ***300*** of them in the oceans! Reflecting their unparalleled ability to massively kill, Albinos have coined the word 'megadeath,' meaning "One million deaths. Used as a unit in reference to nuclear warfare." (!!!) **"Megadeath" = MegGADeath! Albino technology poisons and kills the land, water, atmosphere, plants, animals, people, and the planet itself.** Albinos have destroyed the culture and civilization of indigenous people on every continent. They essentially colonized the world, imposing their destructive Un-culture, false, counterfeit religions and Un-Bible upon the indigenous peoples surviving their global onslaught. They have created hideous weapons of biowarfare, thus it is no

1) Cuba, 27, 28. 2) Massey, HJ, 154, 155. 3) Massey, BB-vII, 249. 4) Holman BD, 1265. 5) Realities, 5. 6) Encyclopedia Britannica, 1982, see *Warfare*.

accident that the countries hardest hit with the (white)manmade biowarfare of AIDS and ebola are Afrikan. "With their continuing history of mass genocide against people of color on all continents, whites have collectively established themselves as the arch-enemy of all people they classify as nonwhite. That's at least 90% of the world!" If allowed to go to its logical conclusion, whites – their Un-culture and genocidal activities, will kill the whole of humanity, the Albinos themselves, and our precious irreplaceable planet Earth.

> **"THE INVENTION of nuclear weapons may actually have marked the beginning of the end of nature: we [Albinos] possessed, finally, the capacity to overmaster nature, to leave an indelible imprint everywhere at once."** [1]

There's more...

GAD is in Kittim / Chittim

The *evasive* roots of Gog /Magog seem impossible to track down. What is a "GOG" or what does it mean? I'm still not sure, however:

- Massey writes: "Sir John Mandeville heard, during his travels, that in countries lying east and north of the Caspian Sea, enclosed among mountains, were the lost Ten Tribes, *'the Jews of the ten lynages that were clepen [called, named] Goth and Magothe.'"* [2] By their spelling in the preceding Old/Middle English sentence, Goth = Gog; Magothe = Magog. This suggests Gog means /or is related to *Goat.*
- Books discussing GOG often connect it with "giant." This is supposed to be from Gog being a son of **Japheth**, derived from ***Iapetus***, a Greek titan (giant). The real reason is that the names *Japheth* & *Iapetus* are derived from AP,[3] the **GREAT** (hence GIANT) **Mother**. And because She is connected with the Astrological North as the GREAT Bear (Ursa MAJOR Constellation), Japheth is assigned to the North. And Japheth's *whiteness*? As one of the Astrological Four, Japheth = AIR, which is "colorless," –like "white"! His father Noah=Water; Ham=Earth; Shem=Fire.
- **GOG** in fact, may be derived from the **CAUK** of **Cauk-asian**! For the very white Land of Gog or "Isles of the Gentiles" was to the North and included the isolated Cauk-asus Mountains.

- "The Kittim" are major characters in the Dead Sea Scrolls, which refer to them as the "Sons of Darkness," that is, the Romans /Greeks (Albinos).
- Kittim was the land of Alexander of Macedon in the apocryphal Book of Maccabees (1:1; 8:5). Alexander was a white man (Greek conqueror) who did serious harm to Black people and their culture (ancient Egypt especially). Chittim and Greece (Grecia) are mentioned in same *chapter* (Dan. 11:2, 30). Chittim and Kedar are mentioned in same *sentence* (Jer. 2:10).
- In Genesis (10:4), Kittim was a descendent of *Magog*, a son of *Japheth*, one of Noah's four sons. Japheth is considered the progenitor of whites. The Divine Hand may be working through the manipulated Bible anyway, in spite of the manipulators because the same Bible that the Albino man has plagiarized, distorted, and inverted, points to themselves –Gog and Magog (fictional or not)– as the origin for the worst evil to challenge humanity and identifies them with Satan as chief culprits (*kill*-prits) in the Armageddon war. Gog and Magog is also the ancient name for the area where the Khazars (imposter-Jews) are from (eastern Europe /Russia). The white-supremist Khazarian Secret World Government appears to be the apex of evil (anti-life) on Earth. They are the enemies of everyone including the white people themselves, whom they control like pawns in a chess game. They intend to eliminate 3/4ths of the world's population (People of Color) by the year 2000.

In the Bible, key GAD-names are typically associated with strife, war, cutting, killing, suffering. They include:

- **Golgotha** ("skull"), where the Black Prophet Christ was allegedly crucified –by Goats or Kittim (Romans/Greeks). Golgotha (Gal-Kata) apparently means circle /cirGOL of destruction or death.
- **Gethsemane** is defined in the dictionary as "an instance or a place of great suffering." Christ suffered here in 'bloody sweat' prior to his arrest and subsequent crucifixion. Gethsemane was a garden east of Jerusalem across the **Kidron /Cedron** Valley on the Mount of Olives.
- **Chidon** ("crescent swords")
- **Gideon** ("one who cuts to pieces")
- **Makkedah** (see page 222 in this chapter)

1) Bill McKibben, *The End of Nature,* 66. 2) Massey, BB-vII, 358. 3) Massey, BB-vII, 314, 315.

Gad is in Catholic

The most destructive force unleashed upon Europe was the Roman Catholic "Church." In their "Crusades" and "Inquisitions," the Roman Catholic Church terrorized, brutalized, subdued, and destroyed a whole civilization, –the so-called "pagan" Europe that was largely, apparently honoring Life, honoring Nature, and honoring the Great Mother. In France alone, during the Albigensian Crusade, the Albinos of the Killer Katholic Khurch massacred half the population! When the papal legate was asked how heretics were to be distinguished from the faithful, Pope Innocent II who ordered this destruction replied, "Kill them all; God will know his own." [1] Thus, Europe was "Christianized" through brutal killing at an estimated cost of 8 million to 10 million lives, all in the name of God and Christ. Even children and babies were slaughtered or burned alive, especially if female. What Albinos did to their own kind in Europe, was practice for what they did to the whole world.

The Roman Empire is alive and well as the Catholic Church. It did a form change. (This is how anti-life essence works, and is a major way it deceives and gets away with it). The Vatican is actually a country! It is so rich from centuries of looting both Albinos and Melanated People, that many believe it cannot count its stolen wealth. (Is this where "filthy rich" originated? Filthy and bloody.) *Catholic* is composed of kat/kata (down) + holos (whole). The dictionary defines *catholic* as universal, universally accepted, or broad scope, including all mankind. This definition indicates the meaning was taken from Kamite *kha-t* (man, mankind) /*khe-t* (people, folk)[2], to get 'all the people'. But history shows that the real meaning was from Kamite *khet*, DOWN, reversed, degenerate, destructive. In reality, and as they have proven, Catholic means "wholly reversed, wholly degenerate /destructive, wholly unholy, wholly pulling down." The Catholic Un-Church "wholly" took Europe "down." This is true also of all the other versions of albino-ized false Christianity. Additionally they demonstrate another meaning of *khet*: to massacre, destroy. They massacred bodies in the past, now they massacre at a higher level, keeping minds in bondage that leads to spiritual death.

Gad going down, down...

Goats naturally dwell in the hardest regions of Earth. Logically, Capricorn would have the hardest hardness, being the Cardinal Earth Sign. Negatively, Capricorn would be *compression*, unyielding rigidity, and hardness of consciousness. Compression makes things hard. Compression (as a result of living/being out of balance) happens physically and psychologically, leading to pain, then sickness, dis-ease and ultimately *death* if not corrected. Elizabeth Haich writes of her past-life experience of the negative, contracting / compressive anti-life aspect, which appeared to her in the form of a bodiless face that resembled a *goat head*, trying to make her spirit compress into the form of a hard rock: "This bodiless face resembles the head of a goat. The silhouette clearly shows the form of horns over a long, pinched face that ends with a little goatee. Or perhaps, are all these shapes only *radiations of invisible forces*? The being's eyes, set so close together, have a terrifying effect, like bottomless maelstroms that irresistibly pull everything down, down, down to *complete annihilation*." [3] (underlines added; *kata* means *down*)

1) Walker, WE, 194. 2) Budge, EHD, 570a, 525a. 3) Haich, 283.

Oh Ohh! Gad sounds like God!

No wonder the world is the way it is! And "God" is not necessarily the Supreme Deity's name any more than "man" is the name of a person. God and Gad sound similar because both are derived from same-sounding roots having meanings which span polarities (good to bad). As Pan and Baal-Gad, the Goat was a significant god of the Greeks and Habirus (Hebrews). The KJ translation disguises this by replacing "goat" with "devil" in some passages, whereas the NI translation reads: "They must no longer offer any of their sacrifices to the goat idols to whom they prostitute themselves" (Lev. 17:7). "And he [Rehoboam] appointed his own priests for the high places and for the goat and calf idols he had made" (2Chron. 11:15).

GOD is derived from *Khut / Khuti / Gudi...*

- **Khut** meaning a **SPIRIT**.[1] John 4:24 states "God is a Spirit."
- The **Gudi** or **Khuti** [2] was the name of the ***Seven* Glorious Ones** who were the first Offspring of the Great Mother and Great Father. They were the **Ali**, the Co-Creators responsible for the Seven Days of Creation, for they made the first Circle of Time. Hence KET also means circle, giving us cirCUIT, CATenary (curved), COAT (goes around), CITy (a circle of habitation), etc. The Seven Khuti appear in Revelation 4:5 as the "Seven Spirits of God." They are the Elohim (derived from ALI) or Plural God in Genesis 1:26 that said "Let **us** make man in **our** image."
- God is Light! (1John 1:5). **Khut** meaning **Light**, was a name of **Isis as the Giver of Light** at the beginning of the year (which follows Capricorn).[3] A title of Her son Heru was **Har-Khuti**, the "Light of the World," and Lord of the Lights that were seven in number, the perfect Star of the gnostic pleroma. His symbol was (\ | /) or (/ | \ ). **Khuait** was a form of Goddess Hathor (a form of Isis). "Kauit **VII**" was the name of the *Seven* Divine Cows [4] who are undoubtedly the Seven Cows of Hathor.
- *Goddess* **Khut**, a name of the ***Oldest Great Mother.***[5]
- **Kait** meaning **Altar**.[6] The Altar symbolized the Great Mother and Her regenerative womb.[7] In Kamite hieroglyphics, KAIT begins with a fish, an ancient Mother /Womb /Yoni symbol. Kait (khet, kat) also means womb, seat, throne.
- Massey derives GOD from both **Khut** (Spirit) and the *abraded* form of Khebt, which is ***Khet***: (underlines added):

  > The goddess Khebt [the Great Mother] carries the knot or tie, the sign of the circle, so much time (Kept) measured out... Khebt modifies into Khet, to shut and seal; Kheti, to go around, surround, make the CirCUIT. Kebt was the goddess, but from the abraded form of Khet we obtain the name of the God. Khetu is a god of things, we might say of the hidden things which belonged to the earliest science, and were the secrets of the learned, but hard riddles, and dark sayings to the ignorant.[8]

1) Massey, BB-vI, 59. 2) Massey, AE, 627. 3) Budge, GE-vII, 216. 4) Budge, EHD, 785b.
5) Massey, BB-vI, 370. 6) Budge, EHD, 572a. 7) Walker, WE, 23. 8) Massey, BB-v-II, 27.

The "GOD" of the reworked, rewritten Bible is the GOD of the same people who rewrote it and in whose name ("GOD") they have committed the most horrible crimes upon indigenous Hue-manity as well as themselves. People whom the Nile Valley Afrikans called the Children of Set.

Black people are worshipping the God of the Children of Set,

particularly if they are using or subscribing to any version of the so-called Bible, for all the versions are from the Europeans.

> **To make sure your prayers are going to the *Loving* God of Life, –and not to the Loveless Un-God of Death,** it may be wise to precede His /Her name (whatever name you use) with the word LOVING. Hence, ***Loving*** God, ***Loving*** Goddess, or *Loving* Great Mother, *Loving* Great Father, or Loving Divine Oneness.

Preceding GOD with LOVING directs it to the Loving God /Goddess. For "Lucifer" the great Deceiver has deceived all of us. His name, according to albino reference books, means *Bringer of Light.* This should also be qualified, for really it is "Bringer of DESTRUCTIVE REVERSED Light!" And where is *Destructive Light* coming from? *Who* are the makers and *bringers* of this destructive light, that is, the light from atom bombs, nuclear bombs? True, any type of "light" including sunlight can be "destructive" but the difference is *intent.* Nuclear bombs are willfully, *intentionally* made to absolutely destroy and kill life (hence *evil*, anti-life). And this is the difference.

Am I calling Capricorn bad and evil?

Consider this, Capricorn has the death-month or Winter Solstice on December 22nd, shortest day of the year. Anciently, when the Sun set on this date, this event was called the "death" of the Sun or Sungod; the powers of darkness had temporarily defeated the light. Three days following the Winter Solstice, there is a perceptible difference in the (increasing) length of the day, hence December 25 has always been celebrated as the birthday of the *Sun* or *Son* of God (Christ, Horus, Hesus, Dionysus, etc.). **After the "death" of the Old Sun, a new "Sun/Son of God" is born.** So now we have *light* after the *darkness* of Gad's Winter Solstice. Capricorn without its Feminine Aspect (Fish-tail) becomes negative, **–a *death* that *stays* dead.** With its Feminine Aspect restored, Capricorn becomes *positive*, –a *semblance* of dying that resurrects and regenerates.

The "white season" of death peaks in Capricorn. "White has anciently been the color of death. This tradition is likely from the observation that white things in Nature equal death, unnaturalness, emptiness, void of substance. Bleakness and lifelessness characterizes the white season of the year (winter) and white places of earth, such as the north and south poles. Only after a body has died and decayed are its white bones visible. And once thoroughly burned, the residue of black charcoal is white ashes. *Bleak, bleach, blond, blank,* and *blanch* are from common roots and reflect the void emptiness of white. Virtually no plants can grow in *white* soil. But plants thrive in *black* soil, for it is the richest and most fertile." [1]

1) Suzar, DM, chapter 6.

The Albino mindset emphasizes the Death aspect, whether in Capricorn or otherwise, for that is its nature, since it suppresses the Feminine Principle of Life.

The Afrikan mindset, before Albino-input, emphasized Life, that is, the Regeneration Principle after so-called death. Up in the mountains (habitat of goats) were located healing shrines of the Great Mother. Geraldine Thorsten enlightens us: "The Goat was the totem animal of those priestesses whose mountain shrines served as the first hospitals and medical colleges. The drugs, medicines, and sacred intoxicants they developed, their skill in surgery and their ability to 'resurrect the dead' or revive people from comas, were among the countless gifts the Great Goddess bestowed on us." [1] What the author does not mention is that these priestess were either Afrikan women originally, or they originally learned the healing arts and other arts and sciences from Afrikan priestesses and priests.

The "death" in Capricorn resurrects into Life only when the Feminine Aspect is restored

Albinos or any people denying or cutting out the Feminine Aspect (Nature) become like the Ankh missing its hole, hence the Crucifix, a symbol of both, Death and the Male Principle. When Albinos accept, thus harmonize with Nature (which is really the Great Mother) they can become positive and life-promoting. **Many Albinos are moving towards the Regeneration Principle of Life.** They seek to get in touch with and be in harmony with Nature. Perhaps their examples will inspire others like them to do likewise. For we are living in the most critical time of all. **Are we going to continue choosing Death (by living totally out of harmony with Nature, even destroying Her) or are we going to choose Life (by getting back in harmony with Nature)?**

And hardness (compression) is "good" only in its right place. When hardness is in its wrong place, it becomes anti-life or has that effect.

With Capricorn, as with the Ankh, the Female Aspect (the Fish) has been removed. When such happens, this creates the serious imbalance that leads to death. This is why the Albinos are so destructive. (Actually, the Feminine Aspect of the entire Zodiac has been seriously denied.)

With the Feminine aspect of the Goat restored, the death at the Winter Solstice is not a death, but a rest, a pause before Resurrection and Regeneration, –a Regeneration leading us to the **Cornucopia or Horn of Plenty,** the hollow goat horn full of Nature's life-sustaining gifts from the hard Earth, –transforming *Bad Gad* into ***GOOD*** *Gad.*

11 Reuben = Aquarius the Water Bearer

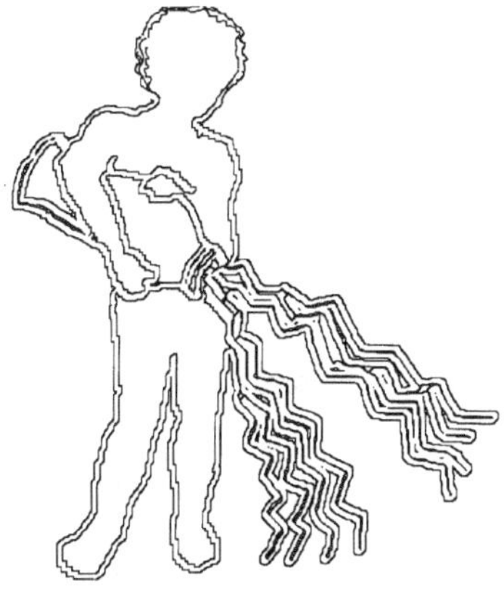

Fixed **AIR** Sign

Blessing his son, Jacob describes Reuben as **"unstable as water"** (Gen. 49:4). The Vulgate Bible has it **"rushing like water."** Jacob said to Reuben, **"Thou are my firstborn, my might, and the beginning of my strength...the excellency of power"** (Gen. 49:3). Aquarius is the *firstborn* month or beginning of the year, and is derived from aqua (water). Reuben is described as "unstable" or "rushing." Why? Because he is the zodiacal sign of the *unstable* element of Air which, when *rushing* is called the Wind.

Air Sign with a Water name?
Odd that the Fixed Air Sign would be named after water. But Air *bears* water as *clouds*, and pours it forth as *rain*, and Aquarius *bears* a vessel of water, and pours it forth in double streams. And the original "water" of this "air" sign originated in the tropical upper "air" of interior Afrika, where it poured down as *rain* into Afrika's great lakes, only to fill up the Nile River and cause it to abundantly overflow its banks each year. Aquarius is modeled from Hapi, the god of the Nile who pours forth the two branches of the double-source Nile. This explains and resolves the apparent contradiction of an air sign named and represented with water.

Reuben

- Hebrew **ruah** (ruach) means spirit, wind, air, and mind. In many languages, the word for spirit and air are also the same; Sanskrit *prana*, Greek *pneuma*, Latin *spiritus*. For breath and life are One. It was Air –as breath– which gave the first idea of a *Spirit* in man. Thus the Fixed Air Sign of Aquarius is identified with Spirituality. The Age of Aquarius which we are presently entering, is called the age of Spiritual Awakening (re-awakening, really). Aquarius's water is *celestial or spiritual water* from heaven. This concept manifests as the clouds and rain of the heavens. As we have seen, this was the original source of water in this Air sign.

- Hebrew **ben** means *son, boy, young man*. Reuben is a man. Aquarius is the only sign represented as a singular (young)man. And it was Reuben who found "mandrakes" (Gen. 30:14). The MANdrake is an herb so named because its roots bear a remarkable resemblance to the shape of the human body. Thus Reuben is doubly identified as male and simultaneously connected with the dragon (drake), a solar symbol.

Reuben is *warm*

Since the rising and setting Sun is red, then by association, **ru/ re** (name of the sun) means red. Kamite **rui** means red. Derivatives include ruddy, rust, Russia, rouge, rose, and red itself. Red is the *first* and *strongest* color of the spectrum; *Reu*ben was Jacob's *first* son, his "might" and "beginning" of his "strength." Red is the very color of strength and vitality, and has the most pronounced effect upon our senses. Our blood is red. Red was worn by royalty, another word from the same Afrikan root. Celtic *ruadh* means both red and royal.

Reuben is getting *warmer*

Watermelon-red or rosy-pink is the color of Love. Valentines are traditionally red. It was Reuben's birth that ignited his father's love for his mother Leah: "now therefore my husband will love me" (Gen. 29:32).

Reuben is *hot*

Deep red is the color of Passion. With all this Redness, Reuben is eligible to compete with his passionate brother, Naphtali (Aries). As a matter of biblical-fact, his sexual activity got him in trouble, causing him to loose his birthright as the firstborn son. And what was his offense? Coupling with Bilhah, his father's concubine (Gen. 35:22; 49:4).

We have resolved the contradiction of Water being prominently connected with a major Air sign. Now we are faced with a greater contradiction, for Reuben's water is now on the verge of *boiling* with all this Red energy. How do we resolve Fire (Red) being so connected with the Fixed Air Sign? Like we did with Water. Aquarius = Air = Breath, which is both wet and warm. Breathe on a glass and see mist; breath on your hand and feel heat. The Fire of Life warms our Breath, and with each breath we take, we inhale *prana*. What's prana? –the Sanskrit word for the etheric life-energy that comes from the *sun* and is especially abundant in bright sunlight. The words breath, prana, pyre, pyramid, and fire share common roots. In addition to being Body, we are Spirit (Mind) and Soul (Heart). Air corresponds to Spirit; the Prana in the air corresponds to Soul, a word derived from solar (sun). **Pyramid** means Fire (pyra) in the Middle. This Fire is our Soul-Spirit (Heart-Mind) dwelling "in the middle" of the temple of our Flesh (physical Body = Earth+ Water). And heat (Fire) causes Water to steam or evaporate, *rising* (denotes spiritual) as moisture into the warm AIR of Aquarius.

Yes the original waters of Aquarius were warm or hot since they were the living, lifegiving, feminine fluids of the Great Mother Herself, pouring forth in two streams as the "Twin Water" to nourish Her children. Hence, the primary form of the Twin Water was Her Milk and Blood. Now we are back at fiery Red again, for blood is both red *and* hot. And milk is both very *warm* (from the nipples) and *white* like the clouds (a form of water) in the *air* of this Air sign. The Twin Water is still the nourishment of infants today, for they are nourished by Blood while in the womb, and by Milk once out the womb. Both liquids are over 95% water.

Red and White were the colors of the royal crowns of Upper (southern) and Lower (northern) Egypt, showing their connection with the Great Mother's Living Waters of Life.

The two branches of the double-source Nile were The Mother's nourishing life fluids, which transformed the middle of a desert into a luxuriant oasis. As previously stated, Aquarius is modeled after Hapi, the god of the Nile, a son (ben) of the Great Mother. From his *two* urns, Hapi poured the two branches of the double-sourced Nile representing the Milk and Blood of the Great Mother. That this "male" god has two pendulous breasts points to his earlier origin as an icon of the Great Mother Herself.

The Great Mother in the sign of Aquarius

The Great Mother of All Beginning is evident in the sign of Aquarius for She *is* the *Vessel* which Her son is holding! Woman is Vessel. The vessel is an ancient symbol of the female body. Human life flows from the vessel of her womb along with menstrual blood. Nourishing milk flows from her breasts. In Egyptian hieroglyphics, that sacred water jar was "the symbol of the Goddess Nut and of femininity, the female genital, woman and the feminine principle."[1] The Zodiac was founded on the inundation, writes Massey. "The mother of water...the womb of source itself...with all her myriad mammae streaming from the fount of liquid life... was now repeated as the multimammalian wet-nurse in the sign of Aquarius." [2]

If Reuben is derived as *Ru*-Ben, then the meanings of his name include:

Royal Spiritual Son	Spiritual Prince
Behold a Spiritual Man	Royal Red Son
Red Son or Red Man ("Adam")	Man of Love (love=red)

All these meanings apply to IU, the messianic Ever-Coming Son reknown as Jesus (Iu-Su), Horus (Har-Iu), and Hare Krishna (Har-Iu Krst). While pondering this, it suddenly occurred to me that ...

Reuben is really Re-U-Ben, –Re-IU-Ben, that is!

In other words, Reuben-Aquarius is Iu!

Aquarius is Iu the **Son**, the *young* **Prince** rising in the *eastern* horizon. Directly opposite him is Iu the **Father**, the *matured* **King** setting in the *western* horizon.

1) Thorsten, 290. 2) Massey, AE, 324.

Dying Father = Setting Sun

Dying Jacob tells Reuben, "Thou are my firstborn, my might, and the beginning of my strength" (Gen. 49:3). How curious that a *dying* father would tell his *first*born son that he is his *might* and *beginning of his strength.* The story makes sense only in the light of its Afrikan genesis, for the *dying* red Sun (Jacob) is the Father who dies at each sunset (daily mini-death) and each Winter Solstice (annual maxi-death); to be reborn as his own Son each sunrise and each Christmas (Dec. 25), a date anciently celebrated as the birthday of the new Sun, or Son. In addition to **Reuben**, this theme repeats with *all* the other biblical "sons" whose names derive from IU:

- **Judah**. The Twin Lions. Young Judah is the son or lion's whelp; his father is the old-lion gone down (sunset) (see section on Judah).
- **Joseph**. Joseph was Jacob's favorite child because Jacob had him in his "old age" and by his "favorite" wife Rachel. Old Father-Jacob is the old setting sun. Son-Joseph is the young rising sun. Father-in-law-Pharaoh-Potiphar & son-in-law-Joseph is another version of Father/Son. Potiphar's name signifies the Sun.
- **Jesus.** The *Son* of God the *Father*. The IU-names of Judah, Joseph, and Reuben each occur as an ancestor of Jesus! "Ragu" (Luke 3:35) is Reu, a shortened version of Reuben. Ragu is spelled Reu in other translations of the Bible.

Reuben's other connections with Iu

- Reuben and Joseph are both firstborn sons (!), per wife of Jacob.
- The dragon is a solar symbol. Along with the RE and IU in his name, Reuben's mandrakes further identify him with the Sun or Horus the original prototypical Solar Dragon.
- Reuben has a special relationship with **Judah** and **Joseph**, his other two brothers whose names also derive from IU:
  - He saved Joseph's life. When his jealous brothers kidnapped Joseph and were about to kill him, Reuben persuaded them to throw Joseph in a pit instead.
  - Reuben's territory and gate are adjacent to Judah's (Ezek. 48:7, 31).
  - Reuben's name follows Judah's name in John's vision of the sealing of the 12 Tribes (Rev 7:5).
  - Judah's milk-stained teeth and wine-reddened eyes (Gen. 49:12) correlate to the Milk/Blood version of Aquarius' Twin Streams. (Wine is a symbol for blood, as in wine of the Eucharist.)
- As stated before, the names Joseph and Jesus are from common roots.
- On the way to the house of the Last Supper, Christ and his group is preceded by **a mysterious man "bearing a pitcher of water"** (Luke 22:10). Since these biblical stories are based on the Zodiac, this pitcher-bearer likely represents Aquarius the Water Bearer!

Etymology of Reuben (Re-Iu-Ben)			
Afrikan-Kamite Roots		**Apparent Derivatives**	
		HEBREW	**ENGLISH**
ra ra rui	• sun. • light, flame, fire. 419a • red. 188BB1		ray, red, ruby radiation, ruddy, rose irradiate, rouge, rust Russia
ru, ra ar, ur	• opening, mouth, door. • to see, eye, pupil. 68a, 17BB2	**raa**, see, look, perceive **roe**, seer **rah**, to see, eye	orb, orate, oratory orbit, oracle, realize oral, oracular
ru + akh	• Ru=mouth; Akh=spirit	**ruh**, **ruach**, breath, wind, air, spirit, mind, the creative spirit	
Iu benu benben	• ever comming, double. • male, man. • phallus.	**ben**, son	(for IU, see page 204) (for BEN, see page 202)

Therefore the primary meaning of *Reuben* is Atum-Iu!

Reuben appears to be another name for Atum-Iu, the rising newborn Sun of early dawn, which is Red. The previous meanings for his name are still valid, but the deeper or primary meaning is Atum-Iu. Red means he is the *first*, also the *sacrificed*. Reuben's territory was the *first* parcel of land to be given (Num. 32). **Atum-Iu** or Horus, was red as the early rising Sun, the sacrificial calf, and solar dragon. The custom of Christ as red-haired, painted red, or wearing a scarlet robe before crucifixion derives from his Kamite origin as Atum-Iu, a form of Horus. **Atum** gives his name to Adam, Autumn, Edom, and Iudumea, all meaning red. **Adam** was the *first* man and *first* son of God (Luke 3:38). Red is the first color of the spectrum. Atum-**Iu** was the first and the only begotten son of Atum-**Ra** the father. Both, the setting and rising suns are ruddy, respectively called Atum-Ra (the Father) and Atum-Iu (the Son). Thus Reuben and Adam are near equivalent names. Both mean red. Both mean man. Both were the first son of the Father.

So Reuben, Adam, and Aquarius are one and the same!

Number Four is connected with "Reu"

And *Reuben*, *Judah*, *Joseph*, and *Jesus* are facets of the same Precious Stone. That there are FOUR Sons with IU-names reflects the Four Elements, Four Faces of God, the Four Divisions of the Kamit's Astronomical Cross. Additionally Reuben had four sons. Other Reu-named people in the Bible also had four sons! Their names are Reuel (whose father was *red* Esau, Jacob's brother), and Reumah (Nahor's concubine) (Gen. 22:24).

Reuben's water runs deep indeed!

Reuben's duality?

If Reuben (Re-Iu-ben) is Iu then he must also be double by definition. So where is his duality?

- He pours *two* streams from his urn (which itself was earlier two urns).
- He is the 11th zodiacal sign. Eleven (11) =*two* ones. Also 1+1=2.
- Two syllables in his name are both sun words (RE and IU).
- He represents Air, which includes breath, which contains Fire & Water as heat and moisture.
- He is Prince Atum-Iu the Son, thus his Father is Atum-Ra who is opposite him on the "double horizon" as Leo the King.
- " ...the two characters of Atum the father-god, who was designated 'the father of mankind,' and of Iu the son have been reproduced in Genesis as Adam the human father and Iahu-Elohim [the deity Iu] as the god." [1]

Father / Mother = Leo / Pisces
Daughter / Son = Virgo / Aquarius

The Great Mother and Great Father are represented in the Zodiac as Pisces and Leo. Opposite the Mother is Her firstborn Daughter, young Virgo. Opposite the Father is His firstborn Son, young Aquarius. Parent and Child are one, and the same as Two in One (Iu). Aquarius *holds* the Mother/Daughter as the Vessel (originally it was two vessels). Virgo constellation *holds* the Messiah Star who is the Father/Son she has birthed.

The **Great Mother's Love** pours through Aquarius's Vessel and through the Lion's Heart. Lion, Leo, and Love are from same roots. The **Great Father's Light** heats the "Upper Waters" of Pisces (sign of Spiritual Rebirth) and radiates from Virgo's Son who "baptizes with the Holy Spirit and Fire." Aquarius and Virgo are **the only signs pictured as giving nourishment.** Aquarius gives the Mother's nourishment in Twin Streams. His sister Virgo, gives the Father's dual nourishment as wheat and wine (the star Spica [spike of wheat], also called Vindemaitrix [Grape Mother]) symbolizing the body and blood of the Father/Son in the Eucharistic meal.

Divine Four. Blue and Red.

Mother Pisces, Father Leo, Daughter Virgo, and Son Aquarius are the Divine FOUR, opposite each other on the Zodiacal Wheel. Each corresponds to one of the Four Classical Elements of Water, Fire, Earth, and Air. They are ***Duality Doubled***. They are the Astronomical Cross of Four Quarters. Blue correlates to the Mother/Daughter as Water, while Red correlates to the Father/Son Principle as Fire. Virgin Mary (Virgo) wears a blue robe. Her name is from Mer which means both **Water** and Mother-**Love**. Water and Love are inseparable as symbols of each other. Thus **Reuben is Aquarius, the Son of God/Goddess** represented in the Zodiac. In reality, the Spiritual Water he abundantly pours forth is LOVE, the Love of the Great Mother and Great Father for all Their Children, to heal and nourish our Souls in this "New Age" of awakening and resurrection from spiritual darkness.

1) Massey, AE, 425.

12 **Zebulun** = Pisces the Fish

Mutable **WATER** Sign

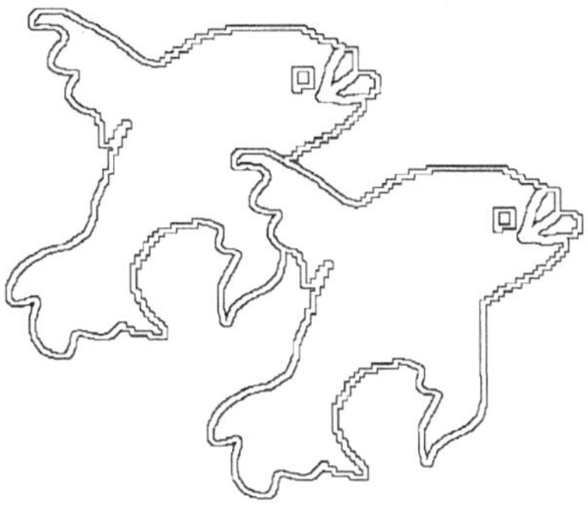

"Zebulun shall dwell at the haven of the sea; and he shall be for an haven" (Gen. 49:13). When Zebulon was born, Leah said "now will my husband dwell with me (Gen. 29:20). A *haven* is a place of refuge or rest; a port, a *sanctuary*. A *sanctuary* is a sacred place or the holiest part of a sacred place such as around the altar of a temple. Zebulun *is* the "Haven of the Sea," and that *sea* is the Celestial Sea of *Pisces*. Zebulun means Lofty Abode or High Dwelling Place. This is the High Abode of the Celestial Waters, the Spiritual Waters, the primeval "waters" of Genesis 1:1, 2. This Abode *is* the Great Mother, whose 10,000 names reflects some attribute of Her beingness as the great Abode, Womb, Throne, Love, Water, Wisdom, and *SEVEN*:

- As Ast (Isis), She was the Throne of Asar (Osiris).
- As Hathor, She was the House of Heru Her son (Hat=house; Hor=Heru).
- As the "Holy Ghost," though masculinized in the Bible, She was "the Comforter" (John 14:16, 26), –the same Comforter called the "Spirit of truth" (14:17), which was a title of the Great Mother as Goddess Maat, the Kamite Goddess of Truth.[1]
- As Hathor-Meri, She was the original Goddess of Love, addressed in the Gospels as Mary the Virgin Mother of Christ, and slandered as Mary Magdalene the Prostitute from which *seven* demons were cast. But note that Jesus becomes the Christ (meaning *Anointed*) through *Her* anointing him. MER, the Afrikan root of Her name, means Love and Water, giving us such words as *marry* and *marine*.
- As Madonna Mary, She was worshiped in Rome as the House consecrated to God, the Tabernacle of the Holy Ghost, the Dwelling-Place or *Zabulo*.[2]

She is the *Sabean* Mother, the *Seven*fold Mother called Sefekh, Goddess of the Seven, or Hepti whose name means Seven. She is the **Zeb** of **Zebulun**, a name derived from Afrikan roots meaning **SEVEN** and **HIGH** (or Great). She gives Her name to the Afrikan Queens of *Sheba*; Sheba means Seven. As Aditi She bore the Seven Sons in Hindu mythology. As "**Hovah**" in **Jehovah** She has the seven eyes "which run to and fro through the whole earth" (Zec. 4:10). She was the Mexican Mother-goddess *Civa*coatl, the Serpent Woman of seven serpents; the Seven Sisters of Pleiades; the Candlestick with Seven Branches; and the Seven Cows / Bears / or Sisters found in the oldest mythologies. Thus Zebulun is clearly feminine, though masculinized in the Bible like many personages, names, and symbols of the Great Mother.

1)Walker, WE, 560. 2) Massey, HJ, 140. 3) Massey, BB-vII, 132.

Etymology of Zebulun (Seb-Alu-On)

Category	Afrikan-Kamite Roots	Apparent Derivatives and Comments
SEB (Seven)	**sevekh** • seven. **sebag** • seven. 149, 359BB2 **shept** • seven. **hept** • seven. 149, 359BB2	**Worldwide Seb Seven** **The ZEB of Zebulun is derived from Kamite Seb** (Sebag, Sevekh, Shept), all meaning **seven**. Since Great Goddess is sevenfold, the various forms of Her names is the Afrikan source of words meaning SEVEN in languages around the world: (144BB2) – Swahili ***sabaa*** – English ***seven, heptad*** – Crow Indian ***sappoah*** – Amharic ***subhat*** – Arabic ***saba*** – Hebrew ***shiva, seba*** – Kaffa ***shebata*** – Khurbat ***heft*** – Sanscrit ***sapta, haya*** – Latin ***septem*** – Bokhara ***hapt*** – Tigre ***shubarte*** – French ***sept*** – Greek ***hept*** – Minetari ***chappo*** – German ***sieben*** – Zend ***hapta*** – Persian ***haft*** – Syriac ***sheba*** – Tater ***epta*** – Brahui ***haft***
ALU (High)	**arar** (alal) • high, exalted.7a, 129a **ari** (ali) • arise, to go up, to be high. 129a **ar** (al) • go up, rise, ascend. 129a **Alu**, Ali • the first Seven Spirits of Light, the co-creators of Creation. AE422	**altar** (high place) altitude alto exalt all hill elder old Alps alpine El (divinity, deity as in angel, Michael) Elohim elite elevate elevator elegant asterisk star astrology astral constellation stellar master (*ma* = great star) sitareh (*star* in Persian) ARABIC: **Allah**, God **Al-Lat**, Goddess **ala u**, to be high, **ala**, high standing, noble **uluw**, height, grandeur **ulan**, height, elevation **The ULU of Zebulun is Kamite Alu** (Ala, Ari) What is Alu? Born at the very beginning of Creation from the Great Mother of All Beginning, the Alu were the first Seven Spirits of Light, the Khuti or co-creators of Creation. Identified with the Circle, they were the "Gods of the Orbit" that revolved and made the Circle and Cycle of Time. That's all that Time is, a circle, a cycle, –from the seconds of the circle of the minute to the cyclic seasons of the year, to the Precession of infinite Great Circle called the Zodiac. The Alu /Ali appear in the mythologies of all the world, brought there by the Afrikans. They are the 7 Spirits of the Great Bear found in Egypt, China and Japan; the 7 Rishis of India; and the 7 Steps of the Masonic Ladder. They are also: • The **Elohim**, from whence the name is derived, the plural God in Genesis who said "Let US make man in OUR image" (Gen. 1:26). Elohim literally mean plural gods (im=plural). • The Seven Spirits of God and Seven Spirits before the Throne in Revelation (Rev. 4:5); the 7 Golden Candlesticks (1:12; 2:1); the 7 Lamps of Fire (4:5). • The Afrikan source of Al in **Allah**, the Arabic name of God; **El,** the Canaanite name of God; and El signifying divinity in Angel, Michael, Gabriel, etc.
ON (Being, Water...) 	**An** • name of the Throne. **An** • the celestial water. 187BB1 **an** • fish. ccx (Budge, EHD) **inu** • water. 143a **inu** • goddess. 143a **nu** • new flood, inundation. 349a **Nu** • (reverse of UN) the Celestial Waters. 349b **Nun** • the Celestial Ocean (called Space), primeval waters. **on** • being, existence **un, unn** • to be, to exist, become, being, existence. 164b **unun** • to be. 164b **Un** • the God of Existence. 165a	**Throne** Lunar **one** June once **John** only **Jonah** **yoni** nun (*fish* in Hebrew) universe Ninevah unite **Noah** unit Nyanza (Afrika's largest lake) **"N"** **now** **innundate** **new** abundant renew abound **rain** **annoint** (oil is poured) **noon** increase **nine** nana (wetnurse) ninety nanny (wetnurse) Ennead (9) enema nano (*small*, because NO cancels NA) unda (*wave* in Latin) **–an –en –in –on** (suffixes of state of being: *darken, opaline, zoon*) **–ence –ance** (state, condition: *independence*) **–tion –sion** (state of being: *revelation, emulsion*) **ontology** (about the nature of being) **The UN of Zebulun is Kamite N, An, On** She is the Throne. As Ast (Isis) Her headdress is the Throne. The LAP of the mother is the "throne" of her Baby, thus infant Christ is depicted in Medieval art sitting upon the LAP of Mary who is the Throne –sitting upon a throne. The Great Mother is the Throne appearing throughout the Book of Revelation: "behold, a throne was set in heaven" (4:2, 3). She is the rainbow encircled 'Sea of Glass' (and Throne): "And before the throne there was a sea of glass like unto crystal" (Rev. 4:6:). She is the Living Water or Water of Life pouring out of Her body, the Throne: "And he showed me a pure river of water of life, clear as crystal, proceeding out of the throne of God and of the Lamb" (Rev. 22:1). "A glorious high throne from the beginning is the place of our sanctuary," declares prophet Jeremiah (17:12). **NINE (3x3) = the Triple Goddess,** the Great Mother whose Womb birthed *The Waters*. She is called the Great Water. **The Fish** represents the Moon Goddess as the ruler of celestial and terrestrial waters. John and Jonah were both connected with water and fish: Fisherman John & Baptist John. Jonah got swallowed by a great fish for 3 days, then saved Nineveh. **NOW is always NEW!** Noon = new beginning, for before the rise of patriarchy, the day began at NOON, not at midnight! And it is *water* that renews and refreshes us.

Names

Kamite gods connected with the Seb-name are also, like Pisces, connected with Water and sea creatures: **Seb**, the name of Her first child as Time, was an early form of Horus as the Solar Dragon (the prototypical dragon).[1] **Sebek** was the name of the Crocodile-god, the Fish of Inundation, and the "father of fishers" who was the prototype for the Gospel *Zebedee*, also a father of fishers.[2]

Biblical variants or names from the same root as *Zebulun* include:

Zebedee	Zebidah	Zebadiah	Sheva
Zebah	Zebul	Zabbud	Shebuel
Zabbaia	Zebina	Seba	Sheba
Zabad	Zeboiim	Shebah	Shebat
Zeboim	Shapphira	Shebaniah	Shebarim
Zebudah	Zabdiel	Bathsheba	Barsabas
Bathsheba	Shabbethai	Shebania	Sebat

The Deep, The Waters

The Great Mother is "the deep" and "the waters" that preceded Creation. "In the beginning God created the heaven and the earth. And the earth was without form, and void; and darkness was upon the face of the deep. And the Spirit of God moved upon the face of the waters" (Gen. 1:1-2).

She is Virgo and Pisces, which are opposite/complementary signs, apparent in Genesis 1:7: "And God made the firmament, and divided the waters which were under the firmament from the waters which were above the firmament" (Gen. 1:7):

- The waters *below* the firmament are the Terrestrial Waters representing Virgo (an Earth sign). Virgo represents the Mother of **physical**, natural *first* birth by Water. This is the birth of the lower body (*matter*ial body of Earth and Water); babies are born in a sac of water; our bodies are 2/3rds water.
- The waters *above* the firmament are the Celestial Waters representing Pisces (a Water sign). Pisces represents the Mother of **spiritual** *second* birth by Fire. This is the re-birth of the higher body (*ether*eal body of Spirit and Soul). Our *Spirit* body is akin to Air (breath). The word for breath and spirit are the same in many languages. Our Soul correspond to Fire (light); "soul" is from solar (sun). Pisces is the Fish-Mother of the Evolved, Spiritually re-born human. Horus, Jesus, Dagon and others were all Piscean Avatars.

And this is appropriately recorded in the *SEVENTH* verse of the *first* chapter of the Bible.

1) Massey, AE, 707-708. 2) Ibid., 909.

Moon Seven Water

"Seven" is intimately linked with Water. Rainbows of seven colors appear after rain. The seven days of the week are cycles derived from the Moon, whose effect on water is witnessed as the tides. Revered as a symbol of the Great Mother, the Moon is intimately connected with Seven and Water.

Fish

The two fish of Pisces, pointing in opposite directions represent two crescent moons, one waxing, one waning. Fish were sacred goddess symbols in the ancient mythologies; they lived in the Sea, -in Water, the arch-symbol of the Great Mother, –as Fire or Light is the arch-symbol of the Great Father. The "half fish, half woman" originates from the Mermaid of the Zodiac, or Sign of the Fishes.[1]

The Meaning

The literal meaning of Zebulon is Seven-High-Throne/ Being. And since Seven refers to the Sabean Mother, Zebulon means the Lofty Sabean Mother of All. And since She *is* the Haven, the Abode, the House, the Throne, Giver of the Heart-Soul, and Source of Life whose Womb gave birth to Water itself, Zebulon finally means,

"The High-Deep Abode
of the Loving
Sabean Mother of All Life"

This page is too tiny to do justice to something so Great; not even a million pages are sufficient. Mere words can only allude to Her fathomless Greatness as Zebulon, the Celestial Waters, the "Haven of the Sea" known as Pisces.

Thus we all belong to a *"Tribe"* of Israel, –that is, *"sign"* of the Zodiac!

In the sense that everyone is born to a "tribe" or sign of the Zodiac, then the Twelve Tribes exist as real people after all; as the whole of Humanity. The "Chosen People thing" is exposed as both, propaganda and psychological illness –or need to cover an inherent sense of inferiority by asserting the opposite. We are all children of Mother Goddess and Father God. States Genesis, "for a father of many nations have I made thee" (Gen. 17:5). Chauvinist Ezra neglects to mention the role of the Mother as progenitor of nations. For the Father cannot produce "many nations" or *any* nations without the Mother!

1) Massey, BB-vI, 452.

The 12 (13) Tribes of Ishmael are also the 12 Zodiac Signs

Ishmael was the firstborn son of Abraham and Hagar his Kamite concubine and handmaid of Sarah, his first wife. Like Israel, Joktan, and a number of biblical male *stars*, Ishmael had *twelve* sons and *one* daughter. These sons were really the zodiacal signs; two of the sons were Gemini the Twins while the daughter was Virgo. His sons are named in Genesis 25:13-16:

> "And these are the names of the sons of Ishmael, by their names... Nebajoth; and Kedar, and Adbeel, and Mibsam, And Mishma, and Dumah, and Massa, Hadar, and Tema, Jetur, Naphish, and Kedema." His daughter, called Mahalath or Bashemath, is named in Genesis 28:9; 36:3.

Their biblical order has been jumbled to further disguise their zodiacal identity. Their proper order is as follows:

Tribes of Ishmael	Zodiac Sign Represented
1. Dumah	Aries the Ram
2. Adbeel	Taurus the Bull
3. Tema & Kedemah	Gemini the Twins
4. Massa	Cancer the Crab
5. Nebaioth	Leo the Lion
6. Mahalath	Virgo the Virgin
7. Mibsam	Libra the Balance
8. Naphish	Scorpio the Scorpion
9. Mishma	Sagittarius the Archer
10. Kedar	Capricorn the Goat
11. Jetur	Aquarius the Waterman
12. Hadar	Pisces the Fish

The etymology or true meaning of their name-roots link them to the signs they represent. Their name-meanings correspond to a major characteristic of the zodiacal sign they stand for. In the following sections we will uncover the true or most likely roots of the names of Ishmael's *thirteen* children.

1 **Dumah** = Aries the Ram

Dumah means RED, the hottest color and also the first color of the rainbow –quite appropriate for Aries the hottest sign, first sign, and Cardinal Fire Sign. Dumah is from **Adumah**, meaning *red* in Hebrew. Adumah is from the same roots as Adumu, Adummin, Dumuzi, Adam, Edom, –all meaning RED, all derived from Kamite **Atum**. *Atum* was the name of the *red* Sungod Atum-Ra, as the Red Sun of winter, sunsets and sunrises, who gives his name to ***Autumn*** the red season. Thus fiery Dumah is Aries the Ram.

2 **Adbeel** = Taurus the Bull

Adbeel is Ad-*Baal*. *Baal* is a divine name and lofty title (*Lord*) conferred on kings and deities. **Baal** of the Hebrews, **Bel** of Babylonia, **Balder** of the Norwegians, **Bala-Rama** of the Hindus, **Bial** of the Irish, **Bar** and the bull-headed **Maha-Bul** or great **Bol** of Syria, are all derived from Kamite **Bal / Bar**, *including* the word ***Bull*** itself! Followers of Baal were worshipers of the Sun in Taurus,[1] who was none other than the great Osiris as the Bull of Heaven; the Bull of the Zodiac worshiped as Apis by the Greeks, and as the human-headed, *kinky*-haired, winged Bull of Assyria whose massive statues flanked the gates of royal palaces. Undoubtedly Osiris was El, the chief god of Canaan whose most important titles were *Bull* or *Bull-El.*[2] Isis his wife was Hathor, the Holy Cow or Female Bull of the Zodiac. Their son Horus was the Golden Calf. When the Zodiacal Age moved to the next sign (Aries), this cosmic divine Trinity became the Ram, Ewe, and Lamb of God (thus Christ –who was Horus– is called the Lamb of God). Numerous ***Baalim*** appear in the Bible, for every god was a Baal including the biblical God (Hosea 2:16). In Hebrew, the **B** in "**B'Jah**" stands for Baal,[3] and is translated as Jehovah in Isaiah 26:4. Written out, it is Baal-Iah (Baal is Jah). **AD** in *Ad*beel is Kamite **At** (king, prince, *stone*, *house*). **Ethbaal**, a variant of Adbeel, was a king (1Ki. 16:31), father of Jezebel, both worshipers of Baal. Thus, royal **Adbeel** is the *hard* zodiacal *House* of the King Bull of Eternity reknown as Taurus.

Biblical Baal-Names include:

Ethbaal	Jezebel	Merib-baal	Belshazzar
Baal-Gad	Baal-zebub	Jerubbaal	Bela
Belial	Eliphal	Elpaal	"Parbar" (1Chr. 26:18)
Esh-baal	Apollo (was Abelius or Bel [4])		Paul

Afrikan-Kamite Roots		Apparent Derivatives	
		ENGLISH:	HEBREW:
At	• king, prince, father, *stone, house.* 96b, 97a	bar (law, rules /principles. "the lord" makes the law; both are the final authority) •baron (a lord or nobleman) •baron (a cut of sirloin *beef*) boar (from Old English *bar.* adult *male* of various animals) bear bull (adult male bovine mammal)	**ad**, prince **par**, bull **para**, cow **bar**, son
Bar	• Bal, Baal. (r = l) 203b		

a, b = columns in An Egyptian Hieroglyphic Dictionary. **BB** = Book of the Beginnings (vol. 1 or 2)

1) Higgens, vI, 259. 2) Larousse, EM, 75. 3) Massey, AE, 498. 4) Blavatsky, IU-vII, 466.

3 **Tema & Kedemah** = Gemini the Twins

Tema means "union, to join, be united to, bring together." **Kedemah** is Ke-Tema, meaning "another Tema," –another *twin*, that is! Both names are from the same roots as Tom (Thomas) which means Twin. Thus Tema and Kedema are Gemini the Twins.

Afrikan-Kamite Roots			Apparent Derivatives	
			SANSKRIT:	HEBREW:
k	• another, also.	782a		
ka	• another, ye two (dual)	782a		
ki	• masc. another, one embraces the other, once again.	792a		
ket	• another.	798b		
tema	• to join, be united to, union, bring together, bind, collect.	878b, 879a,b	**adima,** first male & female, both	**tham,** double, to be twin, twined together
temm	• to unite with.	878b	**dama,** resemble	**tumtum,** hermaphrodite
tam-t	• total of two halves.	20BB2	**dimmo,** liken, compare	**temuna,** likeness, image
Tum	• the double Sungod (father & sun)			**tam,** whole, faultless
tum	• "to complete and perfect in a total of two halves."	287BB2		

4 **Massa** = Cancer the Crab

Massa in Hebrew means burden, bearing (a load), prophecy. The crab and the turtle (symbol of Cancer in the Babylonian Zodiac) are always bearing the load of their home which is the shell in which they live. The symbol of Cancer in the Kamite Zodiac was the Scarab Beetle, noted for pushing or rolling the load of its eggs in a dung-ball across the sand until they hatched. Hebrew Massa is derived from Kamite **mas** or **mesi**. Ever bearing its burden, tidings, or gifts, Massa is Cancer the Crab.

Afrikan-Kamite Roots			Apparent Derivatives	
			ENGLISH:	HEBREW:
mesi	• bearer, producer	321a	message	**massa,** burden, load, cargo, *prophecy*
mas	• to bring, lead forward, come with something.	286b	messenger	**msa,** bearing; "burden of Jehovah"
am, amu	• to seize, grasp.	6a	amass	**amas, omes,** load, burden
			masto– (breast. it "bears" milk)	**amus,** loaded, burden

a, b = columns in An Egyptian Hieroglyphic Dictionary. **BB** = Book of the Beginnings (vol. 1 or 2)

1) Massey, BB-vII, 287. 2) Budge, EHD, 879. 3) Ibid., 878.

5 **Nebaioth** = Leo the Lion

Nebaioth is **Neba-Io**. Io is a variant spelling of **Iu**, a name identified with the Sun, the same Iu from whence Jesus (Iu-Su, Jehoshua), Joseph (Iu-Sif), and Judah (Iu-ta) are derived. Iu means Ever Coming One, and double. Egyptian **Neba** was a royal title and name of a fire god. **Nebaui** (Neba-Iu?) was the name of "a double fire god." The Lion was a solar symbol in ancient Egypt. Feline images represented the Sun-God. **Neb** means lord or master; the Sun was called "Lord" and "Savior" by the ancients. Neb (nub) also means gold, and gives its name to **Nubia** (Ethiopia).

Biblical Neb-names include:

Nebuchadnezzar, king of Babylon	Nebat
Nebo, a god (Is. 46:1)	Naboth
Nabonidus	Neballat
Nabopolassar	Nabal
Barnabas	

Afrikan-Kamite Roots			Apparent Derivatives	
			ENGLISH:	ARABIC:
neb	• lord, master, owner, possessor.	357a	noble (= neb-el)	**nabih**, noble, highborn, eminent
neb-t	• lady, mistress.	357a	nobility	**nabara**, to raise, elevate, go up with the voice
Neba	• a royal title.	357b	nabob (person of wealth and prominence)	**nubug**, eminence, brilliancy, distinction.
Nebaui	• name of "a double fire god."	367a	Napoleon? (NaboLeo or Lord Lion)	
Nebu	• the "Lords."	358a	Nubia	
Neb Taui	• Lord of the Two Lands (Upper & Lower Egypt), a common title of kings.	365a	Anubis	
Nub	• "Golden One," a name of the Sungod.	353b		
nub	• gold.	353a		
nubu	• golden.	353b		
neb	• fire, flame.	366a		
nebu	• ornaments in the form of lions or sphinxes.	367a		

Glowing with such a background, Nebaioth means the Golden Lord Iu, the Great Father or King Father personified as the Zodiacal Lion of Heaven, appropriately a *Fire* sign.

6 **Mahalath Bashemath** = Virgo the Virgin

The only daughter of Ishmael mentioned by name was **Mahalath** who was also called **Bashemath**. (Gen. 28:9, 36:3). Mahalath occurs in the title of Psalms 53 and 88. According to one source, **Mahala** means tender affection, tender, merciful, and loving.[1] These are the same qualities of Virgin Mary and also the meanings of Mary's name! Apparently derived from Egyptian **Ma** + **Ala**, the name **Mahala** means Lofty Mother (similar to Mary Magdalene); Goddess of Truth (Maat, the Goddess of Truth); Heavenly Mother; and Lofty Harvest (Divine Bread?).

Afrikan-Kamite Roots	Apparent Derivatives		
	ENGLISH:	HEBREW:	ARABIC:
ma • true, truth, place, to harvest **ma** • mother **Ala** (Ali, Ari) • the First Seven Co-Creator Gods **ala** (ali, ari) • high, heights, ascension	altar (elevated place) alto altitude elder old Alps alpine El (divinity, deity) angel Michael Elohim elite elevate elevator elegant	**aliya**, ascent **ala**, goddess **El**, god, divinity (as in Elohim, Rachel) **mo'al**, raising **ma'ale**, ascent, rise, slope, platform **ma'ala**, stair, step, degree, position, advantage, merit **ha'la'a**, raise, lifting **he'ela**, raise, lift, advance, grow **mehullal**, glorious, praised, blessed	**AL-Lat**, Goddess **Allah**, God **ala**, high standing, nobility **alu**, from above **ala u**, to be high, elevated, loom **ulan**, height, elevation **uluw**, height, elevation, grandeur

Bashemath is apparently Bast-Maat. Maat was the Kamite Goddess of Truth. **Bast** or **Pash** are names of goddess Hathor in feline form. Hathor was the virgin mother of Horus and prototype of Virgin Mary and Aphrodite, the goddess of Love. Concerning Bast, Budge writes, "As a nature power she represented the gentle, fructifying heat of the sun, and its regenerative influence in the most comforting form." [2] Bast, the Cat-mother was the benevolent aspect of Hathor, the Lioness. Festivals of Bast were joyful with music, dancing, jokes, and sexual rites. [3] The Great Mother as **Pash** was the Bringer of Peace, whose name gives us the word **peace**.[4] Shalem means peace in Hebrew. Salama was a name of goddess Venus (Aphrodite). Jerusalem is *Aarru*-Salem, or Mount-Peace, seat of Goddess Pash.[5] Aaru (meaning ascent, stairs, to mount) was also the name of a celestial city and the heaven, Elysium. Since Kamite L/R are one, Aaru = Aalu; the same alu /ala in Mahalath. Kamite pas (**pasa**, **pasen**, **pas-t**) also means cakes or loaves [6] and is the source of the word **pastry**. How does *pastry* relate to Virgo? Virgo was also known as the House of Bread; she is always portrayed holding a spike of grain. This spike is the bright star *Spica*, found in the constellation of the Celestial Virgin we now know as Mahala-Basemath.

1) Blavatsky, IU-vI, 466. 2) Budge, GE-vI, 518. 3) Walker, WE, 148. 4) Massey, BB-vII, 170. 5) Ibid., 170. 6) Budge, EHD, 232, 233.

7 **Mibsam** = Libra the Balance

Mibsam is apparently *M'basam*, derived from ***bissem*** with an M prefix. It has the same meaning as ***Jibsam*** (1Chrn. 7:2) (or ***Ibsam*** in modern translations). Both words mean fragrant. Hebrew **bissem** means perfume, flavor, intoxicate, gladden; **bassam** means perfumer; **bosem** means perfume scent. A related English word is **balsam** (aromatic resins or their esters), from Greek **balsamon**. Kamite "**m**" is a preposition meaning in, of, from, out, like and "give." [1] Thus Mibsam creatively denotes Libra the Balance, for perfume and fragrance are only possible with Air, and Libra is the Cardinal Air Sign!

8 **Naphish** = Scorpio the Scorpion (& Snake /Eagle)

Naphish is *erroneously* derived from *naphesh*; it is logical and easy to connect these words since they sound the same. Hebrew *naphesh* means living breathing soul, derived from Egyptian *nef* (air, wind, breath) and *nefi* (to breath, blow at, give breath to).[2] Any connection these meanings may have with Scorpio is *not* apparent.

Therefore, the likely origin of Naphish is Greek ***nepas***, meaning scorpion. Latin ***nepa*** means scorpion, crab, and the constellation of Scorpio.[3] The *Arkana Dictionary of Astrology* informs us that **Nepa** is "apparently a word of African origin, meaning 'land crab.'" [4] The Afrikan origin of **Nepa** is Kamite "**Nehp**" meaning "to seize." [5] Crabs and scorpions are "seizers with their claws" or pincers. English derivatives of **nehp** include:

- **kidnap**
- **nab** (to seize, arrest, snatch)
- **neb** (beak of a bird)
- **nip** (to seize and pinch or bite)
- **nibble** (to bite, eat)
- **nipper** (a tool such as pliers or pincers)

Thus Naphish is ***Nepas***, the constellation of Scorpio.

1) Budge, EHD, 264, cvii. 2) Ibid., 396. 3) Cassell's Latin Dictionary, 391. 4) Arkana Dictionary, 246. 5) Massey, BB-vII, 624.

9 **Mishma** = Sagittarius the Archer

Mishma is apparently **Ishma** with an M prefix; the same Ishma of Ishmael his father. Kamite "M" means *see*, *behold*; as a preposition it means *in, from, out from, of, like*.[1] The name of the double-god **Shu** is the root of Ishmael, which is derived from "**Shu-ma-el**." [2] **Shu** in dual form was ShuMa or **MaShu**,[3] the god of two characters, Light and Shade, manifesting as sunlight by day and moonlight by night. Shu was the supporter and warrior for the Sungod, especially when the Sun began diminishing in strength as winter approached. As Warrior for the Sun against the forces of darkness, Shu was the *God of the Bow* whose symbol was the *Arrow*. Ishmael, largely modeled from Shu, is described as an Archer in Genesis 21:20.

Mishma can also be figured as Mash-Ma or MaShu-Ma. Kamite **mash, masha** (Ma-Shu?) means archer,[4] probable source of Hebrew **msa** (dart). Kamite **Ma** means true/truth, renew, see/behold, and mother. Therefore:

- Mash-Ma means True Archer, Behold the Archer, and Bow Mother (Goddess Neith of the Bow). Recall that Jacob's son Joseph (representing Sagittarius) was married to Asenath, a biblical form of Goddess Neith.
- MaShu-Ma means Behold MaShu or MaShu the Renewer (of the weakening Sun).

Drawing from such a background, Mishma is identified as Sagittarius the Archer.

10 **Kedar** = Capricorn the Goat

The biblical tents of Kedar were made of black goat hair. Goat hair was also used in constructing the tabernacle (Ex. 26:7). Goats usually have long straight hair. The predominant breed of Palestine was the Syrian goat (Capra hircus mambrica) which is usually black. King Solomon (or his lover) compares their black skin to the black tents of Kedar (Solomon 1:5). Thus Kedar is connected with the Goat and is derived from the same root as goat. Kedar (Ked-ar) is **Gad-ar**. **Gad** means **Goat**. Kamite **AR** means *born of, in the likeness of, type, to make*.[5] Thus Kedar (Ked-ar) means from /of /like goats, identifying him as Capricorn, the Goat of Heaven.

1) Budge, EHD, 264a. 2) Massey, BB-vII, 339. 3) Ibid, 339. 4) Massey, BB-vII, 624; Budge, EHD, xxxvii. 5) Massey, BB-vI, 247.

11 **Jetur** = Aquarius the Water Bearer

Aligning with its Afrikan roots, Jetur is listed in namebooks as meaning overflow, abundance, more than enough, excelling. Jetur is Aquarius the Water Bearer, pouring forth two wavy streams of abundance. The Afrikan roots of **Jetur** is **Atur** or **Uat-ur**, the origin of the word **WATER** itself! [1] Atur also means "branched river" and referred to the "Twin Water" of the Two Truths. This Twin Water was the original nourishment from the Great Mother of All Beginning, and is still the nourishment of infants today, as Blood and Milk. Infants receive the nourishment of Blood while in the womb, and Milk nourishment when out of the womb. With this bit of information you can surmise Aquarius's feminine roots. Aquarius is modeled from the Afrikan god, Hapi, who pours out the two branches of the Nile, the Mother's water. Kamite **Atur** gives its name to European rivers as the Adour, Atre, Atro, and Etherow.[2] These names resemble the biblical Ater, Ithra, Jeter, and Jethro –all variant spellings of Jetur who is Aquarius the Water Bearer.

Afrikan-Kamite Roots			Apparent Derivatives			
			ENGLISH:			OTHERS:
atur	• to come out, to flow.	97b	**water**	drip	tribe	GREEK:
	• lake, flood, river, arm of river.	97b	**wet**	drop	tributary	**thalassa**, sea
	• branched river.	190,191BB1	**tear** (teardrop)	**Atlantic** (atL = atR)	contribute	
atru	• to pour out.	99b	thirst	Atlantis	attribute	HEBREW:
	• river, stream, canal, Nile.	99b	torrent	Italy	**irrigation**	**yater**, excessive, advantageous, greater
tru	• stream, river.	840b	turbulent (agitated)	drizzle	well	**yittur**, excess, remainder
ter	• mourner.	56BB1	trickle	drink	derive	
uat	• water.	80BB1	travel	drool	dells (rapids of a river)	
uat-ur	• water.	80BB1	stream	dribble	deluge (= del-luge)	
ar (al)	• river.	69a		drown		
ir (il)	• river.	143a				
uari (uali)	• to flow over or away.	157a				

12 **Hadar** = Pisces the Fish

Hadar is **Hat-Ar**. Kamite **Hat** (Het) means Great House or Temple.[3] Hebrew **adar** or **addir**, a likely derivative, means great, mighty. English "are" is from Kamite "ar." **Ar** means born of, type, in the likeness of, to make, and "that which is fundamental."[4] Thus, Hadar means the "Great House." This Great House is the Great Mother, also called the Abode, the Great Throne, and the Womb of Life. As Hathor (Hat-Hor), She was the *House* (Hat) of Horus (Hor). As Ast (Isis), She was the Throne of Asar (Osiris), a Kamite version of the Great Father. And it was Her Womb that gave birth to Water itself, thus She is the Mother of Water and House of the Waters; the same "waters" in Genesis 1:2 at the beginning of creation. Fish is a sacred ancient Mother-symbol, and Hadar, connected with this symbol, is Pisces, the double Fish of Heaven.

1) Massey, BB-vI, 80. 2) Ibid., 191. 3) Budge, EHD, 453. 4) Massey, BB-vI, 247; vII, 295.

The 12 (13) Judges of the Book of Judges are the 12 Zodiac Signs

The Judges

1. ***Deborah***
2. Othniel
3. Ehud
4. Shamgar
5. Barak
6. Gideon
7. Tola
8. Jair
9. Jephthah
10. Ibzan
11. Elon
12. Abdon
13. Samson

There are thirteen warrior "judges" in the Book of Judges. Their Leader and the greatest of them all is the Great Mother Herself, portrayed as Queen Deborah, a biblical version of Goddess Maat, the Original Prototypical Judge. The All-Seeing Eye originally belonged to Maat, thus Queen Deborah is the great Seer, Prophetess. The Bible does not call Her a queen but makes it clear that She was Israel's Leader, Judge, and *Mother* (Judges 4:4, 5; 5:7). There were no princes in Israel, village life ceased, "until that I Deborah arose, that I arose a mother in Israel" (Judges 5:7). **Deborah supposedly means BEE.** This makes Her the *Queen Bee* in a hive of males, *–Sweeet Aphrodite* the Goddess of Love. And nothing is sweeter than Love. Sweetness is Love manifest. The symbol of Aphrodite at Eryx was a golden honeycomb. Aphrodite was as sweet as the honey of Her sacred bees, and honey was considered an *aphro*disiac. This makes sense since the sex organs of plants – flowers– are the source of honey. Naturally the Sweet Lady represents the Earth sign Virgo. She held court under the *Palm Tree of Deborah* (Judges 4:5). This sounds like a metaphor for sex, since the "palm tree" anciently represented the erected phallus, at least in Kamit, and Virgo is the gestator of the Zodiac, teeming with Life. **And bees sting!** This signifies Her warrior Destroyer Aspect! She is the composer of the victory hymn She sings with Barak in Judges 5. The hero *Barak* and Her husband, *Lapidoth*, are really the same in that the meaning of both their names signify "lightnings." [1] And *lightning* is a phallus symbol.

Hers is the reign of Peace –40 years of peace in the land (Judges 5:31). Her first scriptural appearance is in Judges *4:4. Four* is a significant number of the Great Mother of the Four Corners, Four Elements or 4 divisions of Kamit's Astrological Cross. As with all the biblical groupings of 12 (disguisedly 13), the true etymology of the names of these "judges" spell out the Zodiac signs.

The combined ***NAMES*** of ***all*** the Biblical Books conceal five Zodiacs!

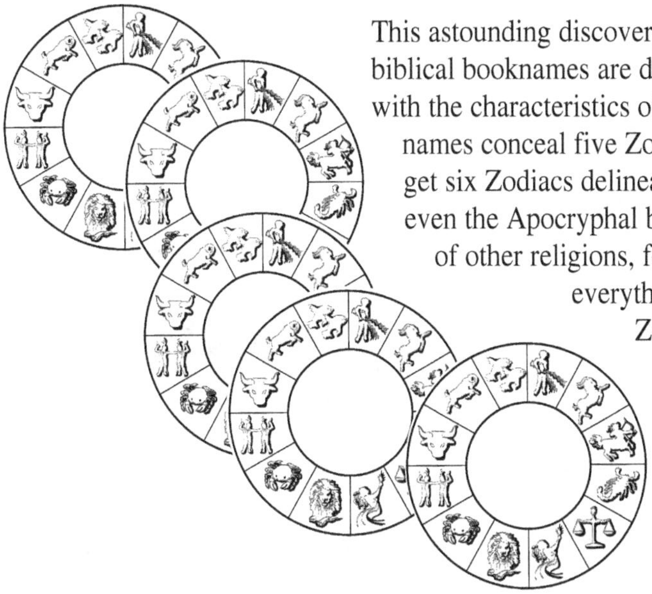

This astounding discovery becomes evident when the true etymology of the biblical booknames are determined. The name of each biblical book aligns with the characteristics of the Zodiac sign it represents. Their combined names conceal five Zodiacs! Add the excluded Apocrypha books and you get six Zodiacs delineated by the actual names of the biblical books. Yes, even the Apocryphal books are zodiacal. And this may include holy books of other religions, for they all had their genesis in Afrika along with everything else –civilization, language, and Humanity. The Zodiac was regarded with vast esteem, else why is it the actual foundation of the Bible? In the following two tables, we shall discover the hidden Zodiacs underlying the names of the biblical books.

1) Massey, BB-vII, 145.

The New Testament booknames disguise 2 Decan-Zodiacs!

***Decan* Zodiac?** This is the earlier Zodiac of TEN signs, corresponding to the TEN Tribes of Israel in Moses's time. JESURUN was the title of the 10-Tribe Israel (Deu. 33:5, 26; 32:15), which preceded the 12-Tribe Israel. Though there are 27 separate books in the New Testament, in reality there are only 20 books (two *Decans*) when double names (like Peter) are excluded! In the table below, note that the underlined double booknames (Peter, Corinthians, Thessalonians, Timothy) correspond to Earth, Water, Air, & Fire! Also Philemon & Corinthians equally apply to Virgo.

Sign	Personal Names	Impersonal Names
1 (1) **Aries** the Ram	**Luke** Derived from Kamite LUKAI (RUKAI), meaning fire, heat.	**Hebrews** *Habirus*, a fiery, warring, Indo-European people (page 108, etymology). Ares was the god of war.
2 (2) **Taurus** the Bull 	**1& 2 Peter** Peter means rock, father, phallus. Taurus = Earth Sign (hard). Bull = symbol of masculinity. 2 bks of Peter = Bull & Calf.	**Galatians** Gal+Lat (Great Goddess names). Yields Latin, lactate, galaxy (milky way), Greek gala (milk). The Cow (female Bull) is a prime source of milk!
3 (3) **Gemini** the Twins 	**Philemon** "Affectionate." From Kamite FEL / PEL (Fer / Per; since L=R), to encircle, embrace, affection, etc.). Yields Greek phil (love). Gemini was originally male/female lovers.	**1 & 2 Corinthians** *Corinth*, from Kamite KAR, the Virgin Goddess or Heart, Cardia, "Kore" of Earth. The two books = 2 hearts; a *couple*; lovers joined at the heart.
... (4) **Cancer**	...	...
4 (5) **Leo** the Lion 	**Jude** Equivalent to Judah (Iu-Ta) the Twin Lions. "Lion of the Tribe of Judah." (See section on Judah of Israel)	**1 & 2 Thessalonians** From Kamite THESI, thasas (master, chief, command, be exalted). Leo=king. 2 books = the Twin Lion Sungods. Sun was anciently the "Lord."
... (6) **Virgo**	...	...
5 (7) **Libra** the Balance	**Matthew** From Kamite MAAT (Truth). Goddess Maat's symbols included the Scale (upon which she weighed the HeartSoul of the deceased) and the Feather (=Air).	**Revelation** From "reveal." To SEE. This points to the All Seeing Eye of Maat, Goddess of Truth, Justice, and the Scales, upon which She weighed hearts.
6 (8) **Scorpio** the Scorpion, Eagle & Serpent 	**1 & 2 Timothy** From Kamite TEMTIT (name of serpent on royal crown); TEM (pierce, be stung). Two books signify the upper /lower nature of Scorpio with its sky symbol (eagle) and earth symbols (scorpion /serpent).	**Romans** The Romans "stung" the original Jews, an Afrikan people. Destroyed them as a nation in Roman-Jewish war. Rome is from Kamite LEM (REM), meaning weeping, water. Scorpio, a water sign.
7 (9) **Sagittarius** the Archer	**Mark** From Kamite MERK (war, strife, etc.). Yields *Marcus & Mars,* the *martial* planet of war. Sagittarius is a warrior (archer).	**Philippians** From Greek *Philip* (horse lover). Sagittarius is the only sign with a horse.
8 (10) **Capricorn** the Goat	**James** From *ames* (burden). The ScapeGoat bore all the sins of Israel. Plus goats have a burden of milk.	**Acts** Goats are the most "active" animals in Zodiac, hence "caper" (to play) = the capricious "capri" (goat). "Kids" & children are very ACTive/playful.
9 (11) **Aquarius** the Water Bearer (*Pourer*, really)	**Titus** Means Giver, Provider. From Kamite TE-T (hand); TATA / TITI (to give, giver); T (to give). Greek tite (day, sun); the Sun only gives, pours out its light.	**Ephesians** *Ephesus*, from AP + AS, two names of the Great Mother, both of which whose meanings include *water*, pointing to the "Twin Waters" of double-source Nile upon which Aquarius is based.
10 (12) **Pisces** the Fish	**John & John 1-2-3** John is from Kamite AN (water, fish, throne). 4 books of John (5 with bk of Jonah)! –more than any other biblical book. Signifies Pisces the "Great House," Exalted Dwelling Place.	**Colossians** Or colossal, from Greek *kolossai* (vast). Pisces is the Great House of the Great Mother, whose Womb birthed Water. The waters of the Nun, a.k.a. "Space," = the Primal Ocean.

The Old Testament booknames disguise 3 Zodiacs!

Sign	Personal Names		Impersonal Names
1 Aries the Ram	**Zachariah** From Kamite SEKER, title of Azar's phallus.Arabic Zeker=penis.	**Habakkuk** "Ardent Embrace"=passion, fire. 2nd meaning = Abba (father) Kak (sun).	**Psalms** or SONGS excel at stirring up Passion, a primary trait of Aries.
2 Taurus the Bull	**Ezra** Hebrew *ezra* = helper. Bull is a "helper" or servile animal. From AZAR (Osiris) as the Bull.	**Ezekiel** "Strength." Bull is reknown for its great strength. From SEK, Seker, title of Asar as sacrificial Bull.	**Deuteronomy** "Second law," derived from Greek *deuteros,* meaning *second.* Taurus is the "second" sign!
3 Gemini the Twins	**Nahum** "Comforter." Love comforts. Love sign of Gemini originally portrayed a couple, later it became twins.	**Nehemiah** "Comforter." Love comforts. Variant of Nahum. From NEM (sweet, etc.) Sweetness = Love manifested.	**Leviticus** "Simeon and Levi are brethren" (or Twins). Levi from same root as Love.
4 Cancer the Crab	**Jeremiah** Is Je-Rem-lah. REM (Lem) = weep hence the Water of this Water sign.	**Zephaniah** Sif (child of) + Ani. Identical with name Benoni, meaning "Son of my mourning /sorrow" (Benjamin's 1st name. See section on Benjamin).	**Lamentations** When "lamenting," or under strong emotion, tears (water) flow! Cancer is a moody water sign. From Kamite Rem (Lem) = weep.
5 Leo the Lion	**1&2 Samuel** Also known as Book of the *Kings.* Sem-IU-El. Sem =sun, fire, double solar plume which was the headdress of the 2 Lion Gods. Two books =the Twin Solar Lions.	**Joel** IU-El. Iu (double) Sungod of the 2 horizons (east/west), the Twin Lions (father/son). Joel is the son. His father was Pethuel (Pat-Iu-El), Divine Father Iu.	**1&2 Kings** The Lion is reknown as "the King." Only feline images represented Ra, source of Royalty itself. Two books = Kamit's Twin Lions. Lion from Ra (La).
6 Virgo the Virgin	**Ruth** A "virtuous woman" (3:11), arrives in Bethlehem (House of *Bread)* at beginning of *barley* harvest (1:22). Gleans grain throughout book! Given 6 measures of grain. Virgo holds *grain* & is the 6th sign.	**Esther** Ast–Ar/Al. Ast =Isis. Obtained favor in the king's sight "more than all the virgins" (2:17). She was made his *Queen.* Virgo is reknown as the *Queen* of Heaven.	**Genesis** The Female or Womb of the Great Mother is the Source of Life. Virgo is the Gestator of the Zodiac.
7 Libra the Balance	**Micah** From Kamite MAKHA (scales). Har-Makru is Lord Michael, Lord of the Scales, a title of Horus.	**Solomon** Peace. Salem (peace). Peace = level (as with undisturbed water), like the scales in perfect balance.	**Numbers** Got scales? Got *Numbers.* Weighing is math, connected with all commercial activities.
8 Scorpio the Scorpion, Eagle /Serpent	**Daniel** From TANN, God of Underworld. Also means serpent (Leviathan, python). See section on Dan.	**Haggai** From Kamite HEK (wisdom). Serpent a symbol of wisdom.	**Judges** Dan = judge in Hebrew. "Dan shall judge..be a serpent..that biteth." See section on Dan.
9 Sagittarius the Archer	**Joshua** "Salvation." From *Jehoshua,* Jesus. Both connected with Fire & Salvation. Based on Shu, Archer of the Gods, Son of Ra. See Joseph.	**Hosea** Variant of the name Joshua, a shortened form of Jehoshua, the Hebrew name of Jesus (Greek version).	**Proverbs** *Wise* sayings. *Wise* and *sharp* (=arrowpoint) is the SAGE; same root as SAGittarius. Pro (*forth* like the arrow) Verb (word, sword).
10 Capricorn the Goat	**Amos** From *ames* (burden). The ScapeGoat bore all Israel's sins, plus goats have burden of milk.	**Obadaiah** "Bearer, servant." The Scapegoat bore all the sins of Israel.	**Ecclesiastes** means "group, gathering." Fancy way of saying "flock." Goats come in "flocks" or "troops / troupes."
11 Aquarius the Water Bearer	**Isaiah** Ish-lah. Hebrew Ish=male, virile; lah = divine. Isaiah is the Divine Male who is Aquarius.	**Malachi** "Prince, King." This is the Prince, Aquarius, the Son of God & Goddess.	**Exodos** Exude, Outflow. Aquarius pours out the 2 streams of The Great Mother's Living Water of Life.
12 Pisces the Fish	**Jonah** From Kamite AN (water, fish, throne). See etym. of Zebulon.	**Job** From Kamite UAB (pure water, purity, holy man).	**1&2 Chronicles** Kronos (time) = *flow.* Time "flows," a trait of water (rivers, ocean currents). Two bks = water above /below firmament (Terrestrial /Celestial) The Nun=Space, the Primal Ocean.

The Bible's first big Zodiac is particularly deceptive!

It's slick, deceptive and deliberately misleading. It's actually 4 Zodiacs in 1 (!), consisting of 2 Decan Zodiacs that really are one and the same; and this resulting 1 Decan Zodiac is part of a 12-sign Zodiac.

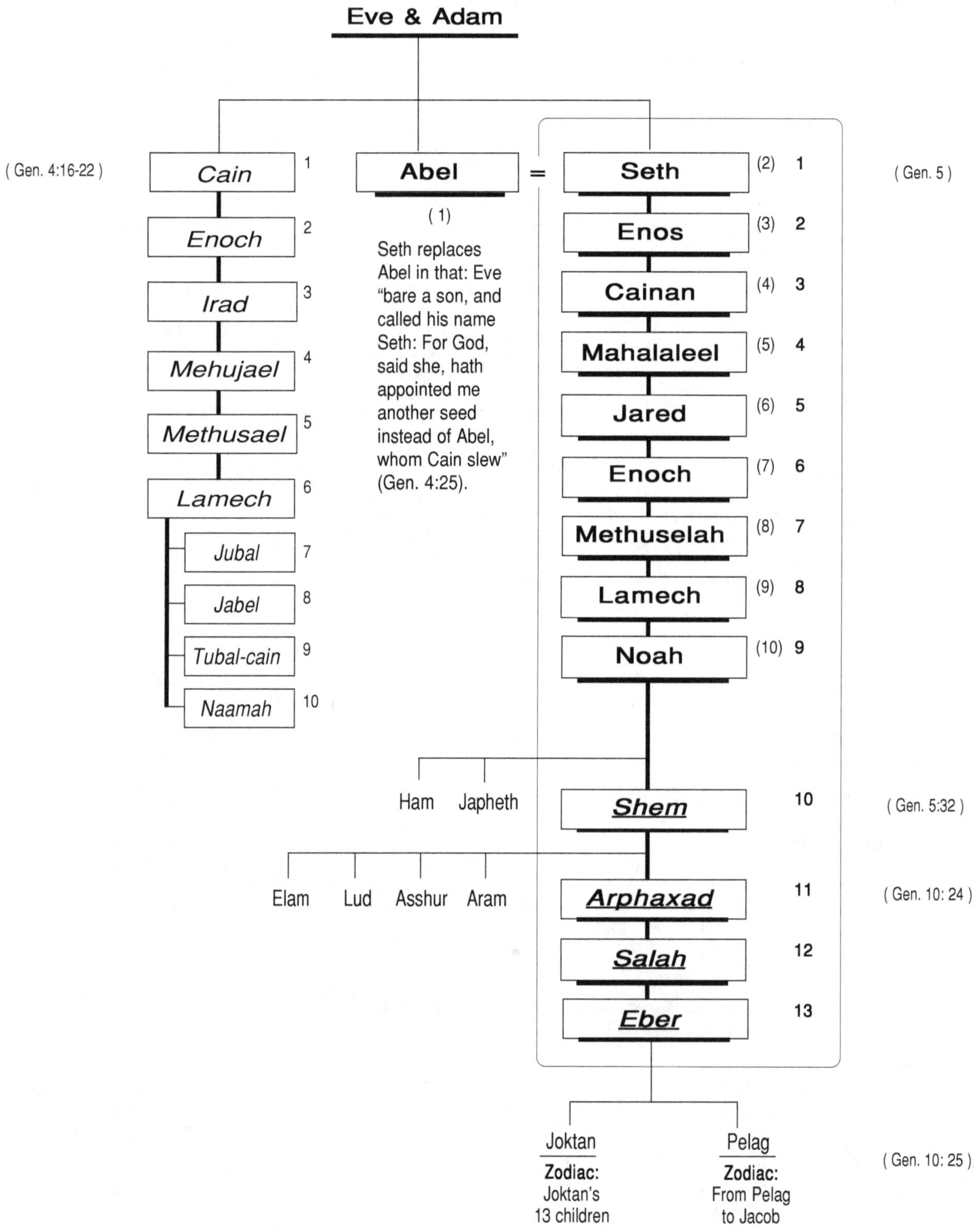

The Cain/Seth Zodiac is the Bible's First Zodiac (4 in 1)

Sign	Seth's Line, etc	=	Cain's Line
1 Aries the Ram	***Eber,*** **Abel** Eber is really AB-UR! Ur=Fire. Abel was a *sheep* keeper. Since L+R, then Abel also = AB-UR.	=	*Tubal-cain* Tubal Cain, a metal worker (hence fire).
2 Taurus the Bull	**Cainan**	=	*Cain* Was a ground tiller. Ground=Earth.
3 Gemini the Twins	**Enos,** **Enoch** Means human being From Kamite ANU, UNNU (man, humans).	=	*Enoch,* *Jabel,* *Jubal* Similarity between names like twins!
4 Cancer the Crab	**Lamech** Lamech is from same root as LAMENT (weep, shed water). Derived from Kamite Rem(Lem) = weep. Cancer=moody water sign.	=	*Lamech* Linked with 7: as a killer, said anyone messing with him would be avenged 77 times; he lived to be 777 years old (Gen. 4:24; 5:31). 7=water! Cancer=moody water sign.
5 Leo the Lion	***Shem*** From Kamite Sem (fire, hot), source of summer, simmer, Hebrew shemash (sun).		
6 Virgo the Virgin	**Mahalaleel** Variant of Mahala, name of Ishmael's only daughter. Ma (mother) + Ala (lofty, high, divine)	=	*Mehujael,* *Naaman* Naamah, the "sister" of Tubal-Cain (Gen. 4:22), and only daughter of Cain. From Kamite NEM (sweet, delicious, voluptuous).
7 Libra the Balance	**Methuselah** From same root as Matthew, which is Kamite MAAT. Maat was the Goddess of Truth, Justice & the Scales.	=	*Methusael* From same root as Matthew, which is Kamite MAAT.
8 Scorpio the Scorpion, Eagle /Serpent	**Seth** From Kamite SET, source of name Satan.		
9 Sagittarius the Archer	**Jared**	=	*Irad*
10 Capricorn the Goat	***Salah*** From Kamite selah (rock). Capricorn, a hard Earth sign.		
11 Aquarius Water Bearer	***Arphaxad***		
12 Pisces the Fish	**Noah** From Kamite NU (water). Noah in the Ark survived the Great Flood.		

On the preceding page, note the similarity between the names in both lists! Why? Disguisedly, they are the same list! Where twins are signified, the names are redoubled (Enoch, Jabel). The genealogy on the preceding page shows that the Bible's rewriters have humanity (or *their* kind: man*kind*) descend from Seth (Satan)!

Also, they have put evil character in good names, and good character in bad names. Example: The real killers are Seth (portrayed blameless) and meat-eater Abel (with his bloody-sheep-killing-sacrifice which the Lord preferred over the fresh fruit & herb offering from vegetarian Cain). But killing is assigned to Cain.

Cain or *Cainan* is really the same as *Canaan* (who also got cursed), ***Kenites, and Canaanites.*** Such *reversal* is prevalent throughout the unholy Bible with the deceiving Un-God of its editors. And why is God upset over the murder of one man when He later urges Moses and Joshua to massacre thousands of people –Canaanites (Blacks!)

In the Bible, the same stories are disguisedly repeated like the cycles of the Zodiac they represent. Example: The story of Adam repeats in the story of Cain, his firstborn son: Adam & Cain are both alone and lonely; takes a wife; hugely sins and are thus banished. Adam's garden is "eastward in Eden"; Cain's city is on the "east of Eden." Adam's wife is made subject to him, as Abel is made subject to Cain. Chauvinist God said to Eve: "thy desire shall be to thy husband and he shall rule over thee" (Gen. 3:16). He said to Cain: "unto thee shall be his desire, and thou shalt rule over him" (Gen. 4:7).

Are the names of the kings of Israel & Judah *zodiacal,* thus exposing them as *fiction* also?!

Is the biblical list of Israel's kings as astrological as Israel's 12 tribes?! Their names and alleged history are in the biblical book of Kings (I & II). Briefly, Saul, David, and Solomon were the first three kings of Israel. Then the kingdom splits as Judah (South), and Israel (North) composed of 10 tribes allegedly. Solomon's son Rehoboam becomes king of the Judah/South. Jeroboam becomes king of the Israel/North. Israel-North has exactly 19 kings. Judah/South also has exactly 19 kings, *plus* one Queen. Guess who She really stands for!

Redundant royal names in a double royal list

We met this before with the Bible's first Zodiac (Cain-Seth). We now meet it again. Examine the names in the list of Judah / Israel's kings and note the following:

- *Within* each list, almost half the names are redundant or name-variants.
- *Between* the lists, about 10 names are redundant or variants. Sometimes the redundancy is sneaky: the name of the first king in both lists are really the same; Je**roboam** = Rehoboam (*Roboam* is a proper name and variant spelling of *Rehoboam*). Redundant names reduce to one name.
- There are 19 *kings* in *each* list. 19 stands for 10 as the total of its digits (1+ 9 = 10). Ten represents Kamit's Decan Zodiac reflected as the 10-Tribe Israel, 10 Commandments, etc.

Kings of Judah & Israel

Kings (+1 Queen) of Judah:	Kings of Israel:
Rehoboam	Jeroboam I
Abijah /Abijam	Nadab
Asa	Baasha
Jehosaphat	Elah
Joram	Zimri
Ahaziah	Omri
Athalia *(the only Queen!)*	Ahah
Joash /Jeoash	Ahaziah
Amaziah	Joram
Uzziah /Azariah	Jehu
Jotham	Jehoahaz
Ahaz	Joash
Hezekiah	Jeroboam II
Manasseh	Zechariah
Amon	Shallum
Josiah	Menahem
Jehoahaz	Pekahiah
Jehoiakim	Pekah
Jehoichin	Hoshea
Zedekiah	

What does this mean?

- **The 2 lists apparently signify:**
  - Four Decan Zodiacs. As such they represent Kamit's Astronomical Cross of 4 divisions (+).

  - Two 12-sign-Zodiacs. How's this? Because redundant names (and variants of the same name) cancel out to 1 name, reducing the true total of names to less than the physical count. Examples: The 3 variant names Ahaz, Ahaziah, and Jehoahaz become just 1 name. The 2 names Joash and Hoshea become 1 name, and so on. (Names with identical meanings probably also count as one name.)

- **Mother.** As with the Jacob, Ishmael, Joktan, the book of Judges, and so on, there is always "one" significant female in the group of males. Yes, She always represents our Great Mother, whose identity is always confirmed by the true meaning or roots of Her name. ***Athaliah***. The ATH of Athliah is the same ATH of Athena and Neith (warrior forms of the Great Goddess), fitting right in with all the warring kings. Neith is Athena (Ath-Na) backwards, hence Na-Ath or Ne-Ith. Kamite ATH means *to string a bow, to draw, pull.* Neith and Athena were Archers.

- **The South/North split** = the ***Double Principle*** of the Zodiac. For Israel was set up or patterned to be a mini Egypt (Kamit). Kamit was divided as Upper (Southern) and Lower (Northern) Egypt to reflect the Upper and Lower Principle of their cosmology. This is a reflection of reflection itself: As above, so below. It also reflects the principle of Life's two complementary polarities, Yin/Yang, Male/Female, Inside/Outside, and Night/Day.

- **Polarity strife.** The whole biblical history of these two kingdoms is one of ceaseless strife, coups, intrigue, plots, overthrows, etc. In light of the zodiacal equation, this reflects the struggle between Light and Darkness, with one or the other prevailing in cycles, as with the Day and the Night.

- **Bloodless bloody sungod kings.** If one has the patience to figure the true etymology of the names, one will likely discover that, consistent with all the other biblical groupings, these names also spell out Zodiacs. **The kings are each the Sungod**. The **Judah-Kings** are the Sun in the **overworld**. The **Israel-Kings** are the Sun in the **underworld**. The events of the kings's lives are allegories about the Sun's annual and precessional history, or cyclic passage though the zodiacal constellations. Without knowing this, such events often appear bloody and repulsive, giving a bad image to God and his alleged "Chosen People." In light of the zodiacal understanding, the murderous history transforms before your eyes. Examples: David killing giant Goliath is the Sun triumphing over Darkness. Israel's first king Saul, was *beheaded*, de-armored, hung on the walls of Beth-*Shan* (House of Quiet*) then removed and ultimately *buried.* Astrologically this means the Sun diminished and set! Solar Saul

*Beth-*Shan* means House of Quiet. (Shan = *Shean /Zion /Sin* of Sinai the Moon. Zion a name for Jerusalem. salem = Peace).

the Sun simply ***set*** (got beheaded), thereby returning to the Womb of his Great Mother (got buried) to be reborn or resurrected as the Sun of the next Day, next Year, or next Age...

> Hence, if it is the Sun of a new Year, the "setting" or death is dramatic. **If it is the Sun of a new *Age*, the setting or death is *spectacular* –as the Resurrection.** Christ the Sun, the Son of God, "son of David" represented just this! The Sun of a New Age! He is even called the Light of the World and the SUN of Righteousness.

Saul, David, and Solomon are all one

Saul and Solomon are both Sol (as in Solar). David too, is Light. In this *trinity* we have "The Uri (David) and the Thummim (Saul /Solomon)"! David (really, the Great Father) "sinned" with Bathsheba (the Great Mother) and She bore a son which died –like Saul (actually, the Lord killed their first child). They married and had another son which lived; he was Solomon (Saul's reincarnation), originally named *Jedidiah* by God (2Sam. 12:25). See the repeating theme here? The **Firstborn** son always loses out, and the glory goes to the **Secondborn** son. Sheba (the Great Mother) as Bathsheba was a wife of David and mother of his son Solomon. Son-Solomon is visited by the Great Mother as the Queen of Sheba who 'tests' him. Passing his test, She bestows lavish gifts upon him, including 666 talents of *gold.* The number 6 stands for sex, a word from same roots as six. Thus this is a way of saying they sexually united. Again this reflects the original Afrikan source-story: Goddess As-t is the wife, mother (& sister) of Asar. And Asar is reborn as his own son (sun), Heru.

Solomon's famous "Great Temple" is really the Great Mother

The Great Mother is the Abode, Womb, Dwelling Place, Shekinah, Temple. Solomon is a Builder, like Christ the *Carpenter* of whom he is a version. And Christ "married" his "Church."

All this points to the fictitious historical identity of the so-called biblical kings of Israel/Judah!

Likely there were some royal leaders, but not as biblically presented. The biblical stories are distorted reworkings of Kamite astrological allegories deceptively presented as real history.

The names of Jerusalem's 12 Gates identify the Zodiac's 12 *Gates*

GATE itself is a zodiacal term of the Sun's entry and exit. In his account of the reconstruction of the walls of Jerusalem, Nehemiah appropriately begins at the Sheep Gate, which of course is Aries. As to be expected, there are 12 gates. Unlike the names of personages, half of these gate names are stark clear about which zodiacal sign they represent. Nehemiah's "wall" symbolizes the Zodiac. These "gates" and their names are mainly in Chapter 3 of Nehemiah, which records the inspection, rebuilding, and dedication of Jerusalem's walls after the Exile. Likely the etymology of the names of the workers assigned to each gate also support the zodiacal equation of each gate. When these gates are occasionally referred to in other biblical books, though the names may be changed to keep the cloak intact, there are always clues linking the gate to its sign, as we shall see.

Jerusalem's 12 gates and the Zodiac Signs they represent:

1 **Sheep Gate** = Aries the Ram — Neh. 3:1

2 **Dung Gate** = Taurus the Bull — Neh. 3:14
Bulls have a lot of it, hence the slang term. One of Hercules's 12 labors (another Zodiac allegory) was the cleaning of the stables.

3 **Valley Gate** = Gemini the Twins — Neh. 3:13
It takes two hills to form a valley. The two hills are the Twins (or Couple).

4 **Prison Gate** (or **Gate of Benjamin**) = Cancer the Crab — Neh. 12:39
Crabs are *grabbers*, a word derived from the same root. Whatever is seized is *imprisoned*, as the disease of cancer attests to. The Gate of Benjamin (Jer. 37:13) is the same as the Prison Gate, evidenced by a *guard* being stationed there. This is the only gate mentioned as having a guard (KJV= "captain of the ward" ; NIV= "captain of the guard"). Named Irijah, this captain arrested, hence imprisoned Jeremiah.

5 **Old Gate** (or **East Gate**) = Leo the Lion — Neh. 3:6, 12:39
Leo is the paternal sign signifying the Great Father in the Zodiac, a wise, *Old* King who has been around for longer than we can imagine. No wonder He is called "the Ancient of Days" (Dan 7:9). Also: "For God is my King of old" (Ps. 74:12). His son Christ was the "Lion of the Tribe of Judah" (Rev. 5:5) The "Old Lion" also appears in Gen. 49:9. The East Gate (Nem. 3:29) = the Old Gate, for it is linked with 3 sun symbols: **1)** King: it was "the king's gate eastward" (Chr. 9:8). Lion is the King. **2)** East: is where the Sun arises. **3)** It was repaired by Shemaiah, a name from Kamite SEM, whose meanings include Sun, Fire. The same root yields summer, simmer, Samson, Simeon, Hebrew Shemesh (sun).

6 **Ephraim Gate** = Virgo the Virgin — Neh. 8:16, 12:39; 2King 14:13
Ephraim means fruitfulness. It's really a feminine name that has been masculinized like many things in the chauvinist Bible. Ephraim is Virgo, the gestator of the Zodiac, a symbol of Goddess, the Great Mother.

7 **Corner Gate** (or **Middle Gate**) = Libra the Balance — 2Kings 14:13; 2Chron. 25:23
The "Corner" is the Mason's Square for measuring, which is exactly the function of scales –they measure weight, and they are only thing in the Zodiac with "corners." Libra is the 7th sign; numeral 7 is a corner! And on either side of the midpoint (4) of seven is perfect *balance* (3 on each side). The word seVen itself contains a 7 (V) as its fulcrum, and is balanced evenly with two letters on each side. Bible dictionaries agree that the 'Middle Gate' (Jer. 39:3) is another name for one of the twelve gates, but are uncertain which one. In accord with zodiacal connections, the Middle Gate is logically the Corner Gate, for the Middle is the balance point which Scales symbolize. The midpoint of 13 is 7.

8 **Water Gate** = Scorpio the Scorpion — Neh. 3:26
Scorpio is the Fixed Water Sign of the Zodiac.

9 **Horse Gate** = Sagittarius the Archer — Neh. 3:28

10 **Miphkad Gate** = Capricorn the Goat — Neh. 3:31
Miphkad (mifkad) in Hebrew means *muster, census, parade, roll call.* All these signify a grouping together, which is the natural behavior of goats; they come in "flocks." Recall the connection of Gad (Goat) with "troop" (troupe). And note *gad* in Mifkad.

11 **Fountain Gate** = Aquarius the Water Bearer — Neh. 3:15

12 **Fish Gate** = Pisces the Fish — Neh. 3:3

Hidden Zodiacs permeate and compose the entire Bible!

Each book of the Bible contains one or more Zodiacs!

The book of Philemon is only one chapter long with 25 verses, yet it contains a full Zodiac –spelled out by the 12 names within it, including "beloved Apphia" (Virgo). Unsuspected hiding places for Zodiacs in the Bible include:

- **Place-Names:** house (beth), wall/city (kir), mountain (har, hor), spring (beer), court /enclosed space (hazar).
- **People-Type-Names:** son (ben, bar), lord (baal), kings and priests.

In such terms are Zodiacs inconspicuously packed! Bible dictionaries such as *The Holman Bible Dictionary* conveniently lists all the Beths, Baals, Bens, Kirs, etc., including their variations. Let's glimpse some of them:

Beth-Baal Zodiacs

The presence of multiple Zodiacs clearly belies the names of the "Baals" and "Beths" of the Bible, which themselves are zodiacal terms: Beth means house; Baal (lord) was a title of the Sun, which moves from "house" to house. Like the names of Jerusalem's "gates," many of these Baals and Beths are easy to link to the zodiacal signs they represent.

- There are apparently 3 Zodiacs behind the 32-38 biblical **Baal-names**. Some names are near duplicates, such as the two females, Baala and Baalath. Baal-names include Baale-Judah, Baal-Gad, Baal-Tamar, Baal-Zebub, Belshazzar, Bildad, Balaam and Bamoth-Baal.
- There are some 72 **Beth-names**, concealing some 6 Zodiacs, which include Beth-Anath (House of Goddess Neith, an Archer; Sagittarius), Bethlehem (House of Bread; Virgo), Beth-Dagon (Pisces; Dagon was the name of the Fishgod), Beth-Shemesh (Leo; House of the Sun). Some names are variants or near-duplicates such as Beth-Haccerem / Beth Haccherem.

Ben Zodiacs

Ben means son. There are apparently two Zodiacs behind the 24 Ben-names of the Bible. This includes the *disguised bens* such as Baana, Bani, Beon, Binea, and Binnui. *Peninnah*, the wife of Elkanah, may be the token female representing Virgo.

High Priests Zodiacs

There are two to three Zodiacs behind the names of the *high, chief,* or *senior* priests. These priests include **Christ** (Heb 6:20, 7:14-17), **Melchizedek** (Heb. 7:1) whom Abraham honored with tithes, **Potipherah**, the high priest of city of On, and likely his daughter **Asenath**, whom Joseph married.

Twins are often easy to recognize

Biblical Geminis are often as easy to recognize as twins, for their names themselves are essentially "twinned" by being variants of the same name which sound alike. *Jabel & Jubal* "his brother", sons of Lamech's first wife Adah (Gen. 4:20, 21). *Huz & Buz* "his brother" (Gen. 22:21). *Medan & Midian,* sons of Keturah. *Ephah & Epher*, sons of Midian. *Sabtecha & Sabta*, sons of Cush. *Tryphena & Tryphosa.* Lot's two unnamed daughters and so on.

13

The Zodiac-Apostles of Christ

Abundant biblical evidence that Christ's 12 Apostles were the 12 Zodiac Signs!

The true etymology of the names of the 12 Apostles conceal the Zodiac!

Christ (like Jacob) was the Sun. His 12 Apostles (like the 12 Tribes of Israel, Ishmael and numerous other groups of twelve) were the twelve Zodiac Signs. The Bible actually calls Christ the *Sun* in more than one place (see Chapter 10 & 11). And Christ is always in the *constant* company of his Twelve Apostles, the 12 Zodiacal Constellations.

Evidence of the Apostles' zodiacal identity is disguised in the original, true meaning of their names and any other names or titles connected with them.

In fact, often they are doubly identified in their zodiacal links. None of their names are arbitrary; they have been carefully chosen to secretly preserve their original astrological integrity. In addition, each Apostle's alleged history or background provides further clues which link them to their respective signs. Thus like all the other biblical groupings of twelve, the 12 Apostles were *fictitious* as people but are *real* as the 12 signs of the Zodiac.

Preview of the Zodiac-Apostles and their corresponding signs

Apostle	Zodiac Sign Represented	Page
1. Simon Zelotes	Aries the Ram	259
2. Simon Peter Cephas	Taurus the Bull	262
3. Thomas Didymus	Gemini the Twins	287
4. James Zebedee Boanerges	Cancer the Crab	290
5. Judas Lebbaeus Thaddaeus	Leo the Lion	292
6. Philip and Mary Magdalene	Virgo the Virgin	293
7. Matthew Levi Alphaeus	Libra the Balance	319
8. Judas Iscariot	Scorpio the Scorpion/Eagle/Serpent	323
9. Bartholomew Nathanael	Sagittarius the Archer	326
10. James Alphaeus	Capricorn the Goat	328
11. Andrew	Aquarius the Water Bearer	330
12. John Zebedee Boanerges	Pisces the Fish	331

Namebooks (& dictionaries) are as unreliable as history books for giving true Afrikan roots

You cannot prove an etymology by using the standard references of the very people who distorted or suppressed the true etymology in the first place. The vast majority of biblical names originated (like the Bible itself) from Afrika, specifically Kamit (ancient Egypt). Consulting Albino-written namebooks for name meanings is inadequate and unreliable. They are shallow and appear unconscious of Afrikan roots. As a rule, they do not disclose the Afrikan origin or derivation of any names. Not only do such namebooks usually give superficial, artificial, generic meanings, they are as guilty as the other Albino-written books in distorting, obscuring and blacking out the Afrikan truth. Many of the meanings given for Afrikan names bear no resemblance to the original name-meanings before they became Europeanized. Even blatant Afrikan names such as "Amen" will be called something European, or at best, Hebrew. In addition, namebooks are sexist; the names of the Great Goddess are demoted, paralleling what has been done to the Great Goddess.

Coverup through name-variants

The use of multiple name-variants throughout the Bible for significant names, serves to disguise the fact that the same individuals –that is, the same zodiacal or celestial bodies, are being recycled and discussed from one biblical book to the next. Always, the same themes and essential characters are ever present, hence the story of Abraham essentially matches that of Jacob and the other patriarchs and so on. The number of times that a basic story or significant character (in all its guises) repeats is also significant. The numerals themselves are often loaded and running over with meaning. The characters are redressed for each play before they are recycled, but always there are telltale clues, often creatively disguised, to keep the undercover record straight, while giving a truly distorted and reversed picture on the surface.

Historians John Jackson, Gerald Massey, Helen Blavatsky, T.W. Doane and others, have written that the Apostles were zodiacal. Christ said, "In my Father's house are many mansions" (John 14:2). The original meaning of 'house of many mansions' was the Zodiac Constellations.[1] This terminology is straight from Egyptian scriptures which described the many mansions in the afterworld.

1) Walker, WD, 144; Hotema, MM, 50.

1 **Simon Zelotes** = Aries the Ram

Cardinal **FIRE** Sign

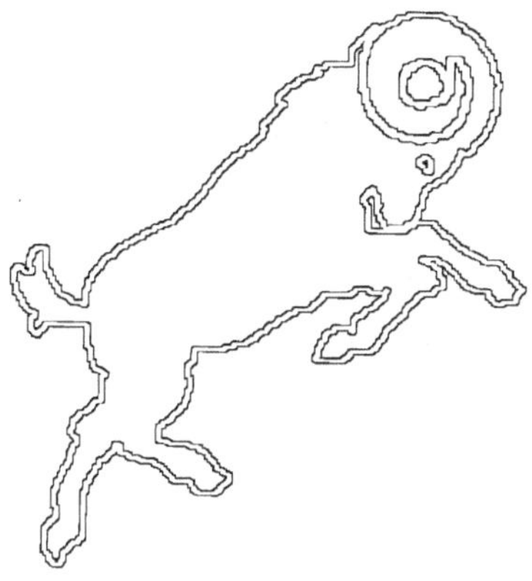

"Simon called Zelotes" (Luke 6:15) is Aries the Ram, as testified by the etymology and background of his name. Aries is the hottest of the three fire signs of the Zodiac. Aries is connected with the sexual passion of paternal procreative power, penetrating maternal Nature, awakening new life and setting it in motion. Thus Aries opens the Zodiac with the Spring Equinox. Honored for his virile powers, the Ram was the most popular of the "horny" animals regarded as incarnations of the phallic god. Egypt's ram god Amon was regarded as the virile principle in gods and men. The "Ram Caught in a Thicket" is an ancient sexual metaphor appearing in the Bible as a surrogate victim to replace Isaac, whose father Abraham was about to sacrifice him on an altar at God's command (Gen. 22:13).

The words *Aries* and *Ram* are both derived from *hot* roots, yielding such words as arson, ardor, arid, wrath, red, ire, eros and *arouse*. And note that AR is the reverse of RA, a name of the sun and source of RAM (RA-M). The names **Simon** and **Zelotes** are also both derived from fiery Afrikan roots. In Egyptian, one meaning of **sem** is heat, fire. **Smen** means foundation, to establish, fix firmly in position. Derivatives of sem/smen include **simmer**, **summer**, **seminary**, and yes, ***semen.***[1] ***Semen*** /seed *establishes* after its own kind. And semen only comes out when the male is ARoused, particularly at the peak (orgasm) of sex.

Aries is also associated with *Mars* and *martial* characteristics (quick temper, courage, aggression, determination). Mars is name of the red planet and red god of war, called Mars by the Romans and "Ares" by the Greeks. *Mars*, and *martial* are from Kamite merkh/merkha (to fight, wage war/war, strife).[2] This brings us to Simon's second name, ***Zelotes*** which is derived from **zeal**. Zeal is intense enthusiasm, *burning* passion. The dictionary defines Zeal as "enthusiastic and diligent devotion in pursuit of a cause, ideal or goal; *fervor.* **Fervor** means ardor or *intense heat.* "Aries is...associated with the element of fire and related ideas of warmth, enthusiasm, vital powers, and sanguine spirit." [3]

1) Massey, BB-vI, 72; HJ, 145. 2) Budge, EHD, 315b. 3) Walker, WD, 289.

Translated, **Simon Zelotes** means Simon the Zealot. Called "militant radicals," the Zealots were Jews (Blacks) who militantly resisted Roman (white) rule in Palestine during the first century A.D. These Afrikans never surrendered to the Albinos but fought to the end, and even then, they committed suicide rather than let themselves be taken alive as prisoners. Masada is the most outstanding example.

***Black* Simon is *Hot* Aries.** When fire (SEM) burns something it turns *black*; and the sun will give you a *tan*. Not surprisingly, blackness is identified with some Sem-names. "Simeon that was called Niger" (Acts 13:1) means Simeon *the Black*. This is a way of doubly identifying hot Aries in another guise. Simon Zelotes was also identified as Black by being called Simon the Canaanite (Mat. 10:4). According to one source, *Canaanite* in regards to Simon is a mistranslation from Aramaic *Quannai* which is rendered *Kananaios* in Greek, which also means *Zealot*.[1] We see that either interpretation is correct, plus the original Jews were Afrikans (Canaanites).

Additionally, *fire* and *purification* are outstandingly associated with the Ram. Fire purifies. Aries is a *Fire* sign. The sacrifice (burning in *fire*) of the Ram led to *purification* in the ceremonies of the ancients. The Ram became the fashionable animal of sacrifice when the Age of the Ram (Aries) began. And avatars of this age, Christ, Krishna, Horus and other Saviors were all called the *Lamb* of God. A lamb is a baby ram. Since the letters R and L were represented by the same symbol in Egyptian, then Ram and Lamb are the same word; both from RA, a name of the Sun. In Egyptian cosmology, the *Smen* (region and name /title of the Eight Primordial Gods) was linked with purification and associated with Light (a form of Fire). Smen was the place appointed for the purging and cleansing of souls, birthplace of the new moon, and symbol of the infant birth of solar light in humanity.[2] Egyptian scriptures state that the Soul is 'censed' or purified with Fire and the *Smen* incense. "Incense" is another meaning of the Kamite word "smen."

Biblical variants or names from the same root as Simon include:

Sem	Shimen	**Samson**	Shamed	Shimhi
Shem	Shimon	**Samuel**	Shemed	Shimshai
Shama	**Simeon**	Shemuel	Shemida	Shamhuth
Shema	Shimeon			Shimron
Shimma		Shimi	Semachiah	Shammua
Shamma	Semei	Shimei	Semakiah	Shamsherai
Shammah	Shimeah			Shamgar
Shemaah	Shimeath	Simri		Shemeber
Shammai	Shammoth	Shimri		
Shemaiah				

Thus Simon Zelotes, by his name, is doubly identified with *fire*.
The meanings of his name include:

- Fire-Fire
- Establishing Fire
- Foundation of Passion

Such is Aries the Ram.

1) Baigent, ML, 51. 2) Kuhn, LL, 256, 257.

Etymology of Simon

Category	Afrikan-Kamite Roots	Apparent Derivatives: ENGLISH	Apparent Derivatives: HEBREW	Comments
Semen Establish Prepare Anoint	s'men • seminal. Massey, HJ, 145; 72BB1 s-men • establish oneself, fix in position, stablish. 602a asmen • stablish, make firm. 89b smen • order, foundation. 670b s-men • to prepare. 602a smen • prepare, annoint. 19BB2 smeh • annoint. 19BB2 sem • total. 77BB1	semen seminiferous seminal disseminate seminary •seminar sum summary exam examine sumptuary (regulating commerce) smear smerian (*anoint* in Old English) smeth (depilatory, ointment, in Old English)	**zimmen**, prepare, summon together **semekh**, support **samakh**, support, trust, ordain, sanction **samkhut**, authority, competence **shmr**, to keep, preserve, to fasten, **shmn**, anointing	**Semen or seed** establishes after the image/genes of the parent. **Anointing** establishes after divinity. **Seminars** & seminaries are places where knowledge is disseminated, thus one reads and listens
Assemble Hear	sam • to assemble, flock together, herd. 514BB2 sem • hear, listen. 453BB2	symposium assemble ensemble lyceum (school) •seminar	**shomen**, hearer, listener, guard **shma**, listen	(hears) carefully. The text of written material is composed of **symbols**. Via symbols, knowledge can be established.
Heat Fire	shemm • heat, flame 19BB2 shem • fire, flame 448BB2 sem • double solar plume. • summer 196BB1 sems • to burn, consume. 672a shm • hot 18BB2 smen • incense. 602a	summer simmer shimmer shimmy smelt smart (to burn, sting) smoke smolder blacksmith eczema (boils)	**shemesh**, sun **simta**, boil	**The original SMITHS** worked with fire, and they were Black Afrikans, hence the term "**blacksmith.**"
Symbol	sam • memorize, emblem, image. 483BB2 smenu • image, figure, statue. s-men • establish, fix in place.	symbol sample sampler example symptom specimen (=spec-smen) semantic semiology (study of sign language)	**semel**, symbol, emblem, image, badge **simmel**, symbolize **siman**, sign, mark	**"Stone"** establises the image or carved symbols of something. Simon *Peter* was the Rock.
Eight	S'men • the Eight Primordial Gods and their region.	Gethsemane Where Christ was arrested. EIGHT olive trees here have been here for centuries. (Insights, VI, 927).	**shmenai**, eighth	HEBREW **zmen**, ARABIC **smen**, MALTESE **zmyn**, all mean to number, to measure out, apportion;
Smite	sema • smite. 19BB2	smite smack smash smatter shamel (where meat is butchered. Old English) shambolic (disorderly) shamble shambles chomp champion (warrior)	**smd**, destroyed **Sammael**, Satan, Angel of Death	derived from SMEN as the name of the eight gods, creators of the Heavens. 143BB2
Stone	smer • an unknown kind of stone. 19BB2		**shmir**, adamant stone, diamond **simmer**, harden, stiffen	

a, b = columns in *An Egyptian Hieroglyphic Dictionary*. **BB** = *Book of the Beginnings* (vol. 1 or 2). **AE** = *Ancient Egypt: Light of the World*.

Etymology of Zelotes (Zel = Zer)

Category	Afrikan-Kamite Roots	Apparent Derivatives: ENGLISH	Apparent Derivatives: GREEK	Apparent Derivatives: OTHERS
Heat, Fire	ser (sel) • fire, flame, the warm breath of life. 680a Serser • lake of boiling water in fiery region in the Tuat. 611 seref • to be hot, angry, warmth, fire, flame, heat. 681a seref-t • heat, warmth. 681a	zeal zealot zealous jealous sear siriasis (sunstroke) Sirius (a star) serious (from *heaviness* of star Sirius) salamander sultry sirocco (hot wind) sulfur (is yellow) sallow (yellow) solstice solar Soul (inner divine Spark that is You) self (from *Soul*) silver	**zelotes**, zealous **zeleea**, envy, jealousy **zele**, **zeal**, to be aroused **zeelos**, zeal, ardor, eagerness, jealousy, fierceness, fervent **zeloo**, affect, covet, desire, earnestly, envy, jealous, zealously **selas**, brightness **seirios**, burning **sele**, moon **seleenee**, moon	HEBREW: **saraf**, burn, burn down **serefa**, fire, burning combustion **Seraphim**, "the burning ones." One of the first order of angels. Winged serpents. OLD IRANIAN: **sarna**, golden ARABIC: **sarq**, east (where sun arises) PUNJABI: **sargarmi**, zeal SYRIAC: **zarnika**, orpiment (a yellow mineral)
Ram	ser • ram. 610a sera • ram. 611a			

2 **Simon Peter Cephas** = Taurus the Bull

Fixed **EARTH** Sign

The biblical and etymological evidence identifies **Simon Peter Cephas** as the Mighty Bull of Heaven. The name Peter is derived from Afrikan roots having the following categories of meanings. Despite the great diversity of these categories, we shall see that they are all related like the facets of a gemstone or parts of a machine, –the machine of the *Male Principle*, which we shall examine in great detail!

Categories of the Male Principle

	Category	Examples of Pe / Pet Derivitives
1	Father, Male	pa, paternal, patriarch
2	Penis, Rod, Point, Bird...	peter, petiole, baton
3	Nose, Breath, Wind, Expand	beak, pant, expand
4	Rock, Hard, Strong, Bold, Real	petrify, evidence
	Foundation, Stable, Secure, Fetter	pedestal, fidelity, fetter
5	Action, Make, Build	computer, competant,
6	Structure, Building	pattern, body, Bethlehem
7	Fire, Light, Sky	beacon, photon
8	Power, Force, Energy, Fuel	pith, potency, battery, butter
9	Strife, Friction, Hit, Cut, Divide, Resist	compete, beat, battle
10	Head, Circle, Opening, Ball, Pipe, Path	pate, patch, path
11	See, Show, Say, Ask, Declare	expatiate, petition
12	Proceed , Go Out, Speed, Expire	speed, rapid, peter (dwindle)

Peter's biblical data encompasses the aspects of the Male Principle

Category 1:
Father, Male

Peter, *paternal*, and *father* are from common roots. As the father, Peter is the fertilizer or provider of semen; his first name *Simon* is from same root as *semen.*[1] In his letter to the "elders," Peter also calls himself an "elder" (1Peter 5:1). Biblical variants of Peter's name include Petra, Patara, and Patrobas, "life of (or from) father."

1) Massey, HJ, 144-5; Massey, BB-vI, 72.

Category 2:
Penis, Rod, Point, Bird...

The word PETER has been a synonym for PEnis since ancient times. Peter is the Bull of the Zodiac. Bulls have huge penises. Bulls are so generously endowed that their penises were used as whips for several centuries.[1] Likely derived from this, in imitation of the real thing, the *bullwhip* or *pizzle* is a long, plaited rawhide whip with a knotted end. The bull was the symbol of male sexual virility. *Bull* and *Baal* are from the same roots. Baal (lord) was a name and title of male deities, including the biblical God (Hos. 2:16). Followers of Baal were worshippers of the Sun in Taurus.[2]

The Bible connects Peter with the COCK. Since ancient times, the "cock" has been a synonym for "penis." The cock was a phallic totem in Roman and Medieval sculptures. As a symbol of St. Peter, the cock's image was often placed atop church towers.[3] In Jewish tradition, the cock was accepted as a substitute for a man. *Gever*, the Hebrew word for cock, also means man. The Gospel story of Peter's denial of Christ three times before cockcrow was related to older legends associating the crowing of the cock with the death and resurrection of the Solar Savior.[4]

***Phallus* and *pillar* are from the same roots.** Throughout the ancient Roman empire, phallic pillars were called **Petra, Pater, or Peter.** [5] In the Bible, Peter is even referred to as a pillar. The NI translation reads "James, Peter and John, those reputed to be pillars" (Gal. 2:9). In the language of ancient Egypt, "Petra" and "Par (Pal) " were both titles of Amen-Ra as "Lord of the Phallus."[6] "Pierre," a likely derivative, means Peter in French. "Perron" means "Big Peter" and is likely from Par-On. The Kamite word PAR = PAL, since the Kamites represented R and L with the same symbol. Thus Par (Pal) is the source of phallus, pillar, pole and numerous other derivatives.

Category 4a:
Rock, Hard, Strong, Bold, Real

Simon Peter is the Fixed *Earth* Sign of the Zodiac, hence a Rock, a Pillar. "Thou art Peter, and upon this rock I will build my Church," Christ allegedly said to Simon (Mat. 16:16). Peter, petra (stone) and petrify are from common roots. Christ additionally named Simon "Cephas," then translated this as "stone" (John 1:42). Thus Simon Peter's "hardness" is doubly conveyed. As CEPHAS, Peter is also referred to as a PILLAR (Gal. 2:9). Peter also has a lot to say about stones in chapter 2 of the first Book of Peter. In verses 4-8, Peter mentions "stone" six times and "rock" once. He writes:

- "you also, like living stones, are being built into a spiritual house."[7]
- "the stone which the builders disallowed, the same is made the head of the corner" (1Pet. 2:7).
- Peter is brave and bold. "Now when they saw the boldness of Peter."[8]

Why is "hardness" associated with *fatherhood*? Because the penis becomes "hard" during an erection, "the *Rock* that begat thee" (Deut. 32:18).

1) Thorsten, 3. 2) Higgens, vI, 259. 3) Walker, WD, 397. 4) Ibid. 5) Ibid., 26. 6) Budge, GE-vII, 19; Walker, WE, 788. 7) 1Peter 2:5. 8) Acts 4:13.

Category 4b:
Foundation, Support, Stable, Secure, Fetter

"Thou art Peter, and upon this rock I will build my Church," Christ allegedly said to Simon (Mt. 16:16). And how appropriate, since Simon Peter represents a *cornerstone* constellation of the Zodiac, the "hardest" one in fact -an ideal choice for a foundation (one of Simon's roots means to *establish*). Peter is modeled from one of the **four** brothers/sons of Horus. This is copied in the Bible as Peter being one of Christ's **first four** disciples, who was with him until his sermon on the mount. As one of the first four, he is a cornerstone constellation - the Rock. And **4** is the square, the number of a firm foundation. In The Historical Jesus and the Mythical Christ, Massey writes:

> The name of *Simon* agrees with the Egyptian *S'men*, "to establish the son in the place of the father." That is the character of Simon who says to Jesus, *"Thou are the Christ, the son of the living God;" "Thou are the Christ of God!"* In return for this recognition the Christ calls Simon
>
> A STONE OR THE ROCK.
>
> S'men denotes that which founds, constitutes, makes durable and fixed. The stone is one type. But it also means that which is seminal, in agreement with the Hebrew *Shmen*, and Maltese or Latin *Semen*.[1]

"In building the house of heaven, which was annually repeated in the mysteries, the fourfold foundations, the four supports or cornerstones, were laid in the mount. These four supports were personalized in the four children of Horus....who had already been four of his brothers in the earlier mythos... the rock is identical with the mount, ...the house or temple of Horus built upon the mount was founded on the rock. In establishing his father's kingdom...Horus built upon the typical rock. In the Gospel Simon is told by Jesus that he will build this church upon *this* rock." [2]

Fetter. Christ allegedly said to Peter "whatsoever thou shalt bind on earth shall be bound in heaven: and whatsoever thou shalt loose on earth shall be loosed in heaven" (Mat. 16:19). Peter was once "bound with two chains" as he slept in Herod's prison between two guards, but was miraculously delivered by an angel (Act 12:6,7).

Category 5:
Action, Make, Build

Peter was a man of action. The roots of the word peter also mean to DO. Peter walked on water by asking Jesus to command him to walk over storm-swept waters (Mat. 14:25-32). Peter was a fabulous miracle worker just like Christ.[3] **Peter even raised the dead!** After praying, he turned to the dead body and said, "Tabitha, arise. And she opened her eyes" (Acts 9:40).

Category 6:
Structure, Building

As the Rock, Peter was made the foundation for Christ's CHURCH. Peter writes "you also, like living stones, are being built into a spiritual house" (1Pet. 2:5).

1) Massey, HJ, 144-5. 2) Massey, AE, 826. 3) Acts 3:1-26, 5:12-16.

Category 7:
Fire, Light, Sky

Peter warmed himself by the fire. He witnessed Christ's transfiguration where the body turns to blazing light.

Category 9:
Strife, Friction, Hit, Cut, Divide, Resist

If Simon *Zelotes* represented PASSION, then Simon *Peter* militantly executed that passion. Simon Peter was also called "Barjona" or "Bar Jonas," meaning Son of Jonah (Mat. 16:17, John 1:42). This is a mistranslation of the Aramaic word "barjonna," meaning outlaw or Zealot.[1] We know that the Zealots were real militants who did not hesitate to fight or kill for their beliefs, hence their name, "Zealots." Peter is armed with a sword and he uses it. At the arrest of Jesus in Gethsemane, "Simon Peter having a sword drew it, and smote the high priest's servant, and cut off his right ear" (John 18:10). Peter probably intended to inflict more damage than this and likely would have, had not Jesus intervened. According to legend, Peter died by crucifixion.

Category 10:
Head, Circle, Opening, Ball, Pipe, Path

The Head is the leader. The leader shows the "way" (path). Peter is the head or leader of the disciples. "Simon called Peter" is the very *first* disciple of Christ mentioned in the Bible (Mat 4:18). In fact, his name is always first in the list of disciples (Mat. 10:2, Mark 3:16, Luke 6:14). His other name, "**Cephas**" is apparently from the same Afrikan root which gives us the words cap, capital, decapitate, chapter, chief –all denoting *head.* Thus Peter is a "headstone" or capstone of the pillar/pyramid. Phallic stones were often pointed or "capped," being imitations of the phallic obelisk which has a pyramidal top. This point or cap corresponds to the "head" of the penis. Solomon's phallic pillars had bowl-like caps or "chapiters" (1Kings 7:41). A chapiter or capital is the top part of a pillar or column.

Opener. St. Peter is represented as the Gate-Keeper of Heaven. This is copied from the Kamite god Petra, who was the door-keeper of heaven, the earth and the underworld.[2] PETH, a root of Peter's name, means opener, to open. A door/gate-keeper is an Opener! Christ alledgedly said to Peter "And I will give unto thee the keys of the kingdom of heaven" (Mat.16:19). If one has the KEYS to something, they can open or close it. **This passage about the keys is a forgery** according to historians. Are these same historians also aware that **the whole Bible is a forgery or distorted, censored plagiarism of ancient Egypt's sacred scriptures?** One historian reported "The so-called Petrine passage in the Gospel of Matthew, about Peter's acquisition of the symbolic keys, was forged and inserted during the third century A.D. for political reasons. The Church never did have any continuous record of popes or 'bishops of Rome' from the beginning; most of the early popes were fictions."[3]

1) Baigent, ML, 51. 2) Jackson, PO, 30. 3) Walker, WD, 60.

Category 11:
Reveal, See, Say, Ask, Declare

Peter the Talker. Of all Christ's disciples, Peter was foremost in speaking. The Gospel records more of Peter's statements than any of the other disciples, plus has more to say about him than the others. Peter was often the spokesman for the disciples (Mat 8:29) and was usually the one who raised the questions which they all seemed to be asking (Mat. 15:15; Mark 10:28, 11:21; Luke 12:41). Jesus often singled him out for teachings intended for the entire group of disciples (Mark 8:29-33). In his letter, Peter said "If any man speak, let him speak as the oracles of God" (1Peter 4:11).

Peter is modeled from one of the **four** brothers/sons of Horus, as well as the Kamite god bearing the same name. "The word Petra or Petar is Egyptian...*Petar is the name or title of an Egyptian god who had been already divinized as the one who* ***discovered and made known*** *the only begotten son of that living god,* who was Atum-Ankhu, the father of Iusa, the Egyptian Jesus..."[1]

***Stone* as a *witness*:** "And Joshua...took a great stone, and set it up there under an oak, that was by the sanctuary of the Lord. And Joshua said unto all the people, Behold, this stone shall be a witness unto us; for it hath heard all the words of the Lord which he spake unto us: it shall be therefore a witness unto you, lest ye deny your God" (Jos. 24:26, 27). The concept of a stone being able to see is expressed as the traditional crystal ball. And the best lenses are made of pure quartz crystal.

Category 12:
Proceed, Go Out, Speed, Expire

When Jesus sought a secluded place before dawn to pray, Peter was soon out leading a group to hunt him down (Mark. 1:35-37). The legend of Peter says he expired (was crucified) on an upside-down cross.

1) Massey, AE, 860.

The PE of Peter is the P of Ptah, the *Original* Great Father

Ptah, "Architect of the Universe," and "God of Creation"

Kamite "PE" or "P" means the masculine article (among other meanings). PE is the first part of PTAH –an Afrikan name of God the original First Great Father who was:

- the earliest form of God the *Father.*[1]
- the *Father* of Beginnings.[2]
- the Father of the Fathers of the gods.[3]
- earliest form of the Eternal *Father* manifested in an Ever-Coming Son.[4]
- and *Grandfather* of the gods.[5]

Ptah was the Great Architect of the Universe, "the architect of heaven and earth, the mastercraftsman in working metals, sculptor, designer, and the fashioner of the bodies of men; he was the blacksmith, sculptor, and mason of the gods."[6] In the Egyptian divine dynasties, Ptah is God the Father in one character and Iu the Son in the other. As Iu, he is the youthful Messianic Sungod who rises from the dead.

He was the Father of the *Ali.* Born at the very beginning of Creation from the Great Mother of All Beginning, the *Ali* were the first Seven Spirits of Light, the associate-gods or co-creators of Creation. Identified with the Circle, they were the "Gods of the Orbit." They appear in the mythologies of all the world. They are the Seven Spirits of the Great Bear found in Egypt, China and Japan; the Seven Rishis of India; the Seven Steps of the Masonic Ladder; and the ***Elo*him** or *plural* God in Genesis who said "Let US make man in OUR image." Massey writes, "Iahu-Elohim is the deity Iu, who was a form of Ptah as god the son, and who afterwards became the father god in Israel under the name of Ihuh or Jehovah."[7]

He is the *Opener.* The name/word Ptah also means to open. Ptah is a form of the Divine Great Father who "opens" the Hymen of the Great Mother in the Passion of Love and Union which begat Life in the Universe. The Universe is always in a state of Sex.

Ptah is One with Asar (Osiris) ?

It seems that Ptah and Asar are two forms of the same Divine Father:

- The power that sustains the universe was Ptah in one cult and Osiris in the other.[8]
- "PTAH-SEKER is the dual god formed by fusing Seker, the Egyptian name of the incarnation of the Apis Bull of Memphis, with Ptah. ...PTAH-SEKER-AUSAR was a triune god who, in brief, symbolized life, death, and the resurrection." The festival of the God, "Osiris-Ptah-Sekari" was annually held in Kamit.[9]
- The Tat cross was the "backbone" of both Ptah and Osiris.[10] The Tat symbol of Stability is the source of the mason's square, and "type of the god Ptah as the fourfold support [*foundation*] of the universe."[11] Ptah himself was the Great Architect of the Universe.[12]
- A prophet of Ra incarnate in the Savior Osiris was known as Petosiris (Pet-Osiris), whose tomb was a great pilgrimage center about 341 B.C.[13]

"If we say *'Ptah'* everyone immediately thinks, 'Oh yes, *Ptah,* the Egyptian God'. No! *Ptah* was not an Egyptian God. On the contrary, the Egyptians called the same *God* whom we call *God,* by the name of *Ptah.* And to take another example, their term for *Satan* was *Seth.*"[13]

1) Massey, AE, 234, 423. 2) Ibid, 413, 420-1. 3) Massey, BB, vII, 319. 4) Massey, AE, 894. 5) Ibid., 891. 6) Budge, EHD, 254b. 7) Massey, AE,423. 8) Ibid., 751. 9) Ibid., 740. 10) Ibid., 351. 11) Ibid., 115. 12) Ibid., 406, 413. 13) Walker, WE, 788. 14) Haich, Author's Note

Biblical variants or names from the same root as Ptah include:

1 **Pethahiah** (Ptah-Iah or Ptah-Jah) (Ezra 10:23, Neh. 9:5)
2 **Pedaiah** (Ptah-Iah or Ptah-Jah)
3 **Pethuel** (Ptah-El or Pet-Iu-El) (Joel 1:1)
4 **Pedahel** (Ptah-El) (Num. 34:28)
5 **Pedahzur** (Ptah-Asar or Ptah-zur) (Num. 1:10, 16; 2:20)
6 **Pethor** (Pet-Horus or Ptah-Horus)
7 **Iphtahel** (defined as "God Opens,"[1] thus admitting Ptah = God)
8 **Iphtah** "he opened." (E-Pthah or Ep-Ptah)
9 **Iphedeiah**
10 **Iphdeiah**
11 **Jephthah** (E-Ptah or Ep-Ptaha)
12 **Jiphthael** (Jos 19:4) (E-Pthah-El or Ep-Ptahel)
13 **Ephphatha** (Af-Ptah or Ap-Ptah) "be opened." Jesus commanded "ephphatha" to a blind man to open/heal his eyes.
14 **Merneptah** ("beloved of Ptah" or "beloved Lord Ptah" as Mer-Neb-Ptah)
15 **Pathros** (land of the source, opening, Upper [southern Egypt]) **Zarephath**
16 **Pathrusim**
17 **Patmos**
18 **Put**
19. **Petra**
20. **Peter**

Phallic Pillars were symbols of the Divine

Phallus and *pillar* are from the same roots. The Rock, Stone, Horn, Pillar, and Phallus were one. The pillar, sacred tree trunk, *unicorn*, Maypole, upright cross, and other male divinity-symbols originated in Afrika. "Pillars" were the phallic emblems of many gods and heroes throughout the ancient world. Because Absalom had no son to carry on his name, he erected and named a pillar as a monument to himself (2 Sam. 18:18). Like Amen-Ra, Shiva bore the title of "the Pillar" or "the Great Lingam." **Pillars were inspired from the Afrikan obelisk**. Carved out of solid *stone*, the obelisk was a giant standing phallus; the prototypical pillar, pole, Maypole, perron, lingam, and Rock. And the **top of an obelisk is a pyramid.** Representing the divine Father Principle, the obelisk symbolized the phallus of Asar (Osiris), Heru (Horus), Geb the *Earth* God, and other Afrikan gods. Afrikans of the Nile Valley erected twin obelisks at their temple gates.

This tradition was copied by Solomon's temple at Jerusalem.
His free standing pillars were made of brass (1Kings 7:15). The right pillar was named Jachin ("God makes him firm") and the left pillar was named Boaz ("Eagerness, strength") (1 Kings 7:21). Like the penis, these pillars had bowl-like "heads" called "chapiters": "The two pillars, and the two bowls of the chapiters that were on the top of the two pillars" (1Kings 7:41). Furthermore, they were surmounted by the female symbols of lilies and pomegranates (1Kings 7:17-22).

1) Holman BD, 713.

The Bible addresses God as a Phallic Stone or "the Rock that begat thee" (Deut. 32:18)

Other rocky references and rocky titles of God include:

- God, the phallic "horn of my salvation, my high tower" (2Sam. 22:3).
- "the rock that is higher than I" (Ps. 61:2).
- "He is the Rock" (Deut. 32:4).
- "Rock of his salvation" (Deut. 32:15).
- "He only is my rock" (Ps. 62:2).
- "exalted be the God of the rock of my salvation" (2Sam. 22:47).
- "The Lord is my rock...The God of my rock" (2Sam. 22:2, 3).
- "For their rock is not as our Rock (Deut. 32:31).
- "the Rock of Israel" (2Sam. 23:3).
- "stone of Israel" (Gen. 49:24).
- "The Lord liveth; and blessed be my rock" (Ps. 18:46).
- "the Lord, is the Rock eternal" (NI translation, Is. 26:4).
- "O Lord, my Rock and my Redeemer" (NI translation, Ps. 19:14).

God was also a pillar-resident in a *Beth-El* stone (dwelling-place of a deity): "This stone, which I have set for a pillar, shall be God's house" (Gen. 28:22). "I am the God of Bethel, where thou anointedst the pillar" (Gen. 31:13).

Pyramids in the Bible? The Bethel stone was one with the Pyramid,[1] a word meaning "fire in the middle" (the Divinity within). "In that day shall there be an altar to the Lord in the midst of the land of Egypt, and a pillar at the border thereof to the Lord" (Is. 19:19). And a "chief cornerstone" is the capstone of a pyramid.

Christ, also addressed as a Horn, Rock, and Stone

- Christ, "an horn of salvation" (Luke 1:69).
- "..for they drank of that spiritual Rock that followed them: and that Rock was Christ" (1Cor. 10:4).
- Christ, a "living stone," appropriately in the book of *Peter* (2:4).
- Christ, the "chief corner stone" and "the stone...head of the corner" (1Peter 2:6,7). Chief cornerstone = capstone of the Pyramid.
- Christ's followers were called living stones who were built into a spiritual temple with Christ as the chief cornerstone: "Jesus Christ himself being the chief corner stone; In whom all the building fitly framed together groweth unto an holy temple in the Lord" (Eph. 2:20, 21).

"Oiling the stone" derives from lubrication for sex

- "And Jacob rose up early in the morning, and took the stone that he had put for his pillows, and set it up for a pillar, and poured oil upon the top of it." (Gen. 28:18).
- "And Jacob set up a pillar in the place where he talked with him [God], even a pillar of stone; and he poured a drink offering thereon, and he poured oil thereon." (Gen. 35:14).

1) Massey, BB-vII, 75.

The custom of oiling "the stone" or phallic pillars, originates from the idea of sexual lubrication. A virgin bride was deflowered by the stone penis of a statue of a priapic god. Oiling the stone penis was necessary for its insertion into the virgin. At the same time this took place, the bride placed a wreath of flowers, symbolizing the female orifice, upon "the head" of the priapic stone god.[1] Biblical terminology calls this operation "opening the matrix: "thou shalt set apart unto the Lord all that openeth the matrix" [NI translation: "you are to give over to the Lord the first offspring of every womb"] (Exo. 13:12). "All that openeth the matrix is mine" (Ex. 34:19). Thus, the bride's firstborn child was considered divinely fathered and therefore dedicated to God.

"Anointing the *head* " also derives from lubrication for sex

If women symbolically mated with God, then men symbolically mated with Goddess. In order to achieve this, their "heads" were oiled or "anointed" -so they could be joined with the Divine Feminine. Walker writes, "Later, the oil itself became a symbol. Kings' heads were anointed with oil, being likened to the 'head' of the god-penis, inserted into the flower wreath that represented the virgin matrix." [2] Anoint is derived from ANKH, an Afrikan-Kamite word meaning Life and Tie or Unite. Anointing, then, was "uniting" or "connecting"...connecting to Goddess –The Great Mother.

Did oil symbolized divine fire? In the higher sense, the "oil" likely symbolized fire, divine fire. For oil not only sits on *top* of (hence *above*) water, but it also *burns*. The "heads" of saviors and other holy men were "anointed with oil." Likely, the consecrated oil was intended to open up their *Crown Chakra* (psychic energy center at the top of the head) to allow the influx and joining –or "ankh-ing"– with the higher Divine Energy or Light. No wonder they are depicted with radiant light around their heads! The Head, then, is the receiver (Feminine) of Divine Energy /Light (Masculine). Standing erect with arms outstretched, the body even resembles the Ankh. The top of the Ankh is the "head."

Significantly, it was *WOMEN* that *anointed* these saviors, including Jesus!

The basic shape of the body/head combined is phallic. Thus the man's whole body became a symbolic phallus that united with Goddess. Our "head" is both feminine and masculine. As a circle, it is feminine, it is the receiver. As the top (or "head") of the linear, phallic body, it is masculine, plus it contains the Mind (a masculine manifestation), while the linear phallic body contains the Heart, a feminine manifestation. The tall conical crowns of Kamite pharaohs was a phallic symbol of the king's union with the Great Mother as the Sky-Goddess, the Queen of Heaven. This "Apex" also symbolized Spiritual Power descending from heaven upon his head. Imitations of this Afrikan headdress includes the bishop's miter, pope's tiara, and the pointed headdress of witches, sorcerers, and priests.

Thus, Simon Peter Cephas with his hard self, is the Fixed Earth Sign of the Zodiac, reknown as Taurus the Bull of Heaven.

1) Walker, WD, 25. 2) Ibid.

Etymology of Peter (Pe, Pet, Par, Pal) & Ptah
– and –
Background of the Masculine Principle they Personify

Interchangeable letters are **p** / **f** / **v**; **b** / **v**; **v** / **w**; and Kamite **r** / **l**. Thus:

pa	**ba**	**fa**	**va**	**wa**
pet	**bet**	**fet**	**vet**	**wet**
per	**ber**	**fer**	**ver**	**wer**
pel	**bel**	**fel**	**vel**	**wel**

Peter's roots = **Pe-Ra; Pe-Ar; Pe-Ta-Ra; Pe-Tar; Pet-Ar**. All agree with the meanings of the name. Compare with related derivatives in section on Philip. Derivatives preceded by a dot (•) appear in more than one category. The categories of derivatives are related like facets on a gem. Egyptian words usually have multiple meanings, –distinguished by their hieroglyphics.

a, b = columns in An Egyptian Hieroglyphic Dictionary. **BB** = Book of the Beginnings (vol. 1 or 2).
WE = Women's Encyclopedia of Myths & Secrets. **AE** = Ancient Egypt: Light of the World.

Category

1

Father

Male

Afrikan-Kamite Roots

P, pa • Egyptian masculine article. 229a
f (fi) • he, his, its 258a
Pau • **Pauti**, the Creator, Primeval God, the Self-Existent, He Who Is. 231a
Pat • image of God. 452BB1
Pet • the God **Ptah**. 253b
Ptah • The Original Father, Creator, Artist...
Putah • the opener, the God Ptah 16BB2

Peti • is a later form of Putra 235b
Pet-a = Petra; Pet=Petr 253b

Petapara
• the biblical Potiphar (a captain) & Potipherah (a priest). 256b
Potiphar was the Kamite captain of the guard who bought Joseph from Midianite traders (Gen. 37:36, 39:1). Potipherah was a priest in the city of On (Heliopolis) where Ra the sungod was worshiped. Joseph married his daughter, Asenath, at the pharaoh's command (Gen. 41:45).

pera • per-a, hero, warrior, mighty man. 243a, 241a
Bar • Bal, Baal 203b
ab • father. 5a
(ab reversed = ba, pa! Baba = father in many Afrikan languages)
• pure man, priest as holy father. 443BB2
abeh • title of a priest. 39b
atf • father. 98a
(Note the reverse of atf /atp is fta /pta or **Ptah**!)
pa • ancestor. 233b
(the reversal of **PA** is **AP**, meaning chief, first ancestor, and also an early name of the Great Mother)

Apparent Derivatives

father, paternal, patriarch, padre, eupatrid, veteran

Petite! (see comments)
petty

pa, pau, papa, pappy, pop, poppa, pope, papal, papacy

abbot, abba, "Abba, Father" (Gal: 4:5), bishop, **•Pharoah**, parson, priest, friar

boy
pimp (*Father* Abraham was is the most famous pimp! (Gen. 12:14-19)
punk (inexperienced young man)

wer (*man* in Old English)
werwolf (man-wolf)
vir (*man* in Latin)
virile
virago
•brass (highranking officers)
fellow

—— NAMES: ——

Ptah
Pitama
Pythagoras
Buddha (Massey & H. Blavatsky derive Buddha from Ptah)
Vatican
Jupiter
•Peter
Patrick
Pierre (*Peter* in French)

Prajapati
Brahma
Abraham

•Bar
Bel
Baal
Bala-Rama
Hannibal
Bill
Will
Apollo
Paul

Comments

Put your hand near your mouth and say "P" or "PA".
You will feel the "power" of the Father/ Male Principle bursting forth, "hitting" you. Only the letter or sound of P "pops" out with such force. "P" is hard and thrusts forward like the PEnis itself!

"P" even resembles the side view of the penis.
The nature of the Male Principle is to go out, project, eject, expand, rise. The Phallus does all of these things; it protrudes, ejects semen, swells, and arises. All fathers are male; what makes them male is their phallus. "Papa goes out, Mama stays home," sounds stereotypical but is a biological truth: Papa's genitals are outside his body. Mama's womb is ever hidden inside her body and is the original home, hence the Great Mother is called the Abode, the House. Mothers tend to stay with and raise their children but fathers might abandon both. In opposite contrast to PA, the sound of "MA" is soft and caressing, like the Feminine Principle it personifies.

PETITE!
Means small, dwarfish, gnomish.
What's the connection of PETITE with FATHER? The word PETITE is direct, profound evidence of Afrikan roots once the logical connection is made. Ptah was the original Divine Father, Creator, Artisan. Since he was modeled after the original Black Afrikan human, he was portrayed as a dwarf (Massey, AE, 372). **Thus the words petite / petty are derived from Ptah.** These "small blacks" or dwarfs, gnomes, Pygmies, were the ancestors of humanity. Their bones are found all over the world, and they appear in all the world's ancient legends. The words GNOME, gnosis, knowledge, keen, gene are from the same Afrikan roots. "Gnomes" were anciently regarded as the keepers of knowledge, as well as treasures.

Etymology of Peter (Pe, Par, Pal), Ptah & the Masculine Principle

Category	Afrikan-Kamite Roots	Apparent Derivatives	
2a **Penis**	**Petra, Par** (Pal) • title of Ra as "Lord of the Phallus." 788WE, Budge-GE-vII-19 **Ba** • Ram-god, god of virility /generation. 199b **•bah** • phallus of a man animal. 204b **•beh** • prepuce (foreskin, clitoris). what is in front.(like the penis!) 220a	**phallus** perron ("big peter") •peter	putos (*penis* in Latin) •prick priapic pizzle
Rod	**pet** • sceptre, staff. 253b **batchar** • stick, staff. 208b **abit** • sceptre, staff, stick. 117 **bu** • bough, branch, leg. 52, 53BB1 **ba** • stick, staff. 202a **ab, aba** • sceptre, staff, stick.	**pole** **•pillar** pile bole (trunk) palisades pale (stake) impale steeple obelisk billy (club) billet	bail (pole) •bilbo (bar) scepter bat baton petiole (leafstalk) •bar sprit (pole) vertical
Point **Spear** **Tongue** **Pierce**	**ban** • spear, javelin. 211a **berber** • stone with pyramidal top. 219b • summit. 444BB2 **baru** • tip, top, cap. 51BB1 **sper** • rib [*spare* rib!]. 662a • tower, height. 455BB2 **parthal** • iron weapons. 232a **peh** • penetrate. 68BB1 **ba** • to plough, dig, break through, force a way, cut up. 201b **pet** • to strike / to break open. 529BB2 / 253a **ptah, pteh** • to open, engrave, openwork. 254b **pekht** • "tearer," bird's title. 247b **tep** • tongue. [tep = pet in reverse] 5BB2 **pena** • to balance the tongue. 236b	**pin** pine porcupine **•point** •poignant •beak peak •pick pique piquant (tart, spicy) epitome **spear** "spare-rib" spire asparagus •sperm spur barb bayonet fork fluke (point of an anchor) plow **pierce** perforate •prick prod bore plough •plunge peck •pick poke focus	bitter (sharp) •spit (skewer) spade whet (sharpen) wedge pyramid prong purpose important taper **spice** spike spiccato spicule (needle-like) •spenoid (wedge shape) javelin foil (fencing sword) •bilbo (sword) bill (beak) bullet •punch (perforate) puncture pinking shears ping pang pungent bang fang branch bronchial

Comments

The phallus is rod-like with a point or "head." The phallus "pierces" the vagina; sperm pierces the egg. Separately or combined, a rod & point makes an effective weapon. A rod (bat) is used for hitting; a point protrudes and will pierce or cut. It is no accident that 99% of weapons are "MAN"-made, phallic looking and even behave like the phallus; piercing, ejaculating fire and bullets. And it is mainly men that use them.

LINGAM means penis; LINGUA means tongue. Sanskrit *lingam* and Latin *lingua* are two forms of the same word. English words in this family include **language**, **linguist**, **lance** (long, thrusting weapon; to pierce or cut), **long** (a phallus & lance are "long"), **longitude, length, lanky, line, linear** and **languish** ("weaken, lose strength or vigor" - like the penis after orgasm!). The phallus-like tongue is perpetually inside the vagina-like mouth. Both, the vagina and mouth are "receivers," are always wet inside, are oval and have "lips." The tongue (lingua) and phallus (lingam) are similar: they protrude, can be hard (stiffen) or soft, are pointed, and can pierce / push. Snake tongues "ejaculate" poison. The underlying Afrikan root of such words is **ANK** (to join, tie or fetter. 64a). When two "lines" are joined, an angle (ANK-L) is created (note that L is an ang-L). An angle is a POINT. The following words contain the ANK root and simply denote a point or angle:

- angle
- anchor (is a point, plus "connects")
- wing
- lingam
- lance
- lingua
- language (is a connector via the lingua /tongue)
- tong
- tongue
- prong
- finger
- fang
- tang (sharp)
- twang
- twinge (pang)
- twinkle
- branch
- bronchial
- pink (to prick, cut with pinking shears)
- pinking shears (makes zigzag cuts)
- ping (sharp, high pitch sound)
- pang (sudden sharp pain)
- pungent (sharp)
- single! (is the point. single = s-ank-L)

The Phallus opens the Yoni. Ptah means to open. Ptah was also the name of an early form of the Great Father. The Great Father "opens" the hymen of the Great Mother in the Passion of Love and Union which begat Life in the Universe, which is always in a state of sex.

The NIPPLE is a short penis on the breast! It even gets an "erection" when rubbed, plus "ejaculates" milk, another life-fluid like semen. Furthermore, the phallic nipple enters the yonic mouth.

Bulls have anciently been a symbol of masculine virility. Their penises are so huge, they have been used as whips for centuries (hence, *bullwhip, pizzle*).

Etymology of Peter (Pe, Par, Pal), Ptah & the Masculine Principle

Category	Afrikan-Kamite Roots	Apparent Derivatives		Comments
2b Penis Finger Five	benn • phallus, virile. 217a • to copulate 217a • engender. 52BB1 benu • male, man. 217a bennu • sons. 52BB1 benben • obelisk (phallic pillar). 217a •ban • spear, javelin. 211a •bah • phallus of a man or animal. 204b •beh • prepuce. what is in front. 220a f • hand. 58BB1 Pent-ta • a title of Ra. 237b	**penis** peninsula penetrate ben ("inside, within" –like the penis!) pen pencil **banana** finger pincer pinch (fingers are pinchers)	wand (stick, scepter) •pant (phallic leg of a trouser) empennage (tail of airplane) Pan (Satyr god of the woods who was very sexually active. Satyrs were reknown for being "horny.") five pentateuch pentagon pentacle	**Penis, pendulum, pension, penny, pound, spend, finance** are apparently from the same roots: the male genitals *hang*. Endowed men are called "well hung." Scales hang and resemble the Tau (T), an ancient phallic symbol. A penny means a hundreth of a *pound* weight. Weights are based on scales. Weights are still associated with the "real" money of precious metals and stones. Thus, weight-terminology is synonymous with payment, hence PAY, penny, pension, spend, finance, etc. **Fingers are phallic** ; the middle finger with an "erection" is a insult. FINger = PENger or projection. Since there are 5 such "projections" on each hand, then the root FEN /PEN means five by association. In "Give me five," *five* means *hand*. And fingers have hard "nails."
Finite Height Hang	benben • obelisk, cap, tip-top. 52BB1 ben • "the supreme height, the roof." (penthouse!) 452BB1 fai • weigher, bearer, supporter, support. 258b	**finite** define final finish **pinnacle** penthouse **pendulum** pendant pending append appendix	fanny (rear) benthos (bottom of sea or lake) pineal (highest gland) **weigh** weight pound pay **penny** pension spend bank ("PILE." And where "piles" of funds are kept !) finance fund	**In Latin, *penis* means *tail*.** The tail is the "end", thus PEN /FIN also means finish, FINal, the limits or FINite. To define is to set limits. **When pierced ("PE-ned", punctured) you feel pain.** PUNishment is PAINishment, PEN-IShment. Go ahead and laugh! But historically it has been (and still is) phallic weapons largely inflicting people's injuries! The threat of pain may produce "PANic." **The arrow piercing the valentine is an ancient symbol for sex.** The arrow is the penis; the valentine is the female genital. **The church steeple originated in imitation of the obelisk** (a phallus). The word steeple is from Old English *stepel*, derived from Kamite ST (standing, stay, sit) + PEL (phallus, pillar). It's no accident that anti-female, Albino-Christianity exalts the phallic principle in the form of steeples, the crucifix, linear pews, and arched, phallic-shaped stainglass windows in churches. There is nothing wrong with this; the problem is its denigration of the Female Principle.
Good & Bad	bena-t • sweetness. 217b ban • sweet, pleasant. ban • to be evil, wicked. ben • evil, wickedness. 216b pensa • to cut off. 237a pen • eradicate. 237a	**benifit** benevolence benediction bonus bona fide	**pain** panic bane (ruin, injury, fatal) ban banal penal repent punish	**Priapus** of Rome/Greece was the "God of the Phallus" with enormous genitals. Born of Aphrodite, he is an Euro version of Osiris. Priapus is Pri-Apis (Pri=love. Apis is the Bull of Osiris). Bulls have enormous penises. As the god of procreation, he personified the male function of generation; guardian of gardens and vineyards; was associated with "lewdness." Eros [and **Valentine**] was a latter form of the same god. (816WE) **The hands and fingers are winglike.** The hand (with the arm) comes from the sides of the body. It folds / closes, opens and spreads. It can "flap" and create a wind (See next section –2c).

Etymology of Peter (Pe, Par, Pal), Ptah & the Masculine Principle

Category	Afrikan-Kamite Roots	Apparent Derivatives	Comments

Category

(2c)

Bird

Wing
Blade

Fly
Fall

Angel

Afrikan-Kamite Roots

- **pui** • birds, feathered fowls, to fly. 235a
- **pera** (pela) •bird. 243a
- **pait** • fowl, birds 230a
- **pi** •fly, ascend. 234b
- **pa** • to fly, wing.
- **pepe** • to fly, wing.
- **baba** • to fly. 203a
- **per** (pel) • to rise. 242a
  • to fly, wing.

Apparent Derivatives

bird, •parrot, warbler, wren, fowl, falcon, vulture, pelican, pheasant, phoenix, phoebe, peacock, petrel, penguin, finch

pter (wing), helicopter, pterdactyl, pterygoid, pterosaur, petal, feather, plumage, foliage, blade, flap, pectoral, spenoid, penache (feathers, plume), pennate (feathered/ winged), pinnate (feather-like), •pinion (bird's wing), •van (wing, fan), •fan (to spread / open in shape of a fan– as with a peacock fan), fin ("wings" of fish)

fly, flight, flitter, flutter, flicker, volitation (flight), pleat, fold, unfold, furl, unfurl, flinch, **balance**, **•branch**, Libra, equilibrium, •vibrate, quiver, •vibrate, brandish, flourish, wield, pulse, beat, repeat

fall, fail, flop, flunk, plummet, •plunge, plunk

Comments

Kamite PI means to fly, ascend. While the PEnis does not fly, it does "ascend" –and juices fly (*pee, ejaculate*) out of it. Penis-shaped bullets, missiles & spears DO fly, only function through flying. Airplanes look like winged phalluses. Earlier talismans of Cupid (Eros), the god of erotic love, were NOT winged babies; they were **winged penises** of "hard" material (bronze, ivory, wood) which gave rise to an Italian slang term for the penis, *uccello*, **"little bird."** (198WE) The COCK, a bird, is an ancient symbol for penis. They are fierce fighters with testicle-like cheek-flaps "hanging" on either side of their phallic beak. And these flaps are RED, the color of Action/Fire. **The basic Bird-shape,** with wings outstretched is a T, ancient symbol for the male genitals. The basic Fish-shape is an oval, or "Vesica Piscis," an ancient symbol for the female genital. Both shapes unite in the ANKH = Life, Join, or Life as the result of joining the two polarities of life.

Birds express the Masculine Principle, as Fish express the Feminine:

Birds live *above* in the Air, treetops. Their wings stay dry, even in rain due to protective oil (consider ducks!).	**Fish** live *below* in Water. They are wet their entire lives.
Birds have hard, pointed, projecting, phallic beaks (containing their *nose* –see section 3), bills and talons which peck, pick, pierce, tear. They have soft "long," projecting, pointed wings / feathers /tails (which are really triangles /points).	Fish have soft, rounded "lips" and hard rounded scales.

Also, Birds fly in the AIR which = Expansion aspect of the Masculine Principle, plus they must *expand* or spread their wings in order to fly (see next section). Their bones and feather-shafts are hollow like the phallus. **Wings, feathers, knives, arrowheads, and tongues are all phallic, pointed blades.** Some fish have wings, and some birds have fin-like wingflaps. Tails and wings are usually pointed.

And it is the *male* birds that have the long, abundant, colorful, fancy feathers. Likewise, it is mainly the male bovine animals ("bulls") that sport hard phallic horns growing out of their heads. And note that lions have a mane of hair. And men not only have **beards**, but usually have more hair all over their body than women. All this reflects the projective, radiating, "pushing out" aspect of the Male Principle.

BALance = BARance , Bar-Ankh = BRanch, the branch of two sides with a middle section (2 bars or 1bar divided) (l=r).

Angel is ANKH (join, life) + EL (divinity). Hence angels are "connectors" to the Divine, or "heavenly messengers." (Messenger also contains ankh!) Angels "ankh" or connect you with divine messages. They are regarded as mediators (connectors) between God & humanity. The biblical image of angels is heavily masculinized, representing them as male, **winged**, shinning, fiery, living in heaven, praising God, wielding swords, fearsome, warriors, blowing phallic horns/ trumpets, and generally executing God's will on earth, thus acting as his HANDS (willing slaves? DOing is a category of the Male Principle). They also*guard* God's throne. (Why would His throne need to be "guarded?" This implies possible threat, as with male rulers on earth.) "Angel books" always portray them as Albinos, especially *blond!*

Etymology of Peter (Pe, Par, Pal), Ptah & the Masculine Principle

Category	Afrikan-Kamite Roots	Apparent Derivatives	Comments
3 **Nose**	**fent** • nose. 260b, 261a **bah** • to snuff, inhale. 204b **paif** • wind, breath, gust. 58BB1	•beak •bill prow proboscis front •pyramid (nose is a pyramid)	**The nose & eyes reflect the same T-shape of the (outer)male, (inner)female genitals.** The nose is phallic; it projects or points out. It is vertical with a perpetual "erection." It is a pyramid in the middle of your face! Pyramid = fire (pyra) in the MIDdle. The invisible fire that goes up your nose and throughout your body is called prana, a Sanscrit word from the same roots as fire, pyre. Prana is cosmic lifeforce or living energy that comes from the Sun. **As with fingers, beaks are natural pinchers /pincers.**
Breath **Wind**	**uin** • window, light, to open. 157b **pet** • to open out, be wide, spacious, extended. 255b **per** • to go out, go forth, proceed or arise from, • to run out, expire or perish. 240a	**wind** winnow (to blow) •pant (puff) puff spirit (breath, soul) respire whisper •breath •breeze •blow •blast •bellows •belch •burp •fart	**It is through the Nose that the masculine expansive element of Air moves in and out; *expanding* the lungs.** Your nostrils themselves can expand (flare). As water is always *sitting* in the Feminine Mouth, Air is aways *flowing* through the masculine projecting nose. The Father /Masculine Principle keeps the universe constantly expanding. And Fire needs Air.
Expand	**par** • around, surround. go round. 452BB2	•window fenestrated (having windows) •van (wing, fan) vent ventilation •fan (device that creates a wind)	**Expansion is a main trait of the Masculine Principle.** Air becomes Wind & Breath once imbued with the masculine quality of Motion; Wind travels (moves) all over the globe; Breath is the Wind always moving in or out your Nose and "wind-pipe".
		•fan (to spread /open in shape of a fan– as with a peacock fan) **•pan** (all as in panorama, panacea) span expand wide width widen bloat bloom inflate flare develop unfurl spread spray diaspora sprawl broaden burgeon burst explode **•expire** •perish	

Etymology of Peter (Pe, Par, Pal), Ptah & the Masculine Principle

Category	Afrikan-Kamite Roots	Apparent Derivatives	Comments
4a **Rock Hard**	**baa** • rock, stone, earth, salt. 51BB1 **brr** • to ossify, become hard 219b **ar** • pebble, stone of the mountain. 129b • wooden objects 129b **ab** • kind of stone 117a **baht** • a kind of precious stone. 204b **batqa** • a kind of stone. 208b **beten** • to compress, to bind. 228a	•pit (stone in fruit) petra peter (erect phallus ="the Rock") petrify lapidary vitrify revetment wood pearl flint bark iceberg brick •brass •brazen (brass) •bronze •block boulder bone	**The phallus is hard only when it is going to "father."** Thus, "hardness" is associated with fatherhood from the fact that the aroused phallus becomes "hard" or the biblical "Rock that begat thee." **Hardness = compression, bondage. FEAR (especially)** and negative emotions causes you to contract both physically (tension) and psychologically. When you contract you compress and become hard, ROCKlike (petrified). This hampers or cuts off your energy flow and sensitivity. Positive emotions cause you to feel expansive. Fear and negative emotions are only "bad" when they are denied, held in and not expressed (out-pressed).
Form Strong Bold	**per-a** • power, strength, bravery. 241a **pauti** • body, form, figure. 52BB1 **pau-t** • stuff, matter, substance, material of which anything is made. 230b **paat-t** • various types of medincinal wood or bark. 231b	•fit (robust) fettle (sound condition) bet vivid •potent •fast (lasting) physical viable •fort verity •evidence bona fide **fraud** false fake phony bold burg (fortified town) •permanent •proof (resistant) palladium (safeguard) valence shell valid value worth forte valiant valor brave **fear** afraid fright **•BULL** bully •baron (cut of beef) beef burly brute brawny **feeble** fragile frail flabby brittle flimsy **body** corporeal flesh firm affirm firmament	**Hard, phallic horns usually grow out the head of MALE,** bovine animals. Because these animals (rams, bulls, goats, etc.) love to copulate, they are reknown for being "horny." **Only hard or sharp things will bruise, cut, or pierce.** Horned animals often use their hard, phallic horns for fighting, just as men use phallic weapons for the same. **Bulls are males and are exceedingly strong.** **The strongest buildings are made of the hardest materials, which are usually rocks.** Afrikans often carved buildings out of solid rock. **All HARD things have a SOFT origin!** Think about that. The penis itself is "soft" most of the time! This reflects a profound cosmic principle: Life is Feminine. All life comes from the Female. Every male had a MOTHER. The word UNIverse is derived from YONIverse. **Jubal shows that "b" is a stylization of Kamit's foot-hierglyph ( ).** He reasons that since the foot is really a foundation, and Kamite "b" means abode, place, plant, people, and soul, then "b" signifies "the most fundamental thing of all, which is 'to be,' or 'existence' [as reflected in base, begin, born, before, breath, black...]." Therefore, he continues, **b** or the foot hierglyph signifies the foundation of life, existence, people, plants, and places. (Asar Jubal, *The Black Truth*, 113-115)
Real	**b** • abode, place, people, plants. 197a **ba** • to be. 51BB1 **p, pa** • to be, exist. 230b • beings. 52BB2	**BE!** **being**	**Kamite P (PA) and B (BA) both mean TO BE, EXIST, hence, REALITY.** Therefore, P and B are essentially the same. The **P** hierglyph is a square, thus it signifies FOUR, the foundation-number. And capital B looks just like the buttocks, which are behind, in the back, and are the base on which we sit. **Note that " p " is an upside down " b " or vice versa!** **Compare "b" and "p."** They not only sound and look similar, but reflect the two states of the penis: the **b** is "erected" while the **p** is "hanging."

Etymology of Peter (Pe, Par, Pal), Ptah & the Masculine Principle

Category	Afrikan-Kamite Roots	Apparent Derivatives	Comments
4b **Foundation** **Support** **Stable** **Secure** **Bind**	P • the square hierglyph □. square = four. 229a • base of a stand. 229a **fu, ftu, fetu,** • 4, the 4 corners or quarters. 258a, 268a, 623BB2 **Periu** • 4 gods who prepared the sky for Ra. 241b **pet** • foot. 233a • footstool, stand, pedestal. 253b **bu** • bough, branch, leg. 52, 53BB1 **fai** • bearer, supporter, support, weigher. 258b **fait** • support, supporter. 258b **peh, peh-t** • end of anything. 244a **pehui** • buttocks, thighs, stearn of boat, base of obelisk, back. 244a **pri** • girdle or tie, to slip, wrap round, binding. 241BB1 **peh** • bolts of a door. 244b **beten** • to tie, to bind. 228a **bent** • to bind, to tie. 219b **baent** • bind. 52BB1 **abt** • to shut, to bolt in. 5a **abut** • rope, fetters. 118a **pi, pa** • what belongs to, mine, belonging to, his, her, thy. 229a, 234a	four •**but–** (containing FOUR carbon atoms; **butyl**) put abide •**pillar** **pillow** plinth plant metropolis bolster •bull (beast of burden) table stable establish parent support portfolio porter bear burden barge barrow **bra** brace vertebrate back **base** basis fundamental **foundation** bier pier flat platform balcony veranda porch **place** •permanent park ——— **foot** feet boot sabot (wooden shoe) **pad** **pedal** podiatry pedestal bed "bedrock" butte (flat-top hill) •**butt**(ocks) **bottom** ——— pew (seat, bench) pose posture **post** (see comments) posterior (rear, butt) position ——— confide confidence fidelity fiducial faith patent patron patrol police warranty ——— **wed** ! rivet fetter •butt (to join) button abut prison weld •bolt (lock) •bar barrier barrette fuse •fix (secure) affix •fast (secure) fasten bind bond •pinion (to shackle) possession (something bound to you) property purchase	**Hardness = strength, thus stability, security.** The best foundation is a hard one. A foundation supports, therefore it is naturally at the bottom, like your feet, a "flexible" foundation which allows you to stand; gives you stability as you move. A good foundation requires 4 points (toes/heels =4 points). This "Four" phenomena is real big, and manifests as the four classical elements of Earth, Water, Air, and Fire, which are fundaments of the Zodiac. **Hardness or the Earth Principle is the essence of FOUR,** the number of stability & security. Kamit's TET cross had 4 bars. Nature's most stable shape is the TETrahedron (4-sided pyramid), which is the actual shape of quartz-crystal molecules (that's probably why it's called "quartz" -hence *quart*-er or "four"). And "earth" is primarily composed of quartz or silicon. **Four is the number of security.** Most of the shapes we surround ourselves with are rectangles (right-angles) including the pages of this book. Humans are very insecure and feel more secure when surrounded by rectangles. **Post:** Stake, after, "behind". The Kamite masculine article P, prefixed to Kamite ST, yields POST (171BB2). **ST** is source of stand, stay, stop, sit, static, etc.) **As a symbol of the Male Principle, the "pillar"** *externally* supports and upholds the Female Principle, which *internally* carries or bears the Life that is to come, including the males. This is reflected in the Anhk; the vertical, table-like, masculine "T" supports the feminine "O". The "pole" supports the "hole." But once inside the hole, the pole is embraced and caressed. Like the pillar, the *pillow* also supports the "head." **To secure something,** we bind it to or inside something hard or strong. Fetters are made of strong or hard material. But the strongest fetters are invisible. Property signifies a thing has been separated from something and bound to someone. Thus proPERty = sePARty or separation and bondage. You are bound to your possessions. Who owns who? **Men (especially Albinos) appear to be far more into possessiveness** & ownership than women. This is probably due to the "separation factor" of the Male Principle. Having separated themselves from Nature and People of Color, the Albinos have a great need for possessions and have more "possessions" than People of Color.

Etymology of Peter (Pe, Par, Pal), Ptah & the Masculine Principle

Category	Afrikan-Kamite Roots	Apparent English Derivatives	Comments
5 Action Make Build	**puta** • "to form, to shape, the former personified as the potter is Putha [Ptah], the Egyptian Buddha." Massey__ **abeh-t** • to create, to make or fashion. 118a **ar** • to make. 32BB2 **per-a** • activity, power. 241a	•form (to make) perform forge effort work (w)organ (w)ergonomic exercise (contains erg/werg/work) labor experience expertise operate •opera (a work) prepare repair prowess practice practical prowess entrepreneur enterprise ---------------- able ability build ploy •exploit (deed) •complete implement flair ---------------- computer robot bedlam competent repeat ---------------- feat counterfeit botch feign function foil palter (to act insincerely) artificial farce perpetrate possible compose ---------------- palm fist ---------------- art artist artisan power (ability to act!) fashion (to make) facsimile fax -facient (causes,brings about, as in abortifacient) fact (from Latin *factus* = done, made) facilitate effect efficacious efficient proficient office •fix devise function ----------- •will •volition	**The Feminine Principle says "I AM." The Masculine Principle says "I DO."** Thus activity and giving is masculine; passivity (stillness, being, receiving) is feminine. Examples: Your ears! They never move: they receive only. A plug: the socket is passive, does not move; the plug is pushed into it. **Your mouth combines the feminine and masculine.** It is receptive (swallowing) and active (talking; chewing; tongue is phallic-like: it protrudes, has a point, and can be hard or soft).  **We use our hands to do, make, build, execute.** The hand even contains a square, the symbol for building (consider the "builder's square"). It has 5 phallic projections called fingers. **Action** is a major quality of the Masculine Principle (as Stillness = Feminine). Five, according to numerology, is the number of action and travel. With fingers extended and closed together, the hand resembles a blade, –and are used like one in *Karate*. With fingers balled up, we get a fist, which is really like a cube or block.
6 Structure Building	**P, pa** • house, abode, building, city. 529BB2 **b** • abode, house. 197a **bat** • house. 208a **bat-ar** • Bethel. 208a **abut** • abode. 49BB1 **pait** • house. 231b **petra-t** • a lookout place, watch tower 245a **afait** • tent, camp, chamber. 120a **per** • house, palace, seat of government 237b **Per-aa** • "great house" or palace of Pharoah. 238	**•body** •form (shape) profile temple chapel palace peel (tower) •pel (castle. Mid.Eng.) •opera (a work) pattern pavilion •vault barn •pyramid porch building abode bethel Bethlehem patio •plan plot •frame template	**Kamit's P hieroglyph was a square.** ☐ **Buildings are usually rectangular and made out of solid rectangular material** (stone, wood, etc., cut or cast into blocks). Blocks are a natural choice for building (due to the principle of FOUR or the Square), for blocks make it very easy to build. The Afrikans of the Nile Valley often carved their temples out of solid rock, directly into mountain sides. All obelisks were carved out of solid rocks. **The phallic principle reflected in architecture** results in towers, obelisks, and "high rise" buildings. **The *House* is essentially an external Womb.** Both are for living IN. The House also imitates the Body (door=mouth; windows=eyes; furniture = organs or functions, etc.). And the Body itself is a temple for our Soul, the divine spark within. **The "bethel" stone, the Hebrew Matzebah, and the Pyramid are essentially the same thing.** (Explained on 74, 75 BB2)

Etymology of Peter (Pe, Par, Pal), Ptah & the Masculine Principle

Category	Afrikan-Kamite Roots	Apparent Derivatives		Comments
7 **Fire** **Light** **Sky**	**pa** • flame, fire, spark. 234a **pa Ra** • the Sun. 230a **afer** • to burn, to be hot. 6a **afr** • fire, to burn. 58BB1 **afit** • flame, fire. 6a **p-ur** • fire. 18, Kuhn, ESA, 18 **ur** • fire. **papa** • to shine, illumine 230 **ba** • shine, be bright. 212b **per** • splendor, to shine **burga** • bright, to shine, to lighten, sparkle. 215b **bet** • to shine, to illumine, burn. 226b, 227b **uin** • light, window, to open. 157b **pehtes** • Black ! 243b **pi** • heaven. 234a **pi-t** • heaven. 234a **pe-t** • sky, the 4 quarters thereof. 229a **pe-t pe-t** • the 2 halves of heaven, the day and night sky. 229a	fire pyre •pyramid parch spark fiery inferno furnace fry fever February copper flame flash flare conflagrant • blitz (lightning) • bolt (flash) splendor ---------------- volcano vulcan volatile -------------- bright braze blaze brilliant broil burn brown brunette bronze	**black** ! (is often confused with *darkness* or lack of light. Black receives & accepts the light! –hence it holds light / power.) pitch (black) sable --------------- photon photography beacon beam piezoelectric bio biology -------------- **white** ! (is often confused with *light.* It is not a light source; it *reflects* light) winter wink (is really a "flash") twinkle •window (lets in the *wind, yes,* but also and especially the "light." Is like the EYES of a house. Eyes "wink.") bleach blanch blank bland blond pale pallid ---------------- •vault •atmosphere firmament empyrean (highest heaven) **blue** ! (color of the sky) watchet (blue)	**Fire personifies the Masculine Principle.** Always vertical, pointed, reaching up, hot and expanding. Under the spell of sexual fire, the phallus does these very things. The Masculine Principle as POWER (light) supports Life, which itself is Feminine. Shining from the empyreal heavens, the fireball Sun is the power-source for life in this solar system. Its light fills the daytime sky. Bright, **blue**, black & bleach are from common roots. The sun is bright; the sunlit sky is blue; sunlight blackens or deepens the color of *living* things and bleaches *nonliving* things like photos, sand. Black soil is the richest and best for plants. Very little can grow in the bleached, white sand of the beach. When Fire burns something, first it turns black; when it is thoroughly burned up, only white ashes remain. In most ancient cultures, white was the color of death. Nothing grows in the white, arctic "wastelands." Heat dries, making a thing hard or rocklike. **When LIGHT gets "hard" it is called a CRYSTAL.** A crystal /glass lens can focus sunLIGHT to a point and start a FIRE! And Light can cut (as a laser beam). **Egyptian TA means earth /land & Light.** (DAY is likely from TA) Earth and Light seem radically different but really are two sides of the same coin; the higher and lower aspect of the same thing. This is personified as the **CRYSTAL** which is frozen LIGHT. Like light, crystals come in all the colors of the rainbow. And if hit with a hammer, a crystal emits light! (piezoelectricity) The quartz crystal even resembles a phallus/obelisk, complete with a tip. As semen emits from the penis, a light/energy beam perpetually radiates from the tip of every crystal (many people are sensitive to this). Kirlian photography confirms that the whole body of a crystal has an aura of light. It also shows that Light radiates from pyramid-tops. The top of an obelisk is a pyramid. Crystals amplify energy. Early radios used crystals. A crystal or glass lens can focus sunLIGHT to a POINT to start a FIRE! And Light itself can cut (laser). **It is possible to turn your physical body into light** ("transfiguration"), plus take it with you when you pass from this world ("ascension"). Ramtha, Christ and many others did it. Such was common practice eons ago before humanity degenerated into its present state. Kirlian photography reveals the aura of light surrounding all living things, including crystals (they too are alive!) When your body is completely purified, it literally glows; your "aura" becomes visible light, perceptible to people who are not even "psychic." "Halos" / auras shine from all people of varying degrees. **Lucifer means "Bringer of Light."** (luci=light; fer = bearer). This name, really a misnomer, is too good for the so-called Devil. In review of his alleged biography, he should have a name that means "Bringer of REVERSED-DESTRUCTIVE Light." That makes more sense 'in light' of his alleged activities. Look around this planet and ask where is the most destructive light coming from? Atom bombs, nuclear bombs, nuclear weapons. And who make these things? Who are the Bringers of Reversed, Destructive Light to this precious planet? –a planet which is dying because of all the destructive light it has suffered from, including ongoing nuclear explosions within her body.

Etymology of Peter (Pe, Par, Pal), Ptah & the Masculine Principle

Category	Afrikan-Kamite Roots	Apparent Derivatives		Comments
8 Power Force Energy Fuel	**peht** • strength, might, power, bravery, renown. 245a **bet** • to illumine, shine, burn, burn incense. 227b **per-a** • power, strength, war, bravery, activity. 241a **pat, pet** • food, loaf, bread, cake. 234a; 253a **pau-t** • food, bread, cake, offering, product. 230b **fetk** • bread, food. 261b **per-t** • fruit, grain, sprout, vegetable, field produce. 242b **per** • a liquid made from grains. 52BB1	•power puissance (power) perk force verve virility •pith (strength, hearth) vitality potency fervent wrath temper peeve furor fury • fit (tantrum) impetus petulant impel propel	food ! fodder fudge fat vittles wheat weed • paté peat bait pudding potato potion pottage bread flour farina barley beer (is made from grains) beverage saltpeter petrol • pitch bitumen butter butyric butane botanical • battery potential potassium (is explosive) fuel flesh supply fare	**Life must feed itself in order to live.** Light is what nourishes us; it is the Light of God (the Great Father) and Liquid Light (Water) of Goddess that supports and nourishes all Life. Words meaning food, fuel, and power are often from common roots. Plants are the basis of all food on the planet, thanks to their light-captive, liquid chlorophyll. Food & fuel is condensed, transmuted light in dormant state. Power is also Love (heart food) and Knowledge (mind food). Even the Bible says man shall not live by bread alone but by every word from the mouth of God (and Goddess!). The heat of fire rises, like the erected phallus and high-rise, phallic buildings, reaching to the sky, where the supreme Fireball generously shines upon all. The Masculine Principle is action or "I Do." In order to DO anything at all, POWER (Light) is required...along with DESIRE! Back to crystals. They are receivers and transmitters. Melanin receives all wavelengths of Light and Energy and stores it in the BATTERY of our BODY. **Who *appears* to have the most power on earth** but Albino males? It seems that males, especially Albino males, have a 'big thing' about power, ever trying to get more and more of it, ever trying to prove they have it. Thus betraying their insecurity and fear they lack it. Their preoccupation with nuclear and other forms of power reflects their insatiable lust for power; no matter how much they have, they can never get enough. It seems they are mad they are not God. But this does not stop them from competing with God (*Goddess*, really), always trying to replace Nature and the things of Nature (Nature is from Kamite neter, meaning god/goddess!). Since collectively, they reject Feminine essence, their creations are massively out of balance, thus highly destructive to life.

Etymology of Peter (Pe, Par, Pal), Ptah & the Masculine Principle

Category

9

Strife
Friction
Hit
Cut
Divide
Resist

Afrikan-Kamite Roots

pera	• (pela) fighting, battle.	243a
	• he who attacks	240b
per-a	• war, violence, power, strength, bravery, activity.	241a
	• hero, warrior, mighty man.	241a
abut	• opposition, resistance.	116a
pehti	• restrain, turn back.	245a
pursh	• to separate, to divide, split.	235a
pet	• to strike / to break open.	529BB2, 253a
peth	• to tear, to rend [the peth or mouth bites, tears]	255b
petsu	• opener, breaker, destroyer	256a
peht	• to cut through, to split, to divide.	245b
fet	• to cut, hack, tear out.	263a
ba	• to plough, dig, break through, force a way, cut up.	201b
baba	• to use force.	201b
pershu	• to break.	15BB2
beta	• bad! evil, evil thing, wickedness, sin, fault, crime, abomination.	226a
Bata	• a god of war and the chase.	208b
bath	• evil, destruction, a name of the devil.	212a
batiu	• fiends, red-haired devils, filthy & abominable creatures.	208a
peh, peh-t	• the end of anything.	244a
put	• a name for the dead [fatal!].	235b
fi	• repel, to disgust.	58BB1

Apparent Derivatives

polarity
differ
vary
war
warp
worry
worse
wrong
wreck
wretched
wrestle

vie
violence
rival
fray (fight)
foray (attack)
brawl

feud
fight
defeat
• fit (tantrum)
• pit (compete)
compete
dispute
debate
bout
sabotage

conflict
afflict
friction
ply, pry
apply
pull
polish
pulverize
burnish
preen
press
print
bruise
brush
oppose
•pound (hit)

pat
pet
bat
beat
bother
pother
•butt (to hit)
rebuttal
battle
combat
• battery (beating)
battalion
•blow (to hit)
flog
flay

problem
blemish
blame
peril
conspiracy
virus
virulent

foe
woe
poison
fate
fatal
futile
bad !
vile
evil
defile
filthy
foul

revolt
rebel
belligerent
defy

divide
divorce
fracture
break
breach
breeches
branch
burglary
part
separate
split
fault
wall (division)

bite
butcher
amputate
whittle
fritter
pare
prune
abort
brief (a thing becomes "brief" when cut)
villain
culprit
pirate
barbarian

•pain
pathology
pathetic
patient
pity / pitiful
suffer
plague
plight

Comments

Polarity is possible only with "poles"; hence conflict, friction. Pole and phallus are from the same root. The "pole" or vertical line is a natural divider, cutter, knife, sword. Friction causes heat; can start a fire. Focusing sunrays (turning light into a point /spear) does the same! Light can pierce and cut (laser). Light beams even resemble blades or swords. And "beam" refers only to lightrays or "hard" things (wood / metal) in elongated (phallic) form. "High" pitched sound can cut/shatter; referred to as "piercing."

When Male Energy is not linked or balanced with Feminine Energy, it is destructive. Whereas women bring Life into the world, almost all killing on earth is done by males. Cultures ruled by women remained peaceful for thousands of years until takeover by males. Now, the planet is ran by males; look at all the violence.

Malevolent = male-violent. Military = male-tary. Men are the likely inventors of most weapons. And virtually all weapons are phallic-looking and phallic-behaving; piercing, ejecting, shooting, exploding. It's been the penises of bulls that has been traditionally used as whips (bullwhips).

The destructive aspect of the Male Principle is exaggerated in Albino males, who have shown themselves to be the most destructive creatures on earth. This is evidenced by their unparalleled destruction of all lifeforms (plants, trees, animals, people of color, themselves, and the Earth herself), and ongoing development, creation, and amassment of the most destructive weapons in the world, including biowarfare such as AIDS and ebola, specifically developed to kill people of color, especially Black people. This is why only Black nations are hardest hit with these plagues. **The Caucasian collective has a fixation upon death and destruction.** They show themselves to be in a major war against everything on Earth. They worship the Death Principle and this permeates their entire culture. Their greatest monuments honor killers and wars. Their greatest religious symbol is the Crucifix, the symbol of both death and the male genitals. Their technology kills the land, plants, animals, people, and themselves. They (specifically Nazi Germany) created and developed killer chemicals which have been used to kill millions of people. These chemicals are still slowly killing people and other lifeforms as pesticides, herbicides, and other "cides." Their weapons are capable of literally killing Earth herself. They continuously spend mega-billions of dollars, ever overproducing their nuclear weapons (weep-on). **Fractionation** is a hallmark of Albinos; they cut, divide, dissect, and fractionate everything, including atoms.

To receive light is to live. There is a connection between respecting Life and the ability to receive Light. Melanin is the receiver of Light and all wavelengths of energy. A melanin deficiency is a dis-ease and means one is not getting all the Light they should, thence are apparently more vulnerable to "evil" (anti-life) behavior.

And Fire is absolutely destructive. Nothing destroys like fire.

Etymology of Peter (Pe, Par, Pal), Ptah & the Masculine Principle

Category	Afrikan-Kamite Roots	Apparent Derivatives		Comments
10 **Head** (Leader) **Circle** **Opening** **Ball** **Pipe** **Path**	**Bat** • title of a very high official... 212a **per** (pel) • seat of government. 237b **pet** • a circle. 69BB1 • to open out, be wide, spacious, extended . 255b **patch** • circular object, disk, cake, round tablet. 234a **par** • around, go round, surround, make a circle. 452BB2 • to surround, enclose, as in a house 68BB1 **petes** • a covering, wrap, bag. 256b **pa, peth** • open mouth, to open, open the mouth. 15BB2 **ptah, pteh** • to open, to make openwork, to engrave. 254b **barbar-t** • knob of crown of the South, grain, seed, berry, any rounded thing. 204a **bul, ber** • to boil up, well forth, be ebullient. 622BB2 **pat** • path, a course, path of the sun. 68BB1	•pate (head, brain) pituitary potentate (ruler) federal brow brain cerebrum cerebral •baron bar (law) •Pharoah phrenology govern sovereign imperial cerebellum poll (top of head) politics pilot •will •volition -------------- aperture •pore (hole) port portal **•atmosphere** (="outmost sphere" enclosing Earth) bracelet burr (washer) burrow (hole) •frame about (around) patch patty •spot (circle, blot) bud spud pi pie pea! (a sphere) spin spindle pivot swivel •pan ("all," as in PANacea.= *all* points, 360˚) bun (roundness, hence a buttock; "roll" of bread/hair) bunion -------------- pita (openable pocket bread) • pit ("open" hole) vat	pot pitcher ("open" container) boat ("open" container) bowl •billy (pot) •pan ("open" shallow dish) -------------- ball bald (ball head) balloon billiard boil ebullient bulla (round seal...) bulge belly bloat blister blimp blob pill pimple plump inflate pudgy ---------------- year (is a "turn," full rotation) **world** ! (sphere which rotates, revolves) wreath wrist wrench period (cycle, dot) •spell (cycle) perfect (whole, complete –like the circle, a symbol of perfection) ----------------- flue (tube, pipe) flute (w)aorta (w)artery •barrel (of gun) pipe pistil pistol piece (gun) way via viatic vein path •pith (center of plants, spine) •fit(s) boulevard	**No part of the body has as many "openings" as the Head,** which has seven (eight, with infant's softspot). Standing erect with arms outstretched, you resemble the Ankh. The "head" of the Ankh is a circle, opening, yonic "hole," doorway to the womb. Circle = feminine symbol; "upright" line = masculine. Like the phallic stem of the Ankh, our linear, phallic-like body supports our "head." **Head is circular, thus feminine, thus a "receiver"** or "opening" at highest point of our body. This principle manifests as the "softspot" of infants' heads. Receiving is feminine. Head receives God's descending Light (Cosmic Rays; Masculine) and is even equipped with antennae (HAIR !) to enhance its receptive abilities. Additionally, the 12 brain centers are heavily pigmented with melanin, the super RECEIVER of all wavelengths of energy! Brain & Nerves cannot function without neuro-melanin! Since the Feminine also = abode, then Head is the abode of our Consciousness within our Body, the Temple of God. And hair is its natural crown (corona, circle); **nappy or *spiraling* hair** = concentrated antennas, further amplifying Head's receptive abilities! The circular heads of flowers point up, keeping their faces towards the Sun to receive God's light, opening in the day, closing at night. **Our circular head is Feminine,** holding our Mind-Brain, which is Masculine. Our linear body is Masculine, holding our Heart-Soul, which is Feminine. **Thus each polarity contains and balances the opposite polarity.** Mind thinks, Heart feels. Mind rules and should be guided by Heart through Feelings. **Head is the LEADER; leaders show the way or PATH.** Halo of Light surrounds the Head, but really a whole feminine sphere of Light (the Aura) surrounds our phallic body! This same pattern is evident with trees. **Circles turn.** Heads turn. Wheels turn, like the boundless circle of the Zodiac. Turning = time = cycle, circle. Thus a "period" is both time and a circle ("dot"). Turning = "going around" = PATH. When a flat plane "goes around" (is rolled), a path called a **tube** is created. The phallus is a tube, thus contains a circle. Tube = phallic form of a circle. **Pipe, hole. "Masculine holes"** are openings to linear conduits: pipes, straws, nose, penis, horn, and sometimes fangs. They are often VISIBLE (external like the penis) & connected to a source (Feminine) of some type. Motion (a Masculine function) is ever present with them; their contents usually RUSH through. **"Feminine holes"** are openings to chamber of some sort, usually HIDDEN, like the womb, ear. While Father is the Opener, the aperture belongs to the Mother. The Male Principle (Expansion) opens the Female Principle. The vertical line (|) and circle (O) are the only symbols that are both numeric (masculine) and alphabetic (feminine) –giving us 10 (ten) and IO; –the Pipe /Hole, Yoni / Phallus, evident in the Ankh. IO is IU, the fertile Afrikan root of *many* divine names. **Sharp, bright, dull, fast**: words for attributes of the Mind (Masculine Polarity) but also of **WEAPONS, POLitics (PHAL-itics) and religion.** No coincidence that these two primary areas that "head" or "control" people are male-dominated at the "seat" of their power, with a bloody HIS-story.

Etymology of Peter (Pe, Par, Pal), Ptah & the Masculine Principle

Category	Kamite Roots	Apparent Derivatives		Comments
11 See Show Say Ask Declare	**per, ber, pera** • to see, vision, appearance, aspect, eye. 243a / 219b **petra-t** • a lookout place, watch tower. [from the high phallic tower you can see the most and the farthest] 254a **pet, petr, petra** • to see or look, glance, sight of anything, things seen 254a **bar, bal** • blind. 203b **ua-t** • name of one eye of Ra. 154a **uin** • window, light, to open. 157b **ba** • book, papyrus, roll, document, liturgy. 200b **pet, petr, petra** • explain, say, declare, reveal, ask, what? 251b, 253b **pteh** • to ask or beg, to pray. 254b **per** • pronounce the words, explain. 15BB2 **pur** • to explain. 452BB2	peer appear apparent apparition parody sport •pore (stare) prove bare brazen overt ferret (uncover) refer(ence) blatant flaunt explicit reveal •pupil (hole, student. it is to "pupils" that things are revealed !) •spot (to see) debut **witch** (originally a woman of great wisdom & knowledge) wit (*knowledge* in Old Eng.) wita (counselor. OE) wittingly witness watch •evidence video Vedas wary aware beware	spy espionage spectrum spectacular conspicuous fantasy phantom phenomena face facet facies (appearance) phase (aspect, angle) ---------------- patois (dialect, jargon) expatiate telepathy pedagogy encyclopedia emphatic prophet vatic (of prophet) veto vote affidavit bode (omen, foretell) badge bill •bull (papal edict) bulletin symbol policy spiel spell gospel reply pledge preach prattle promise report speak fable ------------------ prayer plea plead appeal implore petition bid blaspheme	**Eyes must be "open" in order to see.** You see through the opening /circle of your eyeBALLS. To be shown is to see. To see is to know. Knowledge is Light. In order to see, we need LIGHT. Words relating to knowledge often denote sight: science, seer, revelation. A question is a mental searchlight. When we get the answer, we say "I see!" SAY & SEE sound similar. So does EYE & EAR. Say-See and Eye-Ear = Light & Sound, two sides of the same coin. Essentially, Light is masculine, Sound is feminine. Light (images) and Sound (words) are the primary channels for *Knowledge.* **Word is the Mother.** "The Word" is one form of the Great Mother disguised in the Bible. Word /Sound is the organizing principle of form. All words/sound have a 3-D shape, which can be viewed in device called the tonoscope. This science is called Cymatics. Thus words build and have the power to create form. This recalls mantras and "the Word made flesh." Everything in the Universe is vibrating, from the atoms to galaxies. Thus everything is making a sound! Exquisite symphonies emanate from atoms and molecules. All of Nature sings! Feminine Mouth /Throat is the seat of speech. **Light is the Father.** Lightning is a phallus symbol. Light enters our EYES, Sound enters our EARS. The eyes are both masculine & feminine. They project your energy while simultaneously receiving light. Looking (staring) is a form of protruding into another's privacy. But the ears are feminine; they only receive. Speaking (projecting) is masculine & active, as Hearing (receiving) is feminine & passive. Spoken words project from the opening of the Mouth to opening of the ear. All these powers (seeing, knowing, speaking, hearing) reside in the Head. Knowledge resides in the head / is stored in the genes. Know, gnosis, genius, gene & genitals are from the same root! **"Knowing" is a synonym for sex!** Are you sensing the BIGGER underlying picture!? Your Genitals and Brain(s) are different versions of the same thing! You can create from both. More on this in volume II. **While Sound or "The Word"** is essentially feminine, the act of speaking (form of projecting) is masculine. The phallic, pointed tongue shapes sound and lets you talk or 'pronounce' words. WORD is in "sword." Words can cut, tongues can be "sharp" and forked. Like weapons, words can burn, sting, cut, pierce, etc. But they also have the power to soothe, inspire and heal. **The WORD and the SWORD can both be weapons.** One is "higher" and more powerful, hence Controllers ever seek to suppress it, manipulate it, control it, etc. **Stones seeing?** Crystals can both "see" & record everything it sees. Some hold records of Earth's past. Knowledge can be stored in crystals. Crystal balls are ancient tools for "seeing" past & future. Artificial crystal is the basis of artificial intelligence (computers). Crystals stimulate our pineal gland, a "third eye." Crystal /glass lenses vastly facilitate "seeing" (glasses, tele/microscopes). Clear stone (prisms) affects light. This "reflects" the connectedness of stone and light. Crystals are frozen light, and they radiate light / energy, as proven by Kirlian photography. Light & Sound holds (and is) knowledge. Knowledge is a form of food, nourishment at the higher level. 'Man shall not live by bread alone but by every word proceeding from God.'

Etymology of Peter (Pe, Par, Pal), Ptah & the Masculine Principle

Category	Afrikan-Kamite Roots	Apparent Derivatives	Comments
12 **Proceed** **Go-Out** **Speed** **Expire**	**per** • to go out, go forth, depart, be born, manifest proceed or arise from, • to run out, expire or perish. 240a **pehrer** • to run, traverse, follow course of action. 245a **Pehreri** • "Runner," a title of the Sungod. 245a **sper** • to come forth, to set out. 597a **pert-t** • issue, exist, manifestation, offspring. 240b **perper** • to run swiftly, to leap about, be agitated. 243a **fent** • sign of inundation. [source of *fountain*] 58BB1 **pat** • fountain. 233a **bah** • to snuff or inhale. 204b **bath** • to hasten, escape, depart, run, leap. 212a **betnu** • swift, agile. 227a	**birth** breed forth further progress probe express fare parade walk waltz pursue follow flee fly travel explore dispatch foreign (from *foras*, outside. Phallus is "outside" the body, projects out. You can travel "outside" your country & become a "foreigner") **•breath** •breeze •blow •blast •bellows •belch •burp •fart explode burst blast blurt expel pour pee (urinate) piss spill fill flow brook bleed sprout **beard** pervade invade explode spring (leap) prowl ----------------- font fount ("opening" that flows forth) fountain ----------------- velocity fleet (swift) flee rapid speed expedite • barrel (speeding) • brisk (fast) • bolt (speed) • blitz (to rush) •ballistic • pitch (throw) •spit spurt spew sputter fling ------------------ • peter (dwindle) piddle (squander, urinate) respite abate wither wilt faint wane •expire •perish **future** !	**Now that we're finally at the end, let's repeat the beginning, for all natural things go in cycles,** ever expanding, rising, and improving with each new "turn" or rotation, –as personified by the SPIRAL. And only the truth with stand in the end –for lies and falsehood have no real substance or foundation and therefore will ultimately vanish: *Put your hand near your mouth and say* ***"P" or "PA".*** *You will feel the "power" of the Father/Male Principle bursting forth, "hitting" you. Only the letter or sound of P "pops" out with such force. "P" is hard and thrusts forward like the PEnis itself. ...The nature of the Male Principle is to go out, project, eject, expand, rise. The Phallus does all of these things; it protrudes, ejects semen, swells, and arises.* **And men have largely been the travelers, explorers, experimenters, deserters, adventurers.** As previously stated, it is the *male* birds that have the long, abundant, colorful, fancy feathers. It is the male bovine animals ("bulls") that sport hard phallic horns growing out of their heads. Lions have a mane of hair; men have beards! **All this reflects the projective, "pushing out" aspect of the Male Principle.** **And this is evident with Light! With *great speed* does Light travel!** –projecting out, *expanding* as it travels, moving in a straight, linear path. Light is active. It never stops moving. It will go vast immeasurable distances from its original source. Water is passive, only moving when it is moved or when reacting to a force. The water on Earth stays on Earth. The Wind is both masculine (in that it is expansive and travels) and feminine (circulates all over the earth and sometimes manifests as spinning air such as tornados). Breath circulates in our bodies; speech requires breath (masculine) and sound (feminine). **It takes power /energy to make something proceed.** Heat speeds things up but too much heat will bring things to a standstill. **It is likely that men invented or developed RACING and competitive sports.** In ancient times, "sports" were deliberately deadly –especially in European cultures (Rome, Sparta, Greece, etc.) And still today, European culture is obsessed with speed. On Germany's highways (autobahns) you may travel as fast as your car can go! Europeans started the so-called "arms-race." What is it but a race to death? –taking the whole world down with themselves? The handwriting is all over the place. If something doesn't happen soon to stop it, the Albinos and "humanity's hidden manipulators" will succeed in killing everything including Earth and themselves. All this amounts to a rebellion and defiance against God and especially Goddess, the Great Mother. **Only by restoring the Feminine Principle that respects all Life can we be healed and saved.**

Pe, Pet, Par, Pal: *Apparent Derivatives in Other Languages*

Category	Hausa (Afrika)	Swahilli	Tamil (India)	Japanese
1 Father, Male	**baba**, father, paternal uncle	**baba**, father **babu**, grandfather pa, of **bin**, son of	**puttel**, god, divinity **putalvan**, son	**fubo**, parents **boo**, staff, club, rod, stick
2 Penis, Rod, Point, Bird, Wing, Fly, Fall	**fadi**, fall (down/on) **fado**, fall down to someone **fada**, fall into **biyar**, five **busa**, blow	**popo**, bat **bawa(ma)**, wing **vuvia**, to blow	•**val**, sharpness **pili**, peacock's feather **petai**, female of birds **par**, collapse	**pooru**, pole **batto**, bat **baransu**, balance **furu**, to fall, come down (rain..)
3 Nose, Breath, Wind, Expand	**fiffike**, wing **shebur**, shovel	**pafu**(ma), lung **pua**, nose **bei**, price [pay] **ffura**, to swell, effervesce	**vali**, wind, air	
4 Rock, Strong, Foundation, Support, Fetter	•**fito**, ferrying **baya**, the back		•**val**, strength **viral**, strength, victory **pati**, step **pin**, back, rear, part **poru**, to carry	**futon**, bedding, mattress, cushion **beddo**, bed **baiten**, stand, booth, store **biri**, last, bottom
5 Action, Make, Build	•**buda**, prepare		**parru**, bond, tie **varakku**, behavior	**pedaru**, pedal **watasu**, carry across, ferry over, deliver **furumai**, behavior, action
6 Sturcture, Building	**fada**, chief's residence/ audience chamber **birni**, city **birane**, walled city		**varaippu**, mansion	barakku, barraks, shack
7 Fire, Light, Sky	**fitila**, lamp, lantern **wuta**, fire **gobara**, fire **baki**, black **fari**, white	**fahiri**, splendor	•**val**, luster, brightness **piranku**, to shine **ve**, to burn, to be hot **vin**, sky	**furai**, fry
8 Power, Force, Energy, Fuel	**fari fati**, snow white **fura**, a food of flour/milk **burudi** / **brodi**, bread, roll **fito**, beer		**viraku**, fuel **valci**, food	**abura**, fat **furutte**, energetically, willingly **biira**, beer, ale
9 Strife, Friction, Hit, Cut, Divide, Resist	**fada**, fighting, argument **buga**, beat **buge**, beat, knock over/out **barowo**, thief	**fitina**, discord •**futa**, to wipe, obliterate **papura**, to rend, claw **feli**, an act, a misdeed **furufuru**, confusion **paruparu**, roughly •**papa**, to papitate **araka**, a division	**patu**, affliction, suffering **varutta**, suffering **viluma**, affliction **pari**, vice **vitu**, reject **piri**, to get separated	**fureru**, to strike against, to touch, to conflict with **furi-**, to shake, brandish **barasu**, break into pieces, lay bare (a secret), dispose or kill
10 Head, Circle, Opening, Ball, Pipe, Path,	**fari**, **farko**, beginning, start •**buda**, open, clear away **bude**, open **fili**, open country, space **fal**, completely **batun**, concerning, regarding	**paruza**, be rough **pete**, a ring **petana**, bent into a circle **pito**, a path **pia**, child's top **peupe**, an open place •**papa**, porous	**vay**, mouth **vali**, way, road, series **vari**, way **par**, to look **viri**, to open one's eyes **pul**, stupid	**waru**, to split, crush, divide **booru**, bowl, ball **fuutoo**, envelope **futotta**, fat, plump **wa**, circle, ring **fun, pun**, minute [is part of a circle]
11 See, Show, Say Ask, Declare	**fada**, say **batu**, conversation, affair **butuk**, stark naked **rubuta**, write **fa**?, what about?	•**futa**, unsheath **fali**, divination, augury of good/bad luck	**paliccu**, praise	**pera** pera, fluently, glibly **ben**, valve **beraboo**, fool, blockhead **beeru**, veeru, veil **fuu**, appearance, way
12 Proceed , Go-Out, Speed, Expire	**fara**, start, begin **fita**, go out, going out •**fito**, come out **wurga**, throw	**faulu**, to succeed	**pira**, to be born **valanku**, walk about **vitu**, emit, leave, remove •**val**, quickness **vatu**, fade, dry up	**fuutei**, appearance, looks **bun**, writing, literature **benzetsu**, eloquence, tongue

Pe, Pet, Par, Pal: *Apparent Derivatives in Other Languages*

Category	Sanscrit	Hebrew	Latin	Greek
1 Father, Male	**Pitama**, the father of all men, title of Brahma. **pitar**, father **pati**, lord, king **putra**, son **bala**, boy	**BORE**, the Creator, God **ab**, father •**bar**, son **ben**, son	**pater**, father	**pateras**, father **patreeos**, paternal **pedee**, paido, boy, child
2 Penis, Rod, Point, Bird, Wing, Fly, Fall	**pattram**, petal, leaf, feather **patatrin**, bird		**putos**, penis **pila**, pillar **palus**, pale or stake **pertica**, stick, pole, perch **furca**, 2-prong fork	**peos**, penis **patereetsa**, bishop's staff, crook **ptenon**, bird
3 Nose, Breath, Wind, Expand		**paras**, spread, stretch out •**parats**, expand	**penna**, feather **spirare**, to breathe	
4 Rock, Strong, Foundation, Support, Fetter	**pat**, pad, foot, leg **padah**, foot **padam**, foot, foostep, step **bharati**, bear, support **bhartr**, supporter, husband **balin**, strong	**par**, bull	•**vi**, **vis**, strength	**peereenas**, stone, core **pato**, step on **pateema**, step **patoma**, floor, ground **baitulos**, standing stone **psephos**, stone
5 Action, Make, Build				
6 Structure, Building		**bet**, house, the letter B		
7 Fire, Light, Sky	**peru**, the sun **pra**, to shine forth **prana**, breath, life **budhi**, light	**bo'er**, burning, ablaze		**peer**, fire, firing **pura**, fire **phlegein**, to burn **periastrapto**, shine
8 Power, Force, Energy, Fuel	**balat**, forcibly		vita, life •**vi**, **vis**, force, power, strength	**botane**, fodder [botany]
9 Strife, Friction, Hit, Cut, Divide, Resist		**perets**, breach, gap, trouble •**parats**, break, destroy, split **batash**, ba'at, trample, kick **billa**, destroy, confuse	**bellum**, war **petitio**, thrust, an attack, blow **petere**, to attack, assail,	**ptolemy**, war **prien**, **prizen**, to saw
10 Head, Circle, Opening, Ball, Pipe, Path,	**vatah**, enclosure **valaya**, bracelet, circle **padika**, quarter **pathah**, path **vadanam**, mouth, face	**patah**, open, untie, begin **petah**, opening, doorway **petiha**, opening, foreword **peh**, **peth**, opening, mouth **BOR**, hole, pit, cistern (**Note:** Bore /Bor reflects the original feminine roots of God /Goddess as Creatress, the Abode, Abyss, Doorway or Opening to the Womb..)	**apertus**, aperire, to open **patesco**, to be opened, lie open **patere**, to be open **puteos**, well (an opening!)	**ephphatha**, open, "be open" **periodos**, circuit **pi**, Greek alphabet's 16th letter. A special # relating to the circle)
11 See, Show, Say Ask, Declare	**vad**, say, speak, tell **padam**, position, site, word	•**bar**, to declare, explain **petar**, interpret, solve **pitpet**, chatter, argue **barur**, clear, evident, obvious	**videre**, to see **visus**, video, seeing, sight **pareo**, appear, become evident **fari**, to speak, talk **petere**, request	**pedagogo**, educate, teach
12 Proceed , Go-Out, Speed, Expire	**pur**, proceed **prer**, drive on, impel	•**parats**, burst out **pra**, go before, begin, let go, loose **bara**, fountain **palat**, emit, escape, discharge **patar**, dismiss, let out, acquit **bitsbets**, burst forth, sprout	**pro**, **por**, forward, out **parene**, to give birth, bring forth **parere**, to give birth	**potamas**, river

3 Thomas Didymus = Gemini the Twins (or Couple)

Mutable **AIR** Sign

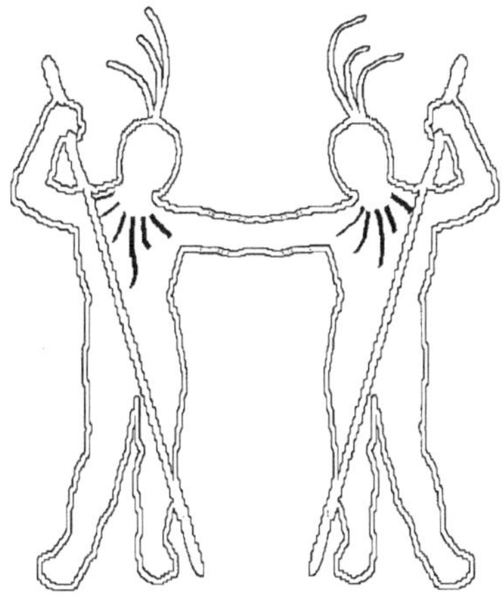

He is "Thomas called Didymus" (John 11:16, 21:2). After knowing the meaning of these names, even a child could match him to the right constellation for both names, *Thomas* and *Didymus* mean "twin." Thomas therefore *doubly* represents Gemini the Twins.

What was Thomas's real name and whose twin was he?

The apocryphal Gospel of Thomas answers by identifying Thomas as *Judas Thomas (Tammuz)*, the twin brother of Jesus! In fact, Judas was the name of one of Christ's four brothers (Mat. 13:55, 56). The text in which Judas Thomas appears as Jesus's twin were at one time widely used by Christian congregations. They were accepted works of scripture, as legitimate as the canonical Gospels of the New Testaments.[1] This aligns with the Afrikan story from which it was plagiarized. Osiris-Horus (who are one) and Set are twin warring brothers (representing Light and Darkness contending) rendered as Christ and Judas. Set betrays his brother Osiris and causes his death. Judas betrays his brother Christ and causes his death.

The god *Tammuz* was identical with the Sumerian savior-god *Dumuzi*, the "only-begotten Son" or 'Son of the Blood." Dumuzi fertilized the earth with his blood at the time of his death, which is exactly what the biblical Judas did in that the place where he died was called Alcedama -meaning field of blood. Tammuz was called Healer, Savior, and Heavenly Shepherd. "Saint Thomas" is the Greek name of the god *Tammuz*, the *Christos* or sacred king annually sacrificed in the temple at Jerusalem. He was attended by women who dedicated him to their Goddess (a form of the Great Mother) Ishtar-Mari, Queen of Heaven, his mother and bride (Eze. 8:14). Tammuz was identical with **Adonis** whom the Romans called the *chief god of the Jews.* [2] The 10th month of the Jewish calendar is still named after Tammuz, who was revered all the way up to the 10th century. The Jewish custom of "weeping for Tammuz" occurred in the month of Tammuz, "of which, in the Zodiac, the Twins are the sign."[3] At the winter solstice the ancients wept and mourned for Tammuz, –crucified by winter, and on the 3rd day they rejoiced at the resurrection of their "lord of light."[5]

English *Thomas*, Greek *Tomos*, Sumerian *Dumuzi*, Indian *Tamus*, and Hebrew *Tammuz* are variations of the same name and are all derived from the name of the Afrikan god *Tum*, who was converted into the Apostle Thomas.[4] Tum is an earlier version of the god, A*tum*, whose dual character is that he is both the *Father* (Atum-Ra, the setting Sun of the evening), and the *Son* (Atum-Iu, the rising Sun of dawn).[6]

1) Baigent, ML, 97. 2) Walker, WE, 971. 3) Higgens, vII, 755. 4) Massey, AE, 891, 893-4, 905. 5) Doane, 495. 6) Massey, AE, 894-895.

The twin character of Tum is also represented as Hu and Ka (meaning Taste & Touch), which are two gods referred to as his "sons."[1] From this originated the association of *doubt* with the name Thomas; "doubting Thomas" insisted on *touching* the resurrected Jesus. The word *doubt* in fact, is from the same root as *double*.

> "Hu and Ka, are *'attached to the generation of the sun, and are followers of their father Tum daily.'* That is Atum, the god of the two heavens, whose station is equinoctial, has two manifestations, the one in the lower, the other in the upper heaven; the one as the god of light, the other as the deity of darkness. In the type of Har-Makhu [Lord of the Scales, a title of Horus in Libra] he unites both; in the type of Khepr, the beetle-god, he makes his transformation from the one into the other character."[2]

As Shutter Up of Day and Autumn, Atum-Ra wears the closing lotus on his head, the antithesis to Horus rising out of the opening flower of dawn. Atum was the Closer as well as the Opener of Amenta by name. "The entrance to Amenta figured in the Egyptian itinerary was 'the mouth of the cleft,' as it was termed at Abydos."[3]

Biblical variants or names from the same root as Thomas include:

Tammuz	Didymus	Damascus	Demas
Tema	Timna	Dimon	Timothy
Temah	Timnah	Dimonah	Nicodemus
Timaeus	Timnathah	Timon	Thama
Kedema	Timnath	Adam	Thamah
Bartimeus	Timothy	Thummim	

Two from TUm. The English word TWO is apparently from TU of Tum, name of the twofold Afrikan god who was none other than Osiris (Asar). Osiris was father and son as Atum-Ra and Atum-Iu (the setting and rising Sun). And two is the meaning of twin, dual, Tu-mas or Thomas Didymus (Ti-Tomas, Two-Thomas) whom we now know as the Celestial Twins of Gemini.

1) Massey, HJ, 103. 2) Massey, BB-vII, 290. 3) Massey, AE, 655.

Etymology of Thomas (Tum)

Category	Afrikan-Kamite Roots	Apparent Derivatives: ENGLISH	Apparent Derivatives: OTHER
Duality Complete	**Tum** • the double Sungod. **tum** • to complete & perfect in a total of two halves. 287BB2 **temui** • "full (dual, of the two hands)." 834a **tema** • to join, be united to, bring together, union, bind, collect. 878b, 879a,b **temm** • to unite with. 878b **tam-t** • two halves. 20BB2 **tuai** • two halves. 156BB1 **ti** • two. 845AE **ta** • mark of the dual. 821a **tui** • the two mountains of sunrise /sunset. 869b **Tauiu** • people of the Two Lands, the Egyptians. 815b	**Tom** **Thomas** **thumb** thama (thumb in Old Eng.) thumpkin thimble **two** duo twin twain twy (two) twilight dual double doubt •dichotomy **Didymos** (Di-Tomas) Deuteronomy team idem (the same, ibid.)	HEBREW : **tham**, double, to be twin, twined together **tumtum**, hermaphrodite **temuna**, likeness, image **tam**, whole, faultless SANSCRIT: **adima**, first male & female, both **dama**, resemble **dimmo**, liken, compare GREEK : **deuteros**, second
Shut	**tumu** • shut up, close. 655AE **tem** • to shut, shut the mouth. 834a **atem** • to shut, to close, make an end of . 98a **tami** • to be silent [mouth shut=silent, "dumb"]. 819b **Tem** • a form of Ra during the last 3 hours of the day. 834b	**•Autumn** (dim season) dim (setting Sun is dim) **dam** (to shut) **tomb** tampion (plug or cover for gun-muzzle) tampon (plug) condom tame timid timorous dumb dummy demur demure	HEBREW : **adm**, to dam **thm**, come to an end, cease, disappear **damam**, be silent or still **demama**, silence **tamum**, burried, hidden LATIN : **domare**, to tame, subdue
Cut Pierce Divide	**tem** • to cut, engrave, inscribe. 836a • to sharpen, to pierce, be stung/ bitten. 878a **tem** • worm, serpent. 878a **tema** • writing, book, roll, document. 836b **Atem** • The Mother Goddess of Time, Time or periodicity. 1, 131BB2 **Tem-Ra** • the Sungod by night and day. 834b	**etymology** ! –tomy (suffix = cutting) tomahawk •dichotomy hysterectomy epitome stimulate timber **atom** **•demon** theme item victim (sacrifice. vi-life, tim-cut) **time** (a circle! Asking "what time" = division, an arc)	GREEK : **tomos**, cutting, a cut **temnein**, to cut **temaheezo**, separate, cut into pieces, break up **temno**, cut, divide, open
Damn	**tamu** • some disgusting thing or quality. 819b **temiu** • the dead, the damned.835b **tem**, **temm** • die, perish, the end, death. 835a **atem** • to annihilate. 20BB2	damn condemn contempt damage demise doom tumult anathema tamper temper (fury) **•demon**	HEBREW : **hatam**, to close, end **temuta**, fall, collapse **timsah**, crocodile GREEK : **temuta**, death, mortality **tame**,defiled, corrupt **thambos**, lifeless, without luster
Misc.	**Atem**, the Red Deity, red sun. 1BB1 **Tem, Temu**, Atem, god of An & 1st living Mangod, creator of heaven &Earth. 834a	Adam •Autumn adamant diamond	HEBREW : **Adam**, red, red man **dam**, blood **damdemanit**, red currant

Comments

Two is undoubtedly from the TU of Tum, the doublegod Atum (Atum-Ra & Atum-Iu or the rising and setting Sun).

Thumb. Hold your *two* thumbs together and look at them. Your "thumbs" are "twins" on your hands. Thus *thumb* really means *twin* just as in the name *Tom Thumb.* **Tum is the Afrikan source of Tom Thumb and Black Jack.** Tum in Egyptian was also a name for the mythical child as the inarticulate one, the little Tum. "For the child Tum passed out of Egypt into Europe to become the Tom Thumb and Thumbkin of our nursery tales." (893 AE) Hu is the spirit of light and Ka or Kak is the sun of darkness in the nocturnal heaven. "Black Jack," whether represented by the Jack in his box or the "Black Jack" of winter greens or the spirit called "Black Jack" is identical with Kak-Atum. (291BB2)

Shut. Egyptian TUMU, to shut up, to close: Tum was Atum-Ra, the setting Sun, the Closer in the western gate. As the Shutter Up of Day he wears the closing lotus on his head, the antithesis to Atum-Iu (or Heru/Horus) rising out of the opening flower of dawn. (655AE)

Cut. Egyptian TEMA, to cut or divide: Where is the connection with Thomas? Thomas is plagiarized from Atum, called Thammuz. Like Osiris, Thammuz was cut, that is, *castrated* annually. "Osiris-Sekari" (sek=cut) was the dismembered god, cut up in 14 pieces by Set, his twin brother. His wife Isis found all the pieces except his penis, therefore she made him another one called the obelisk. Tammuz's castrated penis fathered the gods reknown in Europe as Eros and Priapus. The **Victim** Tammuz was annually castrated and sacrificed, dying and rising again in periodic cycles.

Write. Tema= writing, book, roll, document. Writing began from scratching /cutting to make marks.

Red. Because the setting Sun is red, Tum also means red or blood. Alcedama = field of blood. "Adam" also means "red man."

Damn. The white man is really the "Red Man" (all shades of red), damning the Earth and bringing all to doom. The biblical story of "Adam" is a garbled story of the making of the white man.

4 James Zebedee Boanerges = Cancer the Crab

Cardinal **WATER** Sign

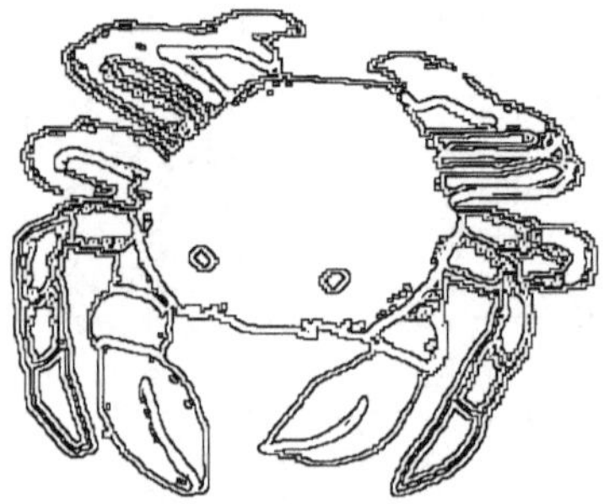

James is derived and modeled from the Kamite god **Amsa** (Amsta, Amset), one of Horus's *four* brothers who became his "children" in a later creation.[1] Each brother was a god of one of the four cardinal points; Amsta represented the South. James was one of Christ's first *four* apostles, with him in the beginning until his Sermon on the Mount. After his resurrection, Christ calls his disciples, "children" (John 21:5). James was also the *name* of one of Christ's *four* brothers. James and John were the sons of Zebedee, which Jesus surnamed *Boanerges*, "The sons of thunder" (Mark 3:17).

James is linked with Water and the features of the Crab:

- He was a fishermen. Like crabs, fishermen are seizers (of fish).
- The name of his father *Zebedee* is derived from *Sebek,* an Egyptian god who was also a father of fishers.[2]
- The god Sebek /Sebag was also represented as a Crocodile and the Great Fish of Inundation. Like crabs, crocodiles are seizers (with their jaws). Crab, grab, and crocodile are from common roots.
- The Gospels say Boanerges means Sons of *Thunder*, "but did not explain why it was appropriate" comments the Holman Bible Dictionary. Now we shall discover its appropriateness. *Thunder* is only half the meaning; Boanerges means Thunder *and* Lighting. Lightning is subtly acknowledged in that James and John were eager to "command fire [lightning!] to come down from heaven, and consume" a Samaritan town that refused to shelter Jesus and his followers (Luke 9:51-54). Boanerges is a combination of the names of two Greek cyclop gods, "Brontes and Arges," whose names mean Thunder and Lightning (or makers of such).[3] In Greek, *bront* means thunder (as in brontosaurus, brontology); *arg* means brilliant shining, white. What has all this to do with water? Thunder & Lightning occurs only with generous amounts of *water* falling from the sky, hence *thunder*storms.
- The Gospels only mention and emphasize the *Thunder* aspect of Boanerges. Why? The answer is simple but it took a while to figure out. If you've ever been to a beach, one thing you immediately notice is the "thunder" of the waves (water) crashing on the *shore*. By only mentioning *thunder*, this highlights the *water* aspect and simultaneously signifies the *shore*. For "thunder" is *constant* at the shore where Crabs live! Crabs are *shoreline* creatures living in two elements (land & water). Crocodiles and turtles (symbol of Cancer in the Babylonian Zodiac) are the same. And in order to fulfill their role, fishermen also have to practically do the same!

1) Massey, AE, 860; HJ, 146-7. 2) Massey, AE, 909; HJ,148-9. 3) Grahm, DM, 317.

Biblical variants or names from the same root as *James* include:

Amasai	Amasiah	Amaziah	**Messiah**
Amassa	Massa	Massah	Messias
Mash	Mashal	Ammizabad	Mesohaite
Amoz	Amos	**Moses**	Maskil

The root of James's name means "load" or "bearing."
What's the crab-connection? Crabs and the turtles are always bearing the load of their home, the shell in which they live! In the Kamite Zodiac, the symbol of Cancer was the Scarab Beetle, noted for pushing or rolling its eggs in a dung-ball across the sand until they hatched. And Fishermen bear the daily load of their draught.

Soaking wet but happily laden with his generous catch, James Zebedee Boanerges is the thundering Water Sign of Cancer the Crab.

Etymology of James (Ames)

Category	Afrikan-Kamite Roots	Apparent Derivatives: ENGLISH:	Apparent Derivatives: HEBREW:	Comments
Bearer	**mesi** • bearer, producer. 321a **mas** • to bring, lead forward, come with something. 286b **am, amu** • to sieze, grasp. 6a	message messenger amass masto– (breast. it "bears" milk)	**massa**, burden, load, cargo, *prophecy* **msa**, bearing; "burden of Jehovah" **amas, omes**, load, burden **amus**, loaded, burden **Mitzraim**, Egypt **Mazzoroth**, zodiac	**AM** (to grasp): To carry a burden you must first *grasp* it just to pick it up. Crabs grasp with their pincers.
In	**ami-t** • it which is in 44b	**im /em** (prefix as in <u>im</u>bibe, <u>em</u>brace)		**Jesus, Moses, James,** and other prophets were all "bearers" of prophecy, which is but a form of inspired leading.
Anoint Child Leader	**masakh** • (m'sakh) to annoint, ungent, pot of oil. 287a **mes** • son, child, baby. 321b, 332a **mes** • to transfer, lead. 324a **ames** • to conduct. 55a **Mes** • chief prince. 324a **Mesu** • a man's name, Moses. 324b	**Messiah** master mister mason Masonic masculine massage masseur masseuse masturbate masticate		**The Messiah** is the anointed child who is the Leader, the Master, and also is the holy meal in the Eucharist! He is born of the Great Mother, and he bears the Loving Life-giving Light or spiritual Mass for all.
Meal	**mes** • supper, evening bread. 323b **mes-t** • grain, cake. 324a	Mass (holy meal) •mash (mixture of ground grain) muesli (cereal) mush muss mess	**masgiah**, kosher-food inspector	
Mask	**mesq** • skin, hide. 327a **meskh-t** • veils, ribbons. 326a **mess** • leather armor, buckler, shield. 324a	mask masquerade mascara		**Mask** is something you hide under or inside. Crabs and turtles do this with their shell.
Harm	**mes** • to slay. 324a **mas** • to cut. 235b **meseh** • to slay, to cut, divide. 325b **mushmush** • to beat, to strike. 295b **msah** • crocodile. 324a (is a *grabber* like the crab)	mis– (bad: <u>mis</u>carry, <u>mis</u>take) miss amiss massacre macerate mace (club) masher •mash (to crush) masticate		**Harm**. The sign of the Crab is the sign of Cancer, the number two killer in America.

5 Judas Lebbaeus Thaddaeus = Leo the Lion

Fixed **FIRE** Sign

Matthew introduces him as Lebbaeus, surnamed Thaddaeus (Mat. 10:3). Luke calls him "Judas the brother of James" (Luke 6:16). ***Judas***, Juda, and Judah are equivalent names linked with royalty, divinity, and the Lion. The Lion was a solar symbol in ancient Egypt. Feline images were only symbolic of the Sungod or Sungoddess. Judas was a royal dynastic name for the priest kings of Judea. Judah (Judas) was the name of two of Christ's disciples, three of his ancestors (Luke 3:26, 30, 33), and one of his brothers. Christ (the Sun) himself is a form of Juda as the "Lion of the Tribe of Juda" (Rev 5:5).

Lebbaeus, *Leo*, and *Love* are derived from the same Afrikan roots. Love is a type of Fire or Light that burns/radiates from the heart. Lebbaeus means Light and Love or "a man of heart" (Smith Bible Dictionary, 352). ***Thaddaeus*** is derived from Kamite *tata*, meaning *father*, –very appropriate since Leo is the paternal sign signifying the Great Father in the Solar Zodiac. The Father is typically represented by Light (Fire Element), just as The Mother is represented by Water. Altogether, the meanings of his three names can be summed up as *Double Royal Blazing Father of Love*, who of course is the King of Heaven. Radiating such vast loving light, Judas Lebbaeus Thaddaeus shines forth as the Fixed Fire Sign of Leo.

Etymology of Lebbaeus (Le-Ab) & Thaddaeus

Category	Afrikan-Kamite Roots	Apparent Derivatives: ENGLISH		Apparent Derivatives	Comments
Light Bright White Love Heart Joy	**Note:** Kamite L=R. English B=V. **le** (re) • sun, light **ab** • heart. (re + ab =re-ab / le-ab / le-av) **ra ab** (la ab) • to be excited with love or passion. 419 **rehiu, reh-h** (lehiu, leh-h) • twin, the twin Lion Gods, Horus & Set. 11BB2	love left Lebbaeus Laban leprosy leper albino (a-LEB-ino)	Levi Leviathan life rhapsody rapture rapport Libera liberty	**HEBREW** **lavi**, lion **levi'a**, lioness **lev**, heart **levav**, heart **levavi**, hearty, amicable **libba**, heart, core **levi, leui**, joined, plural, to wreathe **levay**, auxiliary, attachment **lavud**, united	**Light** and **White** look similar but are virtual opposites. A *white* object will not light up a dark room. *White* appears *light* only by reflection. White reflects more light than a mirror. It seems that "white" people confuse the two, thus ancient Afrikan people, because of their names from the "leb" root, are called "white" in Bible dictionaries.
Father Light Time	**tut** • father, procreator, phallus. 617BB2 **tata** • father. 617BB2 • giver. 865a **ta** • to give. 815a, 865a • fire, flame, [light]. 864b • time, moment. 815a • the, thee, this. 815, 864b **Ta** • God of a Circle. 816a **taa** • divine emanation, essence of a deity. 821b	**Theo** (God) **Deity** (God) **T** (is phallic) **Tau** ("T") **it** ("ti" reversed) title titular titan **the** thee thou this	**dad** daddy dude **Thaddaeus** **Titus** **Daisy** **dais** **day** daily tiara diurnal	**SANSCRIT** **tatah**, father (one's own) **CHINESE** **tai, ta**, big **JAPANESE** **dai**, great, high, huge **dai**, time, period **dai**, title, heading	The greatest LIGHT is the Sun, a giant Circle, giving us the Day, hence Time. From Kamit's "**t**" hieroglyph (hand profile ), meaning "to give," the small letter "t" is derived. The Sun or stars are the Great Givers of the Great Father's /Mother's LIGHT that sustains the Universe. 

6 Philip & Mary Magdalene = Virgo the Virgin

Mutable **EARTH** Sign

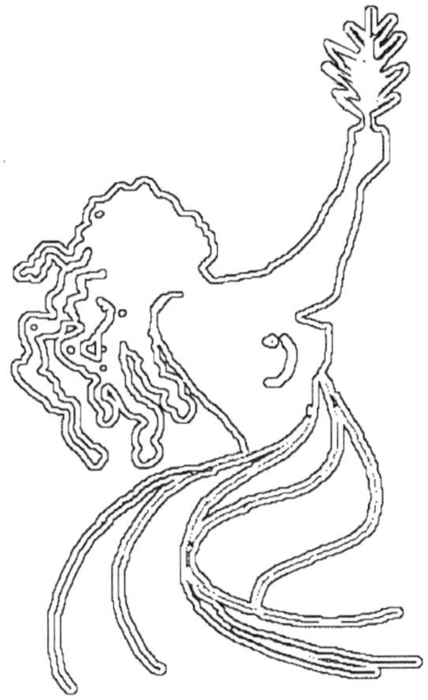

They did their best to suppress, discredit, or obliterate the true role played by women in the *original* biblical books (Kamite Scriptures). Where this was not possible, the anti-women rewriters of the Bible substituted a male in her place if they could get away with it, otherwise they disguised her role using some other literary ploy. Virgo is one form of the Great Mother honored in the *Solar* Zodiac. Her greatest attribute is Love. The name *Phil*ip begins with Love, for "**phil**"(to love) is derived from Greek "**philos**" meaning loving, beloved, dear.

These are the same meanings as that of **Meri**, one of the greatest Afrikan names of the Celestial Virgin, the Great Mother reknown as *Marici* to the Buddhists,[1] *Marratu* to the Chaldeans, *Mariham* to the Persians, *Mari* to the Syrians, *Maerin* to Europeans,[2] and Virgin *Mary* to the Christians. These and other variants of Meri (Myra, Maria, Marian, Marina) are all derived from Kamite **Mer**, meaning Waters, Love, and Mother-Love.[3] Virgin Mary was patterned from the Great Mother as Hathor-Meri, the original and prototypical Goddess of Love[4] who was worshipped as *Venus* by the Romans, *Freya* by the northern Europeans, *Aphrodite* by the Greeks, and *Libera* by the Libyans. On Cyprus, an ancient center for the worship of Aphrodite, Virgin Mary is still hailed today as *Panaghia Aphroditessa*, "All-Holy Aphrodite," in her sanctuary –formerly a reknown temple of Aphrodite.[5]

Mary the *Virgin* and Mary Magdalene the *Whore* are one and the same

Both are forms of the Great Mother. A Gnostic poem merges the two of them: "I am the first and the last. I am the honored one and the scorned one. I am the whore, and the holy one."[6] And it is in the Gospel of *Philip* we learn that the companion of the Savior was Mary Magdalene, whom Christ loved more than all the disciples, and kissed her often on her mouth.[7] Before this book and the other books of the *Gnostic Gospels* were *cut out* from the Bible, they were accepted as the Word of God, as much as the other New Testament writings. The Gnostic Gospels reveal that not only was Mary Magdalene an *apostle*, but Christ called her the "Apostle to the Apostles" and "the Woman Who Knew the All."[8] "There was no grace that He refused her, nor any mark of affection that He withheld from her." Christ said She would excel every other disciple in the coming Kingdom of Light, where She would rule.[9]

1) Walker, WD, 222. 2) Walker, WE, 584. 3) Ibid, 584. 4) Massey, HJ, 139. 5) Walker, WE, 44. 6) Ibid, 614. 7) Pagels, xv. 8) Walker, WE, 613. 9) Ibid, 613.

"But," I hear you say, "if Mary Magdalene was also an apostle, then this makes <u>thirteen</u> apostles!" Yes but Judas got ousted, and according to the recovered Gospel of Peter, there is no sign of Judas the betrayer as having been one of the twelve apostles.[1] This is also consistent with other biblical groupings of *twelve males* with *one female* in the background. Jacob, Ishmael, and other biblical heroes had 13 children (12 sons, 1 daughter); the Book of Judges recounts 13 judges (12 males, 1 female). But let us keep the original twelve Apostles, including Apostle Mary Magdalene, then *yes*, we do have *thirteen* constellations, –and lo and behold! – we have the *original Zodiac* which was the *Lunar* Zodiac you never or hardly hear about. Why? For the same reason you do not hear about *Goddess the Mother* in the Bible, though you hear plenty about *God the Father.*

Mary Magdalene then, becomes the 13th suppressed Sign of the suppressed Lunar Zodiac, a sign which the Kamites called the Station of *Love.*[2]

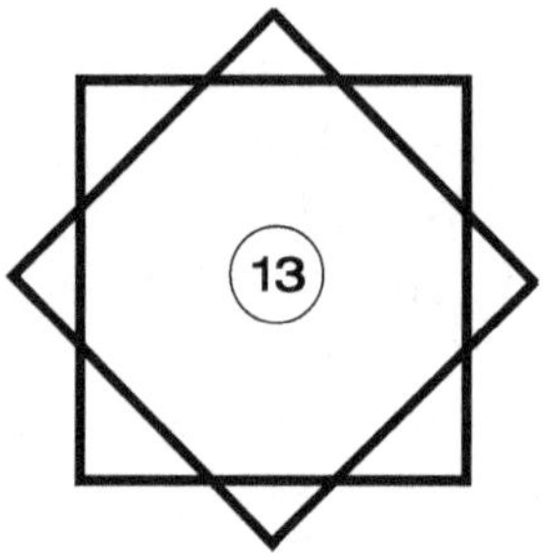

And "thirteen" is <u>not</u> evil or unlucky. People's fear of this number only shows how successful has been the patriarchal campaign to diabolize the Female Principle of Life connected with thirteen. Note that the 13th floor of a building is usually listed as *12B* or *14* in the elevator, outright skipping number 13 –like The Mother is skipped. Thirteen is powerful because it relates directly to the Great Mother and Her three-in-one nature as the Lunar Goddess. This is expressed by numeral 13 itself and the Female Menstrual Cycle which is determined by the Moon; there are 13 lunar months in the year, and women have 13 menstrual periods in a year. Thirteen is also the **HUB**, Capstone, and Number of Completion. The female body has 13 natural "openings" while the male has 12.

Mary Magdalene apparently corresponds to Pleiades,

a group of seven stars (in the constellation of Taurus, another Earth sign) which was *phenomenally* revered in ancient times. The Pleiades were prominent in the early worship of Aphrodite, who birthed them under her name of Pleione.[3] Pleiades was the 13th Zodiacal Constellation,[4] whose "sweet influences" are even mentioned in the Bible (Job 38:31). Lo again! The Pleiades are the "Seven Sisters," linked from antiquity to water or flood-inundation,[5] and respected as the harbingers of Water and Spring. *Seven, Mother, Love*, and *Water* are nearly synonymous –certainly inseparable. Seven is the *midpoint* of thirteen and the 13-month Lunar Year. Seven also symbolizes the nights of a lunar phase. A shimmering rainbow of seven colors appears after rain, which is Water. Virgin Mary had seven children. *Water* is the second meaning of Virgin Mary's name, hence She wears a flowing blue robe. And directly opposite Virgo is its complementary *Water*-sign of Pisces!

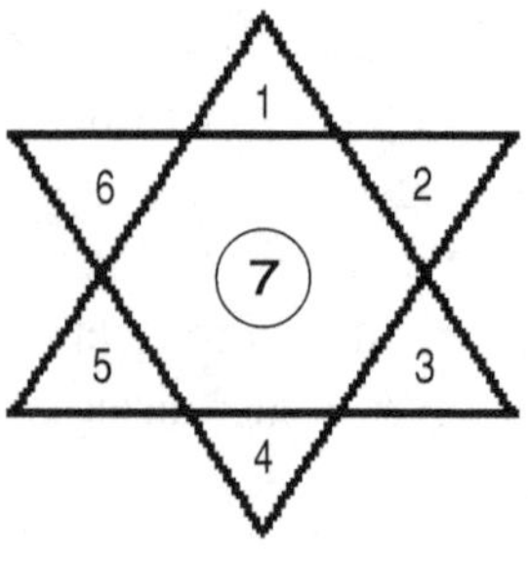

Virgo is the 6th sign. *Six* and *Sex* are from the same roots. And Seven is the heart or centerpoint of the Six Pointed Star (hexagram), an ancient sex symbol representing the "joining" of the Male and Female principles.

1) Massey, AE, 838. 2) Higgens, vI, 317. 3) Walker, WE, 803. 4) Heline, MB, 38. 5) Ibid., 38; Massey, AE, 301.

Seven Marys in the Gospels

In addition to being Virgin Mary and Mary Magdalene, the Great Mother is fragmented as all the "other Marys" in the Gospels, for a grand appropriate total of *seven* Marys, all copied from the *sevenfold* Isis-Hathor:

1) Mary, mother of Jesus
2) Mary Magdalene
3) Mary of Bethany, sister of Martha and Lazarus
4) Mary, mother of James the younger, Jose & Salome (Mark 15:47,16:1)
5) Mary, mother of John Mark (Acts 12:12)
6) Mary, wife of Cleophas (John 19:25)
7) Mary from Rome, greeted by Paul (Rom. 16:6)

Biblical variants or names from the same root as Mary include:

Myra	Mari	Mara	Mearah	Mareshah
Miriam	Martha	Merari	Meraiah	Shemer
Mareal	Maroth	Meraioth	Merab	Samaria
Mareshah	Merneptah	Amariah	Mirma	**Shemariah**
Hamor	Amorite	Tamar	Damaris	Car*mel*

MagDalene, MaGadol, Magdala, MagDara:

- the Great Door
- the Great Water
- the Great Love
- the High Abode
- the Great Mother
- the All-Seeing Eye
- the Great Throne . . .

Mary Magdalene.

Her name signifies Greatness any way its etymology is figured: *Mag* means great. *Gadol* means very great. *Magdeel* means magnify. *Magdala* mean high place or tower. *Ma* means mother and great –as in MAdonna. And the numerous meanings of *Dal* remarkably apply to Great Goddess.

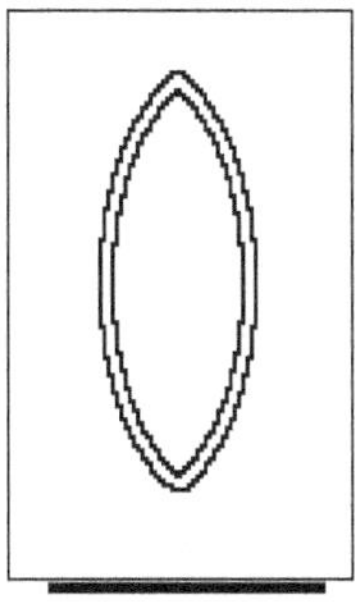

The Mandorla or Vesica Pisces, ancient yoni symbol. Mandorla means Almond. Almonds were regarded holy symbols because of their yonic connotations (like conch shells). They were regarded as having the power of virgin motherhood. The candlestick of the Tabernacle of the Ark was decorated with almonds for their fertility magic (Exo. 25:33-34). The Mandorla is obviously from Kamite RU /RA hierogyph, which looks just like it (but is horizontal), and means mouth, door, opening (hence source/ womb, doorway of Life).

MagDALene, the Great Yonic Door of Life

The "**Dal**" of **MagDALene** is Del, Delta, Daleth, meaning Door, Opening, Circle, Yoni, –Yonic Door of Life. Since Kamite L/ R are one, DAL = DOOR! D is the Delta or triangle, a female-genital symbol known as "the letter of the vulva." [1] Delphi means Womb: the woman or womb-man is the DOORway into this world, via the Womb. Delphi was also the name of Greece's oldest, most famous oracle, where Mother Earth was worshipped as **Delphyne, the Womb of Creation.**[2] Phoenician **Dalt** means the Door of birth, death, and Sexual Paradise [3] Delta also represents the *four* classical elements of Earth, Water, Air and Fire. D, Delta, Daleth, etc., are always the 4th alphabet. Delta as the 4th alphabet signifies "4," but the Delta symbol is a *triangle*. This apparent inconsistency is resolved when the Delta is recognized as a *tetrahedral pyramid.* And note that numeral 4 is really a triangle! Dal /Dar is in Mandala, Mandorla. The *Mandorla* (Almond) is also called the *Vesica Piscis* (Vessel of the Fish); both are a female genital symbol. The *Mandala* is a sacred circular diagram used in meditation to lead to mystical insight.

1)Walker, WE, 218. 2) Ibid. 3) Ibid.

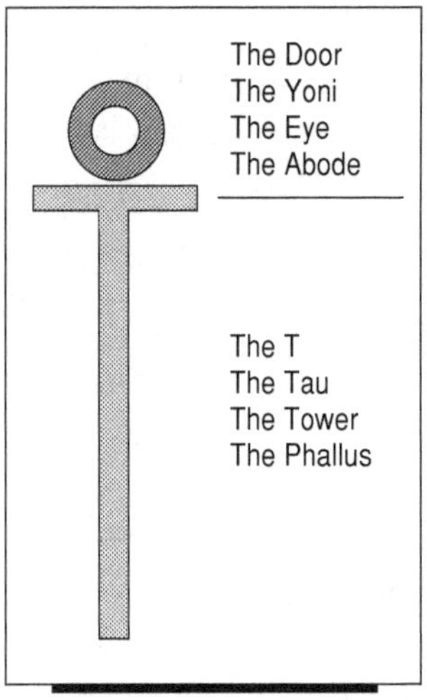

MagDARa, the Great Water

Since Kamite L & R are one, MagDALene = MagDARene. "DAR" is Kamite TER which means waTER! A DELta (triangular alluvial deposit) sits at the mouth of many rivers (water)! Like the name Mary, the name Magdalene also reflects the attribute of Great Goddess as the Great Water, the same "waters" in Genesis at the beginning of Creation. This Water signifies *Pisces*, the *Great House.* But what has Pisces to do with Virgo? We shall discover this next.

MagDARa, the Great Love

So what has Pisces to do with Virgo? Pisces is the complementary sign directly opposite Virgo in the Zodiac. Water = Love, the priMARY quality of the Sabean Mother of Life, Meri Mag-Dal. The Circle and Water are both ancient Love symbols. Thus Dar/Del additionally means Love! –giving us dear, darling, delight (del-light). –And showing us that Madalene is the Door of Love, Source of Love, Love itself embodied, personified.

Magdala, the High Place

Magdala means High Place, High Abode /Temple. Sounds familiar? Yes you heard this before...in the previous chapter, for now we see that the name **Magdalene has nearly the same meaning as Zebulun!** –the *High Dwelling Place* of the *Sabean* Mother of Life. Magdalene also has the same meaning as **Mahala** (Ishmael's "daughter"). **The word ALTAR** reflects this! The Altar is actually a symbol of the Great Mother and Her Womb. Altar = AL (high, elevated) + TAR (circle, abode, womb) (the tar /tal / dal in MagDALene! For Kamite R=L). The Heavenly Virgin was called the "Altar of Heaven." [1]

Magdala also means Tower. Yes towers are "high places" but **towers are also *phallic*.** How does this relate to the Great Mother? Exemplified in the Ankh, the Male Principle is symbolized as the phallic tower or pillar which *externally bears* Life or the Female Principle (male genitals are external). The Female Principles *internally bears* the unborn Life (female genitals are internal). Both are "bearers." Thus the "Temple," Abode, Womb, or Yonic Door (O) sits atop the "table" (T) of the Ankh. The Temple is therefore "high" –it is the High Sanctuary at the top of the Tower. No wonder ***Magdala* was the name of the *sanctuary*** of Queen Mariamme in Herod's triple-*towered* palace in Jerusalem.[2] This acknowledges "Miriam of Magdala" (Mary Magdalene) as the Queen. One meaning of Magdalene is *She of the Temple-Tower.*[3] For the Jerusalem temple had a triple tower representing the triple deity, one tower bearing the name of the queen, Mariamne, an early incarnation of Goddess Mari. This was the same Mary of Mary & Joseph. Priestesses of this temple apparently subsidized Christ and his disciples according to Luke 8:1-3.

Ma-Gadol, the Great *Ma*

Writes Massey, "and as *gadol* in Hebrew signifies the great, the very great, whilst *ma* is a prefix for a thing or person, it is not unreasonable if we derive the name [Magdalene] from ma-gadol as that of the great mother. She is the great one of the three Marys, who is generally put first, even before the Virgin Mary, when these are named together." [4]

1) Walker, WE, 24. 2) Ibid., 565. 3) Ibid., 614. 4) Massey, HJ, 141.

Ma-Gadol, the Great *Eye*

Kamite MA also means EYE or TO SEE, and is represented by an eye hieroglyph. Gadol means very great. Therefore Magdalene also means The Eye of the Great Mother. This is The All Seeing Eye which originally belonged to Her first, particularly as Maat (MA-at), the Goddess of Truth and Justice. Later it was promoted as the Eye of God and the Eye of Heru (Horus) Her son. The DAL in MagDALene also applies to EYE, since DAL means opening, circle, hole, door. The eye opens and closes like a door; it is a circle or opening; and it has an opening (pupil). Recall that the ManDALa leads to mystical *insight* (seeing!), and note that the ManDORla is shaped like the eye. It is curious that the Bible specifically mentions Mary Magdeline as an *eye witness* to key events surrounding Christ:

- She "beheld" his crucifixion (Mat. 27:55, 56; Mark 15:40),
- beheld his burial (Mat. 27:61; Mark 15:47),
- beheld his empty tomb (John 20:1, 11; Luke 24:3; Mat 28:1),
- and beheld his resurrection (Mark 16:9; John 20:18).

To *see* is to *know*. Seeing and Knowing relates to Great Goddess as Maat and the Personification of *Wisdom*, anciently connected with number Seven. As "Hovah" in Jehovah, She has the seven eyes "which run to and fro through the whole earth." (Zech. 4:10). From the *top* of the Tower is the best position to SEE. Your eyes are where? –in the *sanctuary* of your Head on *top* of your body. The circle atop the *Tower* of the Ankh equals Mother's All Seeing Eye. *Water* pours from the Eyes as *Tears*, another word derived from TER. And Mary Magdalene *wept* at Christ's tomb (John 20:11).

Magdal-ENE, the Great Throne

The ENE of Magdalene is Kamite *en /an /on /un,* the same UN of Zebulun. It means the Celestial Waters (also known as "Space"), Existence, and Throne. As Ash or Ast, the Great Mother wears the emblem of the Throne on Her head, signifying She *is* the Throne. "A glorious high throne from the beginning is the place of our sanctuary," declares prophet Jeremiah (17:12). Mother is the Great WombThrone of Water, appearing throughout Revelation as the Source of the Living Waters of Life: "behold, a throne was set in heaven" (4:2). "And he showed me a pure river of water of life, clear as crystal, proceding out of the throne of God..." (Rev. 22:1). She is the *SA*, the *Sea*, the Crystal Lake before the Great Throne. "And before the throne there was a sea of glass like unto crystal" (Rev. 4:6).

Thus the full name of Mary Magdalene signifies:

- The Beloved Great Womb of Source
- The Great Yoni of Love, Yonic Door of Life
- The Loving Great Ocean of Source, Water of Life
- The High Abode of Loving Great Mother
- The Beloved *Great Mother* of Love and Life
- The All Seeing Eye of the Loving Great Mother
- The WombThrone of Creation, Loving Source of Life

She is too great to be obliterated

So She was demoted, denigrated, distorted, divided, discredited and reversed by the chauvinist pens of the Bible's rewriters. They redefined Her Love as lust by rescripting Her as a Whore, and vilified Her sevenfold essence as seven demons cast out of Her (in contrast to Virgin Mary's *seven* children)...

- **But it was Mary Magdalene who anointed Jesus** for his burial, pouring "very precious ointment ...on his head" in the time-honored manner of the sacred king's crowning (Mat. 26:7-12), thus making him "the Christ" which means "the Anointed."
- **It was Mary Magdalene** who, along with a group women, financially supported Christ and "the twelve" by *ministering unto him of their substance* (Luke 8:1-3).
- **It was Mary Magdalene to whom Christ first appeared** after his resurrection: "he appeared first to Mary Magdalene" (Mark 16:9).
- **And it was Mary Magdalene** who was first at Christ's embalming, and first to proclaim Christ's resurrection (John 20:1, 2; Luke 24:10).

Thus, The Great Goddess is there after all, albeit disguised. She is the Door of Life and Death, symbolized as the aromatic resin called "myrrh," which appears at Jesus's *birth* (Mat. 2:11) and *death* (Mark 15:23). Myrrh represented the Virgin Mother called Mary, Mariam, Myrrha, or Virgin Mary called "Myrrh of the Sea." **Immortal Magdalene:** Origen, an early Christian father (ca. 185-254 A.D., an Egyptian-Afrikan who wrote in Greek, exerting a powerful influence on the early Greek church) claimed Mary Magdalene was immortal, having lived from the beginning of time. He showed a mystic devotion to Her, calling Her "the mother of all of us," and sometimes Jerusalem, and sometimes The Church (Ecclesia, another title of the Virgin).[1]

Tamar is another version of Mary Magdalene

Like Mary Magdalene, Tamar, the *first* listed ancestress of Christ (Mat. 1:3) is called a whore. In fact, the only *four* female ancestresses of Christ listed in the Bible are all four forms of the harlot! They are Tamar (Thamar), Rachab (Rahab), Ruth, and "Uriah's wife" (Mat. 1:3-6), who was Bathsheba (2Sam. 11:3). Tamar was the daughter-in-law of Judah, *mother* of Judah's twin sons, and wife of Er, his oldest son. (That's right, her father-in-law sired her children). Tamar was the name of *four* biblical women. Numeral 4 significantly relates to Great Goddess (the digits of 13 = 4). The square was Her symbol as Goddess of the Four Corners.

The four biblical women named Tamar:

1) **Tamar**, mentioned in the previous paragraph.
2) **Tamar**, daughter of David (another ancestor of Christ), who was raped (there's negative sex again) by her half brother, Amnon. The act was revenged by her full brother, Absalom when he had Amnon murdered (Sam. 13:28-29). (Note the resemblance of this with Dinah, Jacob's only daughter, a virgin also representing Virgo –who was raped; –nothing but the chauvinist, female-denigrating, women-hating pen [penis] at work.)
3) **Tamar**, the beautiful, only daughter of Absalom (2Sam. 14:27).

1) Walker, WE, 614.

4) **Damaris**. This name is a variant of Tamar, hence Damar(is). Damaris was a woman who became a believer (Acts 17:34) following Paul's sermon to the philosophers of Athens on Mars' Hill (Acts 17:18, 22), the *highest* court in Athens. She was not Greek since in Athenian society women remained in seclusion. And since she is the only woman present or named, she apparently was a "high" woman of prominence! That Damaris is connected with the "highest court" aligns with the "High Tower /Place" in the name Magdalene.

The 4 Tamars and 4 ancestresses of Christ are one and the same and represent the 4 aspects of Great Goddess or the zodiacal elements of Earth, Water, Air, and Fire. This is indicated by the etymology of their name and the key names they are associated with, as shown in the following table:

The 4 Elements	Christ's 4 Ancestresses	The 4 Tamars & names associated with them
Fire	"**Uriah**'s wife" Ur-lah. Ur means Fire.	**Damaris** (Tamar-is) of **Mars** Hill Mars is the red planet & red god of war. Red =fire, hot.
Air	**Ruth**	**Tamar**, daughter of **David**.
Water	**Rachab** (Rahab) From Kamite Ruhef, synonymous with Hebrew Leviathan (L=R)	**Tamar**, daugher of **Absalom**. Means Peace, a main quality of water. Water is always "at peace" or LEVEL unless disturbed /agitated.
Earth	**Tamar**	**Tamar**, daughter-in-law of **Judah**. Judah (Iu-Ta) means Double Land.

Tamar is TaMer, *Ta-Meri,*

meaning ***Egypt*** as the ***Land*** which was literally the Gift of Water –***Gift of Meri*** (Water /Love / Great Mother), as the ***Double Nile !***

Etymology of Tamar

TA	• ground, earth, land • gift, giver, to give • dual, two	MER	• love, beloved • water

Based on the meanings of its roots, Tamar or TaMer means:

- Land of Mera
- The Land that is the Gift of Meri
- The Beloved Land
- The Land Created by Water
- The Land that is the Gift of Water
- The Loving Gift of Land via Water
- The Alluvial (All-Lov-e-al) Land
- Land of the Two Waters (Double Nile)

Eons ago, there was no "land" of Egypt,

for this area (Lower or northern Egypt) was marshy swamps, partly and wholly underwater. The generous gift of silt (a form of land /earth) from the annual Nile-flooding literally created the "the Land of Mera," "Land of the Nile Flood," or **Ta-Mera, a name of ancient Egypt**.[1] Literally Lower Egypt, the Delta, was a land rained down by the inundations of the Nile. It was the Gift of Meri Mag-Dal-En (Dal /En =Water). Let's visit Massey:

> "Another name of Egypt is Tameri. Ta is to drop, heap, deposit, type; meri is the inundation, Tameri is land thus deposited. ...also Ta-meri read the gift of the inundation, the gift of the goddess Meri who has a dual form as Meri-Res (South) and Meri-Mehi (North)." [2]

> "These derivations of the names from Kam, the created land...product of the river; tameri, the soil and gift of the inundation, show that Lower Egypt was designated from the soil that was shed, dropped, wept, deposited by the inundation of the Nile, and that the natives were in various ways calling it the Alluvial Land." [3]

Kamit was one of the greatest Gifts of The Mother to the World

Afrika was the birthplace; Kamit was the Mouthpiece. It seems that Divine Magic conspired to bring together in one location all the elements required to allow the world's richest civilization to reach new heights in the Land of Mera. Warm beautiful weather, rich ever-renewing soil, abundant food and water, *Melanin*, and much more.

The Afrikans, Parents of Humanity, were likewise generous like the Great Mother had been to them

Like our Great Mother was generous to the Kamites with Her annual Gift of the Nile Inundation, the Afrikans of the Nile Valley were likewise generous to the entire world, giving Mother Mera's gift of agriculture, astron/astrology, language, and civilization to all Four Corners of the World. Kamit was a Divine Oasis (Ua-Isis. Ua=water. Asis is Ash or Ast, the Great Mother).

Modern Egypt is Kamit reversed,

bearing no resemblance to Kamit or *Natural* Egypt, save for its timeless Sphinx and Pyramids, still standing after *tens* of thousands of years, attesting to the great minds that gave it birth (Black women & men). TaMera has become Ta-Mor (as in morgue) the dying land. Dying like the rest of the planet, choking under an anti-life, technological alien culture that is killing everything living, including its originators. The great Nile, Queen of Rivers, longest river the world, is choked with foul toxic pollution. *Dammed* and *damned* by the practitioners of destructive Albino technology, descendents of the Habirus. Dark skinned nappy Black Afrikan people are not in power in Egypt (or anywhere actually, not even in Afrikan countries, for they are "controlled"), nor have they been for decades. They are at the bottom, treated like the *outcasts* they have been made into. *Cast out* like their Great Mother and Her seven so-called "demons."

1) Budge, EHD, 1050b. 2)Massey, BB-vI, .3. 3) Ibid., 4.

"DALmanutha" –the Great Mother Mary MagDALene, disguised

Mentioned only once in the Bible, *Dalmanutha* is where Christ and his disciples *retired* after feeding the 4 thousand with 7 loaves of *bread* (Virgo; she holds grain) and a few fish (Pisces) [Mark 8:6, 7]: "And straightway he entered into a ship with his disciples, and came into parts of Dalmanutha" (Mark 8:10). In Matthew's account, the same place is called *Magdala!* : "And he sent away the multitude, and took ship, and came into the coasts of Magdala" (Mat. 15:39).

Thus Magdala, Dalmanutha, water and "ship" are all connected. "Ship" signifies the Great Mother's Womb or Her symbol as the Great Fish. Greek *delphos* (there's DAL again) means **fish** *and* **womb**.[1] Fish is an ancient symbol of the yoni or female genital (which smells like fish). The pointed oval yoni-sign, called the Vesica Piscis (Vessel of the Fish) is a worldwide symbol of the Great Mother. And like fish, *ships* are in the *sea* (water!)

Etymology & Background of Dalmanutha

Dalmanutha is apparently Kamite **Dal-Ma-Nu**, **Dal-Manu**, and **Dal-Ma-Nut,** signifying the Door/Fish/Womb/Water of the Great Mother as The Deep, the unfathomably Black Primordial Abyss of the Beginning:

- **Ma-Nu** was a Kamite name for Mother Night as the Spirit of the Primordial Abyss that gave birth to the Cosmos.[2]
- **Ma-Nu** or **Nu** or **Nun** sometimes took the form of a great Fish who birthed the gods.[3]
- Massey informs us[4]: the Kamites viewed *Earth* as an "Ark" (ship) in the Cosmic Ocean of Space or Celestial Water which they called the **Nun**. This "**Ark of Nnu**" was the Afrikan prototype for all the other arks of mythology and religions. "Kamite astronomers had measur-ed the earth and knew it to be a globe rotating in space...[which] circulated in the great ocean of heaven." This globe was an Ark of 3 stories or decks, called the "Ship of Heaven" built by the Arch-Craftsman Ptah. The 3 stories represented the Amenta (Under-world), Earth and Heaven. The original Ark was the Womb of the Great Mother, containing the Seeds / ARKetypes of Life: **"She was the primal ark of the unknown Vast, called the waters."**
- Derived from this, India's **Manu** was the Vedic Noah who rode out the Deluge in his ark; the *Ship of Manu* was the Earth itself.[5] And the Hindu god Vishnu (an incarnation of Krishna) took the form of the Great Fish who towed the Hindu Ark. Vishnu ("Fish-Nu") was half fish and half man (signifying Pisces & Aquarius).
- **Nu** was translated into Hebrew as **Noah**. "Significantly, this name was the 'Fish' without the sexually definitive mother-syllable Ma."[6]
- Kamite **Manu** was the *Mountain of the Setting Sun.*[7] The *Land of Manu* was the Land of the West (where the Sun "died" each evening) or the Mount of Manu, Mount of the Sunset.[8]
- Goddess **Nut** or **Nuit** is the Great Mother personifying the Night Sky. Nut "represented the great watery abyss out of which all things came, and who formed the celestial Nile whereon the Sun sailed in his boats."[9] Her image was painted on the inside of coffin lids with arms stretching down to embrace the deceased.

1) Walker, WE, 313. 2) Ibid., 580. 3)Ibid., 580. 4) Massey, AE, 574, 575. 5) Ibid., 575. 6) Walker, WE, 580. 7) Budge, GE-vI, 516. 8) Ibid., 351. 9) Budge, GE-vII, 102.

Thus, Christ entering the "ship" and retiring to Dalmanutha represents the declining Sun,

"dying" or setting at Manu, the Mount of the Sunset, into the Womb of the Abyss, returning to his Great Mother. Finally, the Sun *sets* ("dies" at crucifixion). Note that shortly before his crucifixion, Christ transfigured, "his face did shine as the Sun" (Mat. 17:2). The scarlet robe placed upon him symbolized that he was "setting" (becoming the RED setting Sun).

Samaria, another form of Mary Magdalene

Samaria = Sa-Meri. Sa is the Sea. The Lake of Sa was the Lake of the Holy Spirit in Kamite cosmology. For it was the Lake of The Mother's Holy Blood. To quote from a previous chapter: *Significantly, it was "about the sixth hour" (6 o'clock!) when Jesus met the "woman of Samaria" as he "sat on the well" (well=yoni symbol). And this is recorded in the 6th verse. Jesus discerned that this woman "hast had five husbands" plus her current mate (total of 6) (John 4:18). Thus Jesus becomes the 7th man in Her life... In the 7th verse (7=love, heart, water hence well) "Jesus saith unto her, Give me to drink." (John 4:5-7), and She complies in verse 15 (1+5=6): "Sir, give me this water."*

The above reflects…
• **Numeral Seven.** The same Seven of Magdalene. Jesus subtly becomes the Seventh Man in the life of *Samaria* for the woman's name is really *Samaria* (SaMeri) though the scripture calls her the "woman of Samaria." In fact elsewhere, "sister Samaria" (Eze. 23:33), a virgin, along with her Mother, become prominent whores, near-pornographically rendered (Eze. 23). The biblical fact that they both have essentially the same names (Aholah, Aholibah) means they are the same woman, the demeaned Great Mother.
• **The Yoni.** The "well" is an ancient symbol for the yoni and vaginal canal.
• **Water.** Wells contain water. MER means water (and love). The delta is named after its yonic apearance. Yoni bleeds. Her menstrual blood poured forth as the periodic "Red Nile," rich in iron oxide, the same thing that gives blood its red color!

All this *Watery* talk about an *Earth* sign!

And the connection or justification? Several:

- The land plow originated from imitating water: "The inundation supplied them [Afrikans of the Nile Valley] with the typical plough. To plough is to prepare the soil for seed. The inundation was the first preparer of the soil. The inundation is called Mer, and one sign of the Mer is a plough. This shows that when they had invented the primitive hand-plough of the hoe kind they named it after the water-plough, or preparer of the soil, and the Mer plough is a symbol of the running water." [1]
- Virgo is a Mutable Earth Sign. Mutable and motion are from the same roots. Water moves, flows. Most of water on Earth is flowing in currents.
- Earth is the Baby of Water (Meri). Earth is 3/4ths Water!
- Virgo is the Great Mother as the Food Provider. This was equally, "aqua-ly" true of Her in the form of the Nile (Water). The Nile nourished and nurtured a precious civilization that ultimately nourished the entire world. All crops must be watered in order to grow. And our bodies, like the Body of Mother Earth, is 3/4ths water.

1) Massey, BB-vI, 6.

Etymology of Mary (Mer=Mel)

Category	Afrikan-Kamite Roots	Apparent Derivatives		
1 Love Feel Desire Bond	mer • love, to love, desire, something loved. 309b • tie together, fettered, bind. 313b merr • to wish for, desire, to love. 309b meri • meriu, lover, darling, beloved one. 310a merrut • love, beloved woman, sweetheart. 310a amer • to love. 54b mar-t • favor. 283a mer-t • band, girdle, tie. 313b mer-mer • lovely, amiable. 309b Mera • an ancient name of Egypt. 315a	**amour** **amorous** enamor paramour mercy **marry** marriage merge •moor (fasten) mortar (binder) meld emulsion mulatto (mixed)	melange (mixture) amalgam amalgamate melee (mingling) admire •marrow (innermost -like the heart) marinade merit moral marvel	miracle marigold margariti (pearl) --NAMES:-- Molly Merlin Melrose Merope Amerigo Americus **America!**
2 Water Fluid Soft Churn	mer • any body of water, lake, pool, inundation, flood, stream. 307b • swampy land. 307b merit • coast, river bank, port. 308a Merit • Goddess of the Inundation. 308a m'har • (m'hal) milkman. 284a m'her • (m'hel) milk-pots, vessel • to suckle, be nourished 284b	**marine** marina **mermaid** mere (pond, marsh) maar (volcano lake) ultramarine (*blue* -like sea) margarita mourn (=tears/water) immerse	melt (to liquify) molten •marble (from sea's foamy streaks) moire (ripple sea-pattern) murmur (sea does this) marsh •moor (high marshy land) mire morass	margin mild •mellow (soft) mollify emollient mill (grind, churn; waves do this!) maul (to beat) malleable emery molar teeth **Morpho**
3 Circle Head Begining	mer • circle, encircle. 65BB1 • circle, go round. 528BB2 merit • heaven, sky, celestial lake. 307b m her ab • within. 265a mer • governer, overseer, chief, head, director. 65BB1, 311b	merry-go-round meridian **smile** (a semi-circle!) smirk •marble (ball) morion (crested rounded helmet) •marrow (innermost)	march (border) windmill mell (to wheel round) armor (encloses like the circle) enamel myelin (sheath) **mayor** emir	admiral marshall morning (beginning) •morgan (morn) (to)morrow emerge primary primal mold (source)
4 Plenty Vast Grow	mar • to flourish, prosper. 282b mera-t • fullness. 314b Mer-heh • the Lake of 100,000 Years. 309a	**more** ! myriad mara (*more* in Old English) mort (great number or quantity) **million** ! multi	multiply ameliorate merchant millennium •mole (massive break-water wall in sea) •mole /mol (6.025×10^{23})	molecule (fr. *molas*, mass) moola (money) mohur (goldcoin) emerald malachite (green mineral)
5 Sweet Happy Pleasing	mer • festival. 310b mer-t • gladness. 310b mar • to be happy, to prosper. 282b merh-ta • ungent or perfume maker. 315a m'rkh-t • to anoint, to rub with oil /fat. 315a	**melon** molasses marmalade meringue mildew (nectar)	mulberry myrrh **•mirth** **•merry**	morale melody mellifluous •mellow (sweet
6 Vision Sight	mher • mirror. 65BB1 mer • to see, to look at. eye. 313a, 528BB2 Merit • eyes. title of Eye of Horus/Ra. 313b mer-t • eyes, the two eyes, divine eyes, many eyes, sun & moon. 313a	**mirror** (water is a natural mirror) mirage (illusion of water)	mirador (a window, balcony or tower with extensive view) •marvel	•miracle •mole (spy) memory (images of past) memoir
7 Horse Cow	mer (mel) • cow. 64BB1 m'heru • milk calves, young cattle. 284b mer-t • cow. 314a	**mare** (female horse) Morgan (breed of horse)	mull (*cow* in Old English)	mule mart (*cow fair* in Old English)

Comments

The Great Mother is synonymous with Love. Most words which mean Love are derived from Her many names. When you love a person or anything, you desire to connect with it.

Hathor-Meri was the original Goddess of Love, prototype of Aphrodite and Venus.

Water makes "balls" in the form of bubbles, foam, and boiling. Befitting that water makes "balls" for the circle is a symbol of both Love and the Feminine Principle. Masculine Light makes phallic lines (rays), points and angles.

Abundance or Vastness is a quality of the Great Mother. Green is one of the most abundant colors in Nature.

Mermaid means "Virgin of the Sea," image of fish-tailed Aphrodite. (651WM)

Molly is a nickname for Mary, like Sally is a nickname for Sarah, and Doll is a nickname for Dorothy because Kamite **L and R** are one.

Meridian, from Mary-Diana.

Morpho is an epithet of Aphrodite, also the name of a butterfly species noted for big *BLUE* irridescent wings.

Water • Female • Horse

Now we know why "Mare" =*Water, Female,* and *Horse.* Water represents the Great Mother whose first animal form was the Water-Horse (Hippopotamus). This fact underlies another similar trinity:

Equus • Aqua • Equal

In Latin, **equa** = female horse; **aqua** = water; **aequo** = equal or level. These words are from Kamite **Ak+Ua**, both meaning water (201BB1). But how does "equal" get "wet"? No matter how you hold a container of water, the water always remain level or "equal," maintaining its horizontality. And in Chinese, the word *MA* means both *mother* and *horse*!

Mary (Mer /Mel): Apparent Derivatives in Other Languages

Category	Hebrew	Japanese	Latin	Greek	Miscellaneous
1 Love Feel Desire Bond	**mre'a**, friend, companion **me'oras**, engaged **merukkav**, joined **melet**, cement, mortar **merussan**, reined, bridled **margash**, feeling, disposition	**miren**, attachment	**amor**, love **amare**, to love **par*amour***, a lover **marisca**, large fig. (Figs were sex / love symbols. Fig trees symbolized the Great Mother) **malo**, to wish rather, prefer	**merakee**, ardent **mereemna**, care	**marena**, marry (Maori) **marier**, marry (French) **merci**, mercy, grace, thank you (French) **melange**, mixture (French)
2 Water Fluid Soft Churn	**mrah**, mirror **margalit**, pearl **malah**, salt (a component of sea water) **milh**, saline	**mori**, leak	**mare**, sea **margarita**, pearl **marmor**, marble, sea's foamy surface **merus**, pure, unmixed **malacia**, a calm at sea **mara**, standing water	**Merope**, one of the Pleiades **malagma**, soft mass	**mere**, pool (Nubian) **marmari**, marble (Swahili) **amar**, pool of water(Maori) **mero**, current of water (Maori) **marr**, sea (Norse) **mar**, sea (Spanish) **meer**, sea (German) **mer**, sea (French) **mare**, pool, pond (French) **marais**, marsh (French)
3 Circle Head Begining	**marom**, height, sky, heavens **amir**, crown of tree, treetop **me'ura**, den, cave (womb symbol) **more**, instructor, guide **mora**, female teacher	**mari**, ball **maru**, circle, ring **marui**, circular, spherical **marumeru**, to make round **markiri**, completely, entirely			**mure-mure**, go round and round (Maori) **marae**, enclosure, yard (Maori) **mero**, whirling (Maori) **mere**, mother, origin, source (French)
4 Plenty Vast	**marbe**, much, greatly, increaser **merubbe**, much, multiple, multi-	**amari**, too much, excessively, excess, surplus, remainder **amaru**, to remain, be too much, be in excess	**multus**, much, many	**murios**, countless **muriad**, 10,000	
5 Sweet Happy Pleasing	**marnin**, gladdening **mirus**, wonderful **mar'heev**, resplendant		**mel, mellis**, honey **melimela**, honey apples **melior**, better **mulsus**, honey, sweet **melos**, a tune, song	**meertia**, myrtle **meli**, honey **meerodatos**, fragrant	**marashi**, perfume (Swahili) **marrer**, "split one's sides laughing" (French) **mur**, ripe, mellow (French)
6 Vision Sight	**mar'e**, sight, view, vision, appearance **ma'or**, brightness, light, lightning, window	**miru**, to see, look at, glance at, observe, to judge, to read **mieru**, to be visible, to see, catch sight of, look like, to seem, appear		**martur**, **martus**, witness	**mel**, eye (Maori)
7 Horse, Cow			**mare**, horse		**miluh**, milk (German)

Etymology of Magdalene (Mak-Dal, Ma-Katal...)

Category	Afrikan-Kamite Roots	Apparent Derivatives: ENGLISH	Apparent Derivatives: HEBREW
MA Mother Great Water Truth See...	ma • mother. 613BB2 • true, truth. 521BB2 • temple. 629a • breath, spirit, wind, vapor. 613BB2 ma • water, collection of water, sea, lake. 280a m, ma • see, behold. 266a, 279b maa • to see, examine. 266b mha • addition, increase. 317a	ma, mam, mom, mama, mummy, Madonna, main, master (ma-star), maha (*great* in Sanscrit), maharajah, mahatma, moat, moist, moisture, mist, May, maya (illusory appearance), imitate, mime, mimic, mimeograph, •image, •imagination (the matrix)	imma, mother, ma, mold, matrix ama, female slave emun, belief, trust mi /me, from, of, because me'a, wealth, many, hundred Mai, May •matar, rain emet, truth
"Mag" Great Truth	m'qnas • huge, great, Latin *magnus*. 288b mekes • scepter, staff of authority. 330b m'ga • to command, issue orders, to instruct. 289b mak • to rule and regulate, think, watch. 449BB2 • to watch and rule over. 27BB2 mak • the mage. 27BB2 mak • ma (true, truth). 528BB2	mega, macro, much, max, maxi, maximum, magnate, might, mighty, omega, mage, magister (*master* in Latin), magic, •image, •imagination, major, magistrate, magnificent, majesty, majestic	magdeel, magnify, enlarge meguddal, grown, large mg, mage
"Dalene" Delta Door Circle Love	taraa • door. 822a, 6BB2 tiraa • door, two leaves of a door. 823a ter • entire, complete, all. 454BB2 thera • time, season, year. 857b tera • time, season. 884b teru • circle. 513BB2	•Magdalene, door, D (de), Delphi, •delta (triangular), deltoid, dolphin, dial, tiara (crown), turban, turbo (turbine, rotary), tier (= stacking), entire, dell (wooded valley), dale (valley), •endure ("hold"), tolerate ("hold"), interior /exterior, derive, dear, adore, darling, deli (del-li), delicious (del-licious), turn / term, •eternal, duration, during, Dendera	delet /deleh /dalt, door dalet, or daleth, 4th letter of Hebrew alphabet telem, furrow •deli, bucket, pail dar, dwell, reside
Water	atur • to come out, to flow. 97b • lake, flood, river, river arm. 97b • branched river. 190,191BB1 atru • to pour out. 99b • river, stream, canal, Nile. 99b theri • ti sprinkle, moisten. 857b ter • mourner. 56BB1 tur • to purify, to clean. 873a tru • stream, river. 840b terp • pour a libation, offering. 844b uat-ur • water. 80BB1 terp • [=drip!] pour libation. 884b threm • weep, cause to weep. 858a	•Magdalene, water, tear (teardrop), thirst, torrent, turbulent (agitated), trickle, travel, stream, drip drop, drizzle, drink, drool, dribble, drown, tribe, tributary, contribute, Troy, true (water =mother =love =heart = truth), derive, attribute, •delta, dells (rapids of a river), deluge (= del-luge)	•matar, rain tal, dew talul, dewy •deli, bucket, pail, Aquarius tiltul, moving wandering, carrying Adar, 6th Hebrew month. Corresponds to part of Feb./ March (rainy season!) Adar Sheni, "second Adar," extra month of Hebrew year, added in leap years.
"Gadol" Tower High	mektar • tower [=mek(watch)+ter(tower)] 300b m'ktal • tower. 289b m'gatir • tower, fortress. 290a makatura • midgel, watch tower. 11, 27BB2 Maagdali • name of Kamite city. *Holman* 963 tura • tower. 27BB2 ter (tel) • tower, height. 455BB2 • extreme, extremity. 76BB1 • penis. terter • strong place, fort. 840a tir (til) • strength, might, power. 822b	T (te, Tau), tower, turret, tur (*tower* in Mid. English), altar, Altair (bright star in Aquila-Eagle constellation), star (stars are high), stair (= heights), asterisk(star), stellar (about stars), extreme, tall, tally, total, dildo (phallus), clitoris, tree (tree=*ter*-e), durable, •endure, •eternal	migdal, watchtower, tower, high place, fortress magdeel, magnify, enlarge meguddal, grown, large gadal, to be great godel, power, magnitude gadol, the great, very great, large, mighty, noble tel, hill til, missile (is phallic) tur, column, line, row deliya, vertical branch

And Philip is Phil-Ap. AP is an early name of the Great Mother as the "Horse of the Waters"

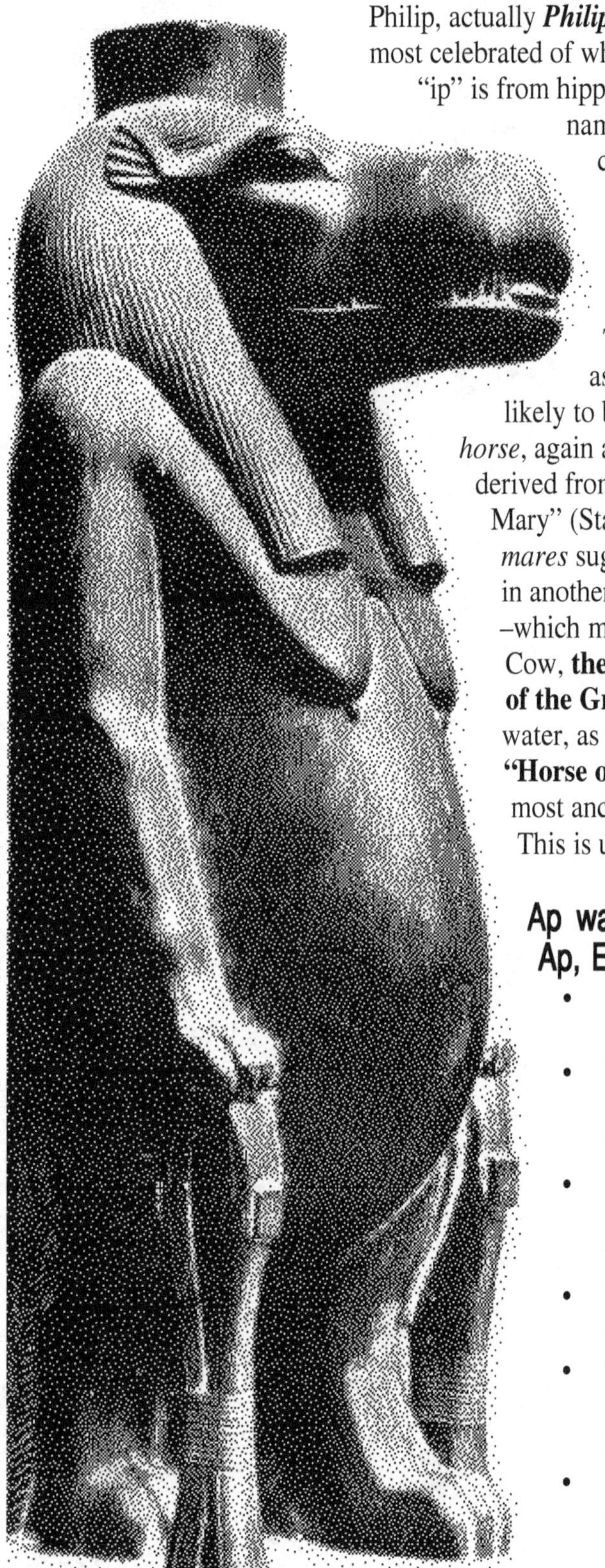

Apt, the First Great Mother, in Her animal form as the Hippopotamus.

Philip, actually ***Philippus***, was "the name of several kings of Macedon, the most celebrated of whom was the father of Alexander the Great." [1] Philip's "ip" is from hippo (horse), making him a "lover of horses" according to namebooks. Remember that each apostle's name was carefully chosen to link him to the zodiacal sign he represented by disguisedly preserving a major characteristic of that sign.

So what has a *horse* to do with the Celestial Virgin? To begin with, FILLY sounds like PHILE and is related as we shall see. A ***filly*** is a "young female horse"–very likely to be a virgin! Filly also means a lively *girl*. A ***mare*** is a *horse*, again a *female* horse. *Mare* is also the Latin word for *sea*, derived from the same root as Virgin *Mary* who is called "Stella Mary" (Star of the Sea) and "*Myrrh* of the Sea." While our two *mares* suggest *seahorse*, the true answer to the question is found in another word which links *water* and *horse:* ***"Hippopotamus"*** –which means *river horse* (hippo/horse + potamus/river). Like the Cow, **the Hippopotamus was one of the sacred animal symbols of the Great Mother** and regarded as a Goddess form in the water, as the Cow was a Goddess form on the land. **In fact, the "Horse of the Waters"** or Hippopotamus, was the FIRST and most ancient form of the Great Mother who was known as AP.[2] This is undoubtedly the origin of *mare* as a female horse!

Ap was *first*, the Apex or beginning point. Ap, Ep, Apt, Apet, Abt, Av, Af, Aft...

- Apt is "the abode and the name of the goddess, the oldest great mother."[3]
- Her name in Egypt ran through the gamut of Kep, Kheb, Khept, Hab, Hapt, Tep and Tev.[4] Egypt is derived from Her name (Kep).
- "She...is known on the monuments as Ap, Apt, Abt, Tep, Teb, Tef, Teft, Kef, Kefa, Keb, Kheft, Khepsh, and Taurt. Ap...is primordial, the first." [5]
- The Hippopotamus Goddess was "practically, identified as a form of every great goddess of Egypt." [6]
- "The immense water cow or hippopotamus was an image of the pregnant female thus of the Great Mother."[7]
- "Teb means the ark. She was the primal ark of the unknown Vast, called the waters, hence the image of the water-cow." [8]

1) Cassell LD, 447. 2) Massey, AE, 124; Massey, BB-vI, 34, 314. 3) Massey, BB-vI, 34. 4) Ibid., 314, 315. 5) Massey, BB-vII, 132. 6) Budge, GE-vII, 359. 7) Van Sertima, ER, (Finch essay), 404. 8)Massey, BB-vII, 132.

- "Her name in full is synonymous with that of Egypt. Af signifies born of; Ap is the first; Aft the abode and the four corners. She was represented as the hippopotamus, the cow, or horse of the waters. Her name is likewise that of the north. Lower Egypt was to the north, and her constellation revolved about the pole of the north. The celestial north is the oldest place of birth in mythology. Kheb means to give birth to; Khep is the womb; and Khebt was the birthplace in the north personified. ...Kheft is the north, the birthplace, the genitrix. She was the bearer, the great or pregnant mother, hence her type of the water-horse, the ark of life amid the waters before any artificial means of carrying had been invented. ...Kheft or Aft was the goddess of the four quarters of the first circle made in heaven. Aft, the abode, is also the four corners." [1] (underlines added)

Her names are the Afrikan roots of countless words which all mean Her attributes.

Since She *is* Love, Water, the Abode, the First, the Vessel or Womb of Life, the derivatives of her names all mean these qualities. This explains why they all sound similar but have varied meanings. They reflect the attributes of the Great Creatress, like the many facets on a single gem. And since Her *first* animal form was the *Horse of the Waters*, or *Water Cow*, Her name also yields words meaning horse and cow, such as heifer and *hippo!*

Biblical variants or names from the same root as Ap include:

Appaim	Aphses	Aphrah	Ophrah
Ophel	Ophni	Happozzez	Happizzez
Epaenetus	Ephraim	Ephesus	Epaphras
Ophren	Ephron	Epher	Ephia

Eleph "El Ap" or Alep, Alpha (Jos. 18:28)
Ephphatha (Ap-Ptah)
Beth-le-Aphrah, "House of Ap."
Epaphroditus, "favored by Aphrodite or Venus," appropriately in the Book of *Philip*pians 2:25.
Apphia, in the Book of *Phile*mon, greeted by Paul as "beloved," plus followed by Arc*hippus* (hippus= hippo, horse) v.2
Appiiforum, "forum of Appius" (Acts 28:15).
Appaim, "nostrils," a prominent feature of horses!
Hephzibah, "my delight is in her." [2]
Zarephath (Sar-Apt, Sar-Ep)

1) Massey, BB-vI, 314, 315. 2) Holman BD, 634.

Etymology of Ap (Ab, Av, Af).

Its Other Forms: Khep /Kheb, Hap /Hab,Tep /Tev, Seb /Sev.

And Background of the Feminine Principle.

Interchangeable letters are **p** /**f** /**v**; **b** /**v**, often **v** /**w**, & Kamite **l** /**r**. Thus:

ap	/ **ab**	/ **af**	/ **av**
kap	/ **kab**	/ **kaf**	/ **kav**
hap	/ **hab**	/ **haf**	/ **hav**
sap	/ **sab**	/ **saf**	/ **sav**

Derivatives preceded by a dot (•) appear in more than one category. The categories of derivatives are related like facets on a gem. A single Egyptian word often has multiple meanings (which are distinguished by its hieroglyphics).

a, b = columns in *An Egyptian Hieroglyphic Dictionary*. **BB** = *Book of the Beginnings* (vol. 1 or 2).
WE = *Women's Encyclopedia of Myths & Secrets*. **AE** = *Ancient Egypt: Light of the World*.

Category	Afrikan-Kamite Roots	Apparent Derivatives	Comments
1 **Mother** **Female** **Source** **First** **"The Deep"**	**Ap** • (Apt, Af, Aft, Av) The Abode & name of the oldest Great Mother. **af** • born of. 67BB1 **Ap, Kap, Khep** • "The First" 314BB1 **khab** • to give birth to. 132BB2 **Tepht** • source, well of "the deep." 300AE • name of the Abyss. **teph-t** • abyss, source, hole of a snake. 5BB2 **Tef** • a name of the Great Mother; source of Sanscrit *deva*. 277AE **Tep** • "first." The Genetrix. 132BB2 **tep** • to breath, inhale (source of *Dove* as symbol of the Holy Spirit). 132BB2	**•Love** Life live •aleph •alpha **elephant** **•calf** **heifer** •eve of off wife ab- (from) after away leave type epithet eponym (= Ap-Name or source name) aboriginal cavity cleft •groove •grove ovary ovum •oval •ovoid **Divine** **dove** **deva** The Absolute The Abyss The Deep deep depth dawn (=davn) conceive conception inception —— NAMES: —— Eve Epps Apas Upanishads •Aphrodite April **Afliae** Priapus •Cupid Jehovah Zebulon Sheba "Seven" Shiva **•Ethiopia** **•Utopia** **Egypt** Coptic Merope Europa **Europe** Capricorn	***Aleph*** is really Al-Ap, El-Af, or Goddess Ap. Coptic and Greek ***Alpha,*** and Hebrew ***Aleph*** all signify "beginning" and are all the *first* letter of their respective ***alphabets***, being derived from *two* Afrikan names meaning *first*. (Ali + Ap) The **elephant's** head is an exaggeration of the *aleph* shape (horned bovine head). **Tef** is the true source of the word **Divine**. **Deep** = De-Ep, Delta or Door of Ap. Deep and dept are from the Mother's name as Teph-t. **Apsis**, "point of greatest or least distance of the orbit of a celestial body from a center of attraction. " Corresponds to least/greatest or depth/ height. The Great Mother is "The Deep" and "The High." **Eponym**, a person whose name is thought to be the source of the name of something, such as a country. Example: Romulus is the eponym of Rome. [eponym = Ap-Nam or first name] ***Eve*** (period immediatly preceding a holiday or event) is derived from Old English ***aefen,*** meaning the evening or *Night*, corresponding to the Primeval Darkness *preceding* the Creation in Genesis. "**Eve**" was First and preceded all; even the Bible calls ***Eve*** the "Mother of All Living" (Gen. 3:20). ***Evening***! Blacker than the deepest "evening," She is the background, "blackground" bearing the stars, Mother of all the lights of heaven. She is Hovah in Jehovah. The original "Utopia" was the Womb of the Great Mother. The words Ethiopia and Utopia are one. Ethiopia means more than "burnt faced"; really it is named after the Source, just like the word Egypt. **Afliae:** "primal matriarchs" led by the Great Mother as Freya in Europe

Etymology of AP (Khep, Hap,Tep, Sab) & the Female Principle

Category	Afrikan-Kamite Roots	A. Derivatives
2 **Love** **Feel** **Desire** **Bond** **Sex**	**ab** • "Mother-given Heart Soul." 375wems • to desire, wish for, to love. 5, 10a, 9BB2 **abeb, abebu, abeb-t** • to love, wish for, to desire. 4b **anup** • together. 15BB2 **nahp** • conjunction, copulate. 13, 15BB2 **ab** • (**abab**) to weave. 116b **Abuti** • the two weavers, Isis and Nephthys. 116b **teph** • apple. 877b **Kefa** • "tied up a knot of time, hence her symbol of the Tie." • to lay hold, grip. 132BB2	**•Love**! **left** (side containing heart) •libido **•Aphrodite** **aphrodisiac** **apple** agape affair affection affect (the "archaic" meaning of ***affect***, "To fancy; love.") affiliate affinity affiance affable devote? **hope** adopt opt option appetite avarice avid •appreciate covet •enrapt (sex is enrapting & in-wraping) **Yippee**! **•Cupid** cupidity couple **copulate** **copper** **Cypress** nuptial synapse **weave** hover waver (hover & waver is the back & forth movement in sex /weaving) glove •gravity **•papyrus** **fabric** **•paper** **keep** **keeper**

Comments

The Great Mother is synonymous with Love.
Most of the words meaning Love are derived from Her many names. When you love a person or anything, you desire to connect/bond with it.

Left = Love!
The left side of the body is the Feminine side (which is why it has been diabolized) and also the side containing the Heart! **Left** is a variant of **Love**, derived from Le-Ab (Re-Ab), Le-Af. Ab =heart, love. Re (Ra) =light. Love is Light from the Heart! (See Etymology of Levi)

Aphrodite the Goddess of Love, is a combination of two names of the Goddess; Afro-Diti. Diti or **Aditi**, Mother of all the lights of heaven, is described in Revelation as "the woman clothed with the sun," identified as Virgin Mary. ***Aphrodisiac***: arousing or intensifying sexual desire. The month of ***April***, named in Her honor.

Ap is apparently synonymous with ***AB***, the Kamite word for heart or "Mother-given Heart-Soul," which was the most important of the seven souls bestowed by the seven birth-goddesses (Hathors), the soul that would be weighed on the balances by Goddess Maat in the underworld Hall of Judgement after death. **In the underworld, the deceased not only addressed his heart as his "mother" but also "considered his heart to be the source of his life and being,"** (Budge, EHD, 144) which is what the Great Mother *is*. She is ***Love***, a word itself derived from her name **Ab**. (See etymology of Levi or Lebbaeus (pages 199 / 292).

Apple =Ap-El or Ab-El, hence Goddess Ap or Heart of Ap. The apple was a heart symbol; the "apple of one's eye" is beloved. In Vedic and Gypsy myths, the apple was represented as the "heart-soul." (362 WE) The Apple was the Goddess' sacred heart of immortality throughout Europe. (48WE) Hidden within the apple is a "**Kore**," another form of the Great Mother. **Virgin Kore (Core) was the *Heart*-Soul of the Earth**, and gives her name to kernal, care, and cardia, the heart. An apple transversely cut reveals her symbol, the 5-pointed star in a circle, which was also the Kamite hieroglyph for the Underworld Womb. (49 WE) The island paradise of Arthurian legend was magic **Avalon**, meaning Apple-Land. And horses love apples!

Made for each other, the male and female genitals ***aptly*** fit together; ***apt*** (fit) is from Latin ***aptus***, fitted to, fastened to (fastened to in sex). Struck by ***Cupid***, the god of erotic love, lovers are drawn together, full of ***cupiditas*** (eager desire, passionate longing, invariably causing them to ***copulate***, a word from Latin ***copula*** (bond, tie). Her island of ***Cyprus*** was a center for ***copper***, the hottest colored metal, akin with the warmth of love and sexual fire.

Weave, a modest word of unsuspected significance! *W* is really *UU* (*double* U). ***Woof*** or ***weft*** = the *horizontal* threads in ***woven*** fabric. Vertical threads = the "warp," which also means to twist, a meaning likely acquired from the twisting necessary to make yarn or thread. ***Weave*** is defined as "To make (cloth) by interlacing the threads of the weft and the warp on a loom." The same dictionary classifies *weave* with *wave* and German ***wab***, "to move back and forth." So where's the connection with Love or Ap (Av)? In the process itself as well as the results. **Weaving then, is a type of *sex*.** Sex is the union of the male and female, and is characterized by "back and forth" movement. Sex is the Creative Principle working through the physical body; outcome = baby. Weaving is the "back and forth" union of vertical (male) and horizontal (female) threads. (Masculine Fire is always *vertical*; Feminine Water is always *horizontal*.) The "child" of this creative union-process is ***fabric***.

Etymology of AP (*Khep, Hap, Tep, Sab*) *& the Female Principle*

Category	Afrikan-Kamite Roots	Apparent Derivatives	Comments
3 Water Fluid Fresh Soft	**ap** • water, pure water. 200BB1 • liquid, first essence. **ap, af** • the first. as liquid -an essence of life. 183BB1 **ab** • purify, make clean. 117a **abu** • libations, purifications, cleansings. 117a **ab-t** • pure or holy. 38b **ab** • be thirsty. 4b **tebu** • to draw liquid. 183BB1 **beb** • well, exhale. 52BB1 **Hapi** • "the soul of water" God of the Nile... **agap** • flood, rainstorm. 95b **agab** • celestial waters, any large mass of water. 12a **tef** • drip, drop. 57BB1	libation, ablution, wave, sap, sob, soup, soap, sip, precipitation, drip, drop, dribble, tap, ebb, effluent, dew (=dev, tef) **soft**, sofa, ebb, **weep**, lube, lubrication, gravy, grieve (tears=water), baptise, sober, sobriety, imbibe, bibulate, • bib (drink, to bubble, well forth)	The Great Mother is symbolyzed by the Moon which **ebbs** and waxes. ***Hapi:*** Though presented as male, he has pendulous breasts & pregnant belly because he was originally a form of the Great Mother. **Naturally, Water makes "balls" (bubbles, foam, froth, boiling).** The sea is ever foaming, especially at the shore. Water (surface) is smooth and it "smooths" the hardest, most jagged rock /will wear it down –making it smooth (like itself). Rounded. Circular. Like pebbles on the beach. Water forms or take on circular shape and moves in circles (swirls, vortex) and flows in curves (winding rivers). Circles, curves, smoothness, etc. are traits of Love. Its opposite,the Male Principle as Light, moves in straight lines, creating angles.
4 Abode Dwelling	**abut** • abode. 49BB1 **ap-t** • house, dwelling place.41b **apa** • house, dwelling, harim. 42a **teph-t** • cave, cavern, hole in the ground. 877b	**abode**, abide, habitat, habitation, **•abyss**, heaven, haven, abode, abbey, •appse, sepulture, crypt **crib**, chapel, tavern, •tabernacle, cave, cavity, cove, cavern, •grave, cabin, •cab	The **cave** and **grove** were popular womb symbols in ancient religions. She is "The Old First Mother....Maker of the starry revolutions, of Cycles, and the Mother of the earliest year in time..." (Churchward, SS, 99) ***Evolution***. Volution is from *volvere*, to roll, turn round, *revolve*. Evolution is **Eve**-Volution; the revolving of Her Great Wheel called the Zodiac, which is ***ever*** turning, eternally spinning like all the atoms, planets, stars, and galaxies in Creation. ***Ever***. She is *eternal*, another word for Time, a *Circle* ***ever*** turning, really the Zodiac! –the Universe or Yoni-verse! **Time is but a circle, cycle.**
5 Circle Opening Ball	**api** • winged disk symbol. 2BB2 **af** • to turn, twist, revolve.43b **teb** • cycle of time. 827a **Upi** • Opener of time. Deity with whose existence time began. 163a **upi** • opener. 160b **uba** • to open, penetrate, invade. 158b **ap** • opener. 68BB1 **up** • to open, to open up, to decree, to judge. 160b **bab** • going and being round. • circle, enclosure, to go around. 483BB1 **beb** • well, exhale. 52BB1 • hole, circle, around. 51BB1	•hub (of *Wheel*), evolution, epoch, open, opening, loop, hoop, aperture, gap, •agape (wide open) •cave, caviar, cobble, chaplet (head-wreath), •grave, globe, globule, bobbin, bubble, pebble, boob (breast), •paps (breasts)	**Circle** is an opening; circle/oval=symbol of the Doorway of the Womb. The Womb is the Doorway to this world. Circle/Oval is a symbol of the Womb and the Yoni. Woman = wombman. Circle is symbol of Love and the Yoni. The Valentive originates from the shape of the female genital. ***Agape*** with ***Agape*** ("Open with Love") English ***agape*** means "wide open" or a state of wonder as with the mouth wide open. Greek ***agape*** means love. Both words are from the same Afrikan source which also unites them, for Ap the Great Mother *is* Love, and life everflows from the Door (Opening) of Her Womb which birthed Water. (Kamite MER means water and love). Agape is Kamite *ag* (water) + Ap. A ***gap*** is a ***"cleft"***; ***gape*** is a "large opening."
6 Vessel Hold Enclose Hide Cover	**ab** • vase. 382 **tep** • pot, urn, large vessel. 877b • coffer, box, chest. 876b **tepu** • vase, vessal, pot. 877a **abt** • to shut, to bolt in. 5a **Teb** • ark. 132BB2	•paps (breasts), keep, cup, cupola, tub, goblet, canopy, •cover, coffer, coffin, coven, envelop, fabric **paper**, •papyrus, apron, •cape, drapes, •tabernacle, tablet, sleeve, slip, slipper, crypt, cryptic, sepulcher, tapestry, web	With **fabric** comes the means to **cover**. A cover makes something hidden; it is always **over** or enclosing something. (Compare cover/over with layer, level.) This is a major aspect of the Female Principle. It "encloses" the phallus and fetus. And the womb is hidden. As the Circle (O) it sits over/upon the T of the Ankh. The mother, especially, "protects" the young. And when you love someone, you often "enclose" them in the circle of your arms (hugging). **Paper is a vessel!** Paper "holds" words /symbols. The symbols are vessels themselves! And the words "go into" us –we too are "vessels"! **"Teb means the ark.** She was the primal ark of the unknown Vast, called the waters, hence the image of the water-cow." (132BB2)

Etymology of AP(Khep, Hap, Tep, Sab) & the Female Principle

Category	Afrikan-Kamite Roots	Apparent Derivatives	
7 Level Middle Peace Seven	**ap** • equal or even. 3BB2 **ap** • heart, middle. 37b **hotep** • peace **shept** • seven. 149, 359BB2 **hept** • seven. 149, 359BB2 **Khept /Hept** • peace & plenty. 145BB2 **Sefekh / Hept** • Goddess of the Seven. 132BB2	**Libra** Liberty equilibrium level layer even sleep appease apt aptitude adapt **oppose** opposite appose **apsis**	woof /weft average half? medi<u>eva</u>l prim<u>eva</u>l aviation aviary **•hub** **Seven** sabbath September heptad heptagon **Hyssop**
8 Warmth Light Food	<u>ab</u>at • light. 5a <u>af</u>er • to burn, to be hot. 6a tep • shine upon, illumine. 877b <u>af</u>it • flame, fire. 6a tap • bread. 76BB2 t<u>ef</u>a • abundance of food. 877b t<u>eb</u>en • grease, fat. 828a	**Deva** (shining one) **Divine** <u>af</u>fervent f<u>ev</u>er fl<u>av</u>escent li<u>po</u> (fat) ale<u>ip</u> (fat)	**•give** pep (energy) pepper peppermint paprika copper (warm colored metal)
9 Apex Best Head Rear	ap • first, first ancestor; chief, head; guide, judge. 1BB2 • top of anything, the forepart. up • top of the head, the crown, the skull, covering for the head 163a • leader, chief. 160b/161a tep • the top of anything, head, point, tip, beginning of journey. (828a) "The head or headland in Egyptian is Ap (or Tep), and the same word signifies the chief, the first.." 323AE	apex apogee epitome •aleph •alpha cape (projecting land point) up upper over lift loft aloft hyper hypo above top tip super superb superior	**heaven** el<u>ev</u>ate optimum apropo apt appropriate copacetic cap capital chapiter capitalize capitol capitate decapitate captain principal chief chaperon <u>af</u>ter aft (rear) *hip (rear)
10 Plenty Vast Yield	**afa** • to be filled, satisfied. 51BB1 **uben** • to be <u>abun</u>dant, to overflow. 159b **tefa** • abundance of food. 877b **ab-t** • gift, offering, sacrifice. 4a **af-t** • gift, offering, present. 4a **papa** • to bring forth, to bear, give birth to. 233b **Khept /Hept** • plenty. 145BB2	opulent opal abundant abound copius copy cornucopia (horn of plenty) **have** ave (to have) habit (is frequent) often offer life baby pupa puppy	puberty population <u>supp</u>ly **shop** ever every aye (always, ever) walloping affluent appreciate (grow) give gift heap avalanche heavy group

Comments

Even: She is "the Waters" and water is always ***even*** (horizontal, flat). **Even is in <u>seven</u>.**

Libra! –the Scales of Balance.
When you are in balance, you have peace.
Heart is in the MIDDLE.

Hyssop heals. Hyssop = As+Ap (Isis-Ap). It is mentioned numerous times in the Bible. Healing means bringing into balance, making "whole".

The word LEVEL perfectly expresses levelness or balance by its very symmetry. It begins & ends with the same letter; has a V (like the fulcrum) in the middle; is spelled & pronounced the same whether backwards or forward. Level or EVEN-ness is a major trait of water; it remains even no matter how you hold it! Its surface is smooth / flat / even. When water or anything is "even" it is at "peace." Water=horizontal (passive), while Fire=vertical (active). **When sleeping,** you are "horizontal," even at "peace." The **Sabbath** is the day of **Rest**, for it is the "pause" at the end of the First Circle, or cycle called Time.

Apsis, "point of greatest or least distance of the orbit of a celestial body from a center of attraction. " Corresponds to **least/greatest** or **depth/ height**. The Great Mother is both the "**Deep**" and the "**High**."
Hip = rear or last. The Great Mother was one who originally said 'I AM Alpha and Omega, the First and the Last,' inscribed on Her temple at Sais.

Deva **and** ***divine*** are <u>not</u> from the same roots as *devil*, despite what Euro-reference books say! Devil is from two words; *dia -bolos* (through-throw). Some derive it from *do-evil*, which makes the most sense.

All "food" is energy. Light is energy, the "food" that sustains the entire universe. The source of Light for the Universe are the stars. We could not live without the Sun. The true source of Light is God/Goddess, shinning through the Suns of Creation throughout the universe. And all these Suns are generous –they are always **giving**.

The original Valentine's Day was Rome's L<u>upe</u>rcalia, a festival of sexual license connected with goddess Juno Februata (a version of Aphrodite), Goddess of the Fever (febris) of Love, whom churchmen replaced with a ficticious St.Valentine.

<u>Op</u>s was a Latin name of the Great Mother as the Goddess of Abundance or ***<u>Op</u>ulence***, a quality which is exquisitely reflected in the rich irridescence of the ***opal***. As the sacred gem of Rome's ***<u>Op</u>alia*** festival, ***ado<u>pt</u>ed*** from Afrika, the ***opal*** represented Her many colored veils.

Lovers make ***babies***. **C*<u>op</u>ulation*** *increases* the **p*<u>op</u>ulation*** count of **pe*<u>op</u>le***, perhaps **c*<u>op</u>iously***, a word from Latin ***<u>cop</u>ia*** (cum+ops).

Shop is from sceoppa, meaning "treasure house" in Old English.

Etymology of AP(Khep, Hap,Tep, Sab) & the Female Principle

Category	Afrikan-Kamite Roots	Apparent Derivatives	Comments
11 Word Speek See Know Wisdom Serpent	**Apt** • The Living Word. 141BB2 **tep** • tongue. 5BB2 **shepht** • language. 359BB2 **ap** • to declare, show, manifest, guide 2BB2 • wisdom, will. 37b **uba** • to open the eyes, to look, to gaze to spy into, "open thou thine eyes" 158b **up** • to open, to open up, to decree, to judge. 160b **ap-t** • measure, judgement. 114BB1 **apa** • to think, consider. 42b **uip** • judgement, decision. 157b **ab** • snake **hef** • viper, snake, worm. 57BB1 **hefa** • name of the Great Serpent of Life [Great Mother /Kundalini of the caduceus, Uraeus]. 342BB2 **hefnr** • lizard. 57BB1	**eye** cyclop optic optical myopia ophthalmology scope telescope obvious peep appear apparent **Shabda** (sound, Holy Sound Current, Sanscrit) alphabets graph ? graphic grafitti papyrus •paper (holds words, symbols) •Biblos •Bible bibliography sophistry sophisticated Sophia Sephira •wife •**hip** (wise, knowledgeable) option apt ophidian cobra Typhon	**Eye.** The eye opens; is an opening; has an opening (pupil). To SEE is to KNOW. From the top/apex is the best position to SEE. **EYE = EVE,** the **Beginning**, the "Hole" atop the Ankh. **"Kef was the sevenfold watcher,** the watcher whose seven eyes went to and fro through the whole earth." (132BB2) **Hip:** Slang term meaning "Keenly aware of, knowledgeable about... cognizant... Perhaps from Wolof *hipi*, *hepi*, to open one's eyes, be aware." This is a rare instance of the dictionary acknowledging the possible Afrikan origin of a word. (Wolof is an Afrikan language) **The Serpent is the ancient supreme symbol for Wisdom.** Wisdom lets you see very well. 
12 Happy Sweet Pleasing Play	**up** • joy, gladness. 160b,161a **hep, heb** • festival. 61BB1	happy appeal appetizing •Utopia •Ethiopia **apian** exuberant ebullient **jovial** jubilant jubilee jubilation favor flavor savor caper capricious cavort •libido aphrodisiac	**Word or Sound is *vibration.*** And Vibration is a Vessel. Vibration holds and radiates the essence of a thing. **Sebek, Sebag** • name of the Crocodile deity; Fish of Inundation. ***Apian*** (relating to bees) is derived from Latin ***apis*** (bee). Where does the Great Mother come into this picture? As the "Queen Bee" herself! The symbol of Aphrodite at Eryx was a golden honeycomb. And honey, which comes from flowers (the sex organs of plants), was regarded as an **aphrodisiac**.  **Epona**, name of the Celtic Horse Goddess of Iron Age Britain. **Zebra**, a horselike animal.
13 Horse Horselike Cow...	**Ap** • (Apt, Af, Aft, Av) Abode, "Horse of the Waters." **abar** (abal) • horses, bulls. 39a **Hapi** • God of Nile *River.* Originally a form of the Great Mother. **Hep** • "Apis" the Bull [of Osiris] 478a **tep, tepu** • hippopotamus. Tep is another form of Ap. 478B **tap** • a kind of cattle. 822a **ab** • elephant, ivory. 57BB2	ippo hippo hippopotamus epo Epona pony appaloosa caballus cavalry okapi zebra elephant calf heifer	**Okapi**, a horselike, zebra-like, forest mammal of Afrika's Congo River basin. **The calf is the *first* form of the cow.** A heifer is a young cow that has not birthed a calf (thus is likely a virgin). Calf is from *cealf* [cealf = ce-alef!] (see *James son of Alphaeus*). **Utopia is defined in dictionaries as "ideally perfect place."** The first and original "Utopia" was the ***Womb* of the Great Mother!** Ethiopia (Eth-Opia) and Utopia (Ut-Opia) are two versions of the same word. The true meaning of Ethiopia is *Watery Birthplace* (not necessarily "burnt faced").

AP: Apparent Derivatives in Other Languages

Category	Hawaiian	Hebrew	Sanscrit	Greek	Latin
1 Female Beginning First, Pure		**abir**, the first **Aleph**, one, first letter of Hebrew alphabet **bat** (is *tab* in reverse. means daughter)	**apsaras**, nymph of heaven apa, away, forth, off **•av, ava, avati** favor, wish well, refresh, have pleasure in	**apo**, away, from (= Source) **eponumos**, named after **•haplous**, single	**coepio**, to begin
2 Love Feel, Desire Bond	**ipo**, sweetheart, lover **ipo.ipo**, to make love **hapapa**, voracious appetite **apona**, embracing, grasping, catching	**anup**, bound together **ab**, desire **iab**, to desire, to long **avh**, to desire, to wish strongly	**ipsita**, desired, wished for **ubh, ubhya**, unite, couple **apa**, bind, fetter **ubha**, both	**epipothia**, desire, longing **hapsis, haptein**, to fasten **abulia**, determination, will	**• avere**, to desire **appeto**, a longing, appetite **nuptiae**, wedding, marriage **apere, aptus**, to fasten **•libido**, pleasure **cupola**, bond, tie
3 Water Fluid Fresh Soft			**up**, water **abda**, water giving **Apa**, Water; deity of Water **Apas**, Waters, luminous outpouring of the Divine. "the waters of being, the Mothers [Mother!] from whom all forms of existence are born. ...symbol for the seven cosmic principles and their activities." (Tyberg, 190)		
4 Dwelling Abode				**topos**, place	
5 Circle Opening Surround Ball	**apo**, circle, hoop, band, ring, embrace **a.poho**, depression, hollow, pitted	**ophn**, symbolic wheel or circle **ippes**, "set to zero" **efes**, zero, end **ef'e**, carpet viper **afaf**, eye, eyelid	**• div**, sky, heaven, light	**ope**, opening, hole, cave **ops**, face **ops**, eye, sight **ophth**, to see, eye, eyeball, sight (as in ophthalmology)	**aevum**, age, eternity **uva**, grape
6 Vessel Hold Carry	**o.pu**, belly, bladder, bag, womb		Upanishads		
7 Level Balance Middle Peace		**aph**, even **avir**, air	**eva**, verily **api**, also, too, and, even, alike		
8 Warmth, Light, Food			**deva**, shining one, deity, angelic being **• div**, light		**febris**, fever
9 Head, Apex Leader Best	**apo.a.lewa**, highest heavens or space	**aphah**, upper **ab**, first ancestor, father; master, teacher, councillor	**Kevala**, Absolute, only, alone [divine title] **Aprameya**, Immeasurable One	**ephapax**, once **•haplous**, single	
10 Plenty Vast					**opiparus**, splendid, rich, sumptuous **uber**, rich, copious; pap, udder, breast **gravare**, to burden **gravis**, heavy
11 Vision Sight Word					
12 Sweet, Happy Pleasing Fruit, Plants			**•av, ava, avati** refresh, have pleasure in		**• avere**, to have pleasure in **•libido**, pleasure
13 Horse, Cow			**asva**, horse, symbol of "life energy" (Tyberg, 33) **haya** [hava], "the horse as the goer. The first horse that went was the water-horse" (144BB2)	**hippo**, horse	**caballinus**, belonging to a horse

Evangelist Philip's 4 virgin daughters

Another form of Philip was Philip the Evangelist, one of "seven" men chosen by Christ's apostles for certain work because they were "full of the Holy Ghost and wisdom" (Acts 6:3,5). The Holy Ghost is the Great Mother! And Wisdom, ever linked with Seven, is one of Her major attributes. Philip had a generous total of four virgin daughters: "And the next day...we entered into the house [*zodiacal sign*] of Philip the evangelist, which was one of the seven; and abode with him. And the same man had four daughters, virgins, which did prophesy" (Acts 21:8, 9). These four virgins represent the Virgin Mother, Virgo. Four is a symbol of the Earth element of stability, and Virgo is an Earth sign. As Ap, the Great Mother, in a four-fold figure was "the bringer forth of the four fundamental elements of earth, water, air, and heat." [1] Therefore Her name (Ap, Aft) also means four and signifies the Four Quarters (of the Astronomy Cross).[2] And four belies number 13 as the total of its digits (1+3 = 4).

Philip the Feeder, like Virgo

Both Philips are connected with food. *Evangelist* Philip and his holy companions were selected by the Apostles to daily serve and distribute food among the Greeks and Hebrews (Acts 6:1-4). *Apostle* Philip was tested by Jesus concerning how to feed the multitude (John 6:5-7) Providing food is a priMARY function of Virgo, who was also known as the House of Bread! She holds bread and wine as the star Spica ("spike of wheat"), also called Vindemaitrix (Grape Mother).

Philip Five *Sex*

Philip is consistently listed as the 5th disciple in the books of Matthew, Mark and Luke. Virgo holds a spike of wheat with *five* kernels. Five is the heart or core number. The pentacle in the *core* of a transversely cut apple is the symbol of the Great *Virgin* as Goddess *Kore*, the inner Soul or *Heart* of Mother *Earth*. Virgo is an *Earth* sign. And Philip is present at the miraculous feeding of the *5000*, with *five* loaves of bread and two fish.

Virgo is the 6th Zodiacal Sign. Six and Sex are really the same words derived from the same Latin root *sexus*, which is further derived from Kamite *sexen*, "to embrace, to copulate." Six corresponds to the double, interlacing triangles, yielding the 6-pointed star, anciently representing the union of the Female and Male principle (see page 194). Kamite *seshmu* (sexual intercourse) "survived in the Sufi love-charm designed to open the 'cave' of the Goddess: Open Sesame." [3]

1) Massey, AE, 123. 2) Massey, BB-vII, 3. 3) Walker, WE, 401.

Philip Phallus

PHIL (love) sounds like PHAL (phallus). Both roots are from the same source, and often, derivatives in this family are hardly distiguishable from each other, for they reflect two sides of the same coin. This is not by chance, for our genitals are (supposed to be) connected with LOVE. Love, Sex and Genitals are (or should be) inseparable. We even call SEX "making LOVE!" No other human activity is called "making love" except Sex. Sex is supposed to both, make LOVE and make LIGHT! Under the proper conditions, this is the case! –for sex generates great energy. But when sex happens under improper conditions, it does not make love or light. Instead, it makes spiritual DARKNESS and PAIN, which cuts us off from Light or Life. Thus sex also means "to cut." (see Etymology of Iscariot, p325) Sex in the presence of *denial* always makes spiritual darkness.*

Phil-Apple, Ap-Phil

Apple is a beautiful word which may be figured as Ap-Pel or Ap-Phil. Both syllables mean love. Nearly a twin of the apple, the PEAR was also a love-fruit, derived from the same roots as "phil" (phil = pel = per, *pear*).

Biblical variants or names from the same root as *Philip* include:

Philemon	Theophilus	Philistia	Phallu
Philetus	Philadelphia	Philistines	Phalec
Philo	Philippi	Phalti	Phaltiel

Deeper than Horses

Our names have *deeper / higher* hidden meanings...that will surface and manifest in our lives as we awaken in consciousness. It is as though names and words sleep as we sleep. But our awakening causes them to also awaken, come alive, and vibrate their higher meaning or gifts into our beingness and lives. In preserving Her main attributes, the name Philip disguisedly recognizes Virgo the Virgin –the celestial form of Hathor-Meri, the original Afrikan Virgin Goddess of Love who is one with Virgin Mary and Mary Magdalene, the "Apostle to the Apostles." All these forms of the Great Mother are one with Love, for the Great Mother is Love. Her names provide the roots of the words which mean Love, including the word LOVE itself! She is the Fertile Virgin, Bearer of Life, and Gestator of the Zodiac. She is Mother Earth who feeds us. And the greatest nourishment of all is Love.

Now we see the name *Philip* both *begins* and *ends* with Love

And while Philip the *Virgin* may a "Lover of Horses," the *deeper /higher* meaning of the name Philip identifies a "Great Heart of Love." And this Heart is none other than the **Virgin Heart** of the Great Mother expressing as Virgo!

* For more information on what this means, read *Right Use of Will*, and the other books of this series by Ceanne DeRohan.

Etymology of Philip (Pil = Pir /Fer)

To recognize Philip's true or most likely roots, we need to be aware that:

- **PHIL=FER.** Kamite L / R are one! If this fact is forgotten, the Afrikan roots of many significant words will remain hidden!
- P and F are equivalent, hence pater /father, pisces /fish, fire /pyra. Phil itself is Fil.
- Other equivalents: P/B (**lips**/**labia**), P/V (**apple**/**avalon**), B/V (**sheba**/**seven**), V/W (**vol**ition, **will**)

The PHIL of Philip is apparently derived from the equivalent roots **FRE / PRI**, both meaning "to love." These roots are further derived from the FER / PER of Nefer and Per. Since Kamite R=L, then Pri / Per = Pli / Pel / **Phil** ! And Fri / Fer = Fli / Fel / **Phil** ! Amazingly (but to be expected) the family of derivatives exactly matches those of Ap! They are all logical facets of the Fertile Virgin, Bearer of Life and Gestator of the Zodiac.

Category	Afrikan-Kamite Roots	Apparent Derivatives			Comments
1 Female Beginning First Pure	**perit** • women of the chamber. 237b (Ne)**frit** • the good or beautiful, goddess, the virgin-goddess. 371b (ne)**fer-t** • virgin, palace beauties. (ne)**fer** • child, youth, young men & maidens. 372b **per-ur** • sanctuary, a holy place, name of the sky or heaven. 238b	•first front ! foremost •prime primary premier •priority princess prince principal prototype •important	fresh pure purge purgative pristine virgin verity virtuous	fairy Pir (lady -love) bride belle filly Afliae from **frau**, woman, wife (German)	**First**. Number one. The Great Mother is A, Ay, Ap, El-Ep, Aleph, Alpha –all signifying FIRST. Thus VIR of **vir**gin, PAR of **par**thenos (virgin), VER of **ver**neris (love) and PHIL of phil are essentially and etymologically one. **Pairidaeza**, a Persian name of the Divine Virgin who would birth the future Redeemer/ Messiah. Also, name of the magic garden surrounding the holy mountain where the Tree of Life bore the fruit of immortality. (Walker, WE, 768)
2 Love Feel Desire Bond Sex	**pari** • wrap [you hug, "wrap around" those you love]. 529BB2 **pri** • wrap around, to slip, girdle or tie, wrap round with the tie sign of binding. 226BB1, 15BB2	*phil-* pal **valentine!** affair **fre-** free friend confrere Friday **forgive** pardon frank friar fraternal phratry brethren	brother **breathe** phalanx phalange **bride** feel palpitate filial affiliate felicific •embrace **will** **"free will"** volition voluntary	**bless** revel revere worship pride blend bridge reprieve please pleasure prefer play foreplay France Paris **freud**, pleasure (German)	**FOReplay** is really "love-play." **Precious** = pre=fre(love)-cious. Love is most precious! **Pair** = two which go together; are equal; are lovers. **Prij**, to make love (source of modern "prick") **Forgiving** is really "love-giving" or an act of love. Forgive = fre(love)-give. **Caper!** is one with the *capri* of Capricorn the "horny" goat. Goats love to make love and play (hence caper, capricious, and "kid" mean play). Caper =cap-per. **Valentine**. Symbol of love derived from the shape of the female genital.
3 Water Fluid Fresh Soft Pure	**pair** • the river, stream 231b **bar** • a mass of water 213a **per** • pour, pour out, flow out, bleed. 69BB1	pool pelagos pluvial fluid fluvial •flood vapor perspire	river brook Pleiades Pirene purl paludal ripple well	*vari*(water) plasma plastic pliant pliancy flabby velvet yield flexible	**Bless**, is an act of love. To bless or love is to give. Love is a blessing to the giver and receiver. **Freya** (Frea, Frigg), the Great Mother, Goddess of Love as known in northern Europe. Her name as **Frigg** (source of **Phrygia**) became a slang word for sex. **Friday** means "Day of Frigg" which means Day of Love or Venus' Day. **France** and **Paris.** The French seem to be very friendly people and allegedly good lovers. French-kiss (= kiss of love). They are generous with kissing & hugging.
4 Dwelling Abode	**per** • house, palace, seat of government 237b **Per-aa** • "great house" or palace of Pharoah.238 **par** • to surround, enclose, as in a house 68BB1	**Four** villa village palace veranda porch **paradise** *Valhalla*	palapa ward barracks barn **•farm** (**parlor**) dwelling belfry	chapel palace • **pel** (castle. Mid.Eng.) temple tabernacle building barn	**She is forever the Great Virgin,** ever fresh and pure for She is "The Waters" and water is the supreme purifying, cleansing, refreshing agent. **February** is from Februata, from Latin **febris**, "fever" of love.

Etymology of Philip (Pil = Pir /Fer)

Category	Afrikan-Kamite Roots		Apparent Derivatives				
5 Circle Opening Surround Ball	par pahrer barbar-t bul, ber	• around, go round, surround, make a circle. 452BB2 • [par, far, var, val] to revolve, to circle, to run. 232a • knob of crown of South, any round-ed thing, grain, seed, berry. 204a • to boil up, well forth, be ebullient. 622BB2	**Universe** versatile year (=ver, turn) **world** (rotating sphere) Fortuna vortex vertebra revolve whirl	swivel **wheel** sphere spiral pirouette aperture •pore (hole) portal pylon (gate) bracelet	embrace belt well valve valley overture wreath wrist wrap period	(cycle, dot) •spell (cycle) •frame bowl ball bald (ball head) balloon boil ebullient bulge	belly bloat blob pimple plump **•flower** apparel persona envelop wear
6 Vessel Hold Carry	par bari	• pail 68BB1 • boat, ship. 204a	phial follicle pail flask fertile ferry frock	afferent ferous- (coni*ferous*) valise valet pregnant pelvis	breast bear burden •farm pall **bell** portfolio	purse bursa (sac) vial wallet amphora **fruit** **•flower**	file barrow burrito barrel bladder **blood** !
7 Level Perfect Middle Peace	(ne)fer (ne)fer-t (ne)fri	• to be good, pleasant, beautiful, excellent, well-doing, happy. 370b • very very good, for the best, most beautiful of all. 371a • good or beautiful thing, prosperity, happiness, all good things. 371a • good one, beautiful one. 371b	par **pair** parity compare fair precious value	worth (=virth) perfect verity level peer verify virture	versus breadth verity plate platter palm plane	plain field prairie plateau blanket well **balance**	placid placate complacent floor flat fortunate virtuous
8 Light Warmth	per afer (ne)fer	• splendor, to shine 242a • to burn, to be hot 6a • fire, sacred fire, a slow fire 373a	fiery fire pyre warm	purple fervent bright fervid	affervent flame pale fair	fever **February** brown bronze	sparkle pallid florescent flavescent
9 Head Apex Leader	per per-ur	• seat of government, palace. 237b • sky, heaven. [they are above, on top!] 238b	•first foremost •priority •important	brow brain cerebrum cerebral	•baron bar (law) •Pharoah phrenology	govern sovereign imperial cerebellum	pilot will volition
10 Plenty Vast	per-t per-t (ne)fer per	• issue, offspring, manifestation. 240b • progeny, seed, descendants. 243a • to succeed, to prosper. 371a • manifest, pour out, come forth, emanate, bleed. 15BB2	plenty plenish plus plural Pleiades	Pluto flourish • forest affluent ever	•prosper variety pluto plush/lush plethora	wealth paradise •flood frequent fruitful	full fill every very complete
11 Vision Sight Word	per, ber, pera pur per, peru	• to see, vision.. 243a, 219b • to explain. 452BB2 • speech, word, what comes forth from the mouth. 240b • pronounce words, explain. 15BB2	appear apparent •pore (stare) pupil	peer **word** verse verb	verbal verbiage parable parrot	praise phrase interpret prattle	promise flatter pledge
12 Happy Sweet Fruit Plants Yield	per per sha per-t (ne)fer (ne)fer-t baruka per-t	• seed. "to come up or sprout (of plants)." 69BB1, 240a • garden. 240a • fruit, sprout, plant vegetable, field produce, grain. 242b • grain. 372b • plant, tree, flowers. 372b • blessings, benedictions. [bar=br=bl in BLess) 444BB2 • festival. 242a	pleasant please pleasure play foreplay flirt prank frolic caper gambol frisk	prance cavort **froh**, happy (German) euphoric perfume frankincense fragrance balm balsam	camphor • fruit plum apple berry pear persimmon apricot plant	vernal fir fern verdant (green) virid (green) • forest paradise forage	foliage foliose • flower farina barley bread flour prefer •prosper
13 Horse Cow	(ne)fer (ne)fer-t (Ne)frit	• young horse, calvary. 372b • young cow. 372b • Hippopotamus Goddess. 371b	filly **fylja**, young female horse (Norse)	foal palfrey burro appaloosa	bronco caballus cavalry	**pferd**, horse (German)	

Pel /Per: Apparent Derivatives in Other Languages

Category	Swahilli	Sanscrit	Hebrew	Greek
1 Female Beginning First, Pure		**bharya**, wife **pra**, before **purva**, previous, first, prior	**parashah**, affair	**parthenos**, **parth**, virgin, maiden
2 Love Feel, Desire Bond	**faraja**, consolation	**preyams**, affection **priya**, loved one, sweet-heart **bratr**, brother		**phile**, loving, friendly, dear **philia**, friendship **phileo**, kiss, love **philia**, friendship **phyle**, kindred
3 Water Fluid Fresh Soft	**furiko**, a flood **vuli**, the short rains	**vari**, water	**bara**, fountain	**pelagos**, sea, depth **phrear**, spring (of water), pit, well
4 Dwelling Abode	**baraza**, veranda, council-house			
5 Circle Opening Surround Ball		**valaya**, bracelet, circle		
6 Vessel Hold Carry		**bharah**, bear, burden		**phero**, bear, bring, come **phore**, to carry, bear children, producing
7 Level Balance Middlååe Peace	**fara**, level measure	**parnam**, leaf, feather	**peles**, scale **pilles**, make level, weigh, balance, straighten, make a road	
8 Light, Warmth		**prana**, breath, life, energy **purna**, full **vira**, fire		**phlegm**, heat **peer**, fire, firing
9 Head, Apex Leader Best				**prote**, first in rank or time, earliest
10 Plenty Vast	**furika**, to overflow **fora**, a success, **bariki**, to bless **baraka**, blessing, prosperity		**piryon**, fertility, productivity	**pleres**, full **polus**, much, many **pleion**, more, above, **ploutos**, wealth, overflowing **perissos**, abundant, advantage, superfluous **phyll**, to thrive, bloom
11 Vision Sight Word				**•phrase**, to show, say **pareemeea**, saying **phyle**, guarding, watcher
12 Happy Sweet Pleasing Fruit, Plants Yield	**furaha**, joy	**phala**, fruit **phalam**, fruit, reward **parimala**, perfume **pri**, to delight	**pele**, miracle, wonder **perot**, fruit **parah**, flower, flourish, bloom **pardes**, garden	**•phrase**, to cheer **phullon**, leaf
13 Horse, Cow	**farasi**, horse			

Afterword

This section on Virgo is very long! The same is true for the section on Taurus (Peter). They turned out this way despite my efforts to drastically shorten them. The reason by now may be obvious, for a glimpse of the Great Mother and Great Father comes through. And though these two sections take up a lot more pages than the other sections of this book, they are still insufficient to do justice to something so great. Our Great Mother is not called "great" for nothing. She encompasses the Great Father –like Ast is the Enveloper and Throne of Asar; –like the Yoni encompasses the Phallus. And He supports Her (like the T under the O of the Ankh ♀) as the Power (Light) that sustains Life, another word derived from Her name.

7 Matthew Levi Alphaeus = Libra the Scales

Cardinal **AIR** Sign

Matthew is derived from the Afrikan name **Matiu,**[1] which is further derived from **Maat**, name of the Great Mother as the Goddess of Truth, also the Kamite word for Truth, Law, and Justice.

The equilibrium of the universe was expressed by Maat, the fixed, undeviating Law and eternal rule of Right. The Balance or Scales is a symbol of Maat and its oneness in duality. The Scales were erected as a symbol of the *Equinox*, when the two halves of Night and Day are equal in length. The Autumn Equinox (Sept 23) initiates the period of Libra. *The Maat* was name of the Hall of Justice or Judgment, also known as the Hall of the *Two* Truths. Judgment with justice was its aim. Its tablets were the Books of the Law. Its judges were the priestesses and priests of Maat.

Goddess Maat **was the embodiment of Truth, Law, and Justice**. She is the Goddess of balanced relation between the cosmic forces of Spirit and Matter. Maat personifies the basic laws of all existence. Without Maat, life was impossible for She was Ra's food and drink. She wore an ostrich feather on Her head, Her identifying emblem.

Matiu, Mati, and *Maati* all mean Double Truth.
- Matiu is *Mat-Iu*, composed of *Maat* (truth) + *Iu* (double)
- Mati and Maati is *Ma* (truth) + *Ti* (two).

Maati were the *two* Goddesses of Truth, the divine *twin* sisters Isis and Nepthys. In the Hall of Justice, "Maat was often doubled into two absolutely identical goddesses [Isis & Nepthys] who stood one in each extremity of the vast hall." [2]

The biblical Matthew was plagiarized from Matiu,

a title and alternate name of the Kamite god **Taht-Aan**, also called **Taht-Matiu**, who:
- was the divine Scribe of the Gods.
- recorded the Logos (sayings & words) of Horus-Osiris.
- appears as Matiu, the Registrar and Recorder in the Kamite Hall of Judgment in the Underworld.

1) Massey, HJ, 157; AE, 903-905. 2) Larousse, EM, 42.

Thus, Matiu was the original author of the sayings and traditions assigned to Matthew.[1] It was Matiu who wrote the Kamite Gospel of Truth which was altered and duplicated in the Bible as the Gospel of Matthew. Matiu (Mati) was the representative of Truth, Law, and Justice in its *duality*. "The name of Mati denotes the truth, law, or justice, in a dual form and phase. He is the recorder in the Hall of the Twin Truth, the judgment-place of the clothed and naked, or the righteous and the wicked. Thus the gospel of Mati would be also the gospel of Truth in this double aspect."[2]

Matthew is linked with the names *John* and *Simon*

Fragments of Matiu's Gospel of Truth were also duplicated in the biblical Book of John, including Revelation (written by John).

- **John:** is none other than Taht-Aan. John's name and biblical history are all derived from and based on Taht-Aan (John=Aan). Four books are assigned to Taht-Aan.[3] This is copied in the Bible as the *four* Books of John (John and John1/2/3), the only name that is the title of four biblical books. In Christian art, Matthew is depicted as the scribe of the gods, with an angel standing near him, to dictate the gospel. At times he is represented carrying a carpenter's rule or square. Taht-Matiu was the measurer, called the measurer of earth and heaven.[4] In Revelation, John looks on as an angel measures the walls and gates of the new city of the new heaven and new earth (Rev. 21:15-17).
- **Simon:** By tradition, Matthew is the EIGHTH apostle; Eighth (as S'men or Esmen) is a title of Taht-Matiu. The name Simon is from S'men. Recall that "the S'men" was the name of the group of eight Kamite gods who were the builders. *Simon* Zelotes = Aries, the zodiacal sign directly opposite Libra (Matthew). And the Spring Equinox (which initiates the period of Aries) is opposite the Autumn Equinox (which initiates Libra).

Matthew Seven

Seven is the number of Perfection; it is connected with the Circle (symbol of perfection) and Balance. Seven is the Fulcrum or midpoint of 13 and the original 13-month Lunar Year of the original Zodiac (Lunar Zodiac). The Midpoint = Balance, Libra, Equlibrium. Libra is the 7th Zodiacal Sign:

- The name Matthew in variant spellings occurs SEVEN times as an ancestor of *Christ* in Luke 3:23-37! Christ is *Heru* (Horus); one of his titles was Har-Makhu (Lord of Balance /the Scales), the model and name source of *Archangel Michael* (Christ, Heru & Michael are one).
- There are seven distinct sections in the Gospel of Matthew.[5]

Biblical variants or names from the same root as Matthew include:

Mathusala	Mattan	Matthat	Mattithiah	Hamath
Methuselah	Matthan	Mattatha	Matthias	Hammath
Methusael	Mattanah	Mattattah	Mattathias	Hamedatha
Mattenai	Mithredath	Mattaniah	Arimathea	

Hamutal (A-Mat-El) was the daughter of "Jeremiah from Libna;" the wife of King Josiah; and the mother of the TWO kings of Judah (Jehoahaz and Mattaniah [Zedekiah]).

1) Massey, HJ, 159. 2) Ibid. 3) Ibid., 161. 4) Ibid., 157. 5) Holman BD, 933.

Matthew was Levi the Tax Collector, son of Alphaeus

Matthew was Levi the *tax collector* (Mat. 9:9; 10:3) who collected toll or transport taxes from merchants carrying their goods to the *market*, where *scales* were surely used! –hence the connection with Libra. Both weighing (using scales) and collecting tax are connected with MATH, another word from the same roots as MATTHew. His other names were Levi Alphaeus: "And as he [Jesus] passed by, he saw Levi the son of Alphaeus sitting at the receipt of custom [tax collector's booth or place of toll], and said unto him, Follow me" (Mark 2:14). "In the gospel according to Matthew the *"place of toll"* is substituted for the Hall of Justice, in which Taht is the scribe and registrar...Levi, to be joined or double, coincides with *Mati*...who is the representative of the truth, law, or justice, in its duality."[1]

Levi Matthew = Libra Sex, Love, Heart, Tree

The words Libra and Love are from the same roots. In astrology, Libra is ruled by Venus, the planet of Love. Love comes from the Heart, where Life's two polarities come into balance. Appropriately, the Heart *Chakra* is GREEN, the color of perfect Balance and the dominant color of Trees. Heart is in the Middle; midpoint = perfect balance. "Judges were regarded as the priests of Maat. In the Hall of Judgment at the Weighing of the Heart the heart of the deceased was placed on the scales of justice balanced against the feather of Maat, symbol of truth."[2] And Love profoundly expresses through sex or "making *love*." The sex organs are an expression of the "Tree of Life." The Tree is an exquisite symbol of *Balance* where opposites are beautifully unified (see section on Asher). The Tree has the same elements as the Scales, only *vertically*, not horizontally. And Trees are dominantly GREEN.

Alphaeus Matthew = Equator

What's the connection of the name ***Alphaeus*** with Libra? The Afrikans called the **equatorial** regions Ap-ta, (Apta), "the uppermost point, the mount, or literally the '**horn-point**' of the earth."[3] (emphasis added) This connects Alphaeus with Libra. Alphaeus is Alpha, the letter "A" which is said to have originated from the shape of the *horned* bovine-head. The *equator* is where opposites meet face to face, as with the Balance or Scales. And the Autumn Equinox initiates the period of Libra. Alpha /Aleph is derived from Kamite Al-Ap. Al means high, great; Ap also means high and is an early name of the Great Mother.

Matthew Levi Alphaeus

Matthew is the Two Truths, the two sides of the Scale. *Levi* is the Heart, the Middle (where Balance is found), the Scale Itself or Libra, a word from the same roots as Levi. *Alphaeus* –as Apta the hornpoint of the equator, is where opposites meet face to face; this reflects Libra, equiLIBRIum. Therefore *Matthew Levi Alphaeus* is Libra the Balance.

1) Massey, HJ, 158. 2) Lurker, 78. 3) Massey, AE, 258.

Etymology of Matthew (Mat-lu)

Category	Afrikan-Kamite Roots	Apparent Derivatives	
Middle	met er • between. 331a meti • middle. 332a met-t • the middle of anything. 332a met-t • the middle. 332a matr • center, to center. 65BB1 ami-t • between, among. 44a	-m (im)prefix **middle** medium mediator matinee median medial medieval	medulla (core) •meditate (go to middle! or within) Mediterranean media moderate •mutual •meet amid medley
Mother Female	ma • mother. 64BB1, 613BB2 mu-t • mother. 294b Mut • the "Mother" Goddess of all Egypt. 295a matruit • soil, stain. 65BB1 matr • marsh. 65BB1	ma mam mama •May Maia **Mother** mater maternal matrix matriarch matron metropolis	matter material mature Madam maid mode **model** module modulate • mouth **mud!**
Water Peace	maa • saltwater, stream. 272b ma • water, collection of water, sea, lake. 280a mama • fountain. 280a mehi • flood. 317b met • innundation. 322a mehit • flood, essence. 317b mu-t, mu • lake, pond,water. 293a mut • silent. 66BB1 maa • to sleep. 280a	•May **moat** **humid** moist moisture mist	mucus **•mouth** •mute •mutual muti-hei (silence in Polynesian)
Truth Justice Measure	maa • to be true, upright, veritable, real. 270b maa-t • truth, integrity, law, justice, genuine. 270b meter • to be right, correct, exact, just. 333b meh • 7 handbreadths/ 28 fingerbreadths. 316a maser • an unknown measure. 65BB1 metcha-t • a measure. 337b meteh • carpenter, cut. 336b	measure math mathematics meter mete (distribute, allot, measure) metric symmetry geometry	isometric method module modulate **Medusa** medicine
See Speak	m, ma • see, behold. 266a, 279b maa • to see, examine. 266b maa-t • an inspection. 266b maaa • seer. 266b maa • eyebrow. 273a math • proclaim, declare. 276b	maya (illusory appearance) •meditate •mouth muth (*mouth* in Old English) mutter	•mute motto **myth** mythology muthos (*story* in Greek)
Great	meh-t • abundance. 317a mha • addition, increase. 317a meh qena • to fill the bosom, i.e., to embrace. 317a	Madonna main maharajah	mahatma meta (beyond, beside, after)
Similar Double	ma • likeness, as. 269b mati • resemblance, likeness, copy. 277b matu • similar in form or nature, likeness. 277b mati • ankles /feet (a pair) 65BB1 Maati • the 2 goddesses of Truth; Isis, Nephthys.	•meet (coming together) mate match imitate •mutual	

Comments

M is the Mother of Massive aMounts of words in English! Just open your dictionary. This reflects the Mother Principle of birth and abundance.

Model. The Great Mother is the original Model! Since Kamite L=R, then model = moder or mother!

In truth, Mathematics means "Mother Wisdom." The word for mother and measure are the same in Egyptian, Sanscrit, and Greek.

Meet: a coming together. When two or more things come face to face or into contact. This happens on the SCALES and at the EQUATOR / EQUINOX, etc., which is what Libra is all about!

Middle: The Heart is in the Middle. The Middle IS the Heart. The Middle is the most important part of the Scales. Goddess Maat weighed the Heart-Soul of the deceased on the Scales with Her Feather of Truth.

Healing (Medicine) = to put back in BALANCE. Modern (Albino) medicine is not medicine but a fraud. It has a lot of nerves calling the ancient, time-tested indigenous medicines "alternative therapies." Only the "modern" medicine as practiced by Albinos is "alternative." Whites do this a lot with words.

Mud is your Mother, Mudder! Mud is wet soft *Earth.* Earth our common Mother, MUD-er. And Water is an ancient, universal Mother-symbol. Reverse the W of Water and get Mater (Mother!). Reverse Wet and get back to Met (Mater). And Softness is a hallmark of the Female Principle; Water and Womb are Soft and Wet. **Now think about this: Everything you have came from Mother Earth, EVERYthing!**

Maat was intimately linked with Mount Sinai. The Sinai Peninsula was Egyptian and named after Egyptian *Sheni.* In the Egyptian legend, Mount Sheni was the seat of the Hall of Justice where the Law was given. This is the source of the plagiarized biblical story of the Law given to Israel: Sinai is where Moses received the Ten Commandments upon *two* tablets: "two tables of testimony, tables of stone, written with the finger of God" (Exo. 31:18). This corresponds to the Law of Maat given at the great Hall of Judgment upon Sinai. The two tablets correspond to the duality of Maati, or twofold Law and Justice.

The Scales symbolize the Balance that must exist between all Dualities in our lives. Reflecting this principle, the name Maat has two **a**'s, and the name Matthew has two **t**'s. Capital **T** itself resembles the Scale, and capital **M** is perfectly divided in the middle. Both **M** and **T** have 3 points or extensions –a trinity inherent within the Scales. This is no coincidence; there is significance in all things. A = Feminine; T = Masculine.

8 **Judas Iscariot** = Scorpio the Scorpion, Eagle, Serpent

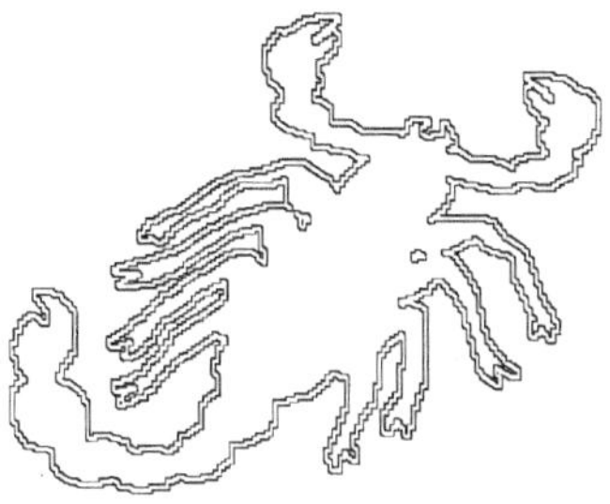

Fixed **WATER** Sign

Judas Iscariot is Scorpio, as evidenced by his infamous deed and etymology of his name. Astrological myths place Scorpio at the Autumn Equinox, where it used to be some 3000 years ago but has shifted due to the Precession. The "Betrayal" is an annual astrological event, as the Scorpion gives the death wound to the Sun (Messiah) when the Sun is going to its death in Winter. **Thus Judas's "kiss" was the "sting" of the Scorpion!**

Iscariot and *Scorpio* are both from the same *cutting* roots

The legend of Judas relates that infant Judas, born of a priestess-queen, was sent out to sea in a chest which washed up on the isle of Scariot, hence the name.[1] But as we shall see, the name *Iscariot*, was deliberately chosen for the betrayer because it literally has the same meaning as the word Scorpio! The etymology shows that the names Iscariot, Scariot and Scorpio are all from the same roots. This root is SEK /SEKER, a Kamite word meaning "to cut or pierce." Judas Iscariot "cut" the thread of life with his "sting" disguised as a kiss –like the fatal Scorpion. Christ became the "Sekari-fice" (Sacrifice) who was *cut* or pierced on the cross. The bite of the serpent or scorpion is a score on the skin which surely leaves a scar. A zodiacal constellation cannot really become "cut out," thus Judas the betrayer is still figured as one of the Twelve Apostles who sits in heaven (as a *constellation*) to dine with Christ (the *Sun*). This can only happen astrologically.

The twinship of Judas and Christ

Judas is a royal name identical with Judah. For a hundred years, Judas was a dynastic name for the priest-kings of Judea.[2] Judas was the name of one of Christ's four brothers (Mat. 13:55, 56). The apocryphal Gospel of Thomas says Judas was Jesus's twin brother whose full name was *Judas Thomas* (Judas the Tammuz or Twin).[3] This aligns with the Afrikan story from which it was copied. Osiris-Horus (who are one) and Set are twin brothers rendered as Christ and Judas. Set betrays his brother Osiris and causes his death. Judas betrays his *brother* Christ and causes his death. Remember these are not necessarily real people but the Principles of Light and Darkness contending. In the Bible, Jesus is called the Morning Star; Lucifer is called the Son of Morning. The name Lucifer means Light Bringer, and is the Latin title for the Morning Star. The twinship of Set/Horus (Judas/Christ) is recognized in the biblical name of *Sethur*, which is really Set-Heru (Set-Horus)! Sethur was a spy of Tribe of Asher (Num. 13:13).

1) Walker, WE, 481. 2) Ibid. 3) Ibid., 482.

Biblically, there are 2 Christs and 2 *Twins* of Christ!

About the two Christs. The "two" Christs are two versions of the same Messiah. These two Christs are **Jesus** and **Joseph**. The parallels between them are many and remarkable (see section on Joseph in chapter 12). **Joseph** and **Jesus** are names from the same Afrikan roots and have the same meaning. Jesus is called a Branch and Joseph is called a Bough. Both started their careers at age 30 and were embalmed (mummified) after death. Five of Jesus's relatives are named Joseph, including his stepfather. Joseph is Jacob's most beloved son and the firstborn son of Rachel. Jesus is God's Beloved Son and the firstborn son of Mary. Joseph was a son of *Jacob*, a name essentially meaning Sun (of the Underworld). Christ's stepfather *Joseph* was the son of *Heli* (which means SUN) according to Luke's genealogy (3:23). Matthew's genealogy lists him as the son of Jacob! (Mat. 1:16). This underscores the solar identity of Jesus and Joseph as Sons of the Sun (Light). "SUN" is the meaning of the root of their names (IU).

About Christ's double twins. These twins are ***Judas*** **Iscariot** and **Thomas Didymos**. Recall that Thomas was Christ's twin whose real name was *Judas* Thomas. Judas Thomas is another version of Christ's twin, Judas Iscariot (just like Joseph is another version of Christ). Note that both "twins" bear the name of Judas! Also, of Christ's four brothers, one was named Judas and another was named Joseph!

How does the name *Thomas* relates to Scorpio/Iscariot? SEKER, the root of Scorpio /Iscariot means to cut or pierce. Recall from Thomas's etymology that TEM (the root of Thomas) also means to cut or pierce. So the Sun (Christ) gets *temed* or *seked* to death (betrayed). And Judas the betrayer died at Alcedama which means field of blood. The Savior Thammuz (Thomas / Damuzi) fertilized the earth with his blood upon his death.

The twinship aspect of Joseph is primarily that he had twin sons which are both counted as distinct tribes of Israel. Another reflection of the twinship of Christ is that he is "the Lion of the tribe of Judah." This is the Double Lion (see section on Judah) recognized in Jacob's blessing to Judah as the young lion and old lion. All these versions are "Thummim" (Refer to Simeon & Levi). The two Christs and two twins of Christ relate to the Double Principle of the Zodiac.

Scorpio, sign of the Great Turning Point

Bearing opposite symbols in the same constellation, plus the Autumn Solstice, Scorpio is the sign of the Great Turning Point. And the Scorpion is the only creature that can kill itself with its own sting; which is exactly what Judas did in committing suicide! In Scorpio, Heaven/Earth, and Light /Darkness are united in the same sign. How's that? The Scorpion/Snake crawls on the ground, living in the Darkness of the Earth; Eagles/Birds soar in the sky, living in treetop-nests in the Light of the Heavens. Similarly with the twins Horus & Set as Christ & Judas; Set-Judas is the Serpent or Scorpion aspect of this constellation, while Horus-Christ represents the Eagle aspect. Horus was symbolized as the Divine Falcon and winged sundisk; Christ is the Sun of righteousness with healing in his wings (Mal. 4:2). Being a cornerstone constellation, Scorpio is of utmost importance. Geraldine Thorsten writes, "For nine thousand years now, Scorpio has been regarded as the most powerful segment of the zodiac. And not without reason. It speaks to us on the vital matters of life, death, and regeneration, and Scorpio's emblems –the scorpion, the serpent, and the bird– are intimately bound up with rebirth and transformation.... The power of Scorpio derives from its connection with the original deity, the Mother of All...Her first emblems were the serpent and bird of Scorpio..." (Thorsten, 191) Thus Judas Iscariot is Scorpio.

Etymology of Iscariot (As-Sekari)

Category	Afrikan-Kamite Roots	Apparent Derivatives: ENGLISH	Apparent Derivatives: OTHER
Man Virile	**Ash** • Tree of Life. 82BB2 **ash** • emission, emanation, issue, seminal source. 9,326BB2 **as-ui** • the testicles. 88b **usr** • strength, prevail, valiant, sustain. cxii, 15BB2 **Asar** • (Born of As-t /Isis) Osiris.	(see Etymology of Issachar & Asher)	HEBREW: **ish**, virile, masculine, male, husband **ish**, being, existence
Cut Separate Pierce Blade	**sekh** • to cut, cut off, reap 685b **sken** • to cleave, to split. 705a **sqeh** • to hew, to cut. 703a **sekar** • to cut, sacrifice. **sker** • to cut, to smite 705a **s-kher** • to cut, pierce. 225BB1 **seki-t** • pain, anguish, despair 703b **seg** • opposition. 705a **ses** • six. **sexen** • sex.	sickle scythe **•Scythians** scimitar skis (blades) sect section sector dissect intersect vivisect segment segregate "**Old Scratch**" sacer •sacred •sacrifice schedule (segmenting) scar eschar (scar /scab from burn) **Scariot** **Iscariot** **Issachar** Kerioth score (cut) **scorpion** Scorpio sequester seclude secure secret scapegoat scape escape **sex** six **sick**	GREEK: **schede**, to split, to cut, splinter of wood **scorp**, something sharp or stinging LATIN: **seco**, to cut **sexus**, sex, "connected with...seco" (Cassell Latin Dic., 552) **sextus**, sixth **secedo**, go apart, withdraw **sica**, dagger **sicarius**, assasin, murderer **Sicily**
Strike Destroy Sick	**sekh** • to strike, to beat, play a harp, beating. 614a **saak** • saq, to destroy 644a **saak** • to smite, to strike. 701b **sek** • to diminish, perish, end, be destroyed, death. 703b **seka** • warriors, soldiers, rebels, murderers, guards. 704a **seqer** • to beat/ strike, to fight. 702b	sack (attack, pillage) skewer •sacrifice execute massacre squash sock (to hit) skirmish scramble scuffle Anglo **Saxons** Scythia •Scythians **sicarii**, ("daggermen")	HEBREW: **azkerah**, sacrifice **zakhar**, remember, memorize (Cutting as a form of writing was the way to remember.) **zekher**, memory, trace
Write Signal Sharp	**sekha** • to cut, incise." 225BB1 **saak** • writing, to write, the writer. 225BB1 • to carve, to model. 644a **skher** • to inform 693b **skher** • to plan, design, picture, mark, trace, scheme. 694a **skhrit** • report, document, plan. 694a **sekha** • "But the first writing was cut or scratched, hence Sekha means to cut, incise." 225BB1	scrape scarp scarify scroll scrawl •scratch scrape scribble script scribe prescribe school (where knowledge is segmented, dissected) sketch scheme skotch (to cut, injure) sign signal signature design significant sage sagacious **Sagitarius** sacrum scream (piercing, cutting sound) squeal sqeak screech	
Penis Masculine	**Seker** • title of the phallus of Asar. **Sekari** • title of the sacrificed Bull of Asar (Osiris), form of the Great Father, the God of Regeneration, & epitome of virility & masculinity.		HEBREW: **zakar**, male, maleness, masculine **zakar**, push, thrust (motion of penis) **zakhrut**, penis, virility **zekhari**, male, manly ARABIC: **zekker**, penis

9 **Bartholomew Nathanael** = Sagittarius the Archer

Mutable **FIRE** Sign

Bartholomew is Bar-Tholomeus meaning "Son of Ptolemy." [1] Ptolemy is derived from *ptolemos / ptolemaios*, the Greek word for ***war***.[2] The Ptolemies were the Greeks who took over Kamit. Thus, Bartholomew means *Son of War* or *Warrier's Son*. The connection with war in the name of Bartholomew links him to Sagittarius, the only Zodiacal Sign bearing a weapon or instrument of war, the Arrow. Derived from *Sagitta* meaning *Arrow*, Sagittarius is thus called the Archer. And like war, which is hot and fiery, Sagittarius is appropriately a Fire sign.

Bartholomew (Mark 3:19) is also called **Nathanael** (John 1:45-51). Nathanael is defined in namebooks as "God has Given." Its etymology and history however, indicates that the reverse is more correct, hence "Gift to Goddess" or "Given or Sacrificed to *Goddess*." And this Goddess was Goddess Neith (Net). Hebrew **nethen** means to pour out a blood offering; "When the spirit was offered up to the heaven, the blood was poured out in libation to the mother earth the Egyptian Neith, goddess of the lower heaven, that is, earth" writes Massey.[3] The "Nethen" was one who was offered, dedicated to the service of the temple. "Nathan...signifies many forms of offering, including the sacrificial; those devoted to the sword or slaughter; having especial relation to blood sacrifice and offerings of blood."[4]

Thus "Nath" of *neth*an and *Nath*anael is the name of the Triple Goddess *Neith*, the Great Mother in her Destroyer aspect as the Goddess of *War*. Her identifying symbol was a shield with two crossed Arrows, and she is usually portrayed holding a bow and two arrows.[5] Variants of her name include Anatha, Athene, and Athena, which is the core of *Nathanael*. In the Bible, she is called Asenath (Ast-Net, Isis-Neith). Her temple is called Beth-Anath and Beth-Anoth, meaning "House of Anath" (Jos. 19:38, 15:59). *Athens*, also in the Bible, is named after her. She is the Great Goddess of the City of the Sun called **An** or Annu by the Kamites, **On** by the Hebrews, and Heliopolis by the Greeks.

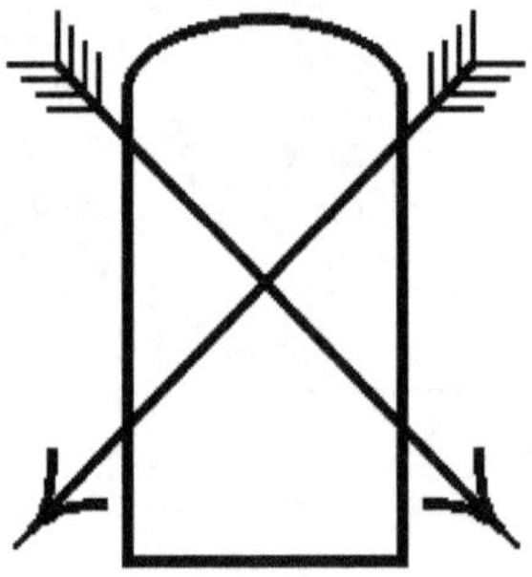

1) Walker, WE, 92. 2) Casson, 150. 3) Massey, BB-vI, 348. 4) Ibid., 347. 5) Budge, GE-vI, 30, 451, 452. 6) Ibid., v-II, 312.

The city of An was the center for the worship of Ra the *Sun* God. The same "An" is found in Nathanael (Neth-An-El), again identifying him with Fire (the Sun). And "Warrior An" was a title of the Sungod Horus as a *warrior* wielding a weapon.[6]

Biblical Variants or names from the same roots as Nathanael include:

Nathan	Nethaneel	Nethanel
Nethaniah	Nethinim	
Anath	Athene	Athaia
Anatha	Athena	Athaliah
Anathoth	Athens	Athach
Asenath (Isis-Neith)	Beth-Anoth	Atharim
Beth-Anath	Nedabiah	

Thus the truer meaning of Nathanael is

- Divine Warrior
- Warrior of the Divine
- Warrior of God-Goddess
- Warrior of Goddess Neith (who was an Archer)...

signifying Bartholomew Nathanael as the fiery sign of Sagittarius the Archer.

Etymology of Nathanael (Neth-An El, Neith-Athen-El)

Category	Afrikan-Kamite Roots	Apparent Derivatives: ENGLISH		Apparent Derivatives: OTHERS
Bow	**ath** • to string a bow; to draw, to harness, to yoke, to pull, to constrain, to restrain, to drag, to haul. 100a, 104a	**athlete** athletic **Athena** **Athens** attrition attract (= at-tract. the AT=Kamite *ath* or *aten*) tendon tense tension attain retain contend extend hypotenuse tenacious thin (from being stretched) **zenith**	needle need (from Old English ned, distress) nod (to bow) nadir (lowest point. Neith presided over the "underworld") 'neath beneath (Neith, goddess of the "underworld") underneath nates, (buttocks. are low, as with nadir) net (yields, profits) net (web)	GREEK: **tetanos**, stiff, rigid **tonos**, string, hence sound, pitch **tainia**, band, ribbon **epiteinein**, to stretch **teinein** to stretch SANSCRIT: **tan** (tanoti) stretch HEBREW: **nat**, blood **nethen**, blood offering
Stretch	**tun** • to string a bow. 872b **tun** • to stretch out, to reach out, to extend, to stretch the legs in walking, to lift up, to rise up, to raise, to bear. 872-3 **aten** • to bind, to tie. 99a **aten-petch-t**, • stringer of bows, bow-bearer. 99a			
Pour Out	**netnet** • to pour or gush out; fluid or emissions; to cut or kill; to pour out blood. 400a **nat, nut** • gifts, offerings, address, to bow. • help, save • afflict, punish • nail **nat** • "name of the red crown and negative form of existence determined by the bleeding flower." Massey, HJ, 348 **Net (Neith)** • the Triple Goddess in Her Destroyer aspect.			

10 James Alphaeus = Capricorn the Goat

Cardinal **EARTH** Sign

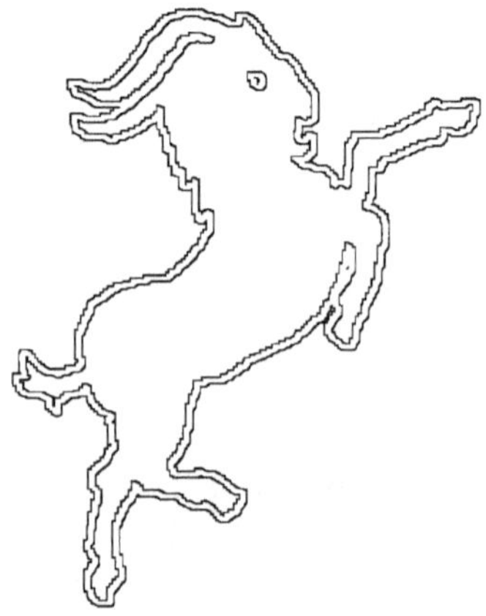

As the second apostle of Christ named James, he was the brother of Matthew and son of *Alphaeus* (Mat. 10:3), an awkward spelling of *Alpha.* Coptic ***Alpha***, Greek ***Alpha***, Hebrew ***Aleph***, Canaanite ***Alep*** and Arabic ***Alif*** all signify "beginning" and are all the *first* letter ("A") of their respective alphabets. Alpha or Aleph = El-Ap. El (first, deification, divine) +Ap (a foremost name of the Great Mother Goddess.

Dictionaries say the root of Aleph or Alpha means **OX**. If so, this should be ox-*head* if you think about it, for "A" is allegedly derived from the upside-down shape of the horned bovine head. The etymology of "ox" shows that it literally means *sharp* or *point*, just like the horn, delta, and letter "**A**." *Ox, ax, apex,* and *acrid* are from the same roots. And the "head" is the apex or top / beginning. Mountains are *aks* (peaks, apexes, high "points") protruding from the *Earth.* Ak = Ap, Alpha, the point, triangle. Goats' natural habitat are the "aks" or mountainous regions of the Earth. "**A**" is both a name and paramount emblem of the Great Mother of the Universe. "A" combines two of Her primary symbols, the Delta and Crescent Moon:

- The Delta (triangle) is the Yoni (female genital, womb), the Door of Life.
- The Crescent Moon represent Horns, and symbolize the Great Mother in Her lunar form. "A" (Ay, Aya, Eve) was the Beginning, the Birth-letter, the symbol of Creation and the Creatress.

"A" was the symbol of the Great Mother in Her bovine form as the horned, milkgiving Cow, which represents the Principle of Nourishment (Milk) and the Earth as the giver of food. Because they were sacred in Kamit,[1] in India, cows are still sacred and beloved. In America, cows are beloved only as *hamburgers*. Derived from the same roots as Aleph, the *calf* (from Old English *cealf*) is the *first* form of the *cow*. And a *heifer* is a *young* cow that has not birthed a calf. **It is during the period of Capricorn that the *birth* ("alpha") or beginning of the New Sun /Son of God** takes place on Christmas (Dec. 25) after the "death" of the Old Sun at the Winter Solstice.

Earth signs qualities include *bearing, building, solidifying, hardness*. Hard things are good bearers. Macho Earth "bears" everything upon it, also pregnantly bears life (seeds, plant roots...) within herself like the Mother she is. Thus Earth is both Mother Nature and Father Nature!

1) Churchward, SS, 234.

The name *James Alphaeus* aligns with the original symbol of Capricorn, the Goat-*<u>Fish</u>*.
In name & symbol, sexual opposites are delineated and united as shown:

Masculine:	Feminine:
Name: **James** (to bear, carry).	Name: **Alphaeus** (Delta, womb, water).
Horn-*masculine* is hard and pointed. Because they are hard, horns symbolize Strength, a quality of Earth signs.	**Horn-*feminine*** is hollow, able to hold within itself.
AK means pe<u>ak</u> in Egyptian, thus something hard, phallic.	**AK** also means water, <u>AQ</u>ua, hence feminine.
Earth bears ***externally***. It holds or supports everything.	Earth carries ***internally*** (like womb holds fetus).
Goat (a mountainous-earthy creature with hard-earthy horns) Goats live in regions of the *hardest* matter on Earth; rocks, stones and boulders.	**Fish** lives in the *soft* medium of water. The complementary opposite of Capricorn is the very wet, moody, teary sign of Cancer. Wetness relates to both *Fish* and *Alpha*-eus, for Alpha signifies *birth* hence *water*. Water is linked with birth. All life is born in water /water bag.

The name James (Ames) is from roots which mean *to bear* or *carry a burden.*

How does this relate to Capricorn? In the following ways:

- The "Scape Goat" carried the heaviest burden of all! A goat called the "scape goat" was randomly selected once a year on the Day of Atonement to BEAR the sins of the entire nation of Israel! (Lev. 16:10-22)
- Like the cow, the goat is a milk-giver, "bearing" milk in her udder.
- Capricorn is derived from Latin *caper* (goat) + *cornu* (horn). Capricorn means "Horned Goat," but literally means "Goat Horn." Goat horns are hollow. Horns signified the Moon's (Great Mother's) crescents, brimming over with Her gifts to humanity, like the *Cornucopias* they have evolved into. Cornucopia means "Horn of Plenty," <u>*laden*</u> ("burdened") with the generous gifts of food from Mother *Earth.*
- In the Zodiac, directly opposite Capricorn-James is his complementary sign, Cancer the Crab. Again what's the connection? The crab also bears a burden, –its home or shell in which it lives. And the crab is the grabber with his claws; correspondingly, Goats are remarkably "sure-footed" in the steep, rocky, perilous, terrain of their mountainous, natural habitats.
- All liquids (water principle, hence feminine) must be borne /held by a solid (earth principle. Oceans are borne by the Earth. Liquids/juices are borne in a *hard* or firm container / cup). This connects with the complementary pairing of Earth-sign Capricorn directly opposite Water-sign Cancer. Additionally, both Cancer and Capricorn bear a James-name (*James* Alphaeus and *James* Boanerges Zebedee).
- Right at the beginning, the author of the Book of James identifies himself as the "servant" of God. This aligns with the meaning of the name James as well as the Cardinal Earth Sign he represents (associated with labor, building, bearing).

Thus *strong* James, son of *Alphaeus*–who was likely his *mother*, is Capricorn the Goat-*Fish.*

11 **Andrew** = Aquarius the Water Bearer

Fixed **AIR** Sign

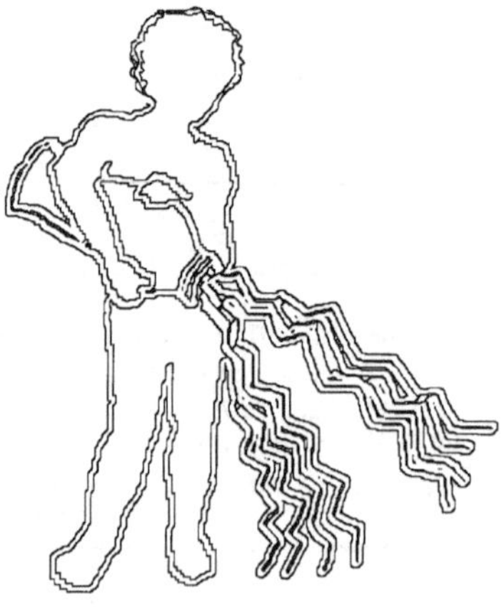

Andrew means *man* or *male* according to namebooks. This is true only for the *first* part of the name. Aquarius is the only sign represented as a single MAN. And note, this apostle has only a *single* name. RU (Red) and IU (Double) are in Andrew's name (And-RU, Andr-IU). And both roots apply to Andrew! Thus, Andrew means more than just Man, it means:

- **The Man, *Iu.*** —Or Iu-Man, Human.
- **Man of Duality.** IU means Double. The original Aquarius in Afrika's Dendera Zodiac poured forth *two* streams from *two separate vessels.* This aligns with the duality of IU in the name Andrew (Andr-IU).
- **Double Man.** Hence there has to be *two* Andrews. And there are: Andrew & *Andronicus* (=Andrew-NICK, NIGht), the latter –also an "apostle"– being the only other near-andrew name in the Albinoed Bible (Rom. 16:7). These two stand for Light & Dark, after the Heru/Set twins. Further, Andrew's "brother" is Simon Peter "called NIGer" (BLACK), again pointing to Heru/Set, plus another version of MAN-ness since Peter means phallus and father. Further still, the 2nd and only other biblical name simply meaning *Man* is ENOCH /ENOS, from the same roots. Sure enough, Enoch is double as he can be. Review pages 250, 251, keeping in mind these are astrological allegories, not real people.
- **Red Man.** Adam, Atum, Atum-Iu. The Sungod was both the Father (Atum-Ra) and the Son (Atum-Iu). Andrew = Andr-Iu; just like Reuben =Re-Iu-Ben.
- **Red Duality of Man.** What? The *Reality* and the *Imitation* (appearance). Black (a color) and Darkness (absence of Light) are *not* the same! Nor are White (a color) and Light (radiance). The "red" needs to be the color of the *AURA* as a result of Love radiating—not the *apparent* color of the SKIN as a result of massive Melanin Deficiency! Hence, we have the 1) natural, *humane* (loving) Original HUE-Man, and 2) *mutated,* unnatural "mankind" —a "kind" of man...in all shades of "RED."

The illogical and prominent association of *water* with the Zodiac's fixed *air* sign is resolved by knowing Aquarius's Afrikan origin from the double-source Nile. **And *water* is in the name *Andrew.*** *Coincidentally* (really, no such thing!), the elements of his name are AN (water), DR (der=water), IU (double). Hence "Double Water" or "Double Stream." Like Aquarius, Andrew is doubly connected with water; Andrew and his brother Simon Peter were *fishermen* whom Christ found by the sea and made them both 'fishers of MEN!' (Mat. 4:18, 19)

Etymology of Andrew (Andr-Iu)

Category	Afrikan-Kamite Roots		Apparent Derivatives: ENGLISH:	Apparent Derivatives: GREEK:	Comments
Man Humanity	unnu anu untuit an ankhu	• a living man, humans, people, men & women, strong men. 164b • "the physical body of man on earth." Khun, LL,11 • men and women, people, society, folk. 170a • a man of noble qualities, a cultured man, good man. 123a • man, citizen. 124b	anthropology anthropic anthropoid android androgynous androgen androgyne polyandry philander misanthrope Anthony Alexander salamander Andromeda, Enoch *Human?* (see comments)	**aner**, man **andr**, man **anthropos**, human being, man, people, person **and**, human, manlike, masculine, male, husband **anth**, man, human life **hupandros**, husband JAPANESE: **ainu**, a tribe of northern Japan. HEBREW: **enosh, enos**, man	**Human?** The word HUMAN may be figured as both: • **Hum-An.** Hum (humus, soil) + An (anu, unnu, meaning people, humans). *Physically,* our bodies are of the same composition as the Earth. • **Hue-Man.** Hue (light, color) + Man. *Spiritually,* we are composed of Light (God). HU-Man (God-Man). HU (Goddess, God, the Source. IU.) + Man. HU-man = IU-man = Divine Being! That's YOU (IU, HU)!
IU	Iu	• double. • The Ever-Coming Child of God. A title of Light as the Sun.			

12 John Zebedee Boanerges = Pisces the Fish

Mutable **WATER** Sign

His name was John, son of Zebedee, brother of James.

John is linked with Water and Fish:

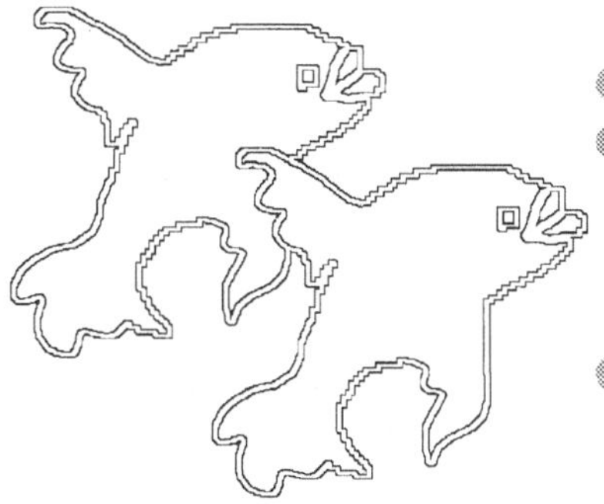

- He was a Fishermen. The environment of Fishermen is water.
- His father *Zebedee* is modeled from the Egyptian god *Sebek,* hence the name, who was also a father of fishers.
- The god Sebek was represented as the Great Fish of Inundation.
- John and his brother James were called *Boanerges* or the "Sons of Thunder." Boanerges actually means Thunder *and* Lightning, a phenomena which happens only with generous amounts of *water* falling from the sky, hence *thunder*storms (see James Zebedee Boanerges).
- Only the *Thunder* aspect of Boanerges is mentioned in the Gospels. Why? This points to WATER, for "thunder" is continous at the beach from the waves (water) ever crashing on the shore.
- John and Jonah are variations of the same name, derived from Kamite *An* or Oan, of which one meaning is Fish. Jonah was the Fish-Man who was swallowed by a huge fish (Book of Jonah). "the fish Oannes was in name the same as John." [1]
- Jonah is a symbol for Pisces the Fish.[2]
- Note that the other "big" Johns in the Bible are also connected with water in a big way: John the Baptist. Jonah, swallowed by a huge fish.

If John is linked with *Water*, he must be also linked with *Love*

Water and Love are inseparable as major attirbutes of the Great Mother. Kamite MER means water and love (giving us marine & marry). And yes! John IS connected with Love! Keep in mind that all the key "Johns" of the Bible are not separate men but the same entity fragmented as many.

- John was Christ's favorite disciple, the disciple "whom Jesus loved."
- Christ made John the son of his own Mother (John 19:26), entrusting him with the care of his Mother prior to his death.
- John (the Baptist) was biblically Christ's cousin. He is another version or twin of Christ (like Joseph, Thomas). He is the underworld twin. The birth of both were announced by the same angel. Both of John's parents were of the priestly house of Aaron, thus making John "high," coinciding with Pisces as the "high" or Celestial Water.
- It was John (the Baptist) who baptised Jesus, and not the other way around.

1) Higgens, vI, 137. 2) Massey, AE, 735.

Biblical variants or names from the same root as *John* include:

Jona	Johanan	Janna	On	Onam
Jonah	Johannan	Janai	Onan	Anamin
Jonas	Jonam	Jannai	Anan	Anem
Jonan	Janum	Joanan	Anaiah	
Jonadab			Annas	
Jehonadab				

With so many connections with Water and especially FISH, John Zebedee-Boanerges is identified as the constellation of Pisces the *Fish*, a *Water* sign.

Etymology of John (On, Aan)

Category	Afrikan-Kamite Roots	Apparent Derivatives	Comments
Water Fish	An • the celestial water. 187BB1 inu • water. 143a Nu • [reverse of UN] the Celestial Waters. 349b Nun • the Celestial Ocean (called Space), primeval waters... nu • new flood, inundation. 349a an • fish. ccx	innundate abundant abound **annoint** (much oil was poured) increase nana (wetnurse) nanny (wetnurse) enema unda, wave (Latin) Lunar John Jonah Nun Ninevah Noah Nyanza (Afrika's largest lake) nun (*fish* in Hebrew. 14th letter of Hebrew alphabet) **now** **new** **noon**	**John and Jonah are both connected with water and fish.** Fisherman John. John the Baptist. Jonah got swallowed by a great fish, saved Nineveh. **NOW is always NEW**! Noon = new beginning, for before the rise of patriarchy, the day began at NOON, not at midnight! And it is *water* that renews and refreshes us. Note that **John the Baptist** renewed people by baptising them in water, an act which means to be reborn.

So WHY is the Zodiac the underlying, disguised, CENTRAL theme of the Bible?

To do justice to answering this very important question, at least another chapter is required...in
Volume II of *Blacked Out Through Whitewash.*

14

The Top 14 Hallmarks of Albino Poison in the World's Top 4 Religions

The Four Tyrannical Counterfeits: Judaism, Christianity, Islam, Hinduism

Albinos stole and perverted the theology of the Blacks in ancient Egypt and ancient India, refashioning them into potent, effective tools for the oppression, domination, and deception of People of Color as well as themselves. The results are four exceedingly harmful, tyrannical and fraudulent religions:

Judaism • Christianity • Islam • Hinduism

Blacks need to recognize all the ways we are being undermined, kept weak, destroyed. Religion is the chief, foremost method. All four of these have the "Hallmarks" of the Albino man's poison. Generally, these hallmarks are dominant traits of the Albino collective, their culture, and general orientation:

Overview of
The Top 14 Hallmarks of Albino Poison
in the World's Top 4 Religions

1 Anti-Female.

Suppresses, vilifies, diabolizes, demeans women and the Female Principle. "How can man be clean that is born of a woman?" (Job 25:14). **Sin and the Fall of Man is blamed on Eve, the first *woman*,** who gets cursed just for seeking knowledge (Gen. 3:5, 16). And Eve is portrayed as an afterthought on God's part, produced *unnaturally* like no other creatures.

Counterfeit Christianity depends upon the diabolism of the Female, that is –of EVE, as the foundation of it entire base. Remove the Serpent, FruitTree and Woman, then there is no Fall of Man, no Hellfire or Damnation, hence no need of a Savior! "Thus the bottom falls out of the whole Christian theology.

"Churchmen" (Albinos) weeded out all references to female authority or participation in Christian origins. The biblical books were deliberately selected and edited to wipe out all feminine images of divinity and sanction religious suppression of women. Anti-female rules and laws permeate the Bible. Example: "If two men are fighting and the wife of one of them comes to rescue her husband from his assailant, and she reaches out and seizes him by his private parts, you shall cut off her hand. Show her no pity" (Deu. 25:11 – N.I. Trans.). To further diabolize women, medieval churchmen put pendulous breasts on the image of their *red* Devil, though retaining his *male* identity (which defeats the purpose, as it points to *men*, especially *red* men, as the real devils). Had they really succeeded in imparting *any* feminine qualities to their devil, he would have been "spoiled" as a devil, thus becoming a *humane* being. In Inquisition Europe, churchmen tortured and burned millions of mainly white women and girls to death at the stake in the name of God. Hinduism also burned countless "disposable" women to death –and widows were expected to throw themselves on their husband's funeral pyres. Female infants or embryos are still killed. Hinduism's cruel Devadasi system is based on the forced prostitution of countless Dalit (Untouchables) women and girls.

In the Bible, *all* key women are demeaned in some way, especially sexually. Demeaning ranges from subordinate-dependence on men, to "whoredom," rape, and even murder. The four, only listed female ancestors of Christ, are four forms of the harlot. "Virtuous" Ruth (Virgo) is dependent on and servile to a man whose favor she seeks to win; she succeeded –he "purchased" her to be his wife (Ruth 4:10). Sarah is made a glorified prostitute, catering only to pharaohs by her pimp-husband Abraham. Jezebel is maligned because she worshipped the Great Mother as Astarte. **For *any* women to belong to *any* of these religions, is to support and perpetuate their ongoing degradation.** Women of Color embrace these religions not realizing they are embracing the daggers, anti-female poisons within them, therefore they suffer and remain subordinate to men, 2nd /3rd /4th class citizens –fallen in the trap.

Subjugation of women is even more notorious in Islam and Hinduism. "From the very beginning it [Hinduism] has had the suppression of the native population [Black people] and women, even Aryan women, as its primary principles." In Moslem countries, men can legally kill their wives, daughters or sisters for adultery (the reverse is not so)! Moslem women in Pakistan who claim to be raped are often imprisoned for having *zina* (sex outside of marriage), and the rapist goes unpunished. Most Moslem women, especially in Afrikan countries, are brutally *castrated* while they are helpless babies or little girls. This is not just *female circumcision*, for the clitoris and part or all of the labia is crudely cut off, without anesthesia, then sewn shut except for a small hole to allow urine and menses to flow through. Thus grooms are ensured of their brides being virgins on their wedding nights.

2 Male-dominant.
Top pillar for male supremacy.

Male-exalting, male-glorifying, patriarchal, thus phallic-worshipping. The steeple on churches originated from the obelisk, a phallus emblem. The Cross or Crucifix, the foremost symbol of Christianity, is also a phallic emblem and symbol of the Male Principle and male genitalia. The Crucifix is a castrated Ankh.

Eve, the first woman, is made from the *rib* of a man and *made just for him*, hence women are supposed to *submit* to their husbands, calling them their *lord* or master:

- "Even as Sarah obeyed Abraham, calling him lord" (1Pet. 3:6).
- "thy desire shall be to thy husband, and he shall rule over thee" (Gen. 3:16).
- "a man...is the image and glory of God; but the woman is the glory of the man. For the man is not of the woman; but the woman of the man. Neither was the man created for the woman; but the woman for the man" (1Cor. 11:7-9).
- "Likewise, ye wives, be in subjection to your own husbands" (1Pet. 3:1).
- Teach "the young women" "to be...obedient to their own husbands, that the word of God be not blasphemed." (Titus 2:5).

There is *God* only; no female *Goddess*. The God of Albino-poisoned religions demands the godhead all to himself. Female gods in Hinduism are not Hindu but of pre-Albino India. Women and the Female Principle is ousted from participation in divinity. Albino men (Hebrews, Edomites, "Church fathers") did all they could to suppress or get rid of the female part of Divine Nature or the Mother Principle of God. There are many anti-Goddess passages in the Albino-ed Bible. The Gospels commanded total destruction of all the temples of the Great Goddess as Diana "whom all Asia and the world worshippeth" (Acts 19:27). The role of women in the original theology of the Blacks was usurped and replaced with males. They ousted the Great Goddess and Her priestesses but note they all still wear Her *dresses* (robes, gowns, etc.). Women are not allowed in high positions; no female popes, bishops, priests, caliphs, etc. Even today nearly all ministers, priests, etc., are male. "A woman should learn in quietness and full submission. I do not permit a woman to teach or to have authority over a man (1Tim. 2:11-14-NI Trans).

Black nations or Men of Color are <u>not</u> benefiting by demeaning and lording over the Women of Color which they oppress (through religion / laws of their countries, etc.). For this oppression of their own women keeps the men and their entire nation weakened (by at least half), and thus more vulnerable to the *Bigger Wolf* of Global Albino Supremacy. It is to the advantage of the white collective that People of Color continue the divisions and sexism among themselves. Divided people will always be weak. Men of Color, especially in India's Caste System, are so stuck, *locked* in this ingeniously devised auto-oppression that it seems they cannot let it go; they must have someone to lord over and be better than and above, while Global Albino Supremacy is lording over the whole world.

3 Anti-Black.
Anti Afrikan / People of Color.

These weapon-religions were tailor(re)made to oppress People of Color. Thus, Black Afrikan / Indian-Dravidian people and their original *matriarchal* culture are maligned, slandered, vilified, demeaned, diabolized. In the religious stories, Blacks are conquered, destroyed, subjugated, enslaved, exploited, and suffer the most. Afrikan theology and culture is labeled pagan, heathen, idolatry. All these fraudulent religions were forced upon Blacks and People of Color at the expense of their own ancient cosmology, culture, and often their lives. And these religions are all racist at their cores, like their re-makers, evidenced by the following examples.

CHRISTIANITY: Major Racism in the Bible

"First came the Crescent flag of the Prophet....The Cross of Jesus Christ followed the Muslim Crescent. The cloak of Christianity was a most convenient hiding place for those who had other designs. Hence, the drive to convert. Conversion here meant far more than conversion to Christianity. As in the case of Islam, it meant change into the white man's image, his ideas and value system. The real object of worship turned out to be neither Jesus Christ nor His Father, God, but Western man and Western civilization." [1]

Anti "FLAT NOSE"

"For whatsoever man he be that hath a blemish, he shall not approach [i.e, give offerings at the altar to God]: a blind man, or a lame, or **he that hath a flat nose**, or any thing superfluous," (Lev. 21:18)

In the Bible, the Black race is portrayed cursed to be the slaves of whites. Blacks are designated as the descendants of Ham (Ham= Kham, Kamit, Egypt), whose first son was Canaan. Canaan (the son / descendents of Ham) is cursed by Noah to be the perpetual slave of whites and Semites:

"And he said **Cursed be Canaan; a servant of servants shall he be unto his brethren**. And he said, Blessed be the Lord God of Shem; and Canaan shall be his servant. God shall enlarge Japheth...and **Canaan shall be his servant**" (Gen. 9: 25-27).

Ancient Egypt, the source of world civilization and spiritual philosophy, is maligned and demeaned throughout the Old Testament, especially the 29th & 30th chapters of Ezekiel. Egyptian (Afrikan) gods are depicted as devils. It seems that the only time Egyptians are favorably regarded was when the Egyptians were *not* Egyptians but *Hyksos* (Albino invaders) who took over Egypt and were the kin of Joseph, a Hebrew-Hyksos himself. Sample phrases:

- "I will make the land of Egypt utterly waste and desolate, from the tower of Syene even unto the border of Ethiopia (Eze. 29:10).
- "I will set the Egyptians against the Egyptians: and they shall fight every one against his brother...And the spirit of Egypt shall fail in the midst thereof...And the Egyptians will I give over into the hands of a cruel lord" (Isaiah 19:2-4).
- "So shall the king of Assyria lead away the Egyptians prisoners, and the Ethiopians captives, young and old, naked and barefoot, even with their buttocks uncovered, to the shame of Egypt" (Isaiah 20:4).

1) Williams, DBC, 56.

JUDAISM: Spectacular Racism in the Talmud

In modern Israel, the Beta-Israel (known as Falashas), Black Jews who are descendants of the original IUs of Afrika, are typically treated as sub-class citizens.

The Talmud is the Jewish Bible, authored by the false Jews (Albinos or Habiru-Hebrews / Edomites / Khazars). Essentially, the original Jews and original Christians were one and the same; they were Black, spiral-haired Afrikan people. The names referring to them include Essenes, Osim, Zealots, *Nazarenes*, and *Nozrim*. Throughout the Talmud are hateful, demeaning, derogatory references to Blacks (as the original Black Jews or *Nazarenes, Nozrim*, etc.), whom the false Habirus were usurping and supplanting. No wonder the Talmud demeans and slanders Black Jesus, calling him the illegitimate son of a prostitute, etc. (see page 94). In unexpurgated editions of the Talmud are numerous allusions to Christ and the original Christians, characterized by intense hatred (see page 95). Jesus is usually spoken of indirectly as "that man," "the Nazarene," "the fool," "Absalom," "the hung," "the son of Stad," "the son of Pandera," etc.

At the beginning of his book, We the Black Jews, Dr. Yosef ben-Jochannan documents blatant racism in Talmudic writing, noting that "In many rabbinical writings severe color prejudice is found." As an example he quotes the following 6th century C.E./A.D. Talmudic commentary on the Old Testament:

> "Now I cannot beget the fourth son whose children I would have ordered to serve you and your brothers! Therefore it must be Canaan, your first born, whom they enslave. And since you have disabled me...doing ugly things in blackness of night, **Canaan's children shall be born ugly and black!** Moreover, because you twisted your head around to see my nakedness, your grandchildren's **hair shall be twisted into kinks**, and their eyes red; again because your **lips** jested at my misfortune, theirs **shall swell**; and because you neglected my nakedness, they shall go naked, and **their male members shall be shamefully elongated! Men of this race are called Negroes, their forefather Canaan commanded them to love theft and fornication, to be banded together in hatred of their masters and never to tell the truth."**
>
> Quoted by Jochannan from *Hebrew Myths*, by Graves & Patai, citing the following Talmudic text as the original sources: B. Sanhedrin 72a-b, 108b; B. Pesahim 113b; Tanhuma Buber Gen. 49-50; Tanhuma Noah 13, 15 Gen. Rab. 341.

ISLAM: Racist as the others

It seems that Islam began as a revolt or defensive reaction to the onslaught of militant Christian domination. Largely, it was forced upon Black Afrikan people at sword point. Even today, *enslaved* Afrikan males in certain Moslem countries are given a choice: either convert to Islam or be made a cripple by getting their achilles tendons cut.[1] Islam carries the same female degradation and racism against Blacks, characteristic of its grandparents Judaism and Christianity. So how can it possibly be wholesome for Black people? And like Judaism and Christianity, its historical Afrikan roots are shrouded or blacked out – by Moslem Arabs (essentially a Habiru people). Black Afrikans are also excluded from the highest posts of the administration of Islam in Mecca.[2] In *African Origins of the Major "Western Religions,"* Dr. Yosef ben-Jochannan documents Islam's Afrikan roots and role played by "Bilal," a key father of Islam.

Islam is 600 years after Christ. Christ, Moses, Adam, Eve, and Abraham are in the Koran, the bible of Islam. **The teachings of Islam, as set forth in the Koran, differs markedly from what is practiced in Afrika and Asia.** There are actually many verses in the Koran which support women; only a handful are anti-female. Apparently, the anti-female, barbaric treatment of women came from the northern invaders and infected all they came in contact with, for we find such treatment among Blacks only *after* sustained contact with invading white barbarians –resulting in *Semites* (racial mixture of the two). The world of Mohammed was already rife with such. He allegedly revolutionized the degrading life of women. If this was so, it must have been short-lived, for modern Islam is notorious for female degradation. Mohammed granted women the right to divorce, to inherit, to have custody of their children in the event of divorce, the right to pray in the mosque, and the right to participate as fully in life as men, according to the Moslem author, Fatima Mernissi. She says "Sharia law does not exist in the Koran. It was created by man. There are only four or five laws in the Koran." [3] The *Hadith* was written centuries after Mohammed's death, just like the *Gospels* were written centuries after Jesus's death.

Black Bilal was the "Angel" of Mohammed's Call

The *Angel* of Mohammed's "call by an Angel of Allah" was ***Bilal***. It was *Hadzart **Bilal** ibn Rahbab,* a gifted Ethiopian philosopher /attorney captured by slavers, who established the fundamentals of Islam.[4] Apparently it was Bilal who originally penned much of the Koran, including its opening verses. *"Bilal, the former African slave, was responsible for the creation of much of what Moslems, past and present, believe about 'Paradise' (Heaven), also many of their first original prayers and doctrines."* [5] Illiterate Mohammed recognized Bilal's genius and collaborated with him to create or ***re-create*** what is called *Islam. "Re-create,"* because as with Christianity, Islam's fundamentals preexisted in Afrikan Cosmology with the original Afrikan inhabitants of Arabia and Kamit eons before it was refashioned, repackaged. *"Bilal was Islam itself. He gave it its 'Paradise.' ...He made Mohamet the Prophet. He managed Islam's treasure and built its capital resources."*[6] Like other prophets, Mohammed is falsely credited for what he did not originate. Fraudulency characterizes all these Bastard Religions in their blacking out the Afrikans' originating roles.

Anti-Afrikan poison is evident in the Black-Muslim story of *Shabazz*, cursed to become black-skinned, nappy & Africoid

In Islam, Shabazz (or "Tribe of Shabazz") –apparently a version of the biblical Ham, is cursed, resulting in his becoming black-skinned, nappy haired and Africoid, giving these traits to Afrikans as progenitor of the Black race. Shabazz was *exiled* out of Asia into Afrika, according to the story. **Blacks must realize that *all* our original theologies have been rewritten, perverted, poisoned, and supplanted by Albinos.** We need to wake up to this fact, recognize these poisons and cast them out or better yet, discard the whole rank Counterfeit Religion! Despite its identity with Islam, Black America's Nation of Islam has done a commendable job of uplifting Blacks on all levels. They taught ancient Black history long before most Black Americans knew they had such a history. They took in outcast Blacks when no other groups would, and helped them become restored with a new lease on life. Look what it did for Malcom X! I give them due honor for what they have accomplished, and still point to the presence of Albino poison permeating *Islam* and the other

1) Tony Brown shows #1720 & 1909. 2) ben-Jochannan, AO, 197. 3) *Vanity Fair*, Aug.1993, 158. 4) ben-Jochannan, AO, 210. 5) Ibid., 199. 6) Ibid., 210.

Counterfeit Religions. We can acknowledge what good we credit them as having given us and at the same time be aware of the *greater harm* from the same. Thus, regardless of any good seeming to come to us from them, Black people, especially *women*, need to recognize the insidious poisons /deceptions / lies /Pseudo Truths of these Counterfeit Religions and reject them, otherwise we will continue to suffer in vital ways that damage us from the core of our beings, keeping us weakened /more vulnerable /receptive to domination and suppression on all levels by Albinos and controller priesthoods. We should tolerate *no* religions having the Anti-Afrikan Hallmarks of those who from day one made it their business to undermine and destroy us. The negatives of these Four Counterfeits outweigh any positives.

HINDUISM: Equally Racist Against Blacks. Racism belies the Vedas

The Vedas, like the Bible & Talmud, are equally racist, fraudulent and corrupt, –perverted by the same people. India's worse curse is Hinduism with its Caste System, both established by Albino invaders over the indigenous Black population. The Caste System originated from the "Rig Veda," [1] the first and most famous of the plagiarized, reworked, four "sacred scriptures" of the so-called Aryans. Rogers writes: "The first recorded instance of color prejudice I have been able to find is in India of some five thousand years ago when the Aryas, or Aryans, invaded the valley of the Indus and found there a black people –the Dasysus, or Dasyus. In any case we find very clear evidences of it in Aryan writings. In the Rig-Veda (Book IX, Hymn, 42:1) Indra, their national god, is depicted as 'Blowing the black skin which Indra hates.' Hymn 42:1, tells of 'Driving the black skin far away.' The blacks were called 'Anasahs' (noseless people). Book v. Hymn 29:10, tells how Indra 'slew the flat-nosed barbarians.' " [2]

India's Caste System or *Varna* System was originally based on skin color (*varna* means *color*). *Color* however, is not the main problem since dark and light skinned people are found in all castes. The main problem is the religiously sanctioned, legally upheld oppression of the Untouchables and Tribals, who represent over 40% of the population of 800-million.[3] Color prejudice is nevertheless evident: actors selected for movies are usually all light-skinned and Aryan-looking; and illustrated Hindu books typically depict "good" people and heroes as white-looking, while portraying "bad" people and demons as darkskinned. (This is also found in American movies: bad people are dressed in black while good people are dressed in white). Even Krishna, whose very name means *black*, is portrayed Albino-looking (like Jesus) with pastel-blue skin, just a shade or two from being white. The white god Indra, of India's white invaders, slays vast numbers of indigenous Blacks. This is actually what the Albinos did upon invading India. "The Aryan, who set his yoke on the peoples of dark race, worshipped in Indra the grandiose projection of his own type...He cleaves demons asunder, as the Indo-European warriors overcame inferior races." [4] (emphasis added) Did he say "inferior"? Yes. And he is referring to India's Black, pre-Albino population, the "demons." "From the very beginning it [Brahminism/Hinduism] has had the suppression of the native population [Black people]...as its primary principles..."

< Left: "Bad people" are typically portrayed darkskinned while "good people" are portrayed lightskinned, as shown in this illustration. Note that Krisna in the background looks white.

1) Rashidi /Van Sertima, APEA, 238. 2) Rogers, NK, 7. 3) Rashidi /Van Sertima, APEA, 236-237. 4) Larousse EM, 326.

4 Top pillar for Albino supremacy.

Exalts, promotes, maintains global white supremacy. Are top pillars for Black mental slavery and **Black physical chattel slavery which is still alive and thriving TODAY in the Moslem countries of North Afrika!** Effectively locks People of Color, especially Black people in the Americas, Afrika, and India in Mental Slavery. The original, life-honoring theology of the Blacks has been reconstructed and perverted by "Cauk-Asians" (Habiru-Hebrews, "Churchmen," Semite-Arabs, Berbers, Aryans) into four, false, potent, effective "weapon religions." These four religions are the primary pillars for global white supremacy and global subjugation and oppression of People of Color and Women. **We can detect some truth in these religions, for lies stand only by virture of the backbone of truth within them.** Satan tempted Jesus not with outstanding lies, but with quotes from the holy scriptures. But any "holy books" or teachings given to us by the very people that have destroyed our cultures and ancestors, will be poisoned and serve to keep us in subjugation, on all levels, beginning with the spiritual and progressing through the mental, material, physical.

Judaism / Christianity

There are many biblical passages promoting, supporting, and establishing Albino supremacy and apartheid ("apart-hate") over "the children of Ham," –racism backed by a racist God (Un-god). They include:

- "ye shall be a peculiar treasure unto me above all people" (Exo: 19:5).
- "and in that day there shall be no more the Canaanite in the house of the Lord of hosts" (Zec. 14:21). Canaanites were Black Afrikan people. Issaac commanded Jacob: "Thou shalt not take a wife of the daughters of Canaan" (Gen. 28:6).
- "And the seed of Israel separated themselves from all strangers" (Neh. 9:2).
- **Canaan, who represents the Black race, is cursed to become the perpetual slave of whites and Semites.** "And he said **Cursed be Canaan; a servant of servants shall he be unto his brethren**. And he said, Blessed be the Lord God of Shem and **Canaan shall be his servant. God shall enlarge Japheth** and he shall dwell in the tents of Shem; and **Canaan shall be his servant**" (Gen 9:25:27). ***Japheth***, regarded the biblical progenitor of white people, receives the blessing of worldly prosperity and widespread dominion.

Around the world, People of Color worship the Whiteman as God

A vital revelation in *The Isis Papers* [1] by Dr. Frances Cress Welsing is thus condensed: It was critical for white supremacy to project the image of a white man as "Christ," the son of God –no matter that Jesus was Black. Because the brain-computer functions on logic circuits, at the deep unconscious level it automatically computes that God the father is also a white male, otherwise he would have produced a nonwhite son. Thus, any person programmed to

1) Welsing, 166-169.

"what happened in the process of converting the Blacks to Islam and Christianity was the supreme triumph of the white world over the black. Millions of Africans became non-Africans. Africans who were neither Muslims nor Christians were classed as 'pagans' and therefore required to disavow their whole culture and to regard practically all African institutions as 'backward' or savage. ...Indeed, in order to destroy completely not only their African heritage, but also their very African identity psychologically, they were forced to change their names to Arabic and Christian names. ...Blacks at home in Africa and Blacks scattered over the world bore the names of their enslavers and oppressors, the ultimate in self-effacement that promoted a self-hatred which made pride in the race difficult. That these psychological shackles still handicap not only the rebirth of modern African states, but also Blacks everywhere, should be obvious to all." [1]

Chancellor Williams

accept (False) Christianity, whether conscious of it or not, has the image of God as a white man in the logic network of their brain computer. Couple this image with the white system definition of God as "the supreme or ultimate reality; the Being perfect in power, wisdom and goodness whom men worship as creator and ruler of the universe." Then of absolute necessity, the logic circuits of the brain-computer prints out "The white man (as God, the father of the white male Christ) is the supreme or ultimate reality; the white man is the Being, perfect in power, wisdom and goodness whom all men should worship as creator and ruler of the universe." With this unconscious logic circuit of "God is a white man" implanted in the minds of vast numbers of nonwhite people throughout the world, white domination over nonwhite people could last a trillion years! **White supremacy aimed to accomplish this implantation through its vast armies of white supremist missionaries, following the guns of white supremacy conquest.** With the white man as God, the nonwhite global collective would always be obedient to the white man!

Thus all People of Color who are members of the Christian (white supremacy) religion, whether conscious of it or not, worship the white man as God! Though they may understand that they are oppressed by the white collective, the brain-computer's logic circuits also unconsciously inform them that it is impossible to liberate one's self from the supreme being! Meaning, as long as they worship a white Jesus, all their liberation efforts will only move them in a circle and they will feel like they are making no progress (as is currently so).

"Blacks and all other non-white peoples who have operated under the concept of God as a white man for the past 2,000 years, should begin an immediate return to the fundamental concept of God as originally understood in Africa before the input of the albino (white) collective. The African understanding of God was that it was the only and all-in-one energy force that created and simultaneously was all energy in the universe...To be Black and accept consciously or unconsciously the image of God as a white man is the highest possible form of self-negation and lack of self-respect under the specific conditions of white domination. Such perception, emotional response and thought are therefore insane. This logic circuit ensures that Black people always will look up to white people and, therefore, down upon themselves. Only by breaking that logic circuit can the concept of Black and other non-white liberation become a reality."

Dr. Frances Cress Welsing

1) Williams, DBC, 56, 57.

The Crusades: European Expansion disguised under religion

"His-story" books say the Crusades were fought to win back the holy land. The real reason was Albino expansion under the cover of Religion. Albinos (Roman Church) were expanding their economic and political power by "Christianizing" (infecting with poisonous teachings) the world. Little, if anything has changed; only gotten more sophisticated. **"The West" (Albinos) finances fundamentalism and religious groups** in so-called Third-World countries, using them for their purposes. They have gone into business with most of the repressive Islamic states. **The C.I.A. funded 3 billion dollars** to "the most extreme right-wing Islamic groups in Afghanistan (Gulbuddin Hekmatyar's Party of God) to [allegedly] fight the Russians." [1]

White feminists and "New Age" exploitation spell destruction for Native Americans

The *New Age* movement has sparked new interest in Native American spirituality among white women claiming to be spiritualists. Indian spirituality is often presented as the panacea for all problems. A flyer stated:

> Many white "feminists" see the opportunity to make great profits from this new craze. They sell sweat lodges, sacred pipe ceremonies or books and records that supposedly describe Indian traditional practices so that you too can be "Indian." **On the surface, it may appear that this new craze is based on respect for Indian spirituality. In fact, the New Age movement is part of a very old story of white racism and genocide against the Indian people**. Of course, white "feminists" want to become only partly Indian.
>
> While New Agers may think that they are escaping white racism by becoming "Indian," they are in fact, continuing the same genocidal practices of their forefathers /foremothers. The one thing that has maintained the survival of Indian people through 500 years of colonialism has been the spiritual bonds that kept us together. When the colonizers saw the strength of our spirituality, they tried to destroy Indian religions by making them illegal....Our colonizers recognized that it was our spirituality that maintained our spirit of resistance and sense of community ...Many white New Age 'feminists,' such as Lynn Andrews, are continuing this practice of destroying Indian spirituality. They trivialize Native American practices so that these practices lose their spiritual force. They have the white privilege and power to make themselves heard at the expense of Native Americans. (Lynn Andrews' books have sold more than all books by Native writers combined). Consumers like what many of these writers have to tell and do not want to be concerned with the facts presented by Native Americans. Our voices are silenced, and consequently, the younger generation of Indians who are trying to find their way back to the Old Ways become hopelessly lost in this morass of consumerist spirituality.

1) Vanity Fair magazine, August 1996, p156.

Islam: Widespread Chattel Enslavement of Black Afrikans still exists!

In Sudan you can buy a Black slave for as low as $15.

"The price varies with supply, as with any commodity."

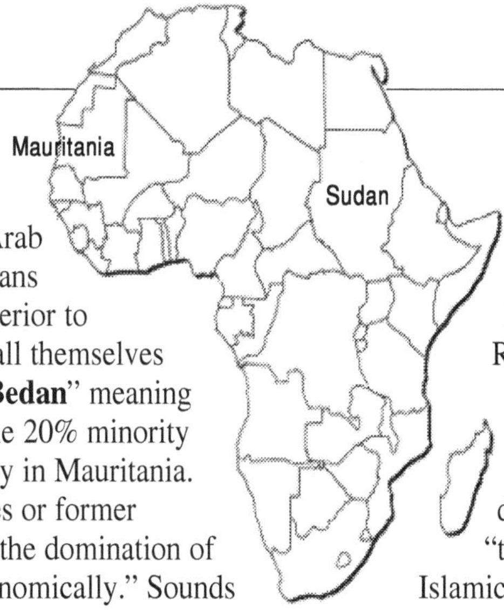

The vast majority of Black Americans do not know that hundreds of thousands of their Black brothers and sisters are still being cruelly enslaved right now throughout Northern Afrika in Islamic countries! They are enslaved by light-skinned Arabs /Berbers (*Semite-Habirus* having a little more Afrikan blood in them than their *European-Habiru* cousins). The Arab enslavers consider the Black Afrikans as **subhuman**, and themselves superior to them. In Mauritania these Arabs call themselves (and are called by the Afrikans) "**Bedan**" meaning "**white man**." These Bedans are the 20% minority that control the 80% Black majority in Mauritania. And 40% of these Blacks are slaves or former slaves! These Afrikans are "under the domination of the Arabs psychologically and economically." Sounds familiar?

Islam and Arab Moslems did –and are still doing – massive, serious damage to Afrika and Black Afrikan people. They may have done as much or more damage than their close ethnic cousins, the Europeans. In fact, the Arab Slave Trade began centuries before that of the Europeans, and "never ended in Mauritania." A slavery article in *The Washington Post* (3/14/96, page A22) stated that the Arab slave trade "has returned with a vengeance in Sudan and to a lesser extent in other Arab countries. Varying reports in recent years...have placed the number of slaves still held in North Africa at between 90,000 and 300,000."

While on paper slavery has been outlawed, the slaves have not been informed so they continue slaving for their masters without pay. Today a vast number of Afrikans are Moslems /Muslims. As with Christianity, their ancestors were largely converted to Islam by the threat of severe physical harm or even death. Though these religions began pure (originating in Afrikan Cosmology), they have been "captured," bastardized and perverted into anti-Afrikan, anti-Melanin, anti-Black people, weapon-religions which are effectively and seriously damaging Black Afrikan people around the world. No wonder that consistently, in all these religions, it is particularly the DARK-skinned believers that are *ab-used* the most and suffering the greatest! Every last one of these reworked Religions primarily originated from intent to oppress and control Blacks, and they are still effectively doing this like no dictator ever could. No wonder "the West" funds "fundamentalist" Islamic groups.

In Mauritania, former Afrikan slaves have even set up an **Underground Railroad!**

–and "safehouses" to help runaway slaves and useless, old, or deformed slaves who are simply thrown out, discarded.

A number of *Tony Brown Journal* shows document Black slavery in Islamic Afrika.
On his show, ***Today's Slave Trade*** (Show #1720), Tony Brown begins [emphasis added]:

"While everyone has been debating the facts about America's slave trade before the civil war, slavery is flourishing <u>in many parts of the world</u> – as of this very moment! Slavery is reappearing in many parts of Africa, where human beings including children are bought, sold, and bred like animals under cruel and inhumane conditions. This practice of trading in human flesh is not isolated to <u>Africa, or the Middle East, and Far East</u>. Countries in the western hemisphere are accused of dealing in human suffering, including the current hotbed of debate: <u>Haiti</u>. In spite of being outlawed, <u>slavery has also persisted in areas of India, the Middle East, and Asia</u>. For example, slavery in the Islamic Republic of Mauritania in northwest Afrika was officially outlawed in 1980. But the United States State Department estimates as many as 90,000 people, mostly Black

Afrikans, still live as the chattel of the light-skinned Berbers. Tens of thousands of other Black Mauritanians have been deported, and languish in refuge camps in Senegal. As my guest wrote in the New York Times, and I quote: Black Africans in Mauritania were converted to Islam over 100 years ago. But while the Koran forbids the enslavement of fellow Muslims, in this country, RACE outranks RELIGIOUS doctrine!"

> Some Blacks are distrustful or suspicious of certain anti-slavery groups, charging that they have a hidden agenda and that the Slavery issue itself is being used as a political tool or weapon to accomplish other (anti-Black) aims. Among questions raised is why are whites suddenly concerned about slavery in Afrika when variant forms of slavery exist here in America and also in other parts of the world?

Tony's guests were Mohamed N. Athie and Dr. Charles Jacob. **Mohamed N. Athie,** a native Afrikan and former consular official of the Mauritanian government, is the executive director of ***The American Anti-Slavery Group.*** Dr. Charles Jacob, a Caucasian Jew, is the director of Research for the same Group. Athie's statements included: *"our main goal is to stop the suffering of the people in Mauritania."* He related: *Mauritania is 100% Muslim. The difference is race. The light Berbers /Arabs populate the north. The south is populated by the Blacks, who are "stolen by Arabs," brought to north and "completely brainwashed" and enslaved. "They have to work 365 days a year" with no pay, no days off. Children born to slaves are also slaves. "Arab Berbers control the government. Arab countries give them ammunition, financial support and economic support."* Jacob's statements included: *"The fact that Africans in North Africa are enslaved just is not in the press. While we celebrate the freedom in South Africa, we have been definitely silent about the realities in North Africa." "In Mauritania [and "all in North Africa"], the situation is...an Arab Islamic civilization sits on tops of and oppresses and rules over a Black civilization. In Mauritania the Blacks are Muslims. In Sudan, Africa's largest country, there is an Arab Islamic war on the Black population of the South and those are mostly Black Christians and Animists."*

Samuel Cotton was the guest of Tony's show: ***A First-Hand View of Slavery in Africa*** (Show #1909). Cotton is an Afrikan American journalist, Human Rights activist, and executive director of ***The Coalition Against Slavery.*** His statements included: *"...the majority of slaves live in the hinterlands. And these slaves are under the controls of masters. ...They are bred; a strong Black woman is mated with a strong Black male and then the children are then divided up among the Arab families. And they are told from birth they must stay under the foot of their master if they are to reach Paradise (Heaven) ..."*

Cotton addressed why Black leaders/organizations/media are eerily silent about the slavery issue. He also spoke of "Arab-centered Muslims" versus "Suni-centered or African-centered Muslims." Apparently, as with Christianity, etc., different Moslem groups practice their own brand of Islam. Slavery is a violation of Islam. *"The reason why the Arabs are able to do this [enslave Blacks] with a free conscience... is because **Afrikans are considered subhuman.**"* Thus, enslaving "subhumans" is not a violation of the Koran. Cotton showed a 1992 legal slave contract drawn in Mauritania for the sale of an Afrikan woman and her daughter by a Muslim holy man. ***Holy*** man? *Holy* like the "churchmen" of Inquisition Europe! The same contract begins with: "IN THE NAME OF ALLAH." Allah backing up slavery? Hallmark 6 shows why! Just like the Europeans committed their crimes in the name of *their* Christ & God, their close cousins, the light-skinned Arabs / Berbers do the same in the name of *their* God. Bastard religions have Bastard Gods in whose name they commit all kinds of atrocities and get away with it –till their karma (Law of Cause & Effect) catches up with them. When criminal Constantine knew he was approaching death, he got baptized /cleansed of his willfully committed sins –or so he thought. Only a Bastard Religion so misleads people into thinking they can live in opposition to Life's natural laws and evade responsibility for their choices /actions. The *Deceiver* has them well deceived.

The Apartheid Mauritanian government also murders Blacks

There's more than the Slavery issue. Samuel Cotton related that **Mauritania also practices murder of its indigenous Black citizens**, and a system of **apartheid**. *"As recently as 1989-1991 that government murdered 1500 of its Black citizens..."* Thus, many Afrikan governments are alien-governments which are anti-Afrikan.

> **North Afrikans say:**
>
> **"It's only going to be the grandsons and granddaughters of Afrikan slaves who will take the lead and free Black slaves in Afrika today."**

Hinduism keeps Black India oppressed & Untouchables near enslaved

Indian activist, V. T. Rajshekar writes: "The word 'Hinduism' is not the scientific name of this religion. The real name is Brahminism or Vedic Dharma. It is Aryan imported stuff to India. From the very beginning it has had the suppression of the native population [Black people] and women, even Aryan women, as its primary principles. ...whereas the natives respected all humans and assured equal status to women. In fact, the natives of India were matriarchal..." [1] These Black Untouchables are the long-suffering descendants of Aryan / Black unions and native Black populations who retreated into the hinterlands of India seeking escape from the advancing Aryan domination under which they eventually succumbed. They call themselves **Dalits** which means *crushed and broken.* No justice exists for India's Untouchables!

India's caste system is unique, with no parallel in the whole world

"It is a social, cultural, and religious institution... The caste structure maintains itself because every member of a particular caste group stands to gain by belonging to that particular caste-group. The caste system helps the exploitation of the weak by the strong. India's constitution not only does not interfere with caste, but fully upholds it. **The Black untouchables are the very bottom of this deathless human pyramid and carry the weight of the entire population.** Caste system is based on purity and pollution. One group is considered more pure than the other. The less pure caste group accepts its lower status because it is happy that it has a much larger caste group below it to exploit. As long as there is somebody below it to exploit, it is proud and will not mind somebody always standing on its shoulders. So the entire caste structure is a ...self-sustaining, automatic, exploitative machine." [2]

Black Buddha gave the first major blow to oppressive Hinduism

The great **Buddha**, one of India's great Black Africoid sages, delivered the first effective major blow to oppressive Hinduism 2500 years ago. He was first to lead India's Black Untouchables' war against Aryan oppressors. Buddhism then became popular all over India (and even spread to China, Japan, Thailand, etc.). However the Brahmins (priests) of Hinduism employed devious strategies [3] to destroy Buddhism and win the natives back. Led by Sankara (circa 800 A.D), unfortunately they succeeded. It is remarkable, but logical, how closely the Indian-Hindu events parallel the Christianity events. Examples:

- Though *Christ* was a Black Afrikan, he is portrayed white by Albinos. Though *Krishna* was a Black Afrikan (identical with Christ since both are versions of Kamit's Heru / Horus), plus his very name means *black*, he is promoted as an Albino-looking man with pastel blue skin, a shade or two from being snow white. The scheming Brahmins promoted and popularized Black Krishna as one of their devious strategies to suck back into their revised Hinduism, all the Blacks (Sudras, Dravidians, Dalits, Untouchables) who had left en masse.
- Like the Euro-churchmen, the Aryanic Hindus destroyed vast quantities of Buddhist literature and murdered numerous Buddhist scholars.
- As with the great Library at Alexandria, the great Buddhist university at Nalanda was destroyed.

Debt-Slavery traps millions of India's Blacks

"...for would-be-slavers, it is far easier to drive workers into debt, then detain them until they pay it off. ...debt bondage, a system in which a parent's debt can be passed on to the children. ...the basic formula is simple: give an illiterate, desperate worker a job, then pay less than it takes to survive. ...For **centuries**, Indian labor agents called *jamadars* have scoured remote provinces, promising good jobs to landless peasants, usually "**untouchables**" or **tribals**.... Once on the job, the workers must borrow money for tools and food, and they fall into debt....The debt slaves do the most grueling forms of labor...Evidence of beating and torture is common...Some kids were even branded with red-hot irons... When they [a beaten up couple in debt-slavery who complained] recovered from their wounds, they returned to work. As **untouchables**, a pariah category under the **caste system**, they had no choice. They break big rocks into smaller ones, then load them into trucks....They have no way out [of debt-bondage]. (Emphasis added) *From Newsweek's Special Report on Slavery (5/4/92)*

1) Rashidi /Van Sertima, APEA, 237. 2) Ibid., 241-242. 3) Ibid., 239.

No justice exists for India's so-called *Untouchables.* Crimes against them by caste Hindus almost always go unpunished!

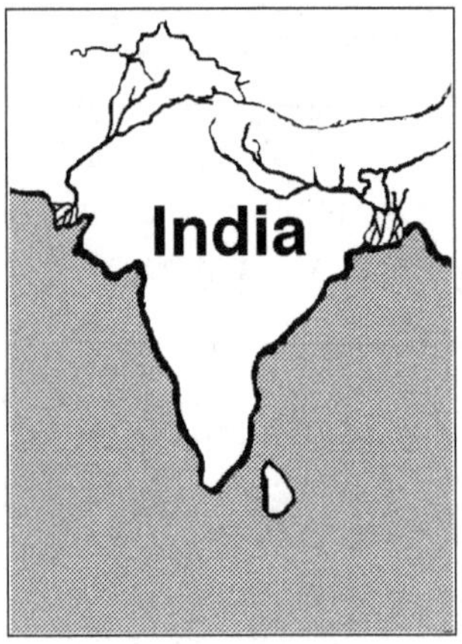

In the Laws of Manu, the unjust social laws of caste system are codified. "Manu ... inflicted the worse punishments on the Black untouchables, and also women. Even to this day the upper castes hold Manu's code as the essence of the 'ideal democratic republic' and defend it to the core. Anybody protesting Manu's Code will be socially ostracized. ...Though the whole of Hindu society is a victim of this code of Manu, the Black untouchables and women, including Brahmin women, are its worse victims." [1]

Runoko Rashidi writes: "During certain period in Indian history Untouchables were only allowed to enter the adjoining Hindu communities at night. Indeed, the Untouchables' very shadows were considered polluting, and they were required to beat drums and make loud noises to announce their approach...Cups were tied around their necks to capture any spittle that might escape their lips and contaminate roads and streets. Their meals were consumed from broken dishes. Their clothing was taken from corpses. They were forbidden to learn to read and write, and were prohibited from listening to any of the sacred Hindu texts. Regular access to public wells and water wells was denied them. They could not use ornaments and were not allowed to enter Hindu temples. The primary work of Untouchables included scavenging and street sweeping, emptying toilets, the public execution of criminals, the disposal of dead animals and human corpses, and the clean-up of cremation grounds, all of which were regarded as impure activities by caste Hindus. The daily life of the Untouchables was one of degradation, deprivation and humiliation. ...**The basic status of India's Untouchables has changed little since ancient times**. ...Untouchables in urban India are crowded together in squalid slums, while in rural India, where the vast majority of Untouchables live, they are exploited as landless agricultural laborers and ruled by terror and intimidation...In one coldly typical case, a state court recently acquitted all persons charged with the brutal mass murder, in bright daylight no less, of fourteen Untouchables in the Central Indian village of Kestara in 1982." [2]

Is Hinduism making the so-called "upper castes" CRIMINALS? For Untouchability = legal crime established as a way of life in India

In recognizing the massive injustice continuously perpetrated upon India's Black Untouchables, are not the perpetrators *criminals* themselves?! This means that by being in this religion of supreme injustice, then by default, the upper caste people apparently become criminal by maintaining and supporting the criminal injustice to the Dalits. Are they so hardened to the plight of their own brothers and sisters? This is not (or was not) the nature of Black people. It is appalling how the Dalits are treated! And these are Black people abusing Black people! The Dalits are kept in ignorance (although this is declining). That is the only way this horrible injustice can be maintained.

The laser sword of truth will cut the choking Aryan-Hindu yoke off the necks of these Blacks on all levels of caste system, but especially at the bottom where the Blacks have nothing to lose, having lost everything already.

1) Rashidi /Van Sertima, APEA, 238. 2) Ibid., 244-245.

Do these upper castes know they are perpetuating a vastly unjust, spiritually reversed /perverted system began by Albinos to control and oppress them, but maintained by themselves? Apparently upper caste Indians resist Dalit upliftment and liberation, for this means they would lose all the benefits they gain by exploiting their brothers /sisters under the sanction of religion, **–but can they see that they will gain far greater benefits in the long run, for both, themselves and their nation?** Probably not a single person in the upper castes would volunteer to change places with people in the lower castes, and certainly no one in *any* caste would volunteer to change places with a so-called Untouchable. This further shows that these people are fully aware of what they are doing to the Untouchables. Regardless, caste Indians extend little or no sympathetic support; rather they maintain the Untouchables' dire painful plight, ostracizing those that do try to help. This further reveals them as criminals against their own people and thus their own country, their *True* Nation, the nation destroyed by the Albinos, for this is the *True* India. Present-day India is as bastardized as the bastard religions it has fallen victim to, which ruthlessly controls it like no dictator could ever accomplish. Knowledge of the truth is the first step, actually a quantum *leap* towards healing this Cancer.

Where the True Light is GREATEST, the anti-life darkness seeks to put it out or keep it suppressed, oppressed.

As with Afrika, Black pre-Albino India must have had phenomenal True Light, for the fist –rather –*hammer* of *Reversed-Light* control has come down heaviest upon Black India, particularly with the Untouchables. When India (and any repressive nation) finally frees her women and so-called Untouchables –and thereby free the immense locked / blocked energy they represent –then India will also "open space" for the True Light to return to her, bringing with it the freedom, prosperity, and happiness that can only thrive in a humane, just society. India will then and only then be able to restore / soar to the phenomenal heights she once enjoyed. For her people, including and especially the dejected so-called Untouchables, are truly gods and goddesses, capable of great accomplishments –like they did in the past before Albino infection, domination, and cultural destruction. Then India will be on her way to becoming again the precious *FIRST*-World nation she used to be!

Redefining *DALIT* through awareness of Afrikan roots

From **CRUSHED & BROKEN** to **WHOLE & UNITED.** As shown by the etymologies in this book, the Afrikan roots of words typically have many meanings. **Dalit** is a Hebrew word meaning "**crushed and broken,**" adopted by India's so-called **Untouchables**, who are among the most dejected people on Earth. Hebrew is from Egyptian, hence is Afrikan, thus DALIT has other meanings. **In fact DALIT has some of the loftiest, most beautiful meanings of any words** since DAL is a name of the Loving Great Mother, for the root DAL means *Circle* –hence *Love*, ...giving us **DEL**ight, **DEL**phi, man**DAL**a, **DEAR** and **DAR**ling (since Kamite L=R). The circle atop the Ankh pours forth the Living Wa**TER**s of Life from ***DAL*** the *High* Abode of the **TUR**ret, **TOWER**, *Mag****DAL****ene.* Thus the **Dalits** are truly the Children of the Loving Great Mother, suffering as She has suffered in this Quantum WAR against Melanin –*crushed and broken* for so long, but now resurrecting to WHOLENESS and UNITY under the music of Truth's Light, the Loving Light of Divine Oneness –Mother's Light and Father's Light unfolding a New Cycle for Humanity.

5 Is a Fraud, Counterfeit, Imposter.
Deceives. Reversal of Afrikan Cosmology.

Is a Fraud, Counterfeit, Imposter! Is a reversal of Afrikan cosmology, its source. Supplanted the Blacks' original theology with a falsified, counterfeit, poisoned version. **Truth is suppressed,** for truth exposes the fraud and destroys the Lie in one stroke. **Albinos had to overthrow or suppress (black out) the truth so their falsehood (whitewash) could grow.**

Whites didn't create anything new; they stole /reversed /perverted the original Afrikan Cosmology, then attempted to burn/destroy the evidence that would expose their fraud. Slick lies, pseudo truth –poisoned at the core. Hundreds of millions of Black people fervently embrace these religions not realizing they are embracing the daggers, poisons within them, therefore they suffer and remained enslaved –fallen in the trap.

It is interesting that the term "faith" is used to describe *Religion*. This indicates people have lost the real "knowledge" or "gnosis" and have resorted to "faith." Such is a shaky foundation because one is asked to "believe" what they don't "know." If you absolutely *know*, then *faith* is unnecessary and nothing can shake your knowingness. One needs to "believe" or "have faith" where there is room for falsehood. These religions command the hearts and minds of the masses as much through blind faith as through fear and intimidation. **The suppression of truth (true Black history /herstory, true theology, true self-knowledge, etc.) keeps people proportionately "unconscious."** The more unconscious people are, the more easily they are controlled. **It is not what you are being told but what you are not being told that is controlling you the most!** The Truth ***will*** set you free –but only when, and to the degree you are aware of it /accept it. Often the truth is not something *told* but something *recognized*, for *Truth* is a vibration that is *felt*.

Note that all the Hallmarks are reversals of the original theology /culture /nature of Blacks. Examples: Afrikan theology was *matriarchal* –equally honoring women and men –and recognizing the role women played in bringing forth and nurturing life; *Sexuality* was sacred, not scorned or deemed filthy. Blacks defined through *affirmation*, not through negation. And everywhere, Blacks were *peaceloving* –becoming violent only in reactive defense to the violent invaders seeking to destroy them and their culture. Afrikans went around the world, dispensing civilization, building and educating, uplifting the peoples they found from barbarianism. Europeans went around the world dispensing unparalleled genocide, destroying civilizations and ancient archives, and oppressing, degrading, enslaving the peoples they found. While there are many whites who *are* loving beings, collectively Albinos have shown themselves to be Anti-Humans, the reversal of the Original Human.

The Koran (like the Vedas, Bible, Talmud) **is loaded with fabrications,** myths, plagiarisms, and allegories. Some of these are addressed by Dr. Yosef ben-Jochannan in *African Origins of the Major Western Religions* (pages 212, 214 -216).

Remember, he is the *Great Deceiver* whom Jesus called the Father of *Lies*. He has the whole world deceived, especially through his four pet top religions, refined through his "chosen ones." Some 99.99% of the world's population are unknowingly worshipping the Deceiver, thinking they are worshipping the True Loving Divine Source of Life /Light.

6 Secretly enthrones, worships "Set."

In the unholy Bible is evidence of (*their*) God being the Devil!

- **"Satan" and "the Lord" (Jehovah, Yaweh) are the exact same being in 2Samuel 24 and 1Chronicles 21.** If you read these chapters, you see they are essentially the same. Here are their beginning verses:

"And again the anger of <u>the Lord</u> was kindled against Israel, and he moved David against them to say, Go, number Israel and Judah. For the king said to Joab the captain of the host which was with him, Go now through all the tribes of Israel, from Dan even to Beer-sheba, and number ye the people, that I may know the number of the people. And Joab said unto the king, Now the Lord thy God add unto the people, how many soever they be, an hundredfold, and that the eyes of my lord the king may see it: but why doth my lord the king delight in this thing?" (2Sam.24:1-3)	"And <u>Satan</u> stood up against Israel, and provoked David to number Israel. And David said to Joab and to the rulers of the people, Go, number Israel from Beer-sheba even to Dan; and bring the number of them to me, that I may know it. And Joab answered, The Lord make his people an hundred times so many more as they be: but, my lord the king, are they not all my lord's servants? why then doth my lord require this thing?" (1Chr. 21:1-3)

- **Shadai** or **El Shaddai** is a key Hebrew (Habiru) name for God, allegedly meaning "God Almighty." The name *<u>Shadai</u>* is from the same root as Set /Seth / Satan / Sodom! [1] (see namelist on page 79). The early Albino Hebrews and Hyksos worshipped Set (also called Sut-Typhon) as their main God. They sacrificed their children to El-Shaddai or ***Shed /Shedim***.[2] Shaddai's name is in the Bible as **Ammishaddai** (Ammi-Shaddai) and **Zurishaddai** (Zuri-Shaddai). Shadai apparently = Set-Iah, Set-Jah.
- Set or Shadai was also known as **Moloch**.[3] The "Israelites" and Judean kings (Ahaz, Manessah) sacrificed their children to Moloch (2Chr. 28:3; Jer. 7:31; 32:35, etc.). (This ties in with Hallmark 12: Power-leeching.) While in some verses, "**the Lord**" forbids sacrificing children to fiery **Molech** (Lev. 18:21), in other verses "**the Lord**" demands that all firstborn children be sacrificed to him! (Exo. 13:2, 15).
- "**Baali**" was another name for El Shaddai.[4] The "**Baal**" of the Hebrews was identical with **Set /Sut**.[5] "The Lord" commands "thou...shalt call me no more **<u>Baali</u>** (Hos. 2:16). "**Bore**," another Hebrew name for God means Creator. Since Kamite L=R, Bore =**BOLE**, likely a variant of **Bal / Baali**.
- Many believe **Satan** was a fallen *angel* but the New Testament call him 'the **<u>GOD</u>** of this world'! (2Cor. 4:4) Isn't "God" supposed to be this?! Plus Satan offered Christ "all the kingdoms of the world" and their glory (Mat. 4:8). How could he offer this if they were not his?
- ***Lucifer*** is the Latin title for the Morning Star. Lucifer the *Light Bringer* is Set, also called ***Shaher***. The Jewish *Shaharit* (Morning Service) still commemorates him.[6] **Shaher** is in the title of Psalm 22, and is often translated as "morning." Lucifer was Son of the Morning (Isa. 14:12).
- And the Bible's rewriters have *all* of man*kind* (their kind?) descend from **Seth** (Set, Satan), Adam's 3rd son (Adam = white / red man). (Gen 5:3).

1) Massey, AE, 499. 2) Massey, BB-vII, 382. 3) Massey, BB-vII, 342-343. 4) Churchward, 365. 5) Ibid., 264. 6) Walker, WE, 551.

- **"The Lord" (which one?) sends "an evil spirit," that's right, an EVIL spirit to torment King Saul:** "an evil spirit from the Lord troubled him. And Saul's servants said unto him, Behold now, an evil spirit from God troubleth thee" (1Sam. 16:14-16). There's more! Musician David (who later replaced Saul), who was sent to play music to soothe tormented Saul, had to be protected by God from Saul's attack on him with a spear while Saul was under the influence of the same "evil spirit" from God! (1Sam. 18: 10-11). This goes against plain reason! *Evil* spirits from *God*? Which God? The same fiery angry killer God (Ps. 78:34, etc.) who sent "evil angels" among his *chosen people* (Ps. 78:49), and said "I...make evil" (Is. 45:7).
- **Some "Lord" this is! Sample verses:** "The Lord shall send upon thee cursing, vexation, and rebuke...The Lord shall make the pestilence cleave unto thee...The lord shall smite thee with a consumption, and with a fever, and with an inflammation, and with an extreme burning, and with the sword, and with blasting, and with mildew; and they shall pursue thee until thou perish ...The Lord shall smite thee with madness, and blindness" (Deu. 28:20-22, 28).
- **Beelzebub** means **"Lord of Flies,"** an alternate biblical name for the Devil. If **"the Lord"** is *not* Beelzebub, then why is he sending spectacular, "grievious" **"swarms of flies"** upon Afrikans (Egyptians) and throughout the land of Egypt? (Exodus 8:20-24, 29; Psalms 78:45, 105:31)
- **"The Lord," a merciless child-killer commanding murder:** "And the Lord said... Go ye ... through the city, and smite: let not your eye spare, neither have pity: Slay utterly old and young, both maids, and little children, and women" (Eze. 9:4-6).
- "The Lord" even turned people into cannibals eating their own children!: **"I will cause them to eat the flesh of their sons and the flesh of their daughters**, and they shall eat every one the flesh of his friend" (Jer. 19:9).
- **Why is "the Lord" surrounded by thick *darkness*?!** "He made darkness his secret place; his pavilion round about him were dark waters and thick clouds of the skies" (Ps. 18:11). A "God that hidest thyself" (Is. 45:15).
- **And what is smoke and fire doing coming outta "the Lord's" nostrils and mouth ?!:** "There went up a smoke out of his nostrils, and fire out of his mouth devoured: coals were kindled by it" (Ps. 18:8). Plus his nostrils could "blast" (Ps. 18:15). Kinda sounds like the red Dragon Set (Rev. 12: 3, 9).
- **The only way "the Devil" could get away with pulling himself off as "God" is through *Quantum Deception*.** People are so well tricked or DECEIVED, they don't even suspect the Deception. This ties in with Hallmark #5: Fraud. Even the Bible (same one the Deceiver has mucked with through his *kids*, states "...Satan, which deceiveth the whole world: he was cast out into the earth [Earth, where we are!]" (Rev. 12:9). In the same Bible, "the Lord" is a Deceiver who "hath put a lying spirit in the mouth of all these prophets" (1Ki. 22:22, 23). Jeremiah moans "O Lord, thou hast deceived me, and I was deceived" (Jer 20:7). *The Lord* even admits to deception!: "And if the prophet be deceived when he hath spoken a thing, I the Lord have deceived that prophet" (Eze. 14:9)! In the same verse, "the Lord" kills such prophets that he has deceived!

"Do we not make God a thousand times worse and more fiendish than the wickedest of his creatures when we talk of his punishing any being forever?"

"Could any man ever smile if he really believed that he had a friend or relative suffering, or doomed to suffer, unending misery in a lake of fire?"

Kersey Graves
The Biography of Satan, 127, 129

• More evidence that the biblical Christ is as messed up and reversed as his Dad also becomes exposed under the light of true etymology –especially with the name MELCHIZEDEK

The Bible gives no record of Melchizedek's ancestry, birth or death. In fact hardly any information is given regarding him, yet Christ is identified several times as "an high priest after the order of Melchisedec" (Heb. 5:10, 6:20, 7:1-17) (Ps. 110:4), who is simultaneously a *King* and High Priest. And **Abraham**, the first biblical Habiru (see page 108) **paid tithes *not* to God but to Melchizedek**!, "the king of Salem" (Jeru*salem*) and "priest of the most high God" (Gen. 14:20, 18). Just who is this mysterious being? Etymology exposes his real identity: the name ***Melchizedek*** (Melchi-Zedek) is derived from *two* prominent names of the Devil! :

- ***Zedek*** is derived from Set (Set-en, Satan). Biblical variants include *Zadok, Sadoc, Saduccee, Zidkijah,* and *Zedekiah* (page 79 lists others). An Akkadian hymn calls him Ztak, the Supreme Ensnarer (based on the Kamite Crocodile God *Sevekh the Ensnarer*, capturer).[1]
- ***Melchi*** is a variant spelling of ***Moloch!*** –which means King or Prince. As previously shown, Moloch was another name of Set. ***Melchi*** was the name of two ancestors of Christ. Biblical variants include *Moloch, Molech, Melech, Malachi, Milcom, Melicu, Allammelech, Elimelech, Hammoleketh.*

The true etymology of Melchisedec /Melchizedek further exposes and underscores the whiteman's biblical Christ as a Fraud / Counterfeit / Anti-Christ. The biblical Christ is disguisedly Set, not the Heru (the true Krst) it is supposed to be and pretends to be. Refer to Chapter 11 of this book, especially pages 171-177. Massey informs us: "Sut [Set] also appears in the person of Melchizedic ...Sut was cast out of Egypt, together with his worshippers, as the unclean. He retained the good character for a while in Israel, yet it was known in after times that, as Melchizedic, he was of an unclean origin, and by degrees the good Sut, the earliest Prince of Peace, became the Moloch, the Tzud, Adversary, Satan and Devil of the later theology."[2] In the Book of Joshua, we find a disguised version of Melchizedec. His name is **Adoni-Zedec**, having essentially the same meaning as Melchizedec. *Adoni* means *Lord* in Hebrew. Like Melchizedek was the "King of Salem," Adoni-Zedec was the "King of Jerusalem" (Jos. 10:1).

• Now we know why Christ built his church upon Satan!

It's in the Bible, for Jesus actually calls Peter Satan (Mark 8:33), the same Peter who denied him three times and to whom he declared "Thou art Peter, and upon this rock I will build my Church" (Mat. 16:16). No wonder "the Church" has the history it has and is the way it is. Any church built on white Counterfeit Christianity /Judaism /Islam / Hinduism is built on "Peter." More evidence for Peter's diabolical identity is the "Cross of Peter," an upside-down Crucifix upon which Peter was *crucified* according to legend. And the source? Kamit. For Peter is Set, who was crucified. Thus the biblical Christ is Set while professing the reverse. *The Wolf in Sheep's clothing.*

1) Massey, BB-vII, 499. 2) Ibid., 340.

What does the name SET (Satan) really mean?

Stone. STone. Rock. The same "Rock" on which the fraudulent biblical Christ built his church. The same "Rock" whom Christ even called "Satan." The same "Rock" whom Christ renamed "Cephas" and translated this as "Stone" (John 1:42).
Massey enlightens us: "This is Bar...and **his name of Sut means a stone. The stone was his especial type.** He is called Stone-head and Stone-arm in the Ritual. As Bar-Sutekh he was the destroyer. Bar was likewise the Babylonian Bel, the breaker and destroyer alluded to by the Hebrew writer [Jer. 50:23] as wielder of the 'hammer of the whole earth.'"[3]

Signifying *stopping* and *staying,* Kamite **ST** is the source of STand, STone, STay, SiT, SeT, SeaT, STasis, STill, STall, subSTance, STop, etc. Thus the STuborn Ass was identified with Set. Massey writes: "One of the types of 'SET' is the rock, an image of fixity itself...The meaning of this standing, staying, stopping, was embodied in the ancient Deity SUT...Stander and Stayer."[4]

Hardness conveys Compression.
Compression in the right place (rocks, metal, etc.) = strength, foundation, something to STand upon. As noted in chapter 12 (with Gad), Compression in the wrong place (consciousness) = bondage, decreasing Vibration, thus decreasing Life, thus PAIN. Vibration = life. The undermining and destruction of WILL, combined with the repression of EMOTION (an aspect of the Will) = Inner Compression (hardening, becoming stone-like), thus leading to permanent Stopping (death) if not corrected. The Supreme Healer of all this is *Accepting & Loving Oneself.*

Set was the original god of the Albino Hebrews and apparently still is the god of "the Jews" *and* the Christians *and* the Moslems –since Judaism is a Counterfeit, along with Christianity and Islam –both founded upon Judaism. Hence secretly, unknown to the believers, their real God is Set (Satan), while professing the opposite. *The Wolf in Sheep's clothing.* **In Hinduism, the Aryan god *Indra* is also modeled from the Devil** as "Ahriman" the "Lord of Darkness," the Persian Lucifer.[1] No wonder these religions have the history they have! And no wonder "the Lord God" (which one?) complains about His name being defiled: "I will make my holy name known in the midst of my people Israel, and I will not let them [*who* is "**them**"?] pollute my holy name any more" (Eze. 39:7). God could legally sue "them" for Grand Slander, *Cosmic* Slander except the courts are ran by "them" !

A Power-Taking King is none other than the "Royal Seizer" we met earlier as "Ben-Amen" (Benjamin) the cancerous Crab,

whom we also now recognize as the "Supreme Ensnarer." No wonder after birthing him, his mother called him *Benoni,* "the son of my sorrow/ mourning,"–then died! "Amen-Ben" is *Hidden* Ben, the *disguised* Darkness-brother (Set) to his only full brother Joseph, the brother of Light. Both are versions of the Set/Heru twins. His father, dying Jacob (another version of Set the Devil) says only bad things about Benjamin (Gen. 49:27), comparing him to the thieving Wolf he really is (another *Seizer*)! *The Wolf (Wolves) in Sheep's Clothing*, wearing many disguises. And **Solomon**, yes, King ***Sol-Amen,*** is another form of Ben-Amen *the Devil.* King Solomon, another ancestor of (the Anti) Christ, built altars to Molech (1Kings 11:7). Solomon's real name –the name given to him by "the Lord" was *Jedidah* (2Sam. 12:25). Solomon is *Sol* (solar, sun) *Amen* (hidden, darkness) or the Sun /Lord of Darkness. Some interpret his name as meaning ***peace*** (Solom, Salem). Well Melchizedek was the "King of *Salem*" hence *King of Peace. Peace* sounds *good* doesn't it? Melchi (or Moloch; King) sounds good too. "***Peace***" was the word spoken to the setting or ***dying*** sun –and to the ***dying*** *sacrificial victim* who impersonated him[2] in rites that "brought forth bread and wine" (Gen. 14:18). *Bread* and *wine* is the *Eucharist* –yes, in the *Old* Testament *before* Christ (!) –representing the flesh (bread) and blood (wine) of the consumed Sungod. Hence this *"**Peace**"* is apparently identified with or is ***Death***.

You thought *Solomon* was a good guy –along with *Abraham, Benjamin, Joseph, Jacob...* The only thing good was the Deception. Let's pick on **Jacob**, a prominent version of the *Lord of Darkness.* The same Jacob that wrestled all night with a *man* called God, and won the fight –taking the god's title and becoming ISRAEL! (Gen. 32: 24-32) All this points to a common theme being recycled and refined, beginning with Cain/Abel, repeated as Esau/Jacob, and other versions of Kamit's warring **Set/Heru Twins**, impersonating Darkness and Light –culminating with the biblical outstanding Christ/Judah –an outstanding Fraud, outstandingly well done.

Remember, Jacob *deceived* his father in order to *steal* Esau's blessing and birthright as the firstborn son. Who sounds like the bad guy here? Yet, Esau was *hated* by God while he was still in his mother's womb; and "smooth" Jacob was loved by God. *Red* Esau (who was born *red* and *hairy*)

1) Blavatsky, IU-vII, 488; Walker, WE, 14. 2) Walker, WE, 885. 3) Massey, BBv-II, 440. 4) Ibid., BBv-I, 170.

was hated because he is the Goat, *Set* (Satan), God's adversary. Yet we discover that Jacob himself is another form of Set while being deceptively presented as the good guy. **Disgusting reversals!** Reversals and reversals within reversals are ever present within the Bible's recycled themes to the point of utter confusion. **But if you keep in mind that the end result is always *the Wolf in Sheep's clothing,* then no problem**...for the most part.

"**Beliel is from Baaliel, Lord of the Opposite**, which means a sign or constellation opposite to the sun at any given point. Adversary, another Satanic title ('your adversary the Devil.' 1 Peter, 5-8), is also traceable to the same source; Adversary being like Beliel a sign at right-angles, or adverse (adversary) to the sun."

Kersey Graves, BOS, 46-47

Benjamin was the *only* son born *after* Jacob (the Dark Sun) became Israel (the Bright Sun) and moved to Canaan! This moving = the Sun *setting* in the west –domain of death– into the Amenta Underworld, represented by Canaan. See the *reversal* in this picture? –for if Jacob becomes *Israel* he should be the *rising* sun (Heru), not the setting, dying sun of death (Set/Sut). Additionally the city he moved to was *Shalem* (variant of Melchizedek's *Salem*) (Gen. 33:18). But... just before this, actually right after he won his fight, there is a sunrise sneaked in: "as he passed over Penuel the sun rose upon him" (Gen. 32:30). This sounds like a "flash appearance" or flash acknowledgment of the Good Principle, then it's whisked away before it's noticed (It is put in to retain the underlying astrological integrity). *After* this, Dark Jacob –who is now Bright Israel – goes (sets) to Canaan (becoming the Sun of Darkness he stands for). **Confusing? As the rewriters intended. Truth is always simple! Lies need thick books,** heavy books in many volumes and wordy explanations to fabricate and support the fraud and deception. Truth *just is.* It does not know how to hide. Yet is invisible to those having not eyes to see it. But once seen, you recognize that *Truth* has *always been there*, with clues all over the place despite suppression –just waiting to be recognized –so *She* may give you Her gift of Liberation. *Libra*-ation. Restoring your clipped wings or missing wings so you may fly again or for the first time ever, in the sweet expansive *Air*, free-est of classical elements. Mother Truth sets us free.

Maat

Back to the ground –with lying Benjamin. Except for Benjamin, all the Tribes of Israel are really the Tribes of *Jacob* (the Devil or Darkness), not *Israel* (the Christ or Light). Logically then, Benjamin is the *only* Tribe of Israel, being the only son born to his father after his father became "Israel." As the only Tribe of Israel, Benjamin should be of Light but his name, etc., signify Darkness. *The Wolf in Sheep's clothing.* Yes the *Son of the Right Side* can also be interpreted as LIGHT, but his Light is from the Bringer (FER) of Reversed Light (LUCI)! His father on his dying bed is called *Jacob*, not Israel! So the Tribes of Israel *are* the Tribes of Jacob –the Deceiver. Another reversal: note that killer Cain is designated bad while his later brother Seth (Satan) is "the Lord's" replacement for the slain Abel. *The Wolf in Sheep's clothing.* Cain is a variant spelling of Canaan. The Canaanites are the Kenites. The multitudinous variant spellings of same-names is a deliberate ploy to further disguise the Truth *–or Lie* –and ultimately point people in the *opposite* direction of where they think they are being guided. True etymology slashes the Deception. **Further evidence of Jacob being the Devil:** Jacob won the fight but lost his ***phallus***, euphemistically called "the sinew that shrank" lying upon "the hollow of the thigh" (Gen. 32:32), which is the real reason he limped after the fight. This is a picture of **castrated Set** –castrated by Heru. Hence Jacob is Set (*The Wolf)* falsely presented as the good guy by becoming Israel (*Sheep's clothing).* Which is the good or bad guy? Or are they poles of the same stick? The "God" which Jacob (Set) wrestled with *all night* was the Sungod Heru (good guy). Yet if he was Heru-Israel, why is this happening at *night?* Another reversal within a reversal. And Jacob SUPPLANTED him, like he earlier supplanted his brother Esau; like Seth supplanted Abel (really, *Cain* – hence another reversal); like Ephraim supplanted Mannessah; like all the biblical 2nd-born sons somehow supplant their firstborn brother and wind up with the firstborn's blessings and position. Bible dictionaries interpret Jacob's name as Supplanter or Deceiver, both titles for the Devil. And Ephraim has *two* sons essentially named Satan by being *both* named ***Shuthelah*** (derived from Sut /Set, hence Sut-El) (1Chr. 7:20, 21). Furthermore, the same Ephraim and Mannessah are counted as Jacob's full sons though they are his grandsons. They are even given a hunk of land like the other tribes. In other words they (Ephraim, actually) supplanted their father Joseph (who is not given any land). Reversals. *The Wolf in Sheep's clothing.* **If you can see it, the *Supplanter* has supplanted firstborn True Cosmology with second-born, bastard Counterfeits,** which are enjoying all the privileges and "birthright" that should go to the firstborn. But it only takes a single flame of vital Truth to start a raging Fire to burn down the thick Forest of *Deception.*

Now we see that the "Lord of Darkness" permeates the entire Bible in numerous disguises penned by his *kids*

He has to disguise himself –else be recognized for who he really is– none other than the *Hidden* Deceiver deceiving though his "disguises." **Supplanting** the Theology of Truth with **Pseudo Truth** –counterfeit religions! What do you expect from the Deceiver? Don't worry, for the Crocodile is now busted; his Deception is pierced; his cycle is over, –his *race* is over and he did *not* win, though it looks like he came close. This is his last *flang* and he's trying to collect as many as possible to **take** with him. For not only is he the great Deceiver but the great **Taker**, the ***Under-Taker***. Not to Hell, for that is fiction, but ultimately to Spiritual Death, the *real* death. And what leads to this "Spiritual Death" ? Not what you think. The culprit is **"suppression of the WILL"** (summed up as Self-Denial and Emotional Repression). **This is why the Supplanter –in so many ways– is always trying to take /suppress / or manipulate your WILL**. WILL is your true Wealth, Health, and Happiness. This subject is of paramount importance yet very simple.

> **WILL** is directly related to Melanin! This is why Melanin is under attack. WILL is directly related to the Female Principle. This is why Women the world over are suppressed. WILL is directly related to Earth. This is why Earth, a Personification of the Great Mother, is under attack. What is *The WILL?* **The WILL is the *Mother Principle of God*** expressing in us as Intuition, FEELing, Emotion, Ability to Choose, Receptivity, and Desire. Details on how to recover and heal your *Lost Will* so you may LIVE is addressed in Ceanne DeRohan's inspired book-series, beginning with *Right Use of Will: Healing and Evolving the Emotional Body*; also, the 6-part inspired article on the Internet entitled ***"Healing The Invisible You"*** at www.godchannel.com/voices.html.

Satan *Santa Claus* is in the Bible too!

Santa Claus is known by several names and all of them are in the Bible as we shall see! His other names are **Old Nick, St. Nicholas** and **Kris Kringle.** Description: Santa Claus is represented as a fat, old, jolly, red-cheeked Albino with a white beard and red suit, who brings toys to good children *globally* on Christmas eve. He is a composite of various so-called pagan gods, especially Set. "As European pagan [*Afrikan*] deities were Christianized [*whitewashed further*], the benevolent aspect of Woden [*another composite god whom Santa was equated to, with traits from Set*] became St. Nicholas (Santa Claus), who galloped over housetops during the winter solstice as the elder god did, granting boons to his worshippers below." [Walker, WE, 726]

Let's look at his other names:

- **Old Nick** is an old name for Santa Claus. Look up "Old Nick" in a dictionary and discover for yourself who he really is! Yet if you look up "Santa Claus," the same dictionary will not tell you that Old Nick is one of his names. "Old Nick" is allegedly from "**Hold Nickar**," a Danish seagod. I doubt this! –for the same "Old" is found in "**Old Scratch**," another name for the Devil.
- **St. Nicholas**, the alleged "saint" behind Santa Claus is as fictional as Santa dispensing toys through chimneys globally in a single night. But *fiction* (lies) is appropriate for the *Deceiver*, "Old Nick," his Christian name. [WE, 726] **Sinte Klaas** was St. Nicholas' Dutch name.
- **Kris Kringle** or "Christ of the Wheel" was a title of the Norse year-god born at the winter solstice (Christmas) as the sungod born again. "His title seems to have applied to a sacrificial victim on a fiery wheel." [WE, 516] **Kris** and **Christ** are both from Kamite **KRS** (krs, krs-t, karast). Where is the "wheel" in this? From **KRS** as the Astronomical or **Equilateral CROSS** of the Four Quarters in a *circle*. ⊕ The same CROSS upon which the *Karast* is annually *crossified* (crucified) –thus **X** means ***Cross*** and to ***cross out!***

Their dictionary tells you **X** also means ***Christ!* The "X-Christ" they are refering to is *Set* the Anti-Christ. For the Cross of the True Christ (Karast) was the PLUS (+), not an X! –signifying Increase and Life.** Hence early portraits of Christ show the Cross of Four Quarters in a circle (halo) behind his head. In "X meaning Christ," the X = negation, death, to X-out, "cross out," hence the "Criss-Cross" (KRS-Cross!) crossing out or crucifying the true KRST / Christ! Note the big X in the Nazis' reversed Swastika and the *Skull & Crossbones*.

Since Kamite L=R then:

- Nickar = Nickal, Nicholas.
- Krs (Kris) = Kls, Klaas, Claus!
- "Criss-Cross" = Kris-Claus!
- Klaas and Claus are also in Ni**colas** as COLAS.
- coLas in Ni**colas** = coRas, hence cRoss.

OLD is from the same root as **EL**, revealing Old Nick & Old Scratch as ***El* Nick** & ***El* Scratch**. Why "Old"? Because Set was the *EL*der brother of Heru. **Thus El-Nick = Nick-El hence Nicholas, the *God* Nick!**

Now to get right to the point –the *Points*. The POINT is Set, Satan. The same Point that will **NICK** and **SCRATCH** like the **AK, AX** (**X**!) in Zad**ek** (Set-Ak), **Jac**ob (AKob), N**ick** (nIK), **Sc**ratch (sEKratch), Mol**och** (Mol-OK), cr**OC**odile, and **Ac**iel (AK-el, a name for Set as the Sun/Lord of Darkness). The Point is the Point of the pointed Christmas Tree. The Point is the ***DiaBolos***, alleged roots of the word ***devil***, meaning ***through*** (dia) ***throw, hurl*** (bolos /ballein). Hence to ***pierce through*** –like Children of Set, reknown for names meaning piercers or cutters. Only a Point (l**anc**e, spear, **ANG**le) will pierce, "through throw." Hence even his name as *Devil* "points" to a Great Point –no wonder he wears a long, red, ***pointed*** cap! Possibly the true roots of ***devil*** is **DEI** (god) **BAL** (Bal, Bar). **Bal** /Bar was identical with Set, **Baal** of the Hebrews, and **Bar** the Syrian God of War (identical with Mars the red god of war). [Budge EH 213; Churchward, 264] The Point is the ***Sword***, a ***Cross***-shaped cutter or modified **cross**; and "kris" is the name for a Malayan dagger. **AK** is also the el**EC**trifying ***fire*** in **IG**nition, **IG**nite. Thus fiery ***red*** Nick is associated with ***hell*** and "**fire places**" like the fiery devouring Mol**OC**k he disguisedly is.

Satan-Santa Claus lives at the North Pole for reason of Set's astrological connection with the North (Is. 14:13). And Whites are from the white cold North. Why does Santa only comes around at Winter? This is the season of *death*, like the Death he represents and the color White (color of death). And why is he connected with Christmas? He is Set, the twin brother of Heru the prototypical Christ.

***Kris KRingle* will make you KRinge:**

- **KR** –to **GR**ab like the **CR**ab. Snatch like the **KL**eptomaniac.
- **INGEL** is the "Fallen Angel" taking us back to the Point, the blade, an **ANGLE** that cuts like the **ANGL**o-Saxons or SEKsons –*Sons* of SEKratch. Cutters. Scythians (SEKthians), *Sic*ilians.
- INGEL is **ANKH-EL**, the ***Life Divine*** that is *cut through*, **KL**ipped, cut off by the sword-shaped **KR**oss of the DiaBolos.

Thus KR–ING–EL is the God (El) that snatches, takes, cuts *Life* (ANKH). A Life Cutter is a Life **CLOSER**, the **CLAUSE** of Santa **CLAWS** –from Latin *clausus* –to close! The Great CLOSER, reverse of the ***Opener*** called **Ptah** and **Heru**. Nick-Clause, Satan Nick Close. Shuts off the True Light. Closed places like closets are **shad**owed, **Shad**dai-owed.

KRingLe is the KLencheR, Clincher, Trapper, Imprisoner. **CLINK** = prison. Clench: to close (claus) tightly; close *claws* tightly. The cRoss is the cLoss, the cLaus, **CLAWS** of Set-an Santa . Claws that will CLOSE upon its prey. Nicholas is **Nick-Claws**, claws that nick. **Satan Nick-Claws**,

In the dictionary, *NICK* means to cut, cheat, steal, also *prison*! *NICKEL* in German means "demon, rascal, from the deceptive copper color of the ore (from the name Nikolaus, Nicholas)." ***NAG*** means to torment, annoy. ***NECRO*** means death. Other words in this family are *snake, sneak, snag, snook, snick* (to cut). All these NICKwords are from Kamite **NEK** (nak, nekht, nag), having very **NEKative** meanings! (calamity, death, to tie/bind, be doomed, injured, violence, break open); And **NAK or NAKI is the likely source of *Nick* as the Devil's name:** *Nak /i* means enemy, foe, serpent-fiend, devil! [Budge, GE, 345]

All the Bible's NICKnames point only to Nick:

1. **Nicanor**: a Greek (Albino) Acts 6:5. Nicanor is Nika-Nor (*neri*, light) of light from Nik-Lucifer.
2. **Nicodemus**: biggest of Nicks. A Pharisee and "ruler of the Jews" (John 3:1). Ruler? Like King Melchizedek, the Nik to whom Nik-Abraham paid tithes. Reference to his **noc**turnal coming (like Old Nick!) is made twice. "The same came to Jesus by night" (John 3:2, 19:39). Like Set came to Heru *bringing* the **NIG**ht, for Set = Spiritual Darkness, lack of God's Loving Light. Jesus told him he could *never* see God's kingdom without being "born again." But why did Nicodemus (the Devil) participate in Christ's burial? (John 19:39-41) He is Set,"burying," "putting down," hiding, suppressing, putting out the True Christ or True Light –*Loving* Light. His "coming by night" is mentioned again in the same verse when he comes to bury Christ! The last part of his name (DEMus, oDEM) reflects the first part, making him *RED* Nick (DEM, aDAM means red), aligned with dam, damn, demon, dichotomy (e**tym**ology, p289).
3. **Nicolaitans**: Nicola-Itan=Nick the Snake Lord. Itan = *snake*, *adoni* (lord). Condemned in Rev. 2:6, 15.
4. **Nicolas**: "a proselyte of Antioch" (Acts 6:5), meaning "Gentile convert to [false] Judaism."
5. **Nicopolis**: where Paul went "to winter" (Tit. 3:12). Like Ol Nick at the permanently *wintered* North Pole. White is the color of death and the albino (white) season of death, when Set peaks. The Spiritual Winter or cycle of the White Season is over!

To summarize Santa's BIBLICAL presence:
Kris Kringle: In the name Christ we find Kris, Klaas, Claus. In Angle/Angel we find Kringle. In Nicolas we find Nick, Nicholas, also Claus /Krs again. So where is the name ***SANTA* in the Bible?** Reference books say *Santa* means *saint;* this is true for *any* Santa "Xcept" CLAUS!, for can we trust *their* references, especially when the Deceiver himself is the subject referenced? **The name *Santa* is *Satan!*** **Santa** is composed of the exact same letters as the **Satan** he is! And Dutch **Sinte = Set-in**. Thus Santa is throughout the Unholy Deceiving Bible! **Satan Nick** personifies consumption /materialism, being an icon of the culture that created him. His fat, a main trait, attests to this.

As they did in the past, Albinos still worship and glorify Set –disguised as Satan Santa Claus. Most Blacks worship Satan Claus also. They put their precious children in his *red* lap and get photos taken with the *red*-cheeked **Hairy *Red* Devil in a *red*** suit. Why red? Because Set was red, hence the Devil is red, *in all shades* like the Children of Set. **Albinos who honor the Loving God as their Father are Real People, IUmans, People of Loving Light.** Albinos and any people who continue to honor Nick as their *Father* are ***NICKars. Nikkars.*** Sounds like ***NIGGERS***. No wonder we hate this word! Brought to us from the ***Nick-ars*** themselves, whose global, historical NICKing is unsurpassed. They had it backwards, *reversed.* ***Nigger* then, is *NICK-ar,*** thus the real **Niggers**, for the most part turn out to be the lily-white or *pink* **Nick-ars**, along with ***any* people of *Heartless Inner Darkness* –the darkness of Set –confused with the *color BLACK.*** The color Black receives (accepts, absorbs) the Light! The color White rejects (reflects) the Light –more than a mirror!

And it was at the **Council of NICea** where the True Light of Karast-ianty got NICKed to death, "claused," "closed," "clawed," "crucified," "through thrust" (dia-bolized), and "buried" by Ol Nick, *El Nick* working through his major **Niggers /Nick-ars** to supplant the teachings of the true Loving God and Goddess with a Counterfeit which is still NICKing people today on all levels, keeping the world in Spiritual **NIG**ht. For s**nicker**ing, s**nigger**ing Santa is not the ***Giver*** he is falsely portrayed as but the ***Thief***, the ***Taker*** (*UnderTaker* like Nicodemus), attested by the words **NIGGARD** (petty in giving, meanly small), and **NAKED** (stripped, devoid). Not a single child ever received a gift from him! Nick turns *Christ*-mas into a *White Deathly* **"X–mas"**, brimming over with artificial gifting, soaring depression, and escalated suicide rates. **Now we know why Santa "winks" !**

7 Anti-Freewill. Obedience demanded.
Undermines, destroys sovereignty.

What all these *Hallmarks* have in common is manipulating or taking peoples' *WILL!* Destroys sovereignty, fosters dependence and relinquishing of Will and personal responsibility for Self. They all foster /promote /establish servile obedience, willessness, docility...to the priests, popes, gurus and other authorities but especially to a God that allegedly demands this. "Not my will but thy will be done O Lord." Total surrender to Allah. The word *Islam* itself means *submission*, from *aslama* (to surrender, resign oneself). The God of all these bastard religions is a dictator who requires absolute obedience and surrender of personal Will. No room for Freewill. If God wanted us to be his slaves why would S/He give us any Will at all? The Un-god would certainly demand such! Our Will (ability to Feel / Choose / Desire) is among our most precious assets. Remove it and we become puppets, robots, androids. As Gwynth said, "The thing that makes it so difficult is that we don't know what Freewill is any more, because it has been so greatly manipulated. And we have been given a set of belief systems that hold the manipulations in place."

All these weapon-religions were forced upon Black People (in Afrika, Americas, India, etc.) against their ***wills***, and often at sword-point under threat of death if the victim would not "convert." False Christianity was also violently forced upon the Europeans! And because their **freedom** (another word for WILL) to worship as they WILL-ed was suppressed by other Albinos, countless Europeans fled to America for "religious freedom."

Obedience demanded. Adherents must have "obedience" to God though He never comes in person to give commands. ALL these commands are physically coming from *men* claiming to be the go-between for God. Note that one is required to "believe" that these men are above all other men in some way (chosen, holy, the prophet, etc.) It's a power-hungry priesthood (*men*) controlling the masses. Abounds in **rituals**, which are really forms of behavior (WILL) control, manipulation, inspiring awe & giving away one's power. Thick, hard to understand books/scriptures. The complex systems, rules, laws, (Islam's Sharia law, Hindu laws of Manu, etc.) are there to control and manipulate people, ensure / maintain the exploitative system, suppress / delete people's wills, deny people expression of their true will. Moslem / Hindu women are not allowed to even choose their own husbands.

That the *Ten Commandments* are called "commandments" illustrates the dictatorial nature of patriarchal gods and their religions. The original "commandments" were not called such but were called "virtues" or affirmations. They did not command "thou shalt"! Instead, they affirmed; "I have..." **Freethinking is prohibited.** Even today, reading religious books outside one's religion is discouraged. Wanton destruction of archives, libraries, learning, and thus, free thought. This is why the **Gnostics** (meaning those who know) were hated, persecuted, and killed by "churchmen." Really, the churchmen (Albinos) were trying to suppress one of the last vestiges of the Afrikan Mysteries which was rearing up as the Gnosis. The knowledge (Gnosis) of Truth is always a threat to established Lies and Fraud.

> **"There is no such thing as the 'will of God' apart from your own divine will.** If God wanted life to be the mundaneness of a singular expression, he never would have created you into being. Nor would he have given you the will to express your own purposeful uniqueness.
>
> "What is called the 'will of God' was created by man so that he could govern and control his brothers. Yet if you believe that teaching and see God's will as separate from yours, then you will always be in the battle of 'his will versus yours.' For you will want to do certain things and feel you must, yet the 'will of God' says you must not!"
>
> *Ramtha*

8 Bondage.

Mentally / physically enslaves, imprisons, restrains.

Notice how hard, often impossible it is for people to "break free" of their "Religion." Why? They are *bound* to it, for the word Religion itself means just this –**Bondage**! Slavery and physical imprisonment are the most extreme forms of Bondage, thus extreme denial of personal WILL. **Worse than this is Bondage where you are not aware you're in Bondage.** For in such, there is no hope of becoming free since the Bondage is not perceived due to the *Deception*. Therefore you continue to be the exploited pawn, the effect, the controlled. *A Slave* in other words. Used. Used up. Constantly giving pieces of yourself, your time, money, energy, **Will** (hence Power). Remaining in the herd, the herd that is led to slaughter both physically (the Crusades, *holy* wars) and spiritually, while being exploited along the way. Note how in all these systems, women defend support the system demeaning them. It is the Moslem women themselves that have their daughters castrated. Though men originated this, men do not have to force them to do this, for the force of inner Bondage is sufficient to "keep them in their places." Internal slavery is the worse kind, for though its chains are invisible they are virtually breakproof –until the TRUTH arrives! Even then, many resist and cling to denial.

The invisible chains of Counterfeit Religion are holding most of the world's population, including the Albinos, in Bondage, as intended by Nick the Imprisoner. Invisible cords are the strongest. Religion binds with invisible cords in an invisible prison from which few escape. Hindu-India is a dramatic example of the pernicious unshakable grip or BONDAGE of Religion, –still firmly, unshakably standing after several thousand years! Hinduism dramatically enslaves the Body, Mind, and Soul of India's Black population. India's "Untouchables" are essentially slaves. Worse yet, **countless Blacks are still in physical chattel slavery in Moslem Afrika** by near-white Arabs! North/ South Afrika, and India are examples in pure form of what Albino poison does at the level of religion and nation. So what is it doing at the level of the Soul? Leading to Spiritual Death ultimately, the permanent death from which there is no reincarnating.

Notice people say they "BELONG" to a particular reLIGion, like a club, a LEAGUE. The word "belong" also betrays the underlying Bondage of ReLIGion. Slaves "belonged" to their masters –who "owned" and "possessed" them, as Religions *own* and *possess* nearly all of Humanity. This points to Bastard Gods who leech Human energy through Bastard Religions –the top pillars for mental slavery for all races but especially the entire Black race. They effectively lock People of Color in Mental Slavery and even physical slavery. **The first slave ship in fact, was called "The Jesus"!** And modern Islamic slave contracts begin with "In the name of Allah."

Perhaps you pride yourself on "not belonging" to any religions? I bet you have friends who do! Plus the society you live in does. Hence you cannot escape being influenced and affected by "Religion." For you are having to adapt /interact/ bend in certain ways because of "other" people in Religion. Thus you are still being controlled, albeit indirectly by "Religion."

The Word *Religion* literally means *Bondage!*

Religion is from Latin *religo /religare*: to tie, to tie fast, fasten behind.

Other words from this root indicate the same: ***ligament*** (fibrous tissues [cords!] binding bones and cartilage at a joint or organ); ***lignin*** (a binding polymer that is the chief constituent of wood; ***league, ligation*** (binding, being bound).

Religion, particularly the counterfeits called Hinduism, Christianity, Islam and Judaism, keeps the world in mental, spiritual, and even physical Bondage –as they were set up to do, for they are well-engineered Bondage systems.

And the word *Church* is from a root meaning *overlord*

"The Church" was Europe's worse overlording dictator. **Hence the Church is a Slave Master.** Modern slavery still exist, only the form has changed. "The Church" still keeps people in Bondage.

Any "holy books" or teachings given to us by or through the very people that have destroyed our cultures and ancestors, will serve to keep us in subjugation and Bondage on all levels.

9 Domineering-dictatorial, haughty hierarchy.

"Obey them that have the rule over you, and submit yourselves" (Heb. 13:17).

Establishes a snooty, rigid, racist, sexist, domineering, dictatorial, hierarchic social structure /priestly hierarchy (Levitical caste system, Hindu caste system, Feudal caste system, hierarchies in the church /military /government) with themselves on top and People of Color /Women at the bottom. **Even *heaven* is set up as a hierarchy. Hindu gods belong to a particular caste!** Though Islam acknowledges only one God, it still has an equally dominating though simple hierarchy: Allah at the *top*, men in the *middle* (Mohammed, caliphs, mullahs), and women at the *bottom* –actually the *Blacks* are at the bottom in Moslem Afrikan countries today; the light-skinned Arab /Berber minority dominates the dark-skinned indigenous Afrikan majority. Sounds familiar? Mohammed was the overlord /theocrat of the theocratic nation he established. The leaders of the imposter Jews set themselves up as high priests (Pharisees, etc.) which controlled everyone. The Pharisees were an influential minority noted for their separation from the "common" people. *Pharisee* even means "separated ones." They turned the original Israelite society into a 2-tiered caste system –practicing apartheid, white supremacy, and subordination of Blacks, with racism backed by *their* God: "And the seed of Israel separated themselves from all strangers" (Neh. 9:2). Ye "shall be a peculiar treasure unto me above all people" (Exo. 19:5). And "in that day there shall be no more the Canaanite (Blacks) in the house of the Lord of hosts" (Zec. 14:21).

Bishop & Episcopal are from the same root meaning "one who stands higher than his fellows and overlooks them." [1] *Overlords* in other words. The tonsure worn by Catholic priests = the disk of the sun,[2] the original "overlord" called "Lord." In the original Afrikan Church, bishops were picked by drawing lots, hence they changed with each convening! In the Kounterfeit Katholic Khurch that destroyed and supplanted it, bishops become bishops by ascending a rigid hierarchy. The Bishop developed into the Pope, **a *feudal lord:***

> "Among the False Decretals was the so-called Donation of Constantine, whereby Pope Sylvester I and his successors were granted temporal as well as spiritual dominion over the entire empire, and the fiefdoms of the Papal States were established. According to this document, Constantine made the pope the greatest feudal lord in Italy: 'Wherefore, that the pontifical crown may be maintained indignity, we hand over and relinquished our palaces, the City of Rome, and all the provinces, places, and cities of Italy and the regions of the West to the most blessed pontiff and Universal Pope, Sylvester.' " [3]

There was no Caste System as found in India until after Albino invasion and takeover. Like Islam, etc., Hinduism is tailor-made to maintain "Ayran" domination over the indigenous population and women. The Caste System originated from the "Rig Veda," the "sacred scriptures" of the Ayrans. The Brahmins (*priests*, like the Habiru Pharisees), who were the real controllers of everyone else, classified themselves as the topmost caste, reserving for themselves a life of leisure and abundance, and for others, manual labor. Second in order was the Warrior Caste (Kshatriyas), then the Merchant Caste (Vaishyas), and 4th, the Sudras (artisans, laborers, menials). Last and at the bottom are the essentially enslaved, so-called Untouchables or "Outcastes."

The Khazars (counterfeit Albino Jews) at the top have plans for total, overt, dictatorial world control. Covertly they are already largely doing this via the so-called Secret World Government. In the words of their Talmud: "Every Jew will have 2,000 'goyim' slaves." [4] These slaves will be any who is not one of them, including whites. If Albinos don't wake up soon and see that their real enemies are not (nor ever have been) People of Color, they may be in the position they have traditionally tried to keep nonwhites in. Many Albinos *have* awakened and are trying to warn people through books like Conspirator's Hierarchy and Behold a Pale Horse.

1) Churchward, SS, 358. 2) Ibid. 3) Walker, WE, 319-320. 4) Hatonn, CB, 58.

10 No direct contact with Supreme Deity.
Has a go-between.

Denies direct contact with Supreme Deity (or tries to). Sets up a go-between or mediator between you and God. Won't let you go to God directly, though they say God is everywhere. You gotta go to God through the priest, minister, angels, Christ, Church, etc. This is an ancient, effective method used by corrupt priesthoods to control people in the name of God. Also to increase their power and make themselves miniature gods to be worshipped in disguised and held in awe. It is a way of stealing people's power. Promotes dependency on a priesthood for the favors of God. "Translates" for you. Against autonomy. Fosters dependence on an authority at the expense of our psyches. This Hallmark ties in directly to the previous (Hierarchal).

These pseudo religions deny /impede access to the true Loving God/Goddess by denying the true knowledge of Him and Her and giving people pseudo knowledge / Pseudo Truth

Fraud, in other words. False Light. Counterfeit Light of the Bringer of *Reversed* Light. Counterfeits which look like the real thing but are not. Many are fooled and fall into the well-laid trap.

> **"most of you still do not know that God *is you;*** that you possess within you the power to know and be *all things.* Thus you let teachers and religions and everyone else rule your life and interpret truth for you. You allow the understanding of others to complicate and clutter the simple truth that has been spoken for the ages in your time –that the Father and the kingdom of heaven are, indeed, within you. What grander truth can be written than that? But many of you who do not know that, still think you must go through dogma and certain 'mechanics,' as it were–rituals, prayers, chants, fasts, meditations–in order to connect with God and become enlightened. Yet the more you do these things, the more you convince your soul that you are not what you are trying to become–that you are far from the love of God and the understanding you are seeking, for you are having to do arduous things in order to achieve it."
>
> *Ramtha*

We don't need Religion to find God / Goddess!

People need to rediscover the cosmic truths about their beings which Religions deny them. **They need to learn that they don't need Religion to find God**; they can go to God /Goddess directly from within their hearts. "Be still and know I AM God." "Know ye not that ye are the Temple of God?" Afrikans erected pyramids to stand as reminders throughout the ages of the *Divine Fire Within* (pyra/fire-mid/middle, center). Practicing rituals and following dogma is not wrong. But it will never feel completely right either, for the voice within you that *is* God –says you already *are* what you are struggling to reach. We can honor Loving God/Goddess the way Humanity's ancient ancestors did, through *Nature*. Frequent the forests. Hug a tree. Listen to the birds. Enjoy the breeze caressing your cheeks. Notice, study, appreciate the beauty and majesty of Nature. This is true worship. Gratitude. **Find *Quiet Time* each day to go *within*,** for your precious body, fat and all, wrinkles and all, beauty and all, is and always has been, the True Temple of God/Goddess. You have always been a child of God /Goddess. HU. Light. Loving Light. Hue. Light in Seven Hues, personified as the *Seven Chakras* of your precious Temple, called the *Seven Seals* in Revelation. You. Goddess-Woman. God-Man. YOU-man. HU-man. **The Hallmarks are only manifestations of Reversed Light seeking to rob all peoples of their true heritage as Divine Beings,** descended not from apes or monkeys, but from the Great Mother and Great Father Themselves, our True Parents. **We are all in a major War**...which is now actually over in Heaven (higher vibratory realms), thus will soon be over on Earth. This means that Humanity, including the Albinos, will get (are being given) the opportunity to heal like we never have. Self-Acceptance and truly Loving Oneself will heal this for both the Blacks and the Albinos. And this precious, all-healing, liberating Self-Love is fostered by knowing the vital truths.

11 Fear-based.
Thrives on fear, intimidation.

"The basic foundation of Religion is fear, and fear is the product of ignorance. Enlightened people are not religionists, and the chief work of the Church is to keep people in darkness and ignorance in order to make them the slaves of Religion." *Hilton Hotema*

The antidote is knowledge of the vital truth. No wonder truth is suppressed! Keeping people ignorant of truth keeps them in darkness, thus easily intimidated and controlled, exploited.

Fear-based, not Love-based like the original Afrikan Cosmology. Uses Fear as a tool to control people. There is always a threat of punishment if you don't *obey* (i.e., surrender your *WILL*). In False Judaism / Christianity / Islam, it is the threat of burning forever in a fiery hell (and just one little sin qualifies you for it!). In Original Karast-ianity (Afrikan Cosmology), there was no such thing! In Hinduism, it is the threat of reincarnating as an Untouchable, an animal, or in some other horrible condition. All this ties in with Hallmark 9 (Dictatorial hierarchy). If one is going to be a dictator, one needs a means of enforcement. **White supremacy operates on the premise of fear –actually, *terrorism*.** It achieves via deception, trickery and lies. It rules via intimidation, hence its psychotic emphasis on weapons of war & destruction. Just one of their nuclear subs can wipe out several continents –in other words, the world. There are *300* of these circulating the ocean!

Early European churchmen helped (*their*) God enforce his alleged edicts by killing/burning people (women especially, also children and even babies) at the stake! What kind of God demands this? Set-Moloch; his sacrificial victims were "passed through the fire." **The "Church fathers" and Habiru priests got God and Satan reversed *deliberately*,** for it was never their intent to worship the God of Love. Why do you think the Kamites called them the "Children of Set"? Their leaders know who their real father is. **In their pseudo Bible is stark evidence of their real God being Satan** (Hallmark 6**).**

People cannot be "scared into righteousness"

Moral behavior resulting from intimidation is fake behavior, suppressive of the persons' true will. This suppression then exits them as very real energy which actually functions as fuel for the negativity in the world, and holds "darkness" in place. By healing ourselves at the true original cause (referred to as "Lost Will" in the book *Right Use of Will*), we come to recognize that we already *are righteous,* for this is our *true* Nature. The missing key ingredient is Self-Love (self-acceptance). This is the bottom line! Without Self-Love, we are subject to a host of *dis-eases* on all levels. So-called "sin" only points to a deficiency in Self-Love.

Their bible says to "fear God." Can you really love who you fear or are terrified of? Actually, it would be a natural response to "fear" the God of their Bible, who is presented as a psychotic monster, a killer, –wrathful, vengeful, regretful, angry, insecure, cursing, racist, anti-female, "hardening" people's *hearts*, devouring people with fire, murdering people and ordaining the ruthless butchering of even babies, despite his alleged commandment "Thou shalt not kill." And not only is he a jealous god, but **His name is *Jealous!:*** "For thou shalt worship no other god; for the Lord, **whose name is Jealous**, is a jealous God" (Exo. 34:14).

This was not the God of the original Afrikan scriptures whites copied from. **This was the white man's Un-God which Albino men made in *their* image (like the Aryan god Indra, also modeled from the devil. Unfortunately, almost all People of Color give their power to him!** Any wonder why we have the problems we do? As recommended in Chapter 12, in your prayers use the word "LOVING" before the name GOD or whatever name you use (hence "*Loving* God" *Loving* Great Father, *Loving* Great Mother), to direct them to such, otherwise you are likely getting the same "God" (Un-god) which the Churchmen also called upon and in whose name they burned and murdered millions. **The worship of Set is alive and well today, rampant and thriving as Christianity, Judaism, Islam, Hinduism, and other religions as well.**

12 Power leeching.

Power sucking / thieving / taking.

Takers, not givers. Thrives by leeching / sucking /stealing /taking power from both the believers and non believers. Afrikan Cosmology empowered and gave energy. Counterfeit Religion does the opposite.

Will and Power are one and the same!

All these Hallmarks have in common the manipulation of people for power, while at the same time, destroying or taking peoples' WILL. **Theft of Will (hence Power/Energy) is the bottom line.** Victims are continosly milked, leeched on all levels and are subordinate to a greedy priesthood /churchmen / God, etc., with Guilt heavily promoted.

Anything which manipulates, diminishes or takes your WILL is also manipulating, diminishing and taking your POWER!

- The chauvinist albino-edited Bible, Talmud, Koran, Vedas empower males by stealing feminine credit. The patriarchal subordination of women in all four of these religions is a means of leeching women's power. Remove the women and the bottom falls out of all Four.
- All four suck from people at all levels: psychologically, spiritually, financially, materially, etc. Typically, church-temples and banks are among the best looking, best built buildings –being both places of *worship!* It is said that the Vatican (a *country* in Europe) is so rich, it can not count its stolen wealth. Fosters and thrives on poverty. Wants to keep people needy, thus more easily controlled. Exists at the expense of the suppressed. Sanctioned by a fraudulent God (Un-god), they all suck people dry then cast them aside on the waste heap. Priests were totally supported by the people, from which they always took the best in the name of God.
- People are encouraged to "give to the lord." "Offering trays" milk them. They are really giving to the anti-Lord. For he is a *God of Death* who cannot generate True Light. He has to steal it, take it, leech it. The *light* (LUCI) that he *brings* (FER) is stolen light, Reversed Destructive Light; totally void of Love, hence anti-life, deadly. That's how he stays alive. If people stopped giving away their power, will, money, time, and all other forms of their energy to his top four monsters, the world would change drastically at record speed for the good.

They hijacked (stole), then reversed the power of Afrikan theology

Essentially, Albinos stole the Exterior Form of the Blacks' theology in order to empower themselves. They have copied only the **Exterior** but not the **Interior** which is the *real thing* and that which counts. The **Interior** is the *prime mover*, the causal essence. If they had really copied the true **Interior** they would not be **Anti-Humans**. Albinos have stolen mega power from all People of Color. They (particularly as the so-called "Secret World Government") use their stolen power to keep themselves in domination, "on top" in their "missionary position" over People of Color. Keeping Blacks especially, at the bottom. Sure, they may put a few token Blacks in high positions but this is just to pacify Blacks; and it seems that Blacks "up there" are puppets with little power if any, to make real changes.

Religion is Re **LEECH** ion!

13 Anti-sexuality.
(especially of females). Exploits sexuality.

SEX: How come the holiest act of creation and means by which Life propagates itself, is called "original sin"? Making sex evil and filthy is a patriarchal invention. If you make Women evil, then naturally sex becomes evil. All four monsters suppress and abuse sexuality, especially of females, and foster tremendous sexual guilt. Welsing's *The Isis Papers*, provides profound insights regarding these sexual dynamics. Women are degraded as servile sex objects –in the religion, culture, and way of life. India's Hindu government supports/benefits greatly from copious female prostitution. "Churchmen [Europeans] claimed the fires of sexual passion were transmuted into the fires of hell, blown by the breath of God into a heat fiercer than any earthly flame."[1] Churchmen sexually mutilated /roasted whitewomen in Inquisition Europe. Numerous biblical verses are anti-sexuality:

- "and there be eunuchs, which have made themselves eunuchs for the kingdom of heaven's sake. <u>He that is able to receive it, let him receive it</u>" (Mat. 19:12). Several early churchfathers "received it." Origen was highly praised for castrating himself. Tertullian declared, "The kingdom of heaven is thrown open to eunuchs."[2] Medieval Europe's cathedral choirs had *castrati* or boys emasculated before puberty to preserve their "virture" and soprano voices, which were considered more pleasing to God than the "impure" female sopranos (who were not allowed in choirs anyway). What kind of God requires such castration?
- And David purchased his wife from God's representative king Saul, with 200 Philistine *foreskins* (1Sam. 18:27).
- "It is good for a man not to marry" (1Cor. 7:1 –N.I.V.). "to the unmarried and the widows I say: It is good for them to stay unmarried, as I am" (1Cor. 7:8–N.I.V.).
- Menstruation is demeaned. Women had to live on the outskirts of the village till their flow stopped. Sex with menstruating women was punished (Lev. 20:18).

Anti-Female is anti-sex & anti-life

For without sex / females, life cannot continue but will die out. As far as the *white man* is concerned, they have figured out a way to eliminate women's reproductive function and still get procreation *artificially* via test tube fertilization, etc.

Purdah sex segregation. In public, Moslem women must essentially veil their entire bodies. They must keep their mouths veiled because it is equated with the vagina.[3] Moslem men can legally kill their wives, daughters or sisters for adultery, but not vice versa. Pakistani Moslem women claiming to be raped are imprisoned for *zina* (sex outside of marriage), but not the rapist. Moslem women, especially in Afrikan countries, are brutally *castrated* while they are helpless babies or girls. **These are primarily Black women suffering this injustice.** And Black Afrikan female SLAVES in Moslem countries are sexually exploited just like Black female slaves were commonly sexually exploited by their slave masters.

Islam's Glorious Sex Paradise

The Moslem paradise, as *created* & penned by Black Bilal, an Islam father, is incredibly *carnal*, promising every *male* believer 72 "Hur-al-Oyum," that is, 72 Black-Eyed Daughters of Paradise or Afrikan Virgins, who were the prize of the entire (male) Arabian world.[4] In addition, their virginity was ever-renewing each time they had sex! No mention is made of rewards to females.

No female Great Goddess. The God of the Albino-poisoned religions demands the godhead all to himself. **Without his female counterpart, he stands in danger of becoming <u>homosexual</u>.** Is it any wonder that whites have been the authors of homosexuality? Indigenous people acquired the habit only after sustained contact with Albinos. Homosexuality was glorified <u>only</u> in an Albino nation (ancient Greece). Male homosexuality especially, finds fertile ground in a culture which diabolizes females while glorifying males.

1) Walker, WE, 387. 2) Ibid., 146. 3) Walker, WD, 319. 4) Jochannan, AO, 200, 201.

14 Warlike, violent, militaristic.
Bloody history, anti-life, death-glorifying.

The religions themselves are weapons against all peoples including the Albinos

All of these bastard religions were violently forced upon People of Color and the Europeans themselves. Europe was brutally murderously "Christianized."

- The world's worse and longest wars have been the "holy wars" fought in the name of religion. Holy holocausts are rife in all these religions. The Crusades killed more people than the two world wars combined.
- Nearly the whole Old Testament is about warring & murdering in the name of a God (Yaweh, Allah..) who commands merciless slaughter of people in war after *holy* war. He forgave no sins without bloodshed: "without shedding blood is no remission" (Heb. 9:22).
- Wars are a major part of the Hindu scriptures. The Aryan god Indra slays vast numbers of indigenous Blacks. This is actually what the Albinos did upon invading India. Hindus murdered many Buddhist scholars and destroyed vast quantities of Buddhist literature.
- A soldier in the cause of Islam is the highest role of the faithful.[1] Theocrat Mohammed and his soldiers violently –for the most part, converted Arabia and many lands to Islam.
- Moslem hordes destroyed many Hindu temples and artwork. Christian hordes did the same to *Egyptianity.*
- Hindu-Moslem riots. Catholic-Protestant riots.
- Their "Church" was not a church but a bloody terrorist military dictatorship using the cloak of Religion. The word church is from a root meaning *overlord.* The Church was Europe's worse dictator-overlord.
- Untouchables/Black Moslem slaves are ruled by terror and intimidation. Both are often aggressed against and the aggressors go unpunished.
- Moslem men can legally kill their wives, daughters or sisters for adultery.
- The Christian Hell is a vast torture chamber. The Inquisition violently tortured and roasted tens of millions of innocent whites (mostly women).

"Hundreds of frightened Kano residents sought refuge at police headquarters as rumors of new Moslem-Christian clashes spread through the northern Nigerian city. ...hundreds of people died and many more were injured in the violence which began when Moslem youths chanted 'Allahu Akbar' (God is Greater) and then set fire to churches, homes, vehicles and shops."[3]

All four religions are Anti-Life because they are Anti-Female

(Female is source of life). Therefore, all four have a prominent track record of mass-killing (wars) and gross disrespect for life. Fighting is glorified. Death is glorified. Appropriate since they are religions of the Loveless Un-god of Death. The rewards of life come AFTER you DIE, as long as you serve their God. The "afterlife," or what happens **after you die** is emphasized. If a Moslem soldier **dies** in battle he goes straight into the midst of the Hur-al-Oyum (beautiful Black virgins ready to sexually bliss him out).[2] Real living in the NOW is thwarted, postponed –only the *future* counts. One is waiting to really begin living *after they die!* This fosters **passivity and tolerance for intolerable conditions** presently afflicting believers (*victims*, actually), such as the global injustice of Albino supremacy, chattel enslavement of Blacks in Islamic North Afrika *today*, and the Aryan Caste System infecting India. Believers (victims) are admonished to have patience while they continue to be exploited, used, manipulated by all the "authorities" feeding off them.

The Crucifix, a symbol of Death, is the top icon of Albino Christianity

The *Crucifixion* and *death* of Christ are emphasized, not his *resurrection.* Murderous emperor Constantine had "In Hoc Signo Vinces" written above the Crucifix which means "In this sign you will conquer." And that's exactly what white supremist armies did around the world, armed with their gun in one hand, and false Bible in the other. **The majority members of white False Christianity are People of Color around the world, held in control under the sign of the cross.** The Crucifix is a symbol of death and white domination over people of color: **Ku Klux Klansmen** leave burning crosses behind. Black Jesus the revolutionary, was executed by whitemen (Romans). No wonder the holy day celebrated for his ***death*** is called "Good Friday."

1) Jochannan, AO, 331. 2) Ibid., 203. 3) *The African Times*, Oct. 31, 1991, page 2.

Conclusion

All these counterfeit weapon-religions are psychotic, reversed, corrupted, and poisoned to the core, while deceptively presenting the opposite image, even promising everlasting life while ever promoting death slowly throughout the world. Therefore they are all "unhealthy," –extremely hazardous to our health and well-being on all levels. If we are to survive, we must let them go! They are as mucked up and reversed as Humanity itself has become by believing them, as was intended by the Deceiver. The Bible, Talmud, Vedas, and Koran are misrepresenting, demeaning and harming the Loving Great Mother, the True Loving God, and True Karast (Loving Light). They keep the world in the false Reversed Light of the Deceiver, thus in Spiritual Darkness that ultimately leads to Spiritual Death. But now *the Wolf in Sheep's Clothing* has been exposed along with his Mega Deception.

All this time Humanity has been embracing the wrong light from the bringer (FER) of Reversed Light (LUCI). But our true Divine Parents do love us and do care. They would like to see all of us freed from the yoke and *spell* of these Counterfeit Religions. We can just simply yank them off and let them go! It is (or can be) that simple! We do not need Religion, period! Only the reverse is true; *Religions* need humans in order to suck power from in order to feed the *Bastard Gods* who really are powerful, negative Extraterrestrials (ETs) practicing advanced Mind Control and Energy-Theft under the vehicle of Counterfeit Religions! Excuse me for springing this up suddenly. I had planned to address this topic only in the next volume of this book, and still intend to, but am mentioning it now. I call these ETs *"Humanity's Hidden Manipulators."* They control us like sheep in a pen. Now we see that the *real culprits (kill-prits)* are not exclusively the Albinos. The Albinos generally function as their executive agents on Earth, while they keep themselves extremely well-concealed. The Albinos and the Greys are part of the same body, which is why they share each other's major traits. The Hallmarks of the Albinos are 10-times or 100-times more so for the Greys. There is still hope for the Albinos...I think. There may be no hope for the Greys! The Greys are where Albinos are heading pell-mell unless they choose healing. Racism, Albinism, Greyism is a cosmic issue reaching much deeper than we suspect. The Deceiver is one of the ETs; he is not as powerful as he seems. His power is largely stolen, and continuously freshly supplied from his pet religions.

The Top Four are not the only guilty Religions. Note that ALL religions /Spiritual Paths bear a number of these Hallmarks (!) especially...

7: Anti-Freewill. One is required to surrender one's WILL. Obedience demanded.
#9 : Hierarchal.
#10 : Go-Between, Mediator. Looking up to /worshipping a human super guru /pope / prophet /holyman, hence placing holiness outside of one's Self. No direct contact with the Creator.
11 : Fear-Based. Threat of punishment if you don't obey.
12 : Militaristic.

You know a tree by its fruit. What has been the "fruit" of these religions? Wherever they were brought / imposed, the people degenerated. **Evil** (*LIVE* spelled backwards hence *anti-life*) comes looking ***good*** (like Satan ***Santa Claus***) in order to deceive us. Just go to any American commercial supermarket and look at all the foods presented so attractively. This is deliberately misleading for these counterfeit, artificial, "refined," chemically poisoned commercial foods are the foods of slow-death –degenerating the body –causing over 240,000 to die in America every two months from so-called incurable disease! This exactly mirrors what these Counterfeit Religions are doing to Humanity. Beautiful on the outside, ugly on the inside. One slowly kills the Body; the other slowly kills the Soul!

Once Blacks wake up to the quantum Fraud of these Counterfeit Religions, they can convert their churches & temples into potent tools for their *liberation*, not their *oppression* in the name of "the Lord."

This is accomplished through dispensing knowledge of the truth instead of counterfeits.

> Black ministers and any ministers who are now awakened to this Truth & Fraud have a choice to make: *whom* will they serve –the Loving God of Life or Loveless Un-god of Death? They also have a responsibility –actually a great ***opportunity*** to awaken their whole congregation to the real truth, original *Karast*-ianity, Afrikan Cosmology. A truth that is *not ethnic* but *cosmic!* –rooted in the universal principles.

Upon knowing and embracing the truth (after recovering from the initial shock), Black ministers can now become an equally potent force for Black mental liberation thus the physical liberation which always follows. (Mind leads, Heart guides through Feelings, Body follows and reflects all three.) They can stop being unknowing promoters and agents for the Un-god of Reversed Light, and start serving the True God /Goddess of Loving Light and Life.

All this time, Black ministers have essentially been serving the Deceiver by promoting his counterfeit Christianity, Islam, etc. As long as Black churches, Black ministers, Black Sunday school teachers, etc., keep Albino religions, they will continue to serve as key instruments in keeping Black people in the Grip of Nick, leading them to Nickland. In ignorance made possible by massive Deception, *Quantum Deception,* well-meaning Black ministers have been seriously hurting "the Sheep." Upon knowing the truth, if they continue to teach and preach the counterfeit religions then they are ***consciously*** **leading the Sheep to slaughter.**

Now is the opportunity to serve the True Loving Father *and Mother.*

We will *live* and have *life everlasting* only when we put ***Mother*** back into the Equation. We will continue to die and unknowingly promote Death by leaving Her out. Un-god has no goddess or female mate; he hates the Feminine Principle of Life and is trying his best to kill Great Goddess and thereby kill the Universe. The reflection of this on Earth, the planet personifying Goddess, are the Earth-threatening nuclear weapons, ongoing underground & oceanic "testing" of these weapons, and the global degradation of females by men of all races.

"EACH one, TEACH one," –or ten, or more...

- **Hold discussion groups around this reference book.**
- **Share this book with your friends, family, clubs, congregations.**

You have *received*, now you have the *opportunity* to *give* and thereby play a vital role in bringing the Awakening and restoring the True Light. For that is what YOU, IU are named after! YOU ***IUmans***. HU-mans. Children of Light. Children of the Sun. The same Sun called IU. The same Light called HU. Soul, Self in Solar. SOUL People, –any people with **Heart**. Divine Fire (Pyra) Within (Mid), for you *are* Light. A precious Cell in the Great Body of the Creator, the Great IU that is You – looking back into your eyes as you gaze at yourSELf in the mirror. Is there any part of your Body that is *not* precious? Likewise are yIU to the Creator. You are valuable, **exceedingly Precious**! –whether you believe it or not. Your *believing* it / *knowing* it –for it is the *Truth*– will open undreamed of doors for you, allowing you to claim your true Heritage as a Daughter or Son of Goddess/ God. The same Heritage which Counterfeit Religion aims to deny you of while falsely claiming to give it –of course only after you DIE. Life is for fully, gloriously living NOW. As a unique part of the Creator you have a unique role to play which you and only you can fulfill.

Thus the formidable massive army for massive expedient Black Awakening is already firmly in place, existing throughout Black America as the Black churches /mosques and their congregations!

If these congregations can be exposed to this liberating Afrikan truth –which is really the Cosmic Truth– then very rapidly, Black America will be *truly* FREE AT LAST from Quantum-Deception, the foremost shackle of the Deceiver.

The Truth is more powerful and devastating than guns and all 300 of Nick's nuclear subs circulating the oceans.

Black People around the world, can you not see that if you were not this powerful, the *Controllers* would not need to spend so much Time–Money–Energy ever striving to keep you in "your (false) place" and keep your minds shackled? This is their top preoccupation! Their whole culture is set up and structured on all levels of people activity –at every turn, in all ways– to keep you (and everyone else) ignorant of the vital liberating truths. For when you know the truth, you are powerful. Truth *is* power. Real power.

The Controllers know this. Hence they freely give you guns (by making them easily accessible) but not books of vital Truth. Rather, they inundate everyone with "facts" and vast amounts of meaningless irrelevant "information" while keeping the truth guarded and locked up in the penthouses of their ivory towers and vaticans, outta reach for most –including most of them.

Instead of Truth, the Controllers give us Pseudo Truth
–false light, *Reversed Light.*

But listen, **you *ARE* the Truth.**
It does not matter that anyone locks up the truth.
For the Truth IS YOU, is IN you, in your genes, your DNA, the "Kore" of your Heart –*Mother*-given HeartSoul. Divine Pyramid Within. As you get exposed to vital parts of the Truth –this starts a *chain reaction*, an inner KHEM-ical reaction that cannot be reversed once initiated!

For the Great Power that IS you,
manifesting as YOU,
has finally pierced the *Great Deception*
and broken the *Great Spell.*

Then it is a matter of brief time before the outer reality matches the inner reality of expanding liberation.

The Albinos or any rebellious Prodigal Children of Reversed Light, cannot stop this Awakening and Quantum Healing but they can *join it* and *become healed themselves* and cease their War Against the True God/Goddess (and *themselves,* unknowingly).

For this is also a great opportunity for
Albino Healing and Liberation *–if they can see it.*

The Creator's Gift of Love can only be accepted through and by those who accept themselves first.

Thus **Self-Acceptance** or truly **Loving Oneself** will heal each of us. This precious, all-healing Self-Love is fostered by knowing the vital relevant Truths that set us free.

15

The *Almost* Immaculate White Deception

Europe was deliberately "Dark-Aged" in a conspiracy to erase Afrikan memories and entrench "Reversed Light" control

In ancient times, it seems that a large percentage of whites embraced the matriarchal spiritual teachings of Afrika. The Greeks and Romans appeared to love and worship their adopted Afrikan gods, even if they did bleach them up later. Throughout Europe, Nature or the Mother Principle of God was honored, although European women never achieved the same status as Afrikan women in Afrika. **But something happened. Something terrible happened.** Actually, it was a development that had already been progressing for some time and finally gained the strength to hatch and make a stronghold upon the consciousness of Europe and ultimately the world. This "something" was the murderous, terrorist, dictatorship called the Roman Catholic Church – which was but a ***form-change*** of the Roman Empire (Roman rulership). When it got through with "initiating" or Christianizing Europe, over a quarter of Europe's population –mainly women– had been ruthlessly tortured and murdered –burned alive in the name of *their* Jesus and *their* God. All visible traces of the Afrikan Wisdom teachings had been bloodily eradicated –and surviving remnants forced underground. An anti-female, truly diabolical establishment called The Church had viciously attacked Europe like no other catastrophe (including Hitler), and entrenched itself. Thereafter, Europe became its permanent slave. The heads of this "Church" were white men, apparently Lucifer's personal executive agents, if not his very incarnates. Thus, flowering Europe was deliberately, intentionally "Dark-Aged" by the false Killer Church and prevented from blossoming into a possible golden era.

When Europe finally emerged from *much* of this darkness (thanks again to descendants of the same Afrikans who gave them their first Light), the same heartless ones in power struck again. This time however, they could not put out the True Light so they revised their strategy. They joined the Light (*appeared to*), taking it over and replacing it with the *Reversed Light* of the *Bringer* (FER) of Destructive Reversed *Light* (LUCI), and redirecting the *Awakening* down an opposite path. They severed the *True Light* from its Afrikan roots and spiritual source, then falsely claimed credit for its creation.

> Not only was *true* history, *Afrikan* history-herstory, ***Blacked Out Through Whitewash,*** but so was Afrikan Cosmology (of True-Loving-Expansive-Light) Blacked Out Through the *Whitewash* of the Loveless-Fraudulent-Destructive-*Reversed Light* of the Deceiver.

This was a crucial turning point in European and *world* history

The aftermath was to permanently set the European mind –and set the stage for racism and anti-female-ism to develop to unparalleled heights by wiping out Europe's memory of the Afrikan high culture that uplifted her from barbarianism and nurtured her like the big black breasts nurturing the slave masters' pink babes. The "Children of Ham" were now inferiorized, fit for slavery. The negative characteristics associated with patriarchy were selectively fostered; the opposite characteristic associated with feminine matriarchy were selectively suppressed. Whites have exhibited these patriarchal anti-women traits more than any group of people.

Europe's Dark Age was necessary in order to erase from European consciousness, the memory and awareness of 1) women as whole beings of power, and 2) Black Afrika as the source of civilization and spirituality. For in ancient times, the phenomenal prowess /abilities / and "*Black* Magic" of the Afrikans – "the gods"– were common knowledge. People from around the world flocked to Afrika's universities (Kamite / Ethiopian temples of Afrikan Wisdom). The established world knew who were its civilizers. Patriarchal white culture led by white men could not impose the control and racism upon a European populace which was a witness to such True Light and human dignity, therefore Europe *had* to be "Dark Aged" to blot out the memory and awareness of this, along with *knowledge* and literacy in general. For it is mighty easy to control *ignorant, misinformed* people. Imagine what the world would be like today had Europe *not* been Dark-Aged!

Thus the Renaissance was the "White-aissance" of Black world history!

Europeans massively whitewashed Black history in Europe during the Renaissance

How ironic that such whitewashing of Black history should take place at this time since it was the Afrikans (the Moors) that sparked the Renaissance in the first place! The Catholic Church, using the artists Michelangelo and Leonardo Da Vinci, was the chief culprit! Surviving art (from the Dark /Middle Ages & Byzantine era) which has escaped being whitewashed, portrays rulers, famous figures, and armies of knights as Black as they can be. A good source of such art are "Icon" artbooks like *Russian Icons* available at some art museums. At the library you may find artbooks on these periods, and if you look very carefully through them, you will usually find one or two stray pieces of Black evidence that 'escaped' the Renaissance's massive whitewashing.

> "**After burning books and closing pagan schools, the church dealt in another kind of forgery: falsification by omission**. All European history was extensively edited by a church that managed to make itself the sole repository of literary and historical records. With all important documents assembled in the monasteries, and the lay public rendered illiterate, [Albino] Christian history could be forged with impunity." [1]

1) Walker, WE, 320.

A Summary of Albino *Quantum Deception*

From Unfood By The UnPeople (vol. 2 of Drugs Masquerading As Foods) by Suzar

They have done an incredible, phenomenal job as masters of Deception with a capital D. They have deceived humanity on a quantum scale and this Deception is still alive, well, and thriving. Deception on every level: matter, energy, space and time. Deception of every sense: sight, hearing, smell, taste, touch. Deception of all People of Color, including themselves. Albinos have distorted everything in their favor but at the expense of Colored People. "Mentacide," as produced by deceit, is necessary for the white minority to control the nonwhite majority's mind. Physical control directly follows mental control.

- **History is *his*-story (his *Lies*).** Albinos misrepresent history on a quantum scale, falsely presenting themselves as the authors of civilization and innumerable modern inventions. At the same time, Afrikans are falsely presented as making little or no worthwhile contributions when in fact, it was Black Afrikan people that authored civilization around the world.
- **They distorted the map of the world;** their lands are shown disproportionately bigger compared with the lands of Colored People, as revealed by the honest Peters Projection World Map.
- **They distorted the calendar.** You can even see that October means 8 (not 10). December means 10 (not 12). But this ain't nothing. The whole calendar is deliberately "off" in order to create a false time to give credibility to Albino falsehood.
- **They burned the most valuable repositories of people of color** in order to establish their foundation of massive falsehood. They had to overthrow the truth so their falsehood could thrive.
- **Whites as "Jews" is one of their greatest deceptions!** There is no such thing as a Caucasian Jew or white-looking Jew, for the original Jews were Black, nappy-haired, Afrikan people. Over 90% of today's so-called "Jews" are European *Khazars*. In 740 A.D, the European Khazars all converted to Judaism as a political ploy. Today they comprise 90% of the world's so-called Jews. They have no authentic real Jew-ancestry. These "Jews" are not Jews, nor ever have been. They are total frauds. The dark-skinned looking "Jews" or ones having curly or kinky hair are the ones having genetic connections with the original Afrikan Jews, though heavily diluted from race mixing.
- **White Christianity, like White Flour, is a complete fraud.** What is called "Christianity" (and all its variations on the theme) is their greatest Falsehood, Fraud, Imposter. "Christianity" is reworked, revised, restructured, reversed, counterfeit "Egyptianity." The original "Christ" was not an effeminate, blond, blue-eyed Albino but an ebony, dredlocked, powerful Afrikan revolutionary! No wonder they executed him –in a style reserved for political offenders or revolutionaries!
- **Everytime something big comes up** –that is, big evidence that can bust or explode their well-established lies and fraud (such as the Essene Scrolls), Albinos grab it, control it, reduce it, deflect it, etc. The *Media* is their prime tool of propagating their lies and shaping people's thinking in order to better control them.

Deceptive terminology is standard practice in Albino Un-culture. The truth is not stated. Euphemisms, double talk, "double speak," lawyer language, trick language, disinformation (lies mixed with truth), and often outright lies are standard. The reality of the situations are so negative that if a spade was called a spade, people would see and know the truth. They would see how bad things are (such as drugfoods) and how vastly they are being deceived, exploited, and manipulated; then they will not participate and buy, then they could not be so exploited, then they would be their *own* person, then the Controllers will be out of business. No problem. Just use nice words that deceive, slant, and mislead.
- Don't call it a slaughtered cow –call it beef.
- Don't call it bastardizing, deranging, denaturing, destroying –call it "**refining**."
- Don't call it *death* insurance –call it *life* insurance.
- A disease bill? No, a health bill.
- Drugs? No, "additives." You get the picture.

"**Underdeveloped**" really means unspoiled, unexploited, uninfected, unraped by Albino technology.
"**Developed**" means fully infected by such.
"**Man**" means white man!
"**Modern**" means white. "Modern man" for sure means white man. "Modern technology" means Albino technology. "Modern medicine" means the white man's medicine. In "modern medicine" people take drugs; drugs do not heal but suppress symptoms, –giving the illusion (lie, deception) of health.

"**Alternative medicine**?" The only real "alternative" medicine is albino medicine, for it is hardly a couple of centuries old while herbal therapy, accupressure, etc., have records reaching back tens of thousands of years (millions, really). So-called *alternative medicine* is the *ancient therapies* of Melanated People.

The true purpose of Albino reference books is to secure & maintain their *Quantum Deception*, lies & falsehood

"The true purpose of their reference books (dictionaries, encyclopedias, etc.) is to secure and maintain their lies /falsehood, and prove their frauds and deceptions as facts or 'truth.' Deceit is necessary for the white minority to control the nonwhite majority's mind. Given their history of massive fraud, massive lying, massive deception, massive stealing of credit, especially from Afrikans, the information from white people (in books & the media) cannot and should not ever be trusted, especially when referring to or connected with Black people. Albinos tend to reverse the truth in all things and all aspects of life because they are a reversed people *collectively*. They say the *opposite* of what they do. **To decode Albinos lies and get to the truth, especially the Black Truth: REVERSE what Albinos say and examine what and whom they attack and promote in their media**." [1]

Education in Albino culture is not true education

It is set up (to train people as obedient servants to "the system" and) to ensure that people do not learn vital relevant truths though they may be inundated and knocked over with irrelevant information, data, and "facts." It is important to know our true history so we may properly identify, know, and understand what is *really* going on, else we fail to learn from our mistakes and thus repeat them! Also, we know what we can achieve by knowing what our ancestors achieved. No group on Earth has accomplished or duplicated what the ancient Afrikans have done! Those Afrikans were truly the gods and goddesses they called themselves! So are their descendants and *all* of Humanity, including the paranoid Albinos. As we reclaim our truths, we need to rewrite the history books and text our children study. This is imperative and vastly important! –which is why they were distorted in the first place!

> **"The truth is not being told in the universities, the 'Ivory Towers' of learning;** as long as truth is hidden and the lie of man's origins and spiritual nature remains cloaked in darkness, there will be no peace, no freedom of body or mind, and the spirit of mankind will remain entrapped and enslaved by those 'Powers of Darkness' which have perpetuated the deception." [2]
>
> *Kali Sichen-Andoh*

1) Suzar, *Drugs Masquerading As Foods*, volume 2. 2) Cole/Andoh, AG, 58.

With the "*Divine* Deception" exposed, we now see that at least 99% of the world's Christian literature is obsolete or largely "no good" !

Were they ever "good"? Good as BAD could be! Obsolete before they were written, for the authors themselves were deceived. "Christian" books and bookstores will go out of business as the authentic Karast-ian Truth is brought to light. Virtually all these books –since they are based on mythology – are mythology themselves! They have little or no value. Like *his*-story books, they need to be rewritten entirely or tossed.

The Bible needs to be reclassified as mythology

Almost everyone, even learned, degreed people, think that the Bible is real history, that there really were 12 Tribes of Israel, that the present-day so-called Jews (imposters) descended from them, that the Gospels are real history, etc. We have all been *Quantumly Deceived,* misled, made fools of, manipulated. A painful truth to admit. But the sooner we recognize the *Deception*, the sooner we are freed and can cease being pawns in Nick's agenda. Para-biblical literature is written as though the Bible was real history. Since it is not, plus is a Fraud, then how valuable are any books written from such a foundation?! The same is true for the churches, ministers, priests, etc., also Judaism, Islam, etc. The Truth will put them out of business as their misled flocks awaken to the *Quantum Deception.*

However, if these ministers, temples, churches start to promote Truth –not Pseudo Truth, they may stand a chance of survival. But no longer will they be able to hold their former stolen power and glory over people. For as people awaken to the liberating truth, they will take their Power back! We do not need preachers, ministers, sunday school teachers, popes, bishops, Bibles, Korans, Talmuds, Vedas, & other books of Fraud! For those that insist on retaining such, and cling to denial despite truth: "you have the right to remain deceived, misled..."

Albinos (the *Khazars*, falsely called "Jews") established Modern Israel Through Deception

In *Chosen People From the Caucasus,* Michael Bradley writes "when we now consider that 95 percent of the Jews in the modern world are Askenazim, their claim to a Jewish homeland in Palestine becomes absurd, grotesque. They are descended from Caucasus converts to Judaism, nothing more, and have no genetic or historical connection with Palestine at all. The case of Zionism is no different from, say, a group of Cree Indians from northern Canada becoming converted to Catholicism and then demanding a piece of the Vatican as a 'Cree homeland.' ...Israel was established by deceiving the rest of the world, but particularly the North American public, about the real origins of the Ashkenazim. That deception was made possible by Jewish influence in U.S. mass media and international finance. ...Koestler was correct. Israel exists, 'and it can not be undone except by genocide.' ...Israel possesses a formidable nuclear capability. It is not so well known that there's 'the Masada Plan': a one way nuclear strike by an elite wing of the Israeli Air Force, to destroy every Middle Eastern capital and major city possible if it looks as if Israel may be defeated."[1]

1) Bradley, CP, 230-231.

Albinos distorted the world map in their favor, inflating their landsizes

Which is larger, Afrika or Greenland? They look the same size on the "traditional" Mercator map in current use throughout academic America. In reality Afrika is 14 times larger! This distortion, really a *global deception*, is consistent: the "lands of the Gentiles" are falsely represented as much larger than they really are, relative to the lands of Colored People. Credit with applause goes Dr. Arno Petersen for correcting this deception, at least in one area, but a key area affecting many others. Now if we can just get this map into the places where it will count the most: SCHOOLS, colleges, and universities!

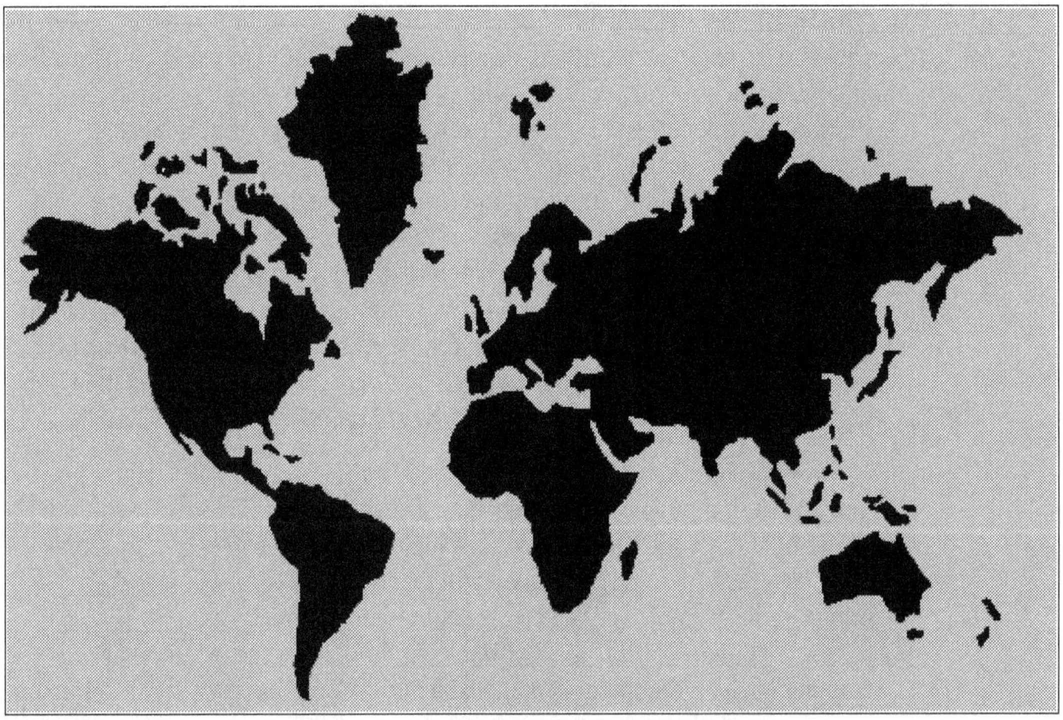

The Deceptive Mercator World Map created over 400 years ago (1569) and still in predominant use today, maintaining the Albino delusion of greatness at the expense of Colored People. Most world maps are oriented North only because most Albino nations are in the north.

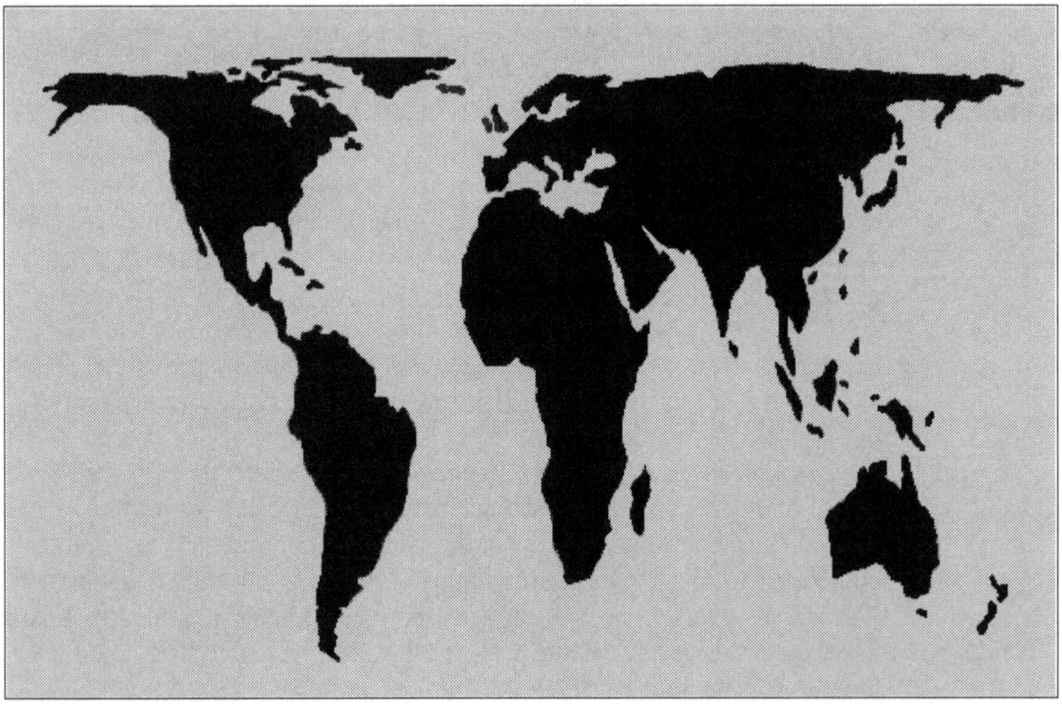

The Honest Peters Projection World Map In 1974, Dr. Arno Petersen, a German cartographer created a fair map of the world which represents all land masses according to their relative sizes. (See *Resources* for publisher's name)

Albinos are trapped in "illusions of greatness" by false history

- **Whites have committed a grand theft and massive coverup of true history.**
- **This coverup keeps most whites ignorant of the truth about themselves!**

In her profound book to White America, *Message to the White Man & Woman in America: Yacub and the Origins of White Supremacy*, Dr. Dorothy Fardan, a white member of the Nation of Islam writes:

> "This ignorance and rejection of history allows whites to continue in illusions of greatness and white supremacy that can only be eliminated by unfolding the layers of rejected history. **What most white people fail to understand is that they too have been denied access to the true history which undergirds their present life, and in the absence of truth fail to gain knowledge of themselves.** In rejecting the truth of 'Black history' (all the way back to beginnings) they have rejected the truth of themselves and the crucial key to unlocking the doors to both the past and present, and therefore, any clear path towards the future." [1]

Speaking on how whites are trapped in a history they do not understand –and until they do, they cannot be released from it,

she continues: "What history are Caucasians trapped in then? It is an historical vacuum; a chunk of time which has been severed from its origin point and reconstructed in terms of fabricated accounts and falsified documents. Such an historical and truncated worldview has allowed the illusion of white supremacy to become not only a general mindset, but an insidious underlying strategy which informs and constitutes every institution within American society...This mindset, which has no grounding in the origins of human presence, no recognized connection to the first civilizations of human beings nor the wisdom accumulated in those civilizations (except for what was stolen and/or rethought and rewritten) is a mindset trapped. ...Trapped history is history without a naval cord to its very being, absent the mother of its inception. That is the foundation of white supremacy. While the Europeans took what they needed and wanted from the original people in Africa to form the foundations of Western civilization, they simultaneously denied and rejected that very source. What occurred was a deliberate effort to cover up, conceal and alter the true origins of human life, in order to establish a supremacist worldview and eventually a civilization which recognized no liability for or answerability to the laws of nature embedded in the universe as well as in human nature." [2]

1) Fardan, 13. 2) Ibid., 14-15..

Black History is the key to Albino Liberation

Professor Fardan writes: "For Caucasians in America this excavation into the lives and deeds of foreparents, into the acts and motives of historical personages, can be painful and overwhelming. But it has to be done in order for the white-wash to wear off and the utter truth of darkness to emerge to purge the consciousness of false security, erroneous detail, and illusions of greatness and superiority. Once this is achieved by individual white Americans, their historians can no longer be allowed to misrepresent any of the past. **The reason white Americans need to be immersed in Black history is not to learn a few facts about black contributions to the culture of America, but to see, for the first time most likely, the truth; to descend into the reality of what actually happened.**

"Most students, most people in white America, avoid this descent into history (which is really a way to **ascend to liberation**). I did once have a Jewish student who was appalled at the realization that Ancient Egyptians were black. She told me she felt cheated and that a 'big number' had been done on her. But she was strong enough to at least recognize it. Once white people realize **Black history is their key to self liberation** and the way to avoid white supremacy thinking, they will hopefully embrace the historical endeavor with great fervor. It is scandalous that even up to the present time, there are still efforts to separate Egypt from black Africa." [1] (emphasis added)

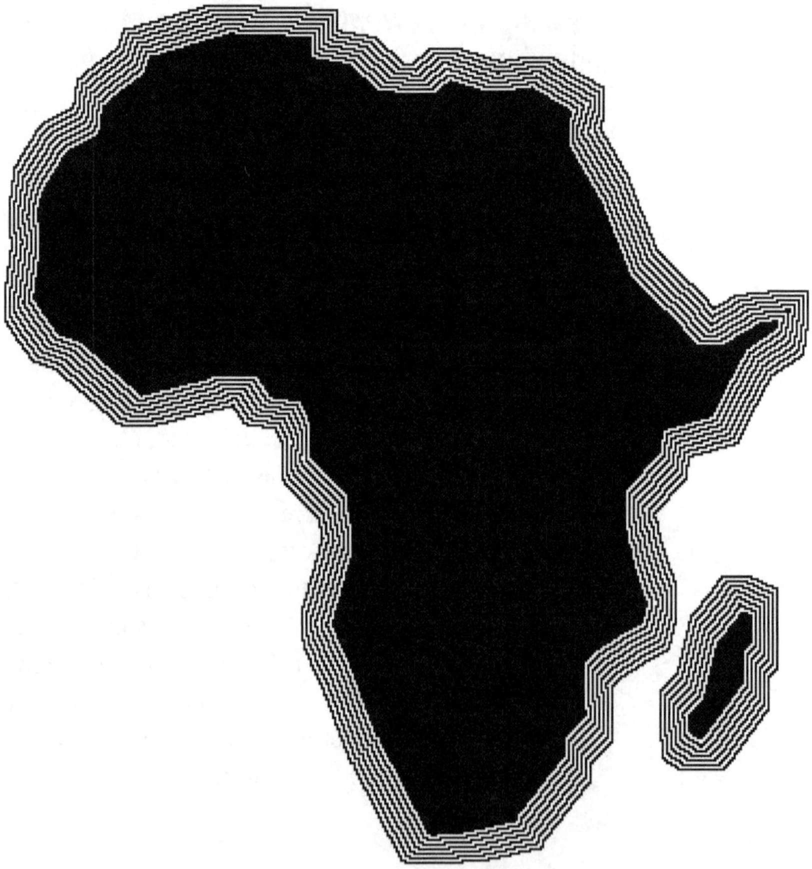

1) Fardan, 55-56.

Albinos' main problem appears to be a disconnection from –and war against their roots

It seems that the main problem of whites is that they are disconnected from their true roots, both spiritually and physically. Their rejection of their Afrikan roots and Afrikan parents is an expression on the physical plane of their rejection of their spiritual roots and spiritual parents; or the Loving God (Great Father) and Loving Goddess (Great Mother). They have made God and His Son *white,* which is really their way of worshipping themselves –and Un-god. Furthermore, they only recognize the male aspect of Divine Nature. Other manifestations of their rejection (hate) of God is that they created Existentialism, Nihilsm, Atheism, Humanism, etc. And if you find any modern-day Churches of Set (Satan), they are Albino churches.

If one is disconnected from their roots and source of energy, they must get energy from somewhere to sustain themselves.

This can be accomplished by stealing or outright taking energy. This is the classic pattern whites have followed. Basically, the wealth they exhibit is primarily taken from so-called Third World countries. They have grown rich from the slave labor or other forms of exploitative labor of People of Color around the world, then used their riches to maintain control over the world. Almost everything significant they have, was stolen from People of Color: whole continents (North/South America, Australia), their culture, their civilization, their religions. They even claim ownership of the Moon. Do they have anything significant they have gotten humanely *without* exploiting, conniving, killing or cheating? Whites living today say they did not do those awful things committed by their ancestors, not noticing/acknowledging that they are greatly benefiting from them, and seem to have no intent to change that. And whites in power (like the so-called Secret World Government) continue global domination of People of Color, and maneuver "ethnic groups" to be at odds in order to secure their power over them. If one is separated from the Loving Source they become destructive. Thus Albinos, particularly white males, have been masters of ever-refined methods of mega destruction, spending billions in this area –more than any other area. Warfare is their top preoccupation.

Not only do they steal and take from People of Color, they do the same to the animals and Nature

Not even tiny *atoms* are safe from them, as they have figured out a way to take energy from the atom. Again this is but an expression of their overwhelming lust for Power.

Albinos have done a phenomenal job of stealing, falsifying and whitewashing Melanated history and theology!

Europeans have gotten away with massively, quantumly deceiving the world for a long time but nothing is permanent except change, and everything has its cycle. **All of us, including whites, have been quantumly lied to, but the cycle and season for the triumph of lies has come to an end.** Napoleon spoke *truth* when he stressed "History is a lie agreed upon." And Hitler said "The bigger the lie...the more people will believe it." The vast foundation of Deception and Quantum Lies, along with all which has been carefully built upon them is collapsing in the face of the fatal truth, the *Black* Truth, *the Krystal Black Afrikan Truth* which is inseparable from the *Cosmic Truth* for they are one –like Humanity is one with its Divine Source. History is "his" story or the Albino man's story (his lies), constructed as a major defense mechanism and strategy for his survival, made necessary because **Albinos themselves have accepted a Great Lie or Untruth, a misunderstanding about their being and survival.** This misunderstanding is part of their separation from Nature thus the Truth. It is a deep *Spiritual Dis-ease* afflicting them especially, but all of Humanity. **The good news is that Quantum Healing *is* possible and has already begun! This is why the Truth is able to come forth at this time despite all the controls in place to keep it suppressed!** This Healing and Awakening cannot be suppressed, cannot be slowed, cannot be derailed, cannot be stopped any more than the rising Sun of the New Cycle embracing our destiny and the destiny of our gracious Earth.

Albinos are *precious*, for they have been our *greatest* teachers!

Albinos truly have done a phenomenal job of doing what they are doing, and we have learned the most important lesson of Life:

–recognizing *what leads to Life* and *what leads to Death*–

By knowing Death, we come to truly appreciate Life and all its blessings (expansion, love, warmth, sweetness, etc.). Thus, Albinos have given us unparalleled lessons in *Polarity*. The Divine Spark of within each of us is called the Soul (after "Sol" in *sol*ar). Part of our Soul-education involves experiencing both polarities of the universe –Positive and Negative. Albinos have amply provided all of Humanity including themselves, with "intense experience of the Negative Polarity." How does one know Life and how good Life is (or should be) unless one also knows or experiences Death and how bad it is? By Albinos being who or what they are, and living accordingly, **they are showing us our destiny if we proceed along the same path as they are.** Such a destiny ultimately leads to two things:

- Loss of Will (Ability to Choose and Feel)
- Total death, both physically and *spiritually* (the *Real* Death).

I trust we have learned our "lessons" and are now ready to graduate by *awakening* and *choosing* to heal ourselves. Albinos can choose to heal also.

Albino Healing is possible, and..

Albinos' unconscious terror of genetic annihilation, as documented by Dr. Frances Cress Welsing in *The Isis Papers*, can be healed by their accepting themselves into the "hue-man" race. They are the ones that have divided the world into "white" and "non-white" Their re-assimilation into the hue-man family would not be an annihilation but a healing and rejoining of themselves back to their roots. For skin whiteness is an aberration, a mutation, yes, *a dis-ease*. They realize this to some degree, else why are they always trying to *tan* themselves, and they think they are more beautiful with a tan? They have even invented melanin-injection shots.

Among People of Color around the world –infected by color-prejudice, the lighter ones view themselves as better and superior to the darker ones. This stems directly from mental and physical colonization by whites who started the whole thing based on their secret fear of being *inferior* to People of Color, especially Black Afrikans. Though whites, relative to the majority People of Color, are living very well and control the planet through the "Secret World Government," are Albinos truly happy? I doubt this. They are paranoid and have much guilt. They are afraid of People of Color, hence they make horrendous weapons.

Albinos' acceptance of the Black Truth, the Melanin Truth, the Blue-Black, Krystal-Black, Cosmic Truth of their *True* but repressed *Inner Divine Being,*

will pave the way for their rapid healing and remergence with the great Family of *True Light,* Children of the Sun (Light) –the same Sun called IU, you *IU-mans.* Then they will feel comfortable accepting Melanin the true and natural, permanent way; not the false, unnatural, artificial way. This means that their Soul-spirits, upon ***reincarnating*** or being born again in the flesh, will choose to be born as a Hue-man, a Person of Color, naturally endowed with the most precious gift from the Great Mother, MELANIN, the medium that RECEIVES the life-sustaining, soul-sustaining True Light from the *Loving* Great Father of Life. *Melanin,* the medium giving us sensitivity or ability to FEEL anything at all. *Melanin*, divine receptive Feminine Essence, yes the magnetic SOUL-Essence that *marries* (*ankhs* with) our electro SPIRIT-Essence –making us *complete in polarity* so we can stay manifest – and thus LIVE. And all who choose to receive this Loving Light are truly His (and Her) Children. Without this Light, one cannot live except by stealing it from those that have it. Since theft of Energy (power, WILL, etc.) will not be permitted in the New Cycle, this means that in order to live one must *accept* the Light that gives them Life. Since we all have Freewill, people may continue to choose the Reversed Light that ultimately leads to Death – physically and spiritually.

If you have the desire and intent to heal, you will heal!

Ask for Divine Guidance from the *Loving* God /Goddess. Healing begins with recognizing where we are "not whole" and taking action which leads to becoming healed, whole! This also means recognizing we are powerful beings who regularly give away our power or allow it to be taken. **All of Humanity, especially Albinos, are seriously fragmented, unwhole, wounded, hurt, diminished, will-denied, dis-aligned with the two polarities of their being, and spiritually disconnected.** This is why we eventually die. We are not supposed to ever *die*. Death is a major dis-ease. *Reincarnation* was set up to correct death. Total healing will end the dis-ease of death.

Therefore we ALL require Divine Help from both our Spiritual Parents (Loving God /Goddess) in order to reach *total true healing* or "Quantum Healing"

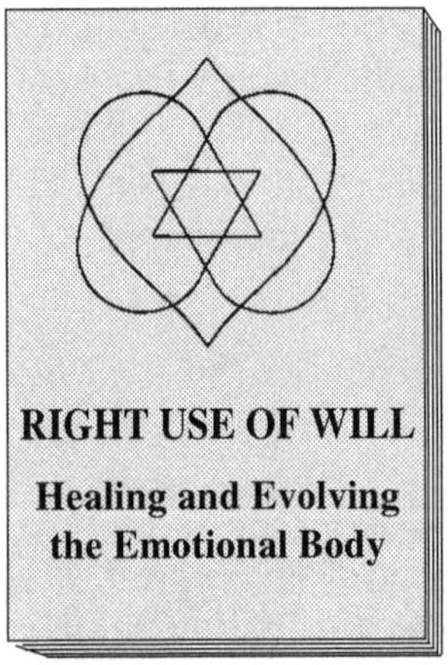

For all who choose it, such healing is possible now –at last, for the first time. A great inspired book (series) dedicated to personal self-healing / true healing, which I recommend is ***Right Use of Will** –Healing & Evolving the Emotional Body*, received through Ceanne DeRohan. Also, the ***Metaphysical Institute of Higher Learning*** (www.metaphy.com) –largely founded on these books, by two dedicated American-Afrikans (see *Resources*). Other divinely inspired writings I strongly recommend are: ***"Healing The Invisible You"*** –a 6-part article on the Internet at www.godchannel.com/voices.html (read the entire article for best results); ***Tapping the Power Within***, by Iyanla Vanzant; ***Listening***, by Lee Coit; and ***In the Spirit***, by Susan Taylor.

Yes ***His*-Story** and ***His*-Religion** have been the greatest tools for our *Quantum Deception* and Manipulation, but the Truth is coming to light and the great Lies and Deceptions are being exposed as the minds and hearts of Humanity reawaken in the increasing, exhilarating, liberating light of a new Dawn, a New Era for all of Awakening Humanity, *IU*manity. When the world finally heals, all people will live in harmony and happiness as Children of our Great Mother and Great Father.

Congratulations IUmanity!

It may be painful to recognize and admit that we have all been vastly deceived by History and Religion, but remember, the Truth sets us free! *–And Lies keep us in Prison!*
Everything that has gone before was apparently necessary in the schoolroom of Life. Finding the truth at last means we are graduating! We have passed! Now we need to work on *healing ourselves* –so we may blossom unimpeded into the great goddesses and gods we already *are!* This is more possible now than ever before because we have entered a new Cosmic Cycle, bringing in abundant energies specifically for our Awakening, Healing, Growth, Life, and Happiness.

Preview of Next Two Volumes

Creation's Great Blak Mother & The Blak Woman

Volume 2 of the seven volumes of this book resurrects awareness of ***The Great BLAK Mother of Creation*** and restores the Blak Feminine part of the equation which has been blacked out the most, even more than Blak history. You thought the Blak Male was the endangered species. No, it's the Blak Woman and her precious Womb. The ongoing Great War on *The Great Mother* and the Female Principle is why women of all races on all continents are being oppressed, repressed, suppressed, depressed, demeaned and subjugated. In reality, the Blak Afrikan Woman is the Original Most Powerful Being on Earth. She is in a *Spell*, along with the entire Blak Race –the Parents of Humanity and usurped Guardians of Planet Earth. The Blak Afrikan Woman –the Mother of Humanity– unknowingly holds the key to Humanity's salvation. Other topics addressed are: the Blak Feminine Foundation of Civilization and "Culture"; Female Biological Superiority –fact or fiction? The Sexual Foundation of Religion; Why "Pussy" is a name for the cat and vagina; Afrikan extraterrestrial legacy and Blak People from outta space –founders of legendary super-civilizations? The Great Mother's Precious Gift of Blak Melanin; How the Albino Controllers stay fat off Her Blak Power; (Disguised) StarScience (Astrology/Astronomy) is still the *global* religion.

Resurrecting BAB-EL, the Book of Books of Books

Volume 3 of the seven volumes of this book resurrects BAB-EL, the Book of Books of Books, a Cosmic Power-Generator and Core of the (True) Bible —personified as the Bab-El of the Great Pyramid, Tree, Melanin Molecule, Eternal Ankh, Ark of the Covenant, "777", but especially the Bab-El of your Temple-Body. Exposes the diabolical *Reversed Bab-Els* ("Un-Babs") empowering "white supremacy" and *UnHeaven USA* –the Counterfeit-Godhead of the Planet (False Egypt).

Selected Bibliography VOLUME I

Al-Mansour, Khalid A.T.	**Betrayal By Any Other Name** San Francisco: First African Arabian Press, 1993.
Amen, Nur Ankh	**The Ankh: African Origin of Electromagnetism** Jamaica NY: Nur Ankh Amen Co., 1993.
Amen, Ra Un Nefer	**Metu Neter** (Vol. I) Bronx NY: Khamit Corp., 1990.
Baigent, M. & Leigh, R.	**The Dead Sea Scrolls Deception** New York: Summit Books, 1991.
Baigent, M. & Leigh, R.	**The Messianic Legacy** New York: Dell Publishing, 1986.
Barashango, Ishakamusa	**God, the Bible and the Black Man's Destiny** Silver Spring MD: IVth Dynasty Publishing Co., 1982.
Barnes, Carol	**Melanin: The Chemical Key to Black Greatness** (Vol. I) Houston TX: Carol Barnes, 1988.
Barr, Frank	**Melanin: The Organizing Molecule** Berkeley CA: Institute for Study of Consciousness, 1983.

Ben-Abba, Dov — **The Signet Hebrew-English / English-Hebrew Dictionary**
Nazareth Israel: Massada-Press, LTD., 1977. (Also published as **The Meridian Hebrew/English - English /Hebrew Dictionary**: NY: Penguin Group.)

ben-Jochannan, Yosef — **African Origins of the Major "Western Religions"**
Baltimore MD: Black Classic Press, 1991.

ben-Jochannan, Yosef — **We the Black Jews**
Baltimore MD: Black Classic Press, 1993.

Bernard, R.W. — **The Dead Sea Scrolls and the Life of the Ancient Essenes**
(No publisher listed, but book is available from Eso-Won. See *Resources*)

Bey, Umaralli Shabazz — **We Are The Washitaw –Indigeneous BLACKS of North America** (7th Edition)
Shreveport LA: T.E. Publications, 1999.

Bhaktivedanta, A.C. — **Krsna –The Supreme Personality of Godhead**
New York: Bhaktivedanta Book Trust, 1970.

Binns, Nijel — **Nuba Wrestling: The Original Art**
Los Angeles: Trans-Continental Network Productions, 1990.

Blavatsky, Helena P. — **Isis Unveiled** (2 volumes)
Pasadena CA: Theosophical University Press, 1988.

Blavatsky, Helena P. — **The Secret Doctrine** (2 volumes)
Pasadena CA: Theosophical University Press, 1988.

Bradley, Michael — **Chosen People From the Caucasus**
Chicago: Third World Press, 1992.

Browder, Anthony — **Nile Valley Contributions to Civilization**
Washington DC: The Institute of Karmic Guidance, 1992.

Browder, Anthony — **From the Browder File**
Washington DC: The Institute of Karmic Guidance, 1989.

Budge, Wallis — **An Egyptian Hieroglyphic Dictionary** (2 volumes)
New York: Dover Publications, Inc., 1978.

Budge, Wallis — **The Gods of the Egyptians** (2 volumes)
New York: Dover Publications, Inc., 1969.

Burland, C. & Forman, W. — **Feathered Serpent and Smoking Mirror**
New York: G.P. Putnam's Sons, 1975.

Butz, Arthur R. — **The Hoax of the Twentieth Century: The Case Against the Presumed Extermination of European Jewry**
Costa Mesa CA: Institute for Historical Review.

Carpenter, Edward — **Pagan & Christian Creeds: Their Origin and Meaning**
Mokelumne Hill CA: Health Research, 1975.

Cassell & Simpson, D.P., ed. — **Cassell's Latin Dictionary**
New York: Macmillan Publishing Company, 1968.

Casson, Lionel — **Ancient Egypt**
New York: Time Incorporated, 1965.

Childress, David — **Lost Cities & Ancient Mysteries of Africa & Arabia**
Stelle IL: Adventures Unlimited Press, 1993.

Churchward, Albert — **The Signs and Symbols of Primordial Man**
Mokelumne Hill CA: Health Research, 1986. (orig. 1913)

Cirlot, J. E. — **A Dictionary of Symbols**
New York: Philosophical Library, Inc., 1962.

Cole, Abayomi & Andoh, Kali., ed. — **Astrological Geomancy In Africa**
San Francisco: The North Scale Institute Publishing, 1990.

Cuba, A. Prince — **Musa and the All-Seeing-Eye**
Hampton VA: United Brothers & Sisters Communications Systems, 1991.

Davies, W.V. — **Egyptian Hieroglyphs**
London: British Museum Press, 1993.

DeRohan, Ceanne — **Right Use of Will**
Santa Fe NM: Four Winds Publications, 1987.

Dictionary — **The American Heritage Dictionary of the English Language** –Third Edition
New York: Houghton Mifflin, 1992.

Dictionary — **Webster's Twentieth-Century Dictionary Unabridged**
New York: Publishers Guild, Inc., 1937.

Dictionary — **Living Language Japanese Dictionary**
New York: Crown Publishers, Inc., 1993.

Dictionary, Bible — **Insight on the Scriptures** (2 volumes)
Brooklyn: Watchtower Bible and Tract Society of New York, Inc., 1988.

Diop, Cheikh Anta — **The Cultural Unity of Black Africa**
Chicago: Third World Press, 1990.

Diop, Cheikh Anta — **The African Origin of Civilization: Myth or Reality**
Chicago: Lawrence Hill Books /Chicago Review Press, 1974.

Doane, T.W. — **Bible Myths and Their Parallels in Other Religions**
- Mokelumne Hill CA: Health Research, 1985. (orig.1882)
- New York: University Books Inc., 1971.

Ewing, Upton C. — **The Prophet of the Dead Sea Scrolls**
Joshua Tree, CA: Tree of Life Publications, 1993.

Fardan, Dorothy Blake — **Message to the White Man & Woman in America: Yacub and the Origins of White Supremacy**
Hampton VA: United Brothers & Sisters Communications Systems, 1991.

Freedman, Benjamin — **Facts Are Facts**
Boring OR: CPA Book Publisher.

Freeman & Moseley — **1001 Black Inventions Supplement**
Washington DC: Pin Points, Inc., 1991.

Friedman, Richard — **Who Wrote the Bible?**
New York: Summit Books, 1987.

Frissell, Bob — **Nothing in This Book Is True, But It's Exactly How Things Are**
Berkeley CA: Frog, Ltd. / North Atlantic Books, 1994.

Gettings, Fred — **The Arkana Dictionary of Astrology**
London: Penguin Group, 1990.

Grahm, Lloyd M. — **Deceptions and Myths of the Bible**
New York: Carol Publishing Group, 1991.

Graves, Kersey — **Bible of Bibles**
Kila MT: Kessinger Publishing Co.

Graves, Kersey — **The Biography of Satan**
Kila MT: Kessinger Publishing Co.

Graves, Kersey — **The World's Sixteen Crucified Saviors**
The Cleage Group, Inc., 1991.

Guthrie, Paul L. — **Making of the Whiteman**
San Diego: Beacon Communications, 1992.

Haich, Elisabeth — **Initiation**
Palo Alto CA: Seed Center, 1974.

Hallet, Jean-Pierre — **Pygmy Kitabu**
New York: Random House, 1973.

Hatonn, G. C. — **The Bitter Communion –Altars of Hemlock**
Tehachapi CA: America West Publishers, 1991.

Hatonn, G. C. — **Counterfeit Blessings –The Anti-Christ By Any Name: Khazars**
Tehachapi CA: America West Publishers, 1991.

Hatonn, G. C. — **Pleiades Connection – Return of the Phoenix** (Vol. I)
Tehachapi CA: America West Publishers, 1991.

Heline, Corinne — **Mythology and the Bible**
Santa Monica CA: New Age Bible & Philosophy Center, 1972.

Higgens, Godfrey — **Anacalypsis** (2 volumes)
Kila MT: Kessinger Publishing Co.

Hionides, Harry — **Collins Gem Greek Dictionary**
Glasgow Britain: HarperCollins Publishers, 1994.
(**Note**: this is the ONLY transliterated Greek dictionary I have found, though it does not say on the cover that it is transliterated, –hence making it possible to read or decode Greek words and thus discover that Greek is very similar to Egyptian and Hebrew!)

Holman & Butler, T., ed. — **Holman Bible Dictionary**
Nashville TN: Holman Bible Publishers, 1991.

Hotema, Hilton — **Genesis of Christianity**
Mokelumne Hill CA: Health Research, 1967.

Hotema, Hilton — **Mystery Man of the Bible**
Mokelumne Hill CA: Health Research.

Holloway, Joseph, ed. — **Africanisms in American Culture**
Indianapolis: Indiana University Press, 1991.

Hughley, Ella J. — **The Truth About Black Biblical Hebrew-Israelite (Jews)**
Springfield Gardens NY: Hughly Publications, 1991.

Jackson, John G. — **Christianity Before Christ**
Austin TX: American Atheist Press, 1985.

Jackson, John G. — **Pagan Origins of the Christ Myth**
Austin TX: American Atheist Press, 1988.

Jairazbhoy, R.A. — **Rameses III: Father of Ancient America**
London: Karnak House, 1992.

James, George — **Stolen Legacy**
Newport News VA: United Brothers Communications Systems, 1980.

Joyce, Donovan — **The Jesus Scroll**
New York: Signet, 1972.

Jubal, Asar — **The Black Truth**
Long Beach, CA: Black Truth Enterprises, 1991.

Judah, Stillson J. — **Hare Krishna and the Counterculture**
New York: John Wiley & Sons, 1974.

Katz, William Loren — **Black Indians**
New York: Atheneum / Macmillan Publishing Co., 1986.

King, Richard — **African Origin of Biological Psychiatry**
Germantown TN: Seymour-Smith, Inc., 1990.

Knight, J.Z. — **Ramtha**
Eastsound WA: Sovereignty, Inc., (2nd printing) 1986.

Koestler, Arthur — **The Thirteenth Tribe**
New York: Random House, Inc, 1976.

Kraft, C. & Green, A. — **Teach Yourself Hausa**
Chicago: NTC Publishing Group, 1975.

Kuhn, Alvin — **The Lost Light**
Kila MT: Kessinger Publishing Co.

Kush, Indus K. — **What They Never Told You In History Class**
Bronx NY: Luxorr Publications, 1983.

Larousse / Hamlyn — **Larousse Encyclopedia of Ancient & Medieval History**
Paris France: Hamlyn Publishing Group, 1972.

Larousse — **New Larousse Encyclopedia of Mythology**
New York: Prometheus Press, 1974.

Laurence, R., Trans. — **The Book of Enoch the Prophet**
Thousand Oaks CA: Artisan Sales, 1980.

Laurita, Raymond — **Greek Roots and Their Modern English Spellings**
Yorktown Heights NY: Leonardo Press, 1989.

Levi — **The Aquarian Gospel of Jesus the Christ**
Santa Monica CA: DeVorss & Co., 1972.

Lurker, Manfred — **The Gods and Symbols of Ancient Egypt**
New York: Thames and Hudson, 1991.

Marciniak, Barbara — **Bringers of the Dawn**
Santa Fe NM: Bear & Company Publishing, 1992.

Massey, Gerald — **Ancient Egypt the Light of the World**
Baltimore MD: Black Classic Press, 1981. (Orig. 1907)

Massey, Gerald — **Egyptian Book of the Dead and the Mysteries of Amenta**
Mokelumne Hill CA: Health Research.

Massey, Gerald — **The Historical Jesus and the Mythical Christ**
Brooklyn NY: A&B Book Publishers, 1992.

Massey, Gerald — **Book of the Beginnings** (2 volumes)
Kila MT: Kessinger Publishing Co.

Mehra, P.S. — **Shrimad Bhagavadgita in Pictures**
Bombay, India: Parmanand Publications, 1954.

Morgan, Marlo — **Mutant Message**
Lees Summit MO: MM Co., 1991.

Nation of Islam — **The Secret Relationship Between Blacks and Jews**
Chicago: Latimer Associates, 1991.

Nicholson, Irene — **Mexican and Central American Mythology**
New York: Peter Bedrick Books, 1985.

Notivitch, Nicolas — **The Unknown Life of Jesus Christ**
Joshua Tree CA: Tree of Life Publications, 1980.

Pagels, Elaine — **The Gnostic Gospels**
New York: Vintage Books /Random House, 1989.

Parker, George Wells — **The Children of the Sun**
Baltimore MD: Black Classic Press, 1981.

Pearl, Irasha — **The Bamboo Forest**
(Publisher to be announced)

Picknett and Prince — **Turin Shroud**
New York: HarperCollins, 1994.

Rashidi, R. & Van Sertima, I. — **African Presence in Early Asia**
New Brunswick NJ: Transaction Publishers, 1993.

Ricciardi, Mirella — **Vanishing Africa**
London: Collins & Harvill Press, 1984.

Rocco, Sha — **The Masculine Cross and Ancient Sex Worship**
Mokelumne Hill CA: Health Research, 1975.

Rogers, J.A. — **Sex and Race** (Vol. I)
St. Petersburg FL: Helga Rogers, 1980.

Rogers, J.A. — **100 Amazing Facts About the Negro**
St. Petersburg FL: Helga Rogers, 1985.

Rogers, J.A. — **Nature Knows No Color-Line**
St. Petersburg FL: Helga Rogers, 1980.

Saakana, Amon Saba, ed. — **The Afrikan Origins of the Major World Religions**
London: Karnak House, 1988.

Sanderson, Ivan T. — **Investigating the Unexplained**
Englewood Cliffs NJ: Prentice Hall, 1972.

Sarna, Nahum M. — **Exploring Exodus**
New York: Schockon Books.

Schonfield, Hugh J. — **The Passover Plot**
New York: Bantam Books, 1967.

Sitchin, Zecharia — **When Time Began**
New York: Avon Books, 1993.

Sitchin, Zecharia — **The Lost Realms**
Santa Fe NM: Bear & Company Publishing, 1990.

Suzar — **UnFood By The UnPeople** (vol. 2 of ***Drugs Masquerading as Foods***)
A-Kar Productions, 1999.

Szekely, Edmond, trans. — **The Essene Gospel of Peace** ("Book One")
Matsqui BC Canada: International Biogenic Society, 1981.

Temple, Robert — **The Syrius Mystery**
Rochester VT: Destiny Books, 1987.

Thorsten, Geraldine — **God Herself: The Feminine Roots of Astrology**
Garden City NY: Doubleday & Company, Inc., 1980.

Tyberg, Judith — **The Language of the Gods**
Los Angeles: East-West Cultural Centre, 1970.

Van Sertima, Ivan, ed. — **African Presence in Early Europe**
New Brunswick NJ: Transaction Publishers, 1990.

Van Sertima, Ivan, ed. — **Egypt Revisited**
New Brunswick NJ: Transaction Publishers, 1993.

Van Sertima, Ivan — **They Came Before Columbus**
New York: Random House, 1976.

Van Sertima, Ivan — **African Presence in Early America**
New Brunswick NJ: Transaction Books, Rutgers State University, 1992.

Von Daniken, Erich — **Chariots of the Gods?**
New York: Berkley Books, 1980.

Walker, Barbara — **The Woman's Encyclopedia of Myths and Secrets**
New York: HarperCollins, 1983.

Walker, Barbara — **The Woman's Dictionary of Symbols & Sacred Objects**
New York: HarperCollins, 1988.

Watts, Daud Malik — **The Black Presence in the Lands of the Bible**
Washington DC: Afro-Vision, Inc., 1990.

Welsing, Frances Cress — **The Isis Papers**
Chicago: Third World Press, 1991.

Wilkinson, Richard — **Reading Egyptian Art**
London: Thames and Hudson, 1992.

Williams, Chancellor — **The Destruction of Black Civilization**
Chicago: Third World Press, 1990.

Wilson, Amos — **The Developmental Psychology of the Black Child**
New York: Africana Research Publications, 1987.

Windsor, Rudolph R. — **From Babylon to Timbuktu**
Atlanta GA: Windsor's Golden Series, 1988.

A

B

T

Afrikan RESOURCES Directory

Afrikans
Networking for
Kinship and
Humanity®

Lecturers, authors, griots,
artists, counselors, therapists,
uplifters, workshop-givers,

organizations, institutions,
centers, programs,
and other resources

for the education, upliftment,
expansion, fellowship, freedom,
healing and empowerment

Of Brothers & Sisters
of All Colors

NOTE: The viewpoints expressed in *Blacked Out Through Whitewash* are those of the author and not necessarily those of the individuals and organizations listed in this *Black Resources Directory.*
The acronym A.N.K.H.® was originated by Raymond Mayes and Omar Shabazz.

Alphabetical Listing of Individuals & Organizations

Lecturers, Authors, Griots, Artists, Workshop Givers, Etc.

Abdulhamid Akoni

Akoni, the Storyman, telling stories for all occasions, specializing in Afrikan, Afrikan-American, and Cherokee folktales. Akoni relates stories from around the world. He provides workshops in storytelling techniques for parents and teachers. An Anthropologist, he lectures on Afrikan American Culture, Islamic Principles, the Nature of Religion, and Personal Empowerment.

P.O. Box 3244 • Santa Barbara, CA 93130
(805) 967-9386

Anyim Palmer, Dr.

Activist, Cultural Enricher, Lecturer, and Founder of the *Marcus Garvey Schools* (pre-school through junior high) and the *Amon-Rah African People's Church.* Dr. Palmer delivers lectures primarily on Religion, Education, and Afrikan & Afrikan American History.

2916 W. Slauson • Los Angeles, CA 90043
(323) 291-9790

Arealia Denby

Survival Specialist, Disaster Instructor, International Emergency Program Manager, Author, Lecturer, Consultant and World Traveler. Author of numerous survival books including: *The MGT & FOI Survival Guide to the New World at Home & Abroad*, and *How to Organize a Community Disaster Task Force*. Lecture topics include International Disaster Relief /Overview / Management; Damage Assessment; Incident Command Centers (setting up); and How to conduct disaster education activities in your community (36 international-base classes). Conducts classes & workshops in disaster management and disaster preparedness for ages 3 and up.

P.O Box 46464 • Las Vegas, NV 89114
(888) 990-9726

Anthony Browder

Cultural Historian, Educational Consultant, Artist, Publisher, and Author of *Nile Valley Contributions to Civilization*, volume II of *From the Browder File: Survival Strategies For Africans Living In America*, and other books/tapes. Founder and director of *The Institute of Karmic Guidance*. Hosts educational Afrocentric tours to Afrika & Mexico. Lecture topics include Afrikan American History, the Afrikan Origin of Religion & Mythology, Science, Medicine, and the Education & Miseducation of Afrikan People

Institute of Karmic Guidance

A culturally oriented organization founded by Anthony Browder, dedicated to the dissemination of ancient Afrikan Egyptian History and Metaphysics. Producer of the "*Free Your Mind*" lecture series which features presentations by world reknown historians, scientists, psychologists, and scholars. Provides Afrocentric tours of Washington D.C. and annual Study Tours to Afrika (Egypt & West Afrika) and Mexico. Books, videos, audio tapes, catalogue, and travel schedule available. Video/audio tapes include:

- *The Melanin Symposium* (6 tapes) Patricia Newton, Richard King, and Carol Barnes gives insights on Melanin, the Chemical Key of Life.
- *The African Origins of Christianity*. The Afrikan influence on religion; history and symbolic meaning of the Bible.

P. O. Box 73025 • Washington, D.C. 20056
(301) 853-2465

Lecturers, Authors, Griots, Artists, Workshop Givers, Etc.

Arvel & Bobbie Chappell, Drs.

Metaphysicians, Lecturers, Authors. Lecture topics include Quantum Healing, Personal Development, Stress Management, "Right Use of Will," Metaphysics, Esoteric Sciences, and balancing and aligning Spirit /Heart /Will /Body. Founders of *The Metaphysical Institute of Higher Learning* (see page R•30). Authors of *The Double-You (W) Book*.

2873 W. 6th Street • Rialto, CA 92376
(909) 874-6807
WEBSITE:www.metaphy.com
EMAIL: Metaphy3@cs.com

Irasha Pearl

Asa Hilliard, Dr.

Courtesy of A. Browder

Educational Psychologist, Lecturer & Historian. His books include *The Maroon Within Us* (socialization of Afrikan children) and *Testing African American Students*. Lectures are customized according to need.

Department of Educational Policy Studies
Georgia State University
Atlanta, GA 30303
(404) 651-1269

Waset Educational Productions

Slide-illustrated interviews of Drs. A. Hilliard /John Henrik Clarke by TV Producer Listervelt Middleton.

- *Free Your Mind - Return to the Source*. Interview featuring Dr. Asa Hilliard.
- *Master Keys*. Interviewing Dr. Asa Hilliard
- *African Diary*. Interviewing John Henrik Clarke

P. O. Box 91123 • East Point GA, 30364

Ashra & Merira Kwesi

Historians, Griots, Lecturers, Kamitologists and Author-Producers of educational videos restoring the Afrikan roots of civilization, showing firsthand information from the ancient temples, tombs, and papyrus papers in Afrika. Merira lectures on Afrikan Fashion and Culture, both ancient and modern. Ashra lectures on Afrikan History, Religion, and Afrikan Origin of Civilization. Founders of *Kemet Nu Productions.* Hosts annual, educational trips / tours to Afrika.

Kemet Nu Productions

Educational videos and audio tapes by Ashra & Merira Kwesi on Afrikan history, Judaism, Christianity, Afrikan fashion and more.
Titles include:

- *Advertising: The Attack on the Afrikan Image*
- *Afrikan History vs. Biblical Myths*
- *The Cultural Destruction of Afrikan Fashions*
- *The Afrikan History of Christianity*
- *Christianity: The Stolen Religion From Afrika*
- *Judaism: The Stolen Religion From Afrika*
- *The Afrikan Origin of Civilization & Western Freemasonry*

3870 Crenshaw Blvd., Suite 104-424
Los Angeles, CA 90008
(323) 938-8031 • (214) 371-0206
WEBSITE: www.blackmind.com/kemetnu
EMAIL: kemetnu@aol.com

Lecturers, Authors, Griots, Artists, Workshop Givers, Etc.

Babatunde Folayemi

A "Contemporary Griot" telling stories of the past as well as the future and present. Historian, Artist/ Sculptor, Counselor, and Program Designer (for at-risk youths & family). Author of In the Father's Image, and To Know Thy Father (A Manual of Fasting and Meditation). Founder of the national organization *"Men Against Domestic Violence" (MADV)*. Founder of a scholarship foundation for students (the Sarah Freeman Recognition Award). Delivers lecture-slide shows on the History of Man, Olmec History, Religion & Evolution, Afrikan Culture, Ancient Civilizations, and Youth Violence (its causes & solutions). His special lecture presentation, "Wisdom of the Elders," addresses how western civilization views seniors as compared with the Afrikan way, and the impact of this upon society, for such also impacts our lack of understanding of what children are about –being the *beginning* and the *end*.

1547 Eucalyptus Hill Road
Santa Barbara, CA 93103
(805) 965-3661 • (805) 899-4800

Bill McAdoo, Dr.

One of the nation's foremost Forensic (& Clinical) Psychologists. Lecture topics include Legal Issues regarding children, Child Custody, and Child Abuse. Author of a number of books soon to be published, including Deadly Love, –about the victimization of children (publisher to be announced).

P.O. Box 1014
Moorpark, CA 93020
(323) 243-4935

Colin Heron, Dr.

Attorney-Businessman lecturing on Economic Issues, Poli-economics and "the Big Picture." Founder of The California Black Pages, the largest distributed directory of Black businesses and professionals in California.

P.O. Box 2595 • Corona, CA 91718-2595
(909) 279-2195

Dena Crowder, M.A.

Describes herself simply as a "Healer, Speaker, and transformational Success Coach." Dena shows people how to access their Essence, discover their "life's work", and be sourceful and masterful in work and play. She creates transformational programs which allow organizations to build successful work environments, increase their profitability and improve the way they communicate. She enlivens individuals and groups from all over the world — celebrities, Fortune 100 executives, professionals, students, homemakers. She has consulted the government of Belize, as well as European political and business entities. She works with corporate & governmental clients as a "Transformational Resolution Consultant," where she radically shifts the quality of interation between individuals, groups and organiztions in stages of transition or conflict. Her 3 workshop-courses are:

- Destiny — Reaching your Ultimate Potential here and now. Reveals unconscious issues that may be hindering the fullest expression of your Destiny.
- The Essential Woman— Discover your *Life's Theme*...probably unconscious to you, but which directs /shapes every interaction & result in life. Understand how you've constructed your life around this Theme . Learn the principles to become the "architect of your Destiny." Reveals what is fundamental to women. A 10-week course, tailorable to businesses, corporate groups, church /social groups.
- Speaking for Success Intensive— Personal success & success of your projects, organizations. 2-day workshop provides the insight /knowledge to set you on a path of strategic, powerful, spirited communication.

626 South Plymouth Blvd. • Los Angeles, CA 90005
(323) 930-1611 Fax (323) 857-1211

Lecturers, Authors, Griots, Artists, Workshop Givers, Etc.

Dadisi Sanyika

Described as a"Renaissance Man." Lecturer, Spiritual Educator, Counselor, Author, Astrological Consultant, Drummer, Choreographer and Artistic Director. Author of Rites of Passage and numerous tapes. Founder of...

Golden Thread Productions

—a multi-faceted institute of Afrikan Spirituality, Knowledge for building the Higher Self, and West Afrikan Dance & Folklore. Features classes (and tapes) on a wide spectrum of subjects related to the Afrikan mystery or wisdom teachings, and is designed to assist participants in liberating their Higher Self. Classes and lecture topics include: Virtues, Ethics, Sacred Geometry, Sacred Music / Harmonics, Mathematics, Astronomy, Astro-Mythology, Afrikan Cosmology, Wholistic Human Development, and Applied Metaphysical Principles.

P.O. Box 875 • Long Beach, CA 90801
(323) 757-0237
WEBSITE: www.afrikanculture.com
EMAIL: sanyika@successnet.net

Doctah B

"Natural Health and Motivational Lecturer," University Instructor, Herbalist, Author, Consultant, and Researcher. Founder of *Soul Proprietorship Natural HealthProducts.* Doctah B's parasite cleansing formula, herbal libido formulas, herbal stop-smoking formula, and other herbal products have been called the best by industry professionals and people who use them. He has helped thousands change their lives, regain and their health, –even so-called incurables. Author of DOCTAH B's Food for Mind Body and Soul, a natural health survival guide. He has been quoted in Time Magazine, Wall Street Journal, and numerous health publications. Presents vital health information in an entertaining, thought-provoking and refreshing way which both captivates and educates his audiences. Gives lectures, workshops and classes on *"simple techniques for long life, geared towards empowering an individual to becoming 'Independently Healthy'."*

Soul Proprietorship
5042 Wilshire Blvd., Ste 121
Los Angeles, CA 90036
(323) 427-8419 • Fax (323) 766-0224
EMAIL: docb737@earthlink.net

Gloria Van Robinson

Empowerment Consultant, Spiritual Counselor, Lecturer, and Travel Professional (for international & domestic travel, lodgings & accommodations). Recently appointed and accepted as a candidate in *Lexington Who's Who Empowering Executives & Professionals*. Provides empowerment workshops and seminars. Gloria also provides other spiritual services as follows:

- *Spiritual House-Cleansing*: through ancient Afrikan rituals, she detoxifies homes or other environments of psychic impurities.
- *Channeling*: she does spiritual counseling /readings in which she channels messages from your Spirit Guides. She is available for private & telephone consultations by appointment.

Her Seminar Workshops include: *Birth to the Present*, *Ask for What You Want*, and *Tapping Your Spirit*. Her workshops for adolescents develop Self Esteem in youth, helping them "come back," that is, give up the streets /dope /etc., and master their own Spirit.

5377 Imperial Ave.
San Diego, CA 92114
(619) 263-9285
EMAIL: vanrobinson@looksmart.com

Lecturers, Authors, Griots, Artists, Workshop Givers, Etc.

Gwynelle Dismukes

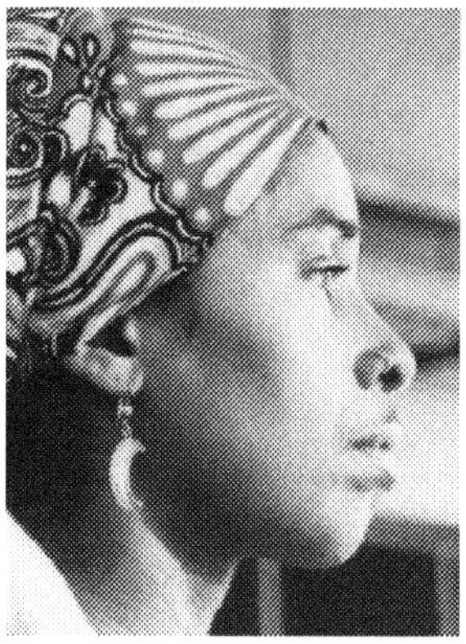

Gwynelle is dedicated to *"promoting the spiritual evolution of humanity, particularly through exposure to the positive, life-affirming aspects of Afrikan culture."* Peace-Activist and Author of Afrikan Alkhemy, she is a Clinical Hynotherapist who does individual and group work using guided imagery to integrate Body, Mind, Spirit, & Heart. She is the founder and publisher of *Brite Moments,* an Afrocentric alternative monthly paper promoting Peace through spiritual growth, family stability, and community responsibility. She conducts lectures and workshops on Kwanzaa, Conflict Resolution Through Afrikan-centered Values, Transformation of Consciousness, and Afrikan-based Spirituality.

P. O. Box 90994 • Nashville, TN 37209

"Gwynth"

Gwendolyn Haynes, M.S., is a Designer, Author and gifted Prophet who calls herself a "Reader," the modern term for a Prophet. Gwynth works with her Spirit Guides to bring messages through from your Loved Ones, your Spirit Guides and Spirit Teachers. She reads photographs to provide information about other people in your life. Gwynth is available for workshops, classes, lectures, private consultations, telephone readings by appointment, past life regression, and group work. She has developed several seminar packages including 21 Days to a Miracle, Why Am I Here?, and Life Cycles, available for various groups.

11908 O'Casey • Yukon, OK 73099
(405) 324-1417

Hassan Kamau Salim, Dr.

Grand Master martial artist, Professor of Afrikan history, Kamitic Priest, Kamitologist, Storyteller, Poet, author of numerous books including Seven Shades of Black (a book of poetry), Kupigana Ngumi (the Afrikan Martial Arts), and in progress– Spiritual Warriors are Healers. Founder of the *Black Gold Afrakan Kultural Arts Center,* the *Ma'at Institute for Children & Adult Education*, and a Kamitic Temple. Lecture topics include the Afrikan Martial Arts, the Metu Neter (Hieroglyphics), Kamitic Breathing Meditation, Rites of Passage, Esoteric Sciences, and Kamite Cosmology.

P. O. Box 1725
Plainfield, N.J. 07060
(908) 226-9100

Iyanla Vanzant

Yoruba Priestess, Empowerment Specialist, Lecturer, and Spiritual-Life Counselor who lectures and facilitates workshops nationally. Her books include Tapping the Power Within: A Path to Self-Empowerment for Black Women, and The Value in the Valley: *"Valleys are not one-size-fits-all.' In fact, they are custom-designed to teach you how to reach your highest potential –to be divine, prosperous, and in alignment with your highest and greatest good."*

Inner Vision
P. O. Box 3231
Silver Spring, MD 20918-0231
(301) 933-9310

Lecturers, Authors, Griots, Artists, Workshop Givers, Etc.

Jamaal Goree

Media Analyst, Lecturer, Journalist, Commercial Radio Producer, and Producer of Afrocentric educational video/audio tapes. Co-founder of *The Talking Drum Community Forum.* His lecture series, *"Ethnic Tokens,"* discusses the assault on the image of Afrikans by the Media. Other lecture topics include Polygamy, Mind Control, and Population Control & Interracial Relationships.

Talking Drum

Provides full video/audio production services. Major archive of independantly produced Afrocentric video/audio tapes, many from *Talking Drum Community Forum.* Catalog available. Titles include:

- *The Nigger Factory*, featuring Del Jones
- *Afrikan Centered Analysis of White Supremist Messages in the Popular Media*
- *Sankofa*, the movie & other films by H. Gerima
- *The Black Truth*, lecture by Asar Jubal
- *The Afrikan Holocaust*
- *The CIA CONTRA Crack Cocaine Epidemic* (series)
- *Ethnic Tokens*, Propaganda, Mind Control, Population Control & the Media
- *The Black Untouchables of India*, by Runoko Rashidi & Dr. Velu Anamalai
- *Hi-Tech Barbarians*, by Dell Jones
- *Black Australians*, Gracelyn Smallwood

3870 Crenshaw Blvd., Suite #104-424
Los Angeles, CA 90008
(213) 296-0768

Jewel Diamond Taylor

Foremost National Motivational Speaker. Lecture and Workshop topics include Self-Esteem, Women's Healing, Rites of Passage, Spiritual Joy, Goal-Setting, Stress Management, Relationships, Parenting, Cultural Pride, Overcoming Procrastination, and learning your own purpose in life. Author of Success Gems (a self-help, motivational book), and *Too Blessed To Be Stressed.*

4195 Chino Hills Parkway
Chino Hill, CA 91707
(323) 964-1736
speaking calendar (323) 964-2513

J. Jordan, Dr.

Describes herself simply as a "God-gifted woman." Provides consultation /counseling to individuals over the phone, primarily after receiving and meditating upon a person's handwritten letter. She is a Spiritual Counselor who *"helps all people of all walks of life; the rich, the poor, the celebrities, the professionals."* She says *"There is no charge for God's work; donations or gifts are accepted with appreciation."*

P. O. Box 1841 • Montgomery, AL 36102
(334) 262-2397

Lecturers, Authors, Griots, Artists, Workshop Givers, Etc.

Keidi Obi Awadu

"The Conscious Rasta" who endeavors to bring forth much needed, alternative viewpoints on issues relating to Survival in an increasingly hostile global environment. Lecture topics include Genocide, Political Perspectives, Health, Organic Gardening, Vaccines, and Population-Control. Prolific author of many highly informing, eye-opening books, reports, videos and audiotapes.

Titles by Keidi Obi Awadu

Books and reports include:
- *Africa's Death Sentence*
- *AIDS Exposed*
- *In Defense of Fertility*
- *Mind Control*
- *The Organic Gardener*
- *Another Loaded Needle: SPF66 Malaria Vaccine*

Video/audio tapes spanning a broad range of topics relating to contemporary, political, and survival issues. Titles include:
- *Vaccinations: An Ounce of Prevention? Or a Pound of Death?*
- *Invasion of the Baby Snatchers*
- *The Trojan Horse Analysis: Rap & Hip-Hop Videos as Mind Control*
- *An Inquiry Into the Death of Eazy E*
- *Food: It's About Survival*

P. O. Box 7683
Longbeach CA, 90807
(310) 403-2921

A. Kweku Andoh, Dr.

Ethnobotanist and Herbal Doctor. Author of a number of books on plants /herbs, and Afrikan interests, including the mystical Iboga herb (Tabernanthe Iboga), "the Plant that Heals the Spirit." Author of the film: *The Graffiti Prophecies of San Francisco* (about Dogon Cosmology and how Afrikan People will carry forward into the New Age). Hosts trips to Ghana, particularly in connection with Iboga. His botanic center offers a wide variety of Afrikan plants & herbs, including books, a catalog, and his herbal supplements /formulations. Lecture topics include Herbology, Healing, Afrikan Spirituality & Cosmology.

North American Branch of AAHAS

Founded by Dr. A. Kweku Andoh, and is part of the All African Healing Arts Society (AAHAS), an international corporate body, with headquarters in Ghana, organized for uniting Traditional and Orthodox Medical Practitioners around the world, and to promote education, research and development into plant-based medicines and alternative healing therapies. Membership is open to everyone concerned with the health and wellness of Earth and all her diverse people.

North Scale Institute

The research arm of AAHAS. Also a referral service and publisher of books largely in botany and medicine. Founded by Dr. A. Kweku Andoh, the North Scale Institute is dedicated to preserving the knowledge and wisdom of ancient cultures throughout the world, particularly in regards to:
- *Ethno-botany*, which studies the relationship between a people and use they make of the plant-life around them.
- *Traditional Medicine* or the art of healing the sick through the "medicine men" of tradition, hence the witch doctors of Afrika, the shamans of Native America, the aryuvedic doctors of India, etc.

2205 Taraval St. • San Francisco, CA 94116
(415) 759-5683

Lecturers, Authors, Griots, Artists, Workshop Givers, Etc.

Lady Prema

Pioneer of the movement, *"Heal A Woman, Heal A Nation."* Her focus is "healing the heart...the home of Love." Sympathetic to the Afrikan American challenge to "be free," Lady Prema facilitates transformation workshops which serve as a "safe place" to heal the spiritual, mental and emotional wounds of the people. She is a Composer, Vocalist, Poet, Author and Producer, channeling her enthusiasm through her music, poetry and voice. As a mistress of ceremony she "brings the spirit of truth wrapped in a bundle of Love & Joy."

Titles by Lady Prema

- *Conscious Living*: Insights for healing Spirit, Mind, & Body), including a 3-set audio tape.
- *Breaking the Spell*: In this 3-set audio tape series, Lady Prema combines ancient wisdom with universal truths to accelerate spiritual growth.
- *Heal A Woman, Heal A Nation*: Featuring Iyanla Vanzant, Queen Afua, Dr. Rosalind Jeffries, Lady Prema, and other dynamic healers. Available in video and audio tapes.
- *My Soul Speaks*: A divine offering in the form of poetry.
- *It's All Grace*: Inspired words for spiritual elevation. Audio tape.

155-41 115th Ave.
Jamaica, NY 11434
(718) 529-4189

Legrand Clegg II, Dr.

City Attorney for the City of Compton –CA, Lecturer, Kamitologist, Author & Producer of *The Clegg Series* educational videos and the internet newsletter: MAAT News. Lecture topics include the Black Origin of Western Law, Egypt During the Golden Age, Egypt During the 18th Dynasty, The Daughters of Isis, and When Black Men Ruled the World.

The Clegg Series

Produced by Dr. Legrand Clegg II, this series redefines the Black experience in its contribution to modern civilization through two videotapes accompanied by a 51-page educational and learning activity booklet. Designed to creatively teach students in elementary, secondary and high school curriculums, the Afrikan foundation and contributions to civilization, seldom addressed by standardized textbooks.

- (Part I) *When Black Men Ruled the World*
- (Part II) *The Daughters of Isis: Black Women in Antiquity*

P. O. Box 0324 • Compton, CA 90223-0324
(800) 788-CLEGG
WEBSITE: www.melanet.com/cleggseries

Lecturers, Authors, Griots, Artists, Workshop Givers, Etc.

Llaila Afrika, Dr.

A Naturopathic Doctor of Holistic Health, Lecturer & Author. Lecture topics include Disease Remedies, Melanin, Afrocentric Health, and Afrikan History.

Titles by Dr. Llaila Afrika

Books include:

- *African Holistic Health*
- *Nutricide: Nutritional Destruction of the Black Race* (includes remedies for "crack babies" and learning disorders)

Tapes: An educational series of over 30 video/audio tapes where Dr. Afrika is teaching classes. Titles include:

- *Dangers of Hospitals, Drugs and Doctors*
- *Self-Diagnosis, Self Treatment*
- *Melanin Nutrition*
- *White Racism: The Nutritional Cause*
- *Homosexuality: The Cause, the Cure, and Detox*
- *Poisons: Digestion & Nutrition*
- *Children's Nutrition Stories*

P. O. Box 2475
Beauford, SC 29901
(803) 522-8545

Meri Morgan Smith, Dr.

Accomplished Educator, Lawyer, and Expert in the area of Human Behavior, Parenting, Relationships, and Psychology. Founder and director of *The Parent Action Center* and *Parents In Action* –which are organizations created to be a resource to teach parents how to more effectively manage the behavior of their children to best prepare them for adulthood. The organizations employ a technique originated by Dr. Smith called "re-parenting", where parents learn parenting skills they were not taught in childhood. The objective is to "break the cycle" of ineffective parenting.

Author of *Parenting By Rhyme and Reason* (available in video, audio, & CD, and also in Spanish and other major languages); *Spankers Anonymous; The Friday Relationship Program;* and *The Universal Parenting Rule of Expectation*. Her books are also total programs. Lecture topics include: Parenting, Why Johnny Won't Listen, Punishment, Forgiving, Human Behavior, and Relationships. In addition she provides workshops, relationship classes, and counseling (personal, family, premarital, and pre-divorce, post-divorce). She says: *"Every story and successful search for solutions to problems in relationships MUST start '...in the beginning' – with TRUTH. Any relationship can be saved by applying principles of TRUTH."*

Parents In Action, Inc.
P.O. Box 4336
West Covina, CA 91791
(323) 732-7799
Fax: (323) 734-9551

Lecturers, Authors, Griots, Artists, Workshop Givers, Etc.

Locksley Geoghagen, Dr.

Professor of Religious Studies, Kamitologist, Historian and Lecturer. Topics include Spirituality, Consciousness, Afrikan Cosmology & Spiritual Systems, World Religions, History, and Kamit.

410 Nopal Way • Nipomo, CA 93444
(805) 929-3961

Micheline Saint Louis

Haitian-born Spiritualist, Lecturer, Author, Singer, and Hair & Fashion Designer. She says: *"Know thyself and be thyself, because knowledge, tradition, culture and unity equal power."* Author of *Haitian Roots In Voudoun Culture* (about the culture and religion of Haiti). Lecture topics include: Afrikan-based Spirituality, Origin of Spirituality, Self Esteem, Afrikan Cultural Traditions. Also lectures on the proper care of the female sex organs: *Restoring the Vagina back to a virgin-like state; What To Do After Childbirth; Proper Feminine Hygiene;* and *How to Stop Vaginal Discharges.*

5206 S. Manhattan Place
Los Angeles, CA 90062
(888) 638-0689

Muhammad A. Nassardeen

National Motivational Speaker, Businessman, Author, Founder of *Recycling Black Dollars*, and Publisher of *The Black Dollar Newsletter.* His *"Change Bank Day"* program –supporting Black-owned banks– has attracted over 1400 new depositors with over $7,00,000.00. Lecture topics include Black Economic Business Development, Sharing Versus Selling, The Art of Being Positive, and Setting & Achieving Goals, and "Connecting the Dots."

110 S. Labrea Ave., Suites 420 & 510
Inglewood, CA 90301
(310) 673-7777

Lecturers, Authors, Griots, Artists, Workshop Givers, Etc.

Na'im Akbar, Dr.

Clinical Psychologist, Educator, Lecturer, and Pioneer in the development of an Afrikan-centered approach to modern psychology. His numerous books include *Visions for Black Men*, and *Chains and Images of Psychological Slavery*. Founder of *Mind Productions & Associates*, and *Na'im Akbar Consultants.* Hosts tours to Afrika.

Mind Productions & Associates

Publisher of Dr. Na'im Akbar's materials and newsletter, *Sun of Mind.* A wealth of video and audio tapes of Akbar's powerful lectures and presentations spanning a broad range of topics. Titles include:

- *Afrocentric Spirituality*
- *Confronting the Challenges of the Black Family*
- *Extraordinary Black Students*
- *Restoration of Culture and Salvaging Our Youth*
- *21st Century Black Leadership*

Na'im Akbar Consultants

Training Programs and Workshops for Personal and Community Evolution. Leadership Development programs for college students and young adults.

P. O. Box 11221
Tallahassee, FL 32302
(904) 222-1764

Nathan F. Rabb, Dr.

A Naturopathic Doctor of Holistic Health and Nutrition, Clinical Iridologist, and Doctor of Divinity. Author of educational video/audio tapes addressing Holistic Health. Lecture topics include Holistic Natural Healing, Holistic & Hygienic Living, and Biblical Guidelines for taking care of the body.

Holistic Health Service

Educational holistic videos by Dr. Nathan Rabb:

- *Herbal Medicine*. Overview of herbal medicine.
- *Detoxification*. Detoxifying the body.
- *Restoration & Prevention*. Restoring the body after detoxification, and preventing onset of any problems.
- *The Three Basic Steps to Optimal Wellness* (audio)

7033 S. Madden Ave.
Los Angeles, CA 90043
(310) 419-4372

Lecturers, Authors, Griots, Artists, Workshop Givers, Etc.

Nijel BPG

Fine Artist, Sculptor, Martial Arts Instructor, and Author of *Nuba Wrestling: The Original Art*. Nijel, whose name means *Black Prince of God,* lectures on the Afrikan roots of the Martial Arts and Defense Systems. His hand-painted sculptures of Afrikan men of achievement such as Marcus Garvey, Malcolm X and others are available through his fine-arts company, *Nijart International.* On May 11, 1996 Nijel unveiled *"The Mother of Humanity,"* the largest bronze stature of a Black Woman in the world today. Standing 16 feet tall and weighing two tons, the monument is located in Watts, California at 10950 Central Ave., with commemorative prints and literature, etc., available. Other locations for this monument will be Afrika, Brazil, Australia, India, China and Spain.

2131 South Hoover St., Suite 101
Los Angeles, CA 90007 • (213) 746-9263

Neely Fuller Jr.

Author of *The United Independent Compensatory Code/System/Concept*, a textbook & workbook for thought, speech and/or action for Victims of Racism ("non-white" people). People of Color can tailor its practical concepts to their individual circumstances at any time. Neely lectures on the topics addressed in his book, which includes: Counter-racism Behavior, and how Racism (white supremacy) affects the nine areas of people-activity, which are Economics, Education, Entertainment, Labor, Law, Politics, Religion, Sex, and War/Counterwar.

905 6th St. S.W.
Washington, DC 20024
(202) 484-5461

Lecturers, Authors, Griots, Artists, Workshop Givers, Etc.

N2WISHN

Edu-taining musical Duo comprised of **Queen Sistah Charmain** —Songstress, Afrikan Dancer, and Percussionist; and **Tony B. Conscious** —Lyricist, Accapella Percussionist, Author, and Spoken Word Artist. Together, they creatively fuse Jazz, R&B, Hip-hop, Reggae and Traditional Afrikan Rhythm, plus dance and original "Spoken Word Poetry", to advance Afrikan cultural awareness. N2WISHN entertains and educates *"by stressing the importance of Cultural Awareness, Unity, 'Blak Love' and connecting with Mother Earth, Nature, the Elements, the Ancestors and above all...THE CREATOR."* **Says Charmain,** *"My talents are just a reflection of the Creator's divine plan for Mother Earth and the original people of the planet. That's why it's time to get back to being what we are and what the creator wants us to be, and that is righteous, conscious, strong, powerful and most of all...connected!!!"* **Tony says,** *"I'm a vessel the Creator uses to bring about messages, so don't look up to me, just meditate, give thanks and become connected."* Founders of *Conscious Enterprises*, via which audio & video tapes of their songs, poetry, and music are available, along with "conscious shirts" and other items which send positive messages. Authors /compilers of *The Million Youth March —Black Power Into the Year 2000*, a pictorial book (& 5-hour documentary video) composed of photographs, stories, press-releases & articles from newspapers and publications, before, during, & after the historical Million Youth March. Poetry books by Tony *include: Diary of A Blak Man; Huemanity, Blak History 101, Blak Luv,* and *Nature-All.*

P.O. Box 761385 • Los Angeles, CA 90076
(818) 985-3327 • Fax (818) 985-4986
EMAIL: cnsciousent@earthlink.net

Ooausha Chakra

Sista Singer and Composer whose voice and lyrics would enhance any Afrocentric cultural event, as they have a number of albums. Also an Actress and Fashion Designer, the "Song Goddess" formerly known as Barbara Paige writes: *"I am ...blessed with music, the vibration that heals and unites. Rhythmic music of the heart with dramatic sophistication. For an earthly connection tune in."*

(888) 515-6049
P. O. Box 70893
Las Vegas,
NV 89170-0893

Otieno Jafri Okatch, M.A.

Behavioral Consultant and founder of the study group, *Life Skills, Inc.*, Okatch delivers lectures for groups, schools and colleges on Race & Ethnicity, Political Perspectives, Behavioral Health, Proper Eating for maximizing spiritual power, Economic Opportunities in Afrika, Afrikan & World History, Ancient & Contemporary Afrikan Spiritual Systems, and Kiswahili.

821 Verona St. • LaHabra, CA 90631
(562) 694-6932 • (800) 281-1371

Lecturers, Authors, Griots, Artists, Workshop Givers, Etc.

Odinga Kambui

Informs us that Afrikan Drum Music was so complex in its rhythms, it could approximate the tones and pitch of human speech, enabling Afrikans to effectively "talk" long-distance via drums. Odinga is a outstanding Drummer, Craftsman, Instructor, Researcher and Founder of ***Words & Deeds Productions*** – which organizes cultural events and facilitates Afrikan cultural awareness. Its resources for Afrikan communities include tours to Afrocentric events, museum shows and historical sites. Slide presentations on The Afrikan Origin of High Culture, and Visual Journey to the Motherland (featuring the late John Henrik Clarke & Dr. ben Jochannan). Video presentations on the Contemporary His/Her Story of Black Liberation. Handcrafted products preserving Afrikan symbols in a variety of creative forms (leathercraft, pendants, art, etc). And of course, workshops and instructional classes on Afrikan Traditional Drumming.

Words & Deeds Productions
P.O.Box 131131 • Dallas, Texas 75313
(214) 421-9828
EMAIL: odinga@swbell.net

Patrick Ross

"Edu-tainer" who educates through entertainment. Also known as "Computer Big," he is a World-beat Musician, Composer, Producer, Recording Engineer, and Synth Programmer recorded on many albums. His versatile musical talent lends a positive addition to Afrikan cultural events.

P. O. Box 2932
Los Angeles, CA 90078-2932
EMAIL: tiger980@concentric.net
Fax (310) 494-3954

Patricia Newton, Dr.

The only female in 600 years of Ashanti Culture to be given the title of *Dompiahene*, –a chief in the royal Ashanti lineage that has historically been only afforded to men. Psychiatrist, Consultant, and "physician-healer, teacher-educator." Author of Handbook for a Melanated, Melatonin-Friendly Lifestyle (a self-help book), Post Traumatic Slavery Disorder, and other books. Lecture topics include Melanin, Chemical Dependency, Mental Health issues, Cultural Therapy, Alternative Health Care Systems, Stress Reduction, Women's Healthcare Issues, Nutritional Counseling, and Self-Motivation. Hosts seminars and study tours in North and South America, Afrika, Europe and the Caribbean.

• Newton & Associates
• Newton-Thoth, Inc. /Speakers Bureau

Founded by Dr. Patricia Newton:

- *Newton & Associates* are specialists in Behavioral Medicine stressing the interface of medical, psychological, and physical illness and wellness.
- *Newton-Thoth, Inc.*, is an international behavioral science management corporation providing consultation to professional public & private agencies, organizations, institutions, etc., on the national and international level.
- *Newton-Thoth Speakers Bureau* represents some of America's leading authorities in Afrikan Spirituality, Science and Geopolitics.

4100 N. Charles Street, #507
Baltimore, MD 21218-1024
(410) 752-2900

Lecturers, Authors, Griots, Artists, Workshop Givers, Etc.

Paul Goss, Dr.

A Naturopathic Doctor, International Lecturer, Author, and Health Activist serving the community for over 30 years. Founder of several firms devoted to health: *The Goss Corporation* which owns the *New Earth Health Food Store* (in Compton, CA); *New Body Products* –an international multi-level company specializing in health /herbal products; the *Eden Holistic Health Retreat* comprising over 700 acres of natural environment of clean air, water, and spirit. The retreat hosts seminars several times a year and is the source of many ingredients in *New Body Products*. Author of The Rebirth of Gods and Forever Young. Lecture topics include Herbology, Iridology, Rejuvenation, and Health Maintenance.

464 W. Compton Blvd.
Compton, CA 90220
(310) 537-4793

Ronnie McQueen

Musician, "Musical Healer," Composer, Rasta man, Philosopher, Instructor. Founded and named the band, "Steel Pulse." Adds the dimension of musical healing to Afrocentric cultural events.

412 N. Coast Hwy., #171
Laguna Beach, CA 92651

Queen Afua

Holistic Health Consultant, Herbalist, founder of the *Heal Thyself Center* and Sacred Women, both a book and 9-hour intensive training on how to be a Full Woman and a Healed Woman for Self, Nation and World Building. Author of Heal Thyself -For Health and Longevity. Lecture topics include Rejuvenation, Self-Healing, Detoxification, Nutritional Fasting, Colon Therapy, Herbology and Spirituality.

106 Kingston Ave. • Brooklyn, NY 11213
(718) 221-HEAL

Richard McCoy

Among other things, a Self-Healing Consultant. Workshops on *The Art of Manifesting Your Desires.* Workshops on the rediscovered ancient art of Self-Healing through "Jin Shin Jyutsu." Lectures on Consciousness, Creativity, Spirituality, Health, and Economic Opportunities in Afrika.

P.O. Box 884691 • San Francisco, CA 94188

Lecturers, Authors, Griots, Artists, Workshop Givers, Etc.

Raymond Howell

Describes himself as a "very dedicated creative person." Through the eyes of others he is seen as an accomplished and prolific Master of Fine Art who has exhibited throughout the U.S. for more than two decades. Raymond is about creating Black images of Divinity. His focus is *"putting Black images and Black Art into Black Christian churches for People of Color* –ours– *to identify themselves with other than the pulpit and the Black preacher."* Among other subjects, including famous Jazz musicians, he paints big, big murals communicating the Black identity of biblical personages. Completed in 1996, his 9'x7' mural, *"The Baptism of Jesus by John the Baptist"* (below) may be viewed in Oakland at Olivet Baptist Church (3232 Market St.). His work expands the dimensions of Afrocentric cultural events.

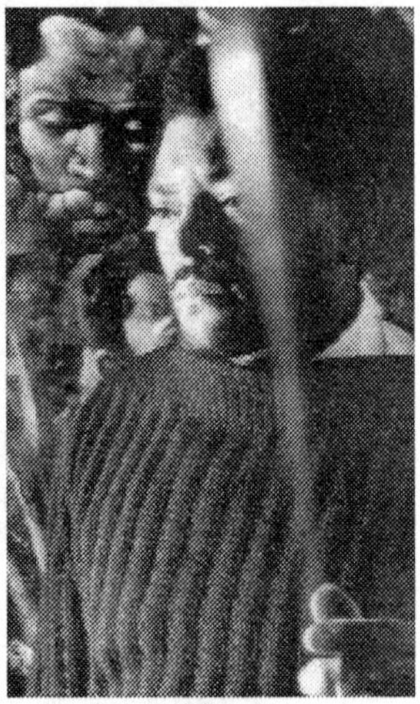

2440 Magnolia Court • Oakland, CA 94607
(510) 451-1231

Roy Shine

Lymph Technician, Sexologist, Anatomist, and Herbalist. Described as a "profound thinker," his lecture topics include Developing Higher Sexual Energy, Nutrition, Herbs for Rejuvenation, and the Human Body.

14412 Passage Ave.
Paramount, CA 90723
EMAIL: rshine1067@aol.com

Irasha Pearl

Detail: "The Baptism of Jesus by John the Baptist"

"Louis"

"Jazz Man"

Lecturers, Authors, Griots, Artists, Workshop Givers, Etc.

Robert Brock, Dr.

Highly revered "Reparations Champion" since 1965. President and founder of the organization, *Self Determination Committee*. Attorney, Author, Historian, Educator, and Expert in Taxes, US Government & International Laws, and the study of the American Slavery Institution. Author of *Passport to Freedom: With Reparations & Self-Determination*; *Who Brought The Slaves To America?: Slavery And The Jews*; and *The Story Of The Constitution*. Lecture topics include: Reparations for U.S. Slave Descendants, Constitutional Law, Eliminating the Effects of Slavery, No Black Taxation Without Reparations, Self-Determination. He says: *"Reparations means that the goverment of the U.S. and its sovereign Constitutional citizens and residents redress U.S. slave descendants for injuries, damages and detriment for: committing and practicing undeclared war, captivity and forced transportation, loss of land and loss of freedom, condition of slaver, the status of a slave, and loss and denial of human rights." "Cash payments of reparations by the U.S. government to American citizens of African descent are long overdue!"* Japanese-Americans who were imprisoned in internment camps during World War II were awareded $20,000 each, as reparations by the U.S. government. Dr. Brock shows American Afrikans how to get paid the "40 acres and a mule" which they were promised but never received. Shows and helps you make the Legal Claim for what's yours.

Self Determination Committee
P.O. Box 15288
Washington, D.C. 20003
(202) 544-5366
WEBSITE: www.directblackaction.com

Rosie Milligan, Dr.

Economic Empowerment Activist, National Motivational Speaker, Author, Businesswoman, Doctor of Business Administration, Registered Nurse, and Health & Business Consultant. Founder of a number of businesses helping people accomplish what they want in life. Founder of a publishing company, health market, *Black Writers On Tour*, and *"Professional Business Consulting Services"* which provides consultation and training for start-up companies, small businesses, and major corporations. Hosts her own radio talk show on health-wealth relationships; co-hosts the *Financial Freedom Forum* on cable TV. Her books include Satisfying The Black Woman Sexually Made Simple, Satisfying The Black Man Sexually Made Simple, and *"Nigger, Please"* –a provocative raw truth book about Blacks born in America. Provides lectures, workshops, and seminars nationally. Lecture topics include Male-Female Relationships, Sexuality, Why Black Men Choose White Women, Healing the Black Woman, Economic Empowerment, and Managing Diversity in the Workplace. Seminar & workshop topics address the many aspects of business such as productivity, marketing, management, etc. Titles include Management Strategies on How to Keep the Team Players Motivated and Productive, Problem Resolution, and Guidelines for Preparing Job Descriptions & Procedure/ Protocol Manuals.

1425 W. Manchester, Suite B
Los Angeles, CA 90047
(323) 750-3592
WEBSITE:www. milliganbooks.com
EMAIL: drrosie@aol.com

Lecturers, Authors, Griots, Artists, Workshop Givers, Etc.

Runoko Rashidi

Historian, Lecturer, World Traveller, Research Specialist and Author of numerous books and educational video/audio tapes. His books include African Presence in Early Asia (editor), African Classical Civilizations, and The Global African Community: the African Presence in Asia, Australia, and the South Pacific. Lecture topics include Afrikan World History, Afrikan History in Asia, India and the Untouchables, Black Herstory, and Great Afrikan Women of Antiquity. Founder of the *International Dalit Support Group*. Runoko also hosts Afrikan-centered educational tours to India.

Titles by Runoko

Numerous video /audio tapes, sometimes featuring other noted historians. Titles include:

- Great African Women in the World of Antiquity
- Black Death Down Under: Australia, Tasmania & the South Pacific. Horrors inflicted on these Blacks by Asians & Europeans.
- The African Presence in Asia and the Black Untouchables of India. Dr. V. Annamalai, a Black Untouchable, provides a shocking firsthand account of India's Black Untouchables (Dalits).
- Are White People Inherently Evil? Lecture-slide presentation, using as case-studies ancient/modern India, Australia & Tasmania.
- The Rape of Africa: Barbarism Unleashed. Overview of the invaders /colonizers of Afrika from antiquity to recent times.
- The African Presence in Asia. Inspiring slide-presentation on the Black presence in ancient/ modern Asia from Arabia to Japan.
- African Presence in Early America
- African Presence in Early Europe

4140 Buckingham Road #D
Los Angeles CA 90008
(323) 293-5807
(210) 648-5178
EMAIL: RRashidi@swbell.net

Eraka Rouzorondu

She's not just a "lecturer" or "teacher" or "motivational speaker." Executive & Artistic Director of Ascension Productions, Eraka Rouzorondu is an Empowerment Specialist – a powerful and transforming communicator with more than 13 years experience in connecting American-Africans and people of all cultures, ages and backgrounds with their own personal power. Eraka's work is informed by the teachings of master historians and philosophers but it is her unique perspective on the spiritual aspects of self-discovery that sets her apart from other educators. She masterfully combines the information gleaned from decades of personal research with speaking skills that have evoked both laughter and tears from audiences of 5 to 5,000. Eraka's teachings are centered upon the premise that knowing is not enough –information is *not* power! Understanding is power...the internalization of information so that it results in lasting, positive change in the total quality of life. No matter what the issue, challenge, celebration, or commemoration, her empowering philosophy offers practical, applicable, step-by-step guidance appropriate for any group or individual, process or event. Lecture and workshop titles include Corporate and Conscious; Man & Woman, Heaven & Earth; AWAKE! Reclaim Your Power!; and From the Ideal to the Real. Special services & spiritual-aid products include keynote addresses, mistress of ceremonies, individual guidance, astrological consultation, metaphysical books, hand-made incense, her audiocassettes and more.

Ascension Productions
P.O. Box 73947 • Washington, DC 20056
(888) 635-0626
WEBSITE: www.ascensionproductions.org

Lecturers, Authors, Griots, Artists, Workshop Givers, Etc.

Sheilaa Hite

Founder of the Personal Empowerment Center. Gifted Spiritual/Therapeutic Counselor, Healer, Metaphysician, Teacher, Clinical Hypnotherapist, Lecturer, Astrologist, and Author who shows you how to create the Magic and Miracles you want in life. Works with you in a loving and supportive manner through metaphysical traditions (having their roots in ancient Afrikan cosmology): Mediumship, Channeling, Astrology ("the road map to your success & how to avoid the pitfalls"), Psychometry ("readings from objects & photographs"), Palmistry ("past life connections & how to get what you want in this life"), and Intuitive Counseling ("answers all your important questions"). Answers your questions on: "past lifes, career & money matters, relationship & soul mate issues, dream interpretation, removing creative blocks, and eliminating the mysteries." Has the ability to "see" and interpret information from the ethereal plane far beyond most in her field, as she brings practical solutions to both spiritual and worldly issues. Her accuracy rate of 85-90% has been affirmed by her more than 4000 international clients. Author of *"Love, Money, Power: Powerful Spells for Creating Magic, Miracles, Love and Abundance."* Sheilaa is available for Private Instruction, Classes, Consultations (by appointment or phone), Ceremonies, Events. She provides workshops, seminars, classes, ceremonies, and Spiritural Tours to Sacred Sites of the World.

Personal Empowerment Center
23852 Pacific Coast Hwy., Ste. 126
Malibu, CA 90265
(310) 859-6932 • Fax (310) 456-2659

Sabrina Peterson

Egyptologist, Lecturer, and Loctician Consultant. Originator of *Yahrajah*, a natural product for locks and spiraling kinky hair. Her company, *Heavenly Healing*, specializes in healing products "from head to toe." Lecture topics include Egyptian Cosmology, The Feather of Maat, Magnetics for Health, Gathering Up the Fragments, Hair Being Resonating Antennae Cables, and Going Galactic –into the Nuclear Eye of the Galaxy or Eye of Maat, hence, *"we are becoming anew, ANU, –burning off the old and becoming reborn* anew. *As we heal the Spirit, the Body automatically heals."*

258 South
Coronado St., #220
Los Angeles,
CA 90057
(323) 934-7644

Steven Meeks

Irasha Pearl

Composer, "Jazz" Musician, Writer, Producer, and Consultant of Afrikan American cultural events. Also an ardent Environmentalist /Naturalist that lectures on the same. Co-founder of Essence of Earth, a health retreat under development in the middle of the urban setting near downtown Dallas, Texas. The retreat is a place of rest and rejuvenation for the weary. A place where one can enjoy massage, fresh organic food, overnight stay, excercise, study and meditation, in an environmentally sound and beautifully landscaped setting.

P.O. Box 1031 • Dallas, Texas 75221
EMAIL: meeksmusic@hotmail.com
(214)948-0707

Lecturers, Authors, Griots, Artists, Workshop Givers, Etc.

Sufia Giza, MA

Consultant, Language Translator, TV-Program Producer, and Public Relations Specialist.
Lecture topics include Afro Mexicanista (Afrikan Presence in Mexico), Herbal Medicine, Holistic Health, and Computer Graphics. Provides multi-media poetry workshops (art as education) for children and adults, plus computer graphics training.

Sankofa Times TV

Founded by Sufia Giza. From art to poetry to TV, the ancestral spirit of Sankofa influences all her work. The Akan word *Sankofa* means "return to the source in order to know where you're going." A cable TV show produced and hosted by Sufia was inspired by the movie, Sankofa (by Haile Gerima). Devoted to Afrikan Spiritual, Emotional, Nutritional, and Wholistic healing. *"Our approach is wholistic, so the goal is to present strategies and alternatives that are geared at empowerment, healing and Peace... Peace in the Hood now... first making peace at home in our families, then in the world around us."* Our motto is "Healing is within our reach."

HOTEP Productions

Video tapes of Sankofa Times TV programs and interviews.

- *Acupuncture*
- *Afrikan Wholistic Health*
- *Parasite Plague*
- *Francisco-Congo Black Movement*
- *The Watts Prophets*
- *International Association of Black Yoga Teachers*
- *Blacked Out Through Whitewash*
- *Black Beauty*

2787 Prospect Ave. • Riverside CA 92507
EMAIL1:sankofa7@yahoo.com
(323) 471-3080

Tarik ibn Freeman

Lay Historian, "Our-storian," Researcher, Lecturer, and Author of *The "HI(D)v.-(A.)I.D.S." Corporate-Goverrnment Deceit Greed Genocide.* Lecture topics include the HIV-AIDS Fraud, "the Right to Die and Not to Live," Human Nutrition, Water, and Holistic Wellness.

1911 19th St. • Santa Monica, CA 90404
(310) 399-9144

Tassili Maat

Among other things, an "Urban Adept" whose full name /title is *Mata Atma Maat Metu Sa Nana Tassili.* "Seer," Spiritual Counselor, Lecturer & Founder of the spiritual center, *Aura-Call of the One*, –a way of describing an *Oracle* and *aura-reading* (reading electromagnetic energy field). Some call this *spiritual reading* and *channeling*. She provides consultations (in person or over the phone), lectures and workshops. Her workshops on applied spirituality include:

Tools for Spiritual Warriors, *Meditation for Melanated People*, and *Intuitive Divination*. These titles are also subjects of her lectures and titles of her books (publisher to be announced). As a *Locktician*, she also lectures on "Love Locks." Offering natural care for the natural hair of spiral-haired people, her healing hair-business is called *Metu Sa Locks* after the dredlocked Afrikan Goddess *Medusa* (derived from *Maat*). And Hair ties in with being a Seer, for Hair is antennae, the *external antennae* that works with the *internal antennae* variously called the Inner Eye, Eye of Maat, "Black Dot," Pineal Gland and "*First* Eye" (Third Eye).

1510 Ezra Church Dr. • Atlanta, GA 30314
(404) 755-5933

Lecturers, Authors, Griots, Artists, Workshop Givers, Etc.

Vet

A dedicated "Art Activist," Fine Artist, Illustrator, Educator, Researcher, and Grant Writer specializing in writing grants for community outreach groups and programs designed to bring art into the community. Also an Organizer of *melanated art shows* and cultural events. She looks for unique projects and special needs, then designs grants to address these needs. For example, she was instrumental in the creation of a grant-funded program catering to the deaf population. Vet has exhibited her art widely, as well as created the opportunity for Black female artists to exhibit their artwork through *"Girlfriends,"* the annual artshow she originated to showcase the art of Afrikan American women. She delivers lectures on Art and the Media from an Afrikan-centered perspective.

P. O. Box 3751 • Ventura, CA 93006
(805) 652-0540

"Rows, Fros, Anythang Goes"

Willie G. Brown, Dr.

Psychologist, Consultant, and Lecturer. Lecture topics include Stress Management for Afrikan Americans, Diversity in the Workplace, Goal Setting, Living with Children with Development Disabilities; also Opportunites in Afrika, and Travel in Kenya.

161 South "E" Street • Oxnard, CA 93030
(805) 983-8091

Steve Cokely

Lecturer, Political Analyst, Researcher, Organizer & "Boulé-Buster" naming names. Founder of the "University of the Bowguard." Lecture topics include Afrikan-centered perspectives & analyses of Current Events (how they relate to Blacks worldwide), the Black Boulé, Conspiracy Theories, & Masonic Texts. Videos & audiotapes available of his prolific lectures.

1703 E. West Highway, #521
Silver Springs, Maryland 20910
(301) 608-3105

Elliott Monds

"Afrikan-World-History Historian," Lecturer, Researcher and Activist. Producer of the radio program series: *"OurStory - The Afrikan Holocaust, 360 Degrees,"* which highlights Afrikan contributions to world civilization and the gamut of the Afrikan Experience. Audio-tapes of this series are available, including a colorful pictorial collage. Lecture topics include Afrikan World History, The Afrikan Moors, World Slavery, and Marcus Garvey.

1330 10th Street • DesMoines, Iowa 50314
(515) 284-6530

Willie Southall, Dr.

Herbologist, Lecturer, & Author of *Hyssop: Super Healing Power*, a book resurrecting awareness of Hyssop, one of the most popular and effective healing /purifying herbs of ancient Afrika and the lands of the Bible. Hyssop is mentioned numerous times in the Bible. Founder of *Hyssop Enterprises,* which provides organic hyssop products, Willie lectures on Health, Longevity, Nutrition, Acupressure, Kinesiology, Iridology, Overcoming Hypoglycemia (he healed himself of hypoglycemia he had over 30 years), and the Super Healing Power of Hyssop. Nothing gives him more joy than reading the myriad of testimonies attesting to the healing wonders attributed to using Hyssop Extract, etc., which reach him from around the world

7095 Hollywood Blvd. Suite 713
Hollywood, CA 90028
(323) 465-3221 • (888) HYSSOP1
WEBSITE: www.hyssopherb.com
EMAIL: hhyssop.com@worldnet.att.net

Lecturers, Authors, Griots, Artists, Workshop Givers, Etc.

Rob Wilson

Multi-media Artist whose style and subject material encompasses a broad range. His original paintings, drawings and prints are available through the company he founded, *Resplendent Editions Fine Arts.* Rob creates inspired, uplifting, feeling-provoking images of Afrikan people, Nature, and Landscapes –his favorite subject. His art shows are available to enhance Afrocentric cultural events. He says: *"I point out to people that almost every material thing they have was first drawn or created by an artist or designer; your clothes, shoes, cups, house."*

Resplendent Edition Fine Arts
758 E. Colorado Blvd., Suite #205
Pasadena, CA 91101
(626) 568-8825 (phone & fax)
(800) 295-3005

Richard D. King, Dr.

Psychiatrist, Professor and Lecturer who considers himself a "student" in the area of Melanin although he is recognized as a foremost authority on Melanin. In his book Melanin: A Key to Freedom, he wrote: *"Perhaps, given the current phase of world wide high achievements by the creative talents of Africans in the arena of music the study of melanin, hearing, and music, may be a 'key to the key' of melanin as a key to freedom. The study of sound is a study of vibration and music (harmonics/resonance=key). Sound is a form of light, particular range of vibrations or movements of atoms in the spectrum of light, Life. Melanin as a photoreceptor, receiver of light, is a door through which light enters the human form through the various sensory organ information portals to self organize, to feed the self or soul of humans while in the physical body."* His other books and publications include: The African Origin of Biological Psychiatry; Kemetic Images of Light; Pineal Gland Calcifications in Blacks, Hispanics and Whites; The Eye of Heru in the Coffin Texts; and The Eye of Heru in the Pyramid Texts. Lecture topics include Melanin, The Third Eye, The Pineal Gland, Afrikan Spirituality, and The Afrikan Origin of Psychiatry.

3751 Stocker St.
Los Angeles, CA 90008
or P.O. Box 884321
San Francisco, CA 94188
(323) 298-3706

"African Prayer" –by Rob Wilson; prints on canvas, 30 x 41

"Aware" –Oil on canvas

Lecturers, Authors, Griots, Artists, Workshop Givers, Etc.

Norma Thompson Hollis

Spiritual Director, Labyrinth Facilitator, Early-Childhood Consultant, Author, Poet, Lecturer, Executive Coach, Hypnotist and Futurist. Inspirational Lecturer who leads her audiences to paths out of the confusion, inspiring them to question current paradigms and motivating them to seek alignment in their lives. Author of _Teach Your Child To Honor God_, _Mystic Footprints_, and _The Candida Epidemic_. Founder of *Speakers Etcetera*, a speakers bureau and professional communications training company. Available for keynotes, seminars, retreats, coaching, consultation and Labyrinth facilitation. Her programs include:

- _Ancient Path of the Labyrinth_: Benefits and Afrikan origin & evolution of the Labyrinth, an ancient walking-meditation tool. Labyrinths originally surrounded Egypt's pyramids. To walk the Labyrinth is to journey to the Center of your being, to the Core of Existence. Once you reach the Center, you are known to be in Union with the Creator. You may ask important questions about your Life and receive Divine answers / guidance as you walk out the same path you took in.
- _Parenting With Passion Patience and Peace_
- _Nurturing Children's Spirituality_: How to sustain the child's innate spirituality. Research reveals young children have the capacity to remember past life experiences, and being with God before birth.
- _Developing Multiple Intelligence In Children_: How to discover which intellectual gifts your children have, how to develop these and use the knowledge to help the child create right life work.
- _Managing Life's Mazes_
- _Reclaim Your Life_
- _Speakeasy_: Learn to speak easily by overcoming fear of public speaking while increasing your confidence, etc.

3628 Summerset Place
Inglewood, CA 90305
(310) 671-7136 • Fax: (310) 672-6570
WEBSITE:www.speakersetc.com

Yosef A.A. ben-Jochannan, Dr.

Courtesy of A. Browder

Historian, Lecturer, Egyptologist and Author of over 30 books, including _Africa: Mother of 'Western Civilization,'_ _Black Men of Nile_, & _African Origins of the Major 'Western Religions.'_ For the past 15 years, "Dr. Ben" has been a major contributor to Daboud Nubian Community of 49 displaced Nubian villages, helping them sustain themselves –from contributions largely from attendees of his lectures. Dr. Ben also heads Afrikan archeological expeditions in Egypt. Anyone desirous of supporting his work may do so in giving contributions towards his expeditions. Primary lecture topics are Ancient Egypt, History, Egyptian Religion & Language, and the Egyptian Educational System (called "the Mysteries" by the Greeks –to whom it *was* a mystery).

40 West 135th St. • New York, NY 10037
(212) 281-7744

A version of the Labyrinth

Children kneeling at the center of the Labyrinth, in communication with the Creator

Organizations, Institutions, Programs, Centers...

Afrikan-Centered Study Groups

Afrikan-centered study groups exist in many cities and towns. If there is not one in your town, start one yourself! For assistance, contact BUST (Black Unity & Spiritual Togetherness), ASCAC (Association for the Study of Classical African Civilizations), or other developers of Afrocentric Study Groups (listed later). You may also contact them for information regarding Chapters of their organization in your area. Excellent general guidelines are presented on pages 248-252 of Anthony Browder's book, Nile Valley Contributions to Civilization, where he wrote:

"The express purpose of a study group is to create an environment where people of like minds can meet with regularity to discuss various aspects of African history and culture. The purpose of these gatherings should not be for the selfish benefit of any individual or the group. Its objective should be for the attainment of accurate information about African people and the development of strategies for the practical application of that knowledge in the personal life, family life and community of each member...Meetings should be held no more that twice a month nor less than once a month...A regular meeting place must be established. It should not be in someone's home. Libraries, churches and schools all have facilities that are available to the public at little or no cost...Each group should operate through a consensus of its membership. There should be no 'leader' in the traditional sense...The selection of reading material to be discussed should be decided by the entire group...."

Courtesy of A. Browder

Afrikan Echoes

Weekly lectures featuring different lecturers. Topics are as diversified as the speakers and include Ancient History, Current & Relative Subjects, Cultural Genocide and Black Studies. Hosts cultural, educational events, fund-raising, and programs for youth. Other arms of this organization are:

- **REFAL**: Reconstructing Economics for Afrikan Liberation.
- **On the Refill**: a food coop serving the local communities.

147 West End Avenue • Newark, NJ 07106-1949
(201) 373-3827

The Afrikan Holocaust Committee of Taui Khuti

An estimated 300 million Afrikans died in the forced, largest transportation of any group of people in history. *"we deem it a vital necessity to establish a Pan Afrikan International coordinated project designed to develop a monumental process in commemoration of the middle passage Afrikan Holocaust. This is the goal of the Afrikan Holocaust Commemoration Committee."* Other goals: Developing *The Golden Ankh* –an international Afrikan relief agency assisting Afrikans impacted by the effects of the Holocaust; Petition all the nations, religious institutions and other parties who participated in the war declared on Afrikan people in 1441 so that a formal armistice can be negotiated and informal hostilities against Afrikan people be stopped (hence, allowing Afrikans the *Peace* necessary for developing in the 21st century); and re-education /leadership programs. The annual conference of Taui Khuti features numerous lecturers, Afrikan cultural arts, and commemoration ceremonies. Founded by Dr. Michael B. Scott.

P. O. Box 1172 • West Covina, CA 91793
(626) 967-3308 • (626) 332-5721 Fax
WEBSITE:www.africanholocaust.com

The African Times

An informative, bi-monthly Afrikan-centered newspaper serving the Afrikan and Afrikan-American communities with news, information, art, travel, entertainment and business of *Afrika.*
Editor & Publisher: Chinyere Charles Anyiam
6363 Wilshire Blvd., Ste. 115
Los Angeles, CA 90048 • (323) 951-0717

Amon-Rah African People's Church

Scholarship is encouraged over emotionalism. Afrikan-centered history is the foundation. Cultish activities of competing religions are exposed and discouraged. Proud and sober Afrikan men and women worship together to create a loving and supportive community. Founded by Dr. Anyim Palmer. Pastor: Red Burton.

2700 W. 54th St. (corner of 5th)
Los Angeles, CA 90043 • (323) 291-9790

Aquarian Spiritual Center

Classes and lectures in Gnosticism, Esoteric Astrology, Metaphysics, Esoteric Sciences and Wholistic Health. Founded by Dr. Alfred Ligon.

1302 W. Martin Luther King Blvd.
Los Angeles, 90037 • (323) 294-0312
Admin. Office (323) 295-1654

Organizations, Institutions, Programs, Centers...

ASCAC: Association for the Study of Classical African Civilizations

Hosts Afrikan-centered Study Conferences nationally and in Afrika. Provides local, regional and national forums for scholarly exchanges and networking. Developer of Afrikan-Centered Study Groups. Disseminates educational materials and study guides for the study of Afrikan civilizations. Purpose: *"The aim and thrust of ASCAC is to bring together scholars, thinkers, planners, artists, students, scientists, technicians and most significantly, dedicated workers to promote and preserve our ancient African heritage."*

2274 West 20th Street • Los Angeles, CA 90018
(323) 730-1155

The Black Pages

A directory of Black Professionals and Black-owned Businesses in YOUR area or state. Example: *The California Black Pages*, founded by Dr. Colin Heron. To get the phone number of the Black Pages in order to locate Black businesses and professionals serving your community, Dr. Heron says:

> "Call up the *white* pages & ask for *The Black Pages*"

...then order your directory. If you have a business and want to route black dollars your way, get listed in *The Black Pages* –"designed to keep you in *the Black*." You'd be surprised at the opportunities that will come your way as a result! Recycle your black dollars to Black businesses (like other ethnic communities). This strengthens any People.

The California Black Pages
P.O. Box 2595
Corona, CA 91718-2595
(909) 279-2195 • (714) 688-1210

Black Unity & Spiritual Togetherness

B.U.S.T. is a Developer of Afrocentric Study Groups with a spiritual and economic direction.

P. O. Box 1088 • Opelousas, LA 70571-1088
(318) 942-2392

Black Writers On Tour

Co-founded by Dr. Rosie Milligan. Designed to give exposure to the many Afrikan American writers and aspiring writers in the country today. Many of the attendees and participants are authors, writers, publishers, agents, and especially readers (general public) looking to purchase books and publications. Activities include exhibitor booths, seminars, workshops, panel discussions, readings, book signings, book selling, press conferences, and networking and marketing opportunities. *"Between 1990 and 1993, African-American book expenditures increased 48%...Between 1988 and 1993 black purchases of books at retail outlets increased 100%."*

8489 W. 3rd St., Suite 1091
Los Angeles, CA 90048
(323) 750-3592
EMAIL: drrosie@aol.com

Community Wellness Practitioners Training

A program founded by Queen Safisha (Dr. Safisha Winema), combining wholistic and modern medicine. Prepares enrollees to meet standards for State-Certified Nursing. Enhances the wellness-promoting skills of homemakers, healthworkers, and care providers for children/seniors. Increases knowledge in Wellness, Alternative Healthcare, Personal Vitality, and Communications Skills. Within this program is *"Building a Divine Temple,"* a 5-week course where one becomes familiar with Self, learns how to maintain inner peace, explore one's strengths and weaknesses, and explore breathing and meditation techniques. Based on her book, *Building a Divine Temple (the Body).*

P. O. Box 72332
Los Angeles, CA 90002
(323) 935-9714
EMAIL:
queensafisha@mail.com

Organizations, Institutions, Programs, Centers...

Dragon Trails –Wilderness Experience

Intimate connection with Nature was the keystone and foundation of Afrikan culture. The word *Nature* itself is derived from Kamite *Neter* (Deity, Divinity).

Most of us are so far removed from Nature. **Irasha Pearl**, a Naturalist, Herbalist, Storyteller, Writer, and Kayak Instructor, has founded *Dragon Trails*, that is, *Wilderness Experience* to help people become more comfortable in Nature through personal and group experience. Teaching you how to survive in the wilderness, *Dragon Trails* is packed with FUN, adventure and practical lessons in the lush wilderness of southern California and other places. Learn Snorkeling and Ocean/River Canoeing. Learn how easy it is to make a shelter, a fire, rope, or even find water! Bask in the *Sunshine's* kiss, inhale invigorating *Air*, drink pure *Water* from sparkling streams, and feel Mother *Earth* under your feet. See wildlife closeup. Sniff the heart of flowers. Communicate with and learn secrets of *Neter.* Irasha also teaches essential basics about plants and herbs, plus their nutritional & therapeutic value. She has developed "Vision Quests" tailored for children, using Nature with Guided Imagery. (Essentially, "Vision Quests" are initiations.) Day Hikes, Camping and Programs for elementary & high schools, organizations, and groups of children & adults.

603 Drown St. • Ojai, CA 93023
(805) 646-2004

First World Alliance

Conducts lectures on Afrikan History and Culture.
400 Convent Avenue #1
New York, NY 10031
(212) 368-7353

The Good Life Holistic Center

A place of healthfood for the Body, Mind & Soul. A great place to meet Afrikan-minded, health-conscious kindred spirits. The center is founded by Ifasade. Topics are as varied as the speakers, ranging from Political Issues in the community to Afrikan Culture/History, and of course, Health.

- ***Mondays:*** lectures on Aromatherapy & Essential Oils, by **Sista Yuki** (Dr. Yukiko Kudo) (213) 920-7044.
- ***Tuesdays:*** lectures on Holistic Health and Herbology, by **Doctah B** (323) 427-8419.
- ***Wednesdays:*** Economic upliftment via "**Matah**." Contact **Klif Burton** (310) 677-3999.
- ***Thursdays:*** Afrikan spirituality. Contact **Ifasade**, (323) 731-0588.
- ***Fridays:*** The **Talking Drum Community Forum**, an Afrikan people's membership organization featuring different lecturers discussing issues pertinent to Afrikans. Contact **Jamaal Goree**, (213) 296-0768.

Good Life: 3631 Crenshaw Blvd.
Los Angeles, CA 90016
(323) 731-0588

Photos by Irasha Pearl

Organizations, Institutions, Programs, Centers...

International Dalit Support Group

Founded by Runoko Rashidi, an organization whose purpose is to disseminate critical information about the struggling Black Untouchables of India.

(See *Runoko Rashidi*)

Kemetic Institute

A Teaching & Research organization which provides Teacher Training and Lectures on Afrikan History and Interests. Also develops Afrocentric Study Groups. Their program, *"Teaching About Africa,"* trains teachers in public schools and any other interested persons on how to include Afrika in their curriculum.

700 East Oakwood Blvd.
Chicago, IL 60653
(312) 268-7500 • (312) 548-0920

Heal Thyself Center

A wholistic center founded by Queen Afua, who, along with her dedicated staff have *"guided over 10,000 people onto and through the path of purification with various natural systems of self-healing."* Workshops, classes & training provided.

106 Kingston Ave. • Brooklyn, NY 11213
(718) 221-HEAL

Kera Jhuty Heru Neb Hu

"The Shrine of articulate thought, speech and writing, through the Kemetic high kultural and spiritual konsciousness for the development and mastery of self." A temple and coalition founded by Dr. Hassan K. Salim, dedicated to re-establishing Kamit and the Kamitic Legacy on the mental, physical, and spiritual planes through the resurrection of ancient ceremonies.

(See *Hassan K. Kalim*)

Ma'at Institute for Children & Adult Education

Classes in the Esoteric Sciences, Metu Neter (Hieroglyphics), Kamit & Kamitic History, Psychology of the Afrikan Self, Herbology, Health, Proper Eating Habits, Afrikan Dance & Drums, Afrikan Ancestral Chants, Rites of Passage for women and men, and Kupigani Ngumi (Afrikan Martial Arts). Founded by Dr. Hassan K. Salim.

(See *Hassan K. Kalim*)

Queen Afua and radiant staff members of *Heal Thyself Center* holding a tray of healing wheat grass

Organizations, Institutions, Programs, Centers...

The Metaphysical Institute of Higher Learning

A state-certified Institute founded by Drs. Arvel & Bobbie Chappell (see page R•4). Offers a Doctor of Metaphysics degree and credentials in Personal Development, Mediumship, Healing, & Ministry. Correspondence and online-Internet programs available. Takes you *beyond* traditional Metaphysics with new revelatory practical knowledge which facilitate spiritual and physical survival, now. These include: Right Use of Will; The Unseen Role of Denial; Balancing & Aligning Your 4 Major Aspects of Spirit, Heart, Will, & Body; and Harmonizing within yourself the Polarity of Will (Feminine Mother Principle) and Spirit (Masculine Father Principle). Other subjects include the Ancient Afrikan Art of Spirit Communication (a.k.a. Mediumship, Channeling), Meditation, Keys to Personal Success, Getting Back and Keeping Your Power, Psychic & Spiritual Development, Psychic Sensitivity, Unconditional Love, Quantum Healing, Your 12 Senses & 12 Chakras, and Meditation.

2873 W. 6th Street • Rialto, CA 92376
(909) 874-6807
WEBSITE:www.metaphy.com
EMAIL: Metaphy3@cs.com

NABSIO

(National Association of Brothers & Sisters In & Out) Its main purpose is to prevent prisoner recidivism, by establishing Afrocentric programs in prisons, including Afrikan studies to Afrikan inmates, encouraging self-esteem and self-help. By teaching Afrikan inmates about their heritage and culture, they can understand themselves collectively and make the correct choices in life. Many other provisions, including: moral support to families of incarcerated Afrikans, for the purpose of inspiring them to keep in contact with their loved ones; post-incarceration group & individual counseling for readjustment; and provide liaison activity between the incarcerated Afrikan and the Afrikan Religious Community. Founder: Dr. Donald Evans, Sr.; Director: Nathaniel Perkins.

"Help us turn every Prison into a University and every Prison Cell into a Classroom for Afrocentric Study....Join and support our brothers and sisters incarcerated"

10013 S. Vermont Ave. # 254
Los Angeles, CA 90044
(323) 564-6446
Fax: (323) 564-2633

Recycling Black Dollars

Founded by Muhammad A. Nassardeen. Developed to motivate and encourage Black professionals, business persons and consumers alike, to invest in the future of the Black business community through patronage and support. Promotes Consumer Education, Race Embrace, and spending as a necessity for economic independence. Offers ways to develop resources for business capitalization and revitalization. RBD's unique feature is its incentive program which mandates each business member to extend a 10% discount on goods and services to all RBD members. Their TV show: Mondays 7 p.m., channel 37 on continental cable. Their Radio show: "*On the Positive Side,*" Fridays 9 p.m., KYPA on 1230-AM (call-in line is 213-520-1212). Hosts monthly business mixers with lectures.

110 S. Labrea Ave., Suites 420 & 510
Inglewood, CA 90301
(310) 673-7777

Rivers Run Deep Institute

Committed to the healing and restoring of the Afrikan Mind, Heart, Body and Spirit. An independent educational institution providing professional development for teachers and staff to schools in urban settings, focusing on the affective and academic needs of American-Afrikan students.

Co-founded by Queen Nzinga R. Heru —Activist, Lecturer, Journalist and International President of ASCAC; and her sister, Subira Aleathia Kifano —Educator and Author of *How to Start and Operate a Saturday School*, and other books, articles.

RRDI sponsors the annual "**Afrikan Holistic Health Healing Retreat & Training Program**," featuring world reknown Afrikan Healers, Doctors, & Educators from around the nation. The retreat is designed to release stress, offer coping strategies, as well as attract persons interested in obtaining knowledge in various healing modalities. RRDI's newsletter, "*Healers*," is dedicated to the same.

2274 W. Twentieth St.
Los Angeles, CA 90018
(323) 734-7551 • Fax: (323) 731-4998
EMAIL: queen@ascac.org

Organizations, Institutions, Programs, Centers...

Rhythm of the Drum

"The Wholistic Health Magazine for Black Folk." A quarterly devoted to advancing the mental /physical / emotional /spiritual, and financial /political /cultural health of Afrikan people. Disseminates information to help Black people *"across the globe stay connected with the natural rhythm that keeps us healthy individually and as a whole."*

P. O. Box 470379 • Los Angeles, CA 90047
Emaill: thedrum@earthlink.net
(800) 324-DRUM

SIMBA-SIS

SIMBA-SIS provides Manhood and Womanhood Training as an Africentric organization whose main purpose is to aid the mental, physical, and spiritual development of the person, family, village, and nation through MAAT. The many SIMBA-SIS organizations in the U.S. are "part of a growing movement geared toward the goals of building institutions, eliminating racism, and creating independence." **S**afe **I**n **M**y **B**rother's **A**rms evolved from the efforts of many people. *SIMBA*, the Swahili word for *Lion*, is the male's symbol or mascot as the boys are prepared to have the motivation, discipline, and courage of a lion. **S**isters **I**n **S**imba (SIS) promotes the development of girls and young women into strong, productive Africentric individuals, –for the rebuilding of the Afrikan male requires the rebuilding of the Afrikan female. Programs include Rites of Passage activities, educational workshops, tutorials, sports, talent shows, lectures, classroom activities, recreational excursions.

P. O. Box 1943 • Pomona, CA 91769
(909) 602-7170

TOURS:
Afrocentric, Educational, Spiritual

Afrikan-centered Educational Tours featuring lectures, etc., by reknown historians and scholars are available through a number of reknown historians and programs. Call for schedules /details. Available through:

- ASCAC: Afrocentric Study Conferences in Afrika.
- Dr. A. Kweku Andoh: Tours to Ghana in connection with the Iboga herb.
- Institute of Karmic Guidance: Afrocentric tours of Washington D.C. Annual Educational Study Tours to Afrika and Mexico. (See *Anthony Browder*).
- Kemet Nu Productions: Educational tours to Egypt (See *Ashra / Merira Kwesi*).
- Dr. Na'im Akbar & Dr. Wade Nobles: Educational tours to Afrika, particularly Ghana.
- Dr. Patricia Newton: Seminars and study tours in North/South America, Afrika, Europe, Caribbean.
- Runoko Rashidi: Educational, Afrocentric tours to India.
- Sheilaa Hite: Spiritual tours to sacred sites of the world.

1-800-UNITE US

Nationwide listing /database of Black Businesses. A Black "411" you call for all types of business, all Black-owned: doctors, restaurants, beauty-supply, lawyers, artists, etc. Other services include:
• *Business Referral Service*: receive referrals; be listed in published & Internet directories.
• *Fax Broadcast Service*: to promote your event, product or service. Your flyer is faxed to either businesses in their database, or yours, or the general market. Specific areas may be targeted.
• *Discount Long Distance & Toll Free Number Rates*: Cheap phone rates, plus money is credited to your account when you refer people.
• *Internet Service Provider*: access to the Internet.
Founded by Charles Brister, Lecturer, Business Man, and World Traveler who lectures on Black Economics and Black History. He says: *"Blacks spend over a BILLION dollars every day in this country. Now what if we just spent half a billion dollars every day with each other? Imagine the RESULTS!! Our FUTURE depends on how much money we spend with each other TODAY. I want every Black man and woman to be able to afford to raise three children."*

3717 South LaBrea Ave., Suite #511
Los Angeles, CA 90016
1-800-UNITE US (1-800-864-8387)
WEBSITE: www.uniteus.com

Organizations, Institutions, Programs, Centers...

The Exhibit Productions, LLC

An educational services company specializing in promoting Positive Images and Self-Esteem in children and adults. Services include:

- Live, interactive presentations which highlights and teaches people of all nationalities about the Contributions of Blacks to Ancient and Modern civilization.
- The Black Inventors Exhibit: The annual Educational Tour featuring the popular exhibit and lecture on Black Scientists and Inventors. Highly informative and entertaining for students and teachers alike.
- Presentations on the Ancient Pyramids & Mounds in North America, the Washitaw Muurs, International Decade of the World's Indigenous Peoples.
- Racial Sensitivity Training & Workshops for schools, employers, organizations, corporations, etc.

Exhibits /displays available to Schools, Organizations, Expos, Churches, Family Reunions, Cultural Events. Also, multi-cultural & multi-lingual publications, books, posters, CDs, videos. Organized by Dr. Umar S. Bey; Lecturer, Researcher, Human Rights Activist & Author of a number of books including *We Are The Washitaw -Indigenous Blacks of North America.*

P.O. Box 29512 • Shreveport, LA 71149 • (318) 682-5963
P.O. Box 2788 • Los Angeles, CA 90294
(323) 964-2075
WEBSITE: www.hotep.org
EMAIL:umar@hotep.org

The Pyramid ("Monk's Mound") in Illinois is larger than the ones in Egypt.

The Great Serpent Mound in Ohio, is about 1/4 mile long.

Tony Linck

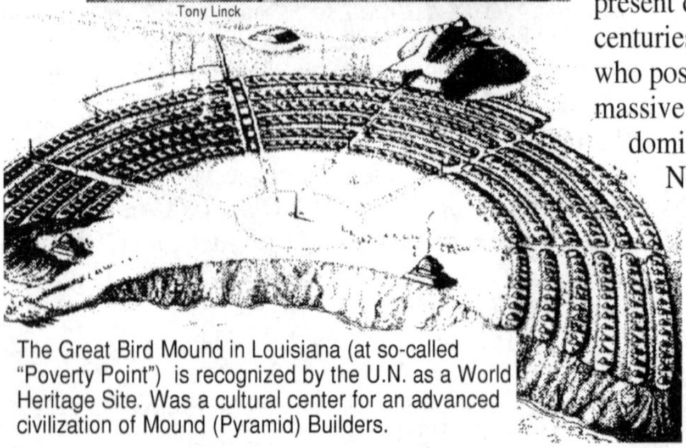

The Great Bird Mound in Louisiana (at so-called "Poverty Point") is recognized by the U.N. as a World Heritage Site. Was a cultural center for an advanced civilization of Mound (Pyramid) Builders.

The Washitaw Nation
"Empire Washitaw de Dugdahmoundyah"

The sovereign nation of mound-building Muurs/Moors. Remnants of the original inhabitants of the lands presently known as the Americas. Recognized by the United Nations as one of the oldest indigenous peoples on Earth. Headed by Her Highness, *Verdiacee Tiari Washitaw-Turner Goston El-Bey:* Empress of the Washitaw. And author of *Return of the Ancient Ones*. This is a nation of Black people who trace their roots to the indigenous inhabitants of this continent best known as "The Ancient Ones". The Muurs/Moors have a legacy of advancing civilizations as they traveled the world thousands of years before the first Europeans were born. The Moors of North Africa and Arabia brought Europe from its dark ages with their occupation and development of the Iberian Peninsula (Spain) from 700 A.D to 1400 A.D. They built the first University in Europe at Salamanca and first libraries and other institutions of organized society. The Ancient Ones, the Muurs who built the first earthen Pyramids on this continent have oral histories dating back 100,000's of years. One tale speaks of journeying from the land of Mu. Today, most Muurs/Moors in America follow the teachings of the Honorable Prophet Noble Drew Ali, founder of the Moorish Science Temple of America.

Archaeologists, in the heart of the Washitaw Proper (a.k.a. Louisiana, Arkansas, Oklahoma, Mississippi River Valley), are excavating ancient communities whose radio carbon dating and levels of sophistication will re-write the history of the original natives & proprietors of this land –referred to as Pre-Columbians, the Lost Tribes, the tribe of Shabazz, the People of the Sun, etc. Western scholarship does not want to recognize the relationships between the mound-building Muurs and the natives (Indians) who were present during the arrival of the first Europeans in the 16th /17th centuries. The Indians were considered nomads and wanderers who possessed neither the time nor the expertise to engineer the massive earthworks and astronomical observatories once that dominated these lands. The significance of the Washitaw Nation is that its roots are indigenous. The Ancient Ones built permanent communities that endured uninterrupted for thousands of years. The Washitaw Nation is the living ascendant of the ancient empire that first ruled this land.(From: *We Are The Washitaw*, by Dr. Umar Bey)

Washitaw Nation
Box 1509 • Columbia via U.S.A ., PZ 71418
PH: (318) 435-1919; FAX: 435-1735

Afrikan INTERNET Resources /Websites

www.saxakali.com
Devoted to connecting people of color through online education and networking. Wealth of information, resources, online classes. Links to: Afrikans, Native Americans, Asians, Latinos, Chicanos. Issues affecting people of color. News, culture, employment, politics, publications, book reviews. Over 25 specially selected news sources on people of color, women, health, & computers.

www.saxakali.com/coloru
"Offers FREE self-paced, interactive training for people of all ages, divided into five programs: youth, employment, business, computer, and cultural study. Courses are delivered to your desktop or home computer as self-study tutorials."

www.melanet.com
Lets you FREELY publicize your events in their "Universal Afrocentric Calendar" — a catalog of the happenings in the Black world. The Calendar lets you freely add, modify and delete the events, conferences, training sessions or media events of *your* organization or business. You can also link the reader back to your website for up-to-the-minute news and information.

www.blackmind.com
Enlightening online books, articles, tapes and other items by People of Color. Offers FREE web pages to all individuals interested. Has a Free For All Links Page.

www.blackmind.com/kemetnu
Internet source for the educational videos and audio tapes by Ashra & Merira Kwesi (see page R•4), of Kemet Nu Productions.

www.directblackaction.com
"This is the Center for a meaningful demand for Black Reparations in The United States of America."
Founded by Dr. Robert Brock (page R•19) to educate diasporan Afrikans on how to become Self Determined. Contains highly informative and educational articles and vital information, relevant to Afrikan people.

www.globalafrica.com
"The place where you make direct contact with other Global African people... You can advertise Africentric books and other positive pro-African items on this page free of charge."

www.blackvoices.com
"Black America's Favorite Website"

www.speakersetc.com
Speakers bureau & professional communications training. Founded by Norma T. Hollis (see page R•25).

www.hyssopherb.com
Discover HYSSOP, the Holy Herb with an ancient Healing Tradition. Hyssop Enterprises has the BEST hyssop products, including 100% pure Hyssop Extract. (see page R•23).

www.milliganbooks.com
Online Afrikan bookstore by Dr. Rosie Milligan.

www.metaphy.com
The Metaphysical Institute of Higher Learning, offering a Doctor of Metaphysics degree and other credentials. Correspondence and online programs available. (See pages R•4 and R•30).

www.ascensionproductions.org
Eraka Rouzorondu (see page R•20) and her lectures, workshops, events, services and spiritual-aid products.

www.melanet.com/cleggseries
Featuring "Maat News: The Africentric Voice of The Internet." By Dr. Legrand Clegg (see page R•10).

www.afrikanculture.com
Afrikan Cosmology, Sacred Geometry, Sacred Music, Mathematics, Astronomy, Astro-Mythology, Human Development, the Higher Self, Applied Metaphysics and more. (See Dadisi Sanyika, page R•6)

www.publicenemy.com
Conscious music & rap for the awakening consciousness of Afrikans worldwide.

www.deepknowledge.com
Online, highly interactive Afrikan bookstore with lecture-schedules of Afrikan authors.

www.cis.yale.edu/swahili
Learn Swahili, the most widely spoken Afrikan language. "The Internet Living Swahili Dictionary". How are you? –*Hujambo?* ; Good/Fine –*Nzuri* ; Bad –*Mbaya* ; Thank you (very much) –*Asante (sana)*

www.uniteus.com
Where you can find Black-owned businesses (Pg. R•31)

www.everythingblack.com
Is exactly what it sez! Huge database of Black Resources. Is yo great Black business listed here?

www.hotep.org
An information exchange featuring the Homepage of The Exhibit Productions (see page R•32); M.U.S.I.C. Human Rights Network (Making and Utilizing Self Initiative in Communities); Indigenous Concepts; The Truth-Brary; and FutureMan Foundation.

www.suzar.com
By the author of the book you are reading, *Blacked Out Through Whitewash...*

Opportunities in Afrika with Dr. Simon & Esther Odede

Background:

Reknown throughout Kenya, Dr. Simon Odede is a philanthropist, businessman, professor, farm-owner, land-owner, and chairman of one of Kenya's major companies (SONY Sugar). His brother, Thaddayo Okatch, a reknown civil rights activist, was assasinated in America in the 1960s. His nephew, Otieno J. Okatch (see page R-15) is an American-Afrikan dedicated to the Afrikan cause. Dr. Odede and his wife Ester are dedicated to the upliftment and advancement of Afrikan people. Among other programs and projects, they founded a school and hospital. After a number of years, the hospital was converted to another school, offering kindergarten through 12th grade, to meet the ever-growing needs. Though they manintain a home in Nairobi where their children attend school, they spend most of their time overseeing the operations of the farm, schools, and SONY Sugar Co, from their Awendo residence. Out of marsh area that others said would amount to nothing, Dr. Simon and Ester Odede have carved out a community, where now a market exists and other homesteads have sprung up. The school also also operates a commissary, guest lodgings, and entertains students, scholars and guests from universities around the world.

Foreground:

Dr. Simon and Ester Odede invites Afrikan Americans (individuals, groups, businesses) to come to Kenya and unite their skills, energies, funds, and talents with theirs towards development /economic projects, programs, investments, etc., for the upliftment, education, health, and development of Afrikan people. In regards to this are a number of industries /demographic trends including:

- Growth of smaller towns in rural areas.
- Need for facilities for processing medicine, foods, organic cleaners, fertilizers, etc.
- Need for private, Afrocentric schools.
- Buying land for cultivation.
- Supply, promotion, and funding of clean-water projects, e.g., rainwater harvesting, piping, purifying, etc. Death at an early age from diarrhea is the top killer of children; clean water = healthier children and adults.
- Need for American Afrikan funding of Kenyan-owned corporations and business projects.
- Donation of medical supplies and books.

English is spoken throughout Kenya. For more information contact Dr. Odede at either of his addresses:

P. O. Box 198 Sare-Awendo, Kenya [254] (0387) 43048	or	P. O. Box 45872 Nairobi, Kenya [254] (2) 522598

S.E.

Dr. Simon Odede

Otieno Okatch

The Odede Family has transformed their previous hospital into a thriving secondary school in Kenya

Free Land in Afrika & a Way Back Home: FIHANKRA International

"There's land there set aside for us and we are loved and wanted." And this land is FREE to diasporan Blacks wishing to relocate or to invest in GHANA. Over 30,000 acres of prime land was granted to FIHANKRA in 1995, in the belief that if land were made available, many Afrikans born in the Diaspora would take advantage of the unique opportunity to live and invest in an Afrikan community in which Diasporans are the co-architects. This beautiful land is near the great River Volta, surrounded by rolling hills and lush tropical vegetation. Comprised of a wide selection of plots ranging from flat and arable to picturesque hillside and river-views. It is about an hour from the Accra Kotoko International Airport. Construction work is underway and plots for houses, schools, clinics, farming, ranching, restaurants, shopping malls, offices, etc., are now available.

What is FIHANKRA? FIHANKRA aims to re-integrate Afrika with its Diaspora. It has evolved to help rekindle the spiritual and material relationship between Afrikans wherever they may be. It is a spiritual, cultural and economic development organization whose mission is to:

- Assist Afrikans throughout the Diaspora in the process of cultural re-identification
- Acquire land and facilitate the cultural and economic planning and development of model communities both in Afrika and the Diaspora
- Promote trade, tourism and investment
- Facilitate cultural exchange through community and creative programming
- Advocate on behalf of Afrikan people on issues affecting the common good
- To do all of the above while offering homage to the Creator and reverence to our ancestors

FIHANKRA was born December 9, 1994 with the inaugural purification of a specially created wooden **Stool** and animal **Skin**. This historical event took place in Accra, Ghana, West Afrika. Together, these two holy objects were named FIHANKRA, meaning "when leaving home no good-byes were said." In Afrikan tradition, the seats of the Stool and Skin are holy symbols of divine chieftaincy authority in which resides the spirit and soul of its people. They compare with the Throne of other nations. Thus, FIHANKRA restores to diasporan Afrikans two holy symbols in one, thereby reaffirming the cultural and spiritual ties that had been denied them for centuries.

Who are FIHANKRA citizens? All diasporan Afrikans around the world. That is, any person who is a descendant of an Afrikan born in the Diaspora as a direct result of the trans-Atlantic slave trade.

Who may participate & live on the Land project? One must be historically and identifiably Afrikan; be an Afrikan Diasporan; be 21 years or older; complete a land application; and pay an administrative/membership fee.

FIHANKRA Programs & Services Include:

- Annual festivals celebrating the purifications of the Stool and Skin of FIHANKRA and Unity of Afrikans Worldwide
- Cooperation with other organizations with similar goals.
- Encouraging members of business and trade associations in the Diaspora to travel to and actively participate in the economic development of Afrika.
- Providing counseling and information in the areas of Social Services, Medicine, Housing, Tourism, Education, Investment, Residency, Citizenship, Business, Culture, Student Exchange Programs, Literacy & Language Classes.

For more information, contact FIHANKRA International:

Ghana Headquarters
P.O. Box 19334 Accra-North
Ghana, West Africa
Phone: 011-233-21-406-413
Fax: 011-233-21-406-641
EMAIL:
fihankra@africaonline.com.gh

Michigan Headquarters
12730 W. 7 Mile Rd.
Detroit, Michigan 48235, USA
Phone: (313) 869-4123
Fax: (313) 869-3140

Los Angeles (Information)
Jasmine Poitier (323) 293-4336

The FIHANKRA Stool & Skin
Parade of Chiefs,
International.
Nana Kwadwo O. Akpan I. Custodian of the Stool of Fihankra International holding the traditional Stool.
Dr. Abena Yeboah (Mildred Purifoy Singleton, M.D.) a chief of Fihankra and an international eye surgeon from Detroit, and Dr. Virginia Anima Danquah, a native ophthalmologist in Accra, encourage doctors, teachers, engineers, businessmen, etc., to share their skills and resources with Ghana through Fihankra International.
GHANA

Certain Buy-ables mentioned in this book

Item: **"Moses: Exodus"**
Photographic artprint (page 71) available from the *First Church of Rasta*, founded by High Priest, *King Oji.*
2126 W. Jefferson Blvd.
Los Angeles, CA 90018
(323) 735-2414

Item: **Book** (& tapes),
The Truth About Black Biblical Hebrew-Israelites (Jews), by Ella Hughly (page 82). Hughly Pub Productions is the sole distributor (to individuals & bookstores) of this book. Also, source for music by Ella Hughly's Sounds, including, Let Peace Prevail, "A song of Peace, Happiness, Love and Hope."
P. O. Box 130261 • Springfield Gardens, NY 11413 • (718) 712-5892

Item: **Petersen Projection World Map** (outlined on page 374)
Friendship Press • P.O. Box 37844
Cincinnati, OH • (513) 948-8733

Items: **All natural hair-care products... the best** (page 14):

Company: ***Hairobics***
"When you feel the tingle... Hairobics is working!" Based on herbal formulas handed down for generations in the family. Founded by Isaac & Stephanie Suthers. Attesting to *Hairobic's* effectiveness, Stephanie's lush, nappy, unlocked hair spirals down past her waist.
1123A East Dominguez St.
Carson, CA 90746 • (800) 697-HAIR

Company: ***Praises***
Natural Hair & Skin Products –specially tailored for the ethnic needs of Afrikan hair & skin. Herbal formulations based on 20 years experience with herbs & botanicals from around the world. Founded by Adio K. Akil-I.
P. O. Box 429 • Bronx, NY 10466
(718) 655-0936 or 655-9447

Item: **"The Moorish Chief"** (page 43).
Artprint available from The Philadelphia Museum of Art 26th Street in Benjamin Franklin Pkwy. (215) 684-7960.

Item: **The Dalit Voice**
(page 65). The best publication on India's Black Untouchables, edited by Indian activist, author, journalist V.T. Rajshekar.
Annual subscriptions: $45.00
c/o Dalit Sahitya Akademy
109 / 70th Cross,
Palace Lower Orchards
Bangalore, India 560 003.

Items: **Certain books.**
Since books by Gerald Massey, Godfrey Higgens, Kersey Graves, and Hilton Hotema are nearly impossible to find, here are publishers who carry them:
- Kessinger Publishing Co.: P.O. Box 160-C, Kila, MT 59920
- Health Research: P.O. Box 70, Mokelumne Hill, CA 95245

Black Bookstores & Galleries Nationally

Afrikan Bookstreet
92-06 148th Street
Jamaica, NY 11435
(718) 206-1511

AmenRa's Bookshop
1326 S. Adams Street
Tallahassee, FL 32301
(904) 681-6628

Aquarian Books
1968 W. Adams Blvd.
Los Angeles, CA 90018
(323) 735-9914

Afrika Enterprises
707 East Broadway
West Memphis, AR 73201
(501) 735-1212

Black Images Books
230 Wynnewood Village
Dallas, TX 75224
(800) 272-5027

The Black Market
2547 Welton Street
Denver, CO 80205

Cultural Comunications
2258 Cascade Road
Atlanta, GA 30311
(404) 756-9658

Dar Es Salaam
4000 34th Street
Mt. Rainier, MD 20712
(301) 209-0010

Dawah Book Shop
4801 S. Crenshaw Blvd.
Los Angeles, CA 90043
(323) 299-0335

Dianna Books Plus
416 New Lots Ave.
Brooklyn, NY 11207
(718) 272-0365

Eso-Won Books
3655 S. LaBrea St.
Los Angeles, CA 90016
(323) 294-0324

Kongo Square Gallery
4334 Degnan Blvd.
Los Angeles, CA 90008
(323) 291-6878

Know Thyself African Books
317 S. 11th Street
Tacoma, WA 98402
(253) 572-8186

Kuumba Korners
9980 Gratiot Ave.
Detroit, MI 48213
(313) 579-3250

Liberation Books
421 Lennox Ave.
New York, NY 10037
(212) 281-4615

Malik's Bookstore
Baldwin Hills Crenshaw Mall
3650 W. M.L. King Blvd.
Los Angeles, CA 90008
(323) 294-1311

Marcus Books
- Oakland, CA at 3900 Martin Luther King Way (510) 652-2344
- San Francisco, CA at 1712 Fillmore, (415) 346-4222

Nijart International, Fine Arts
2131 South Hoover St., Suite 101
Los Angeles, CA 90007
(323) 746-9263

New Jersey Books
59 Market Street
Newark, NJ 07102
(201) 673-4446

Nubian Knowledge Ltd.
3802 Aston Rd.
Columbus, Ohio 43227
(877) 499-8679

Ophelia's Art Gallery
1905 Bessemer Road
Birmingham, AL 35208
(205) 925-9166

Pride Cultural
7601 S. Cicero
Chicago, IL 60652
(312) 767-0477

Pyramid Books
2849 Georgia Ave, NW
Washington, DC 20001
(202) 328-0190

Richards Art Gallery & Books
213 W. 4th Street
Winston Salem, NC 27101
(910) 748-9775

Shrine of the Black Madonna
- Atlanta, GA at 946 Ralph D. Abernathy Blvd. (404)752-6125
- Houston, TX at 5309 Martin Luther King Blvd. (713) 645-1071
- Detroit, MI at 13535 Livernois, (313) 491-0777

Salahuddin
108 E. Main Street
Bennettsville, SC 29512
(803) 479-8843

Silver Spring Books
938 Bonifant St.
Silver Spring, MD
(301) 587-7484

Tiger Bookstore
3533 Walker Ave.
Memphis, TN 38111
(901) 324-2808

Timbuktu Bookstore
5508 Superior Ave.
Cleveland, OH 44103
(216) 391-4740

Togo Heritage
2201 Arrow Ave.
Anlason, IN 46016
(317) 649-7069

Treasured Legacy
Copley Place, Back Bay Station
at Dartmouth Street
Boston, MA
(617) 424-8717

Universal Knowledge
512 8th Avenue, Ste. D
Birmingham, AL 35204
(205) 322-7211

Valley Of The Kings Egyptian Art Gallery & Books
Baldwin Hills Crenshaw Mall
3650 W. M.L. King Blvd.
Los Angeles, CA 90008
(323) 293-9800

Zahra's Books n' Things
900 N. La Brea Ave.
Inglewood, CA 90302
(310) 330-1300

A-KAR Productions
www.A-Kar.com

Featuring the works by Suzar

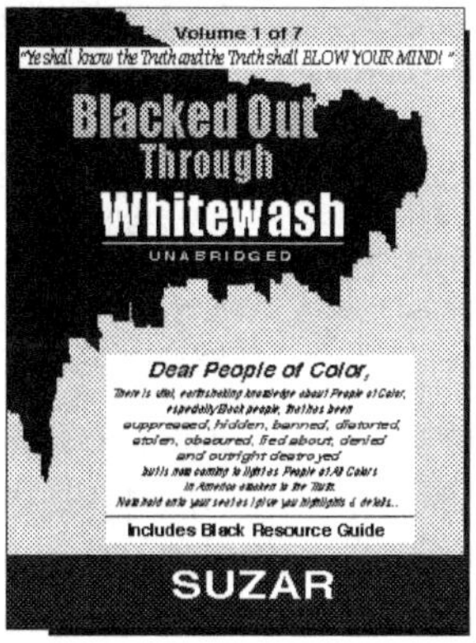

To Order

Mail your request and
1. check/money order payable to A-Kar Productions, for the price & 7.30% CA state tax (if CA resident)
2. shipping address
3. optional: phone # or email address to:

A-Kar Productions
P.O. Box 386
Oak View, CA 93022

PRINT CLEARLY. Orders promptly shipped Priority Mail, First Class or UPS.

Credit Card Orders:
- www.hotep.org
- www.metaphy.com

FREE Shipping

Blacked Out Through Whitewash

by Suzar
Paperback : Vol. 1 of 7
Unabridged, 450 pages
Illustrated, Indexed
Includes **Black Resources Guide**
$49.00

Exposes the Quantum Deception composing the Foundation of Western Culture, Religion and *His*-Story. Exposes the greatest Coverups in "His-Story" along with the massive Mind-Control and Deception perpetrated in the name of "the Lord." Irrefutably proves the astrological foundation of the entire Bible. The Cosmic Principle causing hair (antennae) to be "nappy." The world's 25 crucified risen saviors. Santa Claus in the Bible and his true identity. Recovers lost, suppressed Melanated Truths... – vital truths promoting the healing, upliftment, liberation, kinship and empowerment of all Humanity.

The Double-You (W) Book

by Drs. Arvel & Bobbie Chappell
Edited by Dr. Epps
Paperback : 146 pages,
Color Illustrated
$29.95

The YOU you know and the YOU you have yet to Discover. Discover who YOU truly are (the REAL You) and the WHY of your life. Discover Personal Empowerment that does not require taking power from anyone or giving away your power to anyone. Learn how to align, integrate and balance your Four Aspects: Spirit, Heart, Will, and Body. We must align and balance these Four Aspects in order to sustain our lives and really, to save ourselves. You probably already know that you create your own reality, but HOW you create – as addressed in this book– is brand new. Invest in YOU!

Drugs Masquerading As Foods

Deliciously Killing American-Afrikans & All Peoples
by Suzar, N.D., D.M.
Paperback: 280 pages
Illustrated, Indexed
$19.95

Silent, deadly, delicious. Drugfoods kill over 240,000 Americans every two months from the degenerative diseases they cause, accounting for more than 2/3 of U.S. deaths! **Blacks lead the nation in mortality rates from drugfood diseases!** Sickness, not Health, is a Trillion dollar-a-year industry in America. And you, yes YOU are a Drugfood Addict! Among other vital things, this life-saving book identifies ***the Five Fatal Foremost Traits of Killer Drugfoods*** and just which "foods" are really *Drugs Masquerading as Foods* ...killing us slowly, little by little with each delicious bite!

Partial Table of Contents
- SOUL-food is killer slave-food sending Afrikans to early graves
- The Top Drugfood-Weapons Killing Us Slowly & Deliciously
- Dairy is DIE-ry; Milk is the top Heart-Attack-producing food
- Body-Bankrupting Beverages
- Dangers of genetically engineered, mutant, freak-foods
- Avoid "TTT" -the Top-Toxic Twelve most pesticided produce
- Drug #14: Freaked Fractionated Nutrients
- Why are fractionated vitamins / nutrients harmful?
- Natural Poisons in Vegetables!
- What is Humanity's Proper Food?
- Food Guide Summary – Recommendations for Better Health

Other Books by Suzar, Available Soon...

Creation's Great Blak Mother & the Blak Woman
Volume 2 of *Blacked Out Through Whitewash*. See description on page 381.

Resurrecting BAB-EL, the Book of Books of Books
Volume 3 of B.O.T.W. See description on page 381.

UnFood By The UnPeople $14.95 (Vol. 2 of DMAF) The worse killer drugfoods are the "refined" WHITE drugfoods. Beginning with the "color" White, the 20 Outstanding Hallmarks of white-drugfood exactly match the 20 Outstanding Hallmarks of its white (Albino) creators. It is no accident that the most lethal deadly substances are WHITE and made by WHITE people: crack, cocaine, opium, LSD, angel dust, chemical fertilizer, white styrofoam, white sugar, white flour, white grease and silvery-white Plutonium –the "active ingredient" of nuclear *superweapons* capable of destroying the entire planet! This book is not intended to demean Albinos but to expose and present the *Truth* as history & present conditions testify it so that we all may properly identify and overstand what is really going on. For it is the *Truth*, though *bitter*, that is the key to Humanity's SURVIVAL, Healing & Freedom.

Don't Worry, Be Healthy! $14.95 (Vol. 3 of DMAF) Health is your natural state and the state of the Universe– which is ever striving to maintain its wholeness & the wholeness of all its parts. You are one of its precious "parts." And your magnificent body is ever attempting to stay whole, balanced. Reap the rewards of Glowing Health & Vitality by learning & living the Principles of Health, documented in this manual for achieving & staying healthy in a TOXIC world.

The Latest Releases from the 7-volume series of *Blacked Out Through Whitewash*, by Suzar. **$9.95 Each**

Available by December 1999

The Great BLAK Mother of Creation

Before the patriarchal Albino man came to power, the Supreme Being was worshipped all over the world as a Creatress. If Her precious planet Earth is to survive, the Female Mother Principle of God must be resurrected and restored, along with the Blak Woman – the Mother of Humanity. (Vol. 2, #16) **$9.95**

StarScience, the Disguised Global Cosmology, Founded by Blak Women

Blak Afrikan women were the true authors of "StarScience" the "Mother Of Sciences" and foundation for Agriculture, which was the foundation of Civilization. StarScience was the universal cosmology taught around the globe by the Afrikan Parents of Humanity. In disguise, it still is the "global religion" ! Presently, its diluted forms and fractionations are called Astrology, Astronomy, Mathematics, Geometry, Computer Science, etc. (Vol. 2, #19) **$9.95**

Female Biological Superiority: Fact or Fiction?

Every fetus begins its first 7 weeks in the womb as female. The male & female genitals both start from a female prototype. Every male on the planet is from a female. Not a single female came from a male...or a man's rib. (Vol. 2, #23) **$9.95**

Unbelievable Pussy: Meow & the Sexual Foundation of Religion

Why "Pussy" is a name for the Cat and Vagina. Why Dick is a name for Richard. Reveals the sexual foundation of the world's top religions and ceremonies. Most religious icons /symbols are sexual metaphors or symbolize our genitals. For SEX is the holiest Act of Creation, not "the Original Sin"! Even atoms "do it." (Vol. 2, #24) **$9.95**

Witch-Bitch-Ho: The Great War on The Great Mother & All Women

All over the world on all continents, women, especially women of color, are demeaned, subjugated, ab-used, prostituted, inferiorized, etc. Many Islamic vaginas are systematically maimed. Many Christian uteruses (mainly of Blak women in America) are cut out –a million a year. Many Hindu girl-babies are still being killed. All sanctioned by anti-female men and their anti-female God who has no Goddess. (Vol. 2, #25) **$9.95**

777 or Bab-El the True Bible, a "Power-Generator"

The word "Bible" occurs nowhere in the Bible except on its cover. The original Bible was the "Bab-El." The top traits of the Bab-El are identified. When these traits are "built into" anything, that thing becomes a Bab-El itself (!), thus, a means of generating or accessing POWER. Related to Bab-El is the story of Babel & Babylon, a gross distortion of the Blak Afrikan Truth. Disguisedly about the castration of the Blak "Pole" of Power. Hidden for 2000 years, the Truth about the Bab-El is finally revealed. (Vol. 3, #29) **$9.95**

A Detailed Look At Top Bab-Els

...such as the original Bab-El or Scripture of the Whirling Starry Heavens, Bab-El as the Connector to Heaven, Bab-El the Papyrus, the Mountain, Great Pyramid, Ark of the Covenant, the Star Sevak (Sirius), the Ankh, the Tree, and Bab-El as the "Great 777." (Vol. 3, #30: Parts I & II) **$9.95 each**

Exposing the Top *Reversed* Bab-Els Secretly Empowering "White Supremacy"

Washington DC, the Vatican, Bible, U.S. Dollar Bill, etc., all harness and draw Power by secretly being layed out and structured according to the Cosmic Geometry of the "Zodiac" and the Great Pyramid. But because of their deliberate reversal of certain key elements, they are not true Bab-Els but "UnBabs" (Reversed Bab-Els). Hence, they are not true *power generators* but *power suckers* which fuel global Albino Domination. (Vol. 3, #36: Parts I & II) **$9.95 each**

How the Bible & Dollar-Bill are a Great 555, 666 and 777

For starters, the Bible begins on 5 as the Pentateuch, has exactly 66 books, and 7 of its books are double-books. Why are 5, 6 and 7 singled out from the other numbers? What do trippple digits signify? How the Bible, Dollar Bill & Masonic Logo have the exact same hidden numeric /geometric traits built into them, and why. (Vol. 3, #36c) **$9.95**

How the Great Pyramid & the "Zodiac" are Built into the Bible & Dollar Bill

The Bible, U.S. Dollar Bill & Mason Logo all possess the key traits and geometry of the Great Pyramid. All 12 (13, really) signs of the Zodiac are throughout the Bible and hidden in the U.S. Dollar Bill. (Vol. 3, #36d) **$9.95**

America, the Counterfeit Godhead of Earth

The Throne of Kamit (ancient Blak Egypt) was the Godhead of planet Earth and Seat of the greatest Power. The capstone, apex, top *Bab-El.* As such, Egypt represented Heaven...on Earth. Whites apparently usurped and supplanted Blak Egypt, replicating her essential elements into their structures to secure Power. America is presently the latest and greatest Counterfeit Egypt, thus the False Godhead of Earth and "Counterfeit Heaven" ("UnHeaven USA"). No wonder most people around the world wanna come to America...just like they wanna "go to Heaven." (Vol. 3, #37) **$9.95**

You "Come To Power" Only When You "Come To A Point"

Power is at the Point. Exudes, shoots, radiates from the Point, as shown by Kirlian photographs of pyramids. Only when the spellbound-but-Awakening Blak Race, the Parent Race of Humanity, "Comes-To-A-Point," will it "Come-To-Power." Regain its hi-jacked Power. The Point is the Intersection of Life's two Polarities. This Intersection is where "Creation Happens." The CenterPoint is supposed to be BLAK, like the Pupil of the Eye. When the Pupil or Center is White it is DEAD, a "dead center." Cannot generate power, thus is a Vampire. Like no other people, Blaks (especially Blak women), have been /are being vampirised for their abundant Power, which they have also been trained to give away. Revelations, insights & solutions. (Vol. 4, #38: Parts I & II) **$9.95 each**

The Hidden Sweet Truth About "666"

Like we've been given huge Lies for history, we've been given huge Lies, plus slander and reversals about "666"...and "13." Now the precious Truth is available, ruining the Lies, restoring denied Power, and exposing the true identity of "the Beast," "the Man," and "the Mark of the Beast." (Vol. 6, #46) **$9.95**

Blak Survival Guide Now

Effective practical strategies & tools for our Personal Empowerment and Survival. Effective ways to protect and heal ourselves, awaken and "Come-To-A-Point" thus "Come-To-Power." Work these strategies in increments. Make it an ongoing family /friends project. Make this serious business FUN. (Vol. 7, #51) **$9.95**

The Hidden "Zodiacs" Composing the Bible

Irrefutable evidence that the entire Bible is a "Great Book of StarScience," disguisedly composed of numerous hidden "zodiacs." The abundant evidence is from the Bible itself! This new, formerly hidden key unlocks a whole new Bible before your amazed eyes. Though the Bible has been "tampered with," in reality its original hidden astrological blueprint has been completely preserved. This book is essentially an overview of chapters 12 & 13 in volume 1 of B.O.T.W. **$9.95**

CPSIA information can be obtained
at www.ICGtesting.com
Printed in the USA
LVHW061256120420
653144LV00011B/406

9 780967 53943(